BARRON'S

AP

COMPUTER SCIENCE

2008

Levels A and AB

4TH EDITION

Roselyn Teukolsky, M.S.
Ithaca High School
Ithaca, New York

BARRON'S

All inquiries should be addressed to:
Barron's Educational Series, Inc.
250 Wireless Boulevard
Hauppauge, New York 11788
http://www.barronseduc.com

ISBN-13: 978-0-7641-3709-9
ISBN-10: 0-7641-3709-3
ISBN-13 (with CD-ROM): 978-0-7641-9350-7
ISBN-10 (with CD-ROM): 0-7641-9350-3

Library of Congress Control Number: 2006102317

Library of Congress Cataloging-in-Publication Data
Teukolsky, Roselyn.
    Barron's AP computer science: Levels A and AB / Roselyn Teukolsky.
– 4th ed.
        p. cm.
    Includes index.
    ISBN-13: 978-0-7641-3709-9
    ISBN-10: 0-7641-3709-3
    1. Computer science–Examinations, questions, etc.   I. Title:
QA76.28.T48 2007
004'.076–dc22

                                                    2006102317

PRINTED IN THE UNITED STATES OF AMERICA
9 8 7 6 5 4 3 2

Contents

Preface

This book is aimed at students reviewing for the AP Computer Science exam. It would normally be used at the completion of an AP course. However, it contains a complete summary of all topics for both Level A and AB exams, and it can be used for self-study if accompanied by a suitable textbook.

The book provides a review of object-oriented programming, algorithm analysis, and data structures. It can therefore be used as a supplement to first-year college courses where Java is the programming language, and as a resource for teachers of high school and introductory college courses.

This fourth edition includes some new features of Java 5.0 that were first tested on the May 2007 exam: generic collection classes and the enhanced for loop. Static imports and auto-boxing and -unboxing are also discussed in the book, but these topics will not be tested on the AP exam. The material on object-oriented programming and design has been expanded to reflect the changing emphasis of the AP exam. Similar small changes and improvements have been made throughout the book.

Each review chapter is followed by AP exam-style multiple-choice questions with detailed explanations of the answers.

There is a similarly thorough review of the GridWorld Case Study.

There are four complete practice exams, two Level A and two Level AB. These exams have been revised to be more in keeping with the evolution of the actual exams. The exams follow the format of the AP exam, with multiple-choice and free-response sections. Two are presented after the introduction to the book for possible use as diagnostic tests. Diagnostic charts accompany these tests. Detailed solutions with explanations are provided for all exams. Two additional exams are provided on the optional CD-ROM. This edition contains several new questions. There is no overlap of questions between the exams.

ACKNOWLEDGMENTS

I owe thanks to many people who helped in the creation of this book.

A special thank-you to Chris Nevison and Richard Kick for the care they took in reading the new sections of the manuscript. Their detailed comments and advice were invaluable to me.

I am most grateful to my excellent editor, Linda Turner, of Barron's, for her friendly guidance and moral support throughout this project. Thanks too to Sara Black for her superlative job of copyediting a tough manuscript. I also thank Frank Pasquale and all the other members of the Barron's staff who worked on the production of the book. Thanks too to Tyler DeWall for his patience and perseverance in the development of the CD-ROM.

I am grateful to Steven Andrianoff and David Levine of St. Bonaventure University, New York, for their outstanding workshops over the years that gave me a leg up in computer science. Many ideas from their Java workshop found their way into this book.

A big thank-you goes to my AP computer science students who helped in the debugging of problems. Special thanks to Ben Zax and Ian Lenz for contributing their hours and expertise, and to Johnathon Schultz and Daniel Birman for sharing a couple of clever algorithms.

There is a special place in my heart for Rachel Zax who did an amazing job of checking the practice exams, the GridWorld case study chapter, and the CD-ROM. Her advice and brilliant suggestions are dotted throughout.

Thank-you to Nicole Bohannon of Northern High School in Maryland, for spotting a flaw in a difficult question, and taking the trouble to contact me about it.

Thank you to all of the computer science teachers throughout the country who took time to write to me with suggestions for this new edition.

My husband, Saul, continues to be my partner in this project—typesetting the manuscript, producing the figures, and giving advice and moral support every step of the way. This book is dedicated to him.

Roselyn Teukolsky
Ithaca, NY
March 2007

Introduction

GENERAL INFORMATION ABOUT THE EXAM

The AP Computer Science exam is a three-hour written exam. No books, calculators, or computers are allowed! The exam consists of two parts that have equal weight:

- Section I: 40 multiple-choice questions in 1 hour and 15 minutes.
- Section II: 4 free-response questions in 1 hour and 45 minutes.

Section I is scored by machine—you will bubble your answers with a pencil on a mark-sense sheet. Each question correctly answered is worth 1 point, while incorrect answers get $\frac{1}{4}$ of a point deducted; a question left blank is ignored.

Section II is scored by human readers—you will write your answers in a booklet provided. Free-response questions typically involve writing methods in Java to solve a given problem. Sometimes there are questions analyzing algorithms or designing and modifying data structures. You may be asked to write or design an entire class. To ensure consistency in the grading, each grader follows the same rubric, and each of your four answers may be examined by more than one reader. Each question is worth 9 points, with partial credit awarded where applicable. Your name and school are hidden from the readers.

Your raw score for both sections is converted to an integer score from 1 to 5, where 1 represents "Not at all qualified" and 5 represents "Extremely well qualified." Be aware that the awarding of AP credit varies enormously from college to college.

The exam can be taken at two levels: Level A covers roughly a one-semester introductory college course, while Level AB covers roughly a two-semester course, including data structures. In terms of getting credit at colleges, it makes more sense to get a 4 or 5 on the Level A exam than a 2 or 3 on the Level AB exam.

The language of the AP exam is Java. Only a subset of the Java language will be tested on the exam. In writing your solutions to the free-response questions, however, you may use any Java features, including those that are not in the AP subset. For a complete description of this subset, see the College Board website at *http://www.collegeboard.com/student/testing/ap/subjects.html*. **Every language topic in this review book is part of the AP Java subset unless explicitly stated otherwise. Note that the entire subset is covered in the book, including some new features of Java 5.0 that will be tested on the AP exam, starting in May 2007.**

At least one free-response and five multiple-choice questions will be based on the GridWorld Case Study. The full text of the case study can be found at the College Board website.

At the exam, you will be given

- A copy of the testable case study code.

- A quick reference to the interfaces and "black box" classes of the case study, with lists of their required methods.

- A quick reference to the standard Java interfaces and classes with lists of their required methods.

- (Level AB only) A copy of the `ListNode` and `TreeNode` classes.

HINTS FOR TAKING THE EXAM

The Multiple-Choice Section

- Since $\frac{1}{4}$ of a point is deducted for each wrong answer, don't guess unless you can eliminate at least one choice.

- You have a little less than two minutes per question, so don't waste time on any given question. You can always come back to it if you have time at the end.

- Seemingly complicated array questions can often be solved by hand tracing the code with a small array, two or three elements. The same is true for other data structures such as matrices, stacks, queues, or linked lists.

- Many questions ask you to compare two pieces of code that supposedly implement the same algorithm. Often one program segment will fail because it doesn't handle endpoint conditions properly (e.g., `num == 0` or `list == null`). *Be aware of endpoint conditions throughout the exam.*

- Since the mark-sense sheet is scanned by machine, make sure that you erase completely if you change an answer.

The Free-Response Section

- Each free-response question is worth 9 points. Take a minute to read through the whole exam so that you can start with a question that you feel confident about. It gives you a psychological leg up to have a solid question in the bag.

- Don't omit a question just because you can't come up with a complete solution. Remember, partial credit is awarded. Also, if you can't do part (a) of a question, don't omit part (b)—they are graded independently.

- In writing solutions to a question, you must use the public methods of classes provided in that question wherever possible. If you write a significant chunk of code that can be replaced by a call to one of these methods, you will probably not receive full credit for the question.

- If an algorithm is suggested to solve a problem, just follow it. Don't reinvent the wheel.

- Don't waste time writing comments: the graders generally ignore them. The occasional brief comment that clarifies a segment of code is OK.

- Points are not deducted for inefficient code unless efficiency is an issue in the question.

- Most of the standard Java library methods are not included in the AP subset. They are accepted on the exam if you use them correctly. However, there is always an alternative solution that uses the AP subset and you should try to find it.

- Don't cross out an answer until you have written a replacement. Graders are instructed not to read anything crossed out, even if it would have gotten credit.

- Have some awareness that this section is graded by humans. It is in your interest to have the graders understand your solutions. With this in mind,

  - Use a sharp pencil, write legibly, space your answers, and indent correctly.
  - Use self-documenting names for variables, methods, and so on.
  - Use the identifiers that are given in a question. You will lose a usage point if you persist in using the wrong names.
  - Write clear readable code. This is your goal. Don't write one obscure convoluted statement when you can write two short clear statements. The APCS exam is not the place to demonstrate that you're a genius.

HOW TO USE THIS BOOK

Each chapter in the book contains a comprehensive review of a topic, multiple-choice questions that focus on the topic, and detailed explanations of answers. These focus questions help you to review parts of the Java subset that you should know. A few questions are not typical AP exam questions—for example, questions that test low-level details of syntax. Most of the focus questions, however, and all the multiple-choice questions in the practice exams are representative of actual exam questions.

You should also note that several groups of focus questions are preceded by a single piece of code to which the questions refer. Be aware that the AP exam will usually restrict the number of questions per code example to two.

In both the text and questions/explanations, a special code font is used for parts of the text that are Java code.

```
//This is an example of code font
```

A different font is used for pseudo-code.

< Here is pseudo-code font. >

Sections in the text and multiple-choice questions that are directed at Level AB only are clearly marked as such. Unmarked text and questions are suitable for both Levels A and AB. Chapters 8–11 are for Level AB only. This is stated on the first page of each of these chapters.

Six complete practice exams are provided, three each for Level A and level AB. Two of the exams are at the start of the book and may be used as diagnostic tests. They are accompanied by diagnostic charts that refer you to related topics in the review book. Two of the exams are on the optional CD-ROM provided with the book. The final two exams follow the review chapters near the end of the book.

Each of the six exams has an answer key, complete solutions and explanations for the free-response questions, and detailed explanations for the multiple-choice questions. There is no overlap in the questions, so Level AB students can use the Level A exams for additional practice. Some questions in the Level AB exams are also fair game for Level A students. These are clearly marked as such in the non-CD-ROM exams.

Each practice exam contains at least five multiple-choice questions and one free-response question on the GridWorld Case Study.

An answer sheet is provided for the Section I questions of each exam. When you have completed an entire exam, and have checked your answers, you may wish to calculate your approximate AP score. Use the scoring worksheet provided on the back of the answer sheet.

There are two appendices at the end of the book. Appendix A is a glossary of computer terms that occasionally crop up on the exam. Appendix B contains supplementary material that is not required for the exam.

A final hint about the book: Try the questions before you peek at the answers. Good luck!

PRACTICE EXAM ONE / LEVEL A DIAGNOSTIC TEST

The exam that follows has the same format as that used on the actual AP exam. There are two ways you may use it:

1. As a diagnostic test before you start reviewing. Following the answer key is a diagnostic chart that relates each question to sections that you should review. In addition, complete explanations are provided for each solution.
2. As a practice exam when you have completed your review.

   Complete solutions with explanations are provided for the free-response questions.

Answer Sheet: Practice Exam One

1. Ⓐ Ⓑ Ⓒ Ⓓ Ⓔ
2. Ⓐ Ⓑ Ⓒ Ⓓ Ⓔ
3. Ⓐ Ⓑ Ⓒ Ⓓ Ⓔ
4. Ⓐ Ⓑ Ⓒ Ⓓ Ⓔ
5. Ⓐ Ⓑ Ⓒ Ⓓ Ⓔ
6. Ⓐ Ⓑ Ⓒ Ⓓ Ⓔ
7. Ⓐ Ⓑ Ⓒ Ⓓ Ⓔ
8. Ⓐ Ⓑ Ⓒ Ⓓ Ⓔ
9. Ⓐ Ⓑ Ⓒ Ⓓ Ⓔ
10. Ⓐ Ⓑ Ⓒ Ⓓ Ⓔ
11. Ⓐ Ⓑ Ⓒ Ⓓ Ⓔ
12. Ⓐ Ⓑ Ⓒ Ⓓ Ⓔ
13. Ⓐ Ⓑ Ⓒ Ⓓ Ⓔ
14. Ⓐ Ⓑ Ⓒ Ⓓ Ⓔ

15. Ⓐ Ⓑ Ⓒ Ⓓ Ⓔ
16. Ⓐ Ⓑ Ⓒ Ⓓ Ⓔ
17. Ⓐ Ⓑ Ⓒ Ⓓ Ⓔ
18. Ⓐ Ⓑ Ⓒ Ⓓ Ⓔ
19. Ⓐ Ⓑ Ⓒ Ⓓ Ⓔ
20. Ⓐ Ⓑ Ⓒ Ⓓ Ⓔ
21. Ⓐ Ⓑ Ⓒ Ⓓ Ⓔ
22. Ⓐ Ⓑ Ⓒ Ⓓ Ⓔ
23. Ⓐ Ⓑ Ⓒ Ⓓ Ⓔ
24. Ⓐ Ⓑ Ⓒ Ⓓ Ⓔ
25. Ⓐ Ⓑ Ⓒ Ⓓ Ⓔ
26. Ⓐ Ⓑ Ⓒ Ⓓ Ⓔ
27. Ⓐ Ⓑ Ⓒ Ⓓ Ⓔ
28. Ⓐ Ⓑ Ⓒ Ⓓ Ⓔ

29. Ⓐ Ⓑ Ⓒ Ⓓ Ⓔ
30. Ⓐ Ⓑ Ⓒ Ⓓ Ⓔ
31. Ⓐ Ⓑ Ⓒ Ⓓ Ⓔ
32. Ⓐ Ⓑ Ⓒ Ⓓ Ⓔ
33. Ⓐ Ⓑ Ⓒ Ⓓ Ⓔ
34. Ⓐ Ⓑ Ⓒ Ⓓ Ⓔ
35. Ⓐ Ⓑ Ⓒ Ⓓ Ⓔ
36. Ⓐ Ⓑ Ⓒ Ⓓ Ⓔ
37. Ⓐ Ⓑ Ⓒ Ⓓ Ⓔ
38. Ⓐ Ⓑ Ⓒ Ⓓ Ⓔ
39. Ⓐ Ⓑ Ⓒ Ⓓ Ⓔ
40. Ⓐ Ⓑ Ⓒ Ⓓ Ⓔ

How to Calculate Your (Approximate) AP Score — AP Computer Science Level A

Multiple Choice

Number correct (out of 40)   =   _____

$1/4 \times$ number wrong   =   _____

Raw score = line 1 − line 2   =   _____ $\Longleftarrow$ Multiple-Choice Score
(Do not round. If less than zero, enter zero.)

Free Response

Question 1   _____
(out of 9)

Question 2   _____
(out of 9)

Question 3   _____
(out of 9)

Question 4   _____
(out of 9)

Total   _____   × 1.11 =   _____ $\Longleftarrow$ Free-Response Score
(Do not round.)

Final Score

_____   +   _____   =   _____

Multiple-   Free-   Final Score
Choice   Response   (Round to nearest
Score   Score   whole number.)

Chart to Convert to AP Grade
Computer Science A

Final Score Range	AP Grade[a]
60–80	5
45–59	4
33–44	3
25–32	2
0–24	1

[a]The score range corresponding to each grade varies from exam to exam and is approximate.

Practice Exam One
COMPUTER SCIENCE A
SECTION I

Time—1 hour and 15 minutes
Number of questions—40
Percent of total grade—50

Directions: Determine the answer to each of the following questions or in-complete statements, using the available space for any necessary scratchwork. Then decide which is the best of the choices given and fill in the corresponding oval on the answer sheet. Do not spend too much time on any one problem.

Notes:
- Assume that the classes in the Quick Reference have been imported where needed.
- Assume that variables and methods are declared within the context of an enclosing class.
- Assume that method calls that have no object or class name prefixed, and that are not shown within a complete class definition, appear within the context of an enclosing class.
- Assume that parameters in method calls are not null unless otherwise stated.

1. Consider this inheritance hierarchy, in which `Novel` and `Textbook` are subclasses of `Book`.

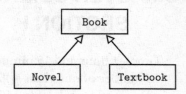

Which of the following is a *false* statement about the classes shown?
(A) The `Textbook` class can have private instance variables that are neither in `Book` nor `Novel`.
(B) Each of the classes—`Book`, `Novel`, and `Textbook`—can have a method `computeShelfLife`, whose code in `Book` and `Novel` is identical, but different from the code in `Textbook`.
(C) If the `Book` class has private instance variables `myTitle` and `myAuthor`, then `Novel` and `Textbook` inherit them but cannot directly access them.
(D) Both `Novel` and `Textbook` inherit the constructors in `Book`.
(E) If the `Book` class has a private method called `readFile`, this method may not be accessed in either the `Novel` or `Textbook` classes.

2. A programmer is designing a program to catalog all books in a library. He plans to have a Book class that stores features of each book: author, title, isOnShelf, and so on, with operations like getAuthor, getTitle, getShelfInfo, and setShelfInfo. Another class, LibraryList, will store an array of Book objects. The LibraryList class will include operations such as listAllBooks, addBook, removeBook, and searchForBook. The programmer plans to implement and test the Book class first, before implementing the LibraryList class. The programmer's plan to write the Book class first is an example of

   (A) top-down development.
   (B) bottom-up development.
   (C) procedural abstraction.
   (D) information hiding.
   (E) a driver program.

GO ON TO THE NEXT PAGE.

Questions 3–5 refer to the Card and Deck classes shown below.

```java
public class Card
{
    private String mySuit;
    private int myValue;        //0 to 12

    public Card(String suit, int value)
    { /* implementation */ }

    public String getSuit()
    { return mySuit; }

    public int getValue()
    { return myValue; }

    public String toString()
    {
        String faceValue = "";
        if (myValue == 11)
            faceValue = "J";
        else if (myValue == 12)
            faceValue = "Q";
        else if (myValue == 0)
            faceValue = "K";
        else if (myValue == 1)
            faceValue = "A";
        if (myValue >= 2 && myValue <= 10)
            return myValue + " of " + mySuit;
        else
            return faceValue + " of " + mySuit;
    }
}

public class Deck
{
    private Card[] myDeck;
    public final static int NUMCARDS = 52;

    public Deck()
    { ...

    //Simulate shuffling the deck.
    public void shuffle()
    { ...

    //other methods not shown ...
}
```

3. Which of the following represents correct /* *implementation* */ code for the constructor in the `Card` class?

   (A) `mySuit = suit;`
   `myValue = value;`

   (B) `suit = mySuit;`
   `value = myValue;`

   (C) `Card = new Card(mySuit, myValue);`

   (D) `Card = new Card(suit, value);`

   (E) `mySuit = getSuit();`
   `myValue = getValue();`

4. Consider this description of the `Deck` constructor:
   A `Deck` object will be constructed as follows:
   `myDeck[0]...myDeck[12]` will contain the spade suit
   `myDeck[13]...myDeck[25]` will contain the heart suit
   `myDeck[26]...myDeck[38]` will contain the diamond suit
   `myDeck[39]...myDeck[51]` will contain the club suit
   In each suit the card values range from 0 to 12. (These are converted to actual card values in the `toString` method of the `Card` class.) Here is the constructor for the `Deck` class:

   ```
   public Deck()
   {
         < declaration of the myDeck array >

         for (int i = 0; i < NUMCARDS; i++)
         {
               /* code to insert the spade cards into myDeck */
               /* code to insert the heart cards into myDeck */
               /* code to insert the diamond cards into myDeck */
               /* code to insert the club cards into myDeck */
         }
   }
   ```

   Which of the following is a correct replacement for /* *code to insert the heart cards into* `myDeck` */, so that the specification for the `myDeck` array is satisfied?

   (A) `if (i / 13 == 1)`
   `myDeck[i / 13] = new Card("hearts", i % 13);`

   (B) `if (i >= 13 && i <= 25)`
   `myDeck[i % 13] = new Card("hearts", i % 13);`

   (C) `if (i / 13 == 1)`
   `myDeck[i] = new Card("hearts", i % 13);`

   (D) `if (i >= 13 && i <= 25)`
   `myDeck[i] = new Card("hearts", i / 13);`

   (E) `if (i / 13 == 1)`
   `myDeck[i % 13] = new Card("hearts", i % 13);`

GO ON TO THE NEXT PAGE.

5. Consider the implementation of a `writeDeck` method that is added to the `Deck` class.

```
//Write the cards in myDeck, one per line.
public void writeDeck()
{
    /* implementation code */
}
```

Which of the following is correct /* *implementation code* */?

  I `System.out.println(myDeck);`

 II `for (Card card : myDeck)`
        `System.out.println(card);`

III `for (Card card : myDeck)`
        `System.out.println((String) card);`

(A) I only
(B) II only
(C) III only
(D) I and III only
(E) II and III only

Refer to the following class for Questions 6 and 7.

```
public class Tester
{
    private int[] testArray = {3, 4, 5};

    //Add 1 to n.
    public void increment (int n)
    { n++; }

    public void firstTestMethod()
    {
        for (int i = 0; i < testArray.length; i++)
        {
            increment(testArray[i]);
            System.out.print(testArray[i] + " ");
        }
    }

    public void secondTestMethod()
    {
        for (int element : testArray)
        {
            increment(element);
            System.out.print(element + " ");
        }
    }
}
```

6. What output will be produced by invoking `firstTestMethod` for a `Tester` object?
    (A) 3 4 5
    (B) 4 5 6
    (C) 5 6 7
    (D) 0 0 0
    (E) No output will be produced. An `ArrayIndexOutOfBoundsException` will be thrown.

7. What output will be produced by invoking `secondTestMethod` for a `Tester` object, assuming that `testArray` contains 3,4,5?
    (A) 3 4 5
    (B) 4 5 6
    (C) 5 6 7
    (D) 0 0 0
    (E) No output will be produced. An `ArrayIndexOutOfBoundsException` will be thrown.

8. Consider the following loop, where n is some positive integer.

```
for (int i = 0; i < n; i += 2)
{
    if (/* test */)
        /* perform some action */
}
```

In terms of n, which Java expression represents the maximum number of times that
/* *perform some action* */ could be executed?
(A) n / 2
(B) (n + 1) / 2
(C) n
(D) n - 1
(E) (n - 1) / 2

9. A method is to be written to search an array for a value that is larger than a given item and return its index. The problem specification does not indicate what should be returned if there are several such values in the array. Which of the following actions would be best?
   (A) The method should be written on the assumption that there is only one value in the array that is larger than the given item.
   (B) The method should be written so as to return the index of every occurrence of a larger value.
   (C) The specification should be modified to indicate what should be done if there is more than one index of larger values.
   (D) The method should be written to output a message if more than one larger value is found.
   (E) The method should be written to delete all subsequent larger items after a suitable index is returned.

10. When will method whatIsIt cause a stack overflow (i.e., cause computer memory to be exhausted)?

```
public static int whatIsIt(int x, int y)
{
    if (x > y)
        return x * y;
    else
        return whatIsIt(x - 1, y);
}
```

(A) Only when $x < y$
(B) Only when $x \le y$
(C) Only when $x > y$
(D) For all values of x and y
(E) The method will never cause a stack overflow.

11. The boolean expression a[i] == max || !(max != a[i]) can be simplified to
(A) a[i] == max
(B) a[i] != max
(C) a[i] < max || a[i] > max
(D) true
(E) false

12. Suppose the characters $0, 1, \ldots, 8, 9, A, B, C, D, E, F$ are used to represent a hexadecimal (base-16) number. Here $A = 10$, $B = 11, \ldots, F = 15$. What is the largest base-10 integer that can be represented with a two-digit hexadecimal number, such as 14 or 3A?
(A) 32
(B) 225
(C) 255
(D) 256
(E) 272

13. Consider a Clown class that has a default constructor. Suppose a list ArrayList<Clown> list is initialized. Which of the following will *not* cause an IndexOutOfBoundsException to be thrown?

(A) for (int i = 0; i <= list.size(); i++)
        list.set(i, new Clown());

(B) list.add(list.size(), new Clown());

(C) Clown c = list.get(list.size());

(D) Clown c = list.remove(list.size());

(E) list.add(-1, new Clown());

GO ON TO THE NEXT PAGE.

Questions 14–16 refer to the Point, Quadrilateral, and Rectangle classes below:

```
public class Point
{
    private int xCoord;
    private int yCoord;

    //constructor
    public Point(int x, int y)
    {
        ...
    }

    //accessors

    public int get_x()
    {
        ...
    }

    public int get_y()
    {
        ...
    }

    //other methods not shown ...

}

public abstract class Quadrilateral
{
    private String myLabels;     //e.g., "ABCD"

    //constructor
    public Quadrilateral(String labels)
    { myLabels = labels; }

    public String getLabels()
    { return myLabels; }

    public abstract int perimeter();
    public abstract int area();
}
```

GO ON TO THE NEXT PAGE.

```
public class Rectangle extends Quadrilateral
{
    private Point myTopLeft;    //coords of top left corner
    private Point myBotRight;   //coords of bottom right corner

    //constructor
    public Rectangle(String labels, Point topLeft, Point botRight)
    { /* implementation code */ }

    public int perimeter()
    { /* implementation not shown */ }

    public int area()
    { /* implementation not shown */ }

    //other methods not shown ...
}
```

14. Which statement about the Quadrilateral class is *false*?
    (A) The perimeter and area methods are abstract because there's no suitable
        default code for them.
    (B) The getLabels method is not abstract because any subclasses of
        Quadrilateral will have the same code for this method.
    (C) If the Quadrilateral class is used in a program, it *must* be used as a super-
        class for at least one other class.
    (D) No instances of a Quadrilateral object can be created in a program.
    (E) Any subclasses of the Quadrilateral class *must* provide implementation
        code for the perimeter and area methods.

15. Which represents correct /* *implementation code* */ for the Rectangle construc-
    tor?

    I super(labels);

    II super(labels, topLeft, botRight);

    III super(labels);
        myTopLeft = topLeft;
        myBotRight = botRight;

    (A) I only
    (B) II only
    (C) III only
    (D) I and II only
    (E) II and III only

GO ON TO THE NEXT PAGE.

16. Refer to the `Parallelogram` and `Square` classes below.

```
public class Parallelogram extends Quadrilateral
{
    //private instance variables and constructor not shown
        . . .

    public int perimeter()
    { /* implementation not shown */ }

    public int area()
    { /* implementation not shown */ }
}

public class Square extends Rectangle
{
    //private instance variables and constructor not shown
        . . .

    public int perimeter()
    { /* implementation not shown */ }

    public int area()
    { /* implementation not shown */ }
}
```

Consider an `ArrayList<Quadrilateral>` `quadList` whose elements are of type `Rectangle`, `Parallelogram`, or `Square`.

Refer to the following method, `writeAreas`:

```
/* Precondition:  quadList contains Rectangle, Parallelogram, or
 *                Square objects in an unspecified order. */
public static void writeAreas(ArrayList quadList)
{
    for (Quadrilateral quad : quadList)
        System.out.println("Area of " + quad.getLabels()
            + " is " + quad.area());
}
```

What is the effect of executing this method?
(A) The area of each `Quadrilateral` in `quadList` will be printed.
(B) A compile-time error will occur, stating that there is no `area` method in abstract class `Quadrilateral`.
(C) A compile-time error will occur, stating that there is no `getLabels` method in classes `Rectangle`, `Parallelogram`, or `Square`.
(D) A `NullPointerException` will be thrown.
(E) A `ClassCastException` will be thrown.

17. Refer to the doSomething method:

```
// postcondition
public static void doSomething(ArrayList<SomeType> list, int i, int j)
{
    SomeType temp = list.get(i);
    list.set(i, list.get(j));
    list.set(j, temp);
}
```

Which best describes the *postcondition* for doSomething?
(A) Removes from list the objects indexed at i and j.
(B) Replaces in list the object indexed at i with the object indexed at j.
(C) Replaces in list the object indexed at j with the object indexed at i.
(D) Replaces in list the objects indexed at i and j with temp.
(E) Interchanges in list the objects indexed at i and j.

18. Consider the NegativeReal class below, which defines a negative real number object.

```
public class NegativeReal
{
    private Double myNegReal;

    //constructor. Creates a NegativeReal object whose value is num.
    //Precondition: num < 0.
    public NegativeReal(double num)
    { /* implementation not shown */ }

    //Postcondition: Returns the value of this NegativeReal.
    public double getValue()
    { /* implementation not shown */ }

    //Postcondition: Returns this NegativeReal rounded to the nearest integer.
    public int getRounded()
    { /* implementation */ }
}
```

Here are some rounding examples:

Negative real number	Rounded to nearest integer
−3.5	−4
−8.97	−9
−5.0	−5
−2.487	−2
−0.2	0

Which /* *implementation* */ of getRounded produces the desired postcondition?
(A) return (int) (getValue() - 0.5);
(B) return (int) (getValue() + 0.5);
(C) return (int) getValue();
(D) return (double) (getValue() - 0.5);
(E) return (double) getValue();

GO ON TO THE NEXT PAGE.

19. Consider the following method.

```
public static void whatsIt(int n)
{
    if (n > 10)
        whatsIt(n / 10);
    System.out.print(n % 10);
}
```

What will be output as a result of the method call whatsIt(347)?
(A) 74
(B) 47
(C) 734
(D) 743
(E) 347

20. A large list of numbers is to be sorted into ascending order. Assuming that a "data movement" is a swap or reassignment of an element, which of the following is a *true* statement?
    (A) If the array is initially sorted in descending order, then insertion sort will be more efficient than selection sort.
    (B) The number of comparisons for selection sort is independent of the initial arrangement of elements.
    (C) The number of comparisons for insertion sort is independent of the initial arrangement of elements.
    (D) The number of data movements in selection sort depends on the initial arrangement of elements.
    (E) The number of data movements in insertion sort is independent of the initial arrangement of elements.

21. Refer to the definitions of ClassOne and ClassTwo below.

```
public class ClassOne
{
    public void methodOne()
    {
        . . .
    }

    //other methods not shown
}

public class ClassTwo extends ClassOne
{
    public void methodTwo()
    {
        . . .
    }

    //other methods not shown
}
```

Consider the following declarations in a client class. You may assume that ClassOne and ClassTwo have default constructors.

```
ClassOne c1 = new ClassOne();
ClassOne c2 = new ClassTwo();
```

Which of the following method calls will cause an error?

  I c1.methodTwo();

 II c2.methodTwo();

III c2.methodOne();

(A) None
(B) I only
(C) II only
(D) III only
(E) I and II only

22. Consider the code segment

```
if (n == 1)
    k++;
else if (n == 4)
    k += 4;
```

Suppose that the given segment is rewritten in the form

```
if (/* condition */)
    /* assignment statement */;
```

Given that n and k are integers and that the rewritten code performs the same task as the original code, which of the following could be used as

 (1) */* condition */*   and (2) */* assignment statement */?*

(A) (1) n == 1 && n == 4   (2) k += n

(B) (1) n == 1 && n == 4   (2) k += 4

(C) (1) n == 1 || n == 4   (2) k += 4

(D) (1) n == 1 || n == 4   (2) k += n

(E) (1) n == 1 || n == 4   (2) k = n - k

23. Which of the following will execute *without* throwing an exception?

 I
```
String s = null;
String t = "";
if (s.equals(t))
    System.out.println("empty strings?");
```

 II
```
String s = "holy";
String t = "moly";
if (s.equals(t))
    System.out.println("holy moly!");
```

 III
```
String s = "holy";
String t = s.substring(4);
System.out.println(s + t);
```

(A) I only
(B) II only
(C) III only
(D) I and II only
(E) II and III only

GO ON TO THE NEXT PAGE.

24. Three numbers a, b, and c are said to be a *Pythagorean Triple* if and only if the sum of the squares of two of the numbers equals the square of the third. A programmer writes a method isPythTriple to test if its three parameters form a Pythagorean Triple:

```
//Returns true if a * a + b * b == c * c; otherwise returns false.
public static boolean isPythTriple(double a, double b, double c)
{
    double d = Math.sqrt(a * a + b * b);
    return d == c;
}
```

When the method was tested with known Pythagorean Triples, isPythTriple sometimes erroneously returned false. What was the most likely cause of the error?

(A) Round-off error was caused by calculations with floating-point numbers.

(B) Type boolean was not recognized by an obsolete version of Java.

(C) An overflow error was caused by entering numbers that were too large.

(D) c and d should have been cast to integers before testing for equality.

(E) Bad test data were selected.

25. Refer to the following class, containing the mystery method.

```
public class SomeClass
{
    private int[] arr;

    //Constructor. Initializes arr to contain nonnegative
    // integers k such that 0 <= k <= 9.
    public SomeClass()
    { /* implementation not shown */ }

    public int mystery()
    {
        int value = arr[0];
        for (int i = 1; i < arr.length; i++)
            value = value * 10 + arr[i];
        return value;
    }
}
```

Which best describes what the mystery method does?

(A) It sums the elements of arr.

(B) It sums the products 10*arr[0]+10*arr[1]+⋯+10*arr[arr.length-1].

(C) It builds an integer of the form $d_1 d_2 d_3 \ldots d_n$, where $d_1 = $ arr[0], $d_2 = $ arr[1], ..., $d_n = $ arr[arr.length-1].

(D) It builds an integer of the form $d_1 d_2 d_3 \ldots d_n$, where $d_1 = $ arr[arr.length-1], $d_2 = $ arr[arr.length-2], ..., $d_n = $ arr[0].

(E) It converts the elements of arr to base-10.

GO ON TO THE NEXT PAGE.

Questions 26 and 27 refer to the search method in the Searcher class below.

```java
public class Searcher
{
    private int[] arr;

    //Constructor. Initializes arr with integers.
    public Searcher()
    { /* implementation not shown */ }

    /* Precondition:  arr[first]...arr[last] sorted in ascending order.
     * Postcondition: Returns index of key in arr. If key not in arr,
     *                returns -1. */
    public int search(int first, int last, int key)
    {
        int mid;
        while (first <= last)
        {
            mid = (first + last) / 2;
            if (arr[mid] == key)        //found key, exit search
                return mid;
            else if (arr[mid] < key)    //key to right of arr[mid]
                first = mid + 1;
            else                        //key to left of arr[mid]
                last = mid - 1;
        }
        return -1;                      //key not in list
    }
}
```

26. Which assertion is true just before each execution of the `while` loop?
    (A) `arr[first]` < key < `arr[last]`
    (B) `arr[first]` ≤ key ≤ `arr[last]`
    (C) `arr[first]` < key < `arr[last]` or key is not in arr
    (D) `arr[first]` ≤ key ≤ `arr[last]` or key is not in arr
    (E) key ≤ `arr[first]` or key ≥ `arr[last]` or key is not in arr

27. Consider the array a with values as shown:

    4, 7, 19, 25, 36, 37, 50, 100, 101, 205, 220, 271, 306, 321

    where 4 is a[0] and 321 is a[13]. Suppose that the search method is called with
    first = 0 and last = 13 to locate the key 205. How many iterations of the `while`
    loop must be made in order to locate it?
    (A) 3
    (B) 4
    (C) 5
    (D) 10
    (E) 13

GO ON TO THE NEXT PAGE.

28. Consider the following RandomList class.

```
public class RandomList
{
    private int[] myList;

    //constructor
    public RandomList()
    { myList = getList(); }

    /* Read random Integers from 0 to 100 inclusive into array list. */
    public int[] getList()
    {
        System.out.println("How many integers? ");
        int listLength = IO.readInt();      //read user input
        int[] list = int[listLength];
        for (int i = 0; i < listLength; i++)
        {
            /* code to add integer to list */
        }
        return list;
    }

    /* Print all elements of this list. */
    public void printList()
    { ...
}
```

Which represents correct /* *code to add* integer *to* list */?

(A) list[i] = (int) (Math.random() * 101);

(B) list.add((int) (Math.random() * 101));

(C) list[i] = (int) (Math.random() * 100);

(D) list.add(new Integer(Math.random() * 100))

(E) list[i] = (int) (Math.random() * 100) + 1;

GO ON TO THE NEXT PAGE.

Questions 29 and 30 refer to method `insert` described here. The `insert` method has two string parameters and one integer parameter. The method returns the string obtained by inserting the second string into the first starting at the position indicated by the integer parameter. For example, if `str1` contains xy and `str2` contains cat, then

```
insert(str1, str2, 0)   returns   catxy
insert(str1, str2, 1)   returns   xcaty
insert(str1, str2, 2)   returns   xycat
```

Here is the header for method `insert`.

```
//Precondition:  0 <= pos <= str1.length().
//Postcondition: Returns /* somestring */.
public static String insert(String str1, String str2, int pos);
```

29. If $str1 = a_0a_1\ldots a_{n-1}$ and $str2 = b_0b_1\ldots b_{m-1}$, which of the following is a correct replacement for /* *somestring* */?

(A) $a_0a_1\ldots a_{pos}b_0b_1\ldots b_{m-1}a_{pos+1}a_{pos+2}\cdots a_{n-1}$

(B) $a_0a_1\ldots a_{pos+1}b_0b_1\ldots b_{m-1}a_{pos+2}a_{pos+3}\cdots a_{n-1}$

(C) $a_0a_1\ldots a_{pos-1}b_0b_1\ldots b_{m-1}a_{pos}a_{pos+1}\cdots a_{n-1}$

(D) $a_0a_1\ldots a_{n-1}b_0b_1\ldots b_{m-1}$

(E) $a_0a_1\ldots a_{pos-1}b_0b_1\ldots b_{pos-1}a_{pos}a_{pos+1}\cdots a_{n-1}$

30. Method `insert` follows:

```
//Postcondition: Returns /* somestring */.
 public static String insert(String str1, String str2, int pos)
 {
     String first, last;
         /* more code */
     return first + str2 + last;
 }
```

Which of the following is a correct replacement for /* *more code* */?

```
(A) first = str1.substring(0, pos);
    last = str1.substring(pos);
```

```
(B) first = str1.substring(0, pos - 1);
    last = str1.substring(pos);
```

```
(C) first = str1.substring(0, pos + 1);
    last = str1.substring(pos + 1);
```

```
(D) first = str1.substring(0, pos);
    last = str1.substring(pos + 1, str1.length());
```

```
(E) first = str1.substring(0, pos);
    last = str1.substring(pos, str1.length() + 1);
```

Use the following program description for Questions 31–33.

A programmer plans to write a program that simulates a small bingo game (no more than six players). Each player will have a bingo card with 20 numbers from 0 to 90 (no duplicates). Someone will call out numbers one at a time, and each player will cross out a number on his card as it is called. The first player with all the numbers crossed out is the winner. In the simulation, as the game is in progress, each player's card is displayed on the screen.

The programmer envisions a short driver class whose main method has just two statements:

```
BingoGame b = new BingoGame();
b.playBingo();
```

The `BingoGame` class will have several objects: a `Display`, a `Caller`, and a `PlayerGroup`. The `PlayerGroup` will have a list of `Players`, and each `Player` will have a `BingoCard`.

31. The relationship between the `PlayerGroup` and `Player` classes is an example of
    (A) an interface.
    (B) encapsulation.
    (C) composition.
    (D) inheritance.
    (E) independent classes.

32. Which is a reasonable data structure for a `BingoCard` object? Recall that a `BingoCard` has 20 integers from 0 to 90, with no duplicates. There should also be mechanisms for crossing off numbers that are called, and for detecting a winning card (i.e., one where all the numbers have been crossed off).

    ```
    I int[] myBingoCard;     //will contain 20 integers
                    //myBingoCard[k] is crossed off by setting it to -1.
       int numCrossedOff;    //player wins when numCrossedOff reaches 20.

    II boolean[] myBingoCard;  //will contain 91 boolean values, of which
                               //20 are true. All the other values are false.
                               //Thus, if myBingoCard[k] is true, then k is
                               //on the card, 0 <= k <= 90. A number k is
                               //crossed off by changing the value of
                               //myBingoCard[k] to false.
       int numCrossedOff;    //player wins when numCrossedOff reaches 20.

    III ArrayList<Integer> myBingoCard;  //will contain 20 integers.
            //A number is crossed off by removing it from the ArrayList.
            //Player wins when myBingoCard.size() == 0.
    ```

    (A) I only
    (B) II only
    (C) III only
    (D) I and II only
    (E) I, II, and III

33. The programmer decides to use an `ArrayList<Integer>` to store the numbers to be called by the `Caller`:

```
public class Caller
{
    private ArrayList<Integer> myNumbers;

    //constructor
    public Caller()
    {
        myNumbers = getList();
        shuffleNumbers();
    }

    //Return the numbers 0...90 in order.
    private ArrayList<Integer> getList()
    { /* implementation not shown */ }

    //Shuffle the numbers.
    private void shuffleNumbers()
    { /* implementation not shown */ }
}
```

When the programmer tests the constructor of the `Caller` class she gets a `NullPointerException`. Which could be the cause of this error?

(A) The `Caller` object in the driver class was not created with `new`.

(B) The programmer forgot the `return` statement in `getList` that returns the list of `Integers`.

(C) The declaration of `myNumbers` is incorrect. It needed to be

    `private ArrayList<Integer> myNumbers = null;`

(D) In the `getList` method, an attempt was made to add an `Integer` to an `ArrayList` that had not been created with `new`.

(E) The `shuffleNumbers` algorithm went out of range, causing a `null Integer` to be shuffled into the `ArrayList`.

Questions 34–40 involve reasoning about the code from the GridWorld Case Study. A Quick Reference to the case study is provided as part of this exam. The actors in GridWorld are represented in this book with the pictures shown below. Each actor is shown facing north. These pictures almost certainly will be different from those used on the AP exam!

`Actor`   `Bug`   `Flower`   `Rock`   `Critter`   `ChameleonCritter`

34. Which is a *false* statement about `Bug` movement?
    (A) A `Bug` can move on a diagonal line across the grid.
    (B) If a `Flower` is directly in front of a `Bug`, the `Bug` will replace the `Flower` in the `Flower`'s location.
    (C) If a `Rock` is directly in front of a `Bug`, the `Bug` will not change its location.
    (D) If a `Bug` is at the edge of the grid, the `Bug` will change its direction to `Location.RIGHT` + its current direction.
    (E) It is possible for a `Bug` to turn through a complete circle without changing its location.

35. Consider an actor whose current direction is `Location.NORTHWEST`. The following method call is made for this actor:

    ```
    setDirection(getDirection() + Location.HALF_LEFT);
    ```

    What is the `int` value of the actor's resulting direction?
    (A) 0
    (B) 45
    (C) 90
    (D) 225
    (E) 270

36. Suppose `Bug` and `BoxBug` behavior will be modified to allow bugs and box bugs to move onto `Rocks` in the same way that they move onto `Flowers`. Which classes will need to be modified to effect this change?

    I `Actor`

    II `Bug`

    III `BoxBug`

    (A) I only
    (B) II only
    (C) III only
    (D) II and III only
    (E) I, II, and III

GO ON TO THE NEXT PAGE.

37. Consider the small bounded grid in the diagram.

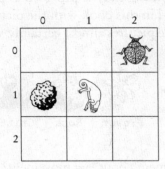

It shows a red `Bug` facing north at (0, 2); a black `Rock` at (1, 0); and a blue `ChameleonCritter` facing south at (1, 1). After one step of the simulation, the bug is facing northeast at location (0, 2), and the rock is still at location (1, 0). Which represents a legitimate state for the `ChameleonCritter`?
   (A) Color is blue, location is (2, 1), and direction is south.
   (B) Color is black, location is (1, 1), and direction is east.
   (C) Color is red, location is (1, 2), and direction is northeast.
   (D) Color is red, location is (0, 0), and direction is northwest.
   (E) Color is black, location is (2, 0), and direction is south.

38. The `moveTo` method of the `Actor` class would *not* be suitable for which of the following operations? You may assume that each scenario below is contained in the context of a two-dimensional grid.
   (A) Capturing a piece in Chess (namely, removing that piece from the board and taking its place on the board).
   (B) Moving a piece on a Checkers board into an empty location.
   (C) Rearranging the furniture in a room that has a rectangular floor plan.
   (D) Changing a reserved seat to another location in a theater that has a rectangular arrangement of seats.
   (E) Placing two monkeys in the same cage at a zoo, where the zoo has a rectangular arrangement of cages.

39. Consider the bounded grid shown, and the `Actor` in location (1, 1).

If it is the `Actor`'s turn to act, which are valid possibilities for a new location, if the `Actor` is a

(1) `Critter`

(2) `ChameleonCritter`

(A) (1) (0, 0), (2, 0), (2, 1), (2, 2), (1, 2), (0, 2)
    (2) (2, 1), (2, 2), (0, 2)

(B) (1) (0, 0), (2, 0), (1, 2)
    (2) (3, 0), (3, 1), (2, 1), (2, 2), (3, 3), (2, 3), (1, 3), (0, 2), (0, 3)

(C) (1) (0, 0), (0, 1), (0, 2), (1, 0), (1, 2), (2, 0), (2, 1), (2, 2)
    (2) (2, 1), (2, 2), (0, 2)

(D) (1) (0, 0), (0, 1), (1, 1), (1, 2), (2, 0), (3, 2)
    (2) (3, 0), (3, 1), (2, 1), (2, 2), (3, 3), (2, 3), (1, 3), (0, 2), (0, 3)

(E) (1) (0, 0), (0, 1), (0, 2), (1, 2), (2, 0), (2, 1), (2, 2)
    (2) (0, 2), (2, 0), (2, 1), (2, 2)

40. Suppose the program is changed so that a `Critter` is allowed to age. A `Critter` will start out at age 1, and have its age incremented by 1 each time it acts. To make this change, a private instance variable age is added to the `Critter` class, as well as an accessor method, `getAge`. A constructor is provided that initializes age to 1. What other changes must be made?

    I The act method of the `Actor` class must be modified.

    II The act method of the `Critter` class must be modified.

    III The act method of the `ChameleonCritter` class must be overridden.

    (A) I only
    (B) II only
    (C) III only
    (D) I and II only
    (E) I, II, and III

END OF SECTION I

COMPUTER SCIENCE A
SECTION II

Time—1 hour and 45 minutes
Number of questions—4
Percent of total grade—50

Directions: SHOW ALL YOUR WORK. REMEMBER THAT
PROGRAM SEGMENTS ARE TO BE WRITTEN IN Java.

Write your answers in <u>pencil only</u> in the booklet provided.

Notes:

- Assume that the classes in the Quick Reference have been imported where needed.

- Unless otherwise stated, assume that parameters in method calls are not `null` and that methods are called only when their preconditions are satisfied.

- In writing solutions for each question, you may use any of the accessible methods that are listed in classes defined in that question. Writing significant amounts of code that can be replaced by a call to one of these methods may not receive full credit.

---

1. Consider the problem of designing a `StockItem` class to model items in stock on the shelf of a store. Each stock item includes the following:

   - A description of the item.
   - An identity number that is a positive integer.
   - A price in dollars, rounded to the nearest cent (two decimal places).
   - The number of this particular item on the shelf.

   When a new stock item is created, it must be assigned a description, an identity number, a price, and the number on the shelf. Operations on a stock item include the following:

   - Retrieve the description of the item.
   - Retrieve the identity number of the item.
   - Retrieve the price of the item.
   - Retrieve the number of this item on the shelf.
   - Set a new price for the item.
   - Remove some quantity of this item from the shelf (if an attempt is made to remove more than the number on the shelf, all are removed).
   - Add some quantity of this item to the shelf.

GO ON TO THE NEXT PAGE.

(a) Write the class declaration for the `StockItem` class. In writing this class you must
  - Choose appropriate method names.
  - Provide the functionality specified above.
  - Provide a data representation consistent with the specification above.

Do not write implementation code for the methods or constructor(s) of the `StockItem` class. Write {*implementation*} under the header. For example, suppose you have a method `changeDescription`. You would indicate it like this:

```
public void changeDescription(String newDescription)
{ implementation }
```

(b) Consider the class `Store`, which represents a list of all the `StockItem` objects in the store. The `Store` class is partially specified below:

```
public class Store
{
    private ArrayList<StockItem> myStockList;    //all stock items
                                                 //in this store
    //constructors and other methods not shown
        ...

    //Precondition:  myStockList contains StockItem with
    //               identity number idNum.
    //Postcondition: All instances of StockItem with identity
    //               number idNum have been completely removed
    //               from the shelf. This StockItem, however,
    //               is still in myStockList.
    public void removeAll(int idNum)
    { /* to be implemented in this part */ }
}
```

Write the `Store` method `removeAll`, which searches for the `StockItem` in `myStockList` whose identity number matches `idNum` and removes all instances of that item from the shelf. You may assume that `myStockList` does contain the `StockItem` with identity number `idNum`.

In writing `removeAll`, you may use any of the methods of the `StockItem` class that you specified in part (a).

Complete method `removeAll` below:

```
//Precondition:  myStockList contains StockItem with
//               identity number idNum.
//Postcondition: All instances of StockItem with identity
//               number idNum have been completely removed
//               from the shelf. This StockItem, however,
//               is still in myStockList.
public void removeAll(int idNum)
```

2. A WordSet, shown in the class declaration below, stores a set of String objects in no particular order and contains no duplicates. Each word is a sequence of capital letters only.

```
public class WordSet
{
    //private data members not shown
        ...
    //Constructor initializes set to empty.
    public WordSet()
    { /* implementation not shown */ }

    //Returns number of words in set.
    public int size()
    { /* implementation not shown */ }

    //Adds word to set (no duplicates).
    public void insert(String word)
    { /* implementation not shown */ }

    //Removes word from set if present, else does nothing.
    public void remove(String word)
    { /* implementation not shown */ }

    //Returns kth word in alphabetical order, where 1 <= k <= size().
    public String findkth(int k)
    { /* implementation not shown */ }

    //Returns true if set contains word, false otherwise.
    public boolean contains(String word)
    { /* implementation not shown */ }
}
```

The findkth method returns the kth word in alphabetical order in the set, even though the implementation of WordSet may not be sorted. The number k ranges from 1 (corresponding to first in alphabetical order) to N, where N is the number of words in the set. For example, if WordSet s stores the words {"GRAPE", "PEAR", "FIG", "APPLE"}, here are the values when s.findkth(k) is called.

k	values of s.findkth(k)
1	APPLE
2	FIG
3	GRAPE
4	PEAR

(a) Write a client method countA that returns the number of words in WordSet s that begin with the letter "A." In writing countA, you may call any of the methods of the WordSet class. Assume that the methods work as specified.

Complete method countA below.

```
//Postcondition: Returns the number of words in s that begin
//                with "A."
public static int countA(WordSet s)
```

(b) Write a client method removeA that removes all words that begin with "A." If there are no such words in s, then removeA does nothing. In writing removeA, you may call method countA specified in part (a). Assume that countA works as specified, regardless of what you wrote in part (a).

Complete method removeA below:

```
//Postcondition: WordSet s contains no words that begin with "A",
//                but is otherwise unchanged.
public static void removeA(WordSet s)
```

(c) Write a client method commonElements that returns the WordSet containing just those elements occurring in both of its WordSet parameters.

For example, if s1 is {"BE", "NOT", "AFRAID"} and s2 is {"TO", "BE", "OR", "NOT"}, then commonElements(s1, s2) should return the WordSet {"BE", "NOT"}. (If you are familiar with mathematical set theory, commonElements returns the intersection of s1 and s2.)

Complete method commonElements below.

```
//Postcondition: Returns the set containing only the elements
//                that occur in both s1 and s2.
public static WordSet commonElements(WordSet s1, WordSet s2)
```

3. This question refers to the `Sentence` class below. Note: A *word* is a string of consecutive nonblank (and nonwhitespace) characters. For example, the sentence

"Hello there!" she said.

consists of the four words

```
"Hello       there!"    she     said.
```

```java
public class Sentence
{
    private String mySentence;
    private int myNumWords;

    //Constructor.  Creates sentence from String str.
    //              Finds the number of words in sentence.
    //Precondition: Words in str separated by exactly one blank.
    public Sentence(String str)
    { /* to be implemented in part (a) */ }

    public int getNumWords()
    { return myNumWords; }

    public String getSentence()
    { return mySentence; }

    //Returns copy of String s with all blanks removed.
    //Postcondition: Returned string contains just one word.
    private static String removeBlanks(String s)
    { /* implementation not shown */ }

    //Returns copy of String s with all letters in lowercase.
    //Postcondition: Number of words in returned string equals
    //               number of words in s.
    private static String lowerCase(String s)
    { /* implementation not shown */ }

    //Returns copy of String s with all punctuation removed.
    //Postcondition: Number of words in returned string equals
    //               number of words in s.
    private static String removePunctuation(String s)
    { /* implementation not shown */ }
}
```

(a) Complete the `Sentence` constructor as started below. The constructor assigns str to mySentence. You should write the subsequent code that assigns a value to myNumWords, the number of words in mySentence.

Complete the constructor below:

```java
//Constructor.  Creates sentence from String str.
//              Finds the number of words in sentence.
//Precondition: Words in str separated by exactly one blank.
public Sentence(String str)
{
    mySentence = str;
```

(b) Consider the problem of testing whether a string is a palindrome. A *palindrome* reads the same from left to right and right to left, ignoring spaces, punctuation, and capitalization. For example,

> A Santa lived as a devil at NASA.
> Flo, gin is a sin! I golf.
> Eva, can I stab bats in a cave?

A public method `isPalindrome` is added to the `Sentence` class. Here is the method and its implementation:

```
//Returns true if mySentence is a palindrome, false otherwise.
public boolean isPalindrome()
{
    String temp = removeBlanks(mySentence);
    temp = removePunctuation(temp);
    temp = lowerCase(temp);
    return isPalindrome(temp, 0, temp.length() - 1);
}
```

The overloaded `isPalindrome` method contained in the code is a private recursive helper method, also added to the `Sentence` class. You are to write the implementation of this method. It takes a "purified" string as a parameter, namely one that has been stripped of blanks and punctuation and is all lowercase letters. It also takes as parameters the first and last index of the string. It returns true if this "purified" string is a palindrome, false otherwise.

A recursive algorithm for testing if a string is a palindrome is as follows:

- If the string has length 0 or 1, it's a palindrome.
- Remove the first and last letters.
- If those two letters are the same, and the remaining string is a palindrome, then the original string is a palindrome. Otherwise it's not.

Complete the `isPalindrome` method below:

```
/* Private recursive helper method that tests whether a substring
 * of string s is a palindrome.
 * start is the index of the first character of the substring.
 * end is the index of the last character of the substring.
 * Precondition:  s contains no spaces, punctuation, or capitals.
 * Postcondition: Returns true if the substring is a palindrome,
 *                false otherwise. */
private static boolean isPalindrome(String s, int start, int end)
```

GO ON TO THE NEXT PAGE.

4. This question involves reasoning about the code from the GridWorld Case Study. A Quick Reference to the case study is provided as part of this exam.

Consider defining a new kind of `ChameleonCritter`, a `HungryChameleon`, that attempts to eat a `Bug` when it acts. If it succeeds in eating a bug, a `HungryChameleon` does not change color. If it fails to eat, then it changes color in the same way a `ChameleonCritter` does. After eating or changing color, a `HungryChameleon` moves like a `ChameleonCritter`. Here is a partial definition of the class `HungryChameleon`.

```
/**
 * A HungryChameleon eats neighboring bugs if there are any;
 * otherwise it takes on the color of neighboring actors as it
 * moves through the grid.
 */
public class HungryChameleon extends ChameleonCritter
{
    /**
     * Gets a list of adjacent bugs.
     * @param actors the list of all adjacent neighbors
     * @return a list of adjacent bugs
     */
    private ArrayList<Bug> getBugs(ArrayList<Actor> actors)
    { /* to be implemented in part (a) */ }

    /**
     * Randomly "eats" one of the bugs in the list of bugs.
     * Precondition: bugs.size() > 0.
     * @param bugs the list of adjacent bugs
     */
    private void eatBug(ArrayList<Bug> bugs)
    { /* to be implemented in part (b) */ }

    /**
     * Gets a list of adjacent neighboring bugs and eats one.
     * If there are no bugs to eat, the HungryChameleon takes
     * on the color of a neighboring actor.
     * @param actors the list of all adjacent neighbors
     */
    public void processActors(ArrayList<Actor> actors)
    { /* to be implemented in part (c) */ }
}
```

(a) Write the private `HungryChameleon` method `getBugs`. This method should return a list of adjacent neighboring actors that are bugs.

   Complete method `getBugs` below.

```
/**
 * Gets a list of adjacent bugs.
 * @param actors the list of all adjacent neighbors
 * @return a list of adjacent bugs
 */
private ArrayList<Bug> getBugs(ArrayList<Actor> actors)
```

(b) Write the private `HungryChameleon` method `eatBug`. Method `eatBug` randomly selects a `Bug` from its bugs parameter and "eats" (i.e. removes) it. Complete method `eatBug` below.

```
/**
 * Randomly "eats" one of the bugs in the list of bugs.
 * Precondition: bugs.size() > 0.
 * @param bugs the list of adjacent bugs
 */
private void eatBug(ArrayList<Bug> bugs)
```

(c) Override the `processActors` method of the `ChameleonCritter` superclass. A `HungryChameleon` processes actors by getting a list of neighboring bugs and randomly selecting one to eat. If there are no bugs to eat, the `HungryChameleon` takes on the color of one of its neighbors, behaving just like a `ChameleonCritter`.
Complete method `processActors` below.

```
/**
 * Gets a list of adjacent neighboring bugs and eats one.
 * If there are no bugs to eat, the HungryChameleon takes
 * on the color of a neighboring actor.
 * @param actors the list of all adjacent neighbors
 */
public void processActors(ArrayList<Actor> actors)
```

END OF EXAMINATION

ANSWER KEY (Section I)

1. D	15. C	29. C
2. B	16. A	30. A
3. A	17. E	31. C
4. C	18. A	32. E
5. B	19. E	33. D
6. A	20. B	34. D
7. A	21. E	35. E
8. B	22. D	36. B
9. C	23. E	37. D
10. B	24. A	38. E
11. A	25. C	39. A
12. C	26. D	40. B
13. B	27. B	
14. E	28. A	

DIAGNOSTIC CHART FOR LEVEL A EXAM

Each multiple-choice question has a complete explanation (p. 40).

The following table relates each question to sections that you should review. For any given question, the topic(s) in the chart represent the concept(s) tested in the question. These topics are explained on the corresponding page(s) in the chart and should provide further insight into answering that question.

Question	Topic	Page
1	Inheritance	190
2	Implementing classes	265
3	Constructors	151
4	Div and mod operators	120
5	The `toString` method	227
	`ClassCastException`	195
6	Passing parameters	291
7	Passing parameters	291
8	`for` loop	128
9	Program specification	261
10	Recursion	339
11	Boolean expressions	123
12	Hexadecimal	119
13	`IndexOutOfBoundsException` for `ArrayList`	298
14	Abstract classes	196
15	Subclass constructors and `super` keyword	190
16	Polymorphism	193
17	`swap` method	292
18	Rounding real numbers	118
19	Recursion	342
20	Selection and insertion sort	524
21	Subclass method calls	195
22	Compound Boolean expressions	123
23	`String` class `equals` method	229
	`String` class `substring` method	231
24	Round-off error	119
25	Array processing	290
26	Assertions about algorithms	269
	Binary search	535
27	Binary search	535
28	Random integers	236
29	Postconditions	270
30	`String` class `substring` method	231
31	Relationships between classes	268
32	Array of objects	294
	`ArrayList`	297
33	`NullPointerException`	158
34	Bug movement	570
35	Location constants	566
36	Bug class	570
	Inheritance	190
37	`ChameleonCritter` description	575
38	`moveTo` method of `Actor` class	570
39	Critter class	573
	`ChameleonCritter` class	575
40	Critter class	573
	Inheritance	190

ANSWERS EXPLAINED (Section I)

1. **(D)** Constructors are never inherited. If a subclass has no constructor, the default constructor for the superclass is generated. If the superclass does not have a default constructor, a compile-time error will occur.

2. **(B)** The programmer is using an object-oriented approach to writing the program and plans to test the simplest classes first. This is bottom-up development. In *top-down* development (choice A), high-level classes are broken down into subsidiary classes. Procedural abstraction (choice C) is the use of helper methods in a class. Information hiding (choice D) is restriction of access to private data and methods in a class. Choice E is wrong because a driver program is one whose sole purpose is to test a given method or class. Implementing the simplest classes first may involve driver programs that test the various methods, but the overall plan is not an example of a driver program.

3. **(A)** In the constructor, the private instance variables `mySuit` and `myValue` must be initialized to the appropriate parameter values. Choice A is the only choice that does this.

4. **(C)** Spades are represented by `myDeck[0]...myDeck[12]`. Hearts are represented by `myDeck[13]...myDeck[25]`. Therefore the correct test for hearts is `if(i/13 == 1)` and the correct assignment is `myDeck[i] = ....` The expression on the right-hand side must use the `Card` constructor. The correct `Card` value (second parameter) is an `int` from 0 to 12. This is correctly obtained with `i % 13`.

5. **(B)** Implementation II invokes the `toString` method of the `Card` class. Implementation I fails because there is no default `toString` method for arrays. Implementation III will cause a `ClassCastException`: You cannot cast a `Card` to a `String`.

6. **(A)** The array will not be changed by the `increment` method. Here are the memory slots:

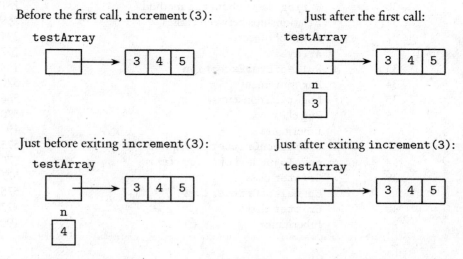

The same analysis applies to the method calls `increment(4)` and `increment(5)`.

7. **(A)** As in the previous question, the array will not be changed by the `increment` method. Nor will the local variable `element`! What *will* be changed by `increment` is the copy of the parameter during each pass through the loop.

8. **(B)** The maximum number will be achieved if /* *test* */ is true in each pass through the loop. So the question boils down to: How many times is the loop executed? Try one odd and one even value of n:

$$\text{If } n = 7, \quad i = 0, 2, 4, 6 \qquad \text{Ans} = 4$$
$$\text{If } n = 8, \quad i = 0, 2, 4, 6 \qquad \text{Ans} = 4$$

Notice that choice B is the only expression that works for both n = 7 and n = 8.

9. **(C)** Here is one of the golden rules of programming: Don't start planning the program until every aspect of the specification is crystal clear. A programmer should never make unilateral decisions about ambiguities in a specification.

10. **(B)** When x ≤ y, a recursive call is made to whatIsIt(x-1, y). If x decreases at every recursive call, there is no way to reach a successful base case. Thus, the method never terminates and eventually exhausts all available memory.

11. **(A)** The expression !(max != a[i]) is equivalent to max == a[i], so the given expression is equivalent to a[i] == max || max == a[i], which is equivalent to a[i] == max.

12. **(C)** A base-b number can be represented with b characters. Thus, base-2 uses 0,1 for example, and base-10 uses $0, 1, \ldots, 8, 9$. A hexadecimal (base-16) number is represented with 16 characters: $0, 1, \ldots, 8, 9, A, B, C, D, E, F$, where $A = 10, B = 11, \ldots, F = 15$. The largest two-place base-2 integer is

$$11 = 1 \times 2^0 + 1 \times 2^1 = 3$$

The largest two-place base-10 integer is

$$99 = 9 \times 10^0 + 9 \times 10^1$$

The largest two-place base-16 integer is

$$FF = F \times 16^0 + F \times 16^1$$

The character F represents 15, so

$$FF = 15 \times 16^0 + 15 \times 16^1 = 255$$

Here's another way to think about this problem: Each hex digit is 4 binary digits (bits), since $16 = 2^4$. Therefore a two-digit hex number is 8 bits. The largest base-10 number that can be represented with 8 bits is $2^8 - 1 = 255$.

13. **(B)** The index range for ArrayList is $0 \le \text{index} \le \text{size()-1}$. Thus, for methods get, remove, and set, the last in-bounds index is size()-1. The one exception is the add method—to add an element to the end of the list takes an index parameter list.size().

14. **(E)** Subclasses of Quadrilateral may also be abstract, in which case they will inherit perimeter and/or area as abstract methods.

15. **(C)** Segment I starts correctly but fails to initialize the additional private variables of the Rectangle class. Segment II is wrong because by using super with topLeft and botRight, it implies that these values are used in the Quadrilateral superclass. This is false—there isn't even a constructor with three arguments in the superclass.

16. **(A)** During execution the appropriate `area` method for each `quad` in `quadList` will be determined (polymorphism or dynamic binding).

17. **(E)** The algorithm has three steps:

    1. Store the object at `i` in `temp`.
    2. Place at location `i` the object at `j`.
    3. Place `temp` at location `j`.

    This has the effect of swapping the objects at `i` and `j`. Notice that choices B and C, while incomplete, are not incorrect. The question, however, asks for the *best* description of the postcondition, which is found in choice E.

18. **(A)** Subtracting 0.5 from a negative real number and then truncating it produces the number correctly rounded to the nearest integer. Note that casting to an `int` truncates a real number. The expression in choice B is correct for rounding a *positive* real number. Choice C won't round correctly. For example, −3.7 will be rounded to −3 instead of −4. Choices D and E don't make sense. Why cast to `double` if you're rounding to the nearest integer?

19. **(E)** The method call `whatsIt(347)` puts on the stack `System.out.print(7)`.
    The method call `whatsIt(34)` puts on the stack `System.out.print(4)`.
    The method call `whatsIt(3)` is a base case and writes out 3.
    Now the stack is popped from the top, and the 3 that was printed is followed by 4, then 7. The result is 347.

20. **(B)** Recall that insertion sort takes each element in turn and (a) finds its insertion point and (b) moves elements to insert that element in its correct place. Thus, if the array is in reverse sorted order, the insertion point will always be at the front of the array, leading to the maximum number of comparisons and data moves—very inefficient. Therefore choices A, C, and E are false.

    Selection sort finds the smallest element in the array and swaps it with `a[0]` and then finds the smallest element in the rest of the array and swaps it with `a[1]`, and so on. Thus, the same number of comparisons and moves will occur, irrespective of the original arrangement of elements in the array. So choice B is true, and choice D is false.

21. **(E)** Method call I fails because `ClassOne` does not have access to the methods of its subclass. Method call II fails because `c2` needs to be cast to `ClassTwo` to be able to access `methodTwo`. Thus, the following would be OK:

    ```
    ((ClassTwo) c2).methodTwo();
    ```

    Method call III works because `ClassTwo` inherits `methodOne` from its superclass, `ClassOne`.

22. **(D)** Notice that in the original code, if `n` is 1, `k` is incremented by 1, and if `n` is 4, `k` is incremented by 4. This is equivalent to saying "if `n` is 1 or 4, `k` is incremented by `n`."

23. **(E)** Segment I will throw a `NullPointerException` when `s.equals...` is invoked, because `s` is a null reference. Segment III looks suspect, but when the `startIndex` parameter of the `substring` method equals `s.length()`, the value returned is the empty string. If, however, `startIndex > s.length()`, a `StringIndexOutOfBoundsException` is thrown.

24. **(A)** Since results of calculations with floating-point numbers are not always represented exactly (round-off error), direct tests for equality are not reliable. Instead of the boolean expression d == c, a test should be done to check whether the difference of d and c is within some acceptable tolerance interval (see the Box on comparing floating-point numbers, p. 122).

25. **(C)** If arr has elements 2, 3, 5, the values of value are

```
2                      //after initialization
2*10 + 3 = 23      //when i = 1
23*10 + 5 = 235    //when i = 2
```

26. **(D)** The point of the binary search algorithm is that the interval containing key is repeatedly narrowed down by splitting it in half. For each iteration of the while loop, if key is in the list, arr[first] ≤ key ≤ arr[last]. Note that (i) the endpoints of the interval must be included, and (ii) key is not necessarily in the list.

27. **(B)**

	first	last	mid	a[mid]
After first iteration	0	13	6	50
After second iteration	7	13	10	220
After third iteration	7	9	8	101
After fourth iteration	9	9	9	205

28. **(A)** The data structure is an array, not an ArrayList, so you cannot use the add method for inserting elements into the list. This eliminates choices B and D. The expression to return a random integer from 0 to k-1 inclusive is

```
(int) (Math.random() * k)
```

Thus, to get integers from 0 to 100 requires k to be 101, which eliminates choice C. Choice E fails because it gets integers from 1 to 100.

29. **(C)** Suppose, for example, str1 is strawberry and str2 is cat. Then insert(str1, str2, 5) will return the following pieces, concatenated:

$$\text{straw} + \text{cat} + \text{berry}$$
$$= a_0a_1a_2a_3a_4 + b_0b_1b_2 + a_5a_6a_7a_8a_9$$
$$= a_0a_1a_2a_3a_4b_0b_1b_2a_5a_6a_7a_8a_9$$

30. **(A)** Recall that s.substring(k, m) (a method of String) returns a substring of s starting at position k and ending at position m-1. Again consider the example in which str1 is strawberry, str2 is cat, and the method call is insert(str1, str2, 5). String str1 must be split into two parts, first and last. Then str2 will be inserted between them. Since str2 is inserted starting at position 5 (the "b"), first = straw, namely str1.substring(0,pos). (Start at 0 and take all the characters up to and including location pos-1, namely 4.) Notice that last, the second substring of str1, must start at the index for "b", which is pos, the index at which str2 was inserted. The expression str1.substring(pos) returns the substring of str1 that starts at pos and continues to the end of the string, which was required. Note that you don't need any "special case" tests. In the cases where str2 is inserted at the front of str1 (i.e., pos is 0) or the back of str1 (i.e., pos is str1.length()), the code for the general case works.

31. **(C)** Composition is the *has-a* relationship. A `PlayerGroup` *has-a* `Player` (several of them, in fact). Inheritance, (choice D) is the *is-a* relationship, which doesn't apply here. None of the choices A, B, or E apply in this example: An interface is a single class composed of only abstract methods (see p. 198); encapsulation is the bundling together of data fields and operations into a single unit, a class (see p. 263); and `PlayerGroup` and `Player` are clearly dependent on each other since `PlayerGroup` contains several `Player` objects (see p. 265).

32. **(E)** All of these data structures are reasonable. They all represent 20 bingo numbers in a convenient way and provide easy mechanisms for crossing off numbers and recognizing a winning card. Notice that data structure II provides a very quick way of searching for a number on the card. For example, if 48 is called, `myBingoCard[48]` is inspected. If it is `true`, then it was one of the 20 original numbers on the card and gets crossed out. If `false`, 48 was not on that player's card. Data structures I and II require a linear search to find any given number that is called. (Note: There is no assumption that the array is sorted, which would allow a more efficient binary search.)

33. **(D)** A `NullPointerException` is thrown whenever an attempt is made to invoke a method with an object that hasn't been created with `new`. Choice A doesn't make sense: To test the `Caller` constructor requires a statement of the form

    ```
    Caller c = new Caller();
    ```

    Choice B is wrong: A missing `return` statement in a method triggers a compile-time error. Choice C doesn't make sense: In the declaration of `myNumbers`, its default initialization is to `null`. Choice E is bizarre. Hopefully you eliminated it immediately!

34. **(D)** `Location.RIGHT` is 90. A `Bug` that doesn't move, however, turns right through 45°, or `Location.HALF_RIGHT`. Choice A could happen if the `Bug` is facing northeast, for example, at its turn to move. If there are no obstacles in its path, the `Bug` will keep moving in that direction, on a diagonal path. For choice B, refer to the bug's `canMove` method, and notice that the `Bug` can move either into an empty location or onto a `Flower`. It may not, however, move onto a `Rock`, so choice C is true. Choice E will happen whenever a `Bug` is blocked in all adjacent locations, either by an actor other than a `Flower` or an edge of the grid. The `Bug` can't move, so it keeps on turning right.

35. **(E)**   getDirection() = Location.NORTHWEST

    $$= 315$$

    Location.HALF_LEFT = −45

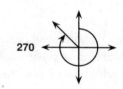

    Answer: $315 − 45 = 270$

36. **(B)** The `canMove` method in the `Bug` class is the only code that needs to be changed. Here is the change:

    ```
    return (neighbor == null) || (neighbor instanceof Flower)
        || (neighbor instanceof Rock);
    ```

    Note that the `BoxBug` class does not need to be changed. In the act method, the inherited canMove method will now return true if the location in front of the BoxBug is empty, or contains a flower, or contains a rock. The Actor class too does not need to be changed. The `moveTo` method specifies that if there is another `Actor` at the new location, that actor will be removed.

37. **(D)** The `ChameleonCritter` randomly picks either the rock or the bug, and changes its color to match that of the selected actor. Eliminate choice A—the `ChameleonCritter` cannot remain blue. Next, the `ChameleonCritter` moves to an empty neighboring location, changing its direction to match the direction in which it moved. Eliminate choice B, since (1, 1) is not an empty neighboring location. Choices C and E both change color correctly and move to a valid location. The `ChameleonCritter`, however, ends up facing the wrong direction. The direction from (1, 1) to (1, 2) is east, not northeast. The direction from (1, 1) to (2, 0) is southwest, not south.

38. **(E)** The specification for `moveTo` states that

- the actor will be moved to a new location.
- if there's already another actor in this location, it will be removed.

The key here is that *two* actors may not occupy the same location simultaneously. Therefore, you cannot use `moveTo` to place two `Monkey` objects in the same location at a zoo.

39. **(A)** The `Critter` will eat the bugs in (0, 0) and (1, 2) and the flower in (2, 0), leaving those locations empty and available. Also available are the other empty locations: (2, 1), (2, 2), and (0, 2). The `ChameleonCritter` doesn't eat its neighbors, so the only available locations are the ones that were empty to begin with: (2, 1), (2, 2), and (0, 2).

40. **(B)** The act method of the `Critter` class must be changed so that the age variable is increased by 1 each time act is called. Statement I is wrong because not all actors age. Statement III is wrong because a `ChameleonCritter` inherits the `Critter`'s act method.

Section II

1. (a) ```java
   public class StockItem
   {
           private String myDescription;
           private int myIdNum;
           private double myPrice;
           private int myNumOnShelf;

           public StockItem(String description, int id,
               double price, int numOnShelf)
           { implementation }

           public String getDescription()
           { implementation }

           public int getIdNum()
           { implementation }

           public double getPrice()
           { implementation }

           public int getNumOnShelf()
           { implementation }

           public void setPrice(double newPrice)
           { implementation }

           public void remove(int quantity)
           { implementation }

           public void add(int quantity)
           { implementation }
   }
   ```

   (b) ```java
   public void removeAll(int idNum)
   {
       int i = 0;
       while (myStockList.get(i).getIdNum() != idNum)
           i++;
       StockItem item = myStockList.get(i);
       item.remove(item.getNumOnShelf());
   }
   ```

   Alternatively,

   ```java
   public void removeAll(int idNum)
   {
       for (StockItem item : myStockList)
       {
           if (item.getIdNum() == idNum)
           {
               item.remove(item.getNumOnShelf());
               break;
           }
       }
   }
   ```

NOTE

- The `while` loop in the first solution for part (b) will not cause an out-of-range error, since the precondition guarantees that a `StockItem` with the given identity number is in the list. If this is not guaranteed, you need to start the `while` loop test with `i<myStockList.size()`.
- In the alternative solution shown for part (b) you want to exit the method as soon as the required `StockItem` has been found and processed. The `break` statement gets you out of the `for` loop and hence out of the method. The `break` construct will not be tested on the AP exam.
- In part (b), don't make the mistake of removing the entire `StockItem` from `myStockList`:

  ```
  myStockList.remove(item);
  ```

  This is not the same as recording that `item` currently has a quantity of zero on the shelf.

2. (a)
```
public static int countA(WordSet s)
{
    int count = 0;
    while (count < s.size() &&
            s.findkth(count + 1).substring(0, 1).equals("A"))
        count++;
    return count;
}
```

Alternatively,

```
public static int countA(WordSet s)
{
    boolean done = false;
    int count = 0;
    while (count < s.size() && !done)
    {
        String nextWord = s.findkth(count + 1);
        if (nextWord.substring(0,1).equals("A"))
            count++;
        else
            done = true;
    }
    return count;
}
```

(b)
```
public static void removeA(WordSet s)
{
    int numA = countA(s);
    for (int i = 1; i <= numA; i++)
        s.remove(s.findkth(1));
}
```

Alternatively,

```
public static void removeA(WordSet s)
{
    while (s.size() != 0 &&
            s.findkth(1).substring(0, 1).equals("A"))
        s.remove(s.findkth(1));
}
```

```
(c) public static WordSet commonElements(WordSet s1, WordSet s2)
    {
        WordSet temp = new WordSet();
        for (int i = 1; i <= s1.size(); i++)
        {
            String nextWord = s1.findkth(i);
            if (s2.contains(nextWord))
                temp.insert(nextWord);
        }
        return temp;
    }
```

NOTE

- To test whether a word starts with "A", you must compare the first letter of word, that is, word.substring(0,1), with "A".
- In part (a), you must check that your solution works if s is empty. For the given algorithm, count < s.size() will fail and short circuit the test, which is desirable since s.findkth(1) will violate the precondition of findkth(k), namely that k cannot be greater than size().
- The parameter for s.findkth must be greater than 0. Hence the use of s.findkth(count+1) in part (a).
- For the first solution in part (b), you get a subtle intent error if your last step is s.remove(s.findkth(i)). Suppose that s is initially {"FLY", "ASK", "ANT"}. After the method call s.remove(s.findkth(1)), s will be {"FLY", "ASK"}. After the statement s.remove(s.findkth(2)), s will be {"ASK"}!! The point is that s is adjusted after each call to s.remove. The algorithm that works is this: If N is the number of words that start with "A", simply remove the first element in the list N times. Note that the alternative solution avoids the pitfall described by simply repeatedly removing the first element if it starts with 'A.' The alternative solution, however, has its own pitfall: The algorithm can fail if a test for s being empty isn't done for each iteration of the while loop.
- Part (c) could also be accomplished by going through each element in s2 and checking if it's included in s1.

3. (a) public Sentence(String str)
```
    {
        mySentence = str;
        myNumWords = 1;
        int k = str.indexOf(" ");
        while (k != -1)   //while there are still blanks in str
        {
            myNumWords++;
            str = str.substring(k + 1); //substring after blank
            k = str.indexOf(" ");       //get index of next blank
        }
    }
```

(b)
```
private static boolean isPalindrome(String s, int start,
            int end)
{
    if (start >= end)  //substring has length 0 or 1
        return true;
    else
    {
        String first = s.substring(start, start + 1);
        String last = s.substring(end, end + 1);
        if (first.equals(last))
            return isPalindrome(s, start + 1, end - 1);
        else
            return false;
    }
}
```

NOTE

- In part (a), for every occurrence of a blank in mySentence, myNumWords must be incremented. (Be sure to initialize myNumWords to 1!)
- In part (a), the code locates all the blanks in mySentence by replacing str with the substring that consists of the piece of str directly following the most recently located blank.
- Recall that indexOf returns –1 if its String parameter does not occur as a substring in its String calling object.
- In part (b), the start and end indexes move toward each other with each subsequent recursive call. This shortens the string to be tested in each call. When start and end meet, the base case has been reached.
- Notice the private static methods in the Sentence class, including the helper method you were asked to write. They are static because they are not invoked by a Sentence object (no dot member construct). The only use of these methods is to help achieve the postconditions of other methods in the class.

4. (a)
```
private ArrayList<Bug> getBugs(ArrayList<Actor> actors)
{
    ArrayList<Bug> bugs = new ArrayList<Bug>();
    for (Actor a : actors)
    {
        if (a instanceof Bug)
            bugs.add((Bug)a);
    }
    return bugs;
}
```

(b)
```
private void eatBug(ArrayList<Bug> bugs)
{
    int n = bugs.size();
    int r = (int) (Math.random() * n);
    Bug b = bugs.get(r);
    b.removeSelfFromGrid();
}
```

```
(c) public void processActors(ArrayList<Actor> actors)
    {
        ArrayList<Bug> bugList = getBugs(actors);
        if (bugList.size() == 0)
            super.processActors(actors);
        else
            eatBug(bugList);
    }
```

NOTE

- In part (a), the bugs ArrayList contains only Bug objects. Notice that in the for loop, the object a that is being examined is an Actor. Therefore you need the cast to Bug in the add statement in the body of the loop.
- In part (c), if there is at least one bug in bugList, the HungryChameleon will eat; otherwise it will do what its superclass, ChameleonCritter, does:

```
super.processActors(actors);
```

PRACTICE EXAM TWO / LEVEL AB DIAGNOSTIC TEST

The exam that follows has the same format as that used on the actual AP exam. There are two ways you may use it:

1. As a diagnostic test before you start reviewing. Following the answer key is a diagnostic chart that relates each question to sections that you should review. In addition, complete explanations are provided for each solution.
2. As a practice exam when you have completed your review.

    Complete solutions with explanations are provided for the free-response questions.

Answer Sheet: Practice Exam Two

1. Ⓐ Ⓑ Ⓒ Ⓓ Ⓔ
2. Ⓐ Ⓑ Ⓒ Ⓓ Ⓔ
3. Ⓐ Ⓑ Ⓒ Ⓓ Ⓔ
4. Ⓐ Ⓑ Ⓒ Ⓓ Ⓔ
5. Ⓐ Ⓑ Ⓒ Ⓓ Ⓔ
6. Ⓐ Ⓑ Ⓒ Ⓓ Ⓔ
7. Ⓐ Ⓑ Ⓒ Ⓓ Ⓔ
8. Ⓐ Ⓑ Ⓒ Ⓓ Ⓔ
9. Ⓐ Ⓑ Ⓒ Ⓓ Ⓔ
10. Ⓐ Ⓑ Ⓒ Ⓓ Ⓔ
11. Ⓐ Ⓑ Ⓒ Ⓓ Ⓔ
12. Ⓐ Ⓑ Ⓒ Ⓓ Ⓔ
13. Ⓐ Ⓑ Ⓒ Ⓓ Ⓔ
14. Ⓐ Ⓑ Ⓒ Ⓓ Ⓔ

15. Ⓐ Ⓑ Ⓒ Ⓓ Ⓔ
16. Ⓐ Ⓑ Ⓒ Ⓓ Ⓔ
17. Ⓐ Ⓑ Ⓒ Ⓓ Ⓔ
18. Ⓐ Ⓑ Ⓒ Ⓓ Ⓔ
19. Ⓐ Ⓑ Ⓒ Ⓓ Ⓔ
20. Ⓐ Ⓑ Ⓒ Ⓓ Ⓔ
21. Ⓐ Ⓑ Ⓒ Ⓓ Ⓔ
22. Ⓐ Ⓑ Ⓒ Ⓓ Ⓔ
23. Ⓐ Ⓑ Ⓒ Ⓓ Ⓔ
24. Ⓐ Ⓑ Ⓒ Ⓓ Ⓔ
25. Ⓐ Ⓑ Ⓒ Ⓓ Ⓔ
26. Ⓐ Ⓑ Ⓒ Ⓓ Ⓔ
27. Ⓐ Ⓑ Ⓒ Ⓓ Ⓔ
28. Ⓐ Ⓑ Ⓒ Ⓓ Ⓔ

29. Ⓐ Ⓑ Ⓒ Ⓓ Ⓔ
30. Ⓐ Ⓑ Ⓒ Ⓓ Ⓔ
31. Ⓐ Ⓑ Ⓒ Ⓓ Ⓔ
32. Ⓐ Ⓑ Ⓒ Ⓓ Ⓔ
33. Ⓐ Ⓑ Ⓒ Ⓓ Ⓔ
34. Ⓐ Ⓑ Ⓒ Ⓓ Ⓔ
35. Ⓐ Ⓑ Ⓒ Ⓓ Ⓔ
36. Ⓐ Ⓑ Ⓒ Ⓓ Ⓔ
37. Ⓐ Ⓑ Ⓒ Ⓓ Ⓔ
38. Ⓐ Ⓑ Ⓒ Ⓓ Ⓔ
39. Ⓐ Ⓑ Ⓒ Ⓓ Ⓔ
40. Ⓐ Ⓑ Ⓒ Ⓓ Ⓔ

How to Calculate Your (Approximate) AP Score — AP Computer Science Level AB

Multiple Choice

Number correct (out of 40)　=　_____

$1/4 \times$ number wrong　=　_____

Raw score = line 1 − line 2　=　_____

Raw score $\times$ 1.25　=　_____　⟸　Multiple-Choice Score
(Do not round. If less than zero, enter zero.)

Free Response

Question 1　_____
　　　　　(out of 9)

Question 2　_____
　　　　　(out of 9)

Question 3　_____
　　　　　(out of 9)

Question 4　_____
　　　　　(out of 9)

Total　_____　$\times$　1.39　=　_____　⟸　Free-Response Score
(Do not round.)

Final Score

_____　+　_____　=　_____
Multiple-　　　Free-　　　Final Score
Choice　　　Response　　(Round to nearest
Score　　　　Score　　　whole number.)

**Chart to Convert to AP Grade
Computer Science AB**

Final Score Range	AP Grade[a]
70–100	5
60–69	4
41–59	3
31–40	2
0–30	1

[a]The score range corresponding to each grade varies from exam to exam and is approximate.

Practice Exam Two

COMPUTER SCIENCE AB
SECTION I

Time—1 hour and 15 minutes
Number of questions—40
Percent of total grade—50

Directions: Determine the answer to each of the following questions or incomplete statements, using the available space for any necessary scratchwork. Then decide which is the best of the choices given and fill in the corresponding oval on the answer sheet. Do not spend too much time on any one problem.

Notes:
- Assume that the classes in the Quick Reference have been imported where needed.
- Assume that the implementation classes ListNode and TreeNode in the Quick Reference are used for any questions referring to linked lists or trees, unless otherwise stated.
- ListNode and TreeNode parameters may be null. Otherwise, unless noted in the question, assume that parameters in method calls are not null, and that methods are called only when their preconditions are satisfied.
- Assume that variables and methods are declared in the context of an enclosing class.
- Assume that method calls that have no object or class name prefixed, and that are not shown within a complete class definition, appear within the context of an enclosing class.

1. A program is to be written that simulates and keeps track of the random motion of a point whose position is represented by coordinates (x, y). The point starts at $(0, 0)$ at time $= 0$. It is to move randomly a large, but unknown, number of times. A record of its (x, y) positions must be kept so as to be able to re-create any part of its path starting from a given previously recorded (x, y) position. The program is to print the point's (x, y) movements, forward or backward in time, from the given (x, y) position. You may assume that no point is visited more than once. Assuming the existence of a Point class that holds a pair of coordinates, which of the following is the best data structure for the task?

   (A) A one-dimensional array of Point objects
   (B) A two-dimensional array of integers in which the array indexes represent the position visited by the point and each integer cell of the array is a counter that keeps track of the number of moves to that position
   (C) A circular doubly linked list of Point objects
   (D) A stack of Point objects
   (E) A queue of Point objects

Questions 2–4 refer to the `TennisPlayer`, `GoodPlayer`, and `WeakPlayer` classes below. These classes are to be used in a program to simulate a game of tennis.

A ALSO

```java
public abstract class TennisPlayer
{
    private String myName;

    //constructor
    public TennisPlayer(String name)
    { myName = name; }

    public String getName()
    { return myName; }

    public abstract boolean serve();
    public abstract boolean serviceReturn();
}

public class GoodPlayer extends TennisPlayer
{
    //constructor
    public GoodPlayer(String name)
    { /* implementation not shown */ }

    //Postcondition: Return true if serve is in (80% probability),
    //               false if serve is out (20% probability).
    public boolean serve()
    { /* implementation not shown */ }

    //Postcondition: Return true if service return is in
    //               (70% probability), false if service return
    //               is out (30% probability).
    public boolean serviceReturn()
    { /* implementation not shown */ }
}

public class WeakPlayer extends TennisPlayer
{
    //constructor
    public WeakPlayer(String name)
    { /* implementation not shown */ }

    //Postcondition: Return true if serve is in (45% probability),
    //               false if serve is out (55% probability).
    public boolean serve()
    { /* implementation not shown */ }

    //Postcondition: Return true if service return is in
    //               (30% probability), false if service return
    //               is out (70% probability).
    public boolean serviceReturn()
    { /* implementation not shown */ }
}
```

GO ON TO THE NEXT PAGE.

A ALSO

2. Which of the following declarations will cause an error? You may assume all the constructors are correctly implemented.
   (A) `TennisPlayer t = new TennisPlayer("Smith");`
   (B) `TennisPlayer g = new GoodPlayer("Jones");`
   (C) `TennisPlayer w = new WeakPlayer("Henry");`
   (D) `TennisPlayer p;`
   (E) `WeakPlayer q = new WeakPlayer("Grady");`

3. Refer to the serve method in the `WeakPlayer` class:

```
//Postcondition: Return true if serve is in (45% probability),
//                false if serve is out (55% probability).
public boolean serve()
{ /* implementation */ }
```

Which of the following replacements for /* *implementation* */ satisfy the postcondition of the serve method?

```
 I  double value = Math.random();
    return value >= 0 || value < 0.45;

 II double value = Math.random();
    return value < 0.45;

III int val = (int) (Math.random() * 100)
    return val < 45;
```

(A) I only
(B) II only
(C) III only
(D) II and III only
(E) I, II, and III

4. Consider the following class definition:

A ALSO

```
public class Beginner extends WeakPlayer
{
    private double myCostOfLessons;

    //methods of Beginner class
        ...
}
```

Refer to the following declarations and method in a client program:

```
TennisPlayer g = new GoodPlayer("Sam");
TennisPlayer w = new WeakPlayer("Harry");
TennisPlayer b = new Beginner("Dick");

public void giveEncouragement(WeakPlayer t)
{ /* implementation not shown */ }
```

Which of the following method calls will *not* cause an error?
(A) `giveEncouragement((WeakPlayer) g);`
(B) `giveEncouragement((WeakPlayer) b);`
(C) `giveEncouragement((Beginner) w);`
(D) `giveEncouragement(w);`
(E) `giveEncouragement(b);`

5. Inorder and postorder traversals yield the same output for which of the following trees?

(A)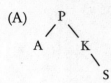

(B)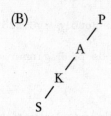

(C)

(D)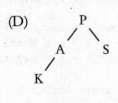

(E)

6. Worst case run time is *never* $O(n^2)$ for which of the following sorting algorithms?

   I Mergesort
  II Heapsort
 III Quicksort

(A) I only
(B) II only
(C) III only
(D) I and II only
(E) I, II, and III

7. An array with no duplicate values is to be sorted into increasing order using heapsort. Step one is to insert the elements of the array sequentially into a max-heap. (Recall that a max-heap with no duplicates is a complete binary tree in which the value in each node is larger than the values in its children's nodes.)

   If the given array is 6 7 1 9 2 0 8, what will the contents of the max-heap be after all the elements are inserted?

(A)
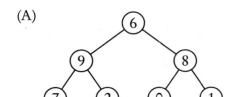

(B)
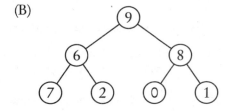

(C)
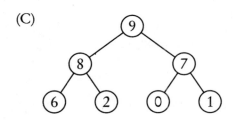

(D)
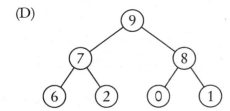

(E)
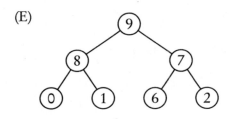

8. Which is true of the following boolean expression, given that x is a variable of type `double`?

   `3.0 == x * (3.0 / x)`

   (A) It will always evaluate to false.
   (B) It may evaluate to false for some values of x.
   (C) It will evaluate to false only when x is zero.
   (D) It will evaluate to false only when x is very large or very close to zero.
   (E) It will always evaluate to true.

A ALSO

GO ON TO THE NEXT PAGE.

9. Refer to the removeWord method below:

```
//Precondition:  wordList is an ArrayList of String.
//Postcondition: All occurrences of word removed from wordList.
public void removeWord(ArrayList<String> wordList, String word)
{
    /* implementation code */
}
```

Which /* *implementation code* */ will produce the required postcondition?

```
I  Iterator<String> itr = wordList.iterator();
   while (itr.hasNext())
   {
       if (itr.next().equals(word))
           itr.remove();
   }
```

```
II Iterator<String> itr = wordList.iterator();
   int i = 0;
   while (itr.hasNext())
   {
       if (itr.next().equals(word))
           wordList.remove(i);
       i++;
   }
```

```
III for (int i = 0; i < wordList.size(); i++)
    {
        if (wordList.get(i).equals(word))
            wordList.remove(i);
    }
```

(A) I only
(B) II only
(C) III only
(D) I and II only
(E) I and III only

Assume that linked lists are implemented with the `ListNode` class provided.

Refer to method `insertBlank` for Questions 10 and 11.

```
//Precondition:   current refers to a node in a linear linked
//                list of character strings. current is not null.
//Postcondition: The node following the node that current
//                refers to contains a blank.
public static void insertBlank(ListNode current)
```

Examples:

Before calling `insertBlank`   After calling `insertBlank`

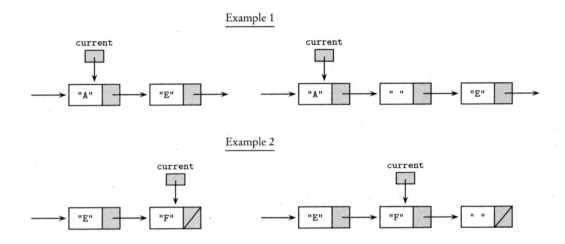

Example 1

Example 2

10. Which of the following could be used as the body of `insertBlank` such that its postcondition is satisfied?

   I `current.setNext(new ListNode(" ", current.getNext()));`

  II `ListNode p = new ListNode(" ", current.getNext());`
      `current = p;`

 III `ListNode p = new ListNode(null, null);`
      `p.setNext(current.getNext());`
      `p.setValue(" ");`
      `current.setNext(p);`

(A) I only
(B) II only
(C) III only
(D) I and II only
(E) I and III only

11. A method `padList`, whose code is given below, is to insert a blank between each pair of existing nodes in its parameter, `list`, a linked list of character strings. For example, if the list is initially

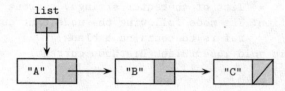

`padList(list)` should result in

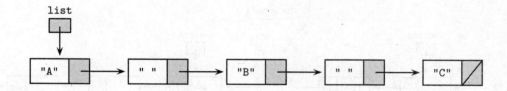

If there are fewer than two nodes in the list, then the list should remain unchanged.

```
//Precondition:  list refers to a linear linked list of n character
//               strings, n >= 0.
//               The list represents the sequence s_1,s_2,...,s_n.
//Postcondition: list refers to the linear linked list representing
//               s_1," ",s_2," ",...," ",s_n. The list remains
//               unchanged if 0 <= n < 2.
public static void padList(ListNode list)
{
    if (list != null)
    {
        ListNode temp = list;
        while (temp.getNext() != null)
        {
            insertBlank(temp);
            temp = temp.getNext();
        }
    }
}
```

Assuming that the precondition for `padList` is satisfied, for which lists will `padList` work correctly?
(A) For all linear linked lists
(B) For no linear linked lists
(C) Only for lists that contain fewer than two nodes
(D) Only for lists that contain exactly one node
(E) Only for empty lists

12. The binary tree shown is traversed preorder. During the traversal, each element, when accessed, is pushed onto an initially empty stack s of String. What output is produced when the following code is executed?

```
while (!s.isEmpty())
    System.out.print(s.pop());
```

(A) AKCPRF
(B) CKRFPA
(C) FPRACK
(D) APFRKC
(E) FRPCKA

Questions 13 and 14 refer to the following class and declaration.

```
public class DigitalClock
{
    //private instance variables and constructors not shown
        ...

    //Returns true if this DigitalClock is defective, false otherwise.
    public boolean isDefective()
    { /* implementation not shown */ }

    //Mutator method. Advances the DigitalClock by one minute.
    public void advanceTime()
    { /* implementation not shown */ }

    //other methods not shown ...
}
```

The declaration below occurs in a client class.

```
ArrayList<DigitalClock> clocks = new ArrayList<DigitalClock>();
```

13. Suppose that the `ArrayList` `clocks` has been initialized and contains a nonempty list of `DigitalClock` objects. Which of the following code segments will correctly remove all defective clocks?

```
I   for (DigitalClock c : clocks)
    {
        if (c.isDefective())
            c.remove();
    }
```

```
II  for (int index = 0; index < clocks.size(); index++)
    {
        if (clocks.get(index).isDefective())
            clocks.remove(index);
    }
```

```
III Iterator<DigitalClock> itr = clocks.iterator();
    while (itr.hasNext())
    {
        if (itr.next().isDefective())
            itr.remove();
    }
```

(A) I only
(B) II only
(C) III only
(D) II and III only
(E) I, II, and III

14. Again, suppose that `clocks` is initialized. Assume that it contains a nonempty list of correctly functioning `DigitalClock` objects. Which of the following code segments will correctly advance the time on every digital clock?

    ```
    I for (DigitalClock c : clocks)
      {
          c.advanceTime();
      }

    II for (int index = 0; index < clocks.size(); index++)
       {
           clocks.get(index).advanceTime();
       }

    III Iterator<DigitalClock> itr = clocks.iterator()
        while (itr.hasNext())
        {
            itr.next().advanceTime();
        }
    ```

    (A) I only
    (B) II only
    (C) III only
    (D) II and III only
    (E) I, II, and III

15. A large charity organization maintains a database of its donors. For each donor, the following information is stored: name, address, phone number, amount and date of most recent contribution, and total contributed so far. Two plans for organizing and modifying the data are considered:

    I A one-dimensional array of `Donor` objects maintained in alphabetical order by name.
    II A hash table of `Donor` objects implemented using an array of linked lists. The hash address for any given `Donor` object will be determined by a hash method that uniformly distributes donors throughout the table.

    Which of the following is *false*? (Assume the most efficient algorithms possible.)
    (A) Plans I and II have roughly the same memory efficiency.
    (B) Insertion of a new donor is more run-time efficient using plan II.
    (C) Modifying an existing donor's record is more run-time efficient using plan II.
    (D) Printing out a mailing list in alphabetical order is more run-time efficient using plan I.
    (E) Printing out a list of donors in decreasing order of total amount contributed is more run-time efficient using plan I.

GO ON TO THE NEXT PAGE.

16. Consider a class that has this private instance variable:

```
private int[][] mat;
```

The class has the following method, alter.

```
public void alter(int c)
{
    for (int i = 0; i < mat.length; i++)
        for (int j = c + 1; j < mat[0].length; j++)
            mat[i][j-1] = mat[i][j];
}
```

If a 3 × 4 matrix mat is

```
1 3 5 7
2 4 6 8
3 5 7 9
```

then alter(1) will change mat to

(A) 1 5 7 7
    2 6 8 8
    3 7 9 9

(B) 1 5 7
    2 6 8
    3 7 9

(C) 1 3 5 7
    3 5 7 9

(D) 1 3 5 7
    3 5 7 9
    3 5 7 9

(E) 1 7 7 7
    2 8 8 8
    3 9 9 9

17. Refer to the following method:

```
/* Deletes maximum item, i.e., item of lowest priority, from
 * PriorityQueue pq.
 * Precondition:  pq is nonempty.
 * Postcondition: Returns a PriorityQueue that contains the same
 *                elements as pq except for the maximum element,
 *                which has been removed.  */
public PriorityQueue<Type> deleteMax(PriorityQueue<Type> pq)
{
    /* code to delete maximum item */
    return priQ;
}
```

Which of the following replacements for /* *code to delete maximum item* */ satisfy the postcondition for the method?

```
I PriorityQueue<Type> priQ = new PriorityQueue<Type>();
  pq.remove();
  priQ = pq;
```

```
II Stack<Type> s = new Stack<Type>();
   while (!pq.isEmpty())
       s.push(pq.remove());
   s.pop();
   PriorityQueue<Type> priQ = new PriorityQueue<Type>();
   while (!s.isEmpty())
       priQ.add(s.pop());
```

```
III Queue<Type> q = new LinkedList<Type>();
    while (!pq.isEmpty())
        q.add(pq.remove());
    q.remove();
    PriorityQueue<Type> priQ = new PriorityQueue<Type>();
    while (!q.isEmpty())
        priQ.add(q.remove());
```

(A) I only
(B) II only
(C) III only
(D) I and II only
(E) I and III only

A ALSO

Use the program description below for Questions 18–20.

A car dealer needs a program that will maintain an inventory of cars on his lot. There are three types of cars: sedans, station wagons, and SUVs. The model, year, color, and price need to be recorded for each car, plus any additional features for the different types of cars. The program must allow the dealer to

- Add a new car to the lot.
- Remove a car from the lot.
- Correct any data that's been entered.
- Display information for any car.

18. The programmer decides to have these classes: `Car`, `Inventory`, `Sedan`, `SUV`, and `StationWagon`. Which statement is *true* about the relationships between these classes and their attributes?

    I There are no inheritance relationships between these classes.
    II The `Inventory` class *has-a* list of `Car` objects.
    III The `Sedan`, `StationWagon`, and `SUV` classes are independent of each other.

  (A) I only
  (B) II only
  (C) III only
  (D) I and II only
  (E) II and III only

19. Suppose that the programmer decides to have a `Car` class and an `Inventory` class. The `Inventory` class will maintain a list of all the cars on the lot. Here are some of the methods in the program:

```
addCar          //adds a car to the lot
removeCar       //removes a car from the lot
displayCar      //displays all the features of a given car
setColor        //sets the color of a car to a given color
                //May be used to correct data
getPrice        //returns the price of a car
displayAllCars  //displays features for every car on the lot
```

In each of the following, a class and a method are given. Which is the *least* suitable choice of class to be responsible for the given method?

  (A) `Car, setColor`
  (B) `Car, removeCar`
  (C) `Car, getPrice`
  (D) `Car, displayCar`
  (E) `Inventory, displayAllCars`

20. Suppose `Car` is a superclass and `Sedan`, `StationWagon`, and `SUV` are subclasses of `Car`. Which of the following is the most likely method of the `Car` class to be overridden by at least one of the subclasses (`Sedan`, `StationWagon`, or `SUV`)?

    (A) `setColor(newColor)` //set color of Car to newColor
    (B) `getModel()`   //return model of Car
    (C) `displayCar()`   //display all features of Car
    (D) `setPrice(newPrice)` //set price of Car to newPrice
    (E) `getYear()`   //return year of Car

A ALSO

21. What is the result of running this code segment?

    ```
    Map<String, String> dwarfs = new HashMap<String, String>();
    dwarfs.put("Sneezy", "sick dwarf");
    dwarfs.put("Happy", "merry dwarf");
    dwarfs.put("Grumpy", "irritable dwarf");
    String s = dwarfs.get("Dopey");
    ```

    (A) A `NoSuchElementException` will be thrown.
    (B) An `IllegalStateException` will be thrown.
    (C) A `ClassCastException` will be thrown.
    (D) The code will run without error, and s will have the value `"Dopey"`.
    (E) The code will run without error, and s will have the value `null`.

22. Assume that `ArrayList` a is initialized with `SomeType` elements. Also, assume the existence of the following method:

    ```
    //Postcondition: Returns a HashSet that contains all the elements
    //               of ArrayList<SomeType> list.
    public HashSet<SomeType> copyListToHashSet(ArrayList<SomeType> list)
    ```

    Consider the following code segment:

    ```
    HashSet<SomeType> s = copyListToHashSet(a);
    System.out.println("Number of elements in ArrayList is " + a.size());
    System.out.println("Number of elements in HashSet is " + s.size());
    ```

    Suppose the output produced by this code segment is

    ```
    Number of elements in ArrayList is 10
    Number of elements in HashSet is 6
    ```

    Which is a valid conclusion?
    (A) List a contains ten distinct (i.e., different) elements, and set s contains six distinct elements.
    (B) There is at least one element in list a that occurs more than once.
    (C) List a contains four more distinct elements than set s.
    (D) There are at least four elements in list a that occur more than once.
    (E) There is one element in list a that occurs five times.

GO ON TO THE NEXT PAGE.

Questions 23–25 are based on the following procedure, which copies items from an array arr containing n distinct numbers into a binary search tree tree and then prints the elements.

Procedure:

Step 1: Initialize tree to be empty.
Step 2: Insert arr[0], arr[1],..., arr[n-1] into tree using a standard algorithm for insertion of item arr[i] into tree. (Assume that the insert operation does no balancing of tree.)
Step 3: Print the elements stored in tree, using an inorder traversal.

23. Which of the following best characterizes the output produced in Step 3 of the above procedure?
    (A) The items are printed in the original order in which they appear in array arr.
    (B) The items are printed in sorted order, from smallest to largest.
    (C) The items are printed in sorted order, from largest to smallest.
    (D) The items are printed in the reverse of the order in which they appear in array arr.
    (E) The items are printed in random order.

24. Which best describes the best case run time of the whole procedure?
    (A) $O(1)$
    (B) $O(n)$
    (C) $O(\log n)$
    (D) $O(n \log n)$
    (E) $O(n^2)$

25. The procedure is most likely to exhibit its best case run time when the numbers are stored in array arr in which of the following ways?

    I   Ascending order
    II Descending order
    III Random order

    (A) I only
    (B) II only
    (C) III only
    (D) I and II only
    (E) I, II, and III

GO ON TO THE NEXT PAGE.

Questions 26 and 27 are based on the `Computable` interface and `LargeInt` class shown below.

A ALSO

```
public interface Computable
{
    Object add(Object obj);         //returns this object + obj
    Object subtract(Object obj);    //returns this object - obj
    Object multiply(Object obj);    //returns this object * obj
}

public class LargeInt implements Comparable, Computable
{
    //private instance variables
        ...

    public LargeInt(int n)      //converts n to LargeInt
    {
        ...
    }

    public String toString()    //returns this LargeInt as a String
    {
        ...
    }

    public Object add(Object obj)  //returns this LargeInt + obj
                                   //precondition: obj of type LargeInt
    {
        ...
    }

    public Object subtract(Object obj)  //returns this LargeInt - obj
                                        //precondition: obj of type LargeInt
    {
        ...
    }

    public Object multiply(Object obj)  //returns this LargeInt * obj
                                        //precondition: obj of type LargeInt
    {
        ...
    }

    //Returns -1 if this LargeInt is less than obj, 1 if it is greater
    // than obj, and 0 if it equals obj.
    public int compareTo(Object obj)
    {
        ...
    }
}
```

A ALSO

26. Of the following pairs of methods, which should be coded and tested first to facilitate testing and debugging the other methods?
    (A) The constructor and `add` method
    (B) The constructor and `compareTo` method
    (C) The constructor and `toString` method
    (D) The `toString` and `compareTo` methods
    (E) The `toString` and one of the `add`, `subtract`, or `multiply` methods

27. Consider the problem of simulating the following loop for `LargeInt` objects:

```
for (int i = 1; i < n; i++)
    System.out.println(i);
```

The following code is used. You may assume that n exists and is of type `LargeInt`.

```
LargeInt i = new LargeInt(1);
LargeInt one = new LargeInt(1);
while (i.compareTo(n) < 0)
{
    System.out.println(i);
    /* statement */
}
```

Which of the following should replace /* *statement* */ to simulate the loop correctly?
    (A) `i = (LargeInt) i.add(one);`
    (B) `i = (LargeInt) i.add(1);`
    (C) `i = (LargeInt) one.add(n);`
    (D) `i = (LargeInt) n.add(one);`
    (E) `i = (LargeInt) i.add(n);`

28. A teacher needs to assess the reading level of a textbook. One measure used is the frequency of words that have six or more letters. A computer program scans the text and keeps track of such words and their corresponding frequencies by storing them in a `TreeMap` data structure.

    Assuming that there are n different words in the key set so far, which is a *true* statement about operations performed on this frequency map?
    (A) Insertion of a new word into the map is $O(1)$.
    (B) To check whether a given word is in the map is $O(\log n)$.
    (C) To update the frequency of an existing word in the map is $O(1)$.
    (D) To print a list of the `keySet` of words in alphabetical order is $O(\log n)$.
    (E) To print a list of all word/frequency pairs is $O(\log n)$.

29. A set set1 is said to be a *subset* of set2, set1 ⊆ set2, if there is no element in set1 that is not in set2. Consider the isSubset method below:

```
//Precondition:  set1 and set2 are initialized with objects of the
//               same type, SomeType.
//Postcondition: Returns true if set1 is a subset of set2, false
//               otherwise.
public boolean isSubset(Set<SomeType> set1, Set<SomeType> set2)
{
    /* implementation code */
}
```

Which /* *implementation code* */ achieves the desired postcondition? Assume the existence of the following method:

```
//Postcondition: Returns a HashSet that contains all the elements
//               of Set s.
public HashSet<SomeType> copySetToHashSet(Set<SomeType> s)
```

```
I  Set<SomeType> temp = copySetToHashSet(set2);
   for (SomeType element : set1)
       temp.add(element);
   return temp.size() == set2.size();
```

```
II for (SomeType element : set1)
       if (!set2.contains(element))
           return false;
   return true;
```

```
III for (SomeType element : set1)
    {
        for (SomeType e : set2)
            if (!element.equals(e))
                return false;
    }
    return true;
```

(A) I only
(B) II only
(C) III only
(D) I and II only
(E) I, II, and III

Refer to the following for Questions 30 and 31.

A word game uses certain five-letter words that are stored in a special dictionary file. In the game, no word may be used more than once. The game is implemented with the `WordStatus` and `WordGame` classes shown:

```
public class WordStatus
{
    private boolean isUsed;

    public WordStatus()
    { isUsed = false; }

    public boolean used() //true if word has been used, false otherwise
    { return isUsed; }

    public void changeStatus()
    { isUsed = !isUsed; }
}


public class WordGame
{
    private Map<String, WordStatus> m;
    //other private instance variables
        ...
    //constructor
    public WordGame()
    {
        m = new HashMap<String, WordStatus>();
        //initialization of other instance variables
            ...
    }

    /* Load hash map with all words in the dictionary,
     * and mark every word as available for use.  */
    public void loadDictionary(String fileName)
    {
        < code to open input file with given fileName >

        while  (< there are words in input file >)
        {
            String word = inFile.readWord(); //read word from input file
            /* code to insert word into Map m */
        }
        //code to close input file not shown
            ...
    }
```

```
    /* Look up word in HashMap m.
     * If present and not yet used, mark as used and return true.
     * Otherwise return false.  */
    public boolean isAvailable(String word, WordStatus status)
    {
        /* implementation code */
    }

    //other methods to implement the game not shown
        ...
}
```

30. Refer to the `loadDictionary` method in the `WordGame` class. Which is correct
    /* *code to insert* word *into* Map m */?
    (A) `m.put(word, new Boolean(true)); //a Boolean object wraps a`
         `boolean value`
    (B) `m.put(word, "true");`
    (C) `m.put(word, true);`
    (D) `m.put(word, new WordStatus(true));`
    (E) `m.put(word, new WordStatus());`

31. Suppose the HashMap m has available words corresponding to a WordStatus where used returns false. When an available word is found in m, it is marked as used by changing its WordStatus. Refer to the isAvailable method of the WordGame class:

```
/* Look up word in HashMap m.
 * If present and not yet used, mark as used and return true.
 * Otherwise return false. */
public boolean isAvailable(String word)
{
    /* implementation code */
}
```

Which represents correct /* implementation code */?

```
I if (m.containsKey(word))
  {
      WordStatus w = m.get(word);
      if (!w.used())
      {
          w.changeStatus();
          return true;
      }
  }
  else
      return false;
```

```
II WordStatus w = m.get(word);
   if (m.containsKey(word))
   {
       WordStatus w = m.get(word);
       if (!w.used())
           w.changeStatus();
   }
   return w.used();
```

```
III if (!m.containsKey(word))
        return false;
    else
    {
        WordStatus w = m.get(word);
        if (!w.used())
        {
            w.changeStatus();
            return true;
        }
    }
```

(A) I only
(B) II only
(C) III only
(D) I and II only
(E) I, II, and III

32. Consider the following binary tree of single-character `String` values:

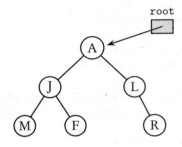

What will be output by the following code segment?

```
Queue<TreeNode> q = new LinkedList<TreeNode>();
//LinkedList implements Queue

if (root == null)
    System.out.println("Empty tree");
else
{
    q.add(root);
    while (!q.isEmpty())
    {
        TreeNode current = q.remove();
        System.out.print(current.getValue());
        if (current.getLeft() != null)
            q.add(current.getLeft());
        if (current.getRight() != null)
            q.add(current.getRight());
    }
}
```

(A) MJFALR
(B) MFRJLA
(C) AJLMFR
(D) MFJRLA
(E) AJMFLR

33. Assume that doubly linked lists are implemented with the `DoublyListNode` class below:

```
public class DoublyListNode
{
    private Object value;
    private DoublyListNode next, prev;

    public DoublyListNode(DoublyListNode initPrev, Object initValue,
                    DoublyListNode initNext)
    {
        prev = initPrev;
        value = initValue;
        next = initNext;
    }

    public DoublyListNode getPrev()
    { return prev; }

    public void setPrev(DoublyListNode theNewPrev)
    { prev = theNewPrev; }

    public Object getValue()
    { return value; }

    public void setValue(Object theNewValue)
    { value = theNewValue; }

    public DoublyListNode getNext()
    { return next; }

    public void setNext(DoublyListNode theNewNext)
    { next = theNewNext; }
}
```

For the doubly linked list shown below, which of the following code segments will remove the node containing b from the list? Following execution of the segment, list may refer to any element of the list. (Note that arrows pointing to the right correspond to next and those to the left correspond to prev.)

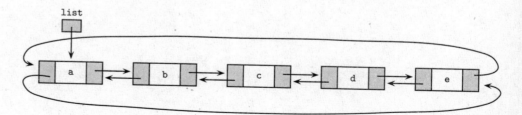

GO ON TO THE NEXT PAGE.

```
  I list.setNext(list.getNext().getNext());
    list.getNext().getNext().setPrev(list);

 II list.getNext().getNext().setPrev(list);
    list.setNext(list.getNext().getNext());

III list = list.getNext().getNext();
    (list.getPrev().getPrev()).setNext(list);
    list.setPrev(list.getPrev().getPrev());
```

(A) I only
(B) II only
(C) III only
(D) I and II only
(E) II and III only

34. Assume that binary trees are implemented with the `TreeNode` class provided. Refer to method `mTree`:

```
//Returns a reference to a newly created tree.
public TreeNode mTree(TreeNode t)
{
    if (t == null)
        return null;
    else
        return new TreeNode(t.getValue(), mTree(t.getRight()),
                mTree(t.getLeft()));
}
```

Suppose p = mTree(t) is invoked for the tree shown.

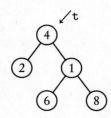

Which of the following trees will be created?

(A)
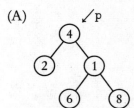

(B)
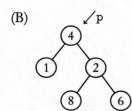

(C)
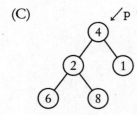

(D)
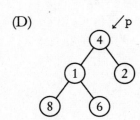

(E)
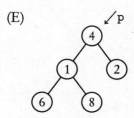

Questions 35–40 involve reasoning about the code from the GridWorld Case Study. A Quick Reference to the case study is provided as part of this exam. The actors in GridWorld are represented in this book with the pictures shown below. Each actor is shown facing north. These pictures almost certainly will be different from those used on the AP exam!

   Actor   Bug   Flower   Rock   Critter   ChameleonCritter

35. Consider a class `PoisonousCritter` that extends `Critter`. A `PoisonousCritter` marks its victims by changing the color of all its adjacent neighbors—except rocks—to green. Rocks remain unchanged. The `PoisonousCritter` then selects one of its victims at random, and "kills" it by moving into its location. Which groups of `Critter` methods will need to be overridden?

> A ALSO

   I `act` and `getActors`

  II `processActors` and `getMoveLocations`

 III `selectMoveLocation` and `makeMove`

(A) I only
(B) II only
(C) III only
(D) II and III only
(E) I, II, and III

A ALSO

36. Consider the bounded grid shown.

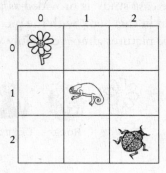

The `Flower` in (0, 0) is yellow. The `ChameleonCritter` in (1, 1) is blue. The `Bug` in (2, 2) is purple. A valid setup after a call to act for the `ChameleonCritter` only is

(A)

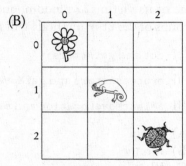

`ChameleonCritter` is purple

(B)

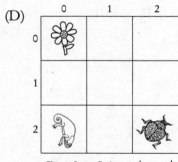

`ChameleonCritter` is yellow

(C)

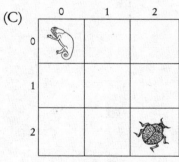

`ChameleonCritter` is yellow

(D)

`ChameleonCritter` is purple

(E)

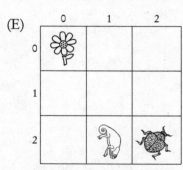

`ChameleonCritter` is yellow

GO ON TO THE NEXT PAGE.

37. During a run of the GridWorld program, in addition to many other actors, a Bug, a Critter, and a ChameleonCritter are created in an UnboundedGrid. While the program is running, it is noticed that these three actors disappear from the visible part of the grid. If the program continues to run, which actor may become visible again, without the screen setting being adjusted?

    I the Bug

    II the Critter

    III the ChameleonCritter

(A) None
(B) I only
(C) II only
(D) III only
(E) I, II, and III

38. Refer to the `getValidAdjacentLocations` method in the `AbstractGrid` class. Lines are numbered for reference.

```
1   public ArrayList<Location> getValidAdjacentLocations(Location loc)
2   {
3       ArrayList<Location> locs = new ArrayList<Location>();
4
5       int d = Location.NORTH;
6       for (int i = 0;
7               i < Location.FULL_CIRCLE / Location.HALF_RIGHT; i++)
8       {
9           Location neighborLoc = loc.getAdjacentLocation(d);
10          if (isValid(neighborLoc))
11              locs.add(neighborLoc);
12          d = d + Location.HALF_RIGHT;
13      }
14      return locs;
15  }
```

Which of the following modifications of the method would be equivalent to the original?

  I Replace lines 5–7 with:

```
int d = 0;
for (int i = 0; i < 8; i++)
```

  II Replace lines 6 and 7 with:

```
for (int i = Location.NORTH;
    i < Location.FULL_CIRCLE / Location.HALF_RIGHT; i++)
```

  III Replace line 12 with:

```
d += 45;
```

(A) None
(B) I only
(C) II only
(D) III only
(E) I, II, and III

39. A slight modification is made to the BoxBug class: One of the turn statements is removed. Here is the modified act method.

A ALSO

```
public void act()
{
    if (steps < sideLength && canMove())
    {
        move();
        steps++;
    }
    else
    {
        turn();
        steps = 0;
    }
}
```

Assuming that there are no impediments in the grid, which is a possible result of executing this code several times?

(A)

(B)

(C)

(D)

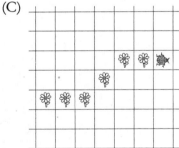

(E)

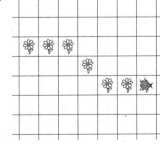

40. Suppose there are n actors in a grid. What is the big-O time complexity for the remove method in
    (1) the BoundedGrid class and (2) the UnboundedGrid class?

    (A) (1) $O(1)$ (2) $O(\log n)$
    (B) (1) $O(n)$ (2) $O(\log n)$
    (C) (1) $O(1)$ (2) $O(n)$
    (D) (1) $O(1)$ (2) $O(1)$
    (E) (1) $O(n)$ (2) $O(n)$

END OF SECTION I

COMPUTER SCIENCE AB
SECTION II

Time—1 hour and 45 minutes
Number of questions—4
Percent of total grade—50

Directions: SHOW ALL YOUR WORK. REMEMBER THAT
PROGRAM SEGMENTS ARE TO BE WRITTEN IN Java.

Write your answers in <u>pencil only</u> in the booklet provided.

Notes:

- Assume that the classes in the Quick Reference have been imported where needed.

- Assume that the implementation classes `ListNode` and `TreeNode` are used for any questions referring to linked lists or trees, unless otherwise specified.

- `ListNode` and `TreeNode` parameters may be `null`. Otherwise, unless noted in the question, assume that parameters in method calls are not `null`, and that methods are called only when their preconditions are satisfied.

- In writing solutions for each question, you may use any of the accessible methods that are listed in classes defined in that question. Writing significant amounts of code that can be replaced by a call to one of these methods may not receive full credit.

---

1. A small zoo has both mammals and birds:

    - Goats that bleat and eat grass.
    - Pigs that squeal and eat swill.
    - Turkeys that gobble and eat grain.
    - Elf owls that hoot and eat insects.
    - Snowy owls that hoot and eat either hares, lemmings, or small birds, whichever are available.

Suppose you are to write a program that simulates the zoo.

GO ON TO THE NEXT PAGE.

(a) Draw a diagram that represents an `Animal` class hierarchy. Your diagram should show the relationship between all the objects in the program, with `Animal` as the superclass for all the other objects. Each class in your design should be represented by a labeled rectangle, and arrows should show the inheritance relationships between classes.

(b) Write the code for the `Animal` class. Each `Animal` has a name, a type of covering (fur, feathers, scales, etc.), and its own particular noise that it makes. When a new animal is constructed, it must be assigned a name, noise, and covering. Each of these can be represented with a `String`. Operations on an `Animal` include the following:
   - Retrieve the name of the animal.
   - Retrieve the noise of the animal.
   - Retrieve the covering of the animal.
   - Retrieve the food of the animal. This should be an abstract method: The appropriate food for each animal will be described in its particular class.

(c) Given the code for a `Bird` class below, write the code for an `Owl` class.

```
public abstract class Bird extends Animal
{
    //constructor
    public Bird(String name, String noise)
    {
        super(name, noise, "feathers");
    }
}
```

An `Owl` is a `Bird` that hoots (its noise!). The food it eats depends on the type of `Owl`. Assuming that the `Animal` and `Bird` classes have been correctly defined, write the `Owl` class below.

(d) Write the code for a `SnowyOwl` class. A `SnowyOwl` is an `Owl` that will randomly eat a hare, a lemming, or a small bird (depending on what's available!). The `SnowyOwl` class should use a random number to help determine which food the `SnowyOwl` will eat.
Assuming that the `Animal`, `Bird`, and `Owl` classes have been correctly defined, write the `SnowyOwl` class below.

2. This question involves reasoning about the code from the GridWorld Case Study. A Quick Reference to the case study is provided as part of this exam.

   Consider defining a new type of `Critter`, a `Frog`, which moves by jumping over other actors. A `Frog` acts by randomly selecting one of its adjacent neighboring actors, and turning to face it. If the location adjacent to that actor in the direction that the `Frog` is facing is valid and empty, the frog jumps over that actor into that location. Otherwise, it does not move. If a frog has no adjacent actors to begin with, it does nothing. The diagram below illustrates what a `Frog` may do.

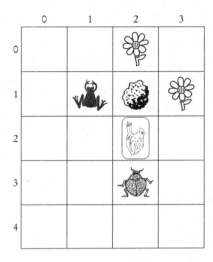

   Note that for the `Frog` in location (2, 2) there are four adjacent neighbors. The table below shows the outcomes for each of the four neighbors, one of which will be randomly selected.

Actor selected	Frog's final location	Frog's final direction
`Critter` in (1, 1)	(0, 0)	northwest
`Rock` in (1, 2)	(2, 2)	north
`Flower` in (1, 3)	(2, 2)	northeast
`Bug` in (3, 2)	(4, 2)	south

   The `Frog` class is defined by extending the `Critter` class and overriding the `processActors` and `act` methods. Two additional methods, `getJumpLocation` and `canJump`, will be defined.

   A partial definition of class `Frog` is shown on the next page.

GO ON TO THE NEXT PAGE.

```
/**
 * A Frog jumps over neighboring actors as
 * it moves through the grid.
 */
public class Frog extends Critter
{
    /**
     * Randomly selects a neighbor and turns to face it.
     * Gets the possible jump location, which is the location
     * adjacent to the selected neighbor in the same direction
     * from the Frog. If the Frog can jump, it will move to the
     * jump location. Otherwise it will not change its location.
     * If the list of actors is empty, the Frog does nothing.
     * @param actors the list of adjacent neighbors
     */
    public void processActors(ArrayList<Actor> actors)
    { /* to be implemented in part (c) */ }


    /**
     * A frog acts by getting a list of its adjacent neighbors,
     * and processing them.
     */
    public void act()
    {
        if (getGrid() == null)
            return;
        ArrayList<Actor> actors = getActors();
        processActors(actors);
    }


    /**
     * Returns the location that is two locations away from this
     * Frog, in the same direction that the Frog is facing. This
     * location may be invalid.
     * Precondition: adjacent is the location of the neighbor to be
     *               jumped over. It is not empty.
     * @param adjacent the location of the neighbor to be jumped
     * over
     * @return the two-away location in the same direction as the
     * frog
     */
    private Location getJumpLocation(Location adjacent)
    { /* to be implemented in part (a) */ }


    /**
     * Returns true if loc is valid and empty;
     * otherwise returns false.
     * @param loc the location to be tested
     * @return true if the location is valid and empty, false
     * otherwise
     */
    private boolean canJump(Location loc)
    { /* to be implemented in part (b) */ }
}
```

GO ON TO THE NEXT PAGE.

(a) Write the private helper method getJumpLocation. This method returns the location that is two locations away from this Frog in the same direction that the Frog is facing. The Location parameter, adjacent, is the location of the actor selected to be jumped over. Note: The Location returned by getJumpLocation may be out of bounds of the grid. (This should not affect the implementation of the method.) For the diagram shown on p. 91, here are some results of the call

```
Location jumpLoc = getJumpLocation(loc);
```

loc	jumpLoc
(3, 2)	(4, 2)
(1, 1)	(0, 0)
(1, 2)	(0, 2)
(1, 3)	(0, 4)

Complete method getJumpLocation below.

```
/**
 * Returns the location that is two locations away from this
 * Frog, in the same direction that the Frog is facing. This
 * location may be invalid.
 * Precondition: adjacent is the location of the neighbor to be
 *               jumped over. It is not empty.
 * @param adjacent the location of the neighbor to be jumped
 * over
 * @return the two-away location in the same direction as the
 * frog
 */
private Location getJumpLocation(Location adjacent)
```

(b) Write the private helper method canJump. Method canJump returns true if loc is valid and empty; otherwise it returns false. For the Frog in the diagram on p. 91, here are some results of a call to canJump(loc):

loc	canJump(loc)
(4, 2)	true
(0, 0)	true
(0, 2)	false (not empty)
(0, 4)	false (not valid)

Complete method canJump below.

```
/**
 * Returns true if loc is valid and empty;
 * otherwise returns false.
 * @param loc the location to be tested
 * @return true if the location is valid and empty, false
 * otherwise
 */
private boolean canJump(Location loc)
```

GO ON TO THE NEXT PAGE.

(c) Override the `processActors` method for the `Frog` class. The `processActors`
method does the following:

- If there are no adjacent neighboring actors, do nothing.
- Select an adjacent neighbor at random and then turn to face it.
- Get the possible "jump location" for the selected actor. This location
  is two locations away from this `Frog`, in the direction that the `Frog` is
  facing.
- If the `Frog` can jump, move to the jump location. Otherwise, do not
  move.

In writing `processActors`, you *must* use the helper methods `canJump` and
`getJumpLocation` defined in parts (a) and (b). You may assume that these
methods work as specified, irrespective of what you wrote.

Complete method `processActors` below.

```
/**
 * Randomly selects a neighbor and turns to face it.
 * Gets the possible jump location, which is the location
 * adjacent to the selected neighbor in the same direction
 * from the Frog. If the Frog can jump, it will move to the
 * jump location. Otherwise it will not change its location.
 * If the list of actors is empty, the Frog does nothing.
 * @param actors the list of adjacent neighbors
 */
public void processActors(ArrayList<Actor> actors)
```

3. Scrabble is a board game played between two players. Players who participate
   in tournaments receive a rating based on their recent performance. Consider
   an interface `ScrabblePlayer` that will be used to represent Scrabble players at a
   Scrabble club. Each player is described by name and current rating.

```
public interface ScrabblePlayer
{
    String name();
    int rating();
}
```

The following `Game` class represents a single game played by a Scrabble player:

```
public class Game
{
    private ScrabblePlayer opponent;
    private boolean won;

    //constructor not shown ...

    public ScrabblePlayer getOpponent()
    { return opponent; }

    public boolean wonGame()
    { return won; }

    //other methods not shown ...
}
```

GO ON TO THE NEXT PAGE.

The following `ScrabbleClub` class is used to store players and the set of games they have played.

```
public class ScrabbleClub
{
    private Map<ScrabblePlayer, Set<Game>> map;

    public ScrabbleClub()
    { map = new HashMap<ScrabblePlayer, Set<Game>>(); }

    //Postcondition: theGame, played by player, has been added to
    //               the map.
    public void addGameToMap(ScrabblePlayer player, Game theGame)
    {
        /* to be implemented in part (a) */
    }

    //Precondition:  player is a key in map.
    //Postcondition: Returns number of games player won against
    //               an expert opponent.
    //(Note that an expert is a ScrabblePlayer whose rating is
    //at least 1600.)
    public int countExpertWins(ScrabblePlayer player)
    {
        /* to be implemented in part (b) */
    }

    //Precondition:  player is a key in map.
    //Postcondition: All games for player in which opponent's
    //               rating is less than 1300 have been removed.
    public void removeWeakOpponents(ScrabblePlayer player)
    {
        /* to be implemented in part (c) */
    }

    //other methods not shown ...
}
```

For example, assume that some of the entries in a `ScrabbleClub` object `clubMap` are as follows:

Key	Value			
Dan Birman 1690	Eli Fabens 1701 false	Khoa Quy 1545 true	Andrea Yonge 1900 true	Mike O'Dell 1635 true
Rachel Zax 1825	Emily Hart 1160 true	Ben Myers 1236 true		
Jon Schultz 1451	Emily Hart 1160 false	Dan Birman 1690 false	Matt Lepage 1270 true	
...	...	...	...	...

GO ON TO THE NEXT PAGE.

This shows, for example, that Dan Birman, with a rating of 1690, had the following record:

Lost against Eli Fabens, rating of 1701
Won against Khoa Quy, rating of 1545
Won against Andrea Yonge, rating of 1900
Won against Mike O'Dell, rating of 1635

(a) Write the `ScrabbleClub` method `addGameToMap`, which adds a single `Game`, played by a specified `ScrabblePlayer`, to the map. For example, suppose `player1` is Rachel Zax with a rating of 1825 and `player2` is Scott Bland with a rating of 2105. If Rachel lost a game against Scott, represented by `game1`, the method call

```
clubMap.addGameToMap(player1, game1);
```

should modify the map as follows:

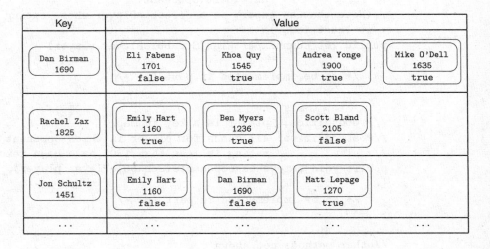

Key	Value			
Dan Birman 1690	Eli Fabens 1701 false	Khoa Quy 1545 true	Andrea Yonge 1900 true	Mike O'Dell 1635 true
Rachel Zax 1825	Emily Hart 1160 true	Ben Myers 1236 true	Scott Bland 2105 false	
Jon Schultz 1451	Emily Hart 1160 false	Dan Birman 1690 false	Matt Lepage 1270 true	
...	...	...	...	...

Complete method `addGameToMap` below.

```
//Postcondition: theGame, played by player, has been added to
//                the map.
public void addGameToMap(ScrabblePlayer player, Game theGame)
```

(b) Write the `ScrabbleClub` method `countExpertWins`, which examines the record of its `player` parameter and returns the number of games that player has won against expert opponents. An expert opponent is a player whose rating is greater than or equal to 1600. For example, if Dan Birman is `player3`, the call `clubMap.countExpertWins(player3)` should return 2, since Dan won games against experts Andrea Yonge and Mike O'Dell.

In writing `countExpertWins`, you may use any of the accessible methods shown in the classes of this question.

GO ON TO THE NEXT PAGE.

Complete method `countExpertWins` below.

```
//Precondition:  player is a key in map.
//Postcondition: Returns number of games player won against
//               an expert opponent.
//(Note that an expert is a ScrabblePlayer whose rating is
//at least 1600.)
public int countExpertWins(ScrabblePlayer player)
```

(c) Write the `ScrabbleClub` method `removeWeakOpponents`, which removes from the map all games for the specified player in which the opponents' ratings were less than 1300. For example, if Jon Schultz is `player4`, the call `clubMap.removeWeakOpponents(player4)` should modify the original map as follows:

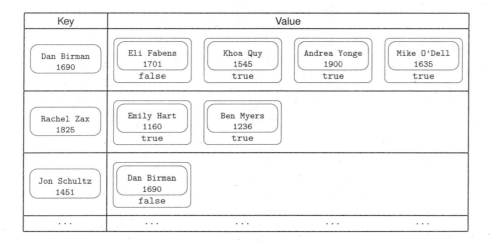

In writing `removeWeakOpponents`, you may use any of the accessible methods shown in the classes of this question.

Complete method `removeWeakOpponents` below.

```
//Precondition:  player is a key in map.
//Postcondition: All games for player in which opponent's
//               rating is less than 1300 have been removed.
public void removeWeakOpponents(ScrabblePlayer player)
```

(d) Suppose `clubMap` has n `ScrabblePlayer` keys, and each player's game set is a `HashSet` that can have c entries, where $c < n$. In terms of n and c, state the big-O running time of each method in the table below:

Method	Big-O run time
addGameToMap	
countExpertWins	
removeWeakOpponents	

GO ON TO THE NEXT PAGE.

4. Consider the following `LinearLinkedList` class that maintains and processes a singly linked linear linked list. The nodes of the list are objects of the `ListNode` class (whose code is provided in the Quick Reference). You will implement two methods of the `LinearLinkedList` class.

```
/*Linear linked list class */
public class LinearLinkedList
{
     private ListNode firstNode;

     //Constructs an empty list.
     public LinearLinkedList()
     { firstNode = null; }

     //Returns true if list is empty, false otherwise.
     public boolean isEmpty()
     { return firstNode == null; }

     //Returns a reference to the first node.
     public ListNode getFirstNode()
     { return firstNode; }

     //Changes first node of list to refer to node.
     public void setFirstNode(ListNode node)
     { firstNode = node; }

     //Changes this LinearLinkedList into a circular linked list.
     //Postcondition: Pointer field of last node refers to first
     //               node of list.
     public void makeCircular()
     { /* to be implemented in part (a) */ }

     //Precondition:  This LinearLinkedList is not circular.
     //Postcondition: Reverses the order of nodes in the list.
     //               firstNode points to the original last node
     //               of the list.
     public void reverse()
     { /* to be implemented in part (b) */ }
}
```

(a) Write the `LinearLinkedList` method `makeCircular`. The `makeCircular` method converts the linear linked list into a circular linked list by setting the pointer field of the last node to refer to the first node of the list. For example, if `list` is of type `LinearLinkedList`, and the state of `list` is

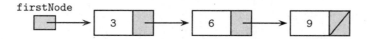

the method call `list.makeCircular()` should change `list` to

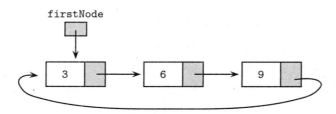

Complete method `makeCircular` below.

```
//Changes this LinearLinkedList into a circular linked list.
//Postcondition: Pointer field of last node refers to first
//        node of list.
public void makeCircular()
```

(b) Write the `LinearLinkedList` method `reverse`. This method reverses pointers in the list. Thus if `list` is of type `LinearLinkedList`, and the state of `list` is

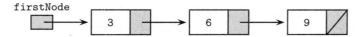

the method call `list.reverse()` should change `list` to

- Notice that if the list is empty, or has just one node, you are done.
- If you are somewhere in the middle of the list, you need at least two adjacent pointers, so that the pointer field of `second` can be changed to refer to `first` (shown below).

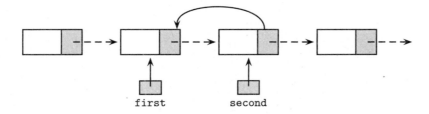

- If you are at the end of the list (base case), the `firstNode` reference must be changed.

In writing `reverse`, you *must* use a private recursive helper method. Your algorithm should not depend on any temporary storage. It must be done by reversing pointers in the current `LinerLinkedList` object.

Complete method reverse below. Then write a private recursive helper method.

```
//Precondition:  This LinearLinkedList is not circular.
//Postcondition: Reverses the order of nodes in the list.
//               firstNode points to the original last node
//               of the list.
public void reverse()
```

END OF EXAMINATION

ANSWER KEY (Section I)

1. C	15. E	29. D
2. A	16. A	30. E
3. D	17. B	31. A
4. B	18. E	32. C
5. B	19. B	33. E
6. D	20. C	34. D
7. D	21. E	35. B
8. B	22. B	36. E
9. A	23. B	37. E
10. E	24. D	38. E
11. C	25. C	39. D
12. E	26. C	40. D
13. C	27. A	
14. E	28. B	

DIAGNOSTIC CHART FOR LEVEL AB EXAM

Each multiple-choice question has a complete explanation (p. 103).

The following table relates each question to sections that you should review. For any given question, the topic(s) in the chart represent the concept(s) tested in the question. These topics are explained on the corresponding page(s) in the chart and should provide further insight into answering that question.

ANSWERS EXPLAINED (Section I)

1. **(C)** A circular doubly linked list works well for this program because of the ability to traverse forward and backward from any given node. Note that a stack (choice D) provides easy backtracking from the current top element but does not allow for convenient access to any other specified position or for easy forward traversal. Similarly, a queue (choice E) allows easy forward traversal from the front position but is awkward for backtracking and random access of elements in the "middle" of the queue. Choice A seems reasonable for both forward and backward traversal. The number of moves, however, is large and unknown, which makes a dynamic data structure preferable. Choice B doesn't satisfy the requirements of the program at all. It also has the problem of representing real-number coordinates (x, y) with the indexes of the array; the indexes must be integers.

2. **(A)** Choice A is illegal because you cannot create an instance of an abstract class.

3. **(D)** The statement

   ```
   double value = Math.random();
   ```

   generates a random `double` in the range $0 \leq$ `value` < 1. Since random doubles are uniformly distributed in this interval, 45 percent of the time you can expect `value` to be in the range $0 \leq$ `value` < 0.45. Therefore, a test for `value` in this range can be a test for whether the serve of a `WeakPlayer` went in. Since `Math.random()` never returns a negative number, the test in implementation II, `value < 0.45`, is sufficient. The test in implementation I would be correct if `||` were changed to `&&` ("or" changed to "and"—both parts must be true). Implementation III also works. The expression

   ```
   (int) (Math.random() * 100)
   ```

   returns a random integer from 0 to 99, each equally likely. Thus, 45 percent of the time, the integer `val` will be in the range $0 \leq$ `val` ≤ 44. Therefore, a test for `val` in this range can be used to test whether the serve was in.

4. **(B)** Choice B is fine: `b`, the `Beginner`, *is-a* `WeakPlayer`. Choices A and C will each cause a `ClassCastException` to be thrown: You can't cast a `GoodPlayer` to a `WeakPlayer` and you can't cast a `WeakPlayer` to a `Beginner`. Choices D and E will each cause a compile-time error: The parameter must be of type `WeakPlayer`, but `w` and `b` are declared to be of type `TennisPlayer`. Each of these choices can be corrected by casting the parameter to `WeakPlayer`.

5. **(B)** Since none of the nodes in choice B has a right subtree, the recursive left-root-right of the inorder traversal becomes left-root. Similarly, the left-right-root of a postorder traversal becomes left-root. In either case, the traversal yields S, K, A, then P.

6. **(D)** Worst case for quicksort is $O(n^2)$. Quicksort recursively partitions the array into two pieces such that elements in the left piece are less than or equal to a pivot element, and those in the right piece are greater than or equal to the pivot. In the worst case, the pivot element repeatedly splits the array into pieces of length 1 and $n - 1$, respectively. In this case, there will be n splits, each using an $O(n)$ partitioning algorithm. Thus, the final run time becomes $O(n^2)$. An example where this could happen is a sorted array in which one of the end elements is repeatedly

chosen as the pivot. Mergesort recursively divides the array into two pieces of roughly the same size until there are n arrays of length 1. This is $O(\log n)$. Then adjacent sorted arrays are recursively merged to form a single sorted array. Thus, the algorithm is $O(n \log n)$, irrespective of the initial ordering of array elements. Heapsort creates a balanced binary tree irrespective of the ordering of the array elements, which leads to an $O(n \log n)$ algorithm in best and worst cases.

7. **(D)** Here are the steps in fixing the heap after the array elements are slotted into a binary tree (see p. 529).

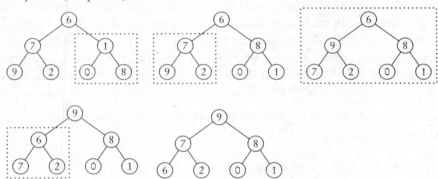

8. **(B)** Although the expression is always algebraically true for nonzero x, the expression may evaluate to false. This could occur because of round-off error in performing the division and multiplication operations. Whether the right-hand side of the expression evaluates to exactly 3.0 depends on the value of x. Note that if x is zero, the expression will be evaluated to `false` because the right-hand side will be assigned a value of `Infinity`.

9. **(A)** Segment II fails because it calls the `ArrayList` method `remove` during iteration. During iteration with an iterator, you may not modify the list with a noniterator method. Segment I correctly invokes the *iterator* `remove` method. Segment III does not use an iterator to cycle through the list. Therefore it is OK to use the `remove` method from `ArrayList`. You must, however, be careful. When you remove the ith item from an `ArrayList`, the $(i + 1)$th item is shifted into that position. Since i is incremented after each loop iteration, consecutive duplicates will not be deleted.

10. **(E)** Segment I correctly uses the `ListNode` constructor. Segment III correctly uses the `setNext` and `setValue` methods to insert the required values in the new node and connect it to the list. Segment II uses the `ListNode` constructor correctly but has an incorrect second statement: It fails to connect the `current` node to the new node (referred to by p). Segment II would be correct if the second statement were changed to

```
current.setNext(p);
```

11. **(C)** The problem with the code is in the last line; change it to

```
temp = temp.getNext().getNext();
```

and the method will work as intended for all cases. As it is, `temp` doesn't advance far enough, and you have an infinite `while` loop that produces an endless stream of blanks:

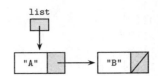

becomes

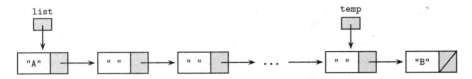

The method works for an empty list because nothing is done. It works for a list with just one node because the `while` test fails immediately and the list remains unchanged.

12. **(E)** A preorder traversal pushes the elements onto `s` in the following order:

    A, K, C, P, R, F.

    The elements will be popped and printed in reverse order, namely

    F, R, P, C, K, A.

13. **(C)** Segment III correctly iterates over the `clocks` list and uses the iterator to remove each defective `DigitalClock`. Segment II will fail whenever two (or more) adjacent clocks are defective. This is because whenever a clock is removed, all subsequent clocks are moved one slot left. The index, however, will move one position *to the right*, which means that a duplicate will be skipped. The main problem with segment I is that an enhanced `for` loop cannot be used to remove an element from a list.

14. **(E)** Contrast this with the previous question. No elements are being removed from or added to the list of clocks. Each element is being accessed and modified, which is fine for each of the three modes of traversal. Take note: You cannot use a for-each loop to remove elements, add elements, or replace elements in the list. You can, however, use it to *modify* objects that have mutator methods.

15. **(E)** To print a list of donors in order of total contributions is equally efficient for plans I and II. Both plans require the same three steps:

    (1) Insert all `Donor` objects into a temporary array.
    (2) Sort the array with respect to total contributions.
    (3) Print the elements.

    Note that simply sorting the existing array in plan I is not a good idea; the array will then need to be "sorted back" into alphabetical order. Choice A is true: All items in the database require the same amount of memory irrespective of data structure. Choices B and C are true: Insertion and searching in a good hash table are both $O(1)$, whereas in a sorted array searching for a given donor or insertion point is $O(\log n)$ (assuming that an efficient method like binary search is used). Choice D is true since plan II requires sorting before printing. Plan I has data items that are already sorted in alphabetical order.

16. **(A)** Method `alter` shifts all the columns, starting at column `c+1`, one column to the left. Also, it does it in a way that overwrites column `c`. Here are the replacements for the method call `alter(1)`:

```
mat[0][1] = mat[0][2]
mat[0][2] = mat[0][3]
mat[1][1] = mat[1][2]
mat[1][2] = mat[1][3]
mat[2][1] = mat[2][2]
mat[2][2] = mat[2][3]
```

17. **(B)** Segment II removes elements form the priority queue in increasing order of priority and pushes each element onto a stack as it is removed. Thus, the maximum element in pq lands on top of the stack. This is the element to be removed, which is carried out by the statement s.pop(). The remaining elements are then placed, with their original ordering, into a new priority queue priQ, which is returned. Segment III is practically identical to segment II, except that it places the elements of pq into a queue. This results in having the *least* element at the front of the queue, which is then deleted by the statement q.remove(). Segment I fails because it too removes the least element instead of the maximum.

18. **(E)** Statement I is false: The Sedan, StationWagon, and SUV classes should all be subclasses of Car. Each one satisfies the *is-a* Car relationship. Statement II is true: The main task of the Inventory class should be to keep an updated list of Car objects. Statement III is true: A class is independent of another class if it does not require that class to implement its methods.

19. **(B)** The Inventory class is responsible for maintaining the list of all cars on the lot. Therefore methods like addCar, removeCar, and displayAllCars must be the responsibility of this class. The Car class should contain the setColor, getPrice, and displayCar methods, since all these pertain to the attributes of a given Car.

20. **(C)** Each subclass may contain additional attributes for the particular type of car that are not in the Car superclass. Since displayCar displays all features of a given car, this method should be overridden to display the original plus additional features.

21. **(E)** The get method of Map returns either the value associated with the key, or null if the map contains no mapping for that key. In the given piece of code, since there is no "Dopey" key, s will be assigned the value null.

22. **(B)** As a counterexample for choices A, C, D, and E, let a be the list

    1, 1, 1, 1, 2, 2, 3, 4, 5, 6

    Then s is the set

    1, 2, 3, 4, 5, 6

    (No duplicates in a set!)

23. **(B)** An inorder traversal of a binary search tree produces the elements in sorted increasing order. (Recall that the leftmost leaf of the binary search tree is the smallest element in the tree and that this is the first element visited.)

24. **(D)** The best case run time occurs when the binary search tree produced is balanced. This means that, for each of the n items in arr, no more than $\log_2 n$ comparisons will need to be made to find its insertion point. Therefore the run time is $O(n \log n)$. Printing the elements is $O(n)$, which is less than $O(n \log n)$. Thus, the overall run time is $O(n \log n)$.

25. **(C)** Any kind of sorted array leads to worst case behavior for insertion into a binary search tree. The tree obtained is completely unbalanced, with a long chain of left links or right links. Run time of insertion becomes $O(n^2)$ (see p. 440). Choice III is thus the most likely of the three choices to lead to a balanced tree and best case behavior.

26. **(C)** Before manipulating `LargeInt` objects, you have to check that they've been correctly constructed, and to do that you need to output them. This means that the `toString` method must be defined in order to read the output easily. Therefore the constructor and `toString` methods should be coded before the others.

27. **(A)** You want to simulate `i++` (or `i=i+1`). Thus, eliminate choices C and D, which don't include `i` in the method calls to `add`. Choice C would be correct if its method call were `one.add(i)`. Eliminate choice B because a `LargeInt` parameter must be used. Choice E is wrong because you're not adding `n` to `i`, you're adding `1` to `i`.

28. **(B)** The `TreeMap` class stores its elements in a balanced binary search tree. This means that `TreeMap` will provide $O(\log n)$ performance for insertion, retrieval, and search. Thus, choices A and C are false. Choices D and E are false because printing a list of all elements involves a simple traversal: $O(n)$.

29. **(D)** In segment I `temp` contains all the elements of `set2`. Then all the elements of `set1` are added to `temp`. If `set1` is a subset of `set2`, all the elements of `set1` will already be in `temp`, which means that the size of `temp` will remain the same as the size of `set2`. (If `set1` is not a subset of `set2`, then `temp.size()` will end up bigger than `set2.size()` because there will be at least one element of `set1` that was not in `set2`.) Segment II checks that `set2` contains each element of `set1`. If it doesn't, the method returns `false`, otherwise `true`. Segment III iterates over both sets `set1` and `set2` and returns `false` as soon as it finds an element in `set1` that is not equal to an element in `set2`. But for `set1` to be a subset of `set2`, all of the elements in `set2` except one will *not* be equal to a given element of `set1`. You would have to modify the code with a more complicated version that searches the entire set `set2` for each element in `set1` and returns `false` only if no element is equal to it.

30. **(E)** The declaration of the map

    ```
    private Map<String, WordStatus> m;
    ```

    shows that the second parameter of the `put` method should be an object of type `WordStatus`. Thus, you can eliminate choices A, B, and C. Choice D is wrong because there is no constructor in `WordStatus` that has a parameter.

31. **(A)** There are two conditions under which the `isAvailable` method should return `false`:

    - Its `word` parameter is not in the map.
    - The `word` parameter is in the map but has already been used.

    Segment I correctly takes care of both these cases. In Segment II, if `word` is not in the map, `m.get(word)` will cause a `NullPointerException`. Segment III fails because it doesn't return `false` if the word is marked as used (i.e., no `else` for the second `if`).

32. **(C)** The algorithm yields a *level-order traversal* of the tree, which visits nodes starting at the root and going from top to bottom, left to right. Suppose that the

`TreeNode` references to the nodes are labeled with small letters as shown:

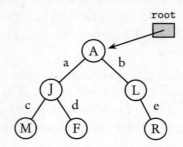

After the first pass through the `while` loop, A has been printed and q is

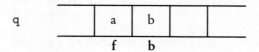

After the second pass, J has been printed and q is

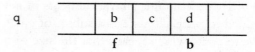

After the third pass, L has been printed and q is

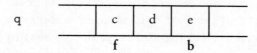

When q is empty, AJLMFR has been printed.

33. **(E)** Segment I fails because it doesn't take into account that the `next` field of `list` was altered in the first line. Here are the faulty pointer connections (dashed lines):

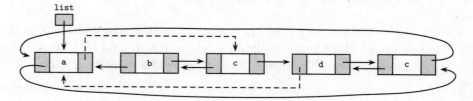

34. **(D)** The method creates a tree that is a mirror image of its parameter. Note the order of the parameters in the `TreeNode` constructor:

```
(initValue, initLeft, initRight)
```

In the method `mTree` the order is

```
(t.getValue(), mTree(t.getRight()), mTree(t.getLeft()))
```

Matching up parameters means that the right subtree of `t` becomes the left connection of the new tree, and the left subtree of `t` becomes the right connection.

35. **(B)** Notice that to do its thing, the `PoisonousCritter` must get the adjacent actors, process them, get a list of possible move locations, randomly select one of these, and then move to it. This is what a regular `Critter` does, so `act` and `getActors` need not be changed. Both of the methods in group II must be changed: `processActors` turns the actors green, whereas the original method removes them. The `getMoveLocations` method must get a list of *occupied* locations, whereas the original method gets empty locations. Group III methods don't change at all: When a `PoisonousCritter` has a list of possible locations, it randomly selects one and moves there. This is what a regular `Critter` does.

36. **(E)** The `ChameleonCritter` randomly chooses a neighboring actor and takes its color. Thus it will end up yellow or purple. It then randomly picks an empty adjacent location, moves into it, and ends up facing the direction in which it moved. Reject choices A and C: A `ChameleonCritter` does not eliminate its neighbors. Choice B is wrong because the `ChameleonCritter` *must* move if it can. Choice D is incorrect because the direction from location (1, 1) to location (2, 0) is southwest, and the `ChameleonCritter` didn't change its direction to southwest.

37. **(E)** All can reappear! When the `Bug` moves out of the grid, going west, say, it will continue to move west until it encounters an obstacle. Depending on the location of obstacles, the `Bug` may have to turn right enough times so that it turns back and reappears on the screen. If the critters move out of the visible part of the grid, on the left of the screen, say, the leftmost visible column could provide empty adjacent locations for the *next* time they act. They then may or may not reappear.

38. **(E)** All of the `Location` constants are `int` values: `Location.NORTH` is 0, `Location.FULL_CIRCLE` is 360, and `Location.HALF_RIGHT` is 45. Thus, the given replacements can be used in the implementation.

39. **(D)** Instead of turning right through 90°, the `BoxBug` now turns right through 45°. This produces the octagon in choice D. Choice A is wrong because the turn is through 90°. Choice B has a 135° turn then a 225° turn. In choice C, the `BoxBug` turns 45° left and then 45° right, while in choice E it turns 45° right and then 45° left. In the code, however, `turn` is a right turn.

40. **(D)** The steps to remove an actor at `loc` in a `BoundedGrid` are:
    - get the occupant at `loc`: $O(1)$
    - Assign `occupantArray[loc.getRow()][loc.getCol()]` to `null`: $O(1)$

    Thus the algorithm is $O(1)$.

    To remove an actor at `loc` in an `UnboundedGrid`:
    - Use the `HashMap` method `remove` to remove the mapping whose key is `loc`:

      ```
      occupantMap.remove(loc);
      ```

    To access any key in a `HashMap` is $O(1)$.

    Therefore the algorithm is $O(1)$.

Section II

1. (a)

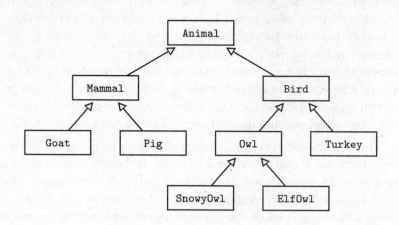

(b)
```
public abstract class Animal
{
    private String myName;
    private String myNoise;
    private String myCovering;

    //constructor
    public Animal(String name, String noise, String covering)
    {
        myName = name;
        myNoise = noise;
        myCovering = covering;
    }

    public String getName()
    { return myName; }

    public String getNoise()
    { return myNoise; }

    public String getCovering()
    { return myCovering; }

    public abstract String getFood();
}
```

(c)
```
public abstract class Owl extends Bird
{
    //constructor
    public Owl(String name)
    {
        super(name, "hoot");
    }
}
```

```
(d) public class SnowyOwl extends Owl
    {
        //constructor
        public SnowyOwl()
        {
            super("Snowy Owl");
        }

        //Returns type of food for this SnowyOwl.
        public String getFood()
        {
            int num = (int) (Math.random() * 3);
            if (num == 0)
                return "hare";
            else if (num == 1)
                return "lemming";
            else
                return "small bird";
        }
    }
```

NOTE

- Since the food type for each `Animal` can't be simply provided in a parameter, the `getFood` method must be abstract in the `Animal` class. This means that the `Animal` class must be abstract.
- Both the `Bird` and `Owl` classes inherit the abstract `getFood` method. Since the food type for a `Bird`, and also for an `Owl`, depends on the type of `Bird` or `Owl`, these classes don't provide implementation code for `getFood`. Therefore both `Bird` and `Owl` must be abstract classes.
- In parts (c) and (d), `super` must be used in the constructors because there's no direct access to the private variables of the `Animal` class.
- Note that the `Bird` constructor has two parameters, `name` and `noise`. The noise for an `Owl`, however, will always be `"hoot"`. Therefore `noise` does not need to be provided as a parameter in the `Owl` constructor. The statement `super(name,"hoot")` will use the superclass (`Bird`) constructor to automatically assign `"hoot"` as an `Owl`'s noise. Similarly, the `SnowyOwl` does not need any parameters in its constructor. Using the superclass (`Owl`) constructor will automatically provide it with its name through the statement `super("SnowyOwl")`.
- The `SnowyOwl` inherits the `"hoot"` noise from `Owl` and the `"feathers"` covering from `Bird`.

2. (a)
```
    private Location getJumpLocation(Location adjacent)
    {
        Location twoAway =
                adjacent.getAdjacentLocation(getDirection());
        return twoAway;
    }
```

(b)
```
private boolean canJump(Location loc)
{
    if (!getGrid().isValid(loc))
        return false;
    Actor occupant = getGrid().get(loc);
    return occupant == null;
}
```

(c)
```
public void processActors(ArrayList<Actor> actors)
{
    int n = actors.size();
    if (n == 0)
        return;
    int r = (int) (Math.random() * n);
    Actor nbr = actors.get(r);
    Location nbrLoc = nbr.getLocation();
    int newDirection =
        getLocation().getDirectionToward(nbrLoc);
    setDirection(newDirection);
    Location jumpLoc = getJumpLocation(nbrLoc);
    if (canJump(jumpLoc))
        makeMove(jumpLoc);
}
```

NOTE

- In part (b), the loc parameter is the prospective "jump location." The isValid test checks that it is not outside the bounds of the grid. The test occupant == null checks whether loc is empty.

3. (a)
```
public void addGameToMap(ScrabblePlayer player, Game theGame)
{
    Set<Game> games = map.get(player);
    if (games == null)
    {
        games = new HashSet<Game>();
        map.put(player, games);
    }
    games.add(theGame);
}
```

(b)
```
public int countExpertWins(ScrabblePlayer player)
{
    Set<Game> games = map.get(player);
    int numWins = 0;
    for (Game g: games)
        if (g.getOpponent().rating() >= 1600 && g.wonGame())
            numWins++;
    return numWins;
}
```

(c)
```
public void removeWeakOpponents(ScrabblePlayer player)
{
    Set<Game> games = map.get(player);
    for (Iterator<Game> itr = games.iterator(); itr.hasNext();)
    {
        ScrabblePlayer opponent = itr.next().getOpponent();
        if (opponent.rating() < 1300)
            itr.remove();
    }
}
```

(d)

Method	Big-O run time
addGameToMap	$O(1)$
countExpertWins	$O(c)$
removeWeakOpponents	$O(c)$

NOTE

- In part (a), you must check the case where `player` is not yet in the key set of the map, in which case games will be `null`. This means you must create a new `HashSet` before you add `theGame` to it.
- In part (b), each game in the set of games for `player` is examined. A for-each loop is used for the traversal. Contrast this with part (c), where an iterator must be used since elements of the set may be removed. A for-each loop cannot be used to traverse a collection where items may be removed.
- In part (d), the get operation in a `HashMap` is $O(1)$, independent of n, the number of keys. The put operation in a `HashSet` is also $O(1)$; thus `addGameToMap` is $O(1)$. The `countExpertWins` method finds the player key, $O(1)$, then traverses the c elements in the corresponding `HashSet`: $O(c)$. Method `removeWeakOpponents` finds the key, $O(1)$, then also traverses the c elements in the corresponding `HashSet`, potentially removing each element. Since removing an item from a `HashSet` is $O(1)$, the method is $O(c)$.
- In part (d), you cannot make any assumptions about the size of c compared with the size of n, other than the fact that $c < n$, which is given. Therefore, it is incorrect to say that the traversals are $O(n)$ (which would be correct if $c \approx n$) or $O(1)$ (which would be correct if c is very small compared to n).

4. (a)
```
public void makeCircular()
{
    if (!isEmpty())
    {
        ListNode p = firstNode;
        while (p.getNext() != null)
        {
            p = p.getNext():
        }
        p.setNext(firstNode);
    }
}
```

(b)
```
    public void reverse()
    {
        if (!isEmpty() && firstNode.getNext() != null)
            reverseHelper(null, firstNode);
    }

    private void reverseHelper(ListNode first, ListNode second)
    {
        if (second.getNext() == null)
        {
            setFirstNode(second);
        }
        else
        {
            reverseHelper(second, second.getNext());
        }
        second.setNext(first);
    }
```

Alternative solution:

```
public void reverse()
{
    if (!isEmpty() && firstNode.getNext() != null)
        setFirstNode(reverseHelper(null, firstNode,
                              firstNode.getNext()));
}

private ListNode reverseHelper(ListNode first,
               ListNode second, ListNode hold)
{
    second.setNext(first);
    if (hold == null)
        return second;
    else
        return reverseHelper(second, hold, hold.getNext());
}
```

NOTE

- In part (a), you are not told that the linear linked list is nonempty. Therefore, you need the isEmpty test.
- The first solution in part (b) uses two consecutive pointers. The alternative solution uses three.
- In the alternative solution reverseHelper eventually returns a reference to the last node in the list, and firstNode is set to it.

Introductory Java Language Features

Fifty loops shalt thou make . . .
—Exodus 26:5

Chapter Goals

- Packages and classes
- Types and identifiers
- Operators
- Input/output
- Storage of numbers

- Binary and hexadecimal numbers
- Control structures
- Errors and exceptions

The AP Computer Science course includes algorithm analysis, data structures, and the techniques and methods of modern programming, specifically, object-oriented programming. A high-level programming language is used to explore these concepts. Java is the language currently in use on the AP exam.

Java was developed by James Gosling and a team at Sun Microsystems in California; it continues to evolve. The AP exam covers a clearly defined subset of Java language features that are presented throughout this book, including some new features of Java 5.0 that were tested for the first time in May 2007. The College Board website, *http://www.collegeboard.com/student/testing/ap/subjects.html*, contains a complete listing of this subset.

Java provides basic control structures such as the `if-else` statement, `for` loop, and `while` loop, as well as fundamental built-in data types. But the power of the language lies in the manipulation of user-defined types called objects, many of which can interact in a single program.

PACKAGES AND CLASSES

A typical Java program has user-defined classes whose objects interact with those from Java class libraries. In Java, related classes are grouped into *packages*, many of which are provided with the compiler. You can put your own classes into a package—this facilitates their use in other programs.

The package `java.lang`, which contains many commonly used classes, is automatically provided to all Java programs. To use any other package in a program, an `import` statement must be used. To import all of the classes in a package called `packagename`, use the form

```
import packagename.*;
```

To import a single class called `ClassName` from the package, use

```
import packagename.ClassName;
```

Java has a hierarchy of packages and subpackages. Subpackages are selected using multiple dots:

```
import packagename.subpackagename.ClassName;
```

The `import` statement allows the programmer to use the objects and methods defined in the designated package. By convention Java package names are lowercase. The AP exam does not require knowledge of packages. You will not be expected to write any `import` statements.

A Java program must have at least one class, the one that contains the *main method*. The java files that comprise your program are called *source files*.

A *compiler* converts source code into machine-readable form called *bytecode*.

Here is a typical source file for a Java program.

```
/* Program FirstProg.java
   Start with a comment, giving the program name and a brief
   description of what the program does. */

import package1.*;
import package2.subpackage.ClassName;

public class FirstProg  //note that the file name is FirstProg.java
{
    public static type1 method1(parameter list)
    {
        < code for method 1 >
    }
    public static type2 method2(parameter list)
    {
        < code for method 2 >
    }
        ...

    public static void main(String[] args)
    {
        < your code >
    }
}
```

NOTE

1. All Java methods must be contained in a class, and all program statements must be placed inside a method.

2. Typically, the class that contains the `main` method does not contain many additional methods.

3. The words `class`, `public`, `static`, `void`, and `main` are *reserved words*, also called *keywords*.

4. The keyword `public` signals that the class or method is usable outside of the class, whereas `private` data members or methods (see Chapter 2) are not.

5. The keyword `static` is used for methods that will not access any objects of a class, such as the methods in the `FirstProg` class in the example on the previous page. This is typically true for all methods in a source file that contains no *instance variables* (see Chapter 2). Most methods in Java do operate on objects and are not static. The `main` method, however, must always be static.

6. The program shown on the previous page is a Java *application*. This is not to be confused with a Java *applet*, a program that runs inside a web browser or applet viewer. Applets are not part of the AP subset.

TYPES AND IDENTIFIERS

Identifiers

An *identifier* is a name for a variable, parameter, constant, user-defined method, or user-defined class. In Java an identifier is any sequence of letters, digits, and the underscore character. Identifiers may not begin with a digit. Identifiers are case-sensitive, which means that `age` and `Age` are different. Wherever possible identifiers should be concise and self-documenting. A variable called `area` is more illuminating than one called `a`.

By convention identifiers for variables and methods are lowercase. Uppercase letters are used to separate these into multiple words, for example `getName`, `findSurfaceArea`, `preTaxTotal`, and so on. Note that a class name starts with a capital letter. Reserved words are entirely lowercase and may not be used as identifiers.

Built-in Types

Every identifier in a Java program has a type associated with it. The *primitive* or *built-in* types that are included in the AP Java subset are

`int`	An integer. For example, 2, -26, 3000
`boolean`	A boolean. Just two values, `true` or `false`
`double`	A double precision floating-point number. For example, `2.718`, `-367189.41`, `1.6e4`

(Note that primitive type `char` is not included in the AP Java subset.)

Integer values are stored exactly. Because there's a fixed amount of memory set aside for their storage, however, integers are bounded. If you try to store a value whose magnitude is too big in an `int` variable, you'll get an *overflow error*. (Java gives you no warning. You just get a wrong result!)

An identifier, for example a *variable*, is introduced into a Java program with a *declaration* that specifies its type. A variable is often initialized in its declaration. Some examples follow:

```
int x;
double y,z;
boolean found;
int count = 1;          //count initialized to 1
double p = 2.3, q = 4.1;    //p and q initialized to 2.3 and 4.1
```

One type can be cast to another compatible type if appropriate. For example,

```
int total, n;
double average;
   ...
average = (double) total/n;    //total cast to double to ensure
                               //real division is used
```

Alternatively,

```
average = total/(double) n;
```

Assigning an `int` to a `double` automatically casts the `int` to `double`. For example,

```
int num = 5;
double realNum = num;    //num is cast to double
```

Assigning a `double` to an `int` without a cast, however, causes a compile-time error. For example,

```
double x = 6.79;
int intNum = x;      //Error. Need an explicit cast to int
```

Note that casting a floating-point (real) number to an integer simply truncates the number. For example,

```
double cost = 10.95;
int numDollars = (int) cost;      //sets numDollars to 10
```

If your intent was to round cost to the nearest dollar, you needed to write

```
int numDollars = (int) (cost + 0.5);   //numDollars has value 11
```

To round a negative number to the nearest integer:

```
double negAmount = -4.8;
int roundNeg = (int) (negAmount - 0.5);    //roundNeg has value -5
```

The strategy of adding or subtracting 0.5 before casting correctly rounds in all cases.

Storage of Numbers

INTEGERS

Integer values in Java are stored exactly, as a string of bits (binary digits). One of the bits stores the sign of the integer, 0 for positive, 1 for negative.

The Java built-in integral type, `byte`, uses one byte (eight bits) of storage.

The picture represents the largest positive integer that can be stored using type byte: $2^7 - 1$.

Type int in Java uses four bytes (32 bits). Taking one bit for a sign, the largest possible integer stored is $2^{31} - 1$. In general, an n-bit integer uses $n/8$ bytes of storage, and stores integers from -2^{n-1} to $2^{n-1} - 1$. (Note that the extra value on the negative side comes from not having to store -0.)

Built-in types in Java are byte (one byte), short (two bytes), int (four bytes), and long (eight bytes). Of these, only int is in the AP Java subset.

FLOATING-POINT NUMBERS

There are two built-in types in Java that store real numbers: float, which uses four bytes, and double, which uses eight bytes. A *floating-point number* is stored in two parts: a *mantissa*, which specifies the digits of the number, and an exponent. The JVM (Java Virtual Machine) represents the number using scientific notation:

$$\text{sign} * \text{mantissa} * 2^{\text{exponent}}$$

In this expression, 2 is the *base* or *radix* of the number. In type double eleven bits are allocated for the exponent, and (typically) 52 bits for the mantissa. One bit is allocated for the sign. This is a *double-precision* number. Type float, which is *single-precision*, is not in the AP Java subset.

When floating-point numbers are converted to binary, most cannot be represented exactly, leading to *round-off error*. These errors are compounded by arithmetic operations. For example,

$$\texttt{0.1*26} \neq \texttt{0.1+0.1+}\cdots\texttt{+0.1} \quad \text{(26 terms)}$$

In Java, no exceptions are thrown for floating-point operations. There are two situations you should be aware of:

- When an operation is performed that gives an undefined result, Java expresses this result as NaN, "not a number." Examples of operations that produce NaN are: taking the square root of a negative number, and 0.0 divided by 0.0.

- An operation that gives an infinitely large or infinitely small number, like division by zero, produces a result of Infinity or -Infinity in Java.

Hexadecimal Numbers

A *hexadecimal number* or *hex number* uses base (radix) 16, and is represented with the symbols 0 – 9 and A – F (occasionally a – f), where A represents 10, and F represents 15. To denote a hex number in Java, the prefix "0x" or "0X" is used, for example, 0xC2A. On the AP exam, the representation is likely to be with the subscript hex: $C2A_{\text{hex}}$. In expanded form, this number means

$$(C)(16^2) + (2)(16^1) + (A)(16^0)$$
$$= (12)(16^2) + (2)(16) + (10)(1)$$
$$= 3114, \text{ or } 3114_{\text{dec}}$$

The advantages of hex numbers are their compactness, and the ease of conversion between hex and binary. Notice that any hex digit expands to four bits. For example,

$$5_{\text{hex}} = 0101_{\text{bin}} \quad \text{and} \quad F_{\text{hex}} = 1111_{\text{bin}}$$

Thus, $5F_{hex} = 01011111_{bin}$, which is 1011111_{bin}.

Similarly, to convert a binary number to hex, convert in groups of four from right to left. If necessary, pad with zeroes to complete the last group of four. For example,

$$1011101_{bin} = 0101 \quad 1101_{bin}$$
$$= 5 \qquad D_{hex}$$
$$= 5D_{hex}$$

Final Variables

A *final variable* or *user-defined constant*, identified by the keyword `final`, is used to name a quantity whose value will not change. Here are some examples of `final` declarations:

```
final double TAX_RATE = 0.08;
final int CLASS_SIZE = 35;
```

NOTE

1. Constant identifiers are, by convention, capitalized.
2. A `final` variable can be declared without initializing it immediately. For example,

   ```
   final double TAX_RATE;
   if (< some condition >)
       TAX_RATE = 0.08;
   else
       TAX_RATE = 0.0;
   // TAX_RATE can be given a value just once: its value is final!
   ```

3. A common use for a constant is as an array bound. For example,

   ```
   final int MAXSTUDENTS = 25;
   int[] classList = new int[MAXSTUDENTS];
   ```

4. Using constants makes it easier to revise code. Just a single change in the `final` declaration need be made, rather than having to change every occurrence of a value.

OPERATORS

Arithmetic Operators

Operator	Meaning	Example
+	addition	3 + x
–	subtraction	p - q
*	multiplication	6 * i
/	division	10 / 4 //returns 2, not 2.5!
%	mod (remainder)	11 % 8 //returns 3

NOTE

1. These operators can be applied to types `int` and `double`, even if both types occur in the same expression. For an operation involving a `double` and an `int`, the `int` is promoted to `double`, and the result is a `double`.
2. The mod operator %, as in the expression a % b, gives the remainder when a is divided by b. Thus 10 % 3 evaluates to 1, whereas 4.2 % 2.0 evaluates to 0.2.
3. Integer division a/b where both a and b are of type `int` returns the integer quotient only (i.e., the answer is truncated). Thus, 22/6 gives 3, and 3/4 gives 0. If at least one of the operands is of type `double`, then the operation becomes regular floating-point division, and there is no truncation. You can control the kind of division that is carried out by explicitly casting (one or both of) the operands from `int` to `double` and vice versa. Thus

```
3.0 / 4          →   0.75
3 / 4.0          →   0.75
(int) 3.0 / 4    →   0
(double) 3 / 4   →   0.75
```

You must, however, be careful:

```
(double) (3 / 4)   →   0.0
```

since the integer division 3/4 is computed first, before casting to `double`.

4. The arithmetic operators follow the normal precedence rules (order of operations):

   (1) parentheses, from the inner ones out (highest precedence)
   (2) *, /, %
   (3) +, – (lowest precedence)

Here operators on the same line have the same precedence, and, in the absence of parentheses, are invoked from left to right. Thus the expression 19 % 5 * 3 + 14 / 5 evaluates to 4 * 3 + 2 = 14. Note that casting has precedence over all of these operators. Thus, in the expression (double) 3/4, 3 will be cast to `double` before the division is done.

Relational Operators

Operator	Meaning	Example
==	equal to	if (x == 100)
!=	not equal to	if (age != 21)
>	greater than	if (salary > 30000)
<	less than	if (grade < 65)
>=	greater than or equal to	if (age >= 16)
<=	less than or equal to	if (height <= 6)

NOTE

1. Relational operators are used in *boolean expressions* that evaluate to true or false.

```
boolean x = (a != b);     //initializes x to true if a != b,
                          // false otherwise
```

```
return p == q;              //returns true if p equals q,
                            // false otherwise
```

2. If the operands are an `int` and a `double`, the `int` is promoted to a `double` as for arithmetic operators.

3. Relational operators should generally be used only in the comparison of primitive types (i.e., `int`, `double`, or `boolean`). User-defined types are compared using the `equals` and `compareTo` methods (see pp. 199 and 227).

4. Be careful when comparing floating-point values! Since floating-point numbers cannot always be represented exactly in the computer memory, they should not be compared directly using relational operators.

> Do not routinely use
> == to test for equality
> of floating-point
> numbers.

Comparing Floating-Point Numbers

Because of round-off errors in floating-point numbers, you can't rely on using the `==` or `!=` operators to compare two `double` values for equality. They may differ in their last significant digit or two because of round-off error. Instead, you should test that the magnitude of the difference between the numbers is less than some number about the size of the machine precision. The machine precision is usually denoted ϵ and is typically about 10^{-16} for double precision (i.e., about 16 decimal digits). So you would like to test something like $|x - y| \le \epsilon$. But this is no good if x and y are very large. For example, suppose $x = 1234567890.123456$ and $y = 1234567890.123457$. These numbers are essentially equal to machine precision, since they differ only in the 16th significant digit. But $|x - y| = 10^{-6}$, not 10^{-16}. So in general you should check the *relative* difference:

$$\frac{|x - y|}{\max(|x|, |y|)} \le \epsilon$$

To avoid problems with dividing by zero, code this as

$$|x - y| \le \epsilon \max(|x|, |y|)$$

An example of code that uses a correct comparison of real numbers can be found in the `Shape` class on p. 199.

Logical Operators

Operator	Meaning	Example
`!`	NOT	`if (!found)`
`&&`	AND	`if (x < 3 && y > 4)`
`||`	OR	`if (age < 2 || height < 4)`

NOTE

1. Logical operators are applied to boolean expressions to form *compound boolean expressions* that evaluate to `true` or `false`.
2. Values of `true` or `false` are assigned according to the truth tables for the logical operators.

&&	T	F		||	T	F		!	
T	T	F		T	T	T		T	F
F	F	F		F	T	F		F	T

For example, F && T evaluates to F, while T \|\| F evaluates to T.

3. *Short-circuit evaluation.* The subexpressions in a compound boolean expression are evaluated from left to right, and evaluation automatically stops as soon as the value of the entire expression is known. For example, consider a boolean OR expression of the form A \|\| B, where A and B are some boolean expressions. If A is `true`, then the expression is `true` irrespective of the value of B. Similarly, if A is `false`, then A && B evaluates to `false` irrespective of the second operand. So in each case the second operand is not evaluated. For example,

```
if (numScores != 0 && scoreTotal/numScores > 90)
```

will not cause a run-time `ArithmeticException` (division-by-zero error) if the value of numScores is 0. This is because numScores != 0 will evaluate to `false`, causing the entire boolean expression to evaluate to `false` without having to evaluate the second expression containing the division.

Assignment Operators

Operator	Example	Meaning
=	x = 2	simple assignment
+=	x += 4	x = x + 4
-=	y -= 6	y = y - 6
*=	p *= 5	p = p * 5
/=	n /= 10	n = n / 10
%=	n %= 10	n = n % 10

NOTE

1. All these operators, with the exception of simple assignment, are called *compound assignment operators*.
2. *Chaining* of assignment statements is allowed, with evaluation from right to left.

```
int next, prev, sum;
next = prev = sum = 0;   //initializes sum to 0, then prev to 0
                         //then next to 0
```

Increment and Decrement Operators

Operator	Example	Meaning
++	i++ or ++i	i is incremented by 1
–	k– or –k	k is decremented by 1

Note that i++ (postfix) and ++i (prefix) both have the net effect of incrementing i by 1, but they are not equivalent. For example, if i currently has the value 5, then System.out.println(i++) will print 5 and then increment i to 6, whereas System.out.println(++i) will first increment i to 6 and then print 6. It's easy to remember: if the ++ is first, you first increment. A similar distinction occurs between k– and –k. (Note: You do not need to know these distinctions for the AP exam.)

Operator Precedence

highest precedence   →   (1)   !, ++, –
                         (2)   *, /, %
                         (3)   +, –
                         (4)   <, >, <=, >=
                         (5)   ==, !=
                         (6)   &&
                         (7) ||
lowest precedence   →   (8)   =, +=, -=, *=, /=, %=

Here operators on the same line have equal precedence. The evaluation of the operators with equal precedence is from left to right, except for rows (1) and (8) where the order is right to left. It is easy to remember: the only "backward" order is for the unary operators (row 1) and for the various assignment operators (row 8).

Example

What will be output by the following statement?

```
System.out.println(5 + 3 < 6 - 1);
```

Since + and – have precedence over <, 5 + 3 and 6 – 1 will be evaluated before evaluating the boolean expression. Since the value of the expression is false, the statement will output false.

INPUT/OUTPUT

Input

Since there are so many ways to provide input to a program, user input is not a part of the AP Java subset. If reading input is a necessary part of a question on the AP exam, it will be indicated something like this:

```
double x = call to a method that reads a floating-point number
```

or

```
double x = IO.readDouble();    //read user input
```

NOTE

The `Scanner` class, new in Java 5.0, simplifies both console and file input. It will not, however, be tested on the AP exam.

Output

Testing of output will be restricted to `System.out.print` and `System.out.println`. Formatted output will not be tested.

`System.out` is an object in the `System` class that allows output to be displayed on the screen. The `println` method outputs an item and then goes to a new line. The `print` method outputs an item without going to a new line afterward. An item to be printed can be a string, or a number, or the value of a boolean expression (`true` or `false`). Here are some examples:

```
System.out.print("Hot");        ⎫  prints  Hotdog
System.out.println("dog");      ⎬

System.out.println("Hot");  ⎫           Hot
System.out.println("dog");  ⎬   prints  dog

System.out.println(7 + 3);      ⎬  prints  10

System.out.println(7 == 2 + 5);  ⎬   prints   true

int x = 27;
System.out.println(x);       ⎬   prints   27
System.out.println("Value of x is " + x);
                        prints  Value of x is 27
```

In the last example, the value of x, 27, is converted to the string `"27"`, which is then concatenated to the string `"Value of x is "`.

To print the "values" of user-defined objects, the `toString()` method is invoked (see p. 226).

Escape Sequences

An *escape sequence* is a backslash followed by a single character. It is used to print special characters. The three escape sequences that you should know for the AP exam are

Escape Sequence	Meaning
\n	newline
\"	double quote
\\	backslash

Here are some examples:

```
System.out.println("Welcome to\na new line");
```

prints

```
Welcome to
a new line
```

The statement

```
System.out.println("He is known as \"Hothead Harry\".");
```

prints

```
He is known as "Hothead Harry".
```

The statement

```
System.out.println("The file path is d:\\myFiles\\..");
```

prints

```
The file path is d:\myFiles\..
```

CONTROL STRUCTURES

Control structures are the mechanism by which you make the statements of a program run in a nonsequential order. There are two general types: decision making and iteration.

Decision-Making Control Structures

These include the if, if...else, and switch statements. They are all selection control structures that introduce a decision-making ability into a program. Based on the truth value of a boolean expression, the computer will decide which path to follow. The switch statement is not part of the AP Java subset.

THE if STATEMENT

```
if (boolean expression)
{
    statements
}
```

Here the *statements* will be executed only if the *boolean expression* is true. If it is false, control passes immediately to the first statement following the if statement.

THE if...else STATEMENT

```
if (boolean expression)
{
    statements
}
else
{
    statements
}
```

Here if the *boolean expression* is true, only the *statements* immediately following the test will be executed. If the *boolean expression* is false, only the *statements* following the else will be executed.

NESTED `if` STATEMENT

If the statement part of an `if` statement is itself an `if` statement, the result is a *nested* if *statement*.

Example 1

```
if  (boolean expr1)
    if  (boolean expr2)
        statement;
```

This is equivalent to

```
if  (boolean expr1 && boolean expr2)
    statement;
```

Example 2

Beware the dangling `else`! Suppose you want to read in an integer and print it if it's positive and even. Will the following code do the job?

```
int n = IO.readInt();          //read user input
if (n > 0)
    if (n % 2 == 0)
        System.out.println(n);
else
    System.out.println(n + " is not positive");
```

A user enters 7 and is surprised to see the output

```
7 is not positive
```

The reason is that `else` always gets matched with the *nearest* unpaired `if`, not the first `if` as the indenting would suggest.

There are two ways to fix the preceding code. The first is to use {} delimiters to group the statements correctly.

```
int n = IO.readInt();          //read user input
if (n > 0)
{
    if (n % 2 == 0)
        System.out.println(n);
}
else
    System.out.println(n + " is not positive");
```

The second way of fixing the code is to rearrange the statements.

```
int n = IO.readInt();          //read user input
if (n <= 0)
    System.out.println(n + " is not positive");
else
    if (n % 2 == 0)
        System.out.println(n);
```

EXTENDED `if` STATEMENT

For example,

```
String grade = IO.readString();          //read user input
if (grade.equals("A"))
    System.out.println("Excellent!");
else if (grade.equals("B"))
    System.out.println("Good");
else if (grade.equals("C") || grade.equals("D"))
    System.out.println("Poor");
else if (grade.equals("F"))
    System.out.println("Egregious!");
else
    System.out.println("Invalid grade");
```

If any of A, B, C, D, or F are entered, an appropriate message will be written and control will go to the statement immediately following the extended `if` statement. If any other string is entered, the final `else` is invoked, and the message `Invalid grade` will be written.

Iteration

Java has three different control structures that allow the computer to perform iterative tasks: the `for` loop, `while` loop, and `do...while` loop. The `do...while` loop is not in the AP Java subset.

THE `for` LOOP

The general form of the `for` loop is

```
for (initialization; termination condition; update statement)
{
    statements           //body of loop
}
```

The termination condition is tested at the top of the loop; the update statement is performed at the bottom.

Example 1

```
//outputs 1 2 3 4
for (i = 1; i < 5; i++)
    System.out.print(i + " ");
```

Here's how it works. The *loop variable* i is initialized to 1, and the termination condition i < 5 is evaluated. If it is true, the body of the loop is executed and then the loop variable i is incremented according to the update statement. As soon as the termination condition is false (i.e., i >= 5), control passes to the first statement following the loop.

Example 2

```
//outputs 20 19 18 17 16 15
for (k = 20; k >= 15; k--)
    System.out.print(k + " ");
```

Example 3

```
//outputs 2 4 6 8 10
for (j = 2; j <= 10; j += 2)
    System.out.print(j + " ");
```

NOTE

1. The loop variable should not have its value changed inside the loop body.
2. The initializing and update statements can use any valid constants, variables, or expressions.
3. The scope (see p. 155) of the loop variable can be restricted to the loop body by combining the loop variable declaration with the initialization. For example,

```
for (int i = 0; i < 3; i++)
{
    ...
}
```

4. The following loop is syntactically valid:

```
for (int i = 1; i <= 0; i++)
{
    ...
}
```

The loop body will not be executed at all, since the exiting condition is true before the first execution.

THE FOR-EACH LOOP

This is used to iterate over an array or collection. The general form of the loop is

```
for (SomeType element : collection)
{
    statements
}
```

(Read the top line as "For each `element` of type `SomeType` in `collection` ...")

Example

```
//Outputs all elements of arr, one per line.
for (int element : arr)
    System.out.println(element);
```

NOTE

1. The for-each loop cannot be used for replacing or removing elements as you traverse.
2. The loop hides the index variable that is used with arrays.
3. The loop hides the iterator that is used with collections other than arrays (see p. 476).

AB ONLY

THE `while` LOOP

The general form of the `while` loop is

```
while (boolean test)
{
    statements          //loop body
}
```

The *boolean test* is performed at the beginning of the loop. If `true`, the loop body is executed. Otherwise, control passes to the first statement following the loop. After execution of the loop body, the test is performed again. If true, the loop is executed again, and so on.

Example 1

```
int i = 1, mult3 = 3;
while (mult3 < 20)
{
    System.out.print(mult3 + " ");
    i++;
    mult3 *= i;
}                           //outputs 3 6 18
```

NOTE

> The body of a `while` loop must contain a statement that leads to termination.

1. It is possible for the body of a `while` loop never to be executed. This will happen if the test evaluates to `false` the first time.
2. Disaster will strike in the form of an infinite loop if the test can never be false. Don't forget to change the loop variable in the body of the loop in a way that leads to termination!

Example 2

```
int power2 = 1;
while (power2 != 20)
{
    System.out.println(power2);
    power2 *= 2;
}
```

Since `power2` will never exactly equal 20, the loop will grind merrily along eventually causing an integer overflow.

Example 3

```
/* Screen out bad data.
 * The loop won't allow execution to continue until a valid
 * integer is entered. */
System.out.println("Enter a positive integer from 1 to 100");
int num = IO.readInt();        //read user input
while (num < 1 || num > 100)
{
    System.out.println("Number must be from 1 to 100.";
    System.out.println("Please reenter");
    num = IO.readInt();
}
```

Example 4

```
/* Uses a sentinel to terminate data entered at the keyboard.
 * The sentinel is a value that cannot be part of the data.
 * It signals the end of the list. */
final int SENTINEL = -999;
System.out.println("Enter list of positive integers," +
    " end list with " + SENTINEL);
int value = IO.readInt();        //read user input
while (value != SENTINEL)
{
    process the value
    value = IO.readInt();        //read another value
}
```

NESTED LOOPS

You create a *nested loop* when a loop is a statement in the body of another loop.

Example 1

```
for (int k = 1; k <= 3; k++)
{
    for (int i = 1; i <= 4; i++)
        System.out.print("*");
    System.out.println();
}
```

Think:

```
for each of 3 rows
{
    print 4 stars
    go to next line
}
```

Output:

```
****
****
****
```

Example 2

This example has two loops nested in an outer loop.

```
for (int i = 1; i <= 6; i++)
{
    for (int j = 1; j <= i; j++)
        System.out.print("+");
    for (int j = 1; j <= 6 - i; j++)
        System.out.print("*");
    System.out.println();
}
```

Output:

```
+*****
++****
+++***
++++**
+++++*
++++++
```

ERRORS AND EXCEPTIONS

An *exception* is an error condition that occurs during the execution of a Java program. For example, if you divide an integer by zero, an `ArithmeticException` will be thrown. If you use a negative array index, an `ArrayIndexOutOfBoundsException` will be thrown.

An *unchecked exception* is one where you don't provide code to deal with the error. Such exceptions are automatically handled by Java's standard exception-handling methods, which terminate execution. You now need to fix your code!

A *checked exception* is one where you provide code to handle the exception, either a `try/catch/finally` statement, or an explicit `throw new ...Exception` clause. These exceptions are not necessarily caused by an error in the code. For example, an unexpected end-of-file could be due to a broken network connection. Checked exceptions are not part of the AP Java subset.

The following exceptions are in the AP Java subset:

Exception	Discussed on page
ArithmeticException	this page
NullPointerException	158
ClassCastException	195
ArrayIndexOutOfBoundsException	288
IndexOutOfBoundsException	298
NoSuchElementException	369, 475, 477, 484
IllegalStateException	476, 477
IllegalArgumentException	next page, 580

Java allows you to write code that throws a standard unchecked exception. Here are typical examples:

Example 1

```
if (numScores == 0)
    throw new ArithmeticException("Cannot divide by zero");
else
    findAverageScore();
```

Example 2

```
public void setRadius(int newRadius)
{
    if (newRadius < 0)
        throw new IllegalArgumentException
                ("Radius cannot be negative");
    else
        radius = newRadius;
}
```

NOTE

1. `throw` and `new` are both reserved words.
2. The error message is optional: The line in Example 1 could have read

   ```
   throw new ArithmeticException();
   ```

   The message, however, is useful, since it tells the person running the program what went wrong.
3. An `IllegalArgumentException` is thrown to indicate that a parameter does not satisfy a method's precondition.
4. Writing code to throw your own exceptions is not part of the Level A subset. Level AB students may be asked to throw a `NoSuchElementException`, an `IllegalStateException`, or an `IllegalArgumentException`.

Chapter Summary

Be sure that you understand the difference between primitive and user-defined types, and between the following types of operators: arithmetic, relational, logical, and assignment. Know which conditions lead to what types of errors.

You should be able to work with numbers—know how to compare them, and how to convert between decimal, binary, and hexadecimal numbers. Know how integers and floating-point numbers are stored in memory, and be aware of the conditions that can lead to round-off error.

Be familiar with each of the following control structures: conditional statements, for loops, while loops, and for-each loops.

Be aware of the AP exam expectations concerning input and output.

MULTIPLE-CHOICE QUESTIONS ON INTRODUCTORY JAVA LANGUAGE CONCEPTS

1. Which of the following pairs of declarations will cause an error message?

    ```
     I  double x = 14.7;
        int y = x;

     II double x = 14.7;
        int y = (int) x;

    III int x = 14;
        double y = x;
    ```

    (A) None
    (B) I only
    (C) II only
    (D) III only
    (E) I and III only

2. What output will be produced by

    ```
    System.out.print("\\* This is not\n a comment *\\");
    ```

    (A) `* This is not a comment *`

    (B) `\* This is not a comment *\`

    (C) `* This is not`
        `a comment *`

    (D) `\\* This is not`
        `a comment *\\`

    (E) `\* This is not`
        `a comment *\`

3. Refer to the following code fragment:

```
double answer = 13 / 5;
System.out.println("13 / 5 = " + answer);
```

The output is

```
13 / 5 = 2.0
```

The programmer intends the output to be

```
13 / 5 = 2.6
```

Which of the following replacements for the first line of code will *not* fix the problem?
(A) `double answer = (double) 13 / 5;`
(B) `double answer = 13 / (double) 5;`
(C) `double answer = 13.0 / 5;`
(D) `double answer = 13 / 5.0;`
(E) `double answer = (double) (13 / 5);`

4. What value is stored in `result` if

```
int result = 13 - 3 * 6 / 4 % 3;
```

(A) −5
(B) 0
(C) 13
(D) −1
(E) 12

5. Suppose that addition and subtraction had higher precedence than multiplication and division. Then the expression

```
2 + 3 * 12 / 7 - 4 + 8
```

would evaluate to which of the following?
(A) 11
(B) 12
(C) 5
(D) 9
(E) −4

6. Let x be a variable of type `double` that is positive. A program contains the boolean expression (`Math.pow(x,0.5)` == `Math.sqrt(x)`). Even though $x^{1/2}$ is mathematically equivalent to $\sqrt{x}$, the above expression returns the value `false` in a student's program. Which of the following is the most likely reason?
(A) `Math.pow` returns an `int`, while `Math.sqrt` returns a `double`.
(B) x was imprecisely calculated in a previous program statement.
(C) The computer stores floating-point numbers with 32-bit words.
(D) There is round-off error in calculating the `pow` and `sqrt` functions.
(E) There is overflow error in calculating the `pow` function.

7. Consider the following code segment

```
if (n != 0 && x / n > 100)
    statement1;
else
    statement2;
```

If n is of type int and has a value of 0 when the segment is executed, what will happen?

(A) An ArithmeticException will be thrown.

(B) A syntax error will occur.

(C) *statement1*, but not *statement2*, will be executed.

(D) *statement2*, but not *statement1*, will be executed.

(E) Neither *statement1* nor *statement2* will be executed; control will pass to the first statement following the if statement.

8. What will the output be for the following poorly formatted program segment, if the input value for num is 22?

```
int num =   call to a method that reads an integer;
if (num > 0)
if (num % 5 == 0)
System.out.println(num);
else System.out.println(num + " is negative");
```

(A) 22

(B) 4

(C) 2 is negative

(D) 22 is negative

(E) Nothing will be output.

9. Look at the following poorly formatted program segment. If a = 7 and c = 6 before execution, which of the following represents the correct values of c, d, p, and t after execution? An undetermined value is represented with a question mark.

```
if (a == 6)
if (c == 6)
{
    c = 9;
    d = 9;
}
else
{
    t = 10;
    if (c == 6)
        c = 5;
}
else p = 9;
```

(A) c = 6, d = ?, p = 9, t = ?
(B) c = 5, d = ?, p = ?, t = 10
(C) c = 6, d = ?, p = ?, t = ?
(D) c = 5, d = 9, p = ?, t = 10
(E) c = 9, d = 9, p = ?, t = ?

10. What values are stored in x and y after execution of the following program segment?

```
int x = 30, y = 40;
if (x >= 0)
{
    if (x <= 100)
    {
        y = x * 3;
        if (y < 50)
            x /= 10;
    }
    else
        y = x * 2;
}
else
    y = -x;
```

(A) x = 30 y = 90
(B) x = 30 y = -30
(C) x = 30 y = 60
(D) x = 3   y = -3
(E) x = 30 y = 40

11. The boolean expression `!A && B || C` is equivalent to
    (A) `!A && (B || C)`
    (B) `((!A) && B) || C`
    (C) `(!A) && (B || C)`
    (D) `!(A && B) || C`
    (E) `!(A && B || C)`

12. Assume that a and b are integers. The boolean expression

    `!(a <= b) && (a * b > 0)`

    will always evaluate to `true` given that
    (A) `a = b`
    (B) `a > b`
    (C) `a < b`
    (D) `a > b and b > 0`
    (E) `a > b and b < 0`

13. Given that a, b, and c are integers, consider the boolean expression

    `(a < b) || !((c == a * b) && (c < a))`

    Which of the following will *guarantee* that the expression is `true`?
    (A) `c < a` is `false`.
    (B) `c < a` is `true`.
    (C) `a < b` is `false`.
    (D) `c == a * b` is `true`.
    (E) `c == a * b` is `true`, and `c < a` is `true`.

14. Given that n and count are both of type `int`, which statement is true about the following code segments?

    ```
    I for (count = 1; count <= n; count++)
          System.out.println(count);
    ```

    ```
    II count = 1;
       while (count <= n)
       {
           System.out.println(count);
           count++;
       }
    ```

    (A) I and II are exactly equivalent for all input values n.
    (B) I and II are exactly equivalent for all input values n ≥ 1, but differ when n ≤ 0.
    (C) I and II are exactly equivalent only when n = 0.
    (D) I and II are exactly equivalent only when n is even.
    (E) I and II are not equivalent for any input values of n.

15. The following fragment intends that a user will enter a list of positive integers at the keyboard and terminate the list with a sentinel:

```
int value;
final int SENTINEL = -999;
while (value != SENTINEL)
{
    //code to process value
    ...
    value = IO.readInt();       //read user input
}
```

The fragment is not correct. Which is a true statement?
(A) The sentinel gets processed.
(B) The last nonsentinel value entered in the list fails to get processed.
(C) A poor choice of SENTINEL value causes the loop to terminate before all values have been processed.
(D) Running the program with this code causes a compile-time error.
(E) Entering the SENTINEL value as the first value causes a run-time error.

16. Suppose that base-2 (binary) numbers and base-16 (hexadecimal) numbers can be denoted with subscripts, as shown below:

$$2A_{hex} = 101010_{bin}$$

Which is equal to $3D_{hex}$?
(A) 111101_{bin}
(B) 101111_{bin}
(C) 10011_{bin}
(D) 110100_{bin}
(E) 101101_{bin}

17. Consider this code segment:

```
int x = 10, y = 0;
while (x > 5)
{
    y = 3;
    while (y < x)
    {
        y *= 2;
        if (y % x == 1)
            y += x;
    }
    x -= 3;
}
System.out.println(x + " " + y);
```

What will be output after execution of this code segment?
(A) 1   6
(B) 7   12
(C) -3   12
(D) 4   12
(E) -3   6

Questions 18 and 19 refer to the following method, checkNumber, which checks the validity of its four-digit integer parameter.

```java
//Precondition:  n is a 4-digit integer.
//Postcondition: Returns true if n is valid, false otherwise.
boolean checkNumber(int n)
{
    int d1,d2,d3,checkDigit,nRemaining,rem;
    //strip off digits
    checkDigit = n % 10;
    nRemaining = n / 10;
    d3 = nRemaining % 10;
    nRemaining /= 10;
    d2 = nRemaining % 10;
    nRemaining /= 10;
    d1 = nRemaining % 10;
    //check validity
    rem = (d1 + d2 + d3) % 7;
    return rem == checkDigit;
}
```

A program invokes method checkNumber with the statement

```java
boolean valid = checkNumber(num);
```

18. Which of the following values of num will result in valid having a value of true?
    (A) 6143
    (B) 6144
    (C) 6145
    (D) 6146
    (E) 6147

19. What is the purpose of the local variable nRemaining?
    (A) It is not possible to separate n into digits without the help of a temporary variable.
    (B) nRemaining prevents the parameter num from being altered.
    (C) nRemaining enhances the readability of the algorithm.
    (D) On exiting the method, the value of nRemaining may be reused.
    (E) nRemaining is needed as the left-hand side operand for integer division.

20. What output will be produced by this code segment? (Ignore spacing.)

```
for (int i = 5; i >= 1; i--)
{
    for (int j = i; j >= 1; j--)
        System.out.print(2 * j - 1);
    System.out.println();
}
```

(A) 9 7 5 3 1
    9 7 5 3
    9 7 5
    9 7
    9

(B) 9 7 5 3 1
    7 5 3 1
    5 3 1
    3 1
    1

(C) 9 7 5 3 1
    7 5 3 1 -1
    5 3 1 -1 -3
    3 1 -1 -3 -5
    1 -1 -3 -5 -7

(D) 1
    1 3
    1 3 5
    1 3 5 7
    1 3 5 7 9

(E) 1 3 5 7 9
    1 3 5 7
    1 3 5
    1 3
    1

21. Which of the following program fragments will produce this output? (Ignore spacing.)

```
2 - - - - -
- 4 - - - -
- - 6 - - -
- - - 8 - -
- - - - 10 -
- - - - - 12
```

```
I for (int i = 1; i <= 6; i++)
  {
      for (int k = 1; k <= 6; k++)
          if (k == i)
              System.out.print(2 * k);
          else
              System.out.print("-");
      System.out.println();
  }

II for (int i = 1; i <= 6; i++)
   {
       for (int k = 1; k <= i - 1; k++)
           System.out.print("-");
       System.out.print(2 * i);
       for (int k = 1; k <= 6 - i; k++)
           System.out.print("-");
       System.out.println();
   }

III for (int i = 1; i <= 6; i++)
    {
        for (int k = 1; k <= i - 1; k++)
            System.out.print("-");
        System.out.print(2 * i);
        for (int k = i + 1; k <= 6; k++)
            System.out.print("-");
        System.out.println();
    }
```

(A) I only
(B) II only
(C) III only
(D) I and II only
(E) I, II, and III

22. Consider this program segment:

```
int newNum = 0, temp;
int num = k;                //k is some predefined integer value ≥ 0
while (num > 10)
{
    temp = num % 10;
    num /= 10;
    newNum = newNum * 10 + temp;
}
System.out.print(newNum);
```

Which is a true statement about the segment?

  I If $100 \le$ num ≤ 1000 initially, the final value of newNum must be in the range $10 \le$ newNum ≤ 100.

 II There is no initial value of num that will cause an infinite while loop.

III If num ≤ 10 initially, newNum will have a final value of 0.

(A) I only
(B) II only
(C) III only
(D) II and III only
(E) I, II, and III

23. Consider the method reverse:

```
//Precondition:  n > 0.
//Postcondition: returns n with its digits reversed.
//Example: If n = 234, method reverse returns 432.
int reverse(int n)
{
    int rem, revNum = 0;

    /* code segment */

    return revNum;
}
```

Which of the following replacements for /* *code segment* */ would cause the method to work as intended?

```
I  for (int i = 0; i <= n; i++)
   {
       rem = n % 10;
       revNum = revNum * 10 + rem;
       n /= 10;
   }

II  while (n != 0)
    {
        rem = n % 10;
        revNum = revNum * 10 + rem;
        n /= 10;
    }

III  for (int i = n; i != 0; i /= 10)
     {
         rem = i % 10;
         revNum = revNum * 10 + rem;
     }
```

(A) I only
(B) II only
(C) I and II only
(D) II and III only
(E) I and III only

ANSWER KEY

1. B	9. A	17. D
2. E	10. A	18. B
3. E	11. B	19. C
4. E	12. D	20. B
5. C	13. A	21. E
6. D	14. A	22. D
7. D	15. D	23. D
8. D	16. A	

ANSWERS EXPLAINED

1. **(B)** When x is converted to an integer, as in segment I, information is lost. Java requires that an explicit cast to an int be made, as in segment II. Note that segment II will cause x to be truncated: the value stored in y is 14. By requiring the explicit cast, Java doesn't let you do this accidentally. In segment III y will contain the value 14.0. No explicit cast to a double is required since no information is lost.

2. **(E)** The string argument contains two escape sequences: '\\', which means print a backslash (\), and '\n', which means go to a new line. Choice E is the only choice that does both of these.

3. **(E)** For this choice, the integer division 13/5 will be evaluated to 2, which will then be cast to 2.0. The output will be 13/5 = 2.0. The compiler needs a way to recognize that real-valued division is required. All the other options provide a way.

4. **(E)** The operators *, /, and % have equal precedence, all higher than -, and must be performed first, from left to right.

   ```
        13 - 3 * 6 / 4 % 3
   =    13 - 18 / 4 % 3
   =    13 - 4 % 3
   =    13 - 1
   =    12
   ```

5. **(C)** The expression must be evaluated as if parenthesized like this:

   ```
   (2 + 3) * 12 / (7 - 4 + 8)
   ```

   This becomes 5 * 12 / 11 = 60 / 11 = 5.

6. **(D)** Anytime arithmetic operations are done with floating-point numbers, round-off error occurs. The Math class methods (see p. 234) such as pow and sqrt use various approximations to generate their answers to the required accuracy. Since they do different internal arithmetic, however, the round-off will usually not result in exactly the same answers. Note that choice A is not correct because both

`Math.pow` and `Math.sqrt` return type `double`. Choice B is wrong because no matter how x was previously calculated, the same x is input to `pow` and `sqrt`. Choice C is wrong since round-off error occurs no matter how many bits are used to represent numbers. Choice E is wrong because if x is representable on the machine (i.e., hasn't overflowed), then its square root, $x^{1/2}$, will not overflow.

7. **(D)** Short-circuit evaluation of the boolean expression will occur. The expression `(n != 0)` will evaluate to `false`, which makes the entire boolean expression `false`. Therefore the expression `(x/n > 100)` will not be evaluated. Hence no division by zero will occur, causing an `ArithmeticException` to be thrown. When the boolean expression has a value of `false`, only the `else` part of the statement, *statement2*, will be executed.

8. **(D)** Each `else` gets paired with the nearest unpaired `if`. Thus when the test `(22 % 5 == 0)` fails, the `else` part indicating that `22 is negative` will be executed. This is clearly not the intent of the fragment, which can be fixed using delimiters:

```
int num =   call to a method that reads an integer;
if (num > 0)
{
    if (num % 5 == 0)
        System.out.println(num);
}
else
    System.out.println(num + " is negative");
```

9. **(A)** Since `(a == 6)` is `false`, the

```
if (c == 6) ...
else
{
    t = 10; ...
```

statement will not be executed. The second `else` matches up with the first `if`, which means that `p = 9` gets executed. Variables `d` and `t` remain undefined.

10. **(A)** Since the first test `(x >= 0)` is `true`, the matching `else` part, `y = -x`, will not be executed. Since `(x <= 100)` is `true`, the matching `else` part, `y = x*2`, will not be executed. The variable y will be set to `x*3` (i.e., 90) and will now fail the test `y < 50`. Thus x will never be altered in this algorithm. Final values are `x = 30` and `y = 90`.

11. **(B)** The order of precedence from highest to lowest is `!`, `&&`, `||`. Thus, the order of evaluation is `(!A)`, `((!A) && B)`, and finally `((!A) && B) || C`.

12. **(D)** To evaluate to `true`, the expression must reduce to `true && true`. We therefore need `!(false) && true`. Choice D is the only condition that guarantees this: `a > b` provides `!(false)` for the left-hand expression, and `a > b` and `b > 0` implies both a and b positive, which leads to `true` for the right-hand expression. Choice E, for example, will provide `true` for the right-hand expression only if a `< 0`. You have no information about a and can't make assumptions about it.

13. **(A)** If `(c < a)` is `false`, `((c == a*b) && (c < a))` evaluates to `false` irrespective of the value of `c == a*b`. In this case, `!(c == a*b && c < a)` evaluates to `true`. Then `(a < b) || true` evaluates to `true` irrespective of the value of the test `(a < b)`. In all the other choices, the given expression *may* be true. There is not enough information given to guarantee this, however.

14. **(A)** If $n \geq 1$, both segments will print out the integers from 1 through n. If $n \leq 0$, both segments will fail the test immediately and do nothing.

15. **(D)** The (value != SENTINEL) test occurs before value is initialized, causing an error at compile time. The code must be fixed by reading the first value before doing the test:

```
final int SENTINEL = -999;
int value = IO.readInt();
while (value != SENTINEL)
{
    //code to process value
    value = IO.readInt();
}
```

Choices A, B, C, and E are all incorrect because if the program doesn't compile, it won't run! A note, however, about choice C: -999 is a fine choice for the sentinel given that only positive integers are valid input data.

16. **(A)** Quick method: Convert each hex digit to binary.

$$3 \qquad D_{hex}$$
$$= 0011 \qquad 1101 \qquad \text{(where D equals 13 in base 10)}$$
$$= 111101_{bin}$$

Slow method: Convert $3D_{hex}$ to base 10.

$$3D_{hex} = (3)(16^1) + (D)(16^0)$$
$$= 48 + 13$$
$$= 61_{dec}$$

Now convert 61_{dec} to binary. Write 61 as a sum of descending powers of 2:

$$61 = 32 + 16 + 8 + 4 + 1$$
$$= 1(2^5) + 1(2^4) + 1(2^3) + 1(2^2) + 0(2^1) + 1(2^0)$$
$$= 111101_{bin}$$

17. **(D)** Here is a trace of the values of x and y during execution. Note that the condition (y % x == 1) is never true in this example.

x	10				7				4
y		3	6	12		3	6	12	

The while loop terminates when x is 4 since the test while (x > 5) fails.

18. **(B)** The algorithm finds the remainder when the sum of the first three digits of n is divided by 7. If this remainder is equal to the fourth digit, checkDigit, the method returns true, otherwise false. Note that (6+1+4) % 7 equals 4. Thus, only choice B is a valid number.

19. **(C)** As n gets broken down into its digits, nRemaining is the part of n that remains after each digit is stripped off. Thus nRemaining is a self-documenting name that helps describe what is happening. Choice A is false because every digit can be stripped off using some sequence of integer division and mod. Choice B is false because num is passed by value and therefore will not be altered when the method is exited (see p. 159). Eliminate choice D: When the method is exited, all local variables are destroyed. Choice E is nonsense.

20. **(B)** The outer loop produces five rows of output. Each pass through the inner loop goes from i down to 1. Thus five odd numbers starting at 9 are printed in the first row, four odd numbers starting at 7 in the second row, and so on.

21. **(E)** All three algorithms produce the given output. The outer for (int i ...) loop produces six rows, and the inner for (int k ...) loops produce the symbols in each row.

22. **(D)** Statement I is false, since if 100 $\leq$ num $\leq$ 109, the body of the while loop will be executed just once. (After this single pass through the loop, the value of num will be 10, and the test if (num > 10) will fail.) With just one pass, newNum will be a one-digit number, equal to temp (which was the original num % 10). Note that statement II is true: there cannot be an infinite loop since num /= 10 guarantees termination of the loop. Statement III is true because if num $\leq$ 10, the loop will be skipped, and newNum will keep its original value of 0.

23. **(D)** The algorithm works by stripping off the rightmost digit of n (stored in rem), multiplying the current value of revNum by 10, and adding that rightmost digit. When n has been stripped down to no digits (i.e., n == 0 is true), revNum is complete. Segment I is wrong because the number of passes through the loop depends on the number of digits in n, not the value of n itself.

Classes and Objects

CHAPTER 2

Work is the curse of the drinking classes.
—*Oscar Wilde*

Chapter Goals

- Objects and classes
- Encapsulation
- References

- Keywords `public`, `private`, and `static`
- Methods

OBJECTS

Every program that you write involves at least one thing that is being created or manipulated by the program. This thing, together with the operations that manipulate it, is called an *object*.

Consider, for example, a program that must test the validity of a four-digit code number that a person will enter to be able to use a photocopy machine. Rules for validity are provided. The object is a four-digit code number. Some of the operations to manipulate the object could be `readNumber`, `getSeparateDigits`, `testValidity`, and `writeNumber`.

Any given program can have several different types of objects. For example, a program that maintains a database of all books in a library has at least two objects:

1. A `Book` object, with operations like `getTitle`, `isOnShelf`, `isFiction`, and `goOutOfPrint`.
2. A `ListOfBooks` object, with operations like `search`, `addBook`, `removeBook`, and `sortByAuthor`.

An object is characterized by its *state* and *behavior*. For example, a book has a state described by its title, author, whether it's on the shelf, and so on. It also has behavior, like going out of print.

Notice that an object is an idea, separate from the concrete details of a programming language. It corresponds to some real-world object that is being represented by the program.

All object-oriented programming languages have a way to represent an object as a variable in a program. In Java, a variable that represents an object is called an object reference.

CLASSES

A *class* is a software blueprint for implementing objects of a given type. An object is a single *instance* of the class. In a program there will often be several different instances of a given class type.

The current state of a given object is maintained in its *data fields* or *instance variables*, provided by the class. The *methods* of the class provide both the behaviors exhibited by the object and the operations that manipulate the object. Combining an object's data and methods into a single unit called a class is known as *encapsulation*.

Here is the framework for a simple bank account class:

```
public class BankAccount
{
    private String myPassword;
    private double myBalance;
    public static final double OVERDRAWN_PENALTY = 20.00;

    //constructors
    /* Default constructor.
     * Constructs bank account with default values. */
    public BankAccount()
    { /* implementation code */ }

    /* Constructs bank account with specified password and balance. */
    public BankAccount(String password, double balance)
    { /* implementation code */ }

    //accessor
    /* Returns balance of this account. */
    public double getBalance()
    { /* implementation code */ }

    //mutators
    /* Deposits amount in bank account with given password. */
    public void deposit(String password, double amount)
    { /* implementation code */ }

    /* Withdraws amount from bank account with given password.
     * Assesses penalty if myBalance is less than amount. */
    public void withdraw(String password, double amount)
    { /* implementation code */ }
}
```

PUBLIC, PRIVATE, AND STATIC

The keyword `public` preceding the class declaration signals that the class is usable by all *client programs*. If a class is not public, it can be used only by classes in its own package. In the AP Java subset, all classes are public.

Similarly, *public methods* are accessible to all client programs. Clients, however, are not privy to the class implementation, and may not access the private instance variables and private methods of the class. Restriction of access is known as *information hiding.* In Java, this is implemented by using the keyword private. *Private methods and variables in a class can be accessed only by methods of that class.* Even though Java allows public instance variables, in the AP Java subset all instance variables are private.

Static final variables (constants) in a class are often declared public (see some examples of Math class constants on p. 234). The variable OVERDRAWN_PENALTY is an example in the BankAccount class. Since the variable is public, it can be used in any client method. The keyword static indicates that there is a single value of the variable that applies to the whole class, rather than a new instance for each object of the class. A client method would refer to the variable as BankAccount.OVERDRAWN_PENALTY. In its own class it is referred to as simply OVERDRAWN_PENALTY.

See p. 153 for static methods.

METHODS

Headers

All method headers, with the exception of constructors (see below) and static methods (p. 153), look like this:

<u>public</u>   <u>void</u>   <u>withdraw</u> <u>(String password, double amount)</u>

  access specifier return type method name   parameter list

NOTE

1. The *access specifier* tells which other methods can call this method (see Public, Private, and Static on the previous page).
2. A *return type* of void signals that the method does not return a value.
3. Items in the *parameter list* are separated by commas.

The implementation of the method directly follows the header, enclosed in a {} block.

Types of Methods

CONSTRUCTORS

A *constructor* creates an object of the class. You can recognize a constructor by its name—always the same as the class. Also, a constructor has no return type.

Having several constructors provides different ways of initializing class objects. For example, there are two constructors in the BankAccount class.

1. The *default constructor* has no arguments. It provides reasonable initial values for an object. Here is its implementation:

```
/* Default constructor.
 * Constructs a bank account with default values */
public BankAccount()
{
    myPassword = "";
    myBalance = 0.0;
}
```

In a client method, the declaration

```
BankAccount b = new BankAccount();
```

constructs a `BankAccount` object with a balance of zero and a password equal to the empty string. The `new` operator returns the address of this newly constructed object. The variable `b` is assigned the value of this address—we say "`b` is a *reference* to the object." Picture the setup like this:

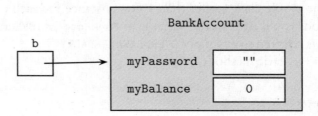

2. The constructor with parameters sets the instance variables of a `BankAccount` object to the values of those parameters.
   Here is the implementation:

```
/* Constructor. Constructs a bank account with
 * specified password and balance */
public BankAccount(String password, double balance)
{
    myPassword = password;
    myBalance = balance;
}
```

In a client program a declaration that uses this constructor needs matching parameters:

```
BankAccount c = new BankAccount("KevinC", 800.00);
```

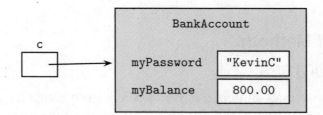

NOTE

`b` and `c` are *object variables* that store the *addresses* of their respective `BankAccount` objects. They do not store the objects themselves (see **References** on p. 156).

ACCESSORS

An *accessor method* accesses a class object without altering the object. An accessor returns some information about the object.

The `BankAccount` class has a single accessor method, `getBalance()`. Here is its implementation:

```
/* Returns the  balance of this account */
public double getBalance()
{ return myBalance; }
```

A client program may use this method as follows:

```
BankAccount b1 = new BankAccount("MattW", 500.00);
BankAccount b2 = new BankAccount("DannyB", 650.50);
if (b1.getBalance() > b2.getBalance())
    ...
```

NOTE

The . *operator* (dot operator) indicates that `getBalance()` is a method of the class to which `b1` and `b2` belong, namely the `BankAccount` class.

MUTATORS

A *mutator method* changes the state of an object by modifying at least one of its instance variables.

Here are the implementations of the `deposit` and `withdraw` methods, each of which alters the value of `myBalance` in the `BankAccount` class:

```
/* Deposits amount in a bank account with the given password. */
public void deposit(String password, double amount)
{
    myBalance += amount;
}
```

```
/* Withdraws amount from a bank account with the given password.
 * Assesses a penalty if myBalance is less than amount. */
public void withdraw(String password, double amount)
{
    if (myBalance >= amount)
        myBalance -= amount;
    else
        myBalance -= OVERDRAWN_PENALTY;  //allows negative balance
}
```

A mutator method in a client program is invoked in the same way as an accessor: using an object variable with the dot operator. For example, assuming valid `BankAccount` declarations for `b1` and `b2`:

```
b1.withdraw("MattW", 200.00);
b2.deposit("DannyB", 35.68);
```

STATIC METHODS

Static Methods vs. Instance Methods   The methods discussed in the preceding sections—constructors, accessors, and mutators—all operate on individual objects of a class. They are called *instance methods*. A method that performs an operation for the entire class, not its individual objects, is called a *static method* (sometimes called a *class method*).

The implementation of a static method uses the keyword `static` in its header. There is no implied object in the code (as there is in an instance method). Thus if the code tries to call an instance method or invoke a private instance variable for this nonexistent object, a syntax error will occur.

Here's an example of a static method that might be used in the BankAccount class:

```
public static double getInterestRate()
{
    System.out.println("Enter interest rate for bank account");
    System.out.println("Enter in decimal form:");
    double rate = IO.readDouble();           // read user input
    return rate;
}
```

Since the rate that's returned by this method applies to all bank accounts in the class, not to any particular BankAccount object, it's appropriate that the method should be static.

Recall that an instance method is invoked in a client program by using an object variable followed by the dot operator followed by the method name:

```
BankAccount b = new BankAccount();
b.deposit(password, amount);        //invokes the deposit method for
                                    //BankAccount object b
```

A static method, by contrast, is invoked by using the *class name* with the dot operator:

```
double interestRate = BankAccount.getInterestRate();
```

Static Methods in a Driver Class   Often a class that contains the main() method is used as a driver program to test other classes. Usually such a class creates no objects of the class. So all the methods in the class must be static. Note that at the start of program execution, no objects exist yet. So the main() method must *always* be static.

For example, here is a program that tests a class for reading integers entered at the keyboard.

```
import java.util.*;
public class GetListTest
{
    /* Return a list of integers from the keyboard. */
    public static List<Integer> getList()
    {
        < code to read integers into a>
        return a;
    }

    /* Write contents of List a. */
    public static void writeList(List<Integer> a)
    {
        System.out.println("List is : " + a);
    }

    public static void main(String[] args)
    {
        List<Integer> list = getList();
        writeList(list);
    }
}
```

NOTE

1. The calls to `writeList(list)` and `getList()` do not need to be preceded by `GetListTest` plus a dot because `main` is not a client program: It is in the same class as `getList` and `writeList`.

2. If you omit the keyword `static` from the `getList` or `writeList` header, you get an error message like the following:

```
Can't make static reference to method getList()
in class GetListTest
```

   The compiler has recognized that there was no object variable preceding the method call, which means that the methods were static and should have been declared as such.

Method Overloading

Overloaded methods are two or more methods in the same class that have the same name but different parameter lists. For example,

```
public class DoOperations
{
    public int product(int n) { return n * n; }
    public double product(double x) { return x * x; }
    public double product(int x, int y) { return x * y; }
        . . .
```

The compiler figures out which method to call by examining the method's *signature*. The signature of a method consists of the method's name and a list of the parameter types. Thus the signatures of the overloaded `product` methods are

```
product(int)
product(double)
product(int, int)
```

Note that for overloading purposes, the return type of the method is irrelevant. You can't have two methods with identical signatures but different return types. The compiler will complain that the method call is ambiguous.

Having more than one constructor in the same class is an example of overloading. Overloaded constructors provide a choice of ways to initialize objects of the class.

SCOPE

The *scope* of a variable or method is the region in which that variable or method is visible and can be accessed.

The instance variables, static variables, and methods of a class belong to that class's scope, which extends from the opening brace to the closing brace of the class definition. Within the class all instance variables and methods are accessible and can be referred to simply by name (no dot operator!).

A *local variable* is defined inside a method. It can even be defined inside a statement. Its scope extends from the point where it is declared to the end of the block in which its declaration occurs. A *block* is a piece of code enclosed in a {} pair. When a block is exited, the memory for a local variable is automatically recycled.

Local variables take precedence over instance variables with the same name. (Using the same name, however, creates ambiguity for the programmer, leading to errors. You should avoid the practice.)

The `this` Keyword

An instance method is always called for a particular object. This object is an *implicit parameter* for the method and is referred to with the keyword `this`.

In the implementation of instance methods, all instance variables can be written with the prefix `this` followed by the dot operator.

Example 1

The `deposit` method of the `BankAccount` class can refer to `myBalance` as follows:

```
public void deposit(String password, double amount)
{
    this.myBalance += amount;
}
```

The use of `this` is unnecessary in the above example.

Example 2

Consider a rational number class called `Rational`, which has two private instance variables:

```
private int num;          //numerator
private int denom;        //denominator
```

Now consider a constructor for the `Rational` class:

```
public Rational(int num, int denom)
{
    this.num = num;
    this.denom = denom;
}
```

It is definitely *not* a good idea to use the same name for the explicit parameters and the private instance variables. But if you do, you can avoid errors by referring to `this.num` and `this.denom` for the current object that is being constructed. (This particular use of `this` will not be tested on the exam.)

REFERENCES

Reference vs. Primitive Data Types

All of the numerical data types, like `double` and `int`, as well as types `char` and `boolean`, are *primitive* data types. All objects are *reference* data types. The difference lies in the way they are stored.

Consider the statements

```
int num1 = 3;
int num2 = num1;
```

The variables num1 and num2 can be thought of as memory slots, labeled num1 and num2, respectively:

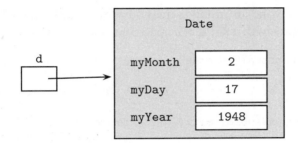

If either of the above variables is now changed, the other is not affected. Each has its own memory slot.

Contrast this with the declaration of a reference data type. Recall that an object is created using new:

```
Date d = new Date(2, 17, 1948);
```

This declaration creates a reference variable d that refers to a Date object. The value of d is the address in memory of that object:

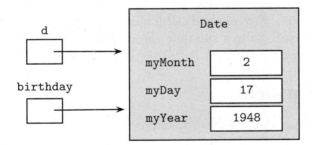

Suppose the following declaration is now made:

```
Date birthday = d;
```

This statement creates the reference variable birthday, which contains the same address as d:

Having two references for the same object is known as *aliasing*. Aliasing can cause unintended problems for the programmer. The statement

```
d.changeDate();
```

will automatically change the object referred to by birthday as well.

What the programmer probably intended was to create a second object called birthday whose attributes exactly matched those of d. This cannot be accomplished without using new. For example,

```
Date birthday = new Date(d.getMonth(), d.getDay(), d.getYear());
```

The statement d.changeDate() will now leave the birthday object unchanged.

The Null Reference

The declaration

```
BankAccount b;
```

defines a reference b that is uninitialized. (To construct the object that b refers to requires the new operator and a BankAccount constructor.) An uninitialized object variable is called a *null reference* or *null pointer*. You can test whether a variable refers to an object or is uninitialized by using the keyword null:

```
if (b == null)
```

If a reference is not null, it can be set to null with the statement

```
b = null;
```

An attempt to invoke an instance method with a null reference may cause your program to terminate with a NullPointerException. For example,

```
public class PersonalFinances
{
    BankAccount b;                       //b is a null reference
        ...
    b.withdraw(password, amt);           //throws a NullPointerException
        ...                              //if b not constructed with new
```

NOTE

If you fail to initialize a local variable in a method before you use it, you will get a compile-time error. If you make the same mistake with an instance variable of a class, the compiler provides reasonable default values for primitive variables (0 for numbers, false for booleans), and the code may run without error. However, if you don't initialize *reference* instance variables in a class, as in the above example, the compiler will set them to null. Any method call for an object of the class that tries to access the null reference will cause a run-time error: The program will terminate with a NullPointerException.

> Do not make a method call with an object whose value is null.

Method Parameters

FORMAL VS. ACTUAL PARAMETERS

The header of a method defines the *parameters* of that method. For example, consider the withdraw method of the BankAccount class:

```
public class BankAccount
{   ...
    public void withdraw(String password, double amount)
        ...
```

This method has two explicit parameters, password and amount. These are *dummy* or *formal parameters*. Think of them as placeholders for the pair of *actual parameters* or *arguments* that will be supplied by a particular method call in a client program.

For example,

```
BankAccount b = new BankAccount("TimB", 1000);
b.withdraw("TimB", 250);
```

Here "TimB" and 250 are the actual parameters that match up with `password` and `amount` for the `withdraw` method.

NOTE

1. The number of arguments in the method call must equal the number of parameters in the method header, and the type of each argument must be compatible with the type of each corresponding parameter.
2. In addition to its explicit parameters, the `withdraw` method has an implicit parameter, `this`, the `BankAccount` from which money will be withdrawn. In the method call

    ```
    b.withdraw("TimB", 250);
    ```

    the actual parameter that matches up with `this` is the object reference `b`.

PASSING PRIMITIVE TYPES AS PARAMETERS

Parameters are *passed by value*. For primitive types this means that when a method is called, a new memory slot is allocated for each parameter. The value of each argument is copied into the newly created memory slot corresponding to each parameter.

During execution of the method, the parameters are local to that method. *Any changes made to the parameters will not affect the values of the arguments in the calling program.* When the method is exited, the local memory slots for the parameters are erased.

Here's an example: What will the output be?

```
public class ParamTest
{
    public static void foo(int x, double y)
    {
        x = 3;
        y = 2.5;
    }

    public static void main(String[] args)
    {
        int a = 7;
        double b = 6.5;
        foo(a, b);
        System.out.println(a + "   " + b);
    }
}
```

The output will be

```
7   6.5
```

The arguments `a` and `b` remain unchanged, despite the method call!

This can be understood by picturing the state of the memory slots during execution of the program.

Just before the `foo(a, b)` method call:

```
   a              b
  ┌───┐          ┌───┐
  │ 7 │          │6.5│
  └───┘          └───┘
```

At the time of the `foo(a, b)` method call:

```
   a              b
  ┌───┐          ┌───┐
  │ 7 │          │6.5│
  └───┘          └───┘

   x              y
  ┌───┐          ┌───┐
  │ 7 │          │6.5│
  └───┘          └───┘
```

Just before exiting the method: Note that the values of x and y have been changed.

```
   a              b
  ┌───┐          ┌───┐
  │ 7 │          │6.5│
  └───┘          └───┘

   x              y
  ┌───┐          ┌───┐
  │ 3 │          │2.5│
  └───┘          └───┘
```

After exiting the method: Note that the memory slots for x and y have been reclaimed. The values of a and b remain unchanged.

```
   a              b
  ┌───┐          ┌───┐
  │ 7 │          │6.5│
  └───┘          └───┘
```

PASSING OBJECTS AS PARAMETERS

In Java both primitive types and object references are passed by value. When an object's reference is a parameter, the same mechanism of copying into local memory is used. The key difference is that the *address* (reference) is copied, not the values of the individual instance variables. As with primitive types, changes made to the parameters will not change the values of the matching arguments. What this means in practice is that it is not possible for a method to replace an object with another one—you can't change the reference that was passed. It is, however, possible to change the state of the object to which the parameter refers through methods that act on the object.

Example 1

A method that changes the state of an object.

```
/* Subtracts fee from balance in b if current balance too low. */
public static void chargeFee(BankAccount b, String password,
        double fee)
{
    final double MIN_BALANCE = 10.00;
    if (b.getBalance() < MIN_BALANCE)
        b.withdraw(password, fee);
}

public static void main(String[] args)
{
    final double FEE = 5.00;
    BankAccount andysAccount = new BankAccount("AndyS", 7.00);
    chargeFee(andysAccount, "AndyS", FEE);
        ...
}
```

Here are the memory slots before the `chargeFee` method call:

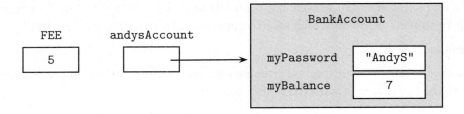

At the time of the `chargeFee` method call, copies of the matching parameters are made:

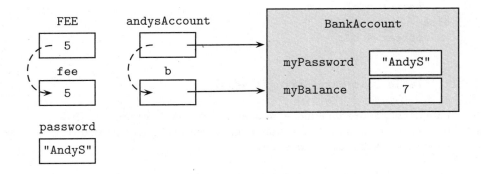

Just before exiting the method: The `myBalance` field of the `BankAccount` object has been changed.

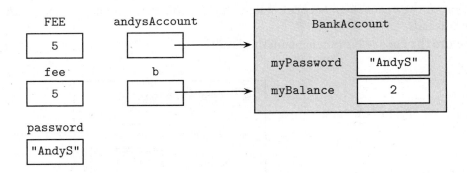

After exiting the method: All parameter memory slots have been erased, but the object remains altered.

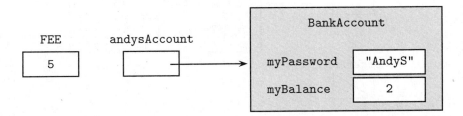

NOTE

The andysAccount reference is unchanged throughout the program segment. The object to which it refers, however, has been changed. This is significant. Contrast this with Example 2 below in which an attempt is made to replace the object itself.

Example 2

A chooseBestAccount method attempts—erroneously—to set its betterFund parameter to the BankAccount with the higher balance:

```
public static void chooseBestAccount(BankAccount better,
        BankAccount b1, BankAccount b2)
{
    if (b1.getBalance() > b2.getBalance())
        better = b1;
    else
        better = b2;
}

public static void main(String[] args)
{
    BankAccount briansFund = new BankAccount("BrianL", 10000);
    BankAccount paulsFund = new BankAccount("PaulM", 90000);
    BankAccount betterFund = null;

    chooseBestAccount(betterFund, briansFund, paulsFund);
        ...
}
```

The intent is that betterFund will be a reference to the paulsFund object after execution of the chooseBestAccount statement. A look at the memory slots illustrates why this fails.

Before the chooseBestAccount method call:

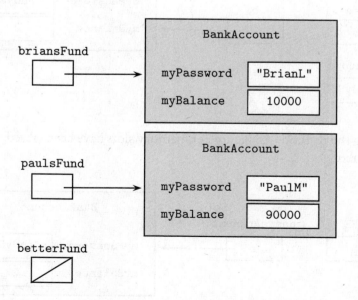

At the time of the chooseBestAccount method call: Copies of the matching references are made.

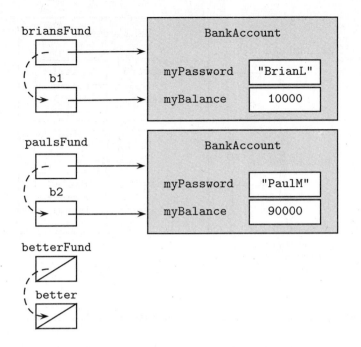

Just before exiting the method: The value of better has been changed; betterFund, however, remains unchanged.

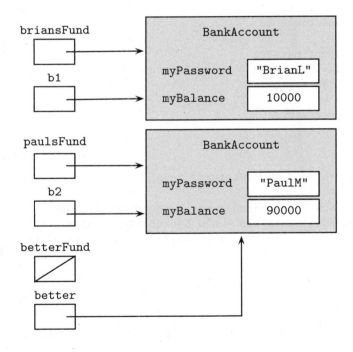

After exiting the method: All parameter slots have been erased.

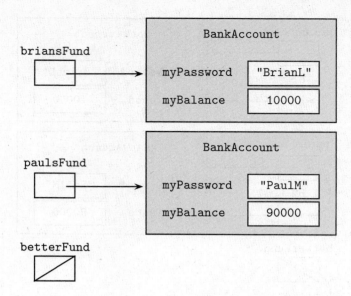

Note that the `betterFund` reference continues to be `null`, contrary to the programmer's intent.

The way to fix the problem is to modify the method so that it returns the better account. Returning an object from a method means that you are returning the address of the object.

```
public static BankAccount chooseBestAccount(BankAccount b1,
        BankAccount b2)
{
    BankAccount better;
    if (b1.getBalance() > b2.getBalance())
        better = b1;
    else
        better = b2;
    return better;
}

public static void main(String[] args)
{
    BankAccount briansFund = new BankAccount("BrianL", 10000);
    BankAccount paulsFund = new BankAccount("PaulM", 90000);
    BankAccount betterFund = chooseBestAccount(briansFund, paulsFund);
        ...
}
```

NOTE

The effect of this is to create the `betterFund` reference, which refers to the same object as `paulsFund`:

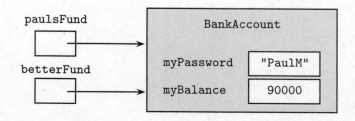

What the method does *not* do is create a new object to which betterFund refers. To do that would require the keyword new and use of a BankAccount constructor. Assuming that a getPassword() accessor has been added to the BankAccount class, the code would look like this:

```
public static BankAccount chooseBestAccount(BankAccount b1,
        BankAccount b2)
{
    BankAccount better;
    if (b1.getBalance() > b2.getBalance())
        better = new BankAccount(b1.getPassword(), b1.getBalance());
    else
        better = new BankAccount(b2.getPassword(), b2.getBalance());
    return better;
}
```

Using this modified method with the same main() method above has the following effect:

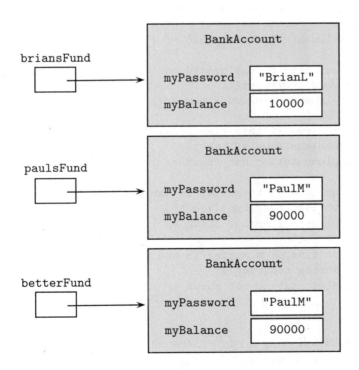

Modifying more than one object in a method can be accomplished using a *wrapper class* (see p. 231).

Chapter Summary

By now you should be able to write code for any given object, with its private data fields and methods encapsulated in a class. Be sure that you know the various types of methods—static, instance, and overloaded.

You should also understand the difference between storage of primitive types and the references used for objects.

MULTIPLE-CHOICE QUESTIONS ON CLASSES AND OBJECTS

Questions 1–3 refer to the Time class declared below:

```
public class Time
{
    private int myHrs;
    private int myMins;
    private int mySecs;

    public Time()
    { /* implementation not shown */ }

    public Time(int h, int m, int s)
    { /* implementation not shown */ }

    //Resets time to myHrs = h, myMins = m, mySecs = s.
    public void resetTime(int h, int m, int s)
    { /* implementation not shown */ }

    //Advances time by one second.
    public void increment()
    { /* implementation not shown */ }

    //Returns true if this time equals t, false otherwise.
    public boolean equals(Time t)
    { /* implementation not shown */ }

    //Returns true if this time is earlier than t, false otherwise.
    public boolean lessThan(Time t)
    { /* implementation not shown */ }

    //Returns time as a String in the form hrs:mins:secs.
    public String toString()
    { /* implementation not shown */ }
}
```

1. Which of the following is a *false* statement about the methods?
   (A) equals, lessThan, and toString are all accessor methods.
   (B) increment is a mutator method.
   (C) Time() is the default constructor.
   (D) The Time class has three constructors.
   (E) There are no static methods in this class.

2. Which of the following represents correct *implementation code* for the constructor with parameters?

(A) ```
myHrs = 0;
myMins = 0;
mySecs = 0;
```

(B) ```
myHrs = h;
myMins = m;
mySecs = s;
```

(C) ```
resetTime(myHrs, myMins, mySecs);
```

(D) ```
h = myHrs;
m = myMins;
s = mySecs;
```

(E) ```
Time = new Time(h, m, s);
```

3. A client class has a `display` method that writes the time represented by its parameter:

```
//Outputs time t in the form hrs:mins:secs.
public void display (Time t)
{
    /* method body */
}
```

Which of the following are correct replacements for /* *method body* */?

I ```
Time T = new Time(h, m, s);
System.out.println(T);
```

II ```
System.out.println(t.myHrs + ":" + t.myMins + ":" + t.mySecs);
```

III ```
System.out.println(t);
```

(A) I only
(B) II only
(C) III only
(D) II and III only
(E) I, II, and III

4. Which statement about parameters is *false*?
   (A) The scope of parameters is the method in which they are defined.
   (B) Static methods have no implicit parameter `this`.
   (C) Two overloaded methods in the same class must have parameters with different names.
   (D) All parameters in Java are passed by value.
   (E) Two different constructors in a given class can have the same number of parameters.

Questions 5–11 refer to the following Date class declaration:

```
public class Date
{
    private int myDay;
    private int myMonth;
    private int myYear;

    public Date()                            //default constructor
    {
        ...
    }

    public Date(int mo, int day, int yr)    //constructor
    {
        ...
    }

    public int month()       //returns month of Date
    {
        ...
    }

    public int day()          //returns day of Date
    {
        ...
    }

    public int year()        //returns year of Date
    {
        ...
    }

    //Returns String representation of Date as "m/d/y", e.g. 4/18/1985.
    public String toString()
    {
        ...
    }
}
```

5. Which of the following correctly constructs a Date object?

   (A) Date d = new (2, 13, 1947);

   (B) Date d = new Date(2, 13, 1947);

   (C) Date d;
       d = new (2, 13, 1947);

   (D) Date d;
       d = Date(2, 13, 1947);

   (E) Date d = Date(2, 13, 1947);

6. Which of the following will cause an error message?

    I ```
    Date d1 = new Date(8, 2, 1947);
    Date d2 = d1;
    ```

    II ```
    Date d1 = null;
    Date d2 = d1;
    ```

    III ```
    Date d = null;
    int x = d.year();
    ```

    (A) I only
    (B) II only
    (C) III only
    (D) II and III only
    (E) I, II, and III

7. A client program creates a `Date` object as follows:

    ```
    Date d = new Date(1, 13, 2002);
    ```

    Which of the following subsequent code segments will cause an error?
    (A) `String s = d.toString();`
    (B) `int x = d.day();`
    (C) `Date e = d;`
    (D) `Date e = new Date(1, 13, 2002);`
    (E) `int y = d.myYear;`

8. Consider the implementation of a `write()` method that is added to the `Date` class:

    ```
    //Write the date in the form m/d/y, for example 2/17/1948.
    public void write()
    {
        /* implementation code */
    }
    ```

    Which of the following could be used as /* *implementation code* */?

    I `System.out.println(myMonth + "/" + myDay + "/" + myYear);`

    II `System.out.println(month() + "/" + day() + "/" + year());`

    III `System.out.println(this);`

    (A) I only
    (B) II only
    (C) III only
    (D) II and III only
    (E) I, II, and III
    ```

9. Here is a client program that uses Date objects:

```
public class BirthdayStuff
{
    public static Date findBirthdate()
    {
        /* code to get birthDate */
        return birthDate;
    }

    public static void main(String[] args)
    {
        Date d = findBirthdate();
            ...
    }
}
```

Which of the following is a correct replacement for
/* *code to get* birthDate */?

```
 I System.out.println("Enter birthdate: mo, day, yr: ");
   int m = IO.readInt();                    //read user input
   int d = IO.readInt();                    //read user input
   int y = IO.readInt();                    //read user input
   birthDate = new Date(m, d, y);
```

```
II System.out.println("Enter birthdate: mo, day, yr: ");
   int birthDate.month() = IO.readInt();        //read user input
   int birthDate.day() = IO.readInt();          //read user input
   int birthDate.year() = IO.readInt();         //read user input
   birthDate = new Date(birthDate.month(), birthDate.day(),
       birthDate.year());
```

```
III System.out.println("Enter birthdate: mo, day, yr: ");
    int birthDate.myMonth = IO.readInt();       //read user input
    int birthDate.myDay = IO.readInt();         //read user input
    int birthDate.myYear = IO.readInt();        //read user input
    birthDate = new Date(birthDate.myMonth, birthDate.myDay,
        birthDate.myYear);
```

(A) I only
(B) II only
(C) III only
(D) I and II only
(E) I and III only

10. A method in a client program for the Date class has this declaration:

    ```
    Date d1 = new Date(month, day, year);
    ```

    where month, day, and year are previously defined integer variables. The same method now creates a second Date object d2 that is an exact copy of the object d1 refers to. Which of the following code segments will *not* do this correctly?

    I Date d2 = d1;

    II Date d2 = new Date(month, day, year);

    III Date d2 = new Date(d1.month(), d1.day(), d1.year());

    (A) I only
    (B) II only
    (C) III only
    (D) I, II, and III
    (E) All will do this correctly.

11. The Date class is modified by adding the following mutator method:

    ```
    public void addYears(int n)     //add n years to date
    ```

    Here is part of a poorly coded client program that uses the Date class:

    ```
    public static void addCentury(Date recent, Date old)
    {
        old.addYears(100);
        recent = old;
    }

    public static void main(String[] args)
    {
        Date oldDate = new Date(1, 13, 1900);
        Date recentDate = null;
        addCentury(recentDate, oldDate);
            . . .
    }
    ```

    Which will be true after executing this code?
    (A) A NullPointerException is thrown.
    (B) The oldDate object remains unchanged.
    (C) recentDate is a null reference.
    (D) recentDate refers to the same object as oldDate.
    (E) recentDate refers to a separate object whose contents are the same as those of oldDate.

Questions 12–15 refer to the following definition of the Rational class:

```
public class Rational
{
    private int myNum;          //numerator
    private int myDenom;        //denominator

    //constructors
    /* default constructor */
    Rational()
    { /* implementation not shown */ }

    /* Constructs a Rational with numerator n and
     * denominator 1. */
    Rational(int n)
    { /* implementation not shown */ }

    /* Constructs a Rational with specified numerator and
     * denominator. */
    Rational(int numer, int denom)
    { /* implementation not shown */ }

    //accessors
    /* Returns numerator. */
    int numerator()
    { /* implementation not shown */ }

    /* Returns denominator. */
    int denominator()
    { /* implementation not shown */ }

    //arithmetic operations
    /* Returns (this + r).
     * Leaves this unchanged. */
    public Rational plus(Rational r)
    { /* implementation not shown */ }

    //Similarly for times, minus, divide
           . . .
    /* Ensures myDenom > 0. */
    private void fixSigns()
    { /* implementation not shown */ }

    /* Ensures lowest terms. */
    private void reduce()
    { /* implementation not shown */ }
}
```

12. The method reduce() is not a public method because
    (A) methods whose return type is void cannot be public.
    (B) methods that change this cannot be public.
    (C) the reduce() method is not intended for use by clients of the Rational class.
    (D) the reduce() method is intended for use only by clients of the Rational class.
    (E) the reduce() method uses only the private data fields of the Rational class.

13. The constructors in the `Rational` class allow initialization of `Rational` objects in several different ways. Which of the following will cause an error?
    (A) `Rational r1 = new Rational();`
    (B) `Rational r2 = r1;`
    (C) `Rational r3 = new Rational(2,-3);`
    (D) `Rational r4 = new Rational(3.5);`
    (E) `Rational r5 = new Rational(10);`

14. Here is the implementation code for the `plus` method:

```
/* Returns (this + r) in reduced form. Leaves this unchanged. */
public Rational plus(Rational r)
{
    fixSigns();
    r.fixSigns();
    int denom = myDenom * r.myDenom;
    int num = myNum * r.myDenom + r.myNum * myDenom;
    /* some more code */
}
```

Which of the following is a correct replacement for /* *some more code* */?

    (A) `Rational rat(num, denom);`
        `rat.reduce();`
        `return rat;`

    (B) `return new Rational(num, denom);`

    (C) `reduce();`
        `Rational rat = new Rational(num, denom);`
        `return rat;`

    (D) `Rational rat = new Rational(num, denom);`
        `Rational.reduce();`
        `return rat;`

    (E) `Rational rat = new Rational(num, denom);`
        `rat.reduce();`
        `return rat;`

15. Assume these declarations:

```
Rational a = new Rational();
Rational r = new Rational(num, denom);
int n = value;
//num, denom, and value are valid integer values
```

Which of the following will cause a compile-time error?
    (A) `r = a.plus(r);`
    (B) `a = r.plus(new Rational(n));`
    (C) `r = r.plus(r);`
    (D) `a = n.plus(r);`
    (E) `r = r.plus(new Rational(n));`

16. Here are the private instance variables for a Frog object:

```
public class Frog
{
    private String mySpecies;
    private int myAge;
    private double myWeight;
    private Position myPosition;       //position (x,y) in pond
    private boolean amAlive;
        ...
```

Which of the following methods in the Frog class is the best candidate for being a static method?

(A) `swim`   `//frog swims to new position in pond`

(B) `getPondTemperature`   `//returns temperature of pond`

(C) `eat`   `//frog eats and gains weight`

(D) `getWeight`   `//returns weight of frog`

(E) `die`   `//frog dies with some probability based`
                                         `//on frog's age and pond temperature`

17. What output will be produced by this program?

```
public class Mystery
{
    public static void strangeMethod(int x, int y)
    {
        x += y;
        y *= x;
        System.out.println(x + " " + y);
    }

    public static void main(String[] args)
    {
        int a = 6, b = 3;
        strangeMethod(a, b);
        System.out.println(a + " " + b);
    }
}
```

(A) 36
    9

(B) 3 6
    9

(C) 9 27
    9 27

(D) 6 3
    9 27

(E) 9 27
    6 3

Questions 18–20 refer to the `Temperature` class shown below:

```
public class Temperature
{
    private String myScale;   //valid values are "F" or "C"
    private double myDegrees;

    //constructors
    /* default constructor */
    public Temperature()
    { /* implementation not shown */ }

    /* constructor with specified degrees and scale */
    public Temperature(double degrees, String scale)
    { /* implementation not shown */ }

    //accessors
    /* Returns degrees for this temperature. */
    public double getDegrees()
    { /* implementation not shown */ }

    /* Returns scale for this temperature. */
    public String getScale()
    { /* implementation not shown */ }

    //mutators
    /* Precondition:  Temperature is a valid temperature
     *                in degrees Celsius.
     * Postcondition: Returns this temperature, which has been
     *                converted to degrees Fahrenheit. */
    public Temperature toFahrenheit()
    { /* implementation not shown */ }

    /* Precondition:  Temperature is a valid temperature
     *                in degrees Fahrenheit.
     * Postcondition: Returns this temperature, which has been
     *                converted to degrees Celsius. */
    public Temperature toCelsius()
    { /* implementation not shown */ }

    /* Raise this temperature by amt degrees and return it. */
    public Temperature raise(double amt)
    { /* implementation not shown */ }

    /* Lower this temperature by amt degrees and return it. */
    public Temperature lower(double amt)
    { /* implementation not shown */ }

    /* Returns true if the number of degrees is a valid
     * temperature in the given scale, false otherwise. */
    public static boolean isValidTemp(double degrees, String scale)
    { /* implementation not shown */ }

    //other methods not shown ...
}
```

18. A client method contains this code segment:

```
Temperature t1 = new Temperature(40, "C");
Temperature t2 = t1;
Temperature t3 = t2.lower(20);
Temperature t4 = t1.toFahrenheit();
```

Which statement is *true* following execution of this segment?
(A) t1, t2, t3, and t4 all represent the identical temperature, in degrees Celsius.
(B) t1, t2, t3, and t4 all represent the identical temperature, in degrees Fahrenheit.
(C) t4 represents a Fahrenheit temperature, while t1, t2, and t3 all represent degrees Celsius.
(D) t1 and t2 refer to the same Temperature object; t3 refers to a Temperature object that is 20 degrees lower than t1 and t2, while t4 refers to an object that is t1 converted to Fahrenheit.
(E) A NullPointerException was thrown.

19. Consider the following code:

```
public class TempTest
{
    public static void main(String[] args)
    {
        System.out.println("Enter temperature scale: ");
        String scale = IO.readString();     //read user input
        System.out.println("Enter number of degrees: ");
        double degrees = IO.readDouble();   //read user input
        /* code to construct a valid temperature from user input */
    }
}
```

Which is a correct replacement for /* *code to construct...* */?

I ```
   Temperature t = new Temperature(degrees, scale);
   if (!t.isValidTemp(degrees,scale))
       /* error message and exit program */
   ```

II ```
   if (isValidTemp(degrees,scale))
       Temperature t = new Temperature(degrees, scale);
   else
       /* error message and exit program */
   ```

III ```
    if (Temperature.isValidTemp(degrees,scale))
        Temperature t = new Temperature(degrees, scale);
    else
        /* error message and exit program */
    ```

(A) I only
(B) II only
(C) III only
(D) I and II only
(E) I and III only
    ```

20. The formula to convert degrees Celsius C to Fahrenheit F is

$$F = 1.8C + 32$$

For example, 30° C is equivalent to 86° F.

An `inFahrenheit()` accessor method is added to the `Temperature` class. Here is its implementation:

```
/* Precondition:  temperature is a valid temperature in
 *                degrees Celsius
 * Postcondition: an equivalent temperature in degrees
 *                Fahrenheit has been returned. Original
 *                temperature remains unchanged */
public Temperature inFahrenheit()
{
    Temperature result;
    /* more code */
    return result;
}
```

Which of the following correctly replaces /* *more code* */ so that the postcondition is achieved?

```
  I result = new Temperature(myDegrees*1.8 + 32, "F");

 II result = new Temperature(myDegrees*1.8, "F");
    result = result.raise(32);

III myDegrees *= 1.8;
    this = this.raise(32);
    result = new Temperature(myDegrees, "F");
```

(A) I only
(B) II only
(C) III only
(D) I and II only
(E) I, II, and III

21. Consider this program:

```
public class CountStuff
{
    public static void doSomething()
    {
        int count = 0;
            ...
        //code to do something - no screen output produced
        count++;
    }

    public static void main(String[] args)
    {
        int count = 0;
        System.out.println("How many iterations?");
        int n = IO.readInt();      //read user input
        for (int  i = 1; i <= n; i++)
        {
            doSomething();
            System.out.println(count);
        }
    }
}
```

If the input value for n is 3, what screen output will this program subsequently produce?

(A) 0
     0
     0

(B) 1
     2
     3

(C) 3
     3
     3

(D) ?
     ?
     ?
     where ? is some undefined value.

(E) No output will be produced.

22. This question refers to the following class:

```
public class IntObject
{
    private int myInt;

    public IntObject()        //default constructor
    { myInt = 0; }
    public IntObject(int n)   //constructor
    { myInt = n; }
    public void increment()   //increment by 1
    { myInt++; }
}
```

Here is a client program that uses this class:

```
public class IntObjectTest
{
    public static IntObject someMethod(IntObject obj)
    {
        IntObject ans = obj;
        ans.increment();
        return ans;
    }

    public static void main(String[] args)
    {
        IntObject x = new IntObject(2);
        IntObject y = new IntObject(7);
        IntObject a = y;
        x = someMethod(y);
        a = someMethod(x);
    }
}
```

Just before exiting this program, what are the object values of x, y, and a, respectively?

(A) 9, 9, 9
(B) 2, 9, 9
(C) 2, 8, 9
(D) 3, 8, 9
(E) 7, 8, 9

23. Consider the following program:

```
public class Tester
{
    public void someMethod(int a, int b)
    {
        int temp = a;
        a = b;
        b = temp;
    }
}

public class TesterMain
{
    public static void main(String[] args)
    {
        int x = 6, y = 8;
        Tester tester = new Tester();
        tester.someMethod(x, y);
    }
}
```

Just before the end of execution of this program, what are the values of x, y, and temp, respectively?

(A) 6, 8, 6

(B) 8, 6, 6

(C) 6, 8, ?, where ? means undefined

(D) 8, 6, ?, where ? means undefined

(E) 8, 6, 8

ANSWER KEY

1. D	9. A	17. E
2. B	10. A	18. B
3. C	11. C	19. C
4. C	12. C	20. D
5. B	13. D	21. A
6. C	14. E	22. A
7. E	15. D	23. C
8. E	16. B	

ANSWERS EXPLAINED

1. **(D)** There are just two constructors. Constructors are recognizable by having the same name as the class, and no return type.

2. **(B)** Each of the private instance variables should be assigned the value of the matching parameter. Choice B is the only choice that does this. Choice D confuses the order of the assignment statements. Choice A gives the code for the *default* constructor, ignoring the parameters. Choice C would be correct if it were resetTime(h, m, s). As written, it doesn't assign the parameter values h, m, and s to myHrs, myMins, and mySecs. Choice E is wrong because the keyword new should be used to create a new object, not to implement the constructor!

3. **(C)** Replacement III will automatically print time t in the required form since a toString method was defined for the Time class. Replacement I is wrong because it doesn't refer to the parameter, t, of the method. Replacement II is wrong because a client program may not access private data of the class.

4. **(C)** The parameter names can be the same—the *signatures* must be different. For example,

```
public void print(int x)       //prints x
public void print(double x)    //prints x
```

The signatures (method name plus parameter types) here are print(int) and print(double), respectively. The parameter name x is irrelevant. Choice A is true: All local variables and parameters go out of scope (are erased) when the method is exited. Choice B is true: Static methods apply to the whole class. Only instance methods have an implicit this parameter. Choice D is true even for object parameters: Their references are passed by value. Note that choice E is true because it's possible to have two different constructors with different signatures but the same number of parameters (e.g., one for an int argument and one for a double).

5. **(B)** Constructing an object requires the keyword new and a constructor of the Date class. Eliminate choices D and E since they omit new. The class name Date should appear on the right-hand side of the assignment statement, immediately following the keyword new. This eliminates choices A and C.

6. **(C)** Segment III will cause a `NullPointerException` to be thrown since d is a null reference. You cannot invoke a method for a null reference. Segment II has the effect of assigning `null` to both d1 and d2—obscure but not incorrect. Segment I creates the object reference d1 and then declares a second reference d2 that refers to the same object as d1.

7. **(E)** A client program cannot access a private instance variable.

8. **(E)** All are correct. Since `write()` is a `Date` instance method, it is OK to use the private data members in its implementation code. Segment III prints `this`, the current `Date` object. This usage is correct since `write()` is part of the `Date` class. The `toString()` method guarantees that the date will be printed in the required format (see p. 226).

9. **(A)** The idea here is to read in three separate variables for month, day, and year and then to construct the required date using `new` and the `Date` class constructor with three parameters. Code segment II won't work because `month()`, `day()`, and `year()` are accessor methods that access existing values and may not be used to read new values into bDate. Segment III is wrong because it tries to access private instance variables from a client program.

10. **(A)** Segment I will not create a second object. It will simply cause d2 to refer to the *same* object as d1, which is not what was required. The keyword `new` *must* be used to create a new object.

11. **(C)** When `recentDate` is declared in `main()`, its value is null. Recall that a method is not able to replace an object reference, so `recentDate` remains null. Note that the intent of the program is to change `recentDate` to refer to the updated `oldDate` object. The code, however, doesn't do this. Choice A is false: No methods are invoked with a null reference. Choice B is false because `addYears()` is a mutator method. Even though a method doesn't change the address of its object parameter, it can change the contents of the object, which is what happens here. Choices D and E are wrong because the `addCentury()` method cannot change the value of its `recentDate` argument.

12. **(C)** The `reduce()` method will be used only in the implementation of the instance methods of the `Rational` class.

13. **(D)** None of the constructors in the `Rational` class takes a real-valued parameter. Thus, the real-valued parameter in choice D will need to be converted to an integer. Since in general truncating a real value to an integer involves a loss of precision, it is not done automatically—you have to do it explicitly with a cast. Omitting the cast causes a compile-time error.

14. **(E)** A new `Rational` object must be created using the newly calculated num and denom. Then it must be reduced before being returned. Choice A is wrong because it doesn't correctly create the new object. Choice B returns a correctly constructed object, but one that has not been reduced. Choice C reduces the current object, `this`, instead of the new object, rat. Choice D is wrong because it invokes `reduce()` for the `Rational` class instead of the specific rat object.

15. **(D)** The `plus` method of the `Rational` class can only be invoked by `Rational` objects. Since n is an `int`, the statement in choice D will cause an error.

16. **(B)** The method `getPondTemperature` is the only method that applies to more than one frog. It should therefore be static. All of the other methods relate directly to one particular `Frog` object. So `f.swim()`, `f.die()`, `f.getWeight()`,

and `f.eat()` are all reasonable methods for a single instance `f` of a Frog. On the other hand, it doesn't make sense to say `f.getPondTemperature()`. It makes more sense to say `Frog.getPondTemperature()`, since the same value will apply to all frogs in the class.

17. **(E)** Here are the memory slots at the start of `strangeMethod(a, b)`:

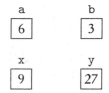

Before exiting `strangeMethod(a, b)`:

```
        a           b
       ┌───┐       ┌───┐
       │ 6 │       │ 3 │
       └───┘       └───┘

        x           y
       ┌───┐       ┌───┐
       │ 9 │       │27 │
       └───┘       └───┘
```

Note that 9 27 is output before exiting. After exiting `strangeMethod(a, b)`, the memory slots are

```
        a           b
       ┌───┐       ┌───┐
       │ 6 │       │ 3 │
       └───┘       └───┘
```

The next step outputs 6 3.

18. **(B)** This is an example of *aliasing*. The keyword `new` is used just once, which means that just one object is constructed. Here are the memory slots after each declaration:

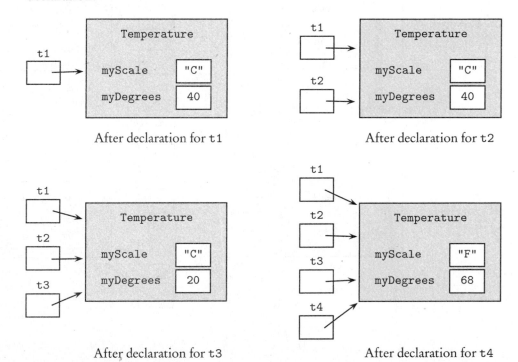

After declaration for `t1`

After declaration for `t2`

After declaration for `t3`

After declaration for `t4`

19. **(C)** Notice that `isValidTemp` is a static method for the `Temperature` class, which means that it cannot be invoked with a `Temperature` object. Thus segment I is incorrect: `t.isValidTemp` is wrong. Segment II fails because `isValidTemp` is not a method of the `TempTest` class. It therefore must be invoked with its class name, which is what happens (correctly) in segment III: `Temperature.isValidTemp`.

20. **(D)** A new `Temperature` object must be constructed to prevent the current `Temperature` from being changed. Segment I, which applies the conversion formula directly to `myDegrees`, is the best way to do this. Segment II, while not the best algorithm, does work. The statement

    ```
    result = result.raise(32);
    ```

    has the effect of raising the `result` temperature by 32 degrees, and completing the conversion. Segment III fails because

    ```
    myDegrees *= 1.8;
    ```

    alters the `myDegrees` instance variable of the current object, as does

    ```
    this = this.raise(32);
    ```

    To be correct, these operations must be applied to the `result` object.

21. **(A)** This is a question about the scope of variables. The scope of the `count` variable that is declared in `main()` extends up to the closing brace of `main()`. In `doSomething()`, `count` is a local variable. After the method call in the `for` loop, the local variable `count` goes out of scope, and the value that's being printed is the value of the `count` in `main()`, which is unchanged from 0.

22. **(A)** Here are the memory slots before the first `someMethod` call:

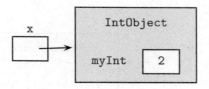 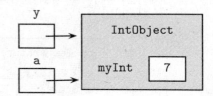

Just before exiting `x = someMethod(y)`:

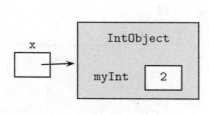 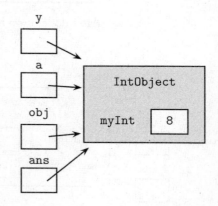

After exiting

```
x = someMethod(y);
```

x has been reassigned, so the object with myInt = 2 has been recycled:

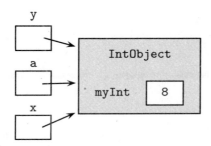

After exiting a = someMethod(x):

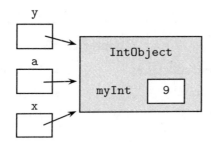

23. **(C)** Recall that when primitive types are passed as parameters, copies are made of the actual arguments. All manipulations in the method are performed on the copies, and the arguments remain unchanged. Thus x and y retain their values of 6 and 8. The local variable temp goes out of scope as soon as someMethod is exited and is therefore undefined just before the end of execution of the program.

Inheritance and Polymorphism

CHAPTER 3

Say not you know another entirely,
till you have divided an inheritance with him.
—*Johann Kaspar Lavatar,* Aphorisms on Man

Chapter Goals

- Superclasses and subclasses
- Inheritance hierarchy
- Polymorphism
- Type compatibility

- Abstract classes
- Interfaces
- The `Comparable` interface

INHERITANCE

Superclass and Subclass

Inheritance defines a relationship between objects that share characteristics. Specifically it is the mechanism whereby a new class, called a *subclass*, is created from an existing class, called a *superclass*, by absorbing its state and behavior and augmenting these with features unique to the new class. We say that the subclass *inherits* characteristics of its superclass.

Don't get confused by the names: a subclass is bigger than a superclass—it contains more data and more methods!

Inheritance provides an effective mechanism for code reuse. Suppose the code for a superclass has been tested and debugged. Since a subclass object shares features of a superclass object, the only new code required is for the additional characteristics of the subclass.

Inheritance Hierarchy

A subclass can itself be a superclass for another subclass, leading to an *inheritance hierarchy* of classes.

For example, consider the relationship between these objects: `Person`, `Employee`, `Student`, `GradStudent`, and `UnderGrad`.

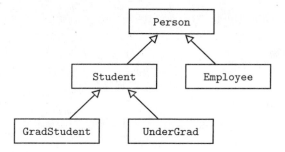

For any of these classes, an arrow points to its superclass. The arrow designates the *is-a* relationship. Thus, an Employee *is-a* Person; a Student *is-a* Person; a GradStudent *is-a* Student; an UnderGrad *is-a* Student. Notice that the opposite is not necessarily true: A Person may not be a Student, nor is a Student necessarily an UnderGrad.

Note that the *is-a* relationship is transitive: If a GradStudent *is-a* Student and a Student *is-a* Person, then a GradStudent *is-a* Person.

Suppose the Person class has instance variables name, socialSecurityNumber, and age, and instance methods getName, getSocSecNum, getAge, and printName. Then every one of the derived classes shown inherits these variables and methods. The Student class may have additional instance variables studentID and gpa, plus a method computeGrade. All of these additional features are inherited by the subclasses GradStudent and UnderGrad. Suppose GradStudent and UnderGrad use different algorithms for computing the course grade. Then the computeGrade implementation can be redefined in these classes. This is called *method overriding*. If part of the original method implementation from the superclass is retained, we refer to the rewrite as *partial overriding*.

Implementing Subclasses

THE extends KEYWORD

The inheritance relationship between a subclass and a superclass is specified in the declaration of the subclass, using the keyword extends. The general format looks like this:

```
public class Superclass
{
    //private instance variables
    //other data members
    //constructors
    //public methods
    //private methods
}

public class Subclass extends Superclass
{
    //additional private instance variables
    //additional data members
    //constructors  (Not inherited!)
    //additional public methods
    //inherited public methods whose implementation is overridden
    //additional private methods
}
```

For example, consider the following inheritance hierarchy:

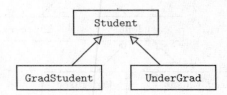

The implementation of the classes may look something like this (discussion follows the code):

```
public class Student
{
    //data members
    public final static int NUM_TESTS = 3;
    private String myName;
    private int[] myTests;
    private String myGrade;

    //constructors
    public Student()
    {
        myName = "";
        myTests = new int[NUM_TESTS];
        myGrade = "";
    }

    public Student(String name, int[] tests, String grade)
    {
        myName = name;
        myTests = tests;
        myGrade = grade;
    }

    public String getName()
    { return myName; }

    public String getGrade()
    { return myGrade; }

    public void setGrade(String newGrade)
    { myGrade = newGrade; }

    public void computeGrade()
    {
        if (myName.equals(""))
            myGrade = "No grade";
        else if (getTestAverage() >= 65)
            myGrade = "Pass";
        else
            myGrade = "Fail";
    }
```

```
    public double getTestAverage()
    {
        double total = 0;
        for (int score : myTests)
            total += score;
        return total/NUM_TESTS;
    }
}

public class UnderGrad extends Student
{
    public UnderGrad()    //default constructor
    { super(); }

    //constructor
    public UnderGrad(String name, int[] tests, String grade)
    { super(name, tests, grade); }

    public void computeGrade()
    {
        if (getTestAverage() >= 70)
            setGrade("Pass");
        else
            setGrade("Fail");
    }
}

public class GradStudent extends Student
{
    private int myGradID;

    public GradStudent()       //default constructor
    {
        super();
        myGradID = 0;
    }

    //constructor
    public GradStudent(String name, int[] tests, String grade,
            int gradID)
    {
        super(name, tests, grade);
        myGradID = gradID;
    }

    public int getID()
    { return myGradID; }

    public void computeGrade()
    {
        //invokes computeGrade in Student superclass
        super.computeGrade();
        if (getTestAverage() >= 90)
            setGrade("Pass with distinction");
    }
}
```

INHERITING INSTANCE METHODS AND VARIABLES

The UnderGrad and GradStudent subclasses inherit all of the methods and variables of the Student superclass. Notice, however, that the Student instance variables my-Name, myTests, and myGrade are private, and are therefore not directly accessible to the methods in the UnderGrad and GradStudent subclasses. A subclass can, however, directly invoke the public accessor and mutator methods of the superclass. Thus, both UnderGrad and GradStudent use getTestAverage. Additionally, both UnderGrad and GradStudent use setGrade to access indirectly—and modify—myGrade.

If, instead of private, the access specifier for the instance variables in Student were protected, then the subclasses could directly access these variables. The keyword protected is not part of the AP Java subset.

Classes on the same level in a hierarchy diagram do not inherit anything from each other (for example, UnderGrad and GradStudent). All they have in common is the identical code they inherit from their superclass.

METHOD OVERRIDING AND THE super KEYWORD

A method in a superclass is overridden in a subclass by defining a method with the same return type and signature (name and parameter types). For example, the computeGrade method in the UnderGrad subclass overrides the computeGrade method in the Student superclass.

Sometimes the code for overriding a method includes a call to the superclass method. This is called *partial overriding*. Typically this occurs when the subclass method wants to do what the superclass does, plus something extra. This is achieved by using the keyword super in the implementation. The computeGrade method in the GradStudent subclass partially overrides the matching method in the Student class. The statement

```
super.computeGrade();
```

signals that the computeGrade method in the superclass should be invoked here. The additional test

```
if (getTestAverage() >= 90)
    ...
```

allows a GradStudent to have a grade Pass with distinction. Note that this option is open to GradStudents only.

CONSTRUCTORS AND super

> Be sure to provide at least one constructor when you write a subclass. Constructors are never inherited from the superclass.

Constructors are never inherited! If no constructor is written for a subclass, the superclass default constructor with no parameters is generated. If the superclass does not have a default (zero-parameter) constructor, but only a constructor with parameters, a compiler error will occur. If there is a default constructor in the superclass, inherited data members will be initialized as for the superclass. Additional instance variables in the subclass will get a default initialization—0 for primitive types and null for reference types.

A subclass constructor can be implemented with a call to the super method, which invokes the superclass constructor. For example, the default constructor in the UnderGrad class is identical to that of the Student class. This is implemented with the statement

```
super();
```

The second constructor in the UnderGrad class is called with parameters that match those in the constructor of the Student superclass.

```
public UnderGrad(String name, int[] tests, String grade)
{ super(name, tests, grade); }
```

For each constructor, the call to super has the effect of initializing the inherited instance variables myName, myTests, and myGrade exactly as they are initialized in the Student class.

Contrast this with the constructors in GradStudent. In each case, the inherited instance variables myName, myTests, and myGrade are initialized as for the Student class. Then the new instance variable, myGradID, must be explicitly initialized.

```
public GradStudent()
{
    super();
    myGradID = 0;
}

public GradStudent(String name, int[] tests, String grade,
            int gradID)
{
    super(name, tests, grade);
    myGradID = gradID;
}
```

NOTE

1. If super is used in the implementation of a subclass constructor, it *must* be used in the first line of the constructor body.
2. If no constructor is provided in a subclass, the compiler provides the following default constructor:

```
public SubClass()
{
    super();        //calls default constructor of superclass
}
```

Since Student and UnderGrad have the same default constructor, it would have been safe to omit the default constructor in the UnderGrad class: The correct default would have been provided.

Rules for Subclasses

- A subclass can add new private instance variables.
- A subclass can add new public, private, or static methods.
- A subclass can override inherited methods.
- A subclass may not redefine a public method as private.
- A subclass may not override static methods of the superclass.
- A subclass should define its own constructors.
- A subclass cannot access the private members of its superclass.

Declaring Subclass Objects

When a variable of a superclass is declared in a client program, that reference can refer not only to an object of the superclass, but also to objects of any of its subclasses. Thus, each of the following is legal:

```
Student s = new Student();
Student g = new GradStudent();
Student u = new UnderGrad();
```

This works because a `GradStudent` *is-a* `Student`, and an `UnderGrad` *is-a* `Student`.

Note that since a `Student` is not necessarily a `GradStudent` nor an `UnderGrad`, the following declarations are *not* valid:

```
GradStudent g = new Student();
Undergrad u = new Student();
```

Consider these valid declarations:

```
Student s = new Student("Brian Lorenzen", new int[] {90,94,99},
        "none");
Student u = new UnderGrad("Tim Broder", new int[] {90,90,100},
        "none");
Student g = new GradStudent("Kevin Cristella",
        new int[] {85,70,90}, "none", 1234);
```

Suppose you make the method call

```
s.setGrade("Pass");
```

The appropriate method in `Student` is found and the new grade assigned. The method calls

```
g.setGrade("Pass");
```

and

```
u.setGrade("Pass");
```

achieve the same effect on g and u since `GradStudent` and `UnderGrad` both inherit the `setGrade` method from `Student`. The following method calls, however, won't work:

```
int studentNum = s.getID();
int underGradNum = u.getID();
```

Neither `Student` s nor `UnderGrad` u inherit the `getID` method from the `GradStudent` class: A superclass does not inherit from a subclass.

Now consider the following valid method calls:

```
s.computeGrade();
g.computeGrade();
u.computeGrade();
```

Since s, g, and u have all been declared to be of type `Student`, will the appropriate method be executed in each case? That is the topic of the next section, *polymorphism*.

NOTE

The initializer list syntax used in constructing the array parameters—for example, `new int[] {90,90,100}`— will not be tested on the AP exam.

POLYMORPHISM

A method that has been overridden in at least one subclass is said to be *polymorphic*. An example is `computeGrade`, which is redefined for both `GradStudent` and `UnderGrad`.

   Polymorphism is the mechanism of selecting the appropriate method for a particular object in a class hierarchy. The correct method is chosen because, in Java, method calls are always determined by the type of the *actual object*, not the type of the object reference. For example, even though s, g, and u are all declared as type `Student`, `s.computeGrade()`, `g.computeGrade()`, and `u.computeGrade()` will all perform the correct operations for their particular instances. In Java, the selection of the correct method occurs *during the run of the program*.

Dynamic Binding (Late Binding)

Making a run-time decision about which instance method to call is known as *dynamic binding* or *late binding*. Contrast this with selecting the correct method when methods are *overloaded* (see p. 155) rather than overridden. The compiler selects the correct overloaded method at compile time by comparing the methods' signatures. This is known as *static binding*, or *early binding*. In polymorphism, the actual method that will be called is not determined by the compiler. Think of it this way: The compiler determines *if* a method can be called (i.e., is it legal?), while the run-time environment determines *how* it will be called (i.e., which overridden form should be used?).

Example 1

```
Student s = null;
Student u = new UnderGrad("Tim Broder", new int[] {90,90,100},
        "none");
Student g = new GradStudent("Kevin Cristella",
        new int[] {85,70,90}, "none", 1234);
System.out.print("Enter student status: ");
System.out.println("Grad (G), Undergrad (U), Neither (N)");
String str = IO.readString();        //read user input
if (str.equals("G"))
    s = g;
else if (str.equals("U"))
    s = u;
else
    s = new Student();
s.computeGrade();
```

When this code fragment is run, the `computeGrade` method used will depend on the type of the actual object s refers to, which in turn depends on the user input.

Example 2

```java
public class StudentTest
{
    public static void computeAllGrades(Student[] studentList)
    {
        for (Student s : studentList)
            if (s != null)
                s.computeGrade();
    }

    public static void main(String[] args)
    {
        Student[] stu = new Student[5];
        stu[0] = new Student("Brian Lorenzen",
                        new int[] {90,94,99}, "none");
        stu[1] = new UnderGrad("Tim Broder",
                        new int[] {90,90,100}, "none");
        stu[2] = new GradStudent("Kevin Cristella",
                        new int[] {85,70,90}, "none", 1234);
        computeAllGrades(stu);
    }
}
```

> Polymorphism applies only to overridden methods in subclasses.

Here an array of five `Student` references is created, all of them initially null. Three of these references, `stu[0]`, `stu[1]`, and `stu[2]`, are then assigned to actual objects. The `computeAllGrades` method steps through the array invoking the appropriate `compute-Grade` method for each of the objects, using dynamic binding in each case. The null test in `computeAllGrades` is necessary because some of the array references could be null.

TYPE COMPATIBILITY

Downcasting

Consider the statements

```java
Student s = new GradStudent();
GradStudent g = new GradStudent();
int x = s.getID();              //compile-time error
int y = g.getID();              //legal
```

Both s and g represent `GradStudent` objects, so why does `s.getID()` cause an error? The reason is that s is of type `Student`, and the `Student` class doesn't have a `getID` method. At compile time, only nonprivate methods of the `Student` class can appear to the right of the dot operator when applied to s. Don't confuse this with polymorphism: `getID` is not a polymorphic method. It occurs in just the `GradStudent` class and can therefore be called only by a `GradStudent` object.

The error shown above can be fixed by casting s to the correct type:

```java
int x = ((GradStudent) s).getID();
```

Since s (of type `Student`) is actually representing a `GradStudent` object, such a cast can be carried out. Casting a superclass to a subclass type is called a *downcast*.

NOTE

1. The outer parentheses are necessary:

   ```
   int x = (GradStudent) s.getID();
   ```

   will still cause an error, despite the cast. This is because the dot operator has higher precedence than casting, so `s.getID()` is invoked before `s` is cast to `GradStudent`.

2. The statement

   ```
   int y = g.getID();
   ```

   compiles without problem because `g` is declared to be of type `GradStudent`, and this is the class that contains `getID`. No cast is required.

Type Rules for Polymorphic Method Calls

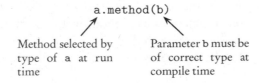

Method selected by type of `a` at run time

Parameter `b` must be of correct type at compile time

- For a declaration like

  ```
  Superclass a = new Subclass();
  ```

  the type of `a` at compile time is `Superclass`; at run time it is `Subclass`.

- At compile time, `method` must be found in the class of `a`, that is, in `Superclass`. (This is true whether the method is polymorphic or not.) If `method` cannot be found in the class of `a`, you need to do an explicit cast on `a` to its actual type.

- For a polymorphic method, at run time the actual type of `a` is determined—`Subclass` in this example—and `method` is selected from `Subclass`. This could be an inherited method if there is no overriding method.

- The type of parameter `b` is checked at compile time. You may need to do an explicit cast to the subclass type to make this correct.

The `ClassCastException`

The `ClassCastException` is a run-time exception thrown to signal an attempt to cast an object to a class of which it is not an instance.

```
Student u = new UnderGrad();
System.out.println((String) u);    //ClassCastException
                                   //u is not an instance of String
int x = ((GradStudent) u).getID(); //ClassCastException
                                   //u is not an instance of GradStudent
```

ABSTRACT CLASSES

Abstract Class

An *abstract class* is a superclass that represents an abstract concept, and therefore should not be instantiated. For example, a maze program could have several different maze components—paths, walls, entrances, and exits. All of these share certain features (e.g., location, and a way of displaying). They can therefore all be declared as subclasses of the abstract class `MazeComponent`. The program will create path objects, wall objects, and so on, but no instances of `MazeComponent`.

An abstract class may contain *abstract methods*. An abstract method has no implementation code, just a header. The rationale for an abstract method is that there is no good default code for the method. Every subclass will need to override this method, so why bother with a meaningless implementation in the superclass? The method appears in the abstract class as a placeholder. The implementation for the method occurs in the subclasses. If a class contains any abstract methods, it *must* be declared an abstract class.

The abstract Keyword

An abstract class is declared with the keyword `abstract` in the header:

```
public abstract class AbstractClass
{   ...
```

The keyword `extends` is used as before to declare a subclass:

```
public class SubClass extends AbstractClass
{   ...
```

If a subclass of an abstract class does not provide implementation code for all the abstract methods of its superclass, it too becomes an abstract class and must be declared as such to avoid a compile-time error:

```
public abstract class SubClass extends AbstractClass
{    ...
```

Here is an example of an abstract class, with two concrete (nonabstract) subclasses.

```
public abstract class Shape
{
    private String myName;

    //constructor
    public Shape(String name)
    { myName = name; }
```

```
        public String getName()
        { return myName; }

        public abstract double area();
        public abstract double perimeter();

        public double semiPerimeter()
        { return perimeter() / 2; }
}

public class Circle extends Shape
{
        private double myRadius;

        //constructor
        public Circle(double radius, String name)
        {
            super(name);
            myRadius = radius;
        }

        public double perimeter()
        { return 2 * Math.PI * myRadius; }

        public double area()
        { return Math.PI * myRadius * myRadius; }
}

public class Square extends Shape
{
        private double mySide;

        //constructor
        public Square(double side, String name)
        {
            super(name);
            mySide = side;
        }

        public double perimeter()
        { return 4 * mySide; }

        public double area()
        { return mySide * mySide; }
}
```

NOTE

1. It is meaningless to define `perimeter` and `area` methods for `Shape`—thus, these are declared as abstract methods.
2. An abstract class can have both instance variables and concrete (nonabstract) methods. See, for example, `myName`, `getName`, and `semiPerimeter` in the `Shape` class.
3. Abstract methods are declared with the keyword `abstract`. There is no method body. The header is terminated with a semicolon.

4. No instances can be created for an abstract class:

```
Shape a = new Shape("blob");  //Illegal.
                    //Can't create instance of abstract class.
Shape c = new Circle(1.5, "small circle");  //legal
```

5. Polymorphism works with abstract classes as it does with concrete classes:

```
Shape circ = new Circle(10, "circle");
Shape sq = new Square(9.4, "square");
Shape s = null;
System.out.println("Which shape?");
String str = IO.readString();        //read user input
if (str.equals("circle"))
    s = circ;
else
    s = sq;
System.out.println("Area of " + s.getName() + " is "
        + s.area());
```

INTERFACES

Interface

An *interface* is a collection of related methods whose headers are provided without implementations. All of the methods are both public and abstract—no need to explicitly include these keywords. As such, they provide a framework of behavior for any class.

The classes that implement a given interface may represent objects that are vastly different. They all, however, have in common a capability or feature expressed in the methods of the interface. An interface called `FlyingObject`, for example, may have the methods `fly` and `isFlying`. Some classes that implement `FlyingObject` could be `Bird`, `Airplane`, `Missile`, `Butterfly`, and `Witch`. A class called `Turtle` would be unlikely to implement `FlyingObject` because turtles don't fly.

An interface called `Computable` may have just three methods: `add`, `subtract`, and `multiply`. Classes that implement `Computable` could be `Fraction`, `Matrix`, `LongInteger`, and `ComplexNumber`. It would not be meaningful, however, for a `TelevisionSet` to implement `Computable`—what does it mean, for example, to multiply two `TelevisionSet` objects?

> A nonabstract class that implements an interface must implement every method of the interface.

A class that implements an interface can define any number of methods. In particular, it contracts to provide implementations for *all* the methods declared in the interface. If it fails to implement any of the methods, the class must be declared abstract.

Defining an Interface

An interface is declared with the `interface` keyword. For example,

```
public interface FlyingObject
{
    void fly();           //method that simulates flight of object
    boolean isFlying();   //true if object is in flight,
                          //false otherwise
}
```

The `implements` Keyword

Interfaces are implemented using the `implements` keyword. For example,

```
public class Bird implements FlyingObject
{
    . . .
```

This declaration means that two of the methods in the `Bird` class must be `fly` and `isFlying`. Note that any subclass of `Bird` will automatically implement the interface `FlyingObject`, since `fly` and `isFlying` will be inherited by the subclass.

A class that extends a superclass can also *directly* implement an interface. For example,

```
public class Mosquito extends Insect implements FlyingObject
{
    . . .
```

NOTE

1. The `extends` clause must precede the `implements` clause.
2. A class can have just one superclass, but it can implement any number of interfaces:

```
        public class SubClass extends SuperClass
                   implements Interface1, Interface2, ...
```

The `Comparable` Interface

The standard `java.lang` package contains the `Comparable` interface, which provides a useful method for comparing objects. Note that the AP Java subset uses the raw `Comparable` interface, not the generic `Comparable<E>` of Java 5.0.

> Classes written for objects that need to be compared should implement `Comparable`.

```
public interface Comparable
{
    int compareTo(Object obj);
}
```

Any class that implements `Comparable` must provide a `compareTo` method. This method compares the implicit object (`this`) with the parameter object (`obj`) and returns a negative integer, zero, or a positive integer depending on whether the implicit object is less than, equal to, or greater than the parameter. If the two objects being compared are not type compatible, a `ClassCastException` is thrown by the method.

Example

The abstract `Shape` class defined previously (p. 196) is modified to implement the `Comparable` interface:

```
public abstract class Shape implements Comparable
{
    private String myName;

    //constructor
    public Shape(String name)
    { myName = name; }
```

```
public String getName()
{ return myName; }

public abstract double area();
public abstract double perimeter();

public double semiPerimeter()
{ return perimeter() / 2; }

public int compareTo(Object obj)
{
    final double EPSILON = 1.0e-15;   //slightly bigger than
                                      //machine precision
    Shape rhs = (Shape) obj;
    double diff = area() - rhs.area();
    if (Math.abs(diff) <= EPSILON * Math.abs(area()))
        return 0;  //area of this shape equals area of obj
    else if (diff < 0)
        return -1; //area of this shape less than area of obj
    else
        return 1;  //area of this shape greater than area of obj
}
}
```

NOTE

1. The Circle, Square, and other subclasses of Shape will all automatically implement Comparable and inherit the compareTo method.

2. It is tempting to use a simpler test for equality of areas, namely

```
if (diff == 0)
    return 0;
```

   But recall that real numbers can have round-off errors in their storage (Box p. 122). This means that the simple test may return false even though the two areas are essentially equal. A more robust test is implemented in the code given, namely to test if the relative error in diff is small enough to be considered zero.

3. The Object class is a universal superclass (see p. 225). This means that the compareTo method can take as a parameter any object reference that implements Comparable.

4. The first step of a compareTo method must cast the Object argument to the class type, in this case Shape. If this is not done, the compiler won't find the area method—remember, an Object is not necessarily a Shape.

5. The algorithm one chooses in compareTo should in general be consistent with the equals method (see p. 227): Whenever object1.equals(object2) returns true, object1.compareTo(object2) returns 0.

Here is a program that finds the larger of two Comparable objects.

```java
public class FindMaxTest
{
    /* Return the larger of two objects a and b. */
    public static Comparable max(Comparable a, Comparable b)
    {
        if (a.compareTo(b) > 0) //if a > b ...
            return a;
        else
            return b;
    }

    /* Test max on two Shape objects. */
    public static void main(String[] args)
    {
        Shape s1 = new Circle(3.0, "circle");
        Shape s2 = new Square(4.5, "square");
        System.out.println("Area of " + s1.getName() + " is " +
                s1.area());
        System.out.println("Area of " + s2.getName() + " is " +
                s2.area());
        Shape s3 = (Shape) max(s1, s2);
        System.out.println("The larger shape is the " +
                s3.getName());
    }
}
```

Here is the output:

```
Area of circle is 28.27
Area of square is 20.25
The larger shape is the circle
```

NOTE

1. The max method takes parameters of type Comparable. Since s1 *is-a* Comparable object and s2 *is-a* Comparable object, no casting is necessary in the method call.
2. The max method can be called with any two Comparable objects, for example, two String objects or two Integer objects (see Chapter 4).
3. The objects must be type compatible (i.e., it must make sense to compare them). For example, in the program shown, if s1 *is-a* Shape and s2 *is-a* String, the compareTo method will throw a ClassCastException at the line

    ```java
    Shape rhs = (Shape) obj;
    ```

4. The cast is needed in the line

    ```java
    Shape s3 = (Shape) max(s1, s2);
    ```

    since max(s1, s2) returns a Comparable.
5. A primitive type is not an object and therefore cannot be passed as Comparable. You can, however, use a wrapper class and in this way convert a primitive type to a Comparable (see p. 231).

ABSTRACT CLASS VS. INTERFACE

Consider writing a program that simulates a game of Battleships. The program may have a Ship class with subclasses Submarine, Cruiser, Destroyer, and so on. The various ships will be placed in a two-dimensional grid that represents a part of the ocean, much like the grid in the GridWorld Case Study.

An abstract class Ship is a good design choice. There will not be any instances of Ship objects because the specific features of the subclasses must be known in order to place these ships in the grid. A Grid interface like that in the case study suggests itself for the two-dimensional grid.

Notice that the abstract Ship class is specific to the Battleships application, whereas the Grid interface is not. You could use the Grid interface in any program that has a two-dimensional grid.

Interface vs. Abstract Class

- Use an abstract class for an object that is application-specific, but incomplete without its subclasses.
- Consider using an interface when its methods are suitable for your program, but could be equally applicable in a variety of programs.
- An interface cannot provide implementations for any of its methods, whereas an abstract class can.
- An interface cannot contain instance variables, whereas an abstract class can.
- An interface and an abstract class can both declare constants.
- It is not possible to create an instance of an interface object or an abstract class object.

Chapter Summary

You should be able to write your own subclasses, given any superclass. Level AB students should be able to write a class that implements Comparable, while all students should be able to use the compareTo method to compare objects.

Be sure you can explain what polymorphism is: Recall that it only operates when methods have been overridden in at least one subclass. You should also be able to explain the difference between the following concepts:

- An abstract class and an interface.
- An overloaded method and an overridden method.
- Dynamic binding (late binding) and static binding (early binding).

MULTIPLE-CHOICE QUESTIONS ON INHERITANCE AND POLYMORPHISM

Questions 1–10 refer to the BankAccount, SavingsAccount, and CheckingAccount classes defined below:

```java
public class BankAccount
{
    private double myBalance;

    public BankAccount()
    { myBalance = 0; }

    public BankAccount(double balance)
    { myBalance = balance; }

    public void deposit(double amount)
    { myBalance += amount; }

    public void withdraw(double amount)
    { myBalance -= amount; }

    public double getBalance()
    { return myBalance; }
}

public class SavingsAccount extends BankAccount
{
    private double myInterestRate;

    public SavingsAccount()
    { /* implementation not shown */ }

    public SavingsAccount(double balance, double rate)
    { /* implementation not shown */ }

    public void addInterest()     //Add interest to balance
    { /* implementation not shown */ }
}

public class CheckingAccount extends BankAccount
{
    private static final double FEE = 2.0;
    private static final double MIN_BALANCE = 50.0;

    public CheckingAccount(double balance)
    { /* implementation not shown */ }

    /* FEE of $2 deducted if withdrawal leaves balance less
     * than MIN_BALANCE. Allows for negative balance. */
    public void withdraw(double amount)
    { /* implementation not shown */ }
}
```

1. Of the methods shown, how many different nonconstructor methods can be invoked by a `SavingsAccount` object?
   (A) 1
   (B) 2
   (C) 3
   (D) 4
   (E) 5

2. Which of the following correctly implements the default constructor of the `SavingsAccount` class?

      I `myInterestRate = 0;`
        `super();`

     II `super();`
        `myInterestRate = 0;`

    III `super();`

   (A) II only
   (B) I and II only
   (C) II and III only
   (D) III only
   (E) I, II, and III

3. Which is a correct implementation of the constructor with parameters in the `SavingsAccount` class?

   (A) `myBalance = balance;`
        `myInterestRate = rate;`

   (B) `getBalance() =  balance;`
        `myInterestRate = rate;`

   (C) `super();`
        `myInterestRate = rate;`

   (D) `super(balance);`
        `myInterestRate = rate;`

   (E) `super(balance, rate);`

4. Which is a correct implementation of the `CheckingAccount` constructor?

      I `super(balance);`

     II `super();`
        `deposit(balance);`

    III `deposit(balance);`

   (A) I only
   (B) II only
   (C) III only
   (D) II and III only
   (E) I, II, and III

5. Which is correct implementation code for the `withdraw` method in the `CheckingAccount` class?

   (A)
```
super.withdraw(amount);
if (myBalance < MIN_BALANCE)
    super.withdraw(FEE);
```

   (B)
```
withdraw(amount);
if (myBalance < MIN_BALANCE)
    withdraw(FEE);
```

   (C)
```
super.withdraw(amount);
if (getBalance() < MIN_BALANCE)
    super.withdraw(FEE);
```

   (D)
```
withdraw(amount);
if (getBalance() < MIN_BALANCE)
    withdraw(FEE);
```

   (E)
```
myBalance -= amount;
if (myBalance < MIN_BALANCE)
    myBalance -= FEE;
```

6. Redefining the `withdraw` method in the `CheckingAccount` class is an example of
   (A) method overloading.
   (B) method overriding.
   (C) downcasting.
   (D) dynamic binding (late binding).
   (E) static binding (early binding).

Use the following for Questions 7–9.

A program to test the `BankAccount`, `SavingsAccount`, and `CheckingAccount` classes has these declarations:

```
BankAccount b = new BankAccount(1400);
BankAccount s = new SavingsAccount(1000, 0.04);
BankAccount c = new CheckingAccount(500);
```

7. Which method call will cause an error?
   (A) `b.deposit(200);`
   (B) `s.withdraw(500);`
   (C) `c.withdraw(500);`
   (D) `s.deposit(10000);`
   (E) `s.addInterest();`

8. In order to test polymorphism, which method must be used in the program?
   (A) Either a `SavingsAccount` constructor or a `CheckingAccount` constructor
   (B) `addInterest`
   (C) `deposit`
   (D) `withdraw`
   (E) `getBalance`

9. Which of the following will *not* cause a ClassCastException to be thrown?
   - (A) `((SavingsAccount) b).addInterest();`
   - (B) `((CheckingAccount) b).withdraw(200);`
   - (C) `((CheckingAccount) c).deposit(800);`
   - (D) `((CheckingAccount) s).withdraw(150);`
   - (E) `((SavingsAccount) c).addInterest();`

10. A new method is added to the BankAccount class.

    ```
    /* Transfer amount from this BankAccount to another BankAccount.
     * Precondition: myBalance > amount */
    public void transfer(BankAccount another, double amount)
    {
        withdraw(amount);
        another.deposit(amount);
    }
    ```

    A program has these declarations:

    ```
    BankAccount b = new BankAccount(650);
    SavingsAccount timsSavings = new SavingsAccount(1500, 0.03);
    CheckingAccount daynasChecking = new CheckingAccount(2000);
    ```

    Which of the following will transfer money from one account to another without error?

    I `b.transfer(timsSavings, 50);`

    II `timsSavings.transfer(daynasChecking, 30);`

    III `daynasChecking.transfer(b, 55);`

    - (A) I only
    - (B) II only
    - (C) III only
    - (D) I, II, and III
    - (E) None

11. Consider these class declarations:

```
public class Person
{
    . . .
}

public class Teacher extends Person
{
    . . .
}
```

Which is a true statement?

    I Teacher inherits the constructors of Person.
   II Teacher can add new methods and private instance variables.
 III Teacher can override existing private methods of Person.

(A) I only
(B) II only
(C) III only
(D) I and II only
(E) II and III only

12. Which statement about abstract classes and interfaces is *false*?
(A) An interface cannot implement any methods, whereas an abstract class can.
(B) A class can implement many interfaces but can have only one superclass.
(C) An unlimited number of unrelated classes can implement the same interface.
(D) It is not possible to construct either an abstract class object or an interface object.
(E) All of the methods in both an abstract class and an interface are public.

13. Consider the following hierarchy of classes:

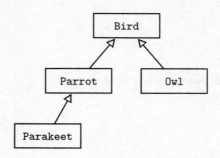

A program is written to print data about various birds:

```
public class BirdStuff
{
    public static void printName(Bird b)
    { /* implementation not shown */ }

    public static void printBirdCall(Parrot p)
    { /* implementation not shown */ }

    //several more Bird methods

    public static void main(String[] args)
    {
        Bird bird1 = new Bird();
        Bird bird2 = new Parrot();
        Parrot parrot1 = new Parrot();
        Parrot parrot2 = new Parakeet();
        /* more code */
    }
}
```

Assuming that none of the given classes is abstract and all have default constructors, which of the following segments of /* *more code* */ will *not* cause an error?

(A) `printName(parrot2);`
    `printBirdCall((Parrot) bird2);`

(B) `printName((Parrot) bird1);`
    `printBirdCall(bird2);`

(C) `printName(bird2);`
    `printBirdCall(bird2);`

(D) `printName((Parakeet) parrot1);`
    `printBirdCall(parrot2);`

(E) `printName((Owl) parrot2);`
    `printBirdCall((Parakeet) parrot2);`

Use the declarations below for Questions 14–16.

```
public abstract class Solid
{
    private String myName;

    //constructor
    public Solid(String name)
    { myName = name; }

    public String getName()
    { return myName; }

    public abstract double volume();
}

public class Sphere extends Solid
{
    private double myRadius;

    //constructor
    public Sphere(String name, double radius)
    {
        super(name);
        myRadius = radius;
    }

    public double volume()
    { return (4.0/3.0) * Math.PI * myRadius * myRadius * myRadius; }
}

public class RectangularPrism extends Solid
{
    private double myLength;
    private double myWidth;
    private double myHeight;

    //constructor
    public RectangularPrism(String name, double l, double w,
            double h)
    {
        super(name);
        myLength = l;
        myWidth = w;
        myHeight = h;
    }

    public double volume()
    { return myLength * myWidth * myHeight; }
}
```

14. A program that tests these classes has the following declarations and assignments:

```
Solid s1, s2, s3, s4;
s1 = new Solid("blob");
s2 = new Sphere("sphere", 3.8);
s3 = new RectangularPrism("box", 2, 4, 6.5);
s4 = null;
```

How many of the above lines of code are incorrect?
(A) 1
(B) 2
(C) 3
(D) 4
(E) 5

15. Which is *false*?
(A) If a program has several objects declared as type `Solid`, the decision about which `volume` method to call will be resolved at run time.
(B) If the `Solid` class were modified to provide a default implementation for the `volume` method, it would no longer need to be an abstract class.
(C) If the `Sphere` and `RectangularPrism` classes failed to provide an implementation for the `volume` method, they would need to be declared as abstract classes.
(D) The fact that there is no reasonable default implementation for the `volume` method in the `Solid` class suggests that it should be an abstract method.
(E) Since `Solid` is abstract and its subclasses are nonabstract, polymorphism no longer applies when these classes are used in a program.

16. Here is a program that prints the volume of a solid:

```
public class SolidMain
{
    /* Output volume of Solid s. */
    public static void printVolume(Solid s)
    {
        System.out.println("Volume = " + s.volume() +
                " cubic units");
    }

    public static void main(String[] args)
    {
        Solid sol;
        Solid sph = new Sphere("sphere", 4);
        Solid rec = new RectangularPrism("box", 3, 6, 9);
        int flipCoin = (int) (Math.random() * 2);   //0 or 1
        if (flipCoin == 0)
            sol = sph;
        else
            sol = rec;
        printVolume(sol);
    }
}
```

Which is a true statement about this program?
(A) It will output the volume of the sphere or box, as intended.
(B) It will output the volume of the default `Solid` s, which is neither a sphere nor a box.
(C) A `ClassCastException` will be thrown.
(D) A compile-time error will occur because there is no implementation code for `volume` in the `Solid` class.
(E) A run-time error will occur because of parameter type mismatch in the method call `printVolume(sol)`.

17. Consider the `Computable` interface below for performing simple calculator operations:

```
public interface Computable
{
    //Return this Object + y.
    Object add(Object y);

    //Return this Object - y.
    Object subtract(Object y);

    //Return this Object * y.
    Object multiply(Object y);
}
```

Which of the following is the *least* suitable class for implementing `Computable`?

(A) `LargeInteger`   //integers with 100 digits or more

(B) `Fraction`   //implemented with numerator and
                       //denominator of type int

(C) `IrrationalNumber` //nonrepeating, nonterminating decimal

(D) `Length`   //implemented with different units, such
                       //as inches, centimeters, etc.

(E) `BankAccount`   //implemented with myBalance

Refer to the `Player` interface shown below for Questions 18–21.

```
public interface Player
{
    /* Return an integer that represents a move in a game. */
    int getMove();

    /* Display the status of the game for this Player after
     * implementing the next move. */
    void updateDisplay();
}
```

18. A class `HumanPlayer` implements the `Player` interface. Another class, `SmartPlayer`, is a subclass of `HumanPlayer`. Which statement is *false*?
    (A) `SmartPlayer` automatically implements the `Player` interface.
    (B) `HumanPlayer` must contain implementations of both the `updateDisplay` and `getMove` methods.
    (C) It is not possible to declare a reference of type `Player`.
    (D) The `SmartPlayer` class can override the methods `updateDisplay` and `getMove` of the `HumanPlayer` class.
    (E) A method in a client program can have `Player` as a parameter type.

19. A programmer plans to write programs that simulate various games. In each case he will have several classes, each representing a different kind of competitor in the game, such as `ExpertPlayer`, `ComputerPlayer`, `RecklessPlayer`, `CheatingPlayer`, `Beginner`, `IntermediatePlayer`, and so on. It may or may not be suitable for these classes to implement the `Player` interface, depending on the particular game being simulated. In the games described below, which is the *least* suitable for having the competitor classes implement the given `Player` interface?

   (A) High-Low Guessing Game: The computer thinks of a number and the competitor who guesses it with the least number of guesses wins. After each guess, the computer tells whether its number is higher or lower than the guess.

   (B) Chips: Start with a pile of chips. Each player in turn removes some number of chips. The winner is the one who removes the final chip. The first player may remove any number of chips, but not all of them. Each subsequent player must remove at least one chip and at most twice the number removed by the preceding player.

   (C) Chess: Played on a square board of 64 squares of alternating colors. There are just two players, called White and Black, the colors of their respective pieces. The players each have a set of pieces on the board that can move according to a set of rules. The players alternate moves, where a move consists of moving any one piece to another square. If that square is occupied by an opponent's piece, the piece is captured and removed from the board.

   (D) Tic-Tac-Toe: Two players alternate placing "X" or "O" on a 3 × 3 grid. The first player to get three in a row, where a row can be vertical, horizontal, or diagonal, wins.

   (E) Battleships: There are two players, each with a 10 × 10 grid hidden from his opponent. Various "ships" are placed on the grid. A move consists of calling out a grid location, trying to "hit" an opponent's ship. Players alternate moves. The first player to sink his opponent's fleet wins.

Consider these declarations for Questions 20 and 21:

```
public class HumanPlayer implements Player
{
    private String myName;

    //constructors not shown ...

    //code to implement getMove and updateDisplay not shown ...

    public String getName()
    { /* implementation not shown */ }
}


public class ExpertPlayer extends HumanPlayer implements Comparable
{
    private int myRating;

    //constructors not shown ...

    public int compareTo(Object obj)
    { /* implementation not shown */ }
}
```

20. Which code segment in a client program will cause an error?

```
    I Player p1 = new HumanPlayer();
      Player p2 = new ExpertPlayer();
      int x1 = p1.getMove();
      int x2 = p2.getMove();

   II int x;
      Comparable c1 = new ExpertPlayer(/* correct parameter list */);
      Comparable c2 = new ExpertPlayer(/* correct parameter list */);
      if (c1.compareTo(c2) < 0)
          x = c1.getMove();
      else
          x = c2.getMove();

  III int x;
      HumanPlayer h1 = new HumanPlayer(/* correct parameter list */);
      HumanPlayer h2 = new HumanPlayer(/* correct parameter list */);
      if (h1.compareTo(h2) < 0)
          x = h1.getMove();
      else
          x = h2.getMove();
```

(A) II only
(B) III only
(C) II and III only
(D) I, II, and III
(E) None

21. Which of the following is correct implementation code for the `compareTo` method in the `ExpertPlayer` class?

```
  I ExpertPlayer rhs = (ExpertPlayer) obj;
    if (myRating == rhs.myRating)
        return 0;
    else if (myRating < rhs.myRating)
        return -1;
    else
        return 1;

 II ExpertPlayer rhs = (ExpertPlayer) obj;
    return myRating - rhs.myRating;

III ExpertPlayer rhs = (ExpertPlayer) obj;
    if (getName().equals(rhs.getName()))
        return 0;
    else if (getName().compareTo(rhs.getName()) < 0)
        return -1;
    else
        return 1;
```

(A) I only
(B) II only
(C) III only
(D) I and II only
(E) I, II, and III

22. Which statement about interfaces is true?

   I An interface contains only public abstract methods and public static final fields.
   II If a class implements an interface and then fails to implement any methods in that interface, then the class *must* be declared abstract.
   III While a class may implement just one interface, it may extend more than one class.

(A) I only
(B) I and II only
(C) I and III only
(D) II and III only
(E) I, II, and III

23. Which of the following classes is the least suitable candidate for implementing the Comparable interface?

(A) ```
public class Point
{
        private double x;
        private double y;

        //various methods follow
            ...
}
```

(B) ```
public class Name
{
        private String firstName;
        private String lastName;

        //various methods follow
            ...
}
```

(C) ```
public class Car
{
        private int modelNumber;
        private int year;
        private double price;

        //various methods follow
            ...
}
```

(D) ```
public class Student
{
        private String name;
        private double gpa;

        //various methods follow
            ...
}
```

(E) ```
public class Employee
{
        private String name;
        private int hireDate;
        private double salary;

        //various methods follow
            ...
}
```
```

24. A programmer has the task of maintaining a database of students of a large university. There are two types of students, undergraduates and graduate students. About a third of the graduate students are doctoral candidates.

   All of the students have the same personal information stored, like name, address, and phone number, and also student information like courses taken and grades. Each student's GPA is computed, but differently for undergraduates and graduates. The doctoral candidates have information about their dissertations and faculty advisors.

   The programmer will write a Java program to handle all the student information. Which of the following is the best design, in terms of programmer efficiency and code reusability? Note: { ... } denotes class code.

   (A) ```
public interface Student { ...}
   public class Undergraduate implements Student { ... }
   public class Graduate implements Student { ... }
   public class DocStudent extends Graduate { ... }
```

   (B) ```
public abstract class Student { ...}
   public class Undergraduate extends Student { ... }
   public class Graduate extends Student { ... }
   public class DocStudent extends Graduate { ... }
```

   (C) ```
public class Student { ...}
   public class Undergraduate extends Student { ... }
   public class Graduate extends Student { ... }
   public class DocStudent extends Graduate { ... }
```

   (D) ```
public abstract class Student { ...}
   public class Undergraduate extends Student { ... }
   public class Graduate extends Student { ... }
   public class DocStudent extends Student { ... }
```

   (E) ```
public interface PersonalInformation { ... }
   public class Student implements PersonalInformation { ...}
   public class Undergraduate extends Student { ... }
   public abstract class Graduate extends Student { ... }
   public class DocStudent extends Graduate { ... }
```
```

25. A certain interface provided by a Java package contains just a single method:

    ```
    public interface SomeName
    {
        int method1(Object o);
    }
    ```

    A programmer adds some functionality to this interface by adding another method to it, method2:

    ```
    public interface SomeName
    {
        int method1(Object ob1);
        void method2(Object ob2);
    }
    ```

    As a result of this addition, which of the following is true?
    (A) A ClassCastException will occur if ob1 and ob2 are not compatible.
    (B) All classes that implement the original SomeName interface will need to be rewritten because they no longer implement SomeName.
    (C) A class that implements the original SomeName interface will need to modify its declaration as follows:

    ```
    public class ClassName implements SomeName extends method2
    {     . . .
    ```
    (D) SomeName will need to be changed to an abstract class and provide implementation code for method2, so that the original and upgraded versions of SomeName are compatible.
    (E) Any new class that implements the upgraded version of SomeName will not compile.

26. Consider the Temperature class defined below:

    ```
    public class Temperature implements Comparable
    {
        private String myScale;
        private double myDegrees;

        //default constructor
        public Temperature ()
        { /* implementation not shown */ }

        //constructor
        public Temperature(String scale, double degrees)
        { /* implementation not shown */ }

        public int compareTo(Object obj)
        { /* implementation not shown */ }

        public String toString()
        { /* implementation not shown */ }
    }
    ```

    Here is a program that finds the lowest of three temperatures:

```
public class TemperatureMain
{
    /* Find smaller of objects a and b. */
    public static Comparable min(Comparable a, Comparable b)
    {
        if (a.compareTo(b) < 0)
            return a;
        else
            return b;
    }

    /* Find smallest of objects a, b, and c */
    public static Comparable minThree(Comparable a,
            Comparable b, Comparable c)
    {
        return min(min(a, b), c);
    }

    public static void main(String[] args)
    {
        /* code to test minThree method */
    }
}
```

Which are correct replacements for /* *code to test* minThree *method* */?

I
```
Temperature t1 = new Temperature("C", 85);
Temperature t2 = new Temperature("F", 45);
Temperature t3 = new Temperature("F", 120);
System.out.println("The lowest temperature is " +
        minThree(t1, t2, t3));
```

II
```
Comparable c1 = new Temperature("C", 85);
Comparable c2 = new Temperature("F", 45);
Comparable c3 = new Temperature("F", 120);
System.out.println("The lowest temperature is " +
        minThree(c1, c2, c3));
```

III
```
Comparable c1 = new Comparable("C", 85);
Comparable c2 = new Comparable("F", 45);
Comparable c3 = new Comparable("F", 120);
System.out.println("The lowest temperature is " +
        minThree(c1, c2, c3));
```

(A) II only
(B) I and II only
(C) II and III only
(D) I and III only
(E) I, II, and III

ANSWER KEY

1. D	10. D	19. C
2. C	11. E	20. C
3. D	12. E	21. E
4. E	13. A	22. B
5. C	14. A	23. A
6. B	15. E	24. B
7. E	16. A	25. B
8. D	17. E	26. B
9. C	18. C	

ANSWERS EXPLAINED

1. **(D)** The methods are `deposit`, `withdraw`, and `getBalance`, all inherited from the `BankAccount` class, plus `addInterest`, which was defined just for the class `SavingsAccount`.

2. **(C)** Implementation I fails because `super()` *must* be the first line of the implementation whenever it is used in a constructor. Implementation III may appear to be incorrect because it doesn't initialize `myInterestRate`. Since `myInterestRate`, however, is a primitive type—`double`—the compiler will provide a default initialization of 0, which was required.

3. **(D)** First, the statement `super(balance)` initializes the inherited private variable `myBalance` as for the `BankAccount` superclass.   Then the statement `myInterestRate = rate` initializes `myInterestRate`, which belongs uniquely to the `SavingsAccount` class. Choice E fails because `myInterestRate` does not belong to the `BankAccount` class and therefore cannot be initialized by a super method. Choice A is wrong because the `SavingsAccount` class cannot directly access the private instance variables of its superclass. Choice B assigns a value to an accessor method, which is meaningless. Choice C is incorrect because `super()` invokes the *default* constructor of the superclass. This will cause `myBalance` of the `SavingsAccount` object to be initialized to 0, rather than `balance`, the parameter value.

4. **(E)** The constructor must initialize the inherited instance variable `myBalance` to the value of the `balance` parameter. All three segments achieve this. Implementation I does it by invoking `super(balance)`, the constructor in the superclass. Implementation II first initializes `myBalance` to 0 by invoking the *default* constructor of the superclass. Then it calls the inherited `deposit` method of the superclass to add `balance` to the account. Implementation III works because `super()` is automatically called as the first line of the constructor code if there is no explicit call to super.

5. **(C)** First the `withdraw` method of the `BankAccount` superclass is used to withdraw `amount`. A prefix of `super` must be used to invoke this method, which eliminates

choices B and D. Then the balance must be tested using the accessor method `getBalance`, which is inherited. You can't test `myBalance` directly since it is private to the `BankAccount` class. This eliminates choices A and E, and provides another reason for eliminating choice B.

6. **(B)** When a superclass method is redefined in a subclass, the process is called *method overriding*. Which method to call is determined at run time. This is called *dynamic binding* (p. 193). *Method overloading* is two or more methods with different signatures in the same class (p. 155). The compiler recognizes at compile time which method to call. This is *early binding*. The process of *downcasting* is unrelated to these principles (p. 194).

7. **(E)** The `addInterest` method is defined only in the `SavingsAccount` class. It therefore cannot be invoked by a `BankAccount` object. The error can be fixed by casting s to the correct type:

   ```
   ((SavingsAccount) s).addInterest();
   ```

   The other method calls do not cause a problem because `withdraw` and `deposit` are both methods of the `BankAccount` class.

8. **(D)** The `withdraw` method is the only method that has one implementation in the superclass and a *different* implementation in a subclass. Polymorphism is the mechanism of selecting the correct method from the different possibilities in the class hierarchy. Notice that the `deposit` method, for example, is available to objects of all three bank account classes, but it's the *same* code in all three cases. So polymorphism isn't tested.

9. **(C)** You will get a `ClassCastException` whenever you try to cast an object to a class of which it is not an instance. Choice C is the only statement that doesn't attempt to do this. Look at the other choices: In choice A, b is not an instance of `SavingsAccount`. In choice B, b is not an instance of `CheckingAccount`. In choice D, s is not an instance of `CheckingAccount`. In choice E, c is not an instance of `SavingsAccount`.

10. **(D)** It is OK to use `timsSavings` and `daynasChecking` as parameters since each of these *is-a* `BankAccount` object. It is also OK for `timsSavings` and `daynasChecking` to call the `transfer` method (statements II and III), since they inherit this method from the `BankAccount` superclass.

11. **(E)** Statement I is false: A subclass must specify its own constructors. Otherwise the default constructor of the superclass will automatically be invoked. Note that statement III is true: It is OK to override private instance methods—they can even be declared public in the subclass implementation. What is *not* OK is to make the access more restrictive, for example, to override a public method and declare it private.

12. **(E)** All of the methods in an interface are by default public (the `public` keyword isn't needed). An abstract class can have both private and public methods.

13. **(A)** There are two quick tests you can do to find the answer to this question:

    (1) Test the *is-a* relationship, namely the parameter for `printName` *is-a* Bird? and the parameter for `printBirdCall` *is-a* Parrot?
    (2) A reference cannot be cast to something it's not an instance of.

    Choice A passes both of these tests: `parrot2` *is-a* Bird, and `(Parrot) bird2` *is-a* Parrot. Also `bird2` is an instance of a `Parrot` (as you can see by looking at the right-hand side of the assignment), so the casting is correct. In choice B `printBirdCall(bird2)` is wrong because `bird2` *is-a* `Bird` and the `printBirdCall` method is expecting a `Parrot`. Therefore `bird2` must be downcast to a `Parrot`. Also, the method call `printName((Parrot) bird1)` fails because `bird1` is an instance of a `Bird` and therefore cannot be cast to a `Parrot`. In choice C, `printName(bird2)` is correct: `bird2` *is-a* `Bird`. However, `printBirdCall(bird2)` fails as already discussed. In choice D, `(Parakeet) parrot1` is an incorrect cast: `parrot1` is an instance of a `Parrot`. Note that `printBirdCall(parrot2)` is OK since `parrot2` *is-a* `Parrot`. In choice E, `(Owl) parrot2` is an incorrect cast: `parrot2` is an instance of `Parakeet`. Note that `printBirdCall((Parakeet) parrot2)` is correct: A `Parakeet` *is-a* `Parrot`, and `parrot2` is an instance of a `Parakeet`.

14. **(A)** The only incorrect line is `s1 = new Solid("blob")`: You can't create an instance of an abstract class. Abstract class references can, however, refer to objects of concrete (nonabstract) subclasses. Thus, the assignments for `s2` and `s3` are OK. Note that an abstract class reference can also be null, so the final assignment, though redundant, is correct.

15. **(E)** The point of having an abstract method is to postpone until run time the decision about which subclass version to call. This is what polymorphism is—calling the appropriate method at run time based on the type of the object.

16. **(A)** This is an example of polymorphism: The correct `volume` method is selected at run time. The parameter expected for `printVolume` is a `Solid` reference, which is what it gets in `main()`. The reference `sol` will refer either to a `Sphere` or a `RectangularPrism` object depending on the outcome of the coin flip. Since a `Sphere` is a `Solid` and a `RectangularPrism` is a `Solid`, there will be no type mismatch when these are the actual parameters in the `printVolume` method. (Note: The `Math.random` method is discussed in Chapter 4.)

17. **(E)** Each of choices A though D represent `Computable` objects: It makes sense to add, subtract, or multiply two large integers, two fractions, two irrational numbers, and two lengths. (One can multiply lengths to get an area, for example.) While it may make sense under certain circumstances to add or subtract two bank accounts, it does not make sense to multiply them!

18. **(C)** You can *declare a reference* of type `Player`. What you cannot do is *construct an object* of type `Player`. The following declarations are therefore legal:

```
SmartPlayer s = new SmartPlayer();
Player p1 = s;
Player p2 = new HumanPlayer();
```

19. **(C)** Remember, to implement the `Player` interface a class must provide implementations for `getMove` and `updateDisplay`. The `updateDisplay` method is suitable for all five games described. The `getMove` method returns a single integer, which works well for the High-Low game of choice A and the Chips game of choice B. In Tic-Tac-Toe (choice D) and Battleships (choice E) a move consists of giving a grid location. This can be provided by a single integer if the grid locations are numbered in a unique way. It's not ideal, but certainly doable. In the Chess game, however, a move cannot be described by a single integer. The player needs to specify both the grid location he is moving the piece to *and* which

piece he is moving. The getMove method would need to be altered in a way that changes its return type. This makes the Player interface unsuitable.

20. **(C)** Segment II has an error in the getMove calls. References c1 and c2 are of type Comparable, which doesn't contain a getMove method. To correct these statements a cast is necessary:

```
x = ((ExpertPlayer) c1).getMove();
```

and similarly for the c2 call. Note that c1.compareTo(c2) is fine, since Comparable does contain the compareTo method and ExpertPlayer implements Comparable. Segment III fails because HumanPlayer does not implement Comparable and therefore does not have a compareTo method. Note that in segment I the getMove calls are fine and require no downcasting, since p1 and p2 are of type Player and Player has the getMove method.

21. **(E)** All implementations are correct. This is *not* a question about whether it is better to compare ExpertPlayers based on their ratings or their names! One might need an alphabetized list of players, or one might need a list according to ranking. In practice, the program specification will instruct the programmer which to use. Note that segment II is correct because compareTo doesn't need to return 1 or -1. Any positive or negative integer is OK.

22. **(B)** Statement III would be correct if it read as follows: While a class may extend just one class, it may implement more than one interface.

23. **(A)** There is no good way to write a compareTo method for a Point class. Two points (x_1, y_1) and (x_2, y_2) are equal if and only if $x_1 = x_2$ and $y_1 = y_2$. But if points P_1 and P_2 are not equal, what will determine if $P_1 < P_2$ or $P_1 > P_2$? You could try using the distance from the origin. Define $P_1 > P_2$ if and only if $OP_1 > OP_2$, and $P_1 < P_2$ if and only if $OP_1 < OP_2$, where O is $(0,0)$. This definition means that points (a, b) and (b, a) are equal, which violates the definition of equals! The problem is that there is no way to map the two-dimensional set of points to a one-dimensional distance function and still be consistent with the definition of equals. The objects in each of the other classes can be compared without a problem. In choice B, two Name objects can be ordered alphabetically. In choice C, two Car objects can be ordered by year or by price. In choice D, two Student objects can be ordered by name or GPA. In choice E, two Employee objects can be ordered by name or seniority (date of hire).

24. **(B)** Here is the hierarchy of classes:

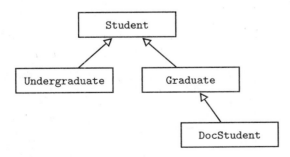

Eliminate choice D which fails to make DocStudent a subclass of Graduate. This is a poor design choice since a DocStudent *is-a* Graduate. Making Student an abstract class is desirable since the methods that are common to all students can go in there with implementations provided. The method to calculate the GPA, which differs among student types, will be declared in Student as an abstract method. Then unique implementations will be provided in both the Graduate and Undergraduate classes. Choice A is a poor design because making Student an interface means that all of its methods will need to be implemented in both the Undergraduate and Graduate classes. Many of these methods will have the same implementations. As far as possible, you want to arrange for classes to inherit common methods and to avoid repeated code. Choice C is slightly inferior to choice B because you are told that all students are either graduates or undergraduates. Having the Student class abstract guarantees that you won't create an instance of a Student (who is neither a graduate nor an undergraduate). Choice E has a major design flaw: making Graduate an abstract class means that you can't create any instances of Graduate objects. Disaster! If the keyword abstract is removed from choice E, it becomes a fine design, as good as that in choice B. Once Student has implemented all the common PersonalInformation methods, these are inherited by each of the subclasses.

25. **(B)** Classes that implement an interface must provide implementation code for all methods in the interface. Adding method2 to the SomeName interface means that all of those classes need to be rewritten with implementation code for method2. (This is not good—it violates the sacred principle of code reusability, and programmers relying on the interface will squeal.) Choices A, C, and D are all meaningless garbage. Choice E *may* be true if there is some other error in the new class. Otherwise, as long as the new class provides implementation code for both method1 and method2, the class will compile.

26. **(B)** Segment III is wrong because you can't construct an interface object. (Remember, Comparable is an interface!) Segments I and II both work because the minThree method is expecting three parameters, each of which is a Comparable. Since Temperature implements Comparable, each of the Temperature objects is a Comparable and can be used as a parameter in this method. Note that the program assumes that the compareTo method is able to compare Temperature objects with different scales. This is an internal detail that would be dealt with in the compareTo method, and hidden from the client. When a class implements Comparable there is always an assumption that the compareTo method will be implemented in a reasonable way.

Some Standard Classes

CHAPTER 4

Anyone who considers arithmetical methods of producing
random digits is, of course, in a state of sin.
—John von Neumann (1951)

Chapter Goals

- The `Object` class
- The `String` class
- Wrapper classes
- The `Math` class
- Random numbers

THE `Object` CLASS

The Universal Superclass

Think of `Object` as the superclass of the universe. Every class automatically extends `Object`, which means that `Object` is a direct or indirect superclass of every other class. In a class hierarchy tree, `Object` is at the top:

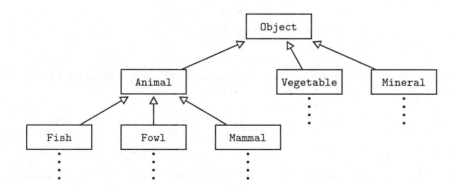

Methods in `Object`

There are many methods in `Object`, all of them inherited by every other class. Since `Object` is not an abstract class, all of its methods have implementations. The expectation is that these methods will be overridden in any class where the default implementation is not suitable. The required methods in the AP Java subset are `toString`, `equals`, and `hashCode` (which is for Level AB only).

225

THE toString METHOD

```
public String toString()
```

This method returns a version of your object in String form.

When you attempt to print an object, the inherited default toString method is invoked, and what you will see is the class name followed by an @ followed by a meaningless number (the address in memory of the object). For example,

```
SavingsAccount s = new SavingsAccount(500);
System.out.println(s);
```

produces something like

```
SavingsAccount@fea485c4
```

To have more meaningful output, you need to override the toString method for your own classes. Even if your final program doesn't need to output any objects, you should define a toString method for each class to help in debugging.

Example 1

```
public class OrderedPair
{
    private double x;
    private double y;

    //constructors and other methods ...

    /* Returns this OrderedPair in String form. */
    public String toString()
    {
        return "(" + x + "," + y + ")";
    }
}
```

Now the statements

```
OrderedPair p = new OrderedPair(7,10);
System.out.println(p);
```

will invoke the overridden toString method and produce output that looks like an ordered pair:

```
(7,10)
```

Example 2

For a BankAccount class the overridden toString method may look something like this:

```
/* Returns this  BankAccount in String form. */
public String toString()
{
    return "Bank Account: balance = $" + myBalance;
}
```

The statements

```
BankAccount b = new BankAccount(600);
System.out.println(b);
```

will produce output that looks like this:

```
Bank Account: balance = $600
```

NOTE

1. The + sign is a concatenation operator for strings (see p. 229).
2. Array objects are unusual in that they do not have a toString method. To print the elements of an array, the array must be traversed and each element must explicitly be printed.

THE equals METHOD

```
public boolean equals(Object other)
```

All classes inherit this method from the Object class. It returns true if this object and other are the same object, false otherwise. Being the same object means referencing the same memory slot. For example,

```
Date d1 = new Date("January", 14, 2001);
Date d2 = d1;
Date d3 = new Date("January", 14, 2001);
```

The test if (d1.equals(d2)) returns true, but the test if (d1.equals(d3)) returns false, since d1 and d3 do not refer to the same object. Often, as in this example, you may want two objects to be considered equal if their *contents* are the same. In that case, you have to override the equals method in your class to achieve this. Some of the standard classes described later in this chapter have overridden equals in this way. You will not be required to write code that overrides equals on the AP exam.

> Do not use == to test objects for equality. Use the equals method.

NOTE

1. The default implementation of equals is equivalent to the == relation for objects: In the Date example above, the test if (d1 == d2) returns true; the test if (d1 == d3) returns false.
2. The operators <, >, and so on, are not overloaded in Java. To compare objects, one must use either the equals method or the compareTo method if the class implements the Comparable interface (see p. 199).

THE hashCode METHOD

AB ONLY

Every class inherits the hashCode method from Object. The value returned by hashCode is an integer produced by some formula that maps your object to an address in a hash table. A given object must always produce the same hash code. Also, two objects that are equal should produce the same hash code; that is, if obj1.equals(obj2) is true, then obj1 and obj2 should have the same hash code. Note that the opposite is not necessarily true. Hash codes do not have to be unique—two objects with the same hash code are not necessarily equal.

To maintain the condition that obj1.equals(obj2) is true implies that obj1 and obj2 have the same hash code, overriding equals means that you should override hashCode at the same time. You will not be required to do this on the AP exam.

You do, however, need to understand that every object is associated with an integer value called its hash code, and that objects that are equal have the same hash code.

THE `String` CLASS

`String` Objects

An object of type `String` is a sequence of characters. All *string literals*, such as `"yikes!"`, are implemented as instances of this class. A string literal consists of zero or more characters, including escape sequences, surrounded by double quotes. (The quotes are not part of the `String` object.) Thus, each of the following is a valid string literal:

```
""                  //empty string
"2468"
"I must\n go home"
```

`String` objects are *immutable*, which means that there are no methods to change them after they've been constructed. You can, however, always create a new `String` that is a mutated form of an existing `String`.

Constructing `String` Objects

A `String` object is unusual in that it can be initialized like a primitive type:

```
String s = "abc";
```

This is equivalent to

```
String s = new String("abc");
```

in the sense that in both cases s is a reference to a `String` object with contents `"abc"` (see Box on p. 230).

It is possible to reassign a `String` reference:

```
String s = "John";
s = "Harry";
```

This is equivalent to

```
String s = new String("John");
s = new String("Harry");
```

Notice that this is consistent with the immutable feature of `String` objects. `"John"` has not been changed; he has merely been discarded! The fickle reference s now refers to a new `String`, `"Harry"`. It is also OK to reassign s as follows:

```
s = s + " Windsor";
```

s now refers to the object `"Harry Windsor"`.

Here are other ways to initialize `String` objects:

```
String s1 = null;           //s1 is a null reference
String s2 = new String();   //s2 is an empty character sequence

String state = "Alaska";
String dessert = "baked " + state;  //dessert has value "baked Alaska"
```

The Concatenation Operator

The `dessert` declaration above uses the *concatenation operator*, +, which operates on `String` objects. Given two `String` operands `lhs` and `rhs`, `lhs + rhs` produces a single `String` consisting of `lhs` followed by `rhs`. If either `lhs` or `rhs` is an object other than a `String`, the `toString` method of the object is invoked, and `lhs` and `rhs` are concatenated as before. If one of the operands is a `String` and the other is a primitive type, then the non-`String` operand is converted to a `String`, and concatenation occurs as before. If neither `lhs` nor `rhs` is a `String` object, an error occurs. Here are some examples:

```
int five = 5;
String state = "Hawaii-";
String tvShow = state + five + "-0";   //tvShow has value
                                       //"Hawaii-5-0"
int x = 3, y = 4;
String sum = x + y;          //error: can't assign int 7 to String
```

Suppose a `Date` class has a `toString` method that outputs dates that look like this: 2/17/1948.

```
Date d1 = new Date(8, 2, 1947);
Date d2 = new Date(2, 17, 1948);
String s = "My birthday is " + d2;  //s has value
                                    //"My birthday is 2/17/1948"
String s2 = d1 + d2;    //error: + not defined for objects
String s3 = d1.toString() + d2.toString();  //s3 has value
                                    //8/2/19472/17/1948
```

Comparison of `String` Objects

There are two ways to compare `String` objects:

1. Use the `equals` method that is inherited from the `Object` class and overridden to do the correct thing:

   ```
   if (string1.equals(string2)) ...
   ```

   This returns `true` if `string1` and `string2` are identical strings, `false` otherwise.

2. Use the `compareTo` method. The `String` class implements `Comparable`, which means that the `compareTo` method is provided in `String`. This method compares strings in dictionary (lexicographical) order:

   - If `string1.compareTo(string2) < 0`, then `string1` precedes `string2` in the dictionary.
   - If `string1.compareTo(string2) > 0`, then `string1` follows `string2` in the dictionary.
   - If `string1.compareTo(string2) == 0`, then `string1` and `string2` are identical. (This test is an alternative to `string1.equals(string2)`.)

Be aware that Java is case-sensitive. Thus, if `s1` is `"cat"` and `s2` is `"Cat"`, `s1.equals(s2)` will return `false`.

Characters are compared according to their position in the ASCII chart. All you need to know is that all digits precede all capital letters, which precede all lowercase letters. Thus "5" comes before "R", which comes before "a". Two strings are compared as follows: Start at the left end of each string and do a character-by-character comparison until you reach the first character in which the strings differ, the *k*th character, say. If the *k*th character of s1 comes before the *k*th character of s2, then s1 will come before s2, and vice versa. If the strings have identical characters, except that s1 terminates before s2, then s1 comes before s2. Here are some examples:

```
String s1 = "HOT", s2 = "HOTEL", s3 = "dog";
if (s1.compareTo(s2) < 0))      //true, s1 terminates first
    ...
if (s1.compareTo(s3) > 0))      //false, "H" comes before "d"
```

Don't Use == to Test Strings!

The expression if(string1 == string2) tests whether string1 and string2 are the same reference. It does not test the actual strings. Using == to compare strings may lead to unexpected results.

Example 1

```
String s = "oh no!";
String t = "oh no!";
if (s == t) ...
```

The test returns true even though it appears that s and t are different references. The reason is that for efficiency Java makes only one String object for equivalent string literals. This is safe in that a String cannot be altered.

Example 2

```
String s = "oh no!";
String t = new String("oh no!");
if (s == t) ...
```

The test returns false because use of new creates a new object, and s and t *are* different references in this example!

The moral of the story? Use equals not == to test strings. It always does the right thing.

Other String Methods

The Java String class provides many methods, only a small number of which are in the AP Java subset. In addition to the constructors, comparison methods, and concatenation operator + discussed so far, you should know the following methods:

```
int length()
```

Returns the length of this string.

```
String substring(int startIndex)
```

Returns a new string that is a substring of this string. The substring starts with the character at `startIndex` and extends to the end of the string. The first character is at index zero. The method throws a `StringIndexOutOfBoundsException` if `startIndex` is negative or larger than the length of the string.

```
String substring(int startIndex, int endIndex)
```

Returns a new string that is a substring of this string. The substring starts at index `startIndex` and extends to the character at `endIndex-1`. (Think of it this way: `startIndex` is the first character that you want; `endIndex` is the first character that you *don't* want.) The method throws a `StringIndexOutOfBoundsException` if `startIndex` is negative, or `endIndex` is larger than the length of the string, or `startIndex` is larger than `endIndex`.

```
int indexOf(String str)
```

Returns the index of the first occurrence of `str` within this string. If `str` is not a substring of this string, –1 is returned. The method throws a `NullPointerException` if `str` is null.

Here are some examples:

```
"unhappy".substring(2)        //returns "happy"
"cold".substring(4)           //returns "" (empty string)
"cold".substring(5)           //StringIndexOutOfBoundsException
"strawberry".substring(5,7)   //returns "be"
"crayfish".substring(4,8)     //returns "fish"
"crayfish".substring(4,9)     //StringIndexOutOfBoundsException
"crayfish".substring(5,4)     //StringIndexOutOfBoundsException

String s = "funnyfarm";
int x = s.indexOf("farm");    //x has value 5
x = s.indexOf("farmer");      //x has value -1
int y = s.length();           //y has value 9
```

WRAPPER CLASSES

A *wrapper class* takes either an existing object or a value of primitive type, "wraps" or "boxes" it in an object, and provides a new set of methods for that type. The point of a wrapper class is to provide extended capabilities for the boxed quantity:

- It can be used in generic Java methods that require objects as parameters.
- It can be used in Java container classes that require the items be objects (see Chapter 11).

In each case, the wrapper class allows

1. Construction of an object from a single value (wrapping or boxing the primitive in a wrapper object).
2. Retrieval of the primitive value (unwrapping or unboxing from the wrapper object).

Java provides a wrapper class for each of its primitive types. The two that you should know for the AP exam are the `Integer` and `Double` classes.

The `Integer` Class

The `Integer` class wraps a value of type `int` in an object. An object of type `Integer` contains just one instance variable whose type is `int`.

Here are the `Integer` methods you should know for the AP exam:

```
Integer(int value)
```

Constructs an `Integer` object from an `int`. (Boxing.)

```
int compareTo(Object other)
```

If `other` is an `Integer`, `compareTo` returns 0 if the value of this `Integer` is equal to the value of `other`, a negative integer if it is less than the value of `other`, and a positive integer if it is greater than the value of `other`.

NOTE

1. The `Integer` class implements `Comparable`.
2. The `compareTo` method throws a `ClassCastException` if the argument `other` is not an `Integer`.

```
int intValue()
```

Returns the value of this `Integer` as an `int`. (Unboxing.)

```
boolean equals(Object obj)
```

Returns `true` if and only if this `Integer` has the same `int` value as `obj`.

NOTE

1. This method overrides `equals` in class `Object`.
2. This method throws a `ClassCastException` if `obj` is not an `Integer`.

```
String toString()
```

Returns a `String` representing the value of this `Integer`.

Here are some examples to illustrate the `Integer` methods:

```
Integer intObj = new Integer(6);   //boxes 6 in Integer object
int j = intObj.intValue();          //unboxes 6 from Integer object

System.out.println("Integer value is " + intObj);
//calls toString() for intObj
//output is
Integer value is 6
```

```
Object object = new Integer(5);    //Integer is a subclass of Object

Integer intObj2 = new Integer(3);
int k = intObj2.intValue();
if (intObj.equals(intObj2))        //OK, evaluates to false
    ...
if (intObj.intValue() == intObj2.intValue())
    ...                 //OK, since comparing primitive types

if (k.equals(j))        //error, k and j not objects
    ...
if ((intObj.intValue()).compareTo(intObj2.intValue()) < 0)
    ...                 //error, can't use compareTo on primitive types

if (intObj.compareTo(object) < 0)  //OK
    ...
if (object.compareTo(intObj) < 0)  //error, no compareTo in Object
    ...
if (((Integer) object).compareTo(intObj) < 0)  //OK
    ...
```

The Double Class

The Double class wraps a value of type double in an object. An object of type Double contains just one instance variable whose type is double.

The methods you should know for the AP exam are analogous to those for type Integer.

> `Double(double value)`

Constructs a Double object from a double. (Boxing.)

> `double doubleValue()`

Returns the value of this Double as a double. (Unboxing.)

> `int compareTo(Object other)`

The Double class implements Comparable. If the argument other is not a Double, the compareTo method will throw a ClassCastException. If other is a Double, compareTo returns 0 if the value of this Double is equal to the value of other, a negative integer if it is less than the value of other, and a positive integer if it is greater than the value of other.

> `boolean equals(Object obj)`

This method overrides equals in class Object and throws a ClassCastException if obj is not a Double. Otherwise it returns true if and only if this Double has the same double value as obj.

> `String toString()`

Returns a String representing the value of this Double.

Here are some examples:

```
Double dObj = new Double(2.5);      //boxes 2.5 in Double object
double d = dObj.doubleValue();      //unboxes 2.5 from Double object

Object object = new Double(7.3);    //Double is a subclass of Object
Object intObj = new Integer(4);
if (dObj.compareTo(object) > 0)     //OK
    ...
if (dObj.compareTo(intObj) > 0)     //ClassCastException
    ...                             //can't compare Integer to Double
```

NOTE

1. Integer and Double objects are immutable: There are no mutator methods in the classes.
2. See the sections on ArrayLists (p. 298) and Collections (Chapter 11) for a discussion of auto-boxing and -unboxing. This is a new feature in Java 5.0 that is very useful and convenient. It will *not*, however, be tested on the AP exam.

THE Math CLASS

This class implements standard mathematical functions such as absolute value, square root, trigonometric functions, the log function, the power function, and so on. It also contains mathematical constants such as π and e.

Here are the functions you should know for the AP exam:

```
static int abs(int x)
```

Returns the absolute value of integer x.

```
static double abs(double x)
```

Returns the absolute value of real number x.

```
static double pow(double base, double exp)
```

Returns base^{exp}. Assumes base > 0, or base $= 0$ and exp > 0, or base < 0 and exp is an integer.

```
static double sqrt(double x)
```

Returns $\sqrt{x}$, $x \geq 0$.

```
static double random()
```

Returns a random number r, where $0.0 \leq r < 1.0$. (See the next section, Random Numbers.)

All of the functions and constants are implemented as static methods and variables, which means that there are no instances of Math objects. The methods are invoked using the class name, Math, followed by the dot operator.

Here are some examples of mathematical formulas and the equivalent Java statements.

1. The relationship between the radius and area of a circle:

$$r = \sqrt{A/\pi}$$

   In code:

   ```
   radius = Math.sqrt(area / Math.PI);
   ```

2. The amount of money A in an account after ten years, given an original deposit of P and an interest rate of 5% compounded annually, is

$$A = P(1.05)^{10}$$

   In code:

   ```
   a = p * Math.pow(1.05, 10);
   ```

3. The distance D between two points $P(x_P, y)$ and $Q(x_Q, y)$ on the same horizontal line is

$$D = |x_P - x_Q|$$

   In code:

   ```
   d = Math.abs(xp - xq);
   ```

NOTE

A new feature of Java 5.0, the static import construct, allows you to use the static members of a class without the class name prefix. For example, the statement

```
import static java.lang.Math.*;
```

allows use of all `Math` methods and constants without the `Math` prefix. Thus, the statement in formula 1 above could be written

```
radius = sqrt(area / PI);
```

Static imports are not part of the AP subset.

Random Numbers

RANDOM REALS

The statement

```
double r = Math.random();
```

produces a random real number in the range 0.0 to 1.0, where 0.0 is included and 1.0 is not.

This range can be scaled and shifted. On the AP exam you will be expected to write algebraic expressions involving `Math.random()` that represent linear transformations of the original interval $0.0 \le x < 1.0$.

Example 1

Produce a random real value x in the range $0.0 \leq x < 6.0$.

```
double x = 6 * Math.random();
```

Example 2

Produce a random real value x in the range $2.0 \leq x < 3.0$.

```
double x = Math.random() + 2;
```

Example 3

Produce a random real value x in the range $4.0 \leq x < 6.0$.

```
double x = 2 * Math.random() + 4;
```

In general, to produce a random real value in the range `lowValue` $\leq x <$ `highValue`:

```
double x = (highValue - lowValue) * Math.random() + lowValue;
```

RANDOM INTEGERS

Using a cast to `int`, a scaling factor, and a shifting value, `Math.random()` can be used to produce random integers in any range.

Example 1

Produce a random integer, from 0 to 99.

```
int num = (int) (Math.random() * 100);
```

In general, the expression

```
(int) (Math.random() * k)
```

produces a random `int` in the range $0, 1, \ldots, k - 1$, where k is called the scaling factor. Note that the cast to `int` truncates the real number `Math.random() * k`.

Example 2

Produce a random integer, from 1 to 100.

```
int num = (int) (Math.random() * 100) + 1;
```

In general, if k is a scaling factor, and p is a shifting value, the statement

```
int n = (int) (Math.random() * k) + p;
```

produces a random integer n in the range $p, p + 1, \ldots, p + (k - 1)$.

Example 3

Produce a random integer from 5 to 24.

```
int num = (int) (Math.random() * 20) + 5;
```

NOTE

There are 20 possible integers from 5 to 24, inclusive.

Chapter Summary

All students should know about overriding the `equals` and `toString` methods of the `Object` class. Level AB should understand about `hashCode`. Everyone should be familiar with the `Integer` and `Double` wrapper classes.

Know the AP subset methods of both the `String` and `Math` classes, especially the use of `Math.random()` for generating both random reals and random integers. Be sure to check where exceptions are thrown in the `String` methods.

MULTIPLE-CHOICE QUESTIONS ON STANDARD CLASSES

1. Here is a program segment to find the quantity base^{exp}. Both base and exp are entered at the keyboard.

    ```
    System.out.println("Enter base and exponent: ");
    double base = IO.readDouble();   //read user input
    double exp = IO.readDouble();     //read user input
    /* code to find power, which equals base^exp */
    System.out.print(base + " raised to the power " + exp);
    System.out.println(" equals " + power);
    }
    ```

    Which is a correct replacement for
    /* code to find power, which equals base^{exp} */?

    ```
    I   double power;
        Math m = new Math();
        power = m.pow(base, exp);

    II  double power;
        power = Math.pow(base, exp);

    III int power;
        power = Math.pow(base, exp);
    ```

    (A) I only
    (B) II only
    (C) III only
    (D) I and II only
    (E) I and III only

2. Consider the `squareRoot` method defined below:

```
public Double squareRoot(Double d)
//Precondition:   value of d >= 0.
//Postcondition: Returns a Double whose value is the square
//               root of the value represented by d.
{
    /* implementation code */
}
```

Which /* *implementation code* */ satisfies the postcondition?

```
I double x = d.doubleValue();
  x = Math.sqrt(x);
  return new Double(x);
```

```
II return new Double(Math.sqrt(d.doubleValue()));
```

```
III return ((Double) Math).sqrt(d.doubleValue());
```

(A) I only
(B) I and II only
(C) I and III only
(D) II and III only
(E) I, II, and III

3. Here are some examples of negative numbers rounded to the nearest integer.

Negative real number	Rounded to nearest integer
−3.5	−4
−8.97	−9
−5.0	−5
−2.487	−2
−0.2	0

Refer to the declaration

```
double d = -4.67;
```

Which of the following correctly rounds `d` to the nearest integer?

(A) `int rounded = Math.abs(d);`

(B) `int rounded = (int) (Math.random() * d);`

(C) `int rounded = (int) (d - 0.5);`

(D) `int rounded = (int) (d + 0.5);`

(E) `int rounded = Math.abs((int) (d - 0.5));`

4. A program is to simulate plant life under harsh conditions. In the program, plants die randomly according to some probability. Here is part of a `Plant` class defined in the program.

```
public class Plant
{
    private double myProbDeath;  //probability that plant dies,
                                 //real number between 0 and 1
    // other private instance variables
            ...

    public Plant(double probDeath, <other parameters >)
    {
        myProbDeath = probDeath;
        < initialization of other instance variables >
    }

    //plant dies
    public void die()
    {
        /* statement to generate random number */
        if (/* test to determine if plant dies */)
            <code to implement plant's death >
        else
            <code to make plant continue living >
    }

    //other methods
            ...
}
```

Which of the following are correct replacements for
(1) /* *statement to generate random number* */ and
(2) /* *test to determine if plant dies* */?

(A)   (1) `double x = Math.random();`
        (2) `x == myProbDeath`

(B)   (1) `double x = (int) (Math.random());`
        (2) `x > myProbDeath`

(C)   (1) `double x = Math.random();`
        (2) `x < myProbDeath`

(D)   (1) `int x = (int) (Math.random()) * 100);`
        (2) `x < (int) myProbDeath`

(E)   (1) `int x = (int) (Math.random()) * 100) + 1;`
        (2) `x == (int) myProbDeath`

5. A program simulates fifty slips of paper, numbered 1 through 50, placed in a bowl for a raffle drawing. Which of the following statements stores in `winner` a random integer from 1 to 50?
   (A) `int winner = (int) (Math.random() * 50) + 1;`
   (B) `int winner = (int) (Math.random() * 50);`
   (C) `int winner = (int) (Math.random() * 51);`
   (D) `int winner = (int) (Math.random() * 51) + 1;`
   (E) `int winner = (int) (1 + Math.random() * 49);`

6. Consider the code segment

   ```
   Integer i = new Integer(20);
   /* more code */
   ```

   Which of the following replacements for `/* more code */` correctly sets `i` to have an integer value of 25?

   I `i = new Integer(25);`

   II `i.intValue() = 25;`

   III `Integer j = new Integer(25);`
   `    i = j;`

   (A) I only
   (B) II only
   (C) III only
   (D) I and III only
   (E) II and III only

7. Consider these declarations:

   ```
   Integer intOb = new Integer(3);
   Object ob = new Integer(4);
   Double doubOb = new Double(3.0);
   ```

   Which of the following will *not* cause an error?
   (A) `if ((Integer) ob.compareTo(intOb) < 0) ...`
   (B) `if (ob.compareTo(intOb) < 0) ...`
   (C) `if (intOb.compareTo(doubOb) < 0) ...`
   (D) `if (doubOb.compareTo(intOb) < 0) ...`
   (E) `if (intOb.compareTo(ob) < 0) ...`

8. Refer to these declarations:

```
Integer k = new Integer(8);
Integer m = new Integer(4);
```

Which test will *not* generate an error?

   I `if (k.intValue() == m.intValue())...`

  II `if ((k.intValue()).equals(m.intValue()))...`

 III `if ((k.toString()).equals(m.toString()))...`

(A) I only
(B) II only
(C) III only
(D) I and III only
(E) I, II, and III

9. Consider the code fragment

```
Object intObj = new Integer(9);
System.out.println((String) intObj);
```

What will be output as a result of running the fragment?
(A) No output. A `ClassCastException` will be thrown.
(B) No output. An `ArithmeticException` will be thrown.
(C) `9`
(D) `"9"`
(E) `nine`

10. Consider these declarations:

```
String s1 = "crab";
String s2 = new String("crab");
String s3 = s1;
```

Which expression involving these strings evaluates to true?

   I `s1 == s2`

  II `s1.equals(s2)`

 III `s3.equals(s2)`

(A) I only
(B) II only
(C) II and III only
(D) I and II only
(E) I, II, and III

11. Suppose that strA = "TOMATO", strB = "tomato", and strC = "tom". Given that "A" comes before "a" in dictionary order, which is true?

    (A) strA.compareTo(strB) < 0 && strB.compareTo(strC) < 0
    (B) strB.compareTo(strA) < 0 || strC.compareTo(strA) < 0
    (C) strC.compareTo(strA) < 0 && strA.compareTo(strB) < 0
    (D) !(strA.equals(strB)) && strC.compareTo(strB) < 0
    (E) !(strA.equals(strB)) && strC.compareTo(strA) < 0

12. This question refers to the following declaration:

    ```
    String line = "Some more silly stuff on strings!";
    //the words are separated by a single space
    ```

    What string will str refer to after execution of the following?

    ```
    int x = line.indexOf("m");
    String str = line.substring(10, 15) + line.substring(25, 25 + x);
    ```

    (A) "sillyst"
    (B) "sillystr"
    (C) "silly st"
    (D) "silly str"
    (E) "sillystrin"

13. Refer to the following method:

    ```
    public static String weirdString(String s, String sub)
    {
        String temp;
        String w = ""; //empty string
        for (int i = 0; i < s.length(); i++)
        {
            temp = s.substring(i, i + 1);
            if (temp.compareTo(sub) < 0)
                w = w + temp;
        }
        return w;
    }
    ```

    What will weirdStr contain after the following code is executed?

    ```
    String str = "conglomeration";
    String weirdStr = weirdString(str, "m");
    ```

    (A) "cglmeai"
    (B) "cgleai"
    (C) "coglloeratio"
    (D) "onomrton"
    (E) No value. StringIndexOutOfBoundsException.

14. A program has a `String` variable `fullName` that stores a first name, followed by a space, followed by a last name. There are no spaces in either the first or last names. Here are some examples of `fullName` values: `"Anthony Coppola"`, `"Jimmy Carroll"`, and `"Tom DeWire"`. Consider this code segment that extracts the last name from a `fullName` variable, and stores it in `lastName` with no surrounding blanks:

```
int k = fullName.indexOf(" ");     //find index of blank
String lastName = /* expression */
```

Which is a correct replacement for /* *expression* */?

   I `fullName.substring(k);`

  II `fullName.substring(k + 1);`

 III `fullName.substring(k + 1, fullName.length());`

(A) I only
(B) II only
(C) III only
(D) II and III only
(E) I and III only

15. One of the rules for converting English to Pig Latin states: If a word begins with a consonant, move the consonant to the end of the word and add "ay". Thus "dog" becomes "ogday," and "crisp" becomes "rispcay". Suppose `s` is a `String` containing an English word that begins with a consonant. Which of the following creates the correct corresponding word in Pig Latin? Assume the declarations

```
String ayString = "ay";
String pigString;
```

(A) `pigString = s.substring(0, s.length()) + s.substring(0,1)`
`            + ayString;`

(B) `pigString = s.substring(1, s.length()) + s.substring(0,0)`
`            + ayString;`

(C) `pigString = s.substring(0, s.length()-1) + s.substring(0,1)`
`            + ayString;`

(D) `pigString = s.substring(1, s.length()-1) + s.substring(0,0)`
`            + ayString;`

(E) `pigString = s.substring(1, s.length()) + s.substring(0,1)`
`            + ayString;`

16. This question refers to the `getString` method shown below:

```
public static String getString(String s1, String s2)
{
    int index = s1.indexOf(s2);
    return s1.substring(index, index + s2.length());
}
```

Which is true about `getString`? It may return a string that

I Is equal to s2.
II Has no characters in common with s2.
III Is equal to s1.

(A) I and III only
(B) II and III only
(C) I and II only
(D) I, II, and III
(E) None is true.

17. Consider this method:

```
public static String doSomething(String s)
{
    final String BLANK = " ";    //BLANK contains a single space
    String str = "";             //empty string
    String temp;
    for (int i = 0; i < s.length(); i++)
    {
        temp = s.substring(i, i + 1);
        if (!(temp.equals(BLANK)))
            str += temp;
    }
    return str;
}
```

Which of the following is the most precise description of what `doSomething` does?
(A) It returns s unchanged.
(B) It returns s with all its blanks removed.
(C) It returns a `String` that is equivalent to s with all its blanks removed.
(D) It returns a `String` that is an exact copy of s.
(E) It returns a `String` that contains `s.length()` blanks.

Questions 18–20 refer to the classes `Position` and `PositionTest` below.

```java
public class Position implements Comparable
{
    private int myRow, myCol;
    /* myRow and myCol are both >= 0 except in
     * the default constructor where they are initialized to -1 */

    public Position()              //constructor
    {
        myRow = -1;
        myCol = -1;
    }

    public Position(int r, int c)         //constructor
    {
        myRow = r;
        myCol = c;
    }

    /* Returns row of Position. */
    public int getRow()
    { return myRow; }

    /* Returns column of Position. */
    public int getCol()
    { return myCol; }

    /* Returns Position north of (up from) this position. */
    public Position north()
    { return new Position(myRow - 1, myCol); }

    //Similar methods south, east, and west
            ...

    /* Compares this Position to another Position object.
     * Returns -1 (less than), 0 (equals), or 1 (greater than). */
    public int compareTo(Object o)
    {
        Position p = (Position) o;
        if (this.getRow() < p.getRow() || this.getRow() == p.getRow()
            && this.getCol() < p.getCol())
                return -1;
        if (this.getRow() > p.getRow() || this.getRow() == p.getRow()
            && this.getCol() > p.getCol())
                return 1;
        return 0;             //row and col both equal
    }

    /* Returns string form of Position. */
    public String toString()
    { return "(" + myRow + "," + myCol + ")"; }
}
```

```
public class PositionTest
{
    public static void main(String[] args)
    {
        Position p1 = new Position(2, 3);
        Position p2 = new Position(4, 1);
        Position p3 = new Position(2, 3);

        //tests to compare positions
            . . .
    }
}
```

18. Which is true about the value of `p1.compareTo(p2)`?
    (A) It equals `true`.
    (B) It equals `false`.
    (C) It equals `0`.
    (D) It equals `1`.
    (E) It equals `-1`.

19. Which boolean expression about p1 and p3 is true?

    I `p1 == p3`

    II `p1.equals(p3)`

    III `p1.compareTo(p3) == 0`

    (A) I only
    (B) II only
    (C) III only
    (D) II and III only
    (E) I, II, and III

20. The Position class is modified so that the equals and hashCode methods of class Object are overridden. Here are the implementations:

```
/* Returns true if this Position equals another Position
 * object, false otherwise. */
public boolean equals(Object o)
{
    Position p = (Position) o;
    return p.myRow == myRow && p.myCol == myCol;
}


/* Returns a hashCode for this Position. */
public int hashCode()
{ return myRow * 10 + myCol; }
```

Which is *false* about the hashCode method?

   I Every Position object has exactly one hashCode value.
  II For two Position objects p1 and p2, if p1.equals(p2) is true, then p1 and p2 have the same hashCode value.
 III A given hashCode value corresponds to exactly one Position object.

(A) I only
(B) II only
(C) III only
(D) I and II only
(E) I, II, and III

Questions 21 and 22 deal with the problem of swapping two integer values. Three methods are proposed to solve the problem, using primitive int types, Integer objects, and IntPair objects, where IntPair is defined as follows:

```
public class IntPair
{
    private int firstValue;
    private int secondValue;

    public IntPair(int first, int second)
    {
        firstValue = first;
        secondValue = second;
    }

    public int getFirst()
    { return firstValue; }

    public int getSecond()
    { return secondValue; }

    public void setFirst(int a)
    { firstValue = a; }

    public void setSecond(int b)
    { secondValue = b;}
}
```

21. Here are three different swap methods, each intended for use in a client program.

```
 I public static void swap(int a, int b)
   {
       int temp = a;
       a = b;
       b = temp;
   }

II public static void swap(Integer obj_a, Integer obj_b)
   {
       Integer temp = new Integer(obj_a.intValue());
       obj_a = obj_b;
       obj_b = temp;
   }

III public static void swap(IntPair pair)
   {
       int temp = pair.getFirst();
       pair.setFirst(pair.getSecond());
       pair.setSecond(temp);
   }
```

When correctly used in a client program with appropriate parameters, which method will swap two integers, as intended?
(A) I only
(B) II only
(C) III only
(D) II and III only
(E) I, II, and III

22. Consider the following program that uses the `IntPair` class:

```
public class TestSwap
{
    public static void swap(IntPair pair)
    {
        int temp = pair.getFirst();
        pair.setFirst(pair.getSecond());
        pair.setSecond(temp);
    }

    public static void main(String[] args)
    {
        int x = 8, y = 6;
        /* code to swap x and y */
    }
}
```

Which is a correct replacement for /* *code to swap* x *and* y */?

```
 I IntPair iPair = new IntPair(x, y);
   swap(x, y);
   x = iPair.getFirst();
   y = iPair.getSecond();

II IntPair iPair = new IntPair(x, y);
   swap(iPair);
   x = iPair.getFirst();
   y = iPair.getSecond();

III IntPair iPair = new IntPair(x, y);
    swap(iPair);
    x = iPair.setFirst();
    y = iPair.setSecond();
```

(A) I only
(B) II only
(C) III only
(D) II and III only
(E) None is correct.

Refer to the `Name` class below for Questions 23 and 24.

```
public class Name implements Comparable
{
    private String firstName;
    private String lastName;

    public Name(String first, String last)  //constructor
    {
        firstName = first;
        lastName = last;
    }

    public String toString()
    { return firstName + " " + lastName; }

    public boolean equals(Object obj)
    {
        Name n = (Name) obj;
        return n.firstName.equals(firstName) &&
                n.lastName.equals(lastName);
    }

    public int hashCode()
    { /* implementation not shown */ }

    public int compareTo(Object obj)
    {
        Name n = (Name) obj;
        /* more code */
    }
}
```

23. The compareTo method implements the standard name-ordering algorithm where last names take precedence over first names. Lexicographic or dictionary ordering of Strings is used. For example, the name Scott Dentes comes before Nick Elser, and Adam Cooper comes before Sara Cooper.

    Which of the following is a correct replacement for /* *more code* */?

    ```
    I  int lastComp = lastName.compareTo(n.lastName);
       if (lastComp != 0)
           return lastComp;
       else
           return firstName.compareTo(n.firstName);

    II  if (lastName.equals(n.lastName))
            return firstName.compareTo(n.firstName);
        else
            return 0;

    III  if (!(lastName.equals(n.lastName)))
             return firstName.compareTo(n.firstName);
         else
             return lastName.compareTo(n.lastName);
    ```

    (A) I only
    (B) II only
    (C) III only
    (D) I and II only
    (E) I, II, and III

AB ONLY

24. Which statement about the Name class is *false*?
    (A) Name objects are immutable.
    (B) It is possible for the methods in Name to throw a NullPointerException.
    (C) The hashCode method should be redefined since the Name class redefines the equals method.
    (D) The compareTo method throws a run-time exception if the parameter is null or the parameter is incompatible with Name objects.
    (E) Since the Name class implements Comparable, it *must* provide an implementation for an equals method.

ANSWER KEY

1. B	9. A	17. C
2. B	10. C	18. E
3. C	11. D	19. C
4. C	12. A	20. C
5. A	13. B	21. C
6. D	14. D	22. B
7. E	15. E	23. A
8. D	16. A	24. E

ANSWERS EXPLAINED

1. **(B)** All the `Math` class methods are static methods, which means there is no instance of a `Math` object that calls the method. The method is invoked using the class name, `Math`, followed by the dot operator. Thus segment II is correct, and segment I is incorrect. Segment III will cause an error: Since the parameters of `pow` are of type `double`, the result should be stored in a `double`.

2. **(B)** The `Math.sqrt` method must be invoked on a primitive type `double`, which is the reason `d.doubleValue()` is needed. A correct segment must create a `Double` object using `new`, which eliminates segment III. Segment III is egregiously bad: It tries to cast `Math` to `Double`. But `Math` is not an object! `Math.sqrt` is a static method.

3. **(C)** The value -4.67 must be rounded to -5. Subtracting 0.5 gives a value of -5.17. Casting to `int` truncates the number (chops off the decimal part) and leaves a value of -5. None of the other choices produces -5. Choice A gives the absolute value of d: 4.67. Choice B is an incorrect use of `Random`. The parameter for `nextInt` should be an integer n, $n \geq 2$. The method then returns a random `int` k, where $0 \leq k < n$. Choice D is the way to round a *positive* real number to the nearest integer. In the actual case it produces -4. Choice E gives the absolute value of -5, namely 5.

4. **(C)** The statement `double x = Math.random();` generates a random `double` in the range $0 \leq x < 1$. Suppose `myProbDeath` is 0.67, or 67%. Assuming that random doubles are uniformly distributed in the interval, one can expect that 67% of the time x will be in the range $0 \leq x < 0.67$. You can therefore simulate the probability of death by testing if x is between 0 and 0.67, that is, if $x < 0.67$. Thus, `x < myProbDeath` is the desired condition for plant death, eliminating choices A and B. Choices D and E fail because `(int) myProbDeath` truncates `myProbDeath` to 0. The test `x < 0` will always be false, and the test `x == 0` will only be true if the random number generator returned exactly 0, an extremely unlikely occurrence! Neither of these choices correctly simulates the probability of death.

5. **(A)** The expression

```
(int) (Math.random() * 50);
```

returns an `int` from 0 to 49. Therefore, adding 1 shifts the range to be 1 to 50, which was required.

6. **(D)** The `Integer` class has no methods that can change the contents of `i`. However, `i` can be reassigned so that it refers to another object. This happens in both segments I and III. Segment II is wrong because `intValue` is an *accessor*—it cannot be used to change the value of object `i`.

7. **(E)** Choice E works because the actual type of `ob` is `Integer`, which is what the `compareTo` method is expecting when the calling object is an `Integer`. Choices C and D will cause a `ClassCastException` since the calling and parameter objects are incompatible types. The `compareTo` method will try erroneously to cast its parameter to the type of the object calling the method. Choice A *almost* works: It fails because the dot operator has higher precedence than casting, which means that `ob.compareTo` is parsed before `ob` is cast to `Integer`, generating a message that the `compareTo` method is not in class `Object`. Choice A can be fixed with an extra pair of parentheses:

```
if (((Integer) ob).compareTo(intOb) < 0) ...
```

Choice B causes the same error message as choice A: no `compareTo` method in class `Object`.

8. **(D)** Test I is correct because it's OK to compare primitive types (in this case `int` values) using `==`. Test III works because `k.toString()` and `m.toString()` are `Strings`, which should be compared with `equals`. Test II is wrong because you can't invoke a method (in this case `equals`) on an `int`.

9. **(A)** An `Integer` cannot be cast to a `String`. Don't confuse this with

```
System.out.println(intObj.toString());     //outputs 9
```

Note that if the first line of the code fragment were

```
Integer intObj = new Integer(9);
```

then the error would be detected at compile time.

10. **(C)** Here are the memory slots:

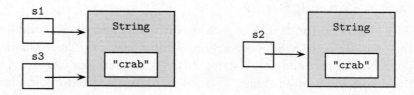

Statements II and III are true because the contents of `s1` and `s2` are the same, and the contents of `s3` and `s2` are the same. Statement I is false because `s1` and `s2` are not the same reference. Note that the expression `s1 == s3` would be true since `s1` and `s3` *are* the same reference.

11. **(D)** Note that `"TOMATO"` precedes both `"tomato"` and `"tom"`, since `"T"` precedes `"t"`. Also, `"tom"` precedes `"tomato"` since the length of `"tom"` is less than the length of `"tomato"`. Therefore each of the following is true:

```
strA.compareTo(strB) < 0
strA.compareTo(strC) < 0
strC.compareTo(strB) < 0
```

So

Choice A is T and F which evaluates to F
Choice B is F or F which evaluates to F
Choice C is F and T which evaluates to F
Choice D is T and T which evaluates to T
Choice E is T and F which evaluates to F

12. **(A)** x contains the index of the first occurrence of "m" in line, namely 2. (Remember that "S" is at index 0.) The method call line.substring(10,15) returns "silly", the substring starting at index 10 and extending though index 14. The method call line.substring(25,27) returns "st" (don't include the character at index 27!). The concatenation operator, +, joins these.

13. **(B)** The statement temp = s.substring(i, i+1) places in temp the string containing the character at position i. The for loop thus cycles through "conglomeration", starting at "c", and compares each single character string to "m". If that character precedes "m", a new String reference "w" is created, which consists of the current value of "w" concatenated with that character.

14. **(D)** The first character of the last name starts at the first character after the space. Thus, startIndex for substring must be k+1. This eliminates expression I. Expression II takes all the characters from position k+1 to the end of the fullName string, which is correct. Expression III takes all the characters from position k+1 to position fullName.length()-1, which is also correct.

15. **(E)** Suppose s contains "cat". You want pigString = "at" + "c" + "ay". Now the string "at" is the substring of s starting at position 1 and ending at position s.length()-1. The correct substring call for this piece of the word is s.substring(1,s.length()), which eliminates choices A, C, and, D. (Recall that the first parameter is the starting position and the second parameter is one position past the last index of the substring.) The first letter of the word—"c" in the example—starts at position 0 and ends at position 0. The correct expression is s.substring(0,1), which eliminates choice B.

16. **(A)** Statement I is true whenever s2 occurs in s1. For example, if strings s1 = "catastrophe" and s2 = "cat", then getString returns "cat". Statement II will never happen. If s2 is not contained in s1, the indexOf call will return -1. Using a negative integer as the first parameter of substring will cause a StringIndexOutOfBoundsException. Statement III will be true whenever s1 equals s2.

17. **(C)** The String temp represents a single-character substring of s. The method examines each character in s and, if it is a nonblank, appends it to str, which is initially empty. Each assignment str += temp assigns a new reference to str. Thus, str ends up as a copy of s but without the blanks. A reference to the final str object is returned. Choice A is correct in that s is left unchanged, but it is not the *best* characterization of what the method does. Choice B is not precise because an object parameter is never modified: Changes, if any, are performed on a copy. Choices D and E are wrong because the method removes blanks.

18. **(E)** The compareTo method returns an int, so eliminate choices A and B. In the

implementation of `compareTo`, the code segment that applies to the particular example is

```
if (this.getRow() < p.getRow() || ...
    return -1;
```

Since $2 < 4$, the value `-1` is returned.

19. **(C)** Expression III is true: the `compareTo` method is implemented to return `0` if two `Position` objects have the same row and column. Expression I is false because `object1 == object2` returns `true` only if `object1` and `object2` are the *same reference*. Expression II is tricky. One would like `p1` and `p3` to be equal since they have the same row and column values. This is not going to happen automatically, however. The `equals` method must explicitly be overridden for the `Position` class. If this hasn't been done, the default `equals` method, which is inherited from class `Object`, will return `true` only if `p1` and `p3` are the same reference, which is not true.

AB ONLY 20. **(C)** Here is a counterexample for statement III: a `hashCode` value of 32 corresponds to $(3, 2)$ and $(2, 12)$.

21. **(C)** Recall that primitive types and object references are passed by value. This means that copies are made of the actual arguments. Any changes that are made are made to the *copies*. The actual parameters remain unchanged. Thus, in methods I and II, the parameters will retain their original values and remain unswapped.

To illustrate, for example, why method II fails, consider this piece of code that tests it:

```
public static void main(String[] args)
{
    int x = 8, y = 6;
    Integer xObject = new Integer(x);
    Integer yObject = new Integer(y);
    swap(xObject, yObject);
    x = xObject.intValue();     //surprise! still has value 8
    y = yObject.intValue();     //surprise! still has value 6
    ...
}
```

Here are the memory slots before `swap` is called:

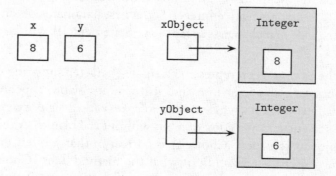

Here they are when `swap` is invoked:

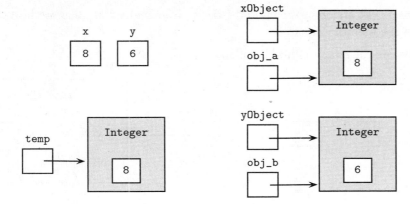

Just before exiting the `swap` method:

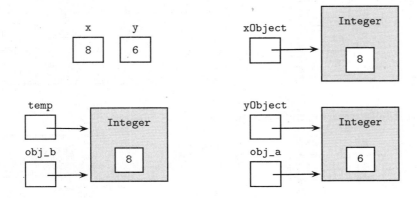

After exiting, `xObject` and `yObject` have retained their original values:

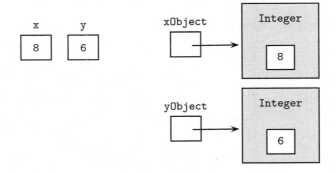

The reason method III works is that instead of the object references being changed, the object *contents* are changed. Thus, after exiting the method, the `IntPair` reference is as it was, but the first and second values have been interchanged. (See explanation to next question for diagrams of the memory slots.) In this question, `IntPair` is used as a wrapper class for a pair of integers whose values need to be swapped.

22. **(B)** The `swap` method has just a single `IntPair` parameter, which eliminates segment I. Segment III fails because `setFirst` and `setSecond` are used incorrectly. These are mutator methods that change an `IntPair` object. What is desired is to return the (newly swapped) first and second values of the pair: Accessor methods

`getFirst` and `getSecond` do the trick. To see why this swap method works, look at the memory slots.

Before the swap method is called:

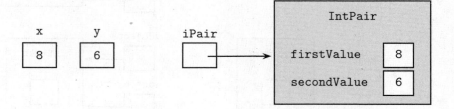

Just after the swap method is called:

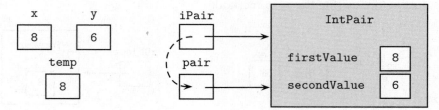

Just before exiting the swap method:

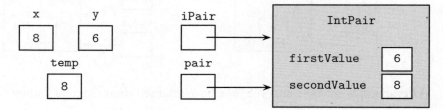

Just after exiting the swap method:

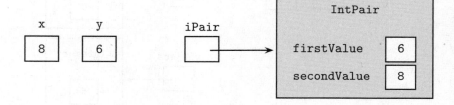

After the statements:

```
x = iPair.getFirst();
y = iPair.getSecond();
```

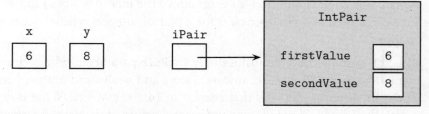

Notice that x and y have been swapped!

23. **(A)** The first statement of segment I compares last names. If these are different, the method returns the `int` value `lastComp`, which is negative if `lastName` precedes `n.lastName`, positive otherwise. If last names are the same, the method returns the `int` result of comparing first names. Segments II and III use incorrect algorithms for comparing names. Segment II would be correct if the `else` part were

```
return lastName.compareTo(n.lastName);
```

Segment III would be correct if the two `return` statements were interchanged.

24. **(E)** The `Comparable` interface has just one method, `compareTo`. Choice E would be true if `equals` were replaced by `compareTo`. Choice A is true. You know this because the `Name` class has no mutator methods. Thus, `Name` objects can never be changed. Choice B is true: If a `Name` is initialized with null references, each of the methods will throw a `NullPointerException`. Choice C is true: `hashCode` must be redefined to satisfy the condition that two equal `Name` objects have the same hash code. Choice D is true: If the parameter is null, `compareTo` will throw a `NullPointerException`. If the parameter is incompatible with `Name` objects, its first statement will throw a `ClassCastException`.

AB ONLY

Program Design and Analysis

CHAPTER 5

Weeks of coding can save you hours of planning.
—Anonymous

Chapter Goals

- Program development, including design and testing
- Object-oriented program design
- Relationships between classes

- Program analysis
- Big-O notation
- Loop invariants

Students of introductory computer science typically see themselves as programmers. They no sooner have a new programming project in their heads than they're at the computer, typing madly to get some code up and running. (Is this you?)

To succeed as a programmer, however, you have to combine the practical skills of a software engineer with the analytical mindset of a computer scientist. A software engineer oversees the life cycle of software development: initiation of the project, analysis of the specification, and design of the program, as well as implementation, testing, and maintenance of the final product. A computer scientist (among other things!) analyzes the implementation, correctness, and efficiency of algorithms. All these topics are tested on the APCS exam.

THE SOFTWARE DEVELOPMENT LIFE CYCLE

The Waterfall Model

The waterfall model of software development came about in the 1960s in order to bring structure and efficiency into the process of creating large programs.

Each step in the process flows into the next: The picture resembles a waterfall.

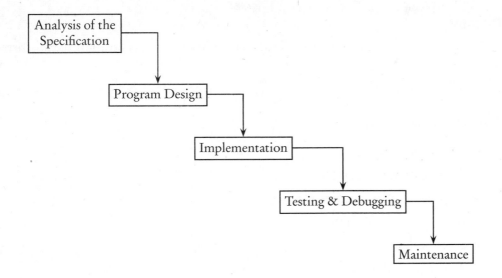

Program Specification

The *specification* is a written description of the project. Typically it is based on a customer's requirements. The first step in writing a program is to analyze the specification, make sure you understand it, and clarify with the customer anything that is unclear.

Program Design

Even for a small-scale program a good design can save programming time and enhance the reliability of the final program. The design is a fairly detailed plan for solving the problem outlined in the specification. It should include all objects that will be used in the solution, the data structures that will implement them, plus a detailed list of the tasks to be performed by the program.

A good design provides a fairly detailed overall plan at a glance, without including the minutiae of Java code.

Program Implementation

Program implementation is the coding phase. Design and implementation are discussed in more detail on p. 263.

Testing and Debugging

TEST DATA

Not every possible input value can be tested, so a programmer should be diligent in selecting a representative set of *test data*. Typical values in each part of a domain of the program should be selected, as well as endpoint values and out-of-range values. If only positive input is required, your test data should include a negative value just to check that your program handles it appropriately.

Example

A program must be written to insert a value into its correct position in this sorted list:

    2   5   9

Test data should include

- A value less than 2
- A value between 2 and 5
- A value between 5 and 9
- A value greater than 9
- 2, 5, and 9
- A negative value

TYPES OF ERRORS (BUGS)

- A *compile-time error* occurs during compilation of the program. The compiler is unable to translate the program into bytecode and prints an appropriate error message. A *syntax error* is a compile-time error caused by violating the rules of the programming language. Examples include omitting semicolons or braces, using undeclared identifiers, using keywords inappropriately, having parameters that don't match in type and number, and invoking a method for an object whose class definition doesn't contain that method.

- A *run-time error* occurs during execution of the program. The Java run-time environment *throws an exception*, which means that it stops execution and prints an error message. Typical causes of run-time errors include attempting to divide an integer by zero, using an array index that is out of bounds, attempting to open a file that cannot be found, and so on. An error that causes a program to run forever ("infinite loop") can also be regarded as a run-time error. (See also Errors and Exceptions, p. 132.)

- An *intent* or *logic error* is one that fails to carry out the specification of the program. The program compiles and runs but does not do the job. These are sometimes the hardest types of errors to fix.

ROBUSTNESS

Always assume that any user of your program is not as smart as you are. You must therefore aim to write a *robust* program, namely one that

- Won't give inaccurate answers for some input data.
- Won't crash if the input data are invalid.
- Won't allow execution to proceed if invalid data are entered.

Examples of bad input data include out-of-range numbers, characters instead of numerical data, and a response of "maybe" when "yes" or "no" was asked for.

Note that bad input data that invalidates a computation won't be detected by Java. Your program should include code that catches the error, allows the error to be fixed, and allows program execution to resume.

Program Maintenance

Program maintenance involves upgrading the code as circumstances change. New features may be added. New programmers may come on board. To make their task easier, the original program must have clear and precise documentation.

OBJECT-ORIENTED PROGRAM DESIGN

Object-oriented programming has been the dominant programming methodology since the mid 1990s. It uses an approach that blurs the lines of the waterfall model. Analysis of the problem, development of the design, and pieces of the implementation all overlap and influence one another.

Here are the steps in object-oriented design:

- Identify classes to be written.
- Identify behaviors (i.e., methods) for each class.
- Determine the relationships between classes.
- Write the interface (public method headers) for each class.
- Implement the methods.

Identifying Classes

Identify the objects in the program by picking out the nouns in the program specification. Ignore pronouns and nouns that refer to the user. Select those nouns that seem suitable as classes, the "big-picture" nouns that describe the major objects in the application. Some of the other nouns may end up as attributes of the classes.

Identifying Behaviors

Find all verbs in the program description that help lead to the solution of the programming task. These are likely behaviors that will probably become the methods of the classes.

Encapsulation

Now decide which methods belong in which classes. Recall that the process of bundling a group of methods and data fields into a class is called *encapsulation*.

You will also need to decide which data fields each class will need and which data structures should store them. For example, if an object represents a list of items, consider an array or `ArrayList` as the data structure.

Determining Relationships Between Classes

INHERITANCE RELATIONSHIPS

Look for classes with common behaviors. This will help identify *inheritance relationships*. Recall the *is-a* relationship—if `object1` *is-a* `object2`, then `object2` is a candidate for a superclass.

COMPOSITION RELATIONSHIPS

Composition relationships are defined by the *has-a* relationship. For example, a `Nurse` *has-a* `Uniform`. Typically, if two classes have a composition relationship, one of them contains an instance variable whose type is the other class.

Note that a wrapper class always implements a *has-a* relationship with any objects that it wraps.

UML Diagrams

An excellent way to keep track of the relationships between classes and show the inheritance hierarchy in your programs is with a UML (Unified Modeling Language) diagram. This is a standard graphical scheme used by object-oriented programmers. Although it is not part of the AP subset, on the AP exam you may be expected to interpret simple UML diagrams and inheritance hierarchies.

Here is a simplified version of the UML rules:

- Represent classes with rectangles.
- Use angle brackets with the word "abstract" or "interface" to indicate either an abstract class or interface.
- Show the *is-a* relationship between classes with an open up-arrow.
- Show the *is-a* relationship that involves an interface with an open, dotted up-arrow.
- Show the *has-a* relationship with a down arrow (indicates composition).

Example

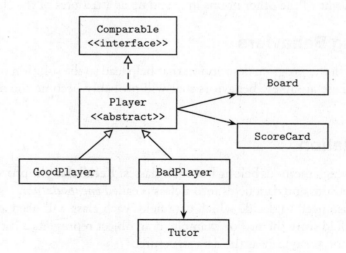

From this diagram you can see at a glance that `GoodPlayer` and `BadPlayer` are subclasses of an abstract class `Player`, and that each `Player` implements the `Comparable` interface. Every `Player` has a `Board` and a `ScoreCard`, while only the `BadPlayer` has a `Tutor`.

Implementing Classes

BOTTOM-UP DEVELOPMENT

For each method in a class, list all of the other classes needed to implement that particular method. These classes are called *collaborators*. A class that has no collaborators is *independent*.

To implement the classes, often an incremental, *bottom-up* approach is used. This means that independent classes are fully implemented and tested before being incorporated into the overall project. These unrelated classes can be implemented by different programmers.

Note that a class can be tested using a dummy `Tester` class that will be discarded when the methods of the class are working. Constructors, then methods, should be added, and tested, one at a time. A *driver class* that contains a `main` method can be used to test the program as you go. The purpose of the driver is to test the class fully before incorporating it as an object in a new class.

When each of the independent classes is working, classes that depend on just one other class are implemented and tested, and so on. This may lead to a working, bare bones version of the project. New features and enhancements can be added later.

Design flaws can be corrected at each stage of development. Remember, a design is never set in stone: It simply guides the implementation.

TOP-DOWN DEVELOPMENT

In a top-down design, the programmer starts with an overview of the program, selecting the highest-level controlling object and the tasks needed. During development of the program, subsidiary classes may be added to simplify existing classes.

Implementing Methods

PROCEDURAL ABSTRACTION

A good programmer avoids chunks of repeated code wherever possible. To this end, if several methods in a class require the same task, like a search or a swap, you should use *helper methods*. The `reduce` method in the `Rational` class on p. 172 is an example of such a method. Also, wherever possible you should enhance the readability of your code by using helper methods to break long methods into smaller tasks. The use of helper methods within a class is known as *procedural abstraction* and is an example of top-down development within a class. This process of breaking a long method into a sequence of smaller tasks is sometimes called *stepwise refinement*.

INFORMATION HIDING

Instance variables and helper methods are generally declared as `private`, which prevents client classes from accessing them. This strategy is called *information hiding*.

STUB METHOD

Sometimes it makes more sense in the development of a class to test a calling method before testing a method it invokes. A *stub* is a dummy method that stands in for a method until the actual method has been written and tested. A stub typically has an output statement to show that it was called in the correct place, or it may return some reasonable values if necessary.

ALGORITHM

An *algorithm* is a precise step-by-step procedure that solves a problem or achieves a goal. Don't write any code for an algorithm in a method until the steps are completely clear to you.

Example 1

A program must test the validity of a four-digit code number that a person will enter to be able to use a photocopy machine. The number is valid if the fourth digit equals the remainder when the sum of the first three digits is divided by seven.

Classes in the program may include an `IDNumber`, the four-digit code; `Display`, which would handle input and output; and `IDMain`, the driver for the program. The data structure used to implement an `IDNumber` could be an instance variable of type `int`, or an instance variable of type `String`, or four instance variables of type `int`—one per digit, and so on.

A top-down design for the program that tests the validity of the number is reflected in the steps of the `main` method of `IDMain`:

Create `Display`
Read in `IDNumber`
Check validity
Print message

Each method in this design is tested before the next method is added to `main`. If the display will be handled in a GUI (graphical user interface), stepwise refinement of the design might look like this:

Create `Display`
    Construct a `Display`
    Create window panels
    Set up text fields
    Add panels and fields to window

Read in `IDNumber`
    Prompt and Read

Check validity of `IDNumber`
    Check input
        Check characters
        Check range
    Separate into digits
    Check validity property

Print message
    Write number
    State if valid

NOTE

1. The `IDNumber` class, which contains the four-digit code, is responsible for the following operations:
    Split value into separate objects
    Check condition for validity

The `Display` class, which contains objects to read and display, must also contain an `IDNumber` object. It is responsible for the following operations:

   Set up display
   Read in code number
   Display validity message

Creating these two classes with their data fields and operations (methods) is an example of encapsulation.

2. The `Display` method `readCodeNumber` needs private helper methods to check the input: `checkCharacters` and `checkRange`. This is an example of procedural abstraction (use of helper methods) and information hiding (making them private).

3. Initially the programmer had just an `IDNumber` class and a driver class. The `Display` class was added as a refinement, when it was realized that handling the input and message display was separate from checking the validity of the `IDNumber`. This is an example of top-down development (adding an auxiliary class to clarify the code).

4. The `IDNumber` class contains no data fields that are objects. It is therefore an independent class. The `Display` class, which contains an `IDNumber` data member, has a composition relationship with `IDNumber` (`Display` *has-a* `IDNumber`).

5. When testing the final program, the programmer should be sure to include each of the following as a user-entered code number: a valid four-digit number, an invalid four-digit number, an n-digit number, where $n \neq 4$, and a "number" that contains a nondigit character. A robust program should be able to deal with all these cases.

Example 2

A program must create a teacher's grade book. The program should maintain a class list of students for any number of classes in the teacher's schedule. A menu should be provided that allows the teacher to

- Create a new class of students.

- Enter a set of scores for any class.

- Correct any data that's been entered.

- Display the record of any student.

- Calculate the final average and grade for all students in a class.

- Print a class list, with or without grades.

- Add a student, delete a student, or transfer a student to another class.

- Save all the data in a file.

IDENTIFYING CLASSES

Use the nouns in the specification as a starting point for identifying classes in the program. The nouns are: program, teacher, grade book, class list, class, student, schedule, menu, set of scores, data, record, average, grade, and file.

   Eliminate each of the following:

> Use nouns in the specification to identify possible classes.

program	(Always eliminate "program" when used in this context.)
teacher	(Eliminate, because he or she is the user.)
schedule	(This will be reflected in the name of the external file for each class, e.g., `apcs_period3.dat`.)
data, record	(These are synonymous with student name, scores, grades, etc., and will be covered by these features.)
class	(This is synonymous with class list.)

The following seem to be excellent candidates for classes: `GradeBook`, `ClassList`, `Student`, and `FileHandler`. Other possibilities are `Menu`, `ScoreList`, and a `GUI_Display`.

RELATIONSHIPS BETWEEN CLASSES

There are no inheritance relationships. There are many composition relationships between objects, however. The `GradeBook` *has-a* `Menu`, the `ClassList` *has-a* `Student` (several, in fact!), a `Student` *has-a* name, average, grade, list_of_scores, etc. The programmer must decide whether to code these attributes as classes or data fields.

IDENTIFYING BEHAVIORS

Use verbs in the specification to identify possible methods.

Use the verbs in the specification to identify required operations in the program. The verbs are: maintain <list>, provide <menu>, allow <user>, create <list>, enter <scores>, correct <data>, display <record>, calculate <average>, calculate <grade>, print <list>, add <student>, delete <student>, transfer <student>, and save <data>.

You must make some design decisions about which class is responsible for which behavior. For example, will a `ClassList` display the record of a single `Student`, or will a `Student` display his or her own record? Who will enter scores—the `GradeBook`, a `ClassList`, or a `Student`? There's no right or wrong answer. You may start it one way and re-evaluate later on.

DECISIONS

Here are some preliminary decisions. The `GradeBook` will `provideMenu`. The menu selection will send execution to the relevant object.

The `ClassList` will maintain an updated list of each class. It will have these public methods: `addStudent`, `deleteStudent`, `transferStudent`, `createNewClass`, `printClassList`, `printScores`, and `updateList`. A good candidate for a helper method in this class is `search` for a given student.

Each `Student` will have complete personal and grade information. Public methods will include `setName`, `getName`, `enterScore`, `correctData`, `findAverage`, `getAverage`, `getGrade`, and `displayRecord`.

Saving and retrieving information is crucial to this program. The `FileHandler` will take care of `openFileForReading`, `openFileForWriting`, `closeFiles`, `loadClass`, and `saveClass`. The `FileHandler` class should be written and tested right at the beginning, using a small dummy class list.

`ScoreList` and `Student` are easy classes to implement. When these are working, the programmer can go on to `ClassList`. This is an example of bottom-up development.

Vocabulary Summary

Know these terms for the AP exam:

Vocabulary	Meaning
software development	Writing a program
object-oriented program	Uses interacting objects
program specification	Description of a task
program design	A written plan, an overview of the solution
program implementation	The code
test data	Input to test the program
program maintenance	Keeping the program working and up to date
top-down development	Implement main classes first, subsidiary classes later
independent class	Doesn't use other classes of the program in its code
bottom-up development	Implement lowest level, independent classes first
driver class	Used to test other classes; contains `main` method
inheritance relationship	*is-a* relationship between classes
composition relationship	*has-a* relationship between classes
inheritance hierarchy	Inheritance relationship shown in a tree-like diagram
UML diagram	Graphical representation of relationship between classes
data structure	Java construct for storing a data field (e.g., array)
encapsulation	Combining data fields and methods in a class
information hiding	Using `private` to restrict access
stepwise refinement	Breaking methods into smaller methods
procedural abstraction	Using helper methods
algorithm	Step-by-step process that solves a problem
stub method	Dummy method called by another method being tested
debugging	Fixing errors
robust program	Screens out bad input
compile-time error	Usually a syntax error; prevents program from compiling
syntax error	Bad language usage (e.g., missing brace)
run-time error	Occurs during execution (e.g., `int` division by 0)
exception	Run-time error thrown by Java method
logic error	Program runs but does the wrong thing

PROGRAM ANALYSIS

Program Correctness

Testing that a program works does not prove that the program is correct. After all, you can hardly expect to test programs for every conceivable set of input data. Computer scientists have developed mathematical techniques to prove correctness in certain cases, but these are beyond the scope of the APCS course. Nevertheless, you are expected to be able to make assertions about the state of a program at various points during its execution.

Assertions

An *assertion* is a precise statement about a program at any given point. The idea is that if an assertion is proved to be true, then the program is working correctly at that point.

An informal step on the way to writing correct algorithms is to be able to make three kinds of assertions about your code.

PRECONDITION

The *precondition* for any piece of code, whether it is a method, loop, or block, is a statement of what is true immediately before execution of that code.

POSTCONDITION

The *postcondition* for a piece of code is a statement of what is true immediately after execution of that code.

AB ONLY

LOOP INVARIANT

A *loop invariant* applies only to a loop. It is a precise statement, in terms of the loop variables, of what is true before and after each iteration of the loop. It includes an assertion about the range of the loop variable. Informally, it describes how much of the loop's task has been completed at each stage.

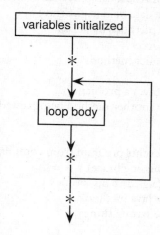

The asterisks show the points at which the loop invariant must be true:

- After initialization
- After each iteration
- After the final exit

Example

```
// method to generate n! //
//Precondition:  n >= 0.
//Postcondition: n! has been returned.
public static int factorial(int n)
{
    int product = 1;
    int i = 0;
    while (i < n)
    {
        i++;
        product *= i;
    }
    return product;
}
```

After initialization	i = 0,	product = 1, i.e., 0!
After first pass	i = 1,	product = 1, i.e., 1!
After second pass	i = 2,	product = 2, i.e., 2!
...		
After kth pass	i = k,	product = k!

The loop invariant for the while loop is

AB *(continued)*

```
    product = i!, 0 ≤ i ≤ n
```

Here is an alternative method body for this method. (Assume the same method header, comment, and pre- and postconditions.)

```
{
    int product = 1;
    for (int i = 1; i <= n; i++)
        product *= i;
    return product;
}
```

The loop invariant for the `for` loop is

```
    product = (i-1)!, 1 ≤ i ≤ n+1
```

Here `(i-1)!` (rather than `i!`) is correct because `i` is incremented at the *end* of each iteration of the loop. Also, `n+1` is needed in the second part of the loop invariant because `i` has a value of `n+1` after the final exit from the loop. Remember, the invariant must also be true after the final exit.

Efficiency

An efficient algorithm is one that is economical in the use of

- CPU time. This refers to the number of machine operations required to carry out the algorithm (arithmetic operations, comparisons, data movements, etc.).

- Memory. This refers to the number and complexity of the variables used.

Some factors that affect run-time efficiency include unnecessary tests, excessive movement of data elements, and redundant computations, especially in loops.

Always aim for early detection of output conditions: Your sorting algorithm should halt when the list is sorted; your search should stop if the key element has been found.

In discussing efficiency of an algorithm, we refer to the *best case*, *worst case*, and *average case*. The best case is a configuration of the data that causes the algorithm to run in the least possible amount of time. The worst case is a configuration that leads to the greatest possible run time. Typical configurations (i.e., not specially chosen data) give the average case. It is possible that best, worst, and average cases don't differ much in their run times.

For example, suppose that a list of distinct random numbers must be searched for a given key value. The algorithm used is a sequential search starting at the beginning of the list. In the best case, the key will be found in the first position examined. In the worst case, it will be in the last position or not in the list at all. On average, the key will be somewhere in the middle of the list.

Big-O Notation

AB ONLY

Big-O notation provides a quantitative way of describing the run time or space efficiency of an algorithm. This method is independent of both the programming language and the computer used.

Let n be the number of elements to be processed. For a given algorithm, express the number of comparisons, exchanges, data movements, and primitive operations as a function of n, $T(n)$. (Primitive operations involve simple built-in types and take one unit of time, for example, adding two `int`s, multiplying two `double`s, assigning an `int`, and performing simple tests.) The type of function that you get for $T(n)$ determines the "order" of the algorithm. For example, if $T(n)$ is a linear function of n, we say the algorithm is $O(n)$ ("order n"). The idea is that for large values of n, the run time will be proportional to n. Here is a list of the most common cases.

Function Type for *T(n)*	Big-O Description
constant	$O(1)$
logarithmic	$O(\log n)$
linear	$O(n)$
quadratic	$O(n^2)$
cubic	$O(n^3)$
exponential	$O(2^n)$

Example 1

An algorithm that searches an unordered list of n elements for the largest value could need n comparisons and n reassignments to a variable max. Thus, $T(n) \approx 2n$, which is linear, so the search algorithm is $O(n)$.

Example 2

An algorithm that prints out the last five elements of a long list stored as an array takes the same amount of time irrespective of the length of the list. Thus, $T(n) = 5$, a constant, and the algorithm is $O(1)$.

Example 3

Algorithm 1 executes with $T(n) = 3n^2 - 5n + 10$ and Algorithm 2 has $T(n) = \frac{1}{2}n^2 - 50n + 100$. Both of these are quadratic, and the algorithms are therefore $O(n^2)$. Constants, low-order terms, and coefficients of the highest order term are ignored in assessing big-O run times.

NOTE

1. Big-O notation is only meaningful for large n. When n is large, there is some value n above which an $O(n^2)$ algorithm will always take longer than an $O(n)$ algorithm, or an $O(n)$ algorithm will take longer than an $O(\log n)$ algorithm, and so on.

> Use average-case behavior to determine the big-O run time of an algorithm.

2. The following table shows approximately how many computer operations could be expected given n and the big-O description of the algorithm. For example, an $O(n^2)$ algorithm performed on 100 elements would require on the order of $100^2 = 10^4$ computer operations, whereas an $O(\log_2 n)$ algorithm would require approximately seven operations.

n	$O(\log_2 n)$	$O(n)$	$O(n^2)$	$O(2^n)$
16	4	16	256	2^{16}
100	7	100	10^4	2^{100}
1000	10	1000	10^6	2^{1000}

3. Notice that one can solve only very small problems with an algorithm that has exponential behavior. At the other extreme, a logarithmic algorithm is very efficient.

Chapter Summary

There's a lot of vocabulary that you are expected to know in this chapter. Learn the words!

Never make assumptions about a program specification, and always write a design before starting to write code. Even if you don't do this for your own programs, these are the answers you will be expected to give on the AP exam. You are certain to get questions about program design. Know the procedures and terminology involved in developing an object-oriented program.

Be sure you understand what is meant by best case, worst case, and average case for an algorithm. There will be many questions about efficiency on the AP exam. Level AB students must know the big-O run time for all standard algorithms.

By now you should know what a precondition and postcondition are. Level AB students only, practice some loop invariants.

MULTIPLE-CHOICE QUESTIONS ON PROGRAM DESIGN AND ANALYSIS

1. A program that reads in a five-digit identification number is to be written. The specification does not state whether zero can be entered as a first digit. The programmer should
   (A) Write the code to accept zero as a first digit since zero is a valid digit.
   (B) Write the code to reject zero as a first digit since five-digit integers do not start with zero.
   (C) Eliminate zero as a possibility for any of the digits.
   (D) Treat the identification number as a four-digit number if the user enters a number starting with zero.
   (E) Check with the writer of the specification whether zero is acceptable as a first digit.

2. Refer to the following three program descriptions:

   I   Test whether there exists at least one three-digit integer whose value equals the sum of the squares of its digits.
   II Read in a three-digit code number and check if it is valid according to some given formula.
   III Passwords consist of three digits and three capital letters in any order. Read in a password, and check if there are any repeated characters.

   For which of the preceding program descriptions would a `ThreeDigitNumber` class be suitable?
   (A) I only
   (B) II only
   (C) III only
   (D) I and II only
   (E) I, II, and III

3. Top-down programming is illustrated by which of the following?
   (A) Writing a program from top to bottom in Java
   (B) Writing an essay describing how the program will work, without including any Java code
   (C) Using driver programs to test all methods in the order that they're called in the program
   (D) Writing and testing the lowest level methods first and then combining them to form appropriate abstract operations
   (E) Writing the program in terms of the operations to be performed and then refining these operations by adding more detail

4. Which of the following should influence your choice of a particular algorithm?

    I The run time of the algorithm
    II The memory requirements of the algorithm
    III The ease with which the logic of the algorithm can be understood

    (A) I only
    (B) III only
    (C) I and III only
    (D) I and II only
    (E) I, II, and III

5. A list of numbers is stored in a sorted array. It is required that the list be maintained in sorted order. This requirement leads to inefficient execution for which of the following processes?

    I Summing the five smallest numbers in the list
    II Finding the maximum value in the list
    III Inserting and deleting numbers

    (A) I only
    (B) III only
    (C) II and III only
    (D) I and III only
    (E) I, II, and III

6. Which of the following is *not* necessarily a feature of a robust program?
    (A) Does not allow execution to proceed with invalid data
    (B) Uses algorithms that give correct answers for extreme data values
    (C) Will run on any computer without modification
    (D) Will not allow division by zero
    (E) Will anticipate the types of errors that users of the program may make

7. A certain freight company charges its customers for shipping overseas according to this scale:

    $80 per ton for a weight of 10 tons or less
    $40 per ton for each additional ton over 10 tons but
        not exceeding 25 tons
    $30 per ton for each additional ton over 25 tons

For example, to ship a weight of 12 tons will cost $10(80) + 2(40) = \$880$. To ship 26 tons will cost $10(80) + 15(40) + 1(30) = \$1430$.

    A method takes as parameter an integer that represents a valid shipping weight and outputs the charge for the shipment. Which of the following is the smallest set of input values for shipping weights that will adequately test this method?
    (A) 10, 25
    (B) 5, 15, 30
    (C) 5, 10, 15, 25, 30
    (D) 0, 5, 10, 15, 25, 30
    (E) 5, 10, 15, 20, 25, 30

8. A code segment calculates the mean of values stored in integers n1, n2, n3, and n4 and stores the result in `average`, which is of type `double`. What kind of error is caused with this statement?

   ```
   double average = n1 + n2 + n3 + n4 / (double) 4;
   ```

   (A) Logic
   (B) Run-time
   (C) Overflow
   (D) Syntax
   (E) Type mismatch

9. A program evaluates binary arithmetic expressions that are read from an input file. All of the operands are integers, and the only operators are +, -, *, and /. In writing the program, the programmer forgot to include a test that checks whether the right-hand operand in a division expression equals zero. When will this oversight be detected?
   (A) At compile time
   (B) While editing the program
   (C) As soon as the data from the input file is read
   (D) During evaluation of the expressions
   (E) When at least one incorrect value for the expressions is output

10. Which best describes the precondition of a method? It is an assertion that
    (A) describes precisely the conditions that must be true at the time the method is called.
    (B) initializes the parameters of the method.
    (C) describes the effect of the method on its postcondition.
    (D) explains what the method does.
    (E) states what the initial values of the local variables in the method must be.

11. Consider the following code fragment:

```
//Precondition:  a1, a2, a3 contain 3 distinct integers.
//Postcondition: max contains the largest of a1, a2, a3.

//first set max equal to larger of a1 and a2
if (a1 > a2)
    max = a1;
else
    max = a2;
//set max equal to larger of max and a3
if (max < a3)
    max = a3;
```

For this algorithm, which of the following initial setups for a1, a2, and a3 will cause
   (1) the least number of computer operations (best case) and
   (2) the greatest number of computer operations (worst case)?

  (A) (1) largest value in a1 or a2   (2) largest value in a3
  (B) (1) largest value in a2 or a3   (2) largest value in a1
  (C) (1) smallest value in a1   (2) largest value in a2
  (D) (1) largest value in a2   (2) smallest value in a3
  (E) (1) smallest value in a1 or a2   (2) largest value in a3

Refer to the following code segment for Questions 12 and 13.

```
//Compute the mean of integers 1 .. N.
//N is an integer >= 1 and has been initialized.
int k = 1;
double mean, sum = 1.0;
while (k < N)
{
    /* loop body */
}
mean = sum / N;
```

12. What is the precondition for the `while` loop?
  (A) $k \geq N$,   sum = 1.0
  (B) sum = 1 + 2 + 3 + ... + k
  (C) k < N,   sum = 1.0
  (D) $N \geq 1$,   k = 1,   sum = 1.0
  (E) mean = sum / N

13. What should replace /* *loop body* */ so that the following is the loop invariant for the `while` loop:

```
sum = 1 + 2 + ... + k, 1 ≤ k ≤ N
```

    (A) `sum += k;`
        `k++;`

    (B) `k++;`
        `sum += k;`

    (C) `sum++;`
        `k += sum;`

    (D) `k += sum;`
        `sum++;`

    (E) `sum += k;`

Questions 14 and 15 refer to the Fibonacci sequence described here. The sequence of Fibonacci numbers is 1, 1, 2, 3, 5, 8, 13, 21, ... The first two Fibonacci numbers are each 1. Each subsequent number is obtained by adding the previous two. Consider this method:

```
//Precondition:  n >= 1.
//Postcondition: The nth Fibonacci number has been returned.
public static int fib(int n)
{
    int prev = 1, next = 1, sum = 1;
    for (int i = 3; i <= n; i++)
    {
        sum = next + prev;
        prev = next;
        next = sum;
    }
    return sum;
}
```

14. Which of the following is a correct assertion about the loop variable `i`?
    (A) `1 ≤ i ≤ n`
    (B) `0 ≤ i ≤ n`
    (C) `3 ≤ i ≤ n`
    (D) `3 ≤ i ≤ n+1`
    (E) `3 < i < n+1`

15. Which of the following is a correct loop invariant for the `for` loop, assuming the correct bounds for the loop variable `i`?
    (A) `sum =` ith Fibonacci number
    (B) `sum = (i+1)`th Fibonacci number
    (C) `sum = (i-1)`th Fibonacci number
    (D) `sum = (prev-1)`th Fibonacci number
    (E) `sum = (next+1)`th Fibonacci number

16. An efficient algorithm that must delete the last two elements in a long list of n elements stored as an array is
    (A) $O(n)$
    (B) $O(n^2)$
    (C) $O(1)$
    (D) $O(2)$
    (E) $O(\log n)$

AB *(continued)*

17. An algorithm to remove all negative values from a list of n integers sequentially examines each element in the array. When a negative value is found, each element is moved down one position in the list. The algorithm is
    (A) $O(1)$
    (B) $O(\log n)$
    (C) $O(n)$
    (D) $O(n^2)$
    (E) $O(n^3)$

18. A certain algorithm is $O(\log_2 n)$. Which of the following will be closest to the number of computer operations required if the algorithm manipulates 1000 elements?
    (A) 10
    (B) 100
    (C) 1000
    (D) 10^6
    (E) 10^9

19. A certain algorithm examines a list of n random integers and outputs the number of times the value 5 appears in the list. Using big-O notation, this algorithm is
    (A) $O(1)$
    (B) $O(5)$
    (C) $O(n)$
    (D) $O(n^2)$
    (E) $O(\log n)$

Refer to the following method for Questions 20 and 21.

```
//Precondition: a and b are initialized integers.
public static int mystery(int a, int b)
{
    int total = 0, count = 1;
    while (count <= b)
    {
        total += a;
        count++;
    }
    return total;
}
```

20. What is the postcondition for method `mystery`?
    (A) $total = a + b$
    (B) $total = a^b$
    (C) $total = b^a$
    (D) $total = a * b$
    (E) $total = a/b$

AB ONLY

21. Which is a loop invariant for the `while` loop?
    (A) total = (count-1)*a, $0 \leq$ count $\leq$ b
    (B) total = count*a, $1 \leq$ count $\leq$ b
    (C) total = (count-1)*a, $1 \leq$ count $\leq$ b
    (D) total = count*a, $1 \leq$ count $\leq$ b+1
    (E) total = (count-1)*a, $1 \leq$ count $\leq$ b+1

22. A program is to be written that prints an invoice for a small store. A copy of the invoice will be given to the customer and will display

    • A list of items purchased.
    • The quantity, unit price, and total price for each item.
    • The amount due.

    Three candidate classes for this program are `Invoice`, `Item`, and `ItemList`, where an `Item` is a single item purchased and `ItemList` is the list of all items purchased. Which class is a reasonable choice to be responsible for the `amountDue` method, which returns the amount the customer must pay?

    I   `Item`

    II `ItemList`

    III `Invoice`

    (A) I only
    (B) III only
    (C) I and II only
    (D) II and III only
    (E) I, II, and III

23. Which is a *false* statement about classes in object-oriented program design?
    (A) If a class C1 has an instance variable whose type is another class, C2, then C1 *has-a* C2.
    (B) If a class C1 is associated with another class, C2, then C1 depends on C2 for its implementation.
    (C) If classes C1 and C2 are related such that C1 *is-a* C2, then C2 *has-a* C1.
    (D) If class C1 is independent, then none of its methods will have parameters that are objects of other classes.
    (E) Classes that have common methods do not necessarily define an inheritance relationship.

24. A Java program maintains a large database of vehicles and parts for a car dealership. Some of the classes in the program are Vehicle, Car, Truck, Tire, Circle, SteeringWheel, and AirBag. The declarations below show the relationships between classes. Which is a poor choice?

    (A)
    ```
    public class Vehicle
    {   ...
        private Tire[] tires;
        private SteeringWheel sw;
        ...
    }
    ```

    (B)
    ```
    public class Tire extends Circle
    {   ...
        //inherits methods that compute circumference
        //and center point
    }
    ```

    (C)
    ```
    public class Car extends Vehicle
    {   ...
        //inherits private Tire[] tires from Vehicle class
        //inherits private SteeringWheel sw from Vehicle class
        ...
    }
    ```

    (D)
    ```
    public class Tire
    {   ...
        private String rating;      //speed rating of tire
        private Circle boundary;
    }
    ```

    (E)
    ```
    public class SteeringWheel
    {   ...
        private AirBag ab;  //AirBag is stored in SteeringWheel
        private Circle boundary;
    }
    ```

25. A Java programmer has completed a preliminary design for a large program. The programmer has developed a list of classes, determined the methods for each class, established the relationships between classes, and written an interface for each class. Which class(es) should be implemented first?
    (A) Any superclasses
    (B) Any subclasses
    (C) All collaborator classes (classes that will be used to implement other classes)
    (D) The class that represents the dominant object in the program
    (E) All independent classes (classes that have no references to other classes)

Use the program description below for Questions 26–28.

A program is to be written that simulates bumper cars in a video game. The cars move on a square grid and are located on grid points (x, y), where x and y are integers between -20 and 20. A bumper car moves in a random direction, either left, right, up, or down. If it reaches a boundary (i.e., x or y is ± 20), then it reverses direction. If it is about to collide with another bumper car, it reverses direction. Your program should be able to add bumper cars and run the simulation. One step of the simulation allows each car in the grid to move. After a bumper car has reversed direction twice, its turn is over and the next car gets to move.

26. To identify classes in the program, the nouns in the specification are listed:

    program, bumper car, grid, grid point, integer, direction, boundary, simulation

    How many nouns in the list should immediately be discarded because they are unsuitable as classes for the program?
    (A) 0
    (B) 1
    (C) 2
    (D) 3
    (E) 4

A programmer decides to include the following classes in the program. Refer to them for Questions 27 and 28.

- `Simulation` will run the simulation.

- `Display` will show the state of the game.

- `BumperCar` will know its identification number, position in the grid, and current direction when moving.

- `GridPoint` will be a position in the grid. It will be represented by two integer fields, `x_coord` and `y_coord`.

- `Grid` will keep track of all bumper cars in the game, the number of cars, and their positions in the grid. It will update the grid each time a car moves. It will be implemented with a two-dimensional array of `BumperCar`.

27. Which operation should not be the responsibility of the `GridPoint` class?

(A) `isEmpty`   returns false if grid point contains a `BumperCar`, true otherwise

(B) `atBoundary`   returns true if x or y coordinate $= \pm 20$, false otherwise

(C) `left`   if not at left boundary, change grid point to 1 unit left of current point

(D) `up`   if not at top of grid, change grid point to 1 unit above current point

(E) `get_x`   return x-coordinate of this point

28. Which method is not suitable for the `BumperCar` class?

(A) `public boolean atBoundary()`
    `//Returns true if BumperCar at boundary, false otherwise.`

(B) `public void selectRandomDirection()`
    `//Select random direction (up, down, left, or right)`
    `// at start of turn.`

(C) `public void reverseDirection()`
    `//Move to grid position that is in direction opposite to`
    `// current direction.`

(D) `public void move()`
    `//Take turn to move. Stop move after two changes`
    `// of direction.`

(E) `public void update()`
    `//Modify Grid to reflect new position after each stage`
    `// of move.`

ANSWER KEY

1. E	11. A	21. E
2. D	12. D	22. D
3. E	13. B	23. C
4. E	14. D	24. B
5. B	15. C	25. E
6. C	16. C	26. C
7. C	17. D	27. A
8. A	18. A	28. E
9. D	19. C	
10. A	20. D	

ANSWERS EXPLAINED

1. **(E)** A programmer should never make unilateral decisions about a program specification. When in doubt, check with the person who wrote the specification.

2. **(D)** In I and II a three-digit number is the object being manipulated. For III, however, the object is a six-character string, which suggests a class other than a `ThreeDigitNumber`.

3. **(E)** Top-down programming consists of listing the methods for the main object and then using stepwise refinement to break each method into a list of subtasks. Eliminate choices A, C, and D: Top-down programming refers to the design and planning stage and does not involve any actual writing of code. Choice B is closer to the mark, but "top-down" implies a list of operations, not an essay describing the methods.

4. **(E)** All three considerations are valid when choosing an algorithm. III is especially important if your code will be part of a larger project created by several programmers. Yet even if you are the sole writer of a piece of software, be aware that your code may one day need to be modified by others.

5. **(B)** A process that causes excessive data movement is inefficient. Inserting an element into its correct (sorted) position involves moving elements to create a slot for this element. In the worst case, the new element must be inserted into the first slot, which involves moving every element up one slot. Similarly, deleting an element involves moving elements down a slot to close the "gap." In the worst case, where the first element is deleted, all elements in the array will need to be moved. Summing the five smallest elements in the list means summing the first five elements. This requires no testing of elements and no excessive data movement, so it is efficient. Finding the maximum value in a sorted list is very fast—just select the element at the appropriate end of the list.

6. **(C)** "Robustness" implies the ability to handle all data input by the user and to give correct answers even for extreme values of data. A program that is not robust

may well run on another computer without modification, and a robust program may need modification before it can run on another computer.

7. **(C)** Eliminate choice D because 0 is an invalid weight, and you may infer from the method description that invalid data have already been screened out. Eliminate choice E because it tests two values in the range 10–25. (This is not wrong, but choice C is better.) Eliminate choice A since it tests only the endpoint values. Eliminate B because it tests *no* endpoint values.

8. **(A)** The statement is syntactically correct, but as written it will not find the mean of the integers. The bug is therefore an intent or logic error. To execute as intended, the statement needs parentheses:

```
double average = (n1 + n2 + n3 + n4) / (double) 4;
```

9. **(D)** The error that occurs is a run-time error caused by an attempt to divide by zero (`ArithmeticException`). Don't be fooled by choice C. Simply reading an expression 8/0 from the input file won't cause the error. Note that if the operands were of type `double`, the correct answer would be E. In this case, dividing by zero does not cause an exception; it gives an answer of `Infinity`. Only on inspecting the output would it be clear that something was wrong.

10. **(A)** A precondition does not concern itself with the action of the method, the local variables, the algorithm, or the postcondition. Nor does it initialize the parameters. It simply asserts what must be true directly before execution of the method.

11. **(A)** The best case causes the fewest computer operations, and the worst case leads to the maximum number of operations. In the given algorithm, the initial test `if (a1 > a2)` and the assignment to `max` will occur irrespective of which value is the largest. The second test, `if (max < a3)`, will also always occur. The final statement, `max = a3`, will occur only if the largest value is in `a3`; thus, this represents the worst case. So the best case must have the biggest value in `a1` or `a2`.

12. **(D)** The precondition is an assertion about the variables in the loop just before the loop is executed. Variables N, k, and sum have all been initialized to the values shown in choice D. Choice C is wrong because k may equal N. Choice A is wrong because k may be less than N. Choice E is wrong because mean is not defined until the loop has been exited. Choice B is wrong because it omits the assertions about N and k.

13. **(B)** Note that A and B are the only reasonable choices. Choice E results in an infinite loop, and choices C and D increment sum by 1 instead of by k. For choice A, 1 is added to sum in the first pass through the loop, which is wrong; 2 should be added. Thus, k should be incremented before updating sum. Note that for choice B after the first pass k = 2 and sum = 1 + 2. After the second pass, k = 3 and sum = 1 + 2 + 3. Also note that k's initial value is 1 and final value on exiting the loop for the last time is N, as in the given loop invariant.

> **AB ONLY**

14. **(D)** Eliminate choices A, B, and E since `i` is initialized to 3 in the `for` loop. Choice C is wrong because the value of `i` after final exit from the loop is n+1.

15. **(C)** Eliminate choices D and E, since the loop invariant should include the loop variable in its statement. Notice that the first exit from the `for` loop has `i = 4` and `sum = 2`, which is the third Fibonacci number. In general, at each exit from the loop, sum is equal to the (i-1)th Fibonacci number.

16. **(C)** Deleting a constant number of elements at the end of an array is independent of n, and therefore $O(1)$. Don't let yourself be caught by choice D: There is no such thing as $O(2)$!

17. **(D)** In the worst case, every element in the array is negative. Thus, the number of data moves will be $(n-1)+(n-2)+\cdots+2+1 = n(n-1)/2$. This is a quadratic function, so the algorithm is $O(n^2)$. Alternatively, you can see that each of the n elements must be examined, and in the average case it is moved about $n/2$ places. So again you get $O(n^2)$. Note that unless you are specifically asked, you should not quote the order of the best case—always assume worst case or average case behavior. Here in the best case there are no negative values in the list and so no data movements. The algorithm is $O(n)$.

18. **(A)** If $n = 1000$, $\log_2 n \approx 10$ since $2^{10} \approx 1000$.

19. **(C)** The entire list of n integers must be examined once; thus, the algorithm is $O(n)$.

20. **(D)** a is being added to total b times, which means that at the end of execution total = a*b.

21. **(E)** Since count is incremented at the end of the loop, total = (count-1)*a, not count*a. Thus, eliminate choices B and D. Choice A is wrong because count is initialized to 1, not 0. Note that after the final exit from the loop, count has value b+1, which eliminates choice C.

22. **(D)** It makes sense for an Item to be responsible for its name, unit price, quantity, and total price. It is *not* reasonable for it to be responsible for other Items. Since an ItemList, however, will contain information for all the Items purchased, it is reasonable to have it also compute the total amountDue. It makes just as much sense to give an Invoice the responsibility for displaying information for the items purchased, as well as providing a final total, amountDue.

23. **(C)** The *is-a* relationship defines inheritance, while the *has-a* relationship defines association. These types of relationship are mutually exclusive. For example, a graduate student *is-a* student. It doesn't make sense to say a student *has-a* graduate student!

24. **(B)** Even though it's convenient for a Tire object to inherit Circle methods, an inheritance relationship between a Tire and a Circle is incorrect: It is false to say that a Tire *is-a* Circle. A Tire is a car part, while a Circle is a geometric shape. Notice that there is an *association* relationship between a Tire and a Circle: A Tire *has-a* Circle as its boundary.

25. **(E)** Independent classes do not have relationships with other classes and can therefore be more easily coded and tested.

26. **(C)** The word "program" is never included when it's used in this context. The word "integer" describes the type of coordinates x and y and has no further use in the specification. While words like "direction," "boundary," and "simulation" may later be removed from consideration as classes, it is not unreasonable to keep them as candidates while you ponder the design.

27. **(A)** A GridPoint object knows only its x and y coordinates. It has no information about whether a BumperCar is at that point. Notice that operations in all of the other choices depend on the x and y coordinates of a GridPoint object. An isEmpty method should be the responsibility of the Grid class that keeps track of

the status of each position in the grid.

28. **(E)** A `BumperCar` is responsible for itself—keeping track of its own position, selecting an initial direction, making a move, and reversing direction. It is not, however, responsible for maintaining and updating the grid. That should be done by the `Grid` class.

Arrays and Array Lists

CHAPTER **6**

Should array indices start at 0 or 1?
My compromise of 0.5 was rejected,
without, I thought, proper consideration.
—S. Kelly-Bootle

Chapter Goals

- One-dimensional arrays
- The `ArrayList<E>` class
- Two-dimensional arrays

ONE-DIMENSIONAL ARRAYS

An array is a data structure used to implement a list object, where the elements in the list are of the same type; for example, a class list of 25 test scores, a membership list of 100 names, or a store inventory of 500 items.

For an array of N elements in Java, index values ("subscripts") go from 0 to $N - 1$. Individual elements are accessed as follows: If `arr` is the name of the array, the elements are `arr[0]`, `arr[1]`, ..., `arr[N-1]`. If a negative subscript is used, or a subscript k where $k \geq N$, an `ArrayIndexOutOfBoundsException` is thrown.

Initialization

In Java, an array is an object; therefore, the keyword `new` must be used in its creation. The size of an array remains fixed once it has been created. As with `String` objects, however, an array reference may be reassigned to a new array of a different size.

Example

All of the following are equivalent. Each creates an array of 25 `double` values and assigns the reference `data` to this array.

```
1.    double[] data = new double[25];

2.    double data[] = new double[25];

3.    double[] data;
      data = new double[25];
```

A subsequent statement like

```
data = new double[40];
```

reassigns `data` to a new array of length 40. The memory allocated for the previous `data` array is recycled by Java's automatic garbage collection system.

When arrays are declared, the elements are automatically initialized to zero for the primitive numeric data types (`int` and `double`), to `false` for boolean variables, or to `null` for object references.

It is possible to declare several arrays in a single statement. For example,

```
int[] intList1, intList2;    //declares intList1 and intList2 to
                             //contain int values
int[] arr1 = new int[15], arr2 = new int[30];   //reserves 15 slots
                                        //for arr1, 30 for arr2
```

INITIALIZER LIST

Small arrays whose values are known can be declared with an *initializer list*. For example, instead of writing

```
int[] coins = new int[4];
coins[0] = 1;
coins[1] = 5;
coins[2] = 10;
coins[3] = 25;
```

you can write

```
int[] coins = {1, 5, 10, 25};
```

This construction is the one case where `new` is not required to create an array.

Length of Array

A Java array has a final public instance variable (i.e., a constant), `length`, which can be accessed when you need the number of elements in the array. For example,

```
String[] names = new String[25];
< code to initialize names >

//loop to process all names in array
for (int i = 0; i < names.length; i++)
    < process names >
```

NOTE

1. The array subscripts go from 0 to `names.length-1`; therefore, the test on `i` in the `for` loop must be strictly less than `names.length`.
2. `length` is not a method and therefore is not followed by parentheses. Contrast this with `String` objects, where `length` *is* a method and *must* be followed by parentheses. For example,

```
String s = "Confusing syntax!";
int size = s.length();    //assigns 17 to size
```

Traversing an Array

Use a for-each loop whenever you need access to every element in an array without replacing or removing any elements. Use a `for` loop in all other cases: to access the index of any element, to replace or remove elements, or to access just some of the elements.

Note that if you have an array of objects (not primitive types), you can use the for-each loop and mutator methods of the object to modify the fields of any instance (see the `shuffleAll` method on p. 294).

Example 1

```
//Return the number of even integers in array arr of integers.
public static int countEven(int[] arr)
{
    int count = 0;
    for (int num : arr)
        if ( num % 2 == 0)    //num is even
            count++;
    return count;
}
```

Example 2

```
//Change each even-indexed element in array arr to 0.
//Precondition:  arr contains integers.
//Postcondition: arr[0], arr[2], arr[4], ... have value 0.
public static void changeEven(int[] arr)
{
    for (int i = 0; i < arr.length; i += 2)
        arr[i] = 0;
}
```

Arrays as Parameters

Since arrays are treated as objects, passing an array as a parameter means passing its object reference. No copy is made of the array. *Thus, the elements of the actual array can be accessed—and modified.*

Example 1

Array elements accessed but not modified:

```
//Return index of smallest element in array arr of integers.
public static int findMin (int[] arr)
{
    int min = arr[0];
    int minIndex = 0;
    for (int i = 1; i < arr.length; i++)
        if (arr[i] < min)     //found a smaller element
        {
            min = arr[i];
            minIndex = i;
        }
    return minIndex;
}
```

To call this method (in the same class that it's defined):

```
int[] array;
< code to initialize array >
int min = findMin(array);
```

NOTE

An alternative header for the method is

```
public static int findMin(int arr[])
```

Example 2

Array elements modified:

```
//Add 3 to each element of array b.
public static void changeArray(int[] b)
{
    for (int i = 0; i < b.length; i++)
        b[i] += 3;
}
```

To call this method (in the same class):

```
int[] list = {1, 2, 3, 4};
changeArray(list);
System.out.print("The changed list is ");
for (int num : list)
    System.out.print(num + " ");
```

The output produced is

```
The changed list is 4 5 6 7
```

Look at the memory slots to see how this happens:

Before the method call:

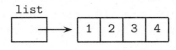

At the start of the method call:

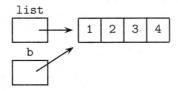

Just before exiting the method:

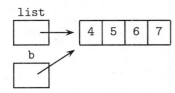

After exiting the method:

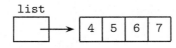

> When an array is passed as a parameter, it is possible to alter the contents of the array.

Example 3

Contrast the `changeArray` method with the following attempt to modify one array element:

```
//Add 3 to an element.
public static void changeElement(int n)
{ n += 3; }
```

Here is some code that invokes this method:

```
int[] list = {1, 2, 3, 4};
System.out.print("Original array: ");
for (int num : list)
    System.out.print(num + " ");
changeElement(list[0]);
System.out.print("\nModified array: ");
for (int num : list)
    System.out.print(num + " ");
```

Contrary to the programmer's expectation, the output is

```
Original array: 1 2 3 4
Modified array: 1 2 3 4
```

A look at the memory slots shows why the list remains unchanged.

The point of this is that primitive types—including single array elements of type `int` or `double`—are passed by value. A copy is made of the actual parameter, and the copy is erased on exiting the method.

Example 4

```
//Swap arr[i] and arr[j] in array arr.
public static void swap(int[] arr, int i, int j)
{
    int temp = arr[i];
    arr[i] = arr[j];
    arr[j] = temp;
}
```

To call the swap method:

```
int[] list = {1, 2, 3, 4};
swap(list, 0, 3);
System.out.print("The changed list is: ");
for (int num : list)
    System.out.print(num + " ");
```

The output shows that the program worked as intended:

```
The changed list is: 4 2 3 1
```

Example 5

```
//Precondition:  Array undefined.
//Postcondition: Returns array containing NUM_ELEMENTS integers
//               read from the keyboard.
public int[] getIntegers()
{
    int[] arr = new int[NUM_ELEMENTS];
    for (int i = 0; i < arr.length; i++)
    {
        System.out.println("Enter integer: ");
        arr[i] = IO.readInt();          //read user input
    }
    return arr;
}
```

To call this method:

```
int[] list = getIntegers();
```

Array Variables in a Class

Consider a simple Deck class in which a deck of cards is represented by the integers 0 to 51.

```
public class Deck
{
    private int[] myDeck;
    public static final int NUMCARDS = 52;

    //constructor
    public Deck()
    {
        myDeck = new int[NUMCARDS];
        for (int i = 0; i < NUMCARDS; i++)
            myDeck[i] = i;
    }

    //Write contents of Deck.
    public void writeDeck()
    {
        for (int card : myDeck)
            System.out.print(card + " ");
        System.out.println();
        System.out.println();
    }

    //Swap arr[i] and arr[j] in array arr.
    private void swap(int[] arr, int i, int j)
    {
        int temp = arr[i];
        arr[i] = arr[j];
        arr[j] = temp;
    }
```

```
        //Shuffle Deck: Generate a random permutation by picking a
        //   random card from those remaining and putting it in the
        //   next slot, starting from the right.
        public void shuffle()
        {
            int index;
            for (int i = NUMCARDS - 1; i > 0; i--)
            {
                //generate an int from 0 to i
                index = (int) (Math.random() * (i + 1));
                swap(myDeck, i, index);
            }
        }
    }
```

Here is a simple driver class that tests the Deck class:

```
    public class DeckMain
    {
        public static void main(String args[])
        {
            Deck d = new Deck();
            d.shuffle();
            d.writeDeck();
        }
    }
```

NOTE

There is no evidence of the array that holds the deck of cards—myDeck is a private instance variable and is therefore invisible to clients of the Deck class.

Array of Class Objects

Suppose a large card tournament needs to keep track of many decks. The code to do this could be implemented with an array of Deck:

```
    public class ManyDecks
    {
        private Deck[] allDecks;
        public static final int NUMDECKS = 500;

        //constructor
        public ManyDecks()
        {
            allDecks = new Deck[NUMDECKS];
            for (int i = 0; i < NUMDECKS; i++)
                allDecks[i] = new Deck();
        }

        //Shuffle the Decks.
        public void shuffleAll()
        {
            for (Deck d : allDecks)
                d.shuffle();
        }
```

```
    //Write contents of all the Decks.
    public void printDecks()
    {
        for (Deck d : allDecks)
            d.writeDeck();
    }
}
```

NOTE

The statement

```
allDecks = new Deck[NUMDECKS];
```

creates an array, allDecks, of 500 Deck objects. The default initialization for these Deck objects is null. In order to initialize them with actual decks, the Deck constructor must be called for each array element. This is achieved with the for loop of the ManyDecks constructor.

Analyzing Array Algorithms

Example 1

(a) Discuss the efficiency of the countNegs method below. What are the best and worst case configurations of the data?

(b) What is the big-O run time?

| **AB ONLY**

```
//Precondition:  arr[0],...,arr[arr.length-1] contain integers.
//Postcondition: Number of negative values in arr has been returned.
public static int countNegs(int[] arr)
{
    int count = 0;
    for (int num : arr)
        if (num < 0)
            count++;
    return count;
}
```

Solution:

(a) This algorithm sequentially examines each element in the array. In the best case, there are no negative elements, and count++ is never executed. In the worst case, all the elements are negative, and count++ is executed in each pass of the for loop.

(b) The run time is $O(n)$, since each element in the list is examined.

| **AB ONLY**

Example 2

The code fragment below inserts a value, num, into its correct position in a sorted array of integers.

(a) Discuss the efficiency of the algorithm.

(b) What is the big-O run time of the algorithm?

(c) What is the loop invariant of the while loop?

| **AB ONLY**

```
//Precondition:  arr[0],...,arr[n-1] contain integers sorted in
//                  increasing order. n < arr.length.
//Postcondition: num has been inserted in its correct position.
{
    //find insertion point
    int i = 0;
    while (i < n && num > arr[i])
        i++;
    //if necessary, move elements arr[i]...arr[n-1] up 1 slot
    for (int j = n; j >= i + 1; j--)
        arr[j] = arr[j-1];
    //insert num in i-th slot and update n
    arr[i] = num;
    n++;
}
```

Solution:

(a) In the best case, num is greater than all the elements in the array: Because it gets inserted at the end of the list, no elements must be moved to create a slot for it. The worst case has num less than all the elements in the array. In this case, num must be inserted in the first slot, arr[0], and every element in the array must be moved up one position to create a slot.

  This algorithm illustrates a disadvantage of arrays: Insertion and deletion of an element in an ordered list is inefficient, since, in the worst case, it may involve moving all the elements in the list.

AB ONLY

(b) Insertion or deletion of a single element in an ordered list is $O(n)$. Note that if n elements must be inserted (or deleted) with this algorithm, the algorithm becomes $O(n^2)$.

(c) The loop invariant for the while loop is

num > arr[0], num > arr[1],...,num > arr[i-1], where $0 \leq i \leq n$

Loop invariants for array algorithms can be nicely illustrated with a diagram showing a snapshot of what is happening. Each rectangle represents a portion of array arr. The labels on top of the rectangle are array indexes for elements at the beginning and end of each portion. Here is the diagram that illustrates this loop invariant:

```
0                              i-1  i              n-1
┌──────────────────────────┬──────────────────────┐
│ num > all elements in here │ still to be examined │
└──────────────────────────┴──────────────────────┘
```

ARRAY LISTS

This section contains the material that Level A students need to know. Level AB students should also see Chapter 11 for a fuller discussion of ArrayList and the other container classes.

The `ArrayList` Class

The `ArrayList` class is part of `java.util`, one of Java's standard packages. An `ArrayList` provides an alternative way of storing a list of objects and has the following advantages over an array:

- An `ArrayList` shrinks and grows as needed in a program, whereas an array has a fixed length that is set when the array is created.

- In an `ArrayList` list, the last slot is always `list.size()-1`, whereas in a partially filled array, you, the programmer, must keep track of the last slot currently in use.

- For an `ArrayList`, you can do insertion or deletion with just a single statement. Any shifting of elements is handled automatically. In an array, however, insertion or deletion requires you to write the code that shifts the elements.

Generics

In Java 5.0, the `ArrayList` class is *generic*, which means that it has a type parameter. Here is part of the class header for `ArrayList`:

```
public class ArrayList<E> ...
```

The type parameter `E` acts as a placeholder for any nonprimitive type. The type must be defined whenever an `ArrayList` is used in a program. The main idea behind this is that you express your intent that the list will be restricted to a particular data type. At compile time, the types are checked and the compiler keeps track of the element type, eliminating the need for casting when you access objects in the list. All this provides built-in type safety for your programs. Note that arrays in Java do not have this generic feature.

> Do not use type parameters with arrays.

The Methods of `ArrayList`

You should know the following methods:

`ArrayList()`

Constructs an empty list.

`int size()`

Returns the number of elements currently in the list.

`boolean add(E obj)`

Appends `obj` to the end of the list. Always returns `true`.

`E get(int index)`

Returns the element at the specified `index` in the list.

```
E set(int index, E element)
```

Replaces the item at a specified `index` in the list with the specified `element`. Returns the element that was previously at `index`.

```
void add(int index, E element)
```

Inserts `element` at the specified `index` in the list. If the insertion is not at the end of the list, shifts the element currently at that position and all elements following it one unit to the right (i.e., adds 1 to their indexes). Adjusts the size of the list.

```
E remove(int index)
```

Removes and returns the element at the specified `index` in the list. Shifts all elements following that element one unit to the left (i.e., subtracts 1 from their indexes). Adjusts the size of the list.

NOTE

Each method above that has an `index` parameter—`add`, `get`, `remove`, and `set`—throws an `IndexOutOfBoundsException` if `index` is out of range. For `get`, `remove`, and `set`, `index` is out of range if

```
index < 0 || index >= size()
```

For `add`, however, it is OK to add an element at the end of the list. Therefore, `index` is out of range if

```
index < 0 || index > size()
```

Auto-Boxing and -Unboxing

Recall that an `ArrayList` must contain *objects*, not primitive types like `double` and `int`. Numbers must therefore be boxed—placed in wrapper classes like `Integer` and `Double`—before insertion into an `ArrayList`.

Auto-boxing is the automatic wrapping of primitive types in their wrapper classes.

To retrieve the numerical value of an `Integer` (or `Double`) stored in an `ArrayList`, the `intValue()` (or `doubleValue()`) method must be invoked.

Auto-unboxing is the automatic conversion of a wrapper class to its corresponding primitive type. Be aware that if a program tries to auto-unbox `null`, the method will throw a `NullPointerException`.

Note that while auto-boxing and -unboxing cut down on code clutter, these operations must still be performed behind the scenes, leading to decreased run-time efficiency. It is much more efficient to assign and access primitive types in an array than an `ArrayList`. You should therefore consider using an array for a program that manipulates sequences of numbers and does not need to use objects.

NOTE

Auto-boxing and -unboxing is a new feature in Java 5.0 and will not be tested on the AP exam. It is OK, however, to use this convenient feature in code that you write in the free-response questions.

Using `ArrayList`

Example 1

```
//Create an ArrayList containing 0 1 4 9.
ArrayList<Integer> list = new ArrayList<Integer>();
for (int i = 0; i < 4; i++)
    list.add(i * i);  //example of auto-boxing
                      //i*i wrapped in an Integer before insertion
Integer intOb = list.get(2); //assigns Integer with value 4 to intOb.
                             //Leaves list unchanged.
int n = list.get(3);  //example of auto-unboxing
                      //Integer is retrieved and converted to int
                      //n contains 9
Integer x = list.set(3, 5);  //list is 0 1 4 5
                             //x contains Integer with value 9
x = list.remove(2);          //list is 0 1 5
                             //x contains Integer with value 4
list.add(1, 7);              //list is 0 7 1 5
list.add(2, 8);              //list is 0 7 8 1 5
```

Example 2

```
//Traversing an ArrayList of Integer.
//Print the elements of list, one per line.
for (Integer i : list)
    System.out.println(i);
```

Example 3

```
/* Precondition:  ArrayList list contains Integer values
 *                sorted in increasing order.
 * Postcondition: value inserted in its correct position in list. */
public static void insert(ArrayList<Integer> list, Integer value)
{
    int index = 0;
    //find insertion point
    while (index < list.size() &&
            value.compareTo(list.get(index)) > 0)
        index++;
    //insert value
    list.add(index, value);
}
```

NOTE

Suppose `value` is larger than all the elements in `list`. Then the `insert` method will throw an `IndexOutOfBoundsException` if the first part of the test is omitted, namely `index < list.size()`.

TWO-DIMENSIONAL ARRAYS

A two-dimensional array (matrix) is often the data structure of choice for objects like board games, tables of values, theater seats, and mazes.

Look at the following 3 × 4 matrix:

AB ONLY

AB *(continued)*

```
2  6  8  7
1  5  4  0
9  3  2  8
```

If mat is the matrix variable, the row subscripts go from 0 to 2 and the column subscripts go from 0 to 3. The element mat[1][2] is 4, whereas mat[0][2] and mat[2][3] are both 8. As with one-dimensional arrays, if the subscripts are out of range an `ArrayIndexOutOfBoundsException` is thrown.

Declarations

Each of the following declares a two-dimensional array:

```
int[][] table;       //table can reference a 2-D array of integers
                     //table is currently a null reference
double[][] matrix = new double[3][4];  //matrix references a 3 × 4
                                       //array of real numbers.
                                       //Each element has value 0.0
String[][] strs = new String[2][5]; //strs references a 2 × 5
                                    //array of String objects.
                                    //Each element is null
```

An *initializer list* can be used to specify a two-dimensional array:

```
int[][] mat = { {3, 4, 5},          //row 0
                {6, 7, 8} };         //row 1
```

This defines a 2 × 3 *rectangular* array (i.e., one in which each row has the same number of elements).

The initializer list is a list of lists in which each inside list represents a row of the matrix. Since a matrix is implemented as an array of rows (where each row is a one-dimensional array of elements), the quantity mat.length represents the number of rows. For any given row k, the quantity mat[k].length represents the number of elements in that row, namely the number of columns. (Java allows a variable number of elements in each row. Since these "jagged arrays" are not part of the AP Java subset, you can assume that mat[k].length is the same for all rows k of the matrix, i.e., that the matrix is rectangular.)

Processing a Two-Dimensional Array

Example 1

Find the sum of all elements in a matrix mat.

```
//Precondition: mat is initialized with integer values.
int sum = 0;
for (int r = 0; r < mat.length; r++)
    for (int c = 0; c < mat[r].length; c++)
        sum += mat[r][c];
```

NOTE

1. mat[r][c] represents the rth row and the cth column.
2. Rows are numbered from 0 to mat.length-1, and columns are numbered from 0 to mat[r].length-1. Any index that is outside these bounds will generate an `ArrayIndexOutOfBoundsException`.
3. Since elements are not being replaced, nested for-each loops can be used instead:

```
        for (int[] row : mat)        //for each row array in mat
            for (int element : row)  //for each element in this row
                sum += element;
```

4. The AP Java subset does not include nested for-each loops for two-dimensional arrays. You can, however, use this construct in free-response questions where applicable—use it for accessing each element, but not for replacing or removing elements.

Example 2

Add 10 to each element in row 2 of matrix `mat`.

```
for (int c = 0; c < mat[2].length; c++)
    mat[2][c] += 10;
```

NOTE

1. In the `for` loop, you can use `c < mat[k].length`, where $0 \le k < mat.length$, since each row has the same number of elements.
2. You cannot use a for-each loop here because elements are being replaced.

Example 3

The major and minor diagonals of a square matrix are shown below:

Major diagonal

Minor diagonal

You can process the diagonals as follows:

```
int[][] mat = new int[SIZE][SIZE];   //SIZE is a constant int value

for (int i = 0; i < SIZE; i++)
    Process mat[i][i];                  //major diagonal
        OR
    Process mat[i][SIZE - i - 1];    //minor diagonal
```

Two-Dimensional Array as Parameter

Example 1

Here is a method that counts the number of negative values in a matrix.

```
//Precondition: mat is initialized with integers.
//Postcondition: Returns count of negative values in mat.
public static int countNegs (int[][] mat)
{
    int count = 0;
    for (int[] row : mat)
        for (int element : row)
            if (element < 0)
                count++;
    return count;
}
```

A method in the same class can invoke this method with a statement such as

```
int negs = countNegs(mat);
```

Example 2

Reading elements into a matrix:

```
//Precondition: Number of rows and columns known.
//Returns matrix containing rows × cols integers
//          read from the keyboard.
public static int[][] getMatrix(int rows, int cols)
{
    int[][] mat = new int[rows][cols];   //initialize slots
    System.out.println("Enter matrix, one row per line:");
    System.out.println();

    //read user input and fill slots
    for (int r = 0; r < rows; r++)
        for (int c = 0; c < cols; c++)
            mat[r][c] = IO.readInt();   //read user input
    return mat;
}
```

To call this method:

```
//prompt for number of rows and columns
int rows = IO.readInt();      //read user input
int cols = IO.readInt();      //read user input
int[][] mat = getMatrix(rows, cols);
```

Chapter Summary

Manipulation of one-dimensional arrays and array lists should be second nature to you by now. Know the Java subset methods for the ArrayList<E> class. You must also know when these methods throw an IndexOutOfBoundsException and when an ArrayIndexOutOfBoundsException can occur.

Be sure you understand that a for-each loop can only be used for traversal if you wish to access each element in a list without replacing or removing any elements.

Level AB students only should be able to manipulate and traverse two-dimensional arrays.

MULTIPLE-CHOICE QUESTIONS ON ARRAYS AND ARRAY LISTS

1. Which of the following correctly initializes an array `arr` to contain four elements each with value 0?

   I `int[] arr = {0, 0, 0, 0};`

   II `int[] arr = new int[4];`

   III
   ```
   int[] arr = new int[4];
   for (int i = 0; i < arr.length; i++)
       arr[i] = 0;
   ```

   (A) I only
   (B) III only
   (C) I and III only
   (D) II and III only
   (E) I, II, and III

2. The following program segment is intended to find the index of the first negative integer in `arr[0] ... arr[N-1]`, where `arr` is an array of N integers.

   ```
   int i = 0;
   while (arr[i] >= 0)
   {
       i++;
   }
   location = i;
   ```

   This segment will work as intended
   (A) always.
   (B) never.
   (C) whenever arr contains at least one negative integer.
   (D) whenever arr contains at least one nonnegative integer.
   (E) whenever arr contains no negative integers.

3. Refer to the following code segment. You may assume that `arr` is an array of `int` values.

   ```
   int sum = arr[0], i = 0;
   while (i < arr.length)
   {
       i++;
       sum += arr[i];
   }
   ```

   Which of the following will be the result of executing the segment?
   (A) Sum of `arr[0], arr[1], ..., arr[arr.length-1]` will be stored in `sum`.
   (B) Sum of `arr[1], arr[2], ..., arr[arr.length-1]` will be stored in `sum`.
   (C) Sum of `arr[0], arr[1], ..., arr[arr.length]` will be stored in `sum`.
   (D) An infinite loop will occur.
   (E) A run-time error will occur.

4. The following code fragment is intended to find the smallest value in
   `arr[0] ... arr[n-1]`.

```
//Precondition:  arr[0]...arr[n-1] initialized with integers.
//               arr is an array, arr.length = n.
//Postcondition: min = smallest value in arr[0]...arr[n-1].
int min = arr[0];
int i = 1;
while (i < n)
{
    i++;
    if (arr[i] < min)
        min = arr[i];
}
```

This code is incorrect. For the segment to work as intended, which of the following modifications could be made?

   I Change the line

```
int i = 1;
```

    to

```
int i = 0;
```

    Make no other changes.

  II Change the body of the `while` loop to

```
{
    if (arr[i] < min)
        min = arr[i];
    i++;
}
```

    Make no other changes.

 III Change the test for the `while` loop as follows:

```
while (i <= n)
```

    Make no other changes.

(A) I only
(B) II only
(C) III only
(D) I and II only
(E) I, II, and III

Questions 5 and 6 refer to the following code segment. You may assume that array
arr1 contains elements arr1[0], arr1[1], ..., arr1[N-1], where N = arr1.length.

```
int count = 0;
for (int i = 0; i < N; i++)
    if (arr1[i] != 0)
    {
        arr1[count] = arr1[i];
        count++;
    }
int[] arr2 = new int[count];
for (int i = 0; i < count; i++)
    arr2[i] = arr1[i];
```

5. If array arr1 initially contains the elements 0, 6, 0, 4, 0, 0, 2 in this order, what
   will arr2 contain after execution of the code segment?
   (A) 6, 4, 2
   (B) 0, 0, 0, 0, 6, 4, 2
   (C) 6, 4, 2, 4, 0, 0, 2
   (D) 0, 6, 0, 4, 0, 0, 2
   (E) 6, 4, 2, 0, 0, 0, 0

6. The algorithm has run time   **AB ONLY**
   (A) $O(N^2)$
   (B) $O(N)$
   (C) $O(1)$
   (D) $O(\log N)$
   (E) $O(N \log N)$

7. Consider this program segment:

```
for (int i = 2; i <= k; i++)
    if (arr[i] < someValue)
        System.out.print("SMALL");
```

   What is the maximum number of times that SMALL can be printed?
   (A) 0
   (B) 1
   (C) k - 1
   (D) k - 2
   (E) k

8. What will be output from the following code segment, assuming it is in the same class as the `doSomething` method?

```
int[] arr = {1, 2, 3, 4};
doSomething(arr);
System.out.print(arr[1] + " ");
System.out.print(arr[3]);
    ...
public void doSomething(int[] list)
{
    int[] b = list;
    for (int i = 0; i < b.length; i++)
        b[i] = i;
}
```

(A) 0 0
(B) 2 4
(C) 1 3
(D) 0 2
(E) 0 3

9. Consider writing a program that reads the lines of any text file into a sequential list of lines. Which of the following is a good reason to implement the list with an `ArrayList` of `String` objects rather than an array of `String` objects?
   (A) The get and set methods of `ArrayList` are more convenient than the `[]` notation for arrays.
   (B) The `size` method of `ArrayList` provides instant access to the length of the list.
   (C) An `ArrayList` can contain objects of any type, which leads to greater generality.
   (D) If any particular text file is unexpectedly long, the `ArrayList` will automatically be resized. The array, by contrast, may go out of bounds.
   (E) The `String` methods are easier to use with an `ArrayList` than with an array.

10. Consider writing a program that produces statistics for long lists of numerical data. Which of the following is the best reason to implement each list with an array of `int` (or `double`), rather than an `ArrayList` of `Integer` (or `Double`) objects?
   (A) An array of primitive number types is more efficient to manipulate than an `ArrayList` of wrapper objects that contain numbers.
   (B) Insertion of new elements into a list is easier to code for an array than for an `ArrayList`.
   (C) Removal of elements from a list is easier to code for an array than for an `ArrayList`.
   (D) Accessing individual elements in the middle of a list is easier for an array than for an `ArrayList`.
   (E) Accessing all the elements is more efficient in an array than in an `ArrayList`.

Refer to the following classes for Questions 11–14.

```
public class Address
{
    private String myName;
    private String myStreet;
    private String myCity;
    private String myState;
    private String myZip;

    //constructors
        . . .

    //accessors
    public String getName()
    { return myName; }
    public String getStreet()
    { return myStreet; }
    public String getCity()
    { return myCity; }
    public String getState()
    { return myState; }
    public String getZip()
    { return myZip; }
}

public class Student
{
    private int idNum;
    private double gpa;
    private Address myAddress;

    //constructors
        . . .

    //accessors
    public Address getAddress()
    { return myAddress; }
    public int getIdNum()
    { return idNum; }
    public double getGpa()
    { return gpa; }
}
```

11. A client method has this declaration, followed by code to initialize the list:

```
Address[] list = new Address[100];
```

Here is a code segment to generate a list of *names only*.

```
for (Address a : list)
    /* line of code */
```

Which is a correct /* *line of code* */?
(A) System.out.println(Address[i].getName());
(B) System.out.println(list[i].getName());
(C) System.out.println(a[i].getName());
(D) System.out.println(a.getName());
(E) System.out.println(list.getName());

12. The following code segment is to print out a list of addresses:

```
for (Address addr : list)
{
    /* more code */
}
```

Which is a correct replacement for /* *more code* */?

```
I  System.out.println(list[i].getName());
   System.out.println(list[i].getStreet());
   System.out.print(list[i].getCity() + ", ");
   System.out.print(list[i].getState() + " ");
   System.out.println(list[i].getZip());
```

```
II System.out.println(addr.getName());
   System.out.println(addr.getStreet());
   System.out.print(addr.getCity() + ", ");
   System.out.print(addr.getState() + " ");
   System.out.println(addr.getZip());
```

```
III System.out.println(addr);
```

(A) I only
(B) II only
(C) III only
(D) I and II only
(E) I, II, and III

13. A client method has this declaration:

```
Student[] allStudents = new Student[NUM_STUDS];  //NUM_STUDS is
                                            //an int constant
```

Here is a code segment to generate a list of Student names only. (You may assume that allStudents has been initialized.)

```
for (Student student : allStudents)
    /* code to print list of names */
```

Which is a correct replacement for /* *code to print list of names* */?
(A) `System.out.println(allStudents.getName());`
(B) `System.out.println(student.getName());`
(C) `System.out.println(student.getAddress().getName());`
(D) `System.out.println(allStudents.getAddress().getName());`
(E) `System.out.println(student[i].getAddress().getName());`

14. Here is a method that locates the Student with the highest idNum:

```
//Precondition:  Array stuArr of Student is initialized.
//Postcondition: Student with highest idNum has been returned.
public static Student locate(Student[] stuArr)
{
    /* method body */
}
```

Which of the following could replace /* *method body* */ so that the method works as intended?

```
I  int max = stuArr[0].getIdNum();
   for (Student student : stuArr)
       if (student.getIdNum() > max)
       {
           max = student.getIdNum();
           return student;
       }
   return stuArr[0];
```

```
II  Student highestSoFar = stuArr[0];
    int max = stuArr[0].getIdNum();
    for (Student student : stuArr)
        if(student.getIdNum() > max)
        {
            max = student.getIdNum();
            highestSoFar = student;
        }
    return highestSoFar;
```

```
III  int maxPos = 0;
     for(int i = 1; i < stuArr.length; i++)
         if(stuArr[i].getIdNum() > stuArr[maxPos].getIdNum())
             maxPos = i;
     return stuArr[maxPos];
```

(A) I only
(B) II only
(C) III only
(D) I and III only
(E) II and III only

Questions 15–17 refer to the `Ticket` and `Transaction` classes below.

```
public class Ticket
{
    private String myRow;
    private int mySeat;
    private double myPrice;

    //constructor
    public Ticket(String row, int seat, double price)
    {
        myRow = row;
        mySeat = seat;
        myPrice = price;
    }

    //accessors getRow(), getSeat(), and getPrice()
        ...
}

public class Transaction
{
    private int myNumTickets;
    private Ticket[] tickList;

    //constructor
    public Transaction(int numTicks)
    {
        myNumTickets = numTicks;
        tickList = new Ticket[numTicks];
        String row;
        int seat;
        double price;
        for (int i = 0; i < numTicks; i++)
        {
            < read user input for row, seat, and price >
                ...

            /* more code */
        }
    }

    //Returns total amount paid for this transaction.
    public double totalPaid()
    {
        double total = 0.0;
        /* code to calculate amount */
        return total;
    }
}
```

15. Which of the following correctly replaces /* *more code* */ in the `Transaction` constructor to initialize the `tickList` array?

   (A) `tickList[i] = new Ticket(getRow(), getSeat(), getPrice());`

   (B) `tickList[i] = new Ticket(row, seat, price);`

   (C) `tickList[i] = new tickList(getRow(), getSeat(), getPrice());`

   (D) `tickList[i] = new tickList(row, seat, price);`

   (E) `tickList[i] = new tickList(numTicks);`

16. Which represents correct /* *code to calculate amount* */ in the `totalPaid` method?

   (A)
```
for (Ticket t : tickList)
    total += t.myPrice;
```

   (B)
```
for (Ticket t : tickList)
    total += tickList.getPrice();
```

   (C)
```
for (Ticket t : tickList)
    total += t.getPrice();
```

   (D)
```
Transaction T;
for (Ticket t : T)
    total += t.getPrice();
```

   (E)
```
Transaction T;
for (Ticket t : T)
    total += t.myPrice;
```

17. Suppose it is necessary to keep a list of all ticket transactions. A suitable declaration would be

   (A) `Transaction[] listOfSales = new Transaction[NUMSALES];`

   (B) `Transaction[] listOfSales = new Ticket[NUMSALES];`

   (C) `Ticket[] listOfSales = new Transaction[NUMSALES];`

   (D) `Ticket[] listOfSales = new Ticket[NUMSALES];`

   (E) `Transaction[] Ticket = new listOfSales[NUMSALES];`

18. Refer to method match below:

```
//Precondition:  v[0]..v[N-1] and w[0]..w[M-1] initialized with
//               integers. v[0] < v[1] < .. < v[N-1] and
//               w[0] < w[1] < .. < w[M-1].
//Postcondition: Returns true if there is an integer k that occurs
//               in both arrays, otherwise returns false.
public static boolean match(int[] v, int[] w, int N, int M)
{
    int vIndex = 0, wIndex = 0;
    while (vIndex < N && wIndex < M)
    {
        if (v[vIndex] == w[wIndex])
            return true;
        else if (v[vIndex] < w[wIndex])
            vIndex++;
        else
            wIndex++;
    }
    return false;
}
```

Assuming that the method has not been exited, which assertion is true at the end of every execution of the while loop?

(A) v[0]..v[vIndex-1] and w[0]..w[wIndex-1] contain no common value, vIndex ≤ N and wIndex ≤ M.

(B) v[0]..v[vIndex] and w[0]..w[wIndex] contain no common value, vIndex ≤ N and wIndex ≤ M.

(C) v[0]..v[vIndex-1] and w[0]..w[wIndex-1] contain no common value, vIndex ≤ N-1 and wIndex ≤ M-1.

(D) v[0]..v[vIndex] and w[0]..w[wIndex] contain no common value, vIndex ≤ N-1 and wIndex ≤ M-1.

(E) v[0]..v[N-1] and w[0]..w[M-1] contain no common value, vIndex ≤ N and wIndex ≤ M.

19. Consider this class:

```
public class Book
{
    private String myTitle;
    private String myAuthor;
    private boolean myCheckoutStatus;

    //constructor
    public Book(String title, String author)
    {
        myTitle = title;
        myAuthor = author;
        myCheckoutStatus = false;
    }

    //Change checkout status.
    public void changeStatus()
    { myCheckoutStatus = !myCheckoutStatus; }

    //other methods not shown ...
}
```

A client program has this declaration:

```
Book[] bookList = new Book[SOME_NUMBER];
```

Suppose `bookList` is initialized so that each `Book` in the list has a title, author, and checkout status. The following piece of code is written, whose intent is to change the checkout status of each book in `bookList`.

```
for (Book b : bookList)
    b.changeStatus();
```

Which is *true* about this code?
(A) The `bookList` array will remain unchanged after execution.
(B) Each book in the `bookList` array will have its checkout status changed, as intended.
(C) A `NullPointerException` may occur.
(D) A run-time error will occur because it is not possible to modify objects using the for-each loop.
(E) A logic error will occur because it is not possible to modify objects in an array without accessing the indexes of the objects.

Consider this class for Questions 20 and 21:

```
public class BingoCard
{
    private int[] myCard;

    /* Default constructor: Creates BingoCard with
     * 20 random digits in the range 1 - 90. */
    public BingoCard()
    { /* implementation not shown */ }

    /* Display BingoCard. */
    public void display()
    { /* implementation not shown */ }
        ...
}
```

A program that simulates a bingo game declares an array of `BingoCard`. The array has `NUMPLAYERS` elements, where each element represents the card of a different player. Here is a code segment that creates all the bingo cards in the game:

```
/* declare array of BingoCard */
/* construct each BingoCard */
```

20. Which of the following is a correct replacement for

    / declare array of `BingoCard` */*?

    (A) `int[] BingoCard = new BingoCard[NUMPLAYERS];`

    (B) `BingoCard[] players = new int[NUMPLAYERS];`

    (C) `BingoCard[] players = new BingoCard[20];`

    (D) `BingoCard[] players = new BingoCard[NUMPLAYERS];`

    (E) `int[] players = new BingoCard[NUMPLAYERS];`

21. Assuming that `players` has been declared as an array of `BingoCard`, which of the following is a correct replacement for

    / construct each `BingoCard` */*

    ```
    I   for (BingoCard card : players)
            card = new BingoCard();

    II  for (BingoCard card : players)
            players[card] = new BingoCard();

    III for (int i = 0; i < players.length; i++)
            players[i] = new BingoCard();
    ```

    (A) I only
    (B) II only
    (C) III only
    (D) I and III only
    (E) I, II, and III

22. Which declaration will cause an error?

    I `ArrayList<String> stringList = new ArrayList<String>();`

    II `ArrayList<int> intList = new ArrayList<int>();`

    III `ArrayList<Comparable> compList = new ArrayList<Comparable>();`

    (A) I only
    (B) II only
    (C) III only
    (D) I and III only
    (E) II and III only

23. Consider these declarations:

    ```
    ArrayList<String> stringList = new ArrayList<String>();
    String ch = " ";
    Integer intOb = new Integer(5);
    ```

    Which statement will cause an error?
    (A) `strList.add(ch);`
    (B) `strList.add(new String("handy andy"));`
    (C) `strList.add(intOb.toString());`
    (D) `strList.add(ch + 8);`
    (E) `strList.add(intOb + 8);`

24. Let `list` be an `ArrayList<Integer>` containing these elements:

    2 5 7 6 0 1

    Which of the following statements would *not* cause an error to occur? Assume that each statement applies to the given list, independent of the other statements.
    (A) `Object ob = list.get(6);`
    (B) `Integer intOb = list.add(3.4);`
    (C) `list.add(6, 9);`
    (D) `Object x = list.remove(6);`
    (E) `Object y = list.set(6, 8);`

25. Refer to method `insert` below:

```
/* Precondition:  ArrayList list contains Comparable values
 *                sorted in decreasing order.
 * Postcondition: Element inserted in its correct position
 *                in list. */
public void insert(ArrayList<Comparable> list,
                   Comparable element)
{
    int index = 0;
    while (element.compareTo(list.get(index)) < 0)
        index++;
    list.add(index, element);
}
```

Assuming that the type of `element` is compatible with the objects in the list, which is a *true* statement about the `insert` method?
(A) It works as intended for all values of `element`.
(B) It fails for all values of `element`.
(C) It fails if `element` is greater than the first item in `list` and works in all other cases.
(D) It fails if `element` is smaller than the last item in `list` and works in all other cases.
(E) It fails if `element` is either greater than the first item or smaller than the last item in `list` and works in all other cases.

26. Consider the following code segment, applied to `list`, an `ArrayList` of `Integer` values.

```
int len = list.size();
for (int i = 0; i < len; i++)
{
    list.add(i + 1, new Integer(i));
    Object x = list.set(i, new Integer(i + 2));
}
```

If `list` is initially 6 1 8, what will it be following execution of the code segment?
(A) 2 3 4 2 1 8
(B) 2 3 4 6 2 2 0 1 8
(C) 2 3 4 0 1 2
(D) 2 3 4 6 1 8
(E) 2 3 3 2

Questions 27 and 28 are based on the Coin and Purse classes given below:

```java
/* A simple coin class */
public class Coin
{
    private double myValue;
    private String myName;

    //constructor
    public Coin(double value, String name)
    {
        myValue = value;
        myName = name;
    }

    //Return the value and name of this coin.

    public double getValue()
    { return myValue; }

    public String getName()
    { return myName; }

    //Define equals method for Coin objects.
    public boolean equals(Object obj)
    { /* implementation not shown */ }

    //Other methods not shown.
        ...
}

/* A purse holds a collection of coins */
public class Purse
{
    private ArrayList<Coin> coins;

    //constructor
    //Creates an empty purse.
    public Purse()
    { coins = new ArrayList<Coin>(); }

    //Adds aCoin to the purse.
    public void add(Coin aCoin)
    { coins.add(aCoin); }

    //Returns total value of coins in purse.
    public double getTotal()
    { /* implementation not shown */}

}
```

27. Here is the getTotal method from the Purse class:

```
//Returns total value of coins in purse.
public double getTotal()
{
    double total = 0;
    /* more code */
    return total;
}
```

Which of the following is a correct replacement for /* *more code* */?

(A)
```
for (Coin c : coins)
{
    c = coins.get(i);
    total += c.getValue();
}
```

(B)
```
for (Coin c : coins)
{
    Coin value = c.getValue();
    total += value;
}
```

(C)
```
for (Coin c : coins)
{
    Coin c = coins.get(i);
    total += c.getValue();
}
```

(D)
```
for (Coin c : coins)
{
    total += coins.getValue();
}
```

(E)
```
for (Coin c : coins)
{
    total += c.getValue();
}
```

28. A boolean method `find` is added to the Purse class:

```
/* Returns true if the purse has a coin that matches aCoin,
 * false otherwise.  */
public boolean find(Coin aCoin)
{
    for (Coin c : coins)
    {
        /* code to find match */
    }
    return false;
}
```

Which is a correct replacement for /* *code to find match* */?

```
 I if (c.equals(aCoin))
        return true;
```

```
 II if ((c.getName()).equals(aCoin.getName()))
        return true;
```

```
III if ((c.getValue()).equals(aCoin.getValue()))
        return true;
```

(A) I only
(B) II only
(C) III only
(D) I and II only
(E) I, II, and III

AB ONLY

29. Which of the following initializes an 8 × 10 matrix with integer values that are perfect squares? (0 is a perfect square.)

```
 I int[][] mat = new int[8][10];
```

```
 II int[][] mat = new int[8][10];
    for (int r = 0; r < mat.length; r++)
        for (int c = 0; c < mat[r].length; c++)
            mat[r][c] = r * r;
```

```
III int[][] mat = new int[8][10];
    for (int c = 0; c < mat[r].length; c++)
        for (int r = 0; r < mat.length; r++)
            mat[r][c] = c * c;
```

(A) I only
(B) II only
(C) III only
(D) I and II only
(E) I, II, and III

AB *(continued)*

30. Consider the following method that will alter the matrix mat:

```
//Precondition: mat is initialized.
public static void matStuff(int[][] mat, int row)
{
    int numCols = mat[0].length;
    for (int col = 0; col < numCols; col++)
        mat[row][col] = row;
}
```

Suppose mat is originally

```
1  4  9  0
2  7  8  6
5  1  4  3
```

After the method call matStuff(mat,2), matrix mat will be

(A) 1 4 9 0
     2 7 8 6
     2 2 2 2

(B) 1 4 9 0
     2 2 2 2
     5 1 4 3

(C) 2 2 2 2
     2 2 2 2
     2 2 2 2

(D) 1 4 2 0
     2 7 2 6
     5 1 2 3

(E) 1 2 9 0
     2 2 8 6
     5 2 4 3

31. Assume that a square matrix mat is defined by

```
int[][] mat = new int[SIZE][SIZE];
//SIZE is an integer constant >= 2
```

What does the following code segment do?

```
for (int i = 0; i < SIZE - 1; i++)
    for (int j = 0; j < SIZE - i - 1; j++)
        swap(mat, i, j, SIZE - j - 1, SIZE - i - 1);
```

You may assume the existence of this swap method:

```
//Interchange mat[a][b] and mat[c][d].
public void swap(int[][] mat, int a, int b, int c, int d)
```

(A) Reflects mat through its major diagonal. For example,

$$2 \quad 6 \qquad\qquad 2 \quad 4$$
$$\longrightarrow$$
$$4 \quad 3 \qquad\qquad 6 \quad 3$$

(B) Reflects mat through its minor diagonal. For example,

$$2 \quad 6 \qquad\qquad 3 \quad 6$$
$$\longrightarrow$$
$$4 \quad 3 \qquad\qquad 4 \quad 2$$

(C) Reflects mat through a horizontal line of symmetry. For example,

$$2 \quad 6 \qquad\qquad 4 \quad 3$$
$$\longrightarrow$$
$$4 \quad 3 \qquad\qquad 2 \quad 6$$

(D) Reflects mat through a vertical line of symmetry. For example,

$$2 \quad 6 \qquad\qquad 6 \quad 2$$
$$\longrightarrow$$
$$4 \quad 3 \qquad\qquad 3 \quad 4$$

(E) Leaves mat unchanged.

32. A square matrix is declared as

    AB *(continued)*

    ```
    int[][] mat = new int[SIZE][SIZE];
    ```

    where SIZE is an appropriate integer constant. Consider the following method:

    ```
    public void mystery(int[][] mat, int value, int top, int left,
        int bottom, int right)
    {
        for (int i = left; i <= right; i++)
        {
            mat[top][i] = value;
            mat[bottom][i] = value;
        }
        for (int i = top + 1; i <= bottom - 1; i++)
        {
            mat[i][left] = value;
            mat[i][right] = value;
        }
    }
    ```

    Assuming that there are no out-of-range errors, which best describes what method mystery does?
    (A) Places value in corners of the rectangle with corners (top, left) and (bottom, right).
    (B) Places value in the diagonals of the square with corners (top, left) and (bottom, right).
    (C) Places value in each element of the rectangle with corners (top, left) and (bottom, right).
    (D) Places value in each element of the border of the rectangle with corners (top, left) and (bottom, right).
    (E) Places value in the topmost and bottommost rows of the rectangle with corners (top, left) and (bottom, right).

33. This question refers to the following method:

```
public static boolean isThere(String[][] mat, int row, int col,
    String symbol)
{
    boolean yes;
    int i, count = 0;
    for (i = 0; i < SIZE; i++)
        if (mat[i][col].equals(symbol))
            count++;
    yes = (count == SIZE);
    count = 0;
    for (i = 0; i < SIZE; i++)
        if (mat[row][i].equals(symbol))
            count++;
    return (yes || count == SIZE);
}
```

Now consider this code segment:

```
public final int SIZE = 8;
String[][] mat = new String[SIZE][SIZE];
```

Which of the following conditions on a matrix mat of the type declared in the code segment will by itself guarantee that

```
isThere(mat, 2, 2, "$")
```

will have the value true when evaluated?

  I The element in row 2 and column 2 is "$"
 II All elements in both diagonals are "$"
III All elements in column 2 are "$"

(A) I only
(B) III only
(C) I and II only
(D) I and III only
(E) II and III only

AB *(continued)*

Questions 34–37 use the nested for-each loop for two-dimensional arrays. This will not be tested on the AP exam.

34. The method `changeNegs` below should replace every occurrence of a negative integer in its matrix parameter with 0.

```
//Precondition: mat is initialized with integers.
//Postcondition: All negative values in mat replaced with 0.
public static void changeNegs(int[][] mat)
{
    /* code */
}
```

Which is correct replacement for /* *code* */?

```
I  for (int r = 0; r < mat.length; r++)
       for (int c = 0; c < mat[r].length; c++)
           if (mat[r][c] < 0)
               mat[r][c] = 0;

II for (int c = 0; c < mat[0].length; c++)
       for (int r = 0; r < mat.length; r++)
           if (mat[r][c] < 0)
               mat[r][c] = 0;

III for (int[] row : mat)
        for (int element : row)
            if (element < 0)
                element = 0;
```

(A) I only
(B) II only
(C) III only
(D) I and II only
(E) I, II, and III

35. This question is based on the Point class below:

```
public class Point
{
    private int x;
    private int y;

    //constructor
    public Point (int x, int y)
    {
        this.x = x;
        this.y = y;
    }

    //accessors
    public int getx()
    { return x; }

    public int gety()
    { return y; }

    //Set x and y to new_x and new_y.
    public void setPoint(int new_x, int new_y)
    {
        x = new_x;
        y = new_y;
    }

    //Return Point in String form.
    public String toString()
    {
        return "(" + x + "," + y + ")";
    }

    //other methods not shown
        ...
}
```

The method changeNegs below takes a matrix of Point objects as parameter and replaces every Point that has as least one negative coordinate with the Point (0,0).

```
/* Precondition:  pointMat is initialized with Point objects.
 * Postcondition: Every point with at least one negative
 *                coordinate has been changed to have both
 *                coordinates equal to zero.  */
public static void changeNegs (Point [][] pointMat)
{
    /* code */
}
```

Which is a correct replacement for /* *code* */?

AB *(continued)*

```
 I for (int r = 0; r < pointMat.length; r++)
       for (int c = 0; c < pointMat[r].length; c++)
          if (pointMat[r][c].getx() < 0
              || pointMat[r][c].gety() < 0)
                 pointMat[r][c].setPoint(0, 0);

 II for (int c = 0; c < pointMat[0].length; c++)
       for (int r = 0; r < pointMat.length; r++)
          if (pointMat[r][c].getx() < 0
              || pointMat[r][c].gety() < 0)
                 pointMat[r][c].setPoint(0, 0);

III for (Point[] row : pointMat)
       for (Point p : row)
          if (p.getx() < 0 || p.gety() < 0)
                 p.setPoint(0, 0);
```

(A) I only
(B) II only
(C) III only
(D) I and II only
(E) I, II, and III

AB *(continued)*

36. A simple Tic-Tac-Toe board is a 3×3 array filled with either X's, O's, or blanks. Here is a class for a game of Tic-Tac-Toe:

```java
public class TicTacToe
{
    private String[][] board;
    private static final int ROWS = 3;
    private static final int COLS = 3;

    //constructor. constructs empty board
    public TicTacToe()
    {
        board = new String[ROWS][COLS];
        for (int r = 0; r < ROWS; r++)
            for (int c = 0; c < COLS; c++)
                board[r][c] = " ";
    }

    /* Precondition:  square on Tic-Tac-Toe board is empty
     * Postcondition: symbol placed in that square */
    public void makeMove(int r, int c, String symbol)
    {
        board[r][c] = symbol;
    }

    /* Creates a string representation of the board, e.g.
     *    |o |
     *    |xx |
     *    | o|
     * Postcondition: returns the string representation */
    public String toString()
    {
        String s = "";       //empty string
        < more code >
        return s;
    }
}
```

Which segment represents a correct replacement for *<more code>* for the `toString` method?

```java
(A) for (int r = 0; r < ROWS; r++)
    {
        for (int c = 0; c < COLS; c++)
        {
            s = s + "|";
            s = s + board[r][c];
            s = s + "|\n";
        }
    }
```

(B)
```
for (int r = 0; r < ROWS; r++)
{
    s = s + "|";
    for (int c = 0; c < COLS; c++)
    {
        s = s + board[r][c];
        s = s + "|\n";
    }
}
```

(C)
```
for (int r = 0; r < ROWS; r++)
{
    s = s + "|";
    for (int c = 0; c < COLS; c++)
        s = s + board[r][c];
}
s = s + "|\n";
```

(D)
```
for (int r = 0; r < ROWS; r++)
    s = s + "|";
    for (int c = 0; c < COLS; c++)
    {
        s = s + board[r][c];
        s = s + "|\n";
    }
```

(E)
```
for (int r = 0; r < ROWS; r++)
{
    s = s + "|";
    for (int c = 0; c < COLS; c++)
        s = s + board[r][c];
    s = s + "|\n";
}
```

37. A two-dimensional array of `double`, `rainfall`, will be used to represent the daily rainfall for a given year. In this scheme, `rainfall[month][day]` represents the amount of rain on the given day and month. For example,

> `rainfall[1][15]`   is the amount of rain on Jan. 15
> `rainfall[12][25]`   is the amount of rain on Dec. 25

The array can be declared as follows:

> `double[][] rainfall = new double[13][32];`

This creates 13 rows indexed from 0 to 12 and 32 columns indexed from 0 to 31, all initialized to 0.0. Row 0 and column 0 will be ignored. Column 31 in row 4 will be ignored, since April 31 is not a valid day. In years that are not leap years, columns 29, 30, and 31 in row 2 will be ignored since Feb. 29, 30, and 31 are not valid days.

Consider the method `averageRainfall` below:

```
/* Precondition:  rainfall is initialized with values
 *                representing amounts of rain on all valid
 *                days. Invalid days are initialized to 0.0.
 *                Feb 29 is not a valid day.
 * Postcondition: Returns average rainfall for the year. */
public double averageRainfall(double rainfall[][])
{
    double total = 0.0;
    /* more code */
}
```

Which of the following is a correct replacement for /* *more code* */ so that the postcondition for the method is satisfied?

```
 I for (int month = 1; month < rainfall.length; month++)
        for (int day = 1; day < rainfall[month].length; day++)
            total += rainfall[month][day];
   return total / (13 * 32);

II for (int month = 1; month < rainfall.length; month++)
        for (int day = 1; day < rainfall[month].length; day++)
            total += rainfall[month][day];
   return total / 365;

III for (double[] month : rainfall)
        for (double rainAmt : month)
            total += rainAmt;
    return total / 365;
```

(A) None
(B) I only
(C) II only
(D) III only
(E) II and III only

38. The following code segment reverses the elements of arr[first] ... arr[last].

AB *(continued)*

```
int k = first, j = last;
while (k < j)
{
    swap(arr, k, j);    //interchanges arr[k] and arr[j]
    k++;
    j--;
}
```

Which of the following diagrams represents the loop invariant for the while loop? (Each rectangle represents a segment of array arr. The labels above the rectangles represent the indexes of array elements at the beginning and end of each segment.)

(A)

first	k k+1	j-1 j	last
swapped	original elements	swapped	

(B)

first	k k+1	j-1 j	last
original elements	swapped	original elements	

(C)

first	k-1 k	j j+1	last
swapped	original elements	swapped	

(D)

first	k-1 k	j j+1	last
original elements	swapped	original elements	

(E)

first	k-1 k	j-1 j	last
swapped	original elements	swapped	

39. The following algorithm sets min equal to the smallest value in arr[0] ... arr[n-1]:

```
min = arr[0];
i = 1;
while (i < n)
{
    if (arr[i] < min)
        min = arr[i];
    i++;
}
```

The loop invariant for the while loop is
(A) min is smallest value in arr[0] ...arr[i], $1 \leq i \leq n$
(B) min is smallest value in arr[0] ...arr[i-1], $1 \leq i \leq n-1$
(C) min is smallest value in arr[0] ...arr[i], $1 \leq i \leq n-1$
(D) min is smallest value in arr[0] ...arr[i-1], $1 < i \leq n$
(E) min is smallest value in arr[0] ...arr[i-1], $1 \leq i \leq n$

ANSWER KEY

1. E	14. E	27. E
2. C	15. B	28. D
3. E	16. C	29. D
4. B	17. A	30. A
5. A	18. A	31. B
6. B	19. B	32. D
7. C	20. D	33. B
8. C	21. C	34. D
9. D	22. B	35. E
10. A	23. E	36. E
11. D	24. C	37. E
12. B	25. D	38. C
13. C	26. A	39. E

ANSWERS EXPLAINED

1. **(E)** Segment I is an initializer list which is equivalent to

```
int[] arr = new int[4];
arr[0] = 0;
arr[1] = 0;
arr[2] = 0;
arr[3] = 0;
```

   Segment II creates four slots for integers, which by default are initialized to 0. The `for` loop in segment III is therefore unnecessary. It is not, however, incorrect.

2. **(C)** If arr contains no negative integers, the value of i will eventually exceed N-1, and `arr[i]` will cause an `ArrayIndexOutOfBoundsException` to be thrown.

3. **(E)** The intent is to sum elements `arr[0]`, `arr[1]`, ..., `arr[arr.length-1]`. Notice, however, that when i has the value `arr.length-1`, it is incremented to `arr.length` in the loop, so the statement `sum += arr[i]` uses `arr[arr.length]`, which is out of range.

4. **(B)** There are two problems with the segment as given:

   1. `arr[1]` is not tested.
   2. When i has a value of n-1, incrementing i will lead to an out-of-range error for the `if(arr[i] < min)` test.

   Modification II corrects both these errors. The change suggested in III corrects neither of these errors. The change in I corrects (1) but not (2).

5. **(A)** The code segment has the effect of removing all occurrences of 0 from array arr1. Then the nonzero elements are transferred to array arr2.

6. **(B)** The algorithm is linear. It passes once through the array, making a single assignment if a nonzero element is found.

7. **(C)** If `arr[i]` < `someValue` for all `i` from 2 to `k`, SMALL will be printed on each iteration of the `for` loop. Since there are `k - 1` iterations, the maximum number of times that SMALL can be printed is `k - 1`.

8. **(C)** Array `arr` is changed by `doSomething`. Here are the memory slots:

Just before `doSomething` is called:

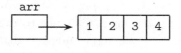

Just after `doSomething` is called, but before the `for` loop is executed:

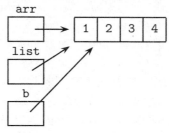

Just before exiting `doSomething`:

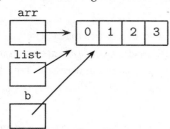

Just after exiting `doSomething`:

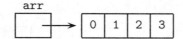

9. **(D)** Arrays are of fixed length and do not shrink or grow if the size of the data set varies. An `ArrayList` automatically resizes the list. Choice A is false: The [] notation is compact and easy to use. Choice B is not a valid reason because an array `arr` also provides instant access to its length with the quantity `arr.length`. Choice C is invalid because an array can also contain objects. Also, generality is beside the point in the given program: The list *must* hold `String` objects. Choice E is false: Whether a `String` object is `arr[i]` or `list.get(i)`, the `String` methods are equally easy to invoke.

10. **(A)** In order for numerical elements to be added to an `ArrayList`, each element must be wrapped in a wrapper class before insertion into the list. Then, to retrieve a numerical value from the `ArrayList`, the element must be unboxed using the `intValue` or `doubleValue` methods. Even though these operations can be taken care of with auto-boxing and -unboxing, there are efficiency costs. In an array, you simply use the [] notation for assignment (as in `arr[i] = num`) or retrieval (`value = arr[i]`). Note that choices B and C are false statements: Both insertion and deletion for an array involve writing code to shift elements. An `ArrayList` automatically takes care of this through its `add` and `remove` methods. Choice D is a poor reason for choosing an array. While the get and set methods of `ArrayList` might be slightly more awkward than using the [] notation, both mechanisms work pretty easily. Choice E is false: Efficiency of access is roughly the same.

11. **(D)** For each `Address` object `a` in `list`, access the name of the object with `a.getName()`.

12. **(B)** Since the `Address` class does not have a `toString` method, each data field must explicitly be printed. Segment III would work if there *were* a `toString` method for the class (but there isn't, so it doesn't!). Segment I fails because of incorrect use of the for-each loop: The array index should not be accessed.

13. **(C)** Each `Student` name must be accessed through the `Address` class accessor `getName()`. The expression `student.getAddress()` accesses the entire address of that student. The `myName` field is then accessed using the `getName()` accessor of the `Address` class.

14. **(E)** Both correct solutions are careful not to lose the student who has the highest `idNum` so far. Segment II does it by storing a reference to the student, `highestSoFar`. Segment III does it by storing the array index of that student. Code segment I is incorrect because it returns the first student whose `idNum` is greater than `max`, not necessarily the student with the highest `idNum` in the list.

15. **(B)** For each `i`, `tickList[i]` is a new `Ticket` object that must be constructed using the `Ticket` constructor. Therefore eliminate choices C, D, and E. Choice A is wrong because `getRow()`, `getSeat()`, and `getPrice()` are accessors for values *that already exist* for some `Ticket` object. Note also the absence of the dot member construct.

16. **(C)** To access the price for each `Ticket` in the `tickList` array, the `getPrice()` accessor in the `Ticket` class must be used, since `myPrice` is private to that class. This eliminates choices A and E. Choice B uses the array name incorrectly. Choices D and E incorrectly declare a `Transaction` object. (The method applies to an existing `Transaction` object.)

17. **(A)** An array of type `Transaction` is required. This eliminates choices C and D. Additionally, choices B and D incorrectly use type `Ticket` on the right-hand side. Choice E puts the identifier `listOfSales` in the wrong place.

18. **(A)** Notice that either `vIndex` or `wIndex` is incremented at the end of the loop. This means that, when the loop is exited, the current values of `v[vIndex]` and `w[wIndex]` have not been compared. Therefore, you can only make an assertion for values `v[0]..v[vIndex-1]` and `w[0]..w[wIndex-1]`. Also, notice that if there is no common value in the arrays, the exiting condition for the `while` loop will be that the end of one of the arrays has been reached, namely `vIndex` equals `N` or `wIndex` equals `M`.

19. **(B)** Objects in an array can be changed in a for-each loop by using mutator methods of the objects' class. The `changeStatus` method, a mutator in the `Book` class, will work as intended in the given code. Choice C would be true if it were not given that each `Book` in `bookList` was initialized. If any given `b` had a value of `null`, then a `NullPointerException` would be thrown.

20. **(D)** The declaration must start with the type of value in the array, namely `BingoCard`. This eliminates choices A and E. Eliminate choice B: The type on the right of the assignment should be `BingoCard`. Choice C is wrong because the number of slots in the array should be `NUMPLAYERS`, not 20.

21. **(C)** Segment III is the only segment that works, since the for-each loop cannot be used to replace elements in an array. After the declaration

```
BingoCard[] players = new BingoCard[NUMPLAYERS];
```

each element in the `players` array is `null`. The intent in the given code is to replace each null reference with a newly constructed `BingoCard`.

22. **(B)** The type parameter in a generic `ArrayList` must be a class type, not a primitive.

23. **(E)** All elements added to `strList` must be of type `String`. Each choice satisfies this except choice E. Note that in choice D, since `ch` is a `String`, the expression `ch + 8` becomes a `String` (just one of the operands needs to be a `String` to convert the whole expression to a `String`). In choice E, neither `intOb` nor 8 is a `String`.

24. **(C)** The effect of choice C is to adjust the size of the list to 7 and to add the `Integer` 9 to the last slot (i.e., the slot with index 6). Choices A, D, and E will all cause an `IndexOutOfBoundsException` because there is no slot with index 6: the last slot has index 5. Choice B will cause a compile-time error, since it is attempting to add an element of type `Double` to a list of type `Integer`.

25. **(D)** If `element` is smaller than the last item in the list, it will be compared with every item in the list. Eventually `index` will be incremented to a value that is out of bounds. To avoid this error, the test in the `while` loop should be

    ```
    while(index < list.size() &&
            element.compareTo(list.get(index)) < 0)
    ```

    Notice that if `element` is greater than or equal to at least one item in `list`, the test as given in the problem will eventually be false, preventing an out-of-range error.

26. **(A)** Recall that `add(index, obj)` shifts all elements, starting at `index`, one unit to the right, then inserts `obj` at position `index`. The `set(index, obj)` method replaces the element in position `index` with `obj`. So here is the state of `list` after each change:

    ```
    i = 0     6 0 1 8
              2 0 1 8
    i = 1     2 0 1 1 8
              2 3 1 1 8
    i = 2     2 3 1 2 1 8
              2 3 4 2 1 8
    ```

27. **(E)** The value of each `Coin` `c` in `coins` must be accessed with `c.getValue()`. This eliminates choice D. Eliminate choices A and B: The loop accesses each `Coin` in the `coins` `ArrayList`, which means that there should not be any statements attempting to get the next `Coin`. Choice B would be correct if the first statement in the loop body were

    ```
    double value = c.getValue();
    ```

28. **(D)** The `equals` method is defined for objects only. Since `getValue` returns a `double`, the quantities `c.getValue()` and `aCoin.getValue()` must be compared either using `==`, or as described in the box on p. 122 (better).

29. **(D)** Segment II is the straightforward solution. Segment I is correct because it initializes all slots of the matrix to 0, a perfect square. (By default, all arrays of `int` or `double` are initialized to 0.) Segment III fails because `r` is undefined in the condition `c < mat[r].length`. In order to do a column-by-column traversal, you need to get the number of columns in each row. The outer `for` loop could be

    ```
    for (int c = 0; c < mat[0].length; c++)
    ```

Now segment III works. Note that since the array is rectangular, you can use any index `k` in the conditional `c < mat[k].length`, provided that k satisfies $0 \le k <$ `mat.length`.

30. **(A)** `matStuff` processes the row selected by the row parameter, 2 in the method call. The row value, 2, overwrites each element in row 2. Don't make the mistake of selecting choice B—the row labels are 0, 1, 2.

31. **(B)** Hand execute this for a 2 × 2 matrix. `i` goes from 0 to 0, `j` goes from 0 to 0, so the only interchange is swap `mat[0][0]` with `mat[1][1]`, which suggests choice B. Check with a 3 × 3 matrix:

    ```
    i = 0   j = 0   swap mat[0][0] with mat[2][2]
            j = 1   swap mat[0][1] with mat[1][2]
    i = 1   j = 0   swap mat[1][0] with mat[2][1]
    ```

    The elements to be interchanged are shown paired in the following figure. The result will be a reflection through the minor diagonal.

32. **(D)** The first `for` loop places `value` in the top and bottom rows of the defined rectangle. The second `for` loop fills in the remaining border elements on the sides. Note that the `top + 1` and `bottom - 1` initializer and terminating conditions avoid filling in the corner elements twice.

33. **(B)** For the method call `isThere(mat, 2, 2, "$")`, the code counts how many times `"$"` appears in row 2 and how many times in column 2. The method returns `true` only if `count == SIZE` for either the row or column pass (i.e., the whole of row 2 or the whole of column 2 contains the symbol `"$"`). This eliminates choices I and II.

34. **(D)** Segment I is a row-by-row traversal; segment II is a column-by-column traversal. Each achieves the correct postcondition. Segment III traverses the matrix but does not alter it. All that is changed is the local variable `element`. You cannot use this kind of loop to replace elements in an array.

35. **(E)** This is similar to the previous question, but in this case segment III is also correct. This is because instead of *replacing* a matrix element, you are *modifying* it using a mutator method.

36. **(E)** There are three things that must be done in each row:

    - Add an opening boundary line:

      ```
      s = s + "|";
      ```

    - Add the symbol in each square:

      ```
      for (int c = 0; c < COLS; c++)
          s = s + board[r][c];
      ```

    - Add a closing boundary line and go to the next line:

```
s = s + "|\n";
```

All of these statements must therefore be enclosed in the outer `for` loop, that is,

```
for (int r = ...)
```

37. **(E)** Since there are 365 valid days in a year, the divisor in calculating the average must be 365. It may appear that segments II and III are incorrect because they include rainfall for invalid days in `total`. Since these values are initialized to `0.0`, however, including them in the total won't affect the final result.

38. **(C)** Since `k` and `j` are changed at the *end* of the loop, the invariant is:

    `arr[first]...arr[k-1]` have been swapped with elements `arr[last]` down to `arr[j+1]`.

    The middle part of the array has not been processed, and these elements are still in their original positions.

39. **(E)** `i` is incremented at the end of the loop, which means that on exiting the loop `arr[i]` has not yet been examined. This eliminates choices A and C. The loop invariant must be true on the final exit from the loop, at which time $i = n$. This eliminates choice B. Choice D is wrong because `i` is initialized to `1`. Thus, $1 \leq i$ ...

Recursion

> recursion *n. See* recursion.
> —*Eric S. Raymond,* The New Hacker's Dictionary *(1991)*

Chapter Goals

- Recursive methods
- Recursion in two-dimensional grids
- Recursive helper methods
- Analysis of recursive algorithms

RECURSIVE METHODS

A *recursive method* is a method that calls itself. For example, here is a program that calls a recursive method stackWords.

```
public class WordPlay
{
    public static void stackWords()
    {
        String word = IO.readString();        //read user input
        if (word.equals("."))
            System.out.println();
        else
            stackWords();
        System.out.println(word);
    }

    public static void main(String args[])
    {
        System.out.println("Enter list of words, one per line.");
        System.out.println("Final word should be a period (.)");
        stackWords();
    }
}
```

Here is the output if you enter

```
hold
my
hand
.
```

You get

```
. .
hand
my
hold
```

The program reads in a list of words terminated with a period, and prints the list in reverse order, starting with the period. How does this happen?

Each time the recursive call to stackWords() is made, execution goes back to the start of a new method call. The computer must remember to complete all the pending calls to the method. It does this by stacking the statements that must still be executed as follows: The first time stackWords() is called, the word "hold" is read and tested for being a period. No it's not, so stackWords() is called again. The statement to output "hold" (which has not yet been executed) goes on a stack, and execution goes to the start of the method. The word "my" is read. No, it's not a period, so the command to output "my" goes on the stack. And so on. The stack looks something like this before the recursive call in which the period is read:

```
|                                    |
|                                    |
|                                    |
| System.out.println("hand");        |
|  System.out.println("my");         |
| System.out.println("hold");        |
```

Imagine that these statements are stacked like plates. In the final stackWords() call, word has the value ".". Yes, it *is* a period, so the stackWords() line is skipped, the period is printed on the screen, and the method call terminates. The computer now completes each of the previous method calls in turn by "popping" the statements off the top of the stack. It prints "hand", then "my", then "hold", and execution of method stackWords() is complete.[1]

NOTE

1. Each time stackWords() is called, a new local variable word is created.
2. The first time the method actually terminates, the program returns to complete the most recently invoked previous call. That's why the words get reversed in this example.

GENERAL FORM OF SIMPLE RECURSIVE METHODS

Every recursive method has two distinct parts:

- A base case or termination condition that causes the method to end.
- A nonbase case whose actions move the algorithm toward the base case and termination.

[1]Actually, the computer stacks the pending statements in a recursive method call more efficiently than the way described. But *conceptually* this is how it is done.

Here is the framework for a simple recursive method that has no specific return type.

```
public void recursiveMeth( ... )
{
    if (base case)
        < Perform some action >
    else
    {
        < Perform some other action >
        recursiveMeth( ... );      //recursive method call
    }
}
```

The base case typically occurs for the simplest case of the problem, such as when an integer has a value of 0 or 1. Other examples of base cases are when some key is found, or an end-of-file is reached. A recursive algorithm can have more than one base case.

In the `else` or nonbase case of the framework shown, the code fragment *< Perform some other action >* and the method call `recursiveMeth` can sometimes be interchanged without altering the net effect of the algorithm. Be careful though, because what *does* change is the order of executing statements. This can sometimes be disastrous. (See the `eraseBlob` example at the end of this chapter, or the tree traversals and recursive tree algorithms in Chapter 10.)

Example 1

```
public void drawLine(int n)
{
    if (n == 0)
        System.out.println("That's all, folks!");
    else
    {
        for (int i = 1; i <= n; i++)
            System.out.print("*");
        System.out.println();
        drawLine(n - 1);
    }
}
```

The method call `drawLine(3)` produces this output:

```
***
**
*
That's all, folks!
```

NOTE

1. A method that has no pending statements following the recursive call is an example of *tail recursion*. Method `drawLine` is such a case, but `stackWords` is not.
2. The base case in the `drawLine` example is n == 0. Notice that each subsequent call, `drawLine(n - 1)`, makes progress toward termination of the method. If your method has no base case, or if you never reach the base case, you will

create *infinite recursion*. This is a catastrophic error that will cause your computer eventually to run out of memory and give you heart-stopping messages like `java.lang.StackOverflowError ...` .

Example 2

```
//Illustrates infinite recursion.
public void catastrophe(int n)
{
    System.out.println(n);
    catastrophe(n);
}
```

Try running the case `catastrophe(1)` if you have lots of time to waste!

> A recursive method must have a base case.

WRITING RECURSIVE METHODS

To come up with a recursive algorithm, you have to be able to frame a process *recursively* (i.e., in terms of a simpler case of itself). This is different from framing it *iteratively*, which repeats a process until a final condition is met. A good strategy for writing recursive methods is to first state the algorithm recursively in words.

Example 1

Write a method that returns *n*! (*n* factorial).

n! defined iteratively	*n*! defined recursively
0! = 1	0! = 1
1! = 1	1! = (1)(0!)
2! = (2)(1)	2! = (2)(1!)
3! = (3)(2)(1)	3! = (3)(2!)
...	...

The general recursive definition for *n*! is

$$n! = \begin{cases} 1 & n = 0 \\ n(n-1)! & n > 0 \end{cases}$$

The definition seems to be circular until you realize that if 0! is defined, all higher factorials are defined. Code for the recursive method follows directly from the recursive definition:

```
/* Compute n! recursively.
 * Precondition:  n >= 0.
 * Postcondition: returns n! */
public static int factorial(int n)
{
    if (n == 0)       //base case
        return 1;
    else
        return n * factorial(n - 1);
}
```

Example 2

Write a recursive method `revDigs` that outputs its integer parameter with the digits reversed. For example,

```
revDigs(147)    outputs    741
revDigs(4)      outputs    4
```

First, describe the process recursively: Output the rightmost digit. Then, if there are still digits left in the remaining number n/10, reverse its digits. Repeat this until n/10 is 0. Here is the method:

```java
/* Precondition:  n >= 0.
 * Postcondition: Outputs n with digits reversed. */
public static void revDigs(int n)
{
    System.out.print(n % 10);  //rightmost digit
    if (n / 10 != 0)                     //base case
        revDigs(n / 10);
}
```

ANALYSIS OF RECURSIVE METHODS

Recall the Fibonacci sequence 1, 1, 2, 3, 5, 8, 13, ... The nth Fibonacci number equals the sum of the previous two numbers if $n \geq 3$. Recursively,

$$\text{Fib}(n) = \begin{cases} 1, & n = 1, 2 \\ \text{Fib}(n-1) + \text{Fib}(n-2), & n \geq 3 \end{cases}$$

Here is the method:

```java
/* Precondition:  n >= 1.
 * Postcondition: Returns the nth Fibonacci number. */
public static int fib(int n)
{
    if (n == 1 || n == 2)
        return 1;
    else
        return fib(n - 1) + fib(n - 2);
}
```

Notice that there are two recursive calls in the last line of the method. So to find Fib(5), for example, takes eight recursive calls to `fib`!

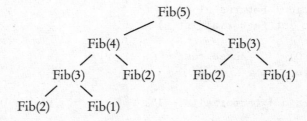

In general, each call to fib makes two more calls, which is the tipoff for an exponential algorithm (i.e., the run time is $O(2^n)$). This is *much* slower than the $O(n)$ run time of the corresponding iterative algorithm (see Chapter 5, preamble to Question 14).

You may ask: Since every recursive algorithm can be written iteratively, when should one use recursion? Bear in mind that recursive algorithms can incur extra run time and memory. Their major plus is elegance and simplicity of code.

General Rules for Recursion

1. Avoid recursion for algorithms that involve large local arrays—too many recursive calls can cause memory overflow.
2. Use recursion when it significantly simplifies code.
3. Avoid recursion for simple iterative methods like factorial, Fibonacci, and the linear search on the next page.
4. Recursion is especially useful for

   - Branching processes like traversing trees or directories.
   - Divide-and-conquer algorithms like mergesort and quicksort.

SORTING ALGORITHMS THAT USE RECURSION

Mergesort and quicksort are discussed in Chapter 12.

RECURSIVE HELPER METHODS

A common technique in designing recursive algorithms is to have a public nonrecursive driver method that calls a private *recursive helper method* to carry out the task. The main reasons for doing this are

- To change the value of an object reference. Recall that in Java if such an object is passed as a parameter in the method, it won't be changed. A helper must be used that returns the object reference (see Recursion That Alters the Tree Structure on p. 444).
- To hide the implementation details of the recursion from the user.
- To enhance the efficiency of the program.

Example 1

Consider the simple example of recursively finding the sum of the first n positive integers.

```
//Returns 1 + 2 + 3 + ... + n.
public static int sum(int n)
{
    if (n == 1)
        return 1;
    else
        return n + sum(n - 1);
}
```

Notice that you get infinite recursion if $n \leq 0$. Suppose you want to include a test for $n > 0$ before you execute the algorithm. Placing this test in the recursive method is inefficient because if n is initially positive, it will remain positive in subsequent recursive calls. You can avoid this problem by using a driver method called getSum, which does the test on *n just once*. The recursive method sum becomes a private helper method.

```
public class FindSum
{
    /* Private recursive helper method.
     * Finds 1 + 2 + 3 + ... + n.
     * Precondition:  n > 0. */
    private static int sum(int n)
    {
        if (n == 1)
            return 1;
        else
            return n + sum(n - 1);
    }

    /* Driver method */
    public static int getSum(int n)
    {
        if (n > 0)
            return sum(n);
        else
        {
            throw new IllegalArgumentException
                ("Error: n must be positive");
        }
    }
}
```

NOTE

This is a trivial method used to illustrate a private recursive helper method. In practice, you would never use recursion to find a simple sum!

Example 2

Consider a recursive solution to the problem of doing a sequential search for a key in an array of elements that are Comparable. If the key is found, the method returns true, otherwise it returns false.

The solution can be stated recursively as follows:

- If the key is in a[0], then the key is found.

- If not, recursively search the array starting at a[1].

- If you are past the end of the array, then the key wasn't found.

Here is a straightforward (but inefficient) implementation:

```
public class Searcher
{
    /* Recursively search array a for key.
     * Postcondition: If a[k] equals key for 0 <= k < a.length
     *                returns true, otherwise returns false.  */
    public boolean search(Comparable[] a, Comparable key)
    {
        if (a.length == 0)  //base case. key not found
            return false;
        else if (a[0].compareTo(key) == 0) //base case
            return true;                    //key found
        else
        {
            Comparable[] shorter = new Comparable[a.length-1];
            for (int i = 0; i < shorter.length; i++)
                shorter[i] = a[i+1];
            return search(shorter, key);
        }
    }

    public static void main(String[] args)
    {
        String[] list = {"Mary", "Joe", "Lee", "Jake"};
        Searcher s = new Searcher();
        System.out.println("Enter key: Mary, Joe, Lee or Jake.");
        String key = IO.readString();  //read user input
        boolean result = s.search(list, key);
        if (!result)
            System.out.println(key + " was not found.");
        else
            System.out.println(key + " was found.");
    }
}
```

Notice how horribly inefficient the search method is: For each recursive call, a new array shorter has to be created! It is much better to use a parameter, startIndex, to keep track of where you are in the array. Replace the search method above with the following one, which calls the private helper method recurSearch:

```
/* Driver method. Searches array a for key.
 * Precondition:  a contains at least one element.
 * Postcondition: If a[k] equals key for 0 <= k < a.length
 *                returns true, otherwise returns false. */
public boolean search(Comparable[] a, Comparable key)
{
    return recurSearch(a, 0, key);
}
```

```
/* Recursively search array a for key, starting at startIndex.
 * Precondition:  a contains at least one element and
 *                0 <= startIndex <= a.length.
 * Postcondition: If a[k] equals key for 0 <= k < a.length
 *                returns true, otherwise returns false. */
private boolean recurSearch(Comparable[] a, int startIndex,
    Comparable key)
{
    if(startIndex == a.length)   //base case. key not found
        return false;
    else if(a[startIndex].compareTo(key) == 0) //base case
        return true;                            //key found
    else
        return recurSearch(a, startIndex+1, key);
}
```

NOTE

Use a recursive helper method to hide private coding details from a client.

1. Using the parameter `startIndex` avoids having to create a new array object for each recursive call. Making `startIndex` a parameter of a helper method hides implementation details from the user.
2. Since `String` implements `Comparable`, it is OK to use an array of `String`. It would also have been OK to test with an array of `Integer` or `Double`, since they too implement `Comparable`.
3. The helper method is private because it is called only by `search` within the `Searcher` class.
4. It's easy to modify the `search` method to return the index in the array where the key is found: Make the return type `int` and return `startIndex` if the key is found, `-1` (say) if it isn't.

RECURSION IN TWO-DIMENSIONAL GRIDS

AB ONLY

A certain type of problem crops up occasionally on the AP exam: using recursion to traverse a two-dimensional array. The problem comes in several different guises. For example,

1. A game board from which you must remove pieces.
2. A maze with walls and paths from which you must try to escape.
3. White "containers" enclosed by black "walls" into which you must "pour paint."

In each case, you will be given a starting position (row, col) and instructions on what to do. The recursive solution typically involves these steps:

> *Check that the starting position is not out of range:*
> > *If (starting position satisfies some requirement)*
> > > *Perform some action to solve problem*
> > > *RecursiveCall(row + 1, col)*
> > > *RecursiveCall(row − 1, col)*
> > > *RecursiveCall(row, col + 1)*
> > > *RecursiveCall(row, col − 1)*

Example

On the right is an image represented as a square grid of black and white cells. Two cells in an image are part of the same "blob" if each is black and there is a sequence of moves from one cell to the other, where each move is either horizontal or vertical to an adjacent black cell. For example, the diagram represents an image that contains two blobs, one of them consisting of a single cell.

Assuming the following Image class declaration, you are to write the body of the eraseBlob method, using a recursive algorithm.

```
public class Image
{
    private final int BLACK = 1;
    private final int WHITE = 0;
    private int[][] image;      //square grid
    private int size;           //number of rows and columns

    public Image()    //constructor
    { /* implementation not shown */ }

    public void display()    //displays Image
    { /* implementation not shown */ }

    /* Precondition:  Image is defined with either BLACK or WHITE
     *                cells.
     * Postcondition: If 0 <= row < size, 0 <= col < size,
     *                and image[row][col] is BLACK, set all cells
     *                in the same blob to WHITE. Otherwise image
     *                is unchanged. */
    public void eraseBlob(int row, int col)
    /* your code goes here */
}
```

Solution:

```
public void eraseBlob(int row, int col)
{
    if (row >= 0 && row < size && col >= 0 && col < size)
        if (image[row][col] == BLACK)
        {
            image[row][col] = WHITE;
            eraseBlob(row - 1, col);
            eraseBlob(row + 1, col);
            eraseBlob(row, col - 1);
            eraseBlob(row, col + 1);
        }
}
```

NOTE

1. The ordering of the four recursive calls is irrelevant.

2. The test

   ```
   if (image[row][col] == BLACK)
   ```

   can be included as the last piece of the test in the first line:

   ```
   if (row >= 0 && ...
   ```

   If `row` or `col` are out of range, the test will short-circuit, avoiding the dreaded `ArrayIndexOutOfBoundsException`.

3. If you put the statement

   ```
   image[row][col] = WHITE;
   ```

   after the four recursive calls, you get infinite recursion if your blob has more than one cell. This is because, when you visit an adjacent cell, one of its recursive calls visits the original cell. If this cell is still `BLACK`, yet more recursive calls are generated, *ad infinitum*.

A final thought: Recursive algorithms can be tricky. Try to state the solution recursively *in words* before you launch into code. Oh, and don't forget the base case!

Chapter Summary

On the AP exam you will be expected to calculate the results of recursive method calls. Recursion becomes second nature when you practice a lot of examples. For the more difficult questions, use box diagrams to untangle the statements. Learn the format for recursion in a two-dimensional array—these questions occasionally come up on the AP exam.

All students should understand that recursive algorithms can be very inefficient. Level AB students should be able to recognize which of these algorithms is exponential, that is, $O(2^n)$.

MULTIPLE-CHOICE QUESTIONS ON RECURSION

1. Which of the following statements about recursion are true?

   I Every recursive algorithm can be written iteratively.
   II Tail recursion is always used in "divide-and-conquer" algorithms.
   III In a recursive definition, an object is defined in terms of a simpler case of itself.

   (A) I only
   (B) III only
   (C) I and II only
   (D) I and III only
   (E) II and III only

2. Which of the following, when used as the /* *body* */ of method sum, will enable that method to compute $1 + 2 + \cdots + n$ correctly for any $n > 0$?

   ```
   public int sum(int n)
   //Precondition:  n > 0.
   //Postcondition: 1 + 2 + ... + n has been returned.
   {
        /* body */
   }
   ```

   I `return n + sum(n - 1);`

   II `if (n == 1)`
   `        return 1;`
   `    else`
   `        return n + sum(n - 1);`

   III `if (n == 1)`
   `        return 1;`
   `    else`
   `        return sum(n) + sum(n - 1);`

   (A) I only
   (B) II only
   (C) III only
   (D) I and II only
   (E) I, II, and III

3. Refer to the method `stringRecur`:

```
public void stringRecur(String s)
{
    if (s.length() < 15)
        System.out.println(s);
    stringRecur(s + "*");
}
```

When will method `stringRecur` terminate without error?
(A) Only when the length of the input string is less than 15
(B) Only when the length of the input string is greater than or equal to 15
(C) Only when an empty string is input
(D) For all string inputs
(E) For no string inputs

4. Refer to method `strRecur`:

```
public void strRecur(String s)
{
    if (s.length() < 15)
    {
        System.out.println(s);
        strRecur(s + "*");
    }
}
```

When will method `strRecur` terminate without error?
(A) Only when the length of the input string is less than 15
(B) Only when the length of the input string is greater than or equal to 15
(C) Only when an empty string is input
(D) For all string inputs
(E) For no string inputs

Questions 5 and 6 refer to method `result`:

```
public int result(int n)
{
    if (n == 1)
        return 2;
    else
        return 2 * result(n - 1);
}
```

5. What value does `result(5)` return?
(A) 64
(B) 32
(C) 16
(D) 8
(E) 2

6. If $n > 0$, how many times will `result` be called to evaluate `result(n)` (including the initial call)?

   (A) 2
   (B) 2^n
   (C) n
   (D) $2n$
   (E) n^2

7. Refer to method `mystery`:

```
public int mystery(int n, int a, int d)
{
    if (n == 1)
        return a;
    else
        return d + mystery(n - 1, a, d);
}
```

   What value is returned by the call `mystery(3, 2, 6)`?

   (A) 20
   (B) 14
   (C) 10
   (D) 8
   (E) 2

8. Refer to method `f`:

```
public int f(int k, int n)
{
    if (n == k)
        return k;
    else
        if (n > k)
            return f(k, n - k);
        else
            return f(k - n, n);
}
```

   What value is returned by the call `f(6, 8)`?

   (A) 8
   (B) 4
   (C) 3
   (D) 2
   (E) 1

9. What does method recur do?

```
//Precondition: x is an array of n integers.
public int recur(int[] x, int n)
{
    int t;
    if (n == 1)
        return x[0];
    else
    {
        t = recur(x, n - 1);
        if (x[n-1] > t)
            return x[n-1];
        else
            return t;
    }
}
```

(A) It finds the largest value in x and leaves x unchanged.
(B) It finds the smallest value in x and leaves x unchanged.
(C) It sorts x in ascending order and returns the largest value in x.
(D) It sorts x in descending order and returns the largest value in x.
(E) It returns x[0] or x[n-1], whichever is larger.

10. Which best describes what the printString method below does?

```
public void printString(String s)
{
    if (s.length() > 0)
    {
        printString(s.substring(1));
        System.out.print(s.substring(0, 1));
    }
}
```

(A) It prints string s.
(B) It prints string s in reverse order.
(C) It prints only the first character of string s.
(D) It prints only the first two characters of string s.
(E) It prints only the last character of string s.

11. Refer to the method power:

```
//Precondition:  expo is any integer, base is not zero.
//Postcondition: base raised to expo power returned.
public double power(double base, int expo)
{
    if (expo == 0)
        return 1;
    else if (expo > 0)
        return base * power(base, expo - 1);
    else
        return /* code */;
}
```

Which /* *code* */ correctly completes method power?
(Recall that $a^{-n} = 1/a^n$, $a \neq 0$; for example, $2^{-3} = 1/2^3 = 1/8$.)
(A) `(1 / base) * power(base, expo + 1)`
(B) `(1 / base) * power(base, expo - 1)`
(C) `base * power(base, expo + 1)`
(D) `base * power(base, expo - 1)`
(E) `(1 / base) * power(base, expo)`

12. Consider the following method:

```
public void doSomething(int n)
{
    if (n > 0)
    {
        doSomething(n - 1);
        System.out.print(n);
        doSomething(n - 1);
    }
}
```

What would be output following the call doSomething(3)?
(A) `3211211`
(B) `1121213`
(C) `1213121`
(D) `1211213`
(E) `1123211`

13. A user enters several positive integers at the keyboard and terminates the list with a sentinel (-999). A `writeEven` method reads those integers and outputs the even integers only, in the reverse order that they are read. Thus, if the user enters

```
3 5 14 6 1 8 -999
```

the output for the `writeEven` method will be

```
8 6 14
```

Here is the method:

```
/* Assume user enters at least one positive integer,
 * and terminates the list with -999.
 * Postcondition: All even integers in the list are
 *                output in reverse order. */
public static void writeEven()
{
    int num = IO.readInt();    //read user input
    if (num != -999)
    {
        /* code */
    }
}
```

Which /* *code* */ satisfies the postcondition of method `writeEven`?

```
I  if (num % 2 == 0)
       System.out.print(num + " ");
   writeEven();
```

```
II  if (num % 2 == 0)
        writeEven();
    System.out.print(num + " ");
```

```
III  writeEven();
     if (num % 2 == 0)
         System.out.print(num + " ");
```

(A) I only
(B) II only
(C) III only
(D) I and II only
(E) I, II, and III

Questions 14–16 refer to method t:

```
//Precondition: n >= 1.
public int t(int n)
{
    if (n == 1 || n == 2)
        return 2 * n;
    else
        return t(n - 1) - t(n - 2);
}
```

14. What will be returned by t(5)?
    (A) 4
    (B) 2
    (C) 0
    (D) −2
    (E) −4

15. For the method call t(6), how many calls to t will be made, including the original call?
    (A) 6
    (B) 7
    (C) 11
    (D) 15
    (E) 25

16. The run time of method t is
    (A) $O(n)$
    (B) $O(n^2)$
    (C) $O(2^n)$
    (D) $O(n^3)$
    (E) $O(\log n)$

AB ONLY

17. This question refers to methods `f1` and `f2` that are in the same class:

```
public int f1(int a, int b)
{
    if (a == b)
        return b;
    else
        return a + f2(a - 1, b);
}

public int f2(int p, int q)
{
    if (p < q)
        return p + q;
    else
        return p + f1(p - 2, q);
}
```

What value will be returned by a call to `f1(5, 3)`?
(A) 5
(B) 6
(C) 7
(D) 12
(E) 15

18. Consider method `foo`:

```
public int foo(int x)
{
    if (x == 1 || x == 3)
        return x;
    else
        return x * foo(x - 1);
}
```

Assuming no possibility of integer overflow, what will be the value of `z` after execution of the following statement?

```
int z = foo(foo(3) + foo(4));
```

(A) (15!)/(2!)
(B) 3!+4!
(C) (7!)!
(D) (3!+4!)!
(E) 15

Questions 19 and 20 refer to the IntFormatter class below.

```
public class IntFormatter
{
    //Write 3 digits adjacent to each other.
    public static void writeThreeDigits(int n)
    {
        System.out.print(n / 100);
        System.out.print((n / 10) % 10);
        System.out.print(n % 10);
    }

    //Insert commas in n, every 3 digits starting at the right.
    //Precondition: n >= 0.
    public static void writeWithCommas(int n)
    {
        if (n < 1000)
            System.out.print(n);
        else
        {
            writeThreeDigits(n % 1000);
            System.out.print(",");
            writeWithCommas(n / 1000);
        }
    }
}
```

19. The method writeWithCommas is supposed to print its nonnegative int argument with commas properly inserted (every three digits, starting at the right). For example, the integer 27048621 should be printed as 27,048,621. Method writeWithCommas does not always work as intended, however. Assuming no integer overflow, which of the following integer arguments will *not* be printed correctly?
    (A) 896
    (B) 251462251
    (C) 365051
    (D) 278278
    (E) 4

20. Which change in the code of the given methods will cause method writeWithCommas to work as intended?
    (A) Interchange the lines System.out.print(n / 100) and System.out.print(n % 10) in method writeThreeDigits.
    (B) Interchange the lines writeThreeDigits(n % 1000) and writeWithCommas(n / 1000) in method writeWithCommas.
    (C) Change the test in writeWithCommas to if (n > 1000).
    (D) In the method writeWithCommas, change the line writeThreeDigits(n % 1000) to writeThreeDigits(n / 1000).
    (E) In the method writeWithCommas, change the recursive call writeWithCommas(n / 1000) to writeWithCommas(n % 1000).

21. Consider triangles that are formed by stacking squares, each with area 1.

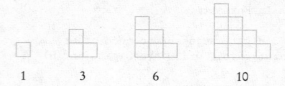

1   3   6   10

The area of each such triangle is a *triangular number*. Note that the area of the *n*th such triangle equals the area of the (*n* − 1)th triangle plus the area of the new base.

Here are two different implementations of a `Triangle` class that provides a recursive method to find the area of these `Triangle` objects, given their base. (The differences between the two implementations are in bold face.)

Implementation I

```
public class Triangle
{
    private int base;

    //constructor
    public Triangle(int b)
    { base = b; }

    public int getArea()
    {
        if (base == 1)
            return 1;
        Triangle smaller =
            new Triangle(base - 1);
        return base +
            smaller.getArea();
    }
}
```

Implementation II

```
public class Triangle
{
    private int base;

    //constructor
    public Triangle(int b)
    { base = b; }

    public int getArea()
    { return area(base); }

    private int area(int b)
    {
        if (b == 1)
            return 1;
        return b + area(b - 1);
    }
}
```

Which of the following is a true statement?

(A) When `getArea` is invoked in a client program, neither Implementation I nor Implementation II will work correctly.

(B) Implementations I and II are equally efficient in speed and memory usage.

(C) Implementation I is more run-time efficient than Implementation II.

(D) Implementation I is more efficient in memory usage than Implementation II.

(E) Implementation II has greater run-time efficiency and memory usage efficiency than Implementation I.

ANSWER KEY

1. D	8. D	15. D
2. B	9. A	16. C
3. E	10. B	17. E
4. D	11. A	18. A
5. B	12. C	19. C
6. C	13. C	20. B
7. B	14. E	21. E

ANSWERS EXPLAINED

1. **(D)** Tail recursion is when the recursive call of a method is made as the last executable step of the method. Divide-and-conquer algorithms like those used in mergesort or quicksort have recursive calls *before* the last step. Thus, statement II is false.

2. **(B)** Code segment I is wrong because there is no base case. Code segment III is wrong because, besides anything else, sum(n) prevents the method from terminating—the base case n == 1 will not be reached.

3. **(E)** When stringRecur is invoked, it calls itself irrespective of the length of s. Since there is no action that leads to termination, the method will not terminate until the computer runs out of memory (run-time error).

4. **(D)** The base case is s.length() $\geq$ 15. Since s gets longer on each method call, the method will eventually terminate. If the original length of s is $\geq$ 15, the method will terminate without output on the first call.

5. **(B)** Letting R denote the method result, we have

$$
\begin{aligned}
R(5) &= 2 * R(4) \\
&= 2 * (2 * (R(3))) \\
&= \cdots \\
&= 2 * (2 * (2 * (2 * R(1)))) \\
&= 2^5 \\
&= 32
\end{aligned}
$$

6. **(C)** For result(n) there will be $(n-1)$ recursive calls before result(1), the base case, is reached. Adding the initial call gives a total of n method calls.

7. **(B)** This method returns the nth term of an arithmetic sequence with first term a and common difference d. Letting M denote method mystery, we have

$$
\begin{aligned}
M(3,2,6) &= 6 + M(2,2,6) \\
&= 6 + (6 + M(1,2,6)) \quad \text{(base case)} \\
&= 6 + 6 + 2 \\
&= 14
\end{aligned}
$$

8. **(D)** Here are the recursive calls that are made, in order: $f(6,8) \rightarrow f(6,2) \rightarrow f(4,2) \rightarrow f(2,2)$, base case. Thus, 2 is returned.

9. **(A)** If there is only one element in x, then recur returns that element. Having the recursive call at the beginning of the else part of the algorithm causes the if part for each method call to be stacked until t eventually gets assigned to x[0]. The pending if statements are then executed, and t is compared to each element in x. The largest value in x is returned.

10. **(B)** Since the recursive call is made directly following the base case, the System.out.print... statements are stacked up. If printString("cat") is called, here is the sequence of recursive calls and pending statements on the stack:

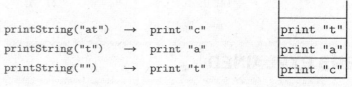

Execution stack

When printString(""), the base case, is called, the print statements are then popped off the stack in reverse order, which means that the characters of the string will be printed in reverse order.

11. **(A)** The required code is for a negative expo. For example, power(2, -3) should return $2^{-3} = 1/8$. Notice that

$$2^{-3} = \tfrac{1}{2}\left(2^{-2}\right)$$
$$2^{-2} = \tfrac{1}{2}\left(2^{-1}\right)$$
$$2^{-1} = \tfrac{1}{2}\left(2^{0}\right)$$

In general:

$$2^{n} = \tfrac{1}{2}(2^{n+1}) \quad \text{whenever} \quad n < 0$$

This is equivalent to (1 / base) * power(base, expo + 1).

12. **(C)** Each box in the diagram below represents a recursive call to doSomething. The numbers to the right of the boxes show the order of execution of the statements. Let D denote doSomething.

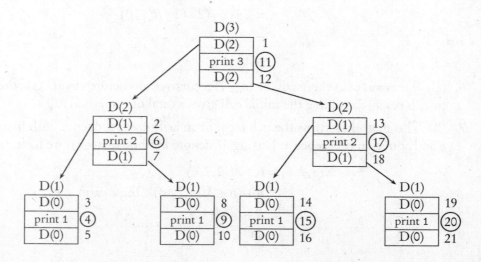

The numbers in each box refer to that method call only. D(0) is the base case, so the statement immediately following it is executed next. When all statements in a given box (method call) have been executed, backtrack along the arrow to find the statement that gets executed next. The circled numbers represent the statements that produce output. Following them in order, statements 4, 6, 9, 11, 15, 17, and 20 produce the output in choice C.

13. **(C)** Since even numbers are printed *before* the recursive call in segment I, they will be printed in the order in which they are read from the keyboard. Contrast this with the correct choice, segment III, in which the recursive call is made before the test for evenness. These tests will be stacked until the last number is read. Recall that the pending statements are removed from the stack in reverse order (most recent recursive call first), which leads to even numbers being printed in reverse order. Segment II is wrong because all numbers entered will be printed, irrespective of whether they are even or not. Note that segment II would work if the input list contained only even numbers.

14. **(E)** The method generates a sequence. The first two terms, $t(1)$ and $t(2)$, are 2 and 4. Each subsequent term is generated by subtracting the previous two terms. This is the sequence: 2, 4, 2, −2, −4, −2, 2, 4, ... Thus, $t(5) = -4$. Alternatively,

$$t(5) = t(4) - t(3)$$
$$= [t(3) - t(2)] - t(3)$$
$$= -t(2)$$
$$= -4$$

15. **(D)** 15. Count them! (Note that you stop at $t(2)$ since it's a base case.)

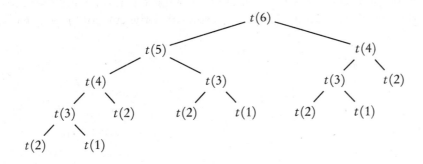

16. **(C)** A simple way of seeing this is that each call makes two more calls. This is the signature of an $O(2^n)$ process.

AB ONLY

17. **(E)** This is an example of *mutual recursion*, where two methods call each other.

$$f_1(5,3) = 5 + f_2(4,3)$$
$$= 5 + (4 + f_1(2,3))$$
$$= 5 + (4 + (2 + f_2(1,3)))$$
$$= 5 + (4 + (2 + 4))$$
$$= 15$$

Note that $f_2(1,3)$ is a base case.

18. **(A)** foo(3) = 3 (This is a base case). Also, foo(4) = 4 × foo(3) = 12. So you need to find foo(foo(3) + foo(4)) = foo(15).

$$
\begin{aligned}
\text{foo}(15) &= 15 \times \text{foo}(14) \\
&= 15 \times (14 \times \text{foo}(13)) \\
&= \cdots \\
&= 15 \times 14 \times \cdots \times 4 \times \text{foo}(3) \\
&= 15 \times 14 \times \cdots \times 4 \times 3 \\
&= (15)!/(2!)
\end{aligned}
$$

19. **(C)** Suppose that $n = 365051$. The method call `writeWithCommas(365051)` will write 051 and then execute the call `writeWithCommas(365)`. This is a base case, so 365 will be written out, resulting in 051,365. A number like 278278 (two sets of three identical digits) will be written out correctly, as will a "symmetrical" number like 251462251. Also, any $n < 1000$ is a base case and the number will be written out correctly as is.

20. **(B)** The cause of the problem is that the numbers are being written out with the sets of three digits in the wrong order. The problem is fixed by interchanging `writeThreeDigits(n % 1000)` and `writeWithCommas(n / 1000)`. For example, here is the order of execution for `writeWithCommas(365051)`.

```
writeWithCommas(365) → Base case. Writes 365
System.out.print(","); → 365,
writeThreeDigits(051) → 365,051 which is correct
```

21. **(E)** Both `getArea` methods should work correctly in a client program. Implementation I, however, is less efficient since it constructs a new `Triangle` object with each recursive call. This slows down the run time and uses more memory than Implementation II, which accesses only the current `Triangle` object.

Linked Lists

CHAPTER 8

But it really doesn't matter whom you put upon the list.
For they'd none of 'em be missed—they'd none of 'em be missed!
—*Gilbert and Sullivan*, The Mikado

Chapter Goals

- Linear linked lists
- The `ListNode` class
- Circular linked lists

- Doubly linked lists
- Run time of linked list vs. array algorithms

LINKED LIST

One way of implementing a list object in Java is as an array. An alternative implementation is as a *linked list*. Unlike an array, the elements of a linked list are not necessarily in contiguous memory slots. Instead, each element stores the address of the next item in the list. We say that it contains a *link* or *pointer* to the next item. In Java a linked list item actually stores a reference to the next object in the list. The last element of the list has a *null reference* in its pointer field to signify the end of the list.

A linked list is a *dynamic data structure*, growing and shrinking during run time. Memory slots are allocated as the need arises. Slots no longer needed are automatically recycled in Java. Contrast this with a built-in Java array, whose size is fixed at construction time.

Implementing a linked list in Java is part of the AB course and is described in this chapter. You also need to understand how to use the class `java.util.LinkedList<E>`, which is discussed with the other "container" classes in Chapter 11.

> Consider a linked list for a program in which the number of list elements is initially unknown.

LINEAR LINKED LISTS

Features of a Linked List

The term "linked list" is often used to mean a *linear linked list*. Picture a linked list as a collection of memory slots called *nodes*, each of which has a data field and a pointer field.

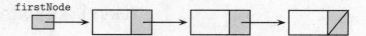

The arrows correspond to reference values in Java. The pointer field in the last item is the null reference. The variable `firstNode` is a reference to the first element in the list.

A linked list can be implemented in Java using a `ListNode` class for each node and a `LinkedList` class for the whole list.

The `ListNode` Class

A `ListNode` class similar to the following will be provided on the AP exam.[1]

```
/* Linked list node */
public class ListNode
{
    private Object value;
    private ListNode next;

    public ListNode(Object initValue, ListNode initNext)
    {
        value = initValue;
        next = initNext;
    }

    public Object getValue()
    { return value; }

    public ListNode getNext()
    { return next; }

    public void setValue(Object theNewValue)
    { value = theNewValue; }

    public void setNext(ListNode theNewNext)
    { next = theNewNext; }
}
```

THE INSTANCE VARIABLES

> `private Object value`

Any `Object` can be placed in a `ListNode`. Primitive types like `int` or `double` will first be auto-boxed. See Example 1 on the next page.

> `private ListNode next`

The `ListNode` class is said to be *self-referential*, since it has an instance variable `next` that refers to itself. Self-referential objects can be linked together to form objects like lists, trees, stacks, and so on. Thus, the variable `next` is called a *link* or *pointer*.

---

[1]Based on the College Board's *AP Computer Science AB: Implementation Classes for Linked Lists and Tree Nodes.*

THE METHODS

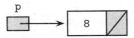

```
public ListNode(Object initValue, ListNode initNext)
```

The ListNode constructor, with initValue and initNext parameters, allows a single statement to assign the value and next fields to a ListNode.

Example 1

The following statement uses the constructor to create a single ListNode containing the value 8.

```
ListNode p = new ListNode(new Integer(8), null); //8 wrapped to
                                       //create an Integer object
```

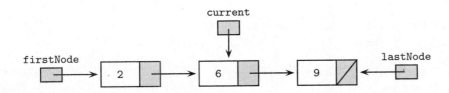

Alternatively,

```
ListNode p = new ListNode(8, null); //8 auto-boxed to create an
                  //Integer object. Not tested on the AP exam.
```

```
public Object getValue()
```

This is an accessor method that returns the value of the current ListNode. Since the type is Object, a cast to Integer, Double, or String, and so on will be needed, unless you plan to assign it to a variable of type Object.

```
public ListNode getNext()
```

This is an accessor method that returns next, the pointer value of the current ListNode.

```
public void setValue(Object theNewValue)
```

This is a mutator method that allows the value of the current ListNode to be changed to theNewValue.

```
public void setNext(ListNode theNewNext)
```

This is a mutator method that allows the next field of the current ListNode to be changed to theNewNext.

Example 2

Consider this linked list of ListNode objects, where firstNode, lastNode, and current are all of type ListNode.

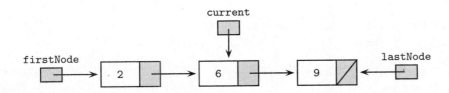

```
Integer first = (Integer) firstNode.getValue(); //first has value 2
ListNode p = current.getNext(); //p refers to ListNode containing 9
int last = ((Integer) current.getNext().getValue()).intValue();
                                                //last has value 9
```

NOTE

An alternative for the last line in Example 2 is

```
int last = (Integer) current.getNext().getValue();
                        //Uses auto-unboxing to create an int.
                        //Not tested on the AP exam.
```

Now consider the statements

```
current.setNext(null);
lastNode = current;
```

These two statements result in this setup:

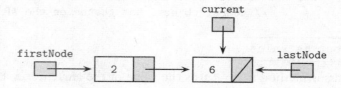

You may wonder what happened to the node containing 9. Java has automatic garbage collection that recycles any memory slot that is no longer in use (i.e., there are no references to the object in that slot).

To change the value in the first node to 5:

```
firstNode.setValue(new Integer(5));
```

Alternatively,

```
firstNode.setValue(5);    //auto-boxing
```

Example 3

Consider a linked list of `ListNode` objects.

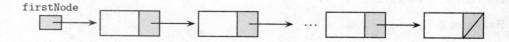

Here is a code segment that traverses the list and outputs the contents to the screen, one element per line.

```
ListNode p = firstNode;
while (p != null)
{
    System.out.println(p.getValue());
    p = p.getNext();
}
```

NOTE

The quantity `p.getValue()` does not need to be cast to the actual object type if the object in the linked list has a `toString` method. Java will polymorphically select the correct `toString` method and print the value accordingly.

A Linear Linked List Class

You are expected to know how to implement linked lists. The `LinearLinkedList` class shown below implements a singly linked list of nodes, in which items are of type `Object`, and the references are of type `ListNode`. A reference to the first node of the list is an instance variable.

Methods provided in the class will allow

- A test for an empty list.
- Elements to be added or removed from either end of the list.
- Printing a list object by providing a `toString` method.
- List traversal by a client, via a `getFirstNode` method.

```
/*Linear linked list class */
import java.util.NoSuchElementException;

public class LinearLinkedList
{
    private ListNode firstNode;

    //Construct an empty list.
    public LinearLinkedList()
    { firstNode = null; }

    //Return true if list is empty, false otherwise.
    public boolean isEmpty()
    { return firstNode == null; }

    //Accesses the first node; needed to traverse the list.
    public ListNode getFirstNode()
    { return firstNode; }

    //Changes first node of list.
    public void setFirstNode(ListNode node)
    { firstNode = node; }

    // Insert object o at front of list.
    public void addFirst(Object o)
    {
        if (isEmpty())
            firstNode = new ListNode(o, null);
        else
            firstNode = new ListNode(o, firstNode);
    }

    // Insert object o at end of list.
    public void addLast(Object o)
    {
        if (isEmpty())
```

```java
            firstNode = new ListNode(o, null);
        else
        {
            ListNode current = firstNode;
            while (current.getNext() != null)
                current = current.getNext();
            current.setNext(new ListNode(o, null));
        }
    }


    //Remove and return first element.
    public Object removeFirst()
    {
        if (isEmpty())
            throw new NoSuchElementException(
                    "Can't remove from empty list");
        Object item = firstNode.getValue();
        firstNode = firstNode.getNext();
        return item;
    }


    //Remove and return last element.
    public Object removeLast()
    {
        if (isEmpty())
            throw new NoSuchElementException(
                    "Can't remove from empty list");
        ListNode current = firstNode;
        ListNode follow = null;
        while (current.getNext() != null)   //at least 2 nodes
        {
            follow = current;
            current = current.getNext();
        }
        if (follow == null)          //list had just 1 node
            firstNode = null;
        else
            follow.setNext(null);
        return current.getValue();
    }


    //Return LinearLinkedList as String.
    public String toString()
    {
        if (isEmpty())
            return "empty.";
        else
        {
            String s = "";
            ListNode current = firstNode;
            while (current != null)
            {
                s = s + current.getValue() + " ";
                current = current.getNext();
            }
            return s;
```

```
            }
        }
    }
```

NOTE

1. You need to know how to throw a `NoSuchElementException`. This error occurs when there's an attempt to access a nonexistent element in a list. (See also the `next()` method of the `Iterator` interface on p. 475.) In the `LinearLinkedList` class, the exception is thrown if an attempt is made to remove an element from an empty list. To throw the exception, you need to include the statement

   ```
   import java.util.NoSuchElementException;
   ```

   in the file with the class whose methods will throw the exception. In the relevant methods, the statement

   ```
   if (isEmpty())
       throw new NoSuchElementException();
   ```

   will cause the program to terminate if the list is empty. Additionally, you can provide your own error message when the exception is thrown:

   ```
   if (isEmpty())
       throw new NoSuchElementException(
               "Can't remove from empty list");
   ```

2. The class shown is not a generic class (i.e., has no type parameter). You do not need to know how to implement generic classes for the AP exam.
3. The Java Collections library provides a class `java.util.LinkedList<E>`. So you may wonder why you need to know how to implement such a class. The answer is that you could tailor your own class to fit any application, by providing additional methods.

Here is a program that tests the `LinearLinkedList` methods:

```
/* Tests LinearLinkedList class. */

public class LinkedListTest
{
    //Return linear linked list of strings.
    public static LinearLinkedList getList()
    {
        final String SENTINEL = "-999";
        LinearLinkedList list = new LinearLinkedList();
        System.out.print("Enter list of words. ");
        System.out.println("Terminate with " + SENTINEL);
        String word = IO.readWord();  //read user input

        while (!(word.equals(SENTINEL)))
        {
            list.addLast(word);
            word = IO.readWord();  //read user input
        }
        return list;
    }
```

```
//Search for key in LinearLinkedList list.
//Return true if found, false otherwise.
public static boolean search(LinearLinkedList list, Object key)
{
    ListNode current = list.getFirstNode();
    while (current != null)
    {
        if (current.getValue().equals(key))
            return true;
        current = current.getNext();
    }
    return false;
}

public static void main(String[] args)
{
    //TESTING getList AND toString
    LinearLinkedList list = getList();
    System.out.print("List is:  ");
    System.out.println(list);

    //TESTING removeFirst AND removeLast
    String first = (String) list.removeFirst();
    System.out.println("First element was: " + first);
    String last = (String) list.removeLast();
    System.out.println("Last element was: " + last);
    System.out.print("List is:  ");
    System.out.println(list);

    //TESTING search
    System.out.print("Enter key word for search: ");
    String key = IO.readWord();   //read user input
    if (search(list, key))
        System.out.println(key + " is in the list.");
    else
        System.out.println(key + " is not in the list.");
}
}
```

Here is some sample output.

```
Enter list of words. Terminate with -999
the cat sat on the mat -999
List is:  the cat sat on the mat
First element was: the
Last element was: mat
List is:  cat sat on the
Enter key word for search: on
on is in the list.
```

NOTE

The method `getFirstNode` in the `LinearLinkedList` class is a crucial method to gain access to the list for traversal outside the class.

CIRCULAR LINKED LISTS

A linear linked list allows easy access to the first node but requires traversal of the whole list to reach the final node. A small change converts a linear linked list into a *circular linked list,* which allows easy access to both the first and last nodes. Let the pointer field of the last node point to the first node, instead of being `null`.

> Consider a circular linked list when frequent access to the first and last elements is required.

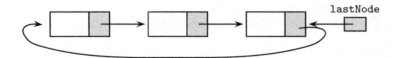

Implementing a Circular Linked List

A circular linked list can be implemented using a `ListNode` class for each node and a `CircularLinkedList` class for the whole list. The `ListNode` class is the same class used for linear linked lists. The `CircularLinkedList` class has the same methods as the `LinearLinkedList` class, but most of the implementation code is different if you use the instance variable

```
private ListNode lastNode;
```

to replace

```
private ListNode firstNode;
```

Also, instead of a `getFirstNode` accessor, the `CircularLinkedList` class would provide a `getLastNode` method.

Having a reference to `lastNode` allows easy access to both the first and last elements of the list. Insertion and deletion operations at both ends of the list can be done in $O(1)$ (constant) time. The data in the first node can be accessed with `lastNode.getNext().getValue()`.

Note that in traversing a circular linked list, there's no longer a null reference in the last node. The `lastNode` reference must therefore be used as a stoplight for list traversal.

Example 1

Here is code for the `addLast` method of a `CircularLinkedList` class.

```
//Insert object o at end of list.
public void addLast(Object o)
{
    if (isEmpty())
    {
        lastNode = new ListNode(o, null);
        lastNode.setNext(lastNode);
    }
    else
    {
        ListNode p = new ListNode(o, lastNode.getNext());
        lastNode.setNext(p);
        lastNode = p;
    }
}
```

NOTE

1. You may think that adding a node to an empty list can be accomplished with the single statement

```
lastNode = new ListNode(o, lastNode);
```

This, however, won't work. Since the current value of lastNode is null, the right-hand side, which is evaluated first, will create a node that has a null reference in its next field.

2. The else part of the addLast method can also be written as follows:

```
lastNode.setNext(new ListNode(o, lastNode.getNext()));
lastNode = lastNode.getNext();
```

Example 2

Here is code for the toString method of the CircularLinkedList class.

```
//Return contents of circular linked list as a string.
public String toString()
{
    if (isEmpty())
        return "empty";
    else
    {
        String s = "";
        ListNode current = lastNode.getNext();
        while (current != lastNode)
        {
            s = s + current.getValue() + " ";
            current = current.getNext();
        }
        s = s + current.getValue();
        return s;
    }
}
```

NOTE

The while loop stops when current refers to the last node:

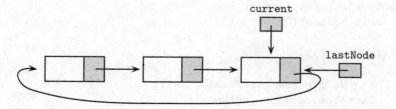

If you omit the final s = s + current.getValue() statement, the returned string s will not have the data from the last node.

DOUBLY LINKED LISTS

Why Doubly Linked Lists?

Singly linked linear and circular lists have several disadvantages:

1. Traversal is in just one direction.
2. To access previous nodes, you must go to one end of the list and start again.
3. Given a reference to a node, you cannot easily delete that node. There is no direct access to the previous pointer field.

A data structure that overcomes these disadvantages is a *doubly linked list*, where each node has three fields: a data field, a reference to the next node, and a reference to the previous node. The price paid for the capability of moving in either direction of the list is the extra memory required for one more instance variable in a doubly linked list node.

Picture a doubly linked list as follows:

> Consider a doubly linked list for an application that requires forward and backward traversal.

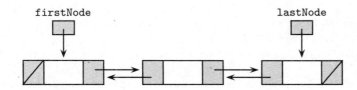

Here is a circular doubly linked list:

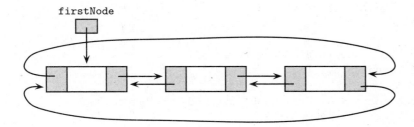

If the pointer fields are `next` and `prev`, notice that `firstNode.prev` refers to the last (rightmost) node in the list. This means that you can dispense with a `lastNode` variable: `firstNode` provides $O(1)$ access to both the first and last nodes of the list.

Header and Trailer Nodes

Header and trailer nodes are nodes at the front and back of a linked list that do not contain elements of the list. Think of them as dummy nodes with no values.

The effect of having header and trailer nodes is that you avoid some special-case testing for the first and last nodes: Insertion and deletion is always done in the "middle" of the list.

Here is an empty doubly linked list with header and trailer nodes:

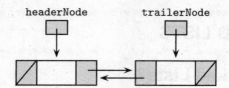

Implementing Doubly Linked Lists

As with linear and circular linked lists, the implementation can be achieved with two classes, one for the node and one for the list.

THE DoublyListNode CLASS

The DoublyListNode class is very similar to the ListNode class. It requires an additional pointer field, prev, and additional methods for accessing and setting values and links for the previous node.

```
/* Doubly linked list node */

public class DoublyListNode
{
    private Object value;
    private DoublyListNode next;
    private DoublyListNode prev;

    public DoublyListNode(DoublyListNode initPrev, Object initValue,
                DoublyListNode initNext)
    {
        prev = initPrev;
        value = initValue;
        next = initNext;
    }

    public DoublyListNode getPrev()
    { return prev; }

    public void setPrev(DoublyListNode theNewPrev)
    { prev = theNewPrev; }

    public Object getValue()
    { return value; }

    public void setValue(Object theNewValue)
    { value = theNewValue; }

    public DoublyListNode getNext()
    { return next; }

    public void setNext(DoublyListNode theNewNext)
    { next = theNewNext; }
}
```

A DoublyLinkedList CLASS

There are several design choices for implementing doubly linked lists—linear, circular, with or without header and/or trailer. The class below is for a linear doubly linked list with header and trailer nodes. Having a header and trailer eliminates many of the special end-of-list cases for insertion and deletion.

```java
/* Doubly linked list class with header and trailer */

import java.util.NoSuchElementException;

class DoublyLinkedList
{
    private DoublyListNode headerNode;
    private DoublyListNode trailerNode;

    //Construct an empty list.
    public DoublyLinkedList()
    {
        headerNode = new DoublyListNode(null, null, null);
        trailerNode = new DoublyListNode(headerNode, null, null);
        headerNode.setNext(trailerNode);
    }

    //Return true if list is empty, false otherwise.
    public boolean isEmpty()
    {
        return headerNode.getNext() == trailerNode;
        //or return trailerNode.getPrev() == headerNode;
    }

    //Return first node in a nonempty list.
    public DoublyListNode getFirstNode()
    { return headerNode.getNext(); }

    //Return last node in a nonempty list.
    public DoublyListNode getLastNode()
    { return trailerNode.getPrev(); }

    //Insert object o at end of list.
    public void addLast(Object o)
    {
        DoublyListNode p = new DoublyListNode(trailerNode.getPrev(),
                        o, trailerNode);
        trailerNode.getPrev().setNext(p);
        trailerNode.setPrev(p);
    }

    //Insert object o at front of list.
    public void addFirst(Object o)
    { /* implementation code similar to addLast */ }

    //Remove and return first element.
    public Object removeFirst()
    {
        if (isEmpty())
            throw new NoSuchElementException
                ("Can't remove from empty list");

        DoublyListNode p = headerNode.getNext();
        Object item = p.getValue();
```

```
            headerNode.setNext(p.getNext());
            p.getNext().setPrev(headerNode);
            return item;
    }


    //Remove and return last element.
    public Object removeLast()
    { /* implementation code similar to removeFirst */ }


    //Add item to the left of node.
    //Precondition: node refers to an element in a nonempty list.
    void addLeft(Object item, DoublyListNode node)
    {
        DoublyListNode p = new DoublyListNode(node.getPrev(),
                              item, node);
        node.setPrev(p);
        p.getPrev().setNext(p);
    }


    //Add item to the right of node.
    //Precondition: node refers to an element in a nonempty list.
    void addRight(Object item, DoublyListNode node)
    { /*implementation code similar to addLeft */ }


    //Remove element referred to by node from list.
    //Precondition: node points to element in list.
    public void remove(DoublyListNode node)
    {
        node.getPrev().setNext(node.getNext());
        node.getNext().setPrev(node.getPrev());
    }


    //Return DoublyLinkedList as String.
    public String toString()
    {
        if (isEmpty())
            return "empty.";
        else
        {
            String s = "";
            DoublyListNode p = headerNode.getNext();
            while (p != trailerNode)
            {
                s = s + p.getValue() + " ";
                p = p.getNext();
            }
            return s;
        }
    }
}
```

NOTE

1. Here's an illustration of the addLeft method. Start with a nonempty doubly linked list, with node pointing to one of the items. Because of the header and trailer nodes, node will not be at either end of the list:

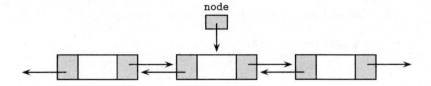

Each statement of the method is illustrated below:

```
DoublyListNode p = new DoublyListNode(node.getPrev(), item, node);
```

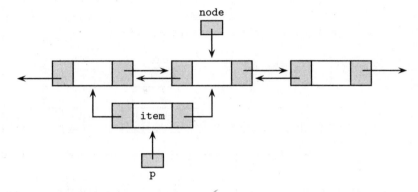

```
node.setPrev(p);
```

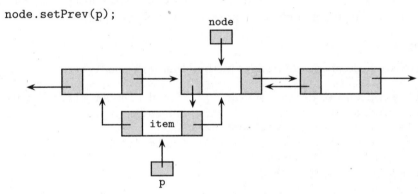

```
p.getPrev().setNext(p);
```

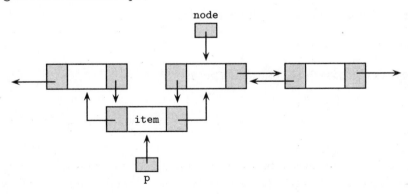

2. Here's an illustration of remove. Again, node points to some element in the "middle" of the list. This is the element that will be removed.

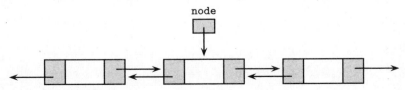

Here are pictures of what happens to the pointers:

```
node.getPrev().setNext(node.getNext());
```

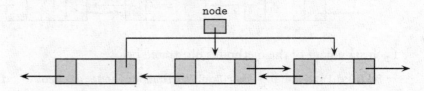

```
node.getNext().setPrev(node.getPrev());
```

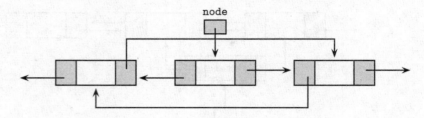

Note that as soon as the method is exited, there will be no references to the deleted element, and its memory slot will be recycled.

Example

Here is a piece of code in a client method that tests `addRight`:

```
DoublyLinkedList dLL = getList();  //reads number strings into dLL
DoublyListNode current = dLL.getFirstNode();
while (current != dLL.getLastNode() &&
    (!((String)current.getValue()).equals("6")))
        current = current.getNext();
dLL.addRight("66", current);
System.out.print("List is: ");
System.out.println(dLL);
```

If the list entered is 2 4 6 8, the output is

```
List is: 2 4 6 66 8
```

If the list entered is 5 10 15, the output is

```
List is: 5 10 15 66
```

NOTE

Because of the symmetry of a doubly linked list, similar results can be achieved by initializing `current` with `dLL.getLastNode()`, and then traveling "left" with

```
current = current.getPrev();
```

RUN TIME OF LINKED LIST VS. ARRAY ALGORITHMS

In each case, assume n elements in a singly linked linear linked list (LLL) and also in an array that has sufficient slots for the operations described below. You may also assume that the linked list implementation has a reference to the first node only.

Algorithm	LLL	Array	Comment
Add or remove element at end	$O(n)$	$O(1)$	For LLL, must traverse whole list. For array, simple assignment: `a[n+1]` = element.
Add or remove element at front	$O(1)$	$O(n)$	For array, must move each element up one slot to create empty slot in `a[0]`. For LLL, simple pointer adjustment.
Linear search for key	$O(n)$	$O(n)$	In worst case, need to search entire LLL or array.
Insert element in correct position in sorted list (a) Find insertion point (b) Insert element	$O(n)$ $O(1)$	$O(\log n)$ $O(n)$	Insertion in LLL requires just pointer adjustments. For array, binary search to find insertion; but then may have to move n elements to create a slot.
Delete all occurrences of value from list	$O(n)$	$O(n)$	For LLL, find value, adjust pointers, find value, adjust pointers, etc. For array, $O(n^2)$ if all elements moved each time you find value. $O(n)$ algorithm in Chapter 6, Question 5.

Chapter Summary

Know the difference between each type of linked list. You could be asked to produce code that manipulates or traverses each type. Know how to use the `ListNode` class and how to write linked list classes of your own.

You should also be able to discuss the types of applications for which each kind of list is suitable as a data structure.

Know the big-O run times for the various operations on linked lists and be able to compare these with similar operations in arrays.

MULTIPLE-CHOICE QUESTIONS ON LINKED LISTS

Assume that all questions on linear and circular linked lists use the ListNode class provided on the AP exam (see p. 364).

1. The following segment is supposed to search for and remove from a linear linked list all nodes whose data fields are equal to val, a previously defined value. Assume that firstNode is accessible and references the first node in the list, and that the list is nonempty.

```
ListNode current = firstNode;
while (current != null)
{
    if (current.getValue().equals(val))
    {
        ListNode q = current.getNext();
        current.setNext(q.getNext());
    }
    else
        current = current.getNext();
}
```

Which is true about this code segment?
(A) It works for all the nodes of the linked list.
(B) It fails for only the first node of the list.
(C) It fails for only the last node of the list.
(D) It fails for the first and last nodes of the list but works for all others.
(E) It fails for all nodes of the list.

2. A circular linked list (CLL) is implemented with a `CircularLinkedList` class that has a private instance variable `lastNode`:

```
ListNode lastNode;      //refers to last node of CLL
```

The `CircularLinkedList` class has a `toString` method that converts the contents of a circular linked list to a string in the correct order. Consider a `writeList` method in the `CircularLinkedList` class:

```
/* Writes elements of CLL to screen.
 * Assumes contents of CLL have a toString method.
 * Precondition:  List is not empty.
 *                lastNode refers to last node in list.
 * Postcondition: All elements printed to screen.  */
public void writeList()
{ /* implementation code */ }
```

Which of the following could replace */* implementation code */* so that `writeList` works as intended?

  I `System.out.println(this);`

  II
```
ListNode current = lastNode.getNext();
while (current != lastNode)
{
    System.out.println(current.getValue() + " ");
    current = current.getNext();
}
System.out.println(current.getValue());
```

  III
```
for (ListNode current = lastNode.getNext();
        current != lastNode; current = current.getNext())
    System.out.println(current.getValue() + " ");
```

(A) I only
(B) II only
(C) III only
(D) I and II only
(E) I, II, and III

3. Consider a `LinearLinkedList` class that has an instance variable `firstNode` of type `ListNode` and an accessor method `getFirstNode` that returns a reference to the first element in the list. Consider a client method `findKey`:

```
/* Search for key in LinearLinkedList a.
 * Return true if found, false otherwise.  */
public static boolean findKey(LinearLinkedList a, Object key)
{
    ListNode current = a.getFirstNode();
    while (current != null && !current.getValue().equals(key))
        current = current.getNext();
    return current != null;
}
```

Which is true about method `findKey`?
(A) `findKey` works as intended only if `key` is in the list.
(B) `findKey` works as intended only if the list is nonempty.
(C) `findKey` works as intended only if `key` is not in the last node of the list.
(D) `findKey` does not work under any circumstances.
(E) `findKey` always works as intended.

4. Consider an insert method in a `LinearLinkedList` class:

```
/* Precondition:  current refers to a node in a nonempty linked
 *                list sorted in increasing order.
 * Postcondition: element inserted directly following node to
 *                which current points.  */
public void insert(ListNode current, Object element)
{
    /* code */
}
```

What is the run time of /* *code* */, assuming the most efficient algorithm?
(A) $O(1)$
(B) $O(n)$
(C) $O(n^2)$
(D) $O(\log n)$
(E) $O(n \log n)$

5. A circular linked list has a reference `firstNode` that points to the first element in the list and is `null` if the list is empty. The following segment is intended to count the number of nodes in the list:

```
int count = 0;
ListNode p = firstNode.getNext();
while (p != firstNode)
{
    count++;
    p = p.getNext();
}
```

Which statement is true?
(A) The segment works as intended in all cases.
(B) The segment fails in all cases.
(C) The segment works as intended whenever the list is nonempty.
(D) The segment works as intended when the list has just one element.
(E) The segment works as intended only when the list is empty.

6. Consider the following method for removing a value from a linear linked list:

```
//Precondition:   p points to a node in a nonempty
//                linear linked list.
//Postcondition: The value that p points to has been removed
//                from the list.
public void remove(ListNode p)
{
    ListNode q = p.getNext();
    p.setValue(q.getValue());
    p.setNext(q.getNext());
}
```

In which of the following cases will the `remove` method fail to work as intended?

   I p points to any node in the list other than the first or last node.
  II p points to the last node in the list.
 III p points to the first node, and there is more than one node in the list.

(A) I only
(B) II only
(C) I and II only
(D) I and III only
(E) I, II, and III

7. Suppose that the precondition of method `remove` in Question 6 is changed so that the method always works as intended. What is the run time of the algorithm?
(A) $O(n)$
(B) $O(\sqrt{n})$
(C) $O(1)$
(D) $O(n^2)$
(E) $O(\log n)$

8. Suppose that `list1` and `list2` refer to the first nodes of two linear linked lists, and that `q` points to some node in the first list. The first piece of the first list, namely all the nodes up to and including the one pointed to by `q`, is to be removed and attached to the front of `list2`, maintaining the order of the nodes. After removal, `list1` should point to the remaining nodes of its original list, and `list2` should point to the augmented list. If neither `q` nor `list1` is originally `null`, then this task is correctly performed by which of the following program segments? Assume that `p` and `q` are both correctly declared to be of type `ListNode`.

```
I q.setNext(list2);
  list2 = list1;
  list1 = q.getNext();
```

```
II while (list1 != q.getNext())
   {
       p = list1;
       list1 = list1.getNext();
       p.setNext(list2);
       list2 = p;
   }
   list1 = p;
```

```
III p = q.getNext();
    q.setNext(list2);
    list2 = list1;
    list1 = p;
```

(A) None
(B) III only
(C) I and III only
(D) II and III only
(E) I, II, and III

9. Refer to method search:

```
/* Returns reference to first occurrence of key in list.
 * Returns null if key not in list.
 * Precondition: node points to first node in list.  */
public static ListNode search(ListNode node, Object key)
{
    /* code */
}
```

Which of the following replacements for /* *code* */ will result in method search working as intended?

```
 I  if (node.getValue().equals(key))
        return node;
    else
        return search(node.getNext(), key);
```

```
 II ListNode current = node;
    while (current != null)
    {
        if(current.getValue().equals(key))
            return current;
        current = current.getNext();
    }
    return null;
```

```
III ListNode current = node;
    while (current != null && !current.getValue().equals(key))
        current = current.getNext();
    return current;
```

(A) I only
(B) II only
(C) III only
(D) II and III only
(E) I and II only

Questions 10 and 11 refer to circular linked lists and a concat method described below. Circular linked lists are implemented with a `CircularLinkedList` class that has a private instance variable `lastNode` of type `ListNode`. The class contains, among others, the following methods:

```
public boolean isEmpty()        //returns true if list is empty
public ListNode getLastNode()   //returns lastNode
public void setLastNode(ListNode node)  //sets lastNode to node
```

Consider two `CircularLinkedList` objects `list1` and `list2`. For example,

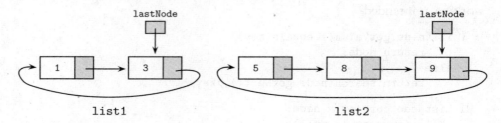

A method `concat` appends `list2` to `list1` and results in an augmented `list1`. The method call `concat(list1, list2)` should produce

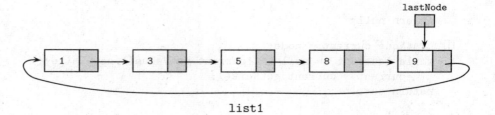

If `list1` is initially empty and `list2` is as shown, `concat(list1, list2)` should produce

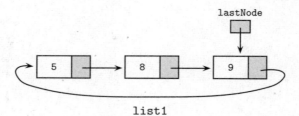

If `list2` is initially empty and `list1` is as shown, `concat(list1, list2)` should produce

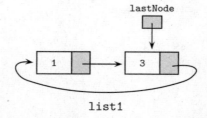

Here is the concat method:

```
/* Precondition:  list1 and list2 are CircularLinkedList objects.
 * Postcondition: list2 has been appended to list1.  */
public static void concat(CircularLinkedList list1,
        CircularLinkedList list2)
{
    ListNode L1 = list1.getLastNode();
    ListNode L2 = list2.getLastNode();
    if (list1.isEmpty())
    {
        /* code */
    }
    else if (!list2.isEmpty())
    {
        /* more code */
    }
}
```

10. Which replacement for /* *code* */ achieves the required postcondition when `list1` is empty?

    I `list1 = list2;`

    II `L1 = L2;`

    III `list1.setLastNode(L2);`

    (A) I only
    (B) II only
    (C) III only
    (D) I and III only
    (E) II and III only

11. Which could replace /* *more code* */ so that the postcondition of concat is satisfied? You may assume the existence of the following swap method:

    ```
    //Interchange ListNode fields of ListNodes p1 and p2.
    public static void swap(ListNode p1, ListNode p2)
    ```

    I `L1.setNext(L2.getNext());`
    `L2.setNext(L1.getNext());`
    `list1.setLastNode(L2);`

    II `ListNode p = L1.getNext();`
    `L1.setNext(L2.getNext());`
    `L2.setNext(p);`
    `list1.setLastNode(L2);`

    III `swap(list1.getLastNode(), list2.getLastNode());`
    `list1.setLastNode(list2.getLastNode());`

    (A) I only
    (B) II only
    (C) III only
    (D) II and III only
    (E) I and II only

For Questions 12–16 assume that linear linked lists are implemented with a class `LinearLinkedList` as shown.

```
public class LinearLinkedList
{
    private ListNode firstNode;

    //constructor and other methods
        ...

    public ListNode getFirstNode()
    { return firstNode; }

    //Change firstNode to node.
    public void setFirstNode(ListNode node)
    { firstNode = node; }

    //Insert Object o at front of list.
    public void addFirst(Object o)
    { /* implementation not shown */ }
}
```

12. This question refers to a client method `mystery`:

```java
public static void mystery(LinearLinkedList list)
{
    ListNode hold = list.getFirstNode();
    list.setFirstNode(null);
    while (hold != null)
    {
        ListNode grab = hold;
        hold = hold.getNext();
        grab.setNext(list.getFirstNode());
        list.setFirstNode(grab);
    }
}
```

Assume an initial list

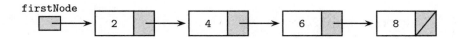

After the method call `mystery(list)`, what will the list look like?

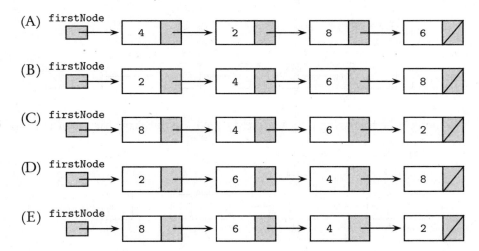

13. A client method `minimum` returns a `ListNode` that contains the smallest value in a linear linked list:

```
/* Precondition:  list is a nonempty linear linked list of
 *                Comparable objects.
 * Postcondition: Reference returned to ListNode with
 *                smallest value.  */
public ListNode minimum(LinearLinkedList list)
{
    ListNode minSoFar = list.getFirstNode();
    ListNode p = minSoFar.getNext();
    while (p != null)
    {
        if (((Comparable) p.getValue()).compareTo
                    (minSoFar.getValue()) < 0)
            minSoFar = p;
        p = p.getNext();
    }
    return minSoFar;
}
```

Suppose `minimum(list)` is called for the following list:

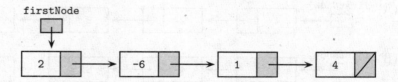

Which of the following does *not* satisfy the loop invariant for the `while` loop?

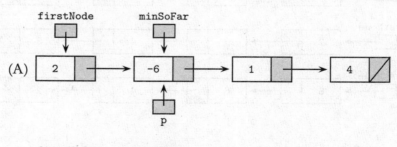

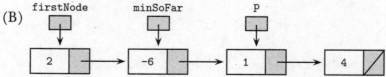

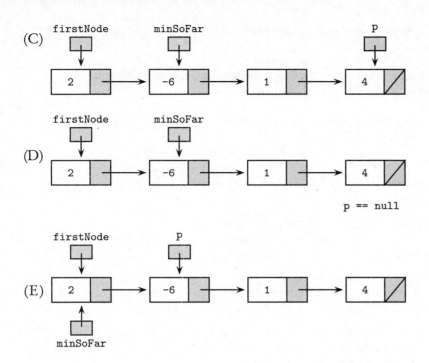

14. Suppose a method `addSecond` is added to the `LinearLinkedList` class:

```
/* Precondition:  list contains at least one element.
 * Postcondition: New node containing Object o inserted at
 *                second position in list.  */
public void addSecond(Object o)
{ /* implementation code */ }
```

Which of the following could replace /* *implementation code* */ so that method `addSecond` works as intended?

(A) `firstNode.getNext(new ListNode(o, firstNode.getNext()));`

(B) `firstNode.setNext(o, firstNode.getNext());`

(C) `firstNode.setNext(new ListNode(o, firstNode.getNext()));`

(D) `firstNode.setNext(ListNode(o, firstNode.setNext()));`

(E) `firstNode = firstNode.getNext();`
    `firstNode.setNext(ListNode(o, firstNode));`

15. Consider an append method for the `LinearLinkedList` class:

```
/* Precondition:  list is not null.
 * Postcondition: Object o added to the end of list.  */
public void append(Object o)
{
    ListNode current = firstNode;
    /* more code */
}
```

Which correctly replaces /* *more code* */ so that the postcondition of append is satisfied?

(A) ```
while (current.getNext() != null)
    current = current.getNext();
current.setNext(new ListNode(o, null));
```

(B) ```
while (current != null)
    current = current.getNext();
current.setNext(new ListNode(o, null));
```

(C) ```
while (current.getNext() != null)
    current = current.getNext();
current = new ListNode(o, null);
```

(D) ```
while (current != null)
    current = current.getNext();
current = new ListNode(o, null);
```

(E) ```
while (current.getNext() != null)
    current = current.getNext();
current.getNext(new ListNode(o, null));
```

16. Consider the following client method, print.

```
//Precondition: list is empty.
public void print(LinearLinkedList list)
{
    for (int i = 1; i <= 5; i++)
        list.addFirst(new Integer(i));
    ListNode p = list.getFirstNode();
    while (p != null)
    {
        System.out.print(p.getValue());
        p = p.getNext();
    }
}
```

What will be printed as a result of calling method print?
(A) 12345
(B) 54321
(C) 2345
(D) 5
(E) 1
```

Questions 17–19 refer to the DoublyListNode class on p. 374.

17. Consider a doubly linked list of String values as shown:

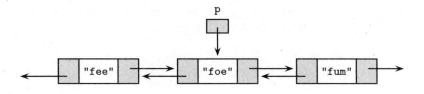

The value "fie" is to be inserted between "fee" and "foe". Here is a code segment that achieves this:

```
DoublyListNode q = new DoublyListNode(p.getPrev(), "fie", p);
/* more code */
```

Which is a correct replacement for /* *more code* */?

   I p.getPrev().setNext(q);
     p.setPrev(q);

  II p.setPrev(q);
     q.getPrev().setNext(q);

 III p.setPrev(q);
     p.getPrev().setNext(q);

(A) I only
(B) II only
(C) III only
(D) I and II only
(E) I, II, and III

18. Suppose a doubly linked list does not have header or trailer nodes. Consider method remove:

```
/* Precondition:  p points to a node in a nonempty
 *                doubly linked list.
 * Postcondition: Node p has been removed from the list. */
public void remove(DoublyListNode p)
{
    p.getPrev().setNext(p.getNext());
    p.getNext().setPrev(p.getPrev());
}
```

In which of the following cases will remove fail to work as intended?

    I p points to the first node in the list.
    II p points to the last node in the list.
    III p points to a node other than the first or last node in the list.

(A) I and II only
(B) III only
(C) I and III only
(D) I, II, and III
(E) None. Method remove will always work as intended.

19. Consider a doubly linked list with three nodes as shown:

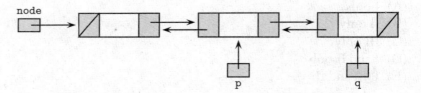

Which of the following code segments converts this list into a doubly linked circular list with three nodes? (Assume that after execution the node reference may point to any node.)

    I q.setNext(node);
       q = q.getNext();
       node.setPrev(q);

    II node.setPrev(p.getNext());
       p.getNext().setNext(node);

    III p.getPrev().setPrev(q);
        q.setNext(p.getPrev());

(A) I only
(B) II only
(C) III only
(D) II and III only
(E) I, II, and III

20. Assume a `DoublyLinkedList` class implements doubly linked lists. Each `DoublyLinkedList` will have a header and trailer node.

```
public class DoublyLinkedList
{
    private DoublyListNode headerNode;
    private DoublyListNode trailerNode;

    //constructor
    //Creates an empty list.
    public DoublyLinkedList()
    { /* implementation not shown */ }

    //Returns first node in list.
    public DoublyListNode getFirstNode()
    { return headerNode.getNext(); }

    //other methods not shown ...
}
```

Suppose the `DoublyLinkedList` class contains an `addRight` method.

```
/* Precondition:  node refers to an element in a nonempty list.
 * Postcondition: item added to the right of node.  */
public void addRight(Object item, DoublyListNode node)
{
    DoublyListNode p = new DoublyListNode(node, item,
            node.getNext());
    /* more implementation code */
}
```

Which of the following represents /* *more implementation code* */ that will result in the desired postcondition?

  I `node.setNext(p);`
    `node.getNext().setPrev(p);`

 II `node.getNext().setPrev(p);`
    `node.setNext(p);`

III `node.setNext(p);`
  . `p.getNext().setPrev(p);`

(A) I only
(B) II only
(C) III only
(D) I and II only
(E) II and III only

21. A list of items is to be maintained in random order. Operations performed on the list include

    (1) Insertion of new items at the front of the list.
    (2) Deletion of old items from the rear of the list.

A programmer considers using a linear singly linked list (LLL), a circular singly linked list (CLL), or an array to store the items. Which of the following correctly represents the run-time efficiency of (1) insertion and (2) deletion for this list? You may assume that

- The array has sufficient slots for insertion.
- Linear linked lists are implemented with a reference to the first node only.
- Circular linked lists are implemented with a reference to the last node only.
- The most efficient algorithm possible is used in each case.

  (A) array: (1) $O(n)$ (2) $O(1)$
           LLL: (1) $O(1)$ (2) $O(n)$
           CLL: (1) $O(1)$ (2) $O(n)$

  (B) array: (1) $O(n)$ (2) $O(1)$
           LLL: (1) $O(1)$ (2) $O(n)$
           CLL: (1) $O(1)$ (2) $O(1)$

  (C) array: (1) $O(1)$ (2) $O(1)$
           LLL: (1) $O(1)$ (2) $O(1)$
           CLL: (1) $O(1)$ (2) $O(1)$

  (D) array: (1) $O(n)$ (2) $O(n)$
           LLL: (1) $O(1)$ (2) $O(n)$
           CLL: (1) $O(1)$ (2) $O(n)$

  (E) array: (1) $O(1)$ (2) $O(n)$
           LLL: (1) $O(n)$ (2) $O(1)$
           CLL: (1) $O(n)$ (2) $O(1)$

22. This question refers to the `remove` method below:

```
public static ListNode remove(ListNode node, Object val)
{
    if (node != null)
    {
        ListNode restOfList = remove(node.getNext(), val);
        if (node.getValue().equals(val))
            return restOfList;
        else
        {
            node.setNext(restOfList);
            return node;
        }
    }
    else
        return null;
}
```

In a test of the method, a client program has this code segment:

```
LinearLinkedList list = new LinearLinkedList();
getList(list);      //read values into list
readValue(val);     //prompt for and read in val
ListNode p = remove(list.getFirstNode(), val);
list.setFirstNode(p);
```

What does `remove` do?
(A) Removes all occurrences of `val` in the list.
(B) Removes all items in the list that are not equal to `val`.
(C) Removes only the first item in the list, if and only if it equals `val`.
(D) Removes all items in the list, irrespective of value.
(E) Leaves the list unchanged.

ANSWER KEY

1. E	9. D	17. D
2. D	10. C	18. A
3. E	11. D	19. D
4. A	12. E	20. E
5. B	13. A	21. A
6. B	14. C	22. A
7. C	15. A	
8. B	16. B	

ANSWERS EXPLAINED

1. (E) Here is what happens if current is pointing to a node that must be removed:

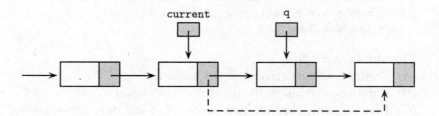

   The algorithm attempts to remove the node *following* the node that should be deleted.

2. (D) Segment I works because the CircularLinkedList class has a toString method. The method will therefore print out the string form of the entire object. In segment II the while loop stops when current refers to the last node. To print the data in the last node, you need the additional statement

   ```
   System.out.println(current.getValue());
   ```

   The for loop in segment III is equivalent to the while loop in segment II. Thus, segment III would have been correct if after the loop it had the additional System.out.println... statement.

3. (E) If current is null, the test will be short-circuited, and there will be no dereferencing of a null pointer in the second half of the test. Also, if current is null, key was not found, and the method will return false, which is correct.

4. (A) The method does not find the insertion point; it merely attaches a new node. This is a constant $O(1)$ operation.

5. (B) When there are no elements in the circular linked list (i.e., firstNode is null), a NullPointerException will be thrown. If there's just one element in the list:

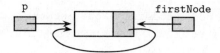

The test will fail immediately, leaving a count of 0. In all other cases, count will have a value one less than the actual number of nodes.

6. **(B)** If p points to the last node, q = p.setNext() will give q a value of null. Referring to q.getValue() will then cause a NullPointerException to be thrown.

7. **(C)** Provided p doesn't point to the last node in the list, this is a nifty algorithm that requires no list traversal. It is independent of the number of nodes in the list and is therefore $O(1)$.

8. **(B)** In segment I the statement q.setNext(list2) maroons the second piece of the first list: list1 can no longer be reassigned. The first statement of segment III, p = q.getNext(), is crucial to avoid losing that piece of the first list. The reference assignments in segment II make no sense.

9. **(D)** Segment I is missing a base case. It would be correct if preceded by

```
if (node == null)
    return null;
else
{ ...
```

10. **(C)** Segment I is wrong because list1 and list2 are passed by value. Therefore when the method is exited, list1 will have its initial value; that is, it will be empty. Segment II fails because the setLastNode method must be used to change the lastNode of list1 as required: getLastNode is an accessor and can't be used for this purpose.

11. **(D)** Segment I fails because the first line breaks the connection to the first node of list1. Now the next field of L2 gets connected to the first node of list2, where it was to begin with! Segment II avoids this problem in its first line by using a temporary reference to hold the address of the first node in list1. Notice that the first three lines of segment II are exactly the code to interchange list1.getNext() and list2.getNext() correctly, so segment III is also correct.

12. **(E)** This breathless-sounding algorithm reverses pointers in the list. Here is a picture of the loop invariant for the while loop:

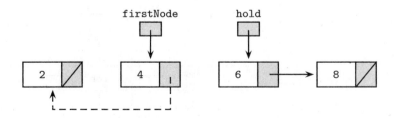

In words, firstNode points to the part of the list that's already been reversed, and hold points to the part of the original list that still needs to be taken care of.

13. **(A)** The loop invariant for the while loop is that minSoFar points to the smallest value up to and excluding the node that p points to. Notice that p is advanced right at the end of the loop (last statement), so the node that p points to on exiting the loop has not yet been examined.

14. **(C)** The correct code needs `firstNode.setNext(...)` because the `next` field of the first node will be altered. It also needs `new ListNode...` because a new node is being created. The expression

```
new ListNode(o, firstNode.getNext());
```

uses the constructor of the `ListNode` class. It will be evaluated first:

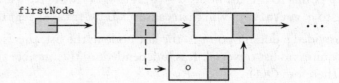

Finally `firstNode.setNext(...)` sets the `next` field of `firstNode` to point to the new node (dashed arrow in the figure above).

15. **(A)** The test must be

```
while (current.getNext() != null)
```

so that `current` eventually points to the last node. This eliminates choices B and D. Choices C and D make the mistake of assigning `current` to the new node, which means that the node won't get attached to the list. Eliminate choice E because `setNext`, not `getNext`, must be used to modify the `next` field of the last node.

16. **(B)** Each pass through the `for` loop creates a new node at the front of the linked list, resulting in

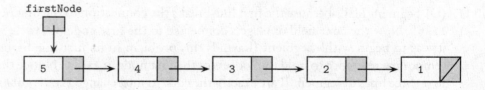

Thus, `54321` will be printed.

17. **(D)** In segment III, here's the situation after `p.setPrev(q)`:

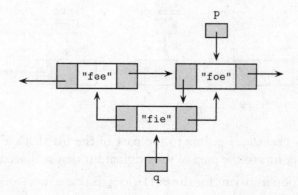

`p.getPrev()` now refers to node q, which means that the node with 7 will not have the correct next pointer connection.

18. **(A)** Cases I and II both fail because a null pointer is being dereferenced. For the first node, `p.getPrev()` is `null`. For the last node, `p.getNext()` is `null`.

19. **(D)** Choice I changes the pointer connections incorrectly, as shown:

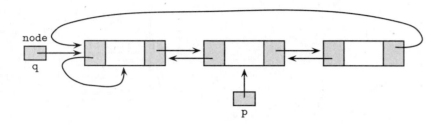

20. **(E)** Here's what goes wrong in segment I: After `node.setNext(p)`, the expression `node.getNext()` no longer refers to the node to the right of `node`. It refers to the new node! Here are the sad pointer connections following execution of segment I:

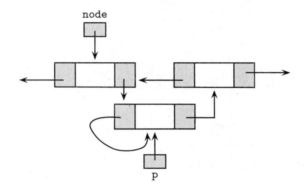

21. **(A)** To insert at the front of an array requires movement of all n elements to create a slot—thus, $O(n)$. Both the LLL and the CLL require just pointer adjustments to insert a node at the front: $O(1)$. To remove at the rear requires simply an adjustment on the number of elements in the array, $O(1)$. To remove from the rear of a LLL requires traversal of the list to reach the last node, $O(n)$. It would seem that a CLL would be $O(1)$ for removing an element from the rear, since the external pointer points to the last element. The problem is that to remove the last element requires accessing the pointer field of the previous node, which requires traversal along the entire list, $O(n)$.

22. **(A)** Here's a recursive description of the `remove` method: If the list is not empty, then if the first node contains `val`, remove that node. Now repeat this procedure for the rest of the list. The tricky part of the algorithm lies in returning the correct reference for each recursive call.

    Suppose the method is called for a linear linked list of three nodes, in which only the second node contains `val`:

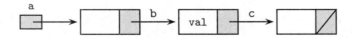

Label the references to the three nodes a, b, and c, as shown. Here's a recursion diagram to execute `remove(a, val)`. In the diagram, r denotes `restOfList`. The circled numbers indicate the order of execution of the statements. Look at the statements in that order.

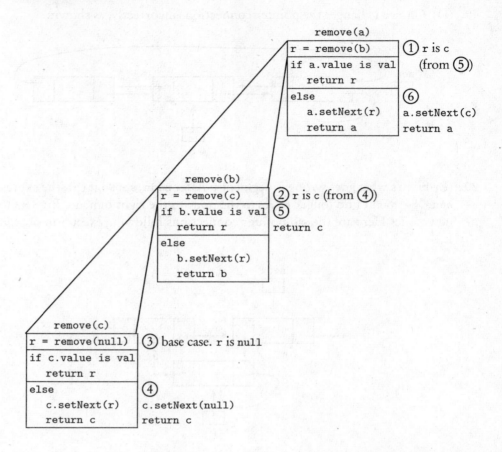

Note: A recursive method like `remove` that alters a linked structure (list or tree) cannot be implemented by passing a `ListNode` parameter that may need to be changed by the method. This is because the parameter is passed by value and will always emerge from the method with its value *unchanged*. The method must be written so that it returns a `ListNode`. This is how changes in the nodes get preserved. Contrast the `remove` method with the `search` method of Question 9. In the `search` method, the list is never changed, so it's OK to have a `ListNode` parameter whose value emerges from the method call unchanged.

Stacks and Queues

The stack sizes should dictate your decision.
—*Paul Ichiban, Poker Website*

Chapter Goals

- Stacks and the Stack<E> class
- Queues and the Queue<E> interface
- Priority queues and the PriorityQueue<E> class
- Run time of stack, queue, and priority queue operations

STACKS

What Is a Stack?

Think of a stack of plates or cafeteria trays. The last one added to the stack is the first one removed: last in first out (LIFO). And you can't remove the second tray without taking off the top one!

A *stack* is a sequence of items of the same type, in which items can be added and removed only at one end. In theory, there is no limit to the number of items on the stack.

Changes to the stack are controlled by two operations, *push* and *pop*. To push an item onto the stack is to add that item to the top of the stack. To pop the stack is to remove an item from the top of the stack. Imagine that the top of the stack floats up and down as items are pushed onto or popped off the stack. Push and pop are ideally $O(1)$ operations.

There are two other useful operations for a stack: an *isEmpty* test, which returns true or false, and *peek*, which inspects the top element and reports what it is. If you try to peek at or pop an empty stack, you get an *underflow* error.

> Use a stack for last-in-first-out applications, like reviewing the most recent moves of a game.

The Stack<E> Class

Stacks are implemented with the Stack<E> class provided in Java 5.0. Stack<E> is a subclass of Vector<E>, which implements an array that can grow and shrink as needed.

THE Stack<E> CLASS METHODS

Here is the subset of Stack methods that you should know for the AP exam:

Stack()

Constructor: creates an empty stack.

boolean isEmpty()

Returns true if the stack is empty, false otherwise. (There is an equivalent method called empty that will not be used on the AP exam.)

E push(E item)

Pushes item onto the top of the stack. Returns item.

E pop()

Pops the top element off the stack. Returns this element. The method throws an EmptyStackException if an attempt is made to pop an empty stack.

E peek()

Returns the top element of the stack but leaves the stack unchanged. Think of it as a method that takes a peek at the top element and returns to tell what it saw. If, however, it peeks and the stack is empty, an EmptyStackException is thrown.

Example

(Statements are numbered for reference.)

```
1   Stack<String> s = new Stack<String>(); //creates empty stack
2   s.push("A");                    //pushes "A" onto s
3   s.push("sunny");                //pushes "sunny" onto s
4   s.push("day");                  //pushes "day" onto s
5   System.out.println( s.pop());   //removes "day" from stack
6                                   // and prints it
7   System.out.println( s.pop());   //removes "sunny" from stack
8                                   //and prints it
9   String str =  s.peek();         //stores "A" in str
10                                  //and leaves stack unchanged
11  if (s.isEmpty())
12      System.out.println("Empty stack");
13  else
14      System.out.println("Stack not empty, " + str + " on top");
15              //outputs "Stack not empty, A on top"
16  s = new Stack<String>();        //empties s
17  if (s.isEmpty())
18      System.out.println("Empty stack");  //this is output
19  else
20      System.out.println("Stack not empty " + s.peek() + " on top");
```

Here are snapshots of the stack s.

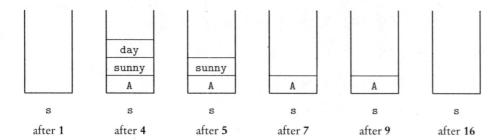

s	s	s	s	s	s
after **1**	after **4**	after **5**	after **7**	after **9**	after **16**

When to Use a Stack

Consider using a stack for any problem that involves backtracking (last in first out). Some examples include retracing steps in a maze and keeping track of nested structures, such as

- Expressions within other expressions.
- Methods that call other methods.
- Traversing directories and subdirectories.

In each case the stack mechanism untangles the nested structure.

Example

Write a method `validParens` to test if a Java expression has valid parentheses. An expression is valid if the number of openers (i.e., left parentheses "`(`") equals the number of enders (right parentheses "`)`"). For example, 3 / (a + (b * 2)) is valid, but (x - (y * (z + 4) is invalid. Note that simply checking if the number of openers equals the number of enders is insufficient: the expression)3 + 4(is not valid. To be valid, each ender must be preceded by a matching opener.

Assume that the expression is a `String` in an `Expression` class. The `validParens` method returns `true` if the parentheses in the `Expression` are valid, `false` otherwise. Here's where the stack comes in. Do a character-by-character processing. If any character substring is an opener, push it onto the stack `s`. If it's an ender and the stack is empty, the expression is invalid since there is no matching opener. If the stack is not empty, however, pop the stack. When the end of the expression is reached, the stack should be empty if the expression is valid.

Suppose that the expression to be examined is (3 + 4 * (5 % 3)). Here is the state of the stack at various stages of the processing:

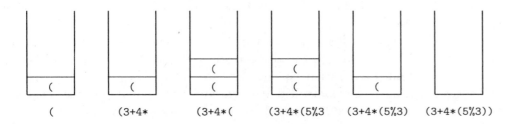

(	(3+4*	(3+4*(	(3+4*(5%3	(3+4*(5%3)	(3+4*(5%3))

Notice that the given expression is valid.

Here is part of an `Expression` class that contains the `validParens` method.

```
/* Tests the validity of an expression */

public class Expression
{
    private String myExpression;
    private final String OPENER = "(";
    private final String ENDER = ")";

    //constructor
    public Expression()
    { /* code to read myExpression */ }

    //Returns true if parentheses valid, false otherwise.
    public boolean validParens()
    {
        Stack<String> s = new Stack<String>();
        for (int i = 0; i < expr.length(); i++)
        {
          String ch = expr.substring(i,i + 1);
          if (ch.equals(OPENER))
            s.push(ch);
          else
            if (ch.equals(ENDER))
                if (s.isEmpty())  //no matching opener
                    return false;
                else
                    s.pop();        //pop matching opener
        }
        return s.isEmpty();       //if false, too many openers
    }

    //other methods not shown
      ...
}
```

QUEUES

What Is a Queue?

Use a queue for first-in-first-out applications, like serving customers in a bank line.

Think of a line of well-behaved people waiting to board a bus. New arrivals go to the back of the line. The first one in line arrived first and is the first to board the bus: first in first out (FIFO).

A *queue* is a sequence of items of the same type in which items are removed at one end, the front, and new items are added at the other end, the back. In theory, there is no limit to the number of items in a queue.

Changes to the queue are controlled by operations *add* (sometimes called *enqueue*) and *remove* (sometimes called *dequeue*). To add an item is to add that item to the *back* of the queue. To remove is to remove an item from the *front* of the queue. If you try to remove from or peek at an empty queue you get an underflow error. As for a stack, an `isEmpty` operation tests for an empty queue, and a `peek` method reports what's at the front.

The `Queue<E>` Interface

The Java Collections Framework contains a queue interface, `Queue<E>`. This interface is implemented with the `LinkedList<E>` class, which can be used for all the standard queue operations.

THE QUEUE METHODS

Here is the AP Java subset of methods that you should know:

```
boolean isEmpty()
```

Returns `true` if the queue is empty, `false` otherwise.

```
boolean add(E item)
```

Inserts `item` at the back of the queue. Returns `true` if `item` successfully added, `false` otherwise.

```
E remove()
```

Removes an element from the front of the queue. Returns this element. The method throws a `NoSuchElementException` if an attempt is made to `remove` from an empty queue.

```
E peek()
```

Returns the front element of the queue, leaving the queue unchanged. The method returns `null` if the queue is empty. (Note that this method is analogous to `peek()` in the `Stack` class. The stack, however, throws an exception for peeking at an empty stack.)

Queue Implementation

On the AP exam, code such as the following will be used:

```
Queue<String> q = new LinkedList<String>();
                        //LinkedList implements Queue
```

Example

(Statements are numbered for reference.)

```
1   Queue<String> q = new LinkedList<String>();  //q is empty
2   String st = "ghijkl";
3   for (int i = 0; i < st.length(); i++)
4       q.add(st.substring(i, i + 1)); //add "g", "h", "i",
5                                      //"j", "k", "l"
6   System.out.println(q);             //prints [g, h, i, j, k, l]
7   for (int i = 1; i < 3; i++)
8       q.remove();                    //remove "g", "h"
9   System.out.println(q);             //prints [i, j, k, l]
10  q.add("r");
11  System.out.println(q);             //prints [i, j, k, l, r]
12  String str = q.peek();             //str contains "i"
```

The state of the queue is shown below. The labels **f** and **b** underneath each figure denote the front and back of the queue.

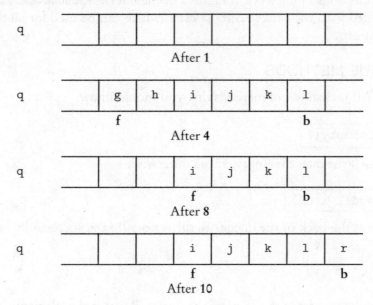

When to Use a Queue

Think of a queue for any problem that involves processing data in the order in which it was entered. Some examples include

- Going back to the beginning and retracing steps.
- Simulating lines—cars waiting at a car wash, people standing in line at a bank, and so on.

Example

Here is a code segment that simulates the redial feature of a telephone. Each digit that is entered is treated as a separate element and placed in a queue. When it's time to redial, the queue is emptied, and the digits are printed in the order that they were entered.

```
/* Simulate redial features of a phone. */
final String PERIOD = ".";
Queue<String> q = new LinkedList<String>();
System.out.println("Enter digits of phone number" +
        " separated by spaces");
System.out.println("Terminate with a space then a period.");
String digit = IO.readString();    //read user input
while (!digit.equals(PERIOD))
{
    q.add(digit);
    digit = IO.readString();       //read user input
}
System.out.println();
System.out.println("The number dialed was: ");
while (!q.isEmpty())
{
    System.out.print(q.remove());
}
```

PRIORITY QUEUES

What Is a Priority Queue?

A *priority queue* is a collection of items of the same type, each of which contains a data field and a priority. Items are ordered by priority, in the sense that items with the highest priority are removed first. The head of a priority queue is the *least* element with respect to its ordering. This means that elements in a priority queue must be `Comparable`, with the smallest element having the highest priority. A priority queue does not allow insertion of `null` elements.

> Use a priority queue when removal of items depends only on item priority, not on order of insertion.

The `PriorityQueue<E>` Class

Priority queues are implemented with the `PriorityQueue<E>` class provided in Java 5.0. The `PriorityQueue<E>` class is implemented with a heap (see #5 in Implementation of a Priority Queue, below).

THE `PriorityQueue<E>` CLASS METHODS

Here is the subset of `PriorityQueue` class methods that you should know.

`PriorityQueue()`

Constructor: Creates a priority queue with default initial capacity.

`boolean isEmpty()`

Returns `true` if the priority queue is empty, `false` otherwise.

`boolean add(E item)`

Adds `item` to the priority queue and returns `true`. Throws a `NullPointerException` if `item` is `null`. Throws a `ClassCastException` if `item` cannot be compared to items in the priority queue.

`E remove()`

Removes and returns the item at the head of the priority queue. This is the least element, the one with the highest priority. If an attempt is made to remove an item from an empty priority queue, `remove` throws a `NoSuchElementException`.

`E peek()`

Returns, but does not remove, the smallest item in the priority queue. The method returns `null` if the priority queue is empty.

Implementation of a Priority Queue

You are not expected to be familiar with the black box code in the `PriorityQueue` class. You should, however, understand the following general principles about implementing a priority queue.

The data structure selected for a priority queue should allow for

- Rapid insertion of elements that arrive in arbitrary order.
- Rapid retrieval of the element with highest priority.

Some possible data structures for a priority queue follow:

1. A linear linked list with elements in random order. Insertion is done at the front of the list, $O(1)$. Deletion requires a linear search for the element with highest priority, $O(n)$.
2. A linear linked list with elements sorted by priority, smallest elements in front. Deletion means removal of the first node, $O(1)$. Insertion requires a linear scan to find the insertion point, $O(n)$.
3. An array with elements in random order. Insertion is done at the end of the list, $O(1)$. Deletion requires a linear search, $O(n)$.
4. An array with elements sorted by priority, smallest elements at the end. Deletion means removing the last element in the array, $O(1)$. Insertion requires finding the insertion point and then creating a slot by moving array elements—$O(n)$ irrespective of the type of search.
5. The classic data structure for a priority queue: a *binary heap*. (See Chapter 12 for a description of a heap and an array representation of a heap.) For a priority queue, a *minimum heap* is used. The value in every node is less than or equal to the value in each of its children. For example,

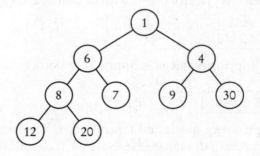

The numbers in the heap represent the *priorities* of the elements. (The lower the number, the higher the priority.) Notice that the element with the highest priority is kept in the root of the tree. Deleting an element means removing the root element, then restoring the heap ("reheaping"), which is $O(\log n)$. Insertion of an element also requires reheaping, $O(\log n)$. To peek at the least element means to report the root value: $O(1)$.

When to Use a Priority Queue

Think of using a priority queue in any problem where elements enter in a random order but are removed according to their priority. For example,

- A database of patients awaiting liver transplants, where the sickest patients have the highest priority.
- Scheduling events. Events are generated in random order and each event has a time stamp denoting when the event will occur. The scheduler retrieves the events in the order they will occur.

Example

Here is a program that illustrates how a priority queue may be used. Imagine that patients awaiting an organ transplant are placed on a list. When an organ becomes available, the patient with the highest priority is contacted.

```java
public class Patient implements Comparable
{
    private String myName;
    private int myPriority;

    public Patient(String name, int priority)
    {
        myName = name;
        myPriority = priority;
    }

    public int compareTo(Object o)
    {
        Patient rhs = (Patient) o;
        if (myPriority < rhs.myPriority)
            return -1;
        else if (myPriority > rhs.myPriority)
            return 1;
        else
            return 0;
    }

    public String toString()
    {
        String s = myName + " with priority " + myPriority;
        return s;
    }
}

/* Illustrates priority queue. */

public class PriQueueTest
{
    public static void main(String args[])
    {
        PriorityQueue<Patient> pq = new PriorityQueue<Patient>();
        Patient p1 = new Patient("John Smith", 3);
        Patient p2 = new Patient("Mary Jones", 1);
        Patient p3 = new Patient("Kathy Gibb", 2);
        pq.add(p1);
        pq.add(p2);
        pq.add(p3);

        while (!pq.isEmpty())
        {
          System.out.println("The next patient for liver" +
                " transplant is ");
          System.out.println(pq.remove());
        }
    }
}
```

The output for this program is

```
The next patient for liver transplant is
Mary Jones with priority 1
The next patient for liver transplant is
Kathy Gibb with priority 2
The next patient for liver transplant is
John Smith with priority 3
```

RUN TIME OF STACK, QUEUE, AND PRIORITY QUEUE OPERATIONS

In each case, assume n elements and the following implementations:

- Stack s: an array with sufficient slots.
- Queue q: a doubly linked list (DLL) with reference at each end.
- Priority queue pq: a minimum heap.

Algorithm	Stack (Array)	Queue (DLL)	Priority Queue (Min-heap)	Comment
Insert element	push(x) $O(1)$	add(x) $O(1)$	add(x) $O(\log n)$	s: Insert at end of array. q: Simple pointer adjustment at end of LL. pq: Fix the heap after insertion.
Remove element	pop() $O(1)$	remove() $O(1)$	remove() $O(\log n)$	s: Remove at end of array. q: Pointer adjustment at front of LL. pq: Remove root element of heap. Fix heap.
Peek	peek() $O(1)$	peek() $O(1)$	peek() $O(1)$	s: $O(1)$ access to any array element: top of stack = last element in array. q: $O(1)$ access to first element in LL, front of q. pq: $O(1)$ access to root node in heap, the least element.

Chapter Summary

Be familiar with the differences between stacks, queues, and priority queues, and the types of applications for which each data structure is suitable.

You must also be able to use the standard Java classes Stack<E>, Queue<E>, and PriorityQueue<E> to implement stacks, queues, and priority queues. Know how to call each method associated with each data structure. You must also know the big-O run time for each of these methods.

MULTIPLE-CHOICE QUESTIONS ON STACKS AND QUEUES

Assume that stacks are implemented with the Stack<E> class (p. 404), and queues with the Queue<E> interface and LinkedList<E> class (p. 407).

1. A stack s of strings contains "Stan", "Nan", "Fran", "Jan", "Dan" in the order given, with "Stan" on top. What will be output by the following code segment?

    ```
    while (s.peek().length() % 2 == 0)
    {
        String str = s.pop();
        System.out.print(s.peek());
    }
    ```

    (A) Stan
    (B) Nan
    (C) Fran
    (D) StanNan
    (E) NanFran

2. What is the output from the following code segment?

    ```
    Stack<String> s = new Stack<String>();
    String str = "cat";
    for (int i = 0; i < str.length(); i++)
        s.push(str.substring(i));
    while (!s.isEmpty())
        System.out.print(s.pop());
    ```

    (A) catatt
    (B) tac
    (C) ttatac
    (D) tatcat
    (E) cattat

3. Assume these declarations:

    ```
    Queue<SomeClass> q = new LinkedList<SomeClass>();
                               //LinkedList implements Queue
    SomeClass obj;
    ```

    If q is initialized, which of the following code segments will correctly access the
    elements of q and leave q unchanged? You may assume that the access method
    does not change the SomeClass objects.

    ```
     I  Queue<SomeClass> temp = new LinkedList<SomeClass>();
        while (!q.isEmpty())
        {
            obj = q.remove();
            obj.access();
            temp.add(obj);
        }
        q = temp;

    II  while (!q.isEmpty())
        {
            obj = q.remove();
            obj.access();
            q.add(obj);
        }

   III  Queue<SomeClass> temp = q;
        while (!temp.isEmpty())
        {
            obj = temp.remove();
            obj.access();
        }
    ```

    (A) I only
    (B) II only
    (C) III only
    (D) I and III only
    (E) II and III only

4. Consider the following sequence of statements:

```
Queue<String> q = new LinkedList<String>();
                        //LinkedList implements Queue
String str1 = "ab", str2 = "cd", str3 = "ef";

q.add(str1);
q.add(str2);
q.add(str3);
str1 = str3.substring(0, 1);
str2 = q.remove();
q.add(str1);
q.add(str2);
str2 = str1;
q.add(str2);
while (!q.isEmpty())
    System.out.print(q.remove());
```

What output will be produced?
(A) abcdeefe
(B) abcdefefabef
(C) abcdefeabe
(D) cdefeabe
(E) cdefefabef

5. Suppose that a queue q contains the Integer values 1, 2, 3, 4, 5, 6 in that order, with 1 at the front of q. Suppose that there are just three operations that can be performed using only one stack, s.

(i) Remove x from q then print x.
(ii) Remove x from q then push x onto s.
(iii) Pop x from s then print x.

Which of the following is not a possible output list using just these operations?
(A) 123456
(B) 654321
(C) 234561
(D) 125643
(E) 345612

6. Let `intStack` be a stack of `Integer` values and `opStack` be a character stack of arithmetic operators, where each operator is a single-character `String`. A method `doOperation()` exists that

    (i)   Pops two values from `intStack`.
    (ii) Pops an operator from `opStack`.
    (iii) Performs the operation.
    (iv) Pushes the result onto `intStack`.

    Assume that the `Integer` values 5, 8, 3, and 2 are pushed onto `intStack` in that order (2 pushed last), and "*", "-", and "+" are pushed onto `opStack` in that order ("+" pushed last). The `doOperation()` method is invoked three times. The top of `intStack` contains the result of evaluating which expression?
    (A) $((2*3)-8)+5$
    (B) $((2+3)-5)*8$
    (C) $((2+3)-8)*5$
    (D) $((5*8)-3)+2$
    (E) $((5+8)-3)*2$

7. Suppose that `s` and `t` are both stacks of type `T` and that `x` is a variable of type `T`. Assume that `s` initially contains n elements, where n is large, and that `t` is initially empty. Assume further that `length(s)` gives the number of elements in `s`. Which is true after execution of the following code segment?

    ```
    int len = length(s) - 2;
    for (int i = 1; i <= len; i++)
    {
        x = s.pop();
        t.push(x);
    }
    len = length(s) - 2;
    for (int i = 1; i <= len; i++)
    {
        x = t.pop();
        s.push(x);
    }
    ```

    (A) `s` is unchanged, and `x` equals the third item from the bottom of `s`.
    (B) `s` is unchanged, and `x` equals `s.peek()`.
    (C) `s` contains two elements, and `x` equals `s.peek()`.
    (D) `s` contains two elements, and `x` equals the bottom element of `s`.
    (E) `s` contains two elements, and `x` equals `t.peek()`.

8. Refer to the following program segment:

```
Queue<Integer> q = new LinkedList<Integer>();
                        //LinkedList implements Queue
Integer x;
for (int i = 1; i < 6; i++)
    q.add(new Integer(i * i));
while (!q.isEmpty())
{
    if (q.peek().intValue() % 2 == 0)
    {
        System.out.print(q.peek() + " ");
        x = q.remove();
    }
    else
    {
        x = q.remove();
        q.add(x);
    }
}
```

Which will be true after this segment is executed?

(A) 4 16 has been printed, and the queue contains 1 9 25, with 1 at the front and 25 at the back.

(B) 16 4 has been printed, and the queue contains 1 9 25, with 1 at the front and 25 at the back.

(C) 1 4 9 16 25 has been printed, and the queue is empty.

(D) 4 16 has been printed, and the segment continues to run without termination.

(E) 4 16 4 16 4 16 ... has been printed, and the segment continues to run without termination.

9. Consider a stack `s` and queue `q` of integers. What must be true following execution of this code segment?

```
q = new LinkedList<Integer>();
s = new Stack<Integer>();
Integer x;
for (int i = 1; i <= 4; i++)
    s.push(new Integer(i));
for (int i = 1; i <= 4; i++)
{
    x = s.pop();
    if (x.intValue() % 2 == 0)
        q.add(x);
    else
    {
        x = q.remove();
        s.push(x);
    }
}
```

(A) 2 is at the back of q.
(B) `s.peek()` is 2.
(C) s is empty.
(D) q is empty.
(E) An error has occurred.

Consider the following code segment for Questions 10 and 11.

```
Stack<String> s = new Stack<String>();
String str = "racketeer";
for (int i = 0; i < str.length(); i++)
    s.push(str.substring(i, i + 1));
for (int i = 0; i < str.length(); i++)
{
    String ch = str.substring(i, i + 1);
    if (isVowel(ch))   //test if ch is a lowercase vowel,
                       //"a", "e", "i", "o", or "u"
    {
        System.out.print(s.pop());
    }
    else
        s.push(ch);
}
```

10. What output will be produced by the segment?
(A) `aeee`
(B) `eeea`
(C) `ctkr`
(D) `rktc`
(E) `rkct`

11. Suppose the segment is modified to omit the first `for` loop, in which the letters of `str` are pushed onto stack `s`. Additionally, string `str` is assigned to be a random string of lowercase letters. Under which circumstances will the code cause an `EmptyStackException`?

    I Whenever `str` starts with a consonant.

    II Whenever `str` starts with a vowel.

    III Whenever the number of vowels in `str` exceeds the number of consonants.

(A) I only
(B) II only
(C) III only
(D) II and III only
(E) I, II, and III

12. Methods `add(s)` and `multiply(s)` do the following to a stack `s` when invoked:

    The stack is popped twice.
    The two popped items are added or multiplied accordingly.
    The `Integer` result is pushed onto the stack.

What will stack `s` contain following execution of the following code segment?

```
int x = 3, y = 5, z = 7, w = 9;
s.push(new Integer(x));
s.push(new Integer(y));
add(s);
s.push(new Integer(w));
s.push(new Integer(z));
multiply(s);
add(s);
```

(A) Nothing
(B) 31
(C) 71
(D) 78
(E) 128

13. Assume that

- Linked lists are implemented with the `ListNode` class (p. 364).
- Stack s and queue q are initially empty and have been declared to hold objects of the same type as the linked list.
- Objects in the linked list have a `toString` method.

Refer to the following method, `reverse`:

```
/* Precondition:  first refers to the first node of a linear
 *                linked list.
 * Postcondition: List elements printed in reverse order.  */
public void reverse(ListNode first)
{
    /* code */
}
```

Which /* *code* */ will successfully achieve the postcondition of reverse?

```
I   if (first != null)
    {
        System.out.print(first.getValue() + " ");
        reverse(first.getNext());
    }
```

```
II  while (first != null)
    {
        s.push(first.getValue());
        first = first.getNext();
    }
    while (!s.isEmpty())
        System.out.print(s.pop() + " ");
```

```
III while (first != null)
    {
        q.add(first.getValue());
        first = first.getNext();
    }
    while (!q.isEmpty())
        System.out.print(q.remove() + " ");
```

(A) I only
(B) II only
(C) III only
(D) I and II only
(E) I and III only

14. Suppose the `Stack` class added another pop method, one that changes the stack but does not return the object that's being removed:

    ```
    public void pop(E item)    //remove top item without saving it
    ```

    This is an example of
    (A) polymorphism.
    (B) method overriding.
    (C) method overloading.
    (D) a helper method.
    (E) a `NoSuchElementException`.

15. Suppose stacks are implemented with a linear linked list that has just one private instance variable, `firstNode`, which refers to the first element of the list:

    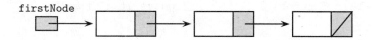

    In the diagram, `firstNode` points to the top of the stack. Which of the following correctly gives the run time of (1) push and (2) pop in this implementation?

    (A)   (1) $O(1)$ (2) $O(1)$

    (B)   (1) $O(1)$ (2) $O(n)$

    (C)   (1) $O(n)$ (2) $O(1)$

    (D)   (1) $O(n)$ (2) $O(n)$

    (E)   (1) $O(\log n)$ (2) $O(1)$

16. Which of the following is true of a priority queue?
    (A) If elements are inserted in increasing order of priority (i.e., lowest priority element inserted first), and all elements are inserted before any are removed, it works like a queue.
    (B) If elements are inserted in increasing order of priority (i.e., lowest priority element inserted first), and all elements are inserted before any are removed, it works like a stack.
    (C) If all elements are inserted before any are removed, it works like a queue.
    (D) If elements are inserted in decreasing order of priority (i.e., highest priority element inserted first), and all elements are inserted before any are removed, it works like a stack.
    (E) If elements are inserted in increasing order of priority, then it works like a queue whether or not all insertions precede any removals.

Questions 17–19 refer to the following interface and class definition. You may assume that type T is Comparable.

```
public interface Container<T>
{
    void insert(T x);    //insert x into Container
    T remove();          //remove item from Container
}

public class C<T> implements Container<T>
{
    public C()           //constructor
    { ...

    public void insert(T x)    //insert x into C
    { ...

    public T remove()          //remove item from C
    { ...

    //appropriate private instance variables to implement C
        ...
}
```

Here is a program segment that uses class C above:

```
Container<String> words = new C<String>();
String w1 = "Tom";
String w2 = "Dick";
String w3 = "Harry";
String w4 = "Moe";
words.insert(w1);
words.insert(w2);
words.insert(w3);
words.insert(w4);
String str = words.remove();
str = words.remove();
System.out.println(str);
```

17. What will the output be if C is a stack?
    (A) Tom
    (B) Dick
    (C) Harry
    (D) Moe
    (E) There is insufficient information to determine the output.

18. What will the output be if C is a queue?
    (A) Tom
    (B) Dick
    (C) Harry
    (D) Moe
    (E) There is insufficient information to determine the output.

19. What will the output be if C is a priority queue? You may assume that priorities are assigned using the fact that items are `Comparable`.
    (A) `Tom`
    (B) `Dick`
    (C) `Harry`
    (D) `Moe`
    (E) There is insufficient information to determine the output.

20. In the package `java.util`, the `Stack<E>` class extends Java's `Vector<E>` class. Thus, `Stack` inherits all the methods of `Vector`. Here are three of the methods that `Stack` inherits:

    I `void add(int i, E x)` //insert x into stack at index i

    II `E get(int i)`   //return element at index i
                             //leave stack unchanged

    III `E remove(int i)`   //remove element at index i from stack

    Which of these methods are *not* consistent with the definition of a stack?
    (A) I only
    (B) II only
    (C) III only
    (D) II and III only
    (E) I, II, and III

21. Refer to the following declaration:

    ```
    PriorityQueue<Integer> pq = new PriorityQueue<Integer>();
    ```

    The elements of the priority queue pq will be `Integer` values. These values will also represent the priorities of the items: smallest value = *highest* priority. Assuming that the code works as intended, what output will be produced by the following segment?

    ```
    pq.add(new Integer(4));
    pq.add(new Integer(1));
    pq.add(new Integer(3));
    pq.add(new Integer(2));
    pq.add(new Integer(5));
    while (!pq.isEmpty())
        System.out.print(pq.remove());
    ```

    (A) `54321`
    (B) `41325`
    (C) `12345`
    (D) `52314`
    (E) `11111`

22. Consider the following client method for the Stack class:

```
/* Precondition:  Stack s is defined.
 * Postcondition: Returns the bottom element of s.
 *                s remains unchanged.  */
public ItemType bottom(Stack<ItemType> s)
{
    /* code */
}
```

Which replacements for /* *code* */ will achieve the required postcondition?

```
I  ItemType item;
   while (!s.isEmpty())
       item = s.pop();
   return item;

II ItemType item;
   Stack<ItemType> t = s;
   while (!t.isEmpty())
       item = t.pop();
   return item;

III ItemType item;
    Stack<ItemType> t = new Stack<ItemType>();
    while (!s.isEmpty())
        t.push(s.pop());
    item = t.peek();
    while (!t.isEmpty())
        s.push(t.pop());
    return item;
```

(A) I only
(B) II only
(C) III only
(D) I and II only
(E) I and III only

23. Consider the following programming assignments:

    I Maintain a waiting list for reservations at a hotel. Rooms are assigned on a first-come, first-served basis.

    II Maintain a list of violin players who auditioned for a major orchestra. The players were ranked during their auditions, and the top-ranked player will get offered any job that opens up.

    III Attempt to find an escape route for a mouse in a maze. The mouse should be able to retrace its steps while attempting to escape.

    IV Store the moves in a chess game. The program should allow a user to view the game later on.

    In applications I and II, the programmer must select a suitable data structure for storing the names of people. For III and IV, moves must be stored. Select the best choice of data structures for each application.

    (A) I priority queue II priority queue III array   IV queue
    (B) I priority queue II priority queue III priority queue IV stack
    (C) I queue   II priority queue III stack   IV queue
    (D) I stack   II queue   III queue   IV stack
    (E) I queue   II queue   III stack   IV priority queue

ANSWER KEY

1. B	9. A	17. C
2. D	10. D	18. B
3. A	11. D	19. C
4. D	12. C	20. E
5. E	13. B	21. C
6. C	14. C	22. C
7. E	15. A	23. C
8. D	16. B	

ANSWERS EXPLAINED

1. **(B)** When "Stan" is s.peek(), it passes the while test (having an even number of characters) and gets popped. The current s.peek() is then "Nan", which gets printed. Now the test fails on "Nan", and the while loop is not executed again.

2. **(D)** Here is the stack after the for loop has been executed:

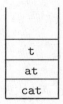

(Recall that str.substring(i) returns the substring of str starting at the *i*th position of str and extending to the end of the string.) The while loop pops and prints "t", then "at", then "cat", resulting in "tatcat".

3. **(A)** Placing the elements in a temporary queue works because the elements will have the same order as in the original queue. Segment II seems to have a fine idea—take an element out of q, access it, and then insert it back. Trouble is, the while loop will be infinite since q will never be empty! Segment III fails because temp is not a separate queue: It refers to the same queue as q. Any changes made to temp will therefore change q.

4. **(D)** Here is the state of the queue just before it is emptied:

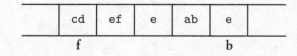

The queue is a first-in-first-out structure, which means that elements are removed in the order they were inserted, from front to back as shown.

5. **(E)** For 3456 to have been printed means that 1 and 2 were removed and pushed onto s in that order. The order of printing would then have to be 21, not 12. Note that this means that 345621 would have been OK.

6. **(C)** The first call to doOperation() pops 2 and 3, pops +, and pushes 5, the result. The second call pops 5 and 8, pops -, and pushes -3. The third call pops -3 and 5, pops *, and pushes -15. The expression in C is the only choice that evaluates to -15.

   Alternatively, work from the inside out:

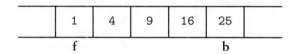

$$
\begin{aligned}
\text{pop 2, 3, and } + &\quad\rightarrow\quad (2+3) \\
\text{pop } (2+3),\ 8,\ \text{and } - &\quad\rightarrow\quad ((2+3)-8) \\
\text{pop } ((2+3)-8),\ 5,\ \text{and } * &\quad\rightarrow\quad ((2+3)-8)*5)
\end{aligned}
$$

7. **(E)** The first `for` loop removes the top `length(s)` - 2 elements from s, leaving two elements. Therefore, `length(s)` equals 2. Also, x currently equals the top element of t, `t.peek()`. The second `for` loop is for i equals 1 to 0, so nothing is done in this loop! This leaves s with two elements, and x equal to `t.peek()`.

8. **(D)** Here is q initially:

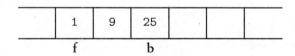

1 fails the test, is removed from the front, and is inserted at the back of the queue.
4 passes the test and is printed and removed.
9 fails and is removed and inserted at the back.
16 passes and is printed and removed.
25 fails and is removed and inserted at the back.
q now looks like this:

None of the elements in the queue will now pass the `if` test, which means that there will be an infinite sequence of removals and insertions in q. The `while` loop never terminates.

9. **(A)** Initially s contains 1, 2, 3, 4 with 4 on top. Here is the state of s and q after each pass through the second `for` loop:

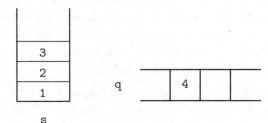

After 1st pass

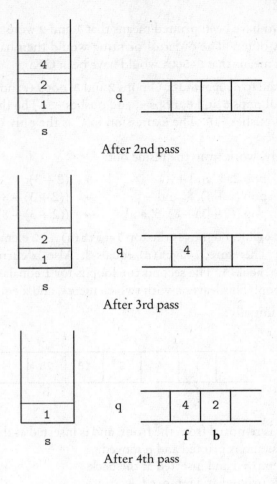

After 2nd pass

After 3rd pass

After 4th pass

10. **(D)** Initially, each letter in `"racketeer"` is pushed onto the stack (first `for` loop). Here's what happens for each letter of the word (second `for` loop):

   r: r pushed onto stack
   a: stack popped and <u>r</u> printed
   c: c pushed onto stack
   k: k pushed onto stack
   e: stack popped and <u>k</u> printed
   t: t pushed onto stack
   e: stack popped and <u>t</u> printed
   e: stack popped and <u>c</u> printed
   r: r pushed onto stack

11. **(D)** Notice that every time a vowel is encountered, the stack is popped. Therefore, if the stack is initially empty, condition II will cause an immediate failure. Condition III will cause an eventual failure, when all consonants have been popped and another vowel is encountered. Notice that condition I will not cause a failure provided there's a consonant on the stack every time a vowel is reached in `str`. Thus, `"lap"` will work, but `"leap"` will not.

12. **(C)** After the first call to `add(s)`, the stack will contain 8. After the call to `multiply(s)`, it will contain 63 (on top), then 8. Therefore, after the second `add(s)`, it will contain 71.

13. **(B)** Remember that a stack is a last-in-first-out structure, which means that ele-

ments placed in it are retrieved in reverse order. So segment II is correct. A queue is a first-in-first-out structure, so the elements will be printed in the order they were received. Thus, segment III is wrong. Segment I would be correct if the print and reverse statements were interchanged. As it is, an element is printed *before* the recursive call, which means that elements will be printed out in the given order rather than being reversed.

14. **(C)** Two (or more) forms of the same method in a given class is an example of method overloading. The compiler distinguishes the methods by matching parameter types. Note that the item parameter is necessary; otherwise, the two pop methods would have the same signature, and the compiler could not distinguish them. The return type is not part of the signature.

15. **(A)** Simple pointer adjustments independent of the number of nodes achieve both push and pop, making them both $O(1)$:

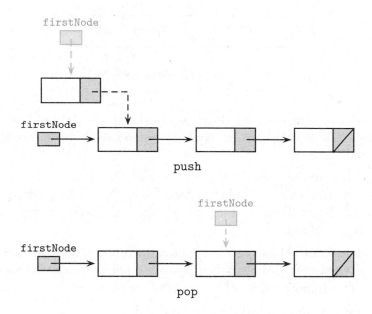

16. **(B)** If elements are inserted in increasing order of priority, the last one in will have top priority and will be the first one out, and so on. Thus, the priority queue will work just like a stack. Choice C would be correct only if the elements were inserted in decreasing order of priority, since the first one in would then be the first one out. Choice D is wrong because the first element entered (top priority) would have to be the first one out—not a stack! Choices A and E are both wrong because higher priority elements would land at the back of the queue. Removing these would violate the first-in-first-out property of a queue.

17. **(C)** Here is the stack:

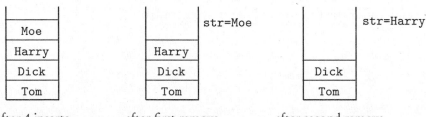

after 4 inserts   after first remove   after second remove

18. **(B)** Here is the queue:

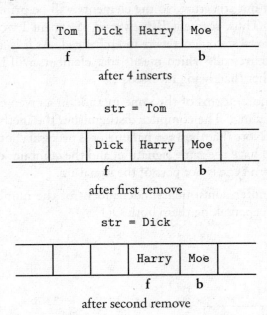

after 4 inserts

str = Tom

after first remove

str = Dick

after second remove

19. **(C)** For type `String`, the ordering of priorities is alphabetical. Thus, the first `remove` call removes `"Dick"`, and the second removes `"Harry"`, which is then printed.

20. **(E)** None of these methods are valid stack operations! Method I violates the principle that a value should be added to a stack only by pushing it onto the top. Methods II and III violate the principle that only the top element is accessible for peeking and removal.

21. **(C)** The smaller the integer, the higher the priority. Elements are deleted from a priority queue according to their priority number, highest priority (lowest value) first. This is independent of the order of the insertion.

22. **(C)** Suppose the original stack looks like this:

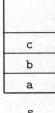

s

You will need a temporary stack to access the bottom element. Here are stacks s and t after the first `while` loop in segment III:

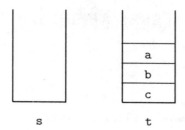

Notice that the required item, a, is now at the top of t. The second `while` loop restores s to its original state.

Segment I returns the correct item, but leaves s with no elements. Even though s is passed by value and the reference s remains unchanged, this doesn't protect the *contents* of s. Segment II also returns the correct element but leaves s with no elements. Assigning t to s means that any changes made to t will also be made to s.

23. **(C)** Application I: "First-come, first-served" is a classic queue situation. The first name in the queue is the first one out.

Application II: Players are ranked, and will be removed from the list according to their ranking or priority. They should therefore be stored in a priority queue.

Application III: "Retracing steps" is that phrase that tells you to store the moves in a stack. The last move in will be first move out.

Application IV: To replay a game means to retrieve the moves in the order in which they were stored—a classic queue.

Trees

TREE: A tall vegetable...
—*Ambrose Bierce,* The Devil's Dictionary *(1911)*

Chapter Goals

- Binary trees
- The TreeNode class
- Binary search trees
- Tree traversals

- Recursive tree algorithms
- Binary expression trees
- Run time of binary search tree algorithms

In arrays and matrices, there is a certain equality to the elements, with easy and speedy access to any given element. A tree, on the other hand, is a hierarchy in the way it represents data, with some elements "higher" and easier to access than others. A tree is also a structure that allows branching.

BINARY TREES

Definitions

A *binary tree* is a finite set of elements that is either empty or contains a single element called the *root*, and whose remaining elements are partitioned into two disjoint subsets. Each subset is itself a binary tree, called the left or right *subtree* of the original tree.

Binary trees are often represented schematically as shown below.

Here is some vocabulary you should know:

- A is the *root* of the tree. B and C are the roots of the left and right subtrees of A, and so on down the tree.

- Each element is a *node* of the tree. The tree shown has nine nodes.

- Any node whose left and right subtrees are empty is called a *leaf*. Thus D, G, H, and I are leaves.

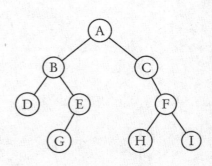

432

- Note the following family relationships among nodes. A is the *parent* of B and C. B and C are the *children* of A, called the left and right child, respectively. C has no left child, just a right child, F. A leaf is a node with no children.

- Any node that occurs in a subtree of node k is a *descendant* of k. Thus, every node except A is a descendant of A. Node I is a descendant of C but not of B.

- If node k is a descendant of node j, then j is an *ancestor* of node k. Thus, B is an ancestor of D, E, and G, but not of F, H, and I.

- The *depth* of a node is the length of the path (or number of edges) from the root to that node. Thus, the depth of A is 0, of B is 1, and of H and I is 3.

- The *level of a node* is equal to its depth. Thus, nodes D, E, and F are all at level 2. The *level of a tree* is equal to the level of its deepest leaf. Thus, the level of the tree shown is 3.

- The *height* of a tree is the maximum distance of any leaf from the root. The height is defined to be 0 for a single node tree. The height of the tree shown on the previous page is 3.

- A *balanced tree* has approximately the same number of nodes in the left and right subtrees at each level. The tree on the previous page is balanced.

- A *perfect binary tree* has every leaf on the same level; and every nonleaf node has two children.

- A *complete binary tree* is either perfect or perfect through the next-to-last level, with the leaves as far left as possible in the last level.

NOTE

Textbooks vary in their definitions of tree features. Any question on the AP exam that requires you to use an attribute of a tree will provide the definition.

Implementation of Binary Trees

A binary tree can be implemented in Java using a `TreeNode` class for the nodes and a `BinaryTree` class for the tree.

The TreeNode Class

A `TreeNode` class similar to the following will be provided on the AP exam.[1]

```
/* TreeNode class for the AP exam */
public class TreeNode
{
    private Object value;
    private TreeNode left, right;
```

---

[1]Based on the College Board's *AP Computer Science AB: Implementation Classes for Linked Lists and Tree Nodes*.

```
    public TreeNode(Object initValue)
    {
        value = initValue;
        left = null;
        right = null;
    }

    public TreeNode(Object initValue, TreeNode initLeft,
        TreeNode initRight)
    {
        value = initValue;
        left = initLeft;
        right = initRight;
    }

    public Object getValue()
    { return value; }

    public TreeNode getLeft()
    { return left; }

    public TreeNode getRight()
    { return right; }

    public void setValue(Object theNewValue)
    { value = theNewValue; }

    public void setLeft(TreeNode theNewLeft)
    { left = theNewLeft; }

    public void setRight(TreeNode theNewRight)
    { right = theNewRight; }
}
```

THE INSTANCE VARIABLES

```
private Object value
```

This is exactly like the data field of a `ListNode`. Primitive types like `int` or `double` will first be auto-boxed.

```
private TreeNode left, right
```

Like the `ListNode` class, the `TreeNode` class is self-referential. The variables `left` and `right` for any given `TreeNode` are pointers to the left and right subtrees of that node.

THE METHODS

```
public TreeNode(Object initValue)
public TreeNode(Object initValue, TreeNode initLeft,
    TreeNode initRight)
```

These constructors initialize `value` to `initValue`. The variables `left` and `right` are initialized to `null` in the first constructor and to `initLeft` and `initRight` in the second.

```
public Object getValue()
```

This is an accessor method that returns the value of the current `TreeNode`. You may need to cast this value to `Integer`, `Double`, or `String`, and so on, unless you plan to assign it to a variable of type `Object`.

```
public TreeNode getLeft()
public TreeNode getRight()
```

These are accessor methods that return `left` or `right`, the left or right pointer of the current `TreeNode`.

```
public void setValue(Object theNewValue)
```

This is a mutator method that changes the current `value` of `TreeNode` to `theNewValue`.

```
public void setLeft(TreeNode theNewLeft)
public void setRight(TreeNode theNewRight)
```

These are mutator methods that change the `left` or `right` field of the current `TreeNode` to `theNewLeft` or `theNewRight`.

A BinaryTree Class

To represent a binary tree, it makes sense to have an abstract class, since searching and insertion methods depend on the type of binary tree. Notice that these methods are declared `abstract` in the `BinaryTree` class below. A `BinarySearchTree` class, which is derived from `BinaryTree`, is shown on the next page. Implementations for `insert` and `find` are provided in that class.

Here is the abstract superclass, `BinaryTree`.

```
public abstract class BinaryTree
{
    private TreeNode root;

    public BinaryTree()
    { root = null; }

    public TreeNode getRoot()
    { return root; }

    public void setRoot(TreeNode theNewNode)
    { root = theNewNode; }

    public boolean isEmpty()
    { return root == null; }

    public abstract void insert(Comparable item);

    public abstract TreeNode find(Comparable key);
}
```

NOTE

1. A binary tree class will not be provided on the AP exam, but you are expected to know how to implement binary trees.
2. The class shown here is not generic (has no type parameter).

BINARY SEARCH TREES

A *binary search tree* is a binary tree that stores elements in an ordered way that makes it efficient to find a given element and easy to access the elements in sorted order. The ordering property is conventional. The following definition of a binary search tree gives the ordering property used most often.

A binary search tree is either empty or has just one node, the root, with left and right subtrees that are binary search trees. Each node has the property that all nodes in its left subtree are less than it, and all nodes in its right subtree are greater than or equal to it. This is a binary search tree that allows duplicates. Some do not.

Here is an example:

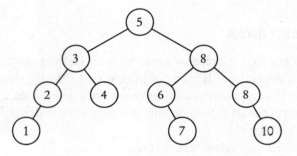

A BinarySearchTree Class

The class shown below is a subclass of the abstract `BinaryTree` class given on the previous page.

```
public class BinarySearchTree extends BinaryTree
{
    //Insert item in BinarySearchTree.
    public void insert(Comparable item)
    { /* implementation code on the next page */ }

    //Returns TreeNode with key.
    //If key not in tree, returns null.
    public TreeNode find(Comparable key)
    { /* implementation code on p. 439 */ }
}
```

NOTE

1. Only the abstract methods of the `BinaryTree` class, insert and find, are provided in the `BinarySearchTree` class. All the other methods of `BinaryTree`, namely `getRoot`, `setRoot`, and `isEmpty`, are inherited.

2. No constructor is provided in `BinarySearchTree`, which means that the compiler will provide the default constructor of the `BinaryTree` superclass:

```
public BinarySearchTree()
{ super(); }      //initializes root to null.
```

3. The `getRoot` and `setRoot` methods in `BinarySearchTree` are used to access the private instance variable `root` of the superclass.
4. The parameters of both `insert` and `find` need to be `Comparable`, since the methods require you to compare objects.

Inserting an Element into a Binary Search Tree

INSERTION ALGORITHM

Suppose that you wish to insert the element 9 into the preceding tree. Start by comparing with the root:

    9 > 5, go right
    9 > 8, go right
    9 > 8, go right
    9 < 10, insert to left of 10

Here is the resulting binary search tree.

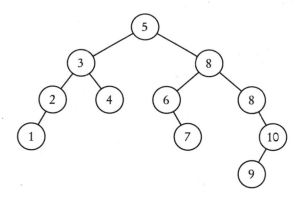

An algorithm for inserting an element uses two `TreeNode` pointers, p and q, say, following each other to find the insertion point. The "front" pointer q is like a kamikaze pilot plunging downward until it is `null`, at which point p points to the node at which the new data will be attached. A simple comparison tells whether the new node goes left or right.

THE `insert` METHOD

Here is the `insert` method for the `BinarySearchTree` class:

```
//Insert item in BinarySearchTree.
public void insert(Comparable item)
{
    if (getRoot() == null)
        setRoot(new TreeNode(item));
```

```
        else
        {
            TreeNode p = null, q = getRoot();
            while (q != null)
            {
                p = q;
                if (item.compareTo(p.getValue()) < 0)
                    q = p.getLeft();
                else
                    q = p.getRight();
            }
            if (item.compareTo(p.getValue()) < 0)
                p.setLeft(new TreeNode(item));
            else
                p.setRight(new TreeNode(item));
        }
    }
```

RUN-TIME ANALYSIS

To insert a single element in an existing binary search tree of n elements:

> A balanced binary search tree leads to efficient algorithms for insertion and searching.

1. Balanced tree: Insertion will require at most one comparison per level (i.e., no more than $\log_2 n$ comparisons). Thus, the algorithm is $O(\log n)$.
2. Unbalanced tree: As many as n comparisons may be required if the tree consists of a long chain of children. Thus, the algorithm is $O(n)$ in the worst case. For example,

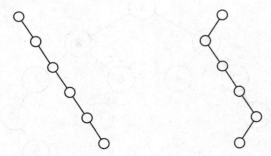

NOTE

See p. 445 for a recursive version of `insert`.

Finding a Target Element in a Binary Search Tree

The special ordering property of a binary search tree allows for quick and easy searching for any given element. If the target is less than the current node value, go left, otherwise go right.

The following method returns a `TreeNode` with the key value. It returns `null` if the key is not in the tree.

THE find METHOD

Here is the `find` method from the `BinarySearchTree` class:

```
//Returns TreeNode with key.
//If key not in tree, returns null
public TreeNode find(Comparable key)
{
    TreeNode p = getRoot();
    while (p != null && key.compareTo(p.getValue())!= 0)
    {
        if (key.compareTo(p.getValue()) < 0)
            p = p.getLeft();
        else
            p = p.getRight();
    }
    return p;
}
```

RUN-TIME ANALYSIS

To find a single element in a binary search tree of n elements: The analysis is practically identical to that for insertion.

1. Balanced tree: A search will require at most one comparison per level (i.e., no more than $\log_2 n$ comparisons). Thus, the algorithm is $O(\log n)$.
2. Unbalanced tree: As many as n comparisons may be required to search a long chain of nodes. Thus, the algorithm is $O(n)$ in the worst case.

NOTE

See Question 35 on p. 679 for a recursive version of find.

Creating a Binary Search Tree

CREATING THE TREE

The following program

- Creates a binary search tree of single-character strings.
- Tests the find method.

```
/* Accesses a file of character strings, one per line,
   and inserts them into a binary search tree. */
public class BinarySearchTreeTest
{
    public static void main(String[] args)
    {
        //code to open inFile
        BinaryTree tree = new BinarySearchTree();
        String ch;
        while (< there are still elements in inFile >)
        {
            ch = inFile.readLine();
            tree.insert(ch);
        }
        System.out.println("Enter character key: ");
        ch = IO.readLine();     //read user input
        TreeNode t = tree.find(ch);
```

```
            if (t == null)
                System.out.println(ch + " was not in the tree.");
            else
                System.out.println(ch + " was found in the tree!");
        }
    }
```

RUN-TIME ANALYSIS FOR CREATING A BINARY SEARCH TREE

1. The best case occurs if the elements are in random order, leading to a tree that is reasonably balanced, with the level of the tree approximately equal to $\log_2 n$. To create the tree, each of the n elements will require no more than $\log_2 n$ comparisons, so the run time is $O(n \log n)$.

2. An example of the worst case occurs if the elements are initially sorted or sorted in reverse order. The tree thus formed is a sequence of left or right links as shown. To create the tree, insertion of nodes requires $0 + 1 + 2 + \cdots + n - 1 = n(n-1)/2$ comparisons, which is $O(n^2)$.

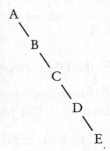

TREE TRAVERSAL

Three Methods of Traversal

There is no natural order for accessing all the elements of a binary tree. Three different methods of traversal are used, each with its own applications.

Inorder:	left - root - right	A
Recursively:	If root is not `null`:	/ \
	Traverse the left subtree inorder	B C
	Visit the root	
	Traverse the right subtree inorder	BAC
Preorder:	root - left - right	
Recursively:	If root is not `null`:	
	Visit the root	
	Traverse the left subtree preorder	
	Traverse the right subtree preorder	ABC
Postorder:	left - right - root	
Recursively:	If root is not `null`:	
	Traverse the left subtree postorder	
	Traverse the right subtree postorder	
	Visit the root	BCA

Example 1

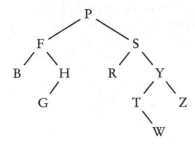

Inorder: BFGHPRSTWYZ
Preorder: PFBHGSRYTWZ
Postorder: BGHFRWTZYSP

Example 2

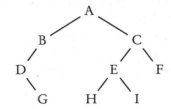

Inorder: DGBAHEICF
Preorder: ABDGCEHIF
Postorder: GDBHIEFCA

Implementing the Traversal Algorithms

The traversals described apply to all binary trees. It therefore makes sense to add them to the `BinaryTree` superclass with their implementations. Each traversal will have a recursive helper method. Each recursive helper method follows the definition for its particular traversal and has a `TreeNode` parameter. The base case is when this parameter is `null`. The "Visit the root" step of the definition simply writes out the data in the node with `System.out.println...`

Here is the code for the `postorder` method.

```
public void postorder()
{ doPostorder(root); }

private void doPostorder(TreeNode t)
{
    if (t != null)
    {
        doPostorder(t.getLeft());
        doPostorder(t.getRight());
        System.out.print(t.getValue());
    }
}
```

NOTE

1. Similar methods can be written for inorder and preorder traversals—be sure to put the statements in the correct order!
2. Using the private helper methods (`doPostorder`, for example) allows the root parameter to remain hidden in the `BinaryTree` class. A client method can call a traversal method as follows:

```
BinaryTree tree = new BinarySearchTree();
< code to read elements into tree >
System.out.print("POSTORDER: ");
tree.postorder();     //prints the elements postorder
```

3. If the tree is a binary search tree (as in Example 1 on the previous page), an inorder traversal will print out the elements in increasing sorted order.

RECURSIVE TREE ALGORITHMS

Most algorithms that involve binary trees are recursive because the trees themselves are recursive structures. Many of these algorithms traverse the tree and then report some result about the tree. Some change the contents of the nodes without altering the structure of the tree (i.e., no nodes are added or removed). Other algorithms change the structure of the tree.

A typical recursive method that does not change the structure of the tree has this scheme (in pseudo-code):

```
doTreeStuff
{
    if (root != null)            //handles base case
    {
        Handle the root           //Don't forget to visit the root.
        doTreeStuff to left subtree    //recursive call
        doTreeStuff to right subtree   //recursive call
    }
}
```

NOTE

1. This is just a general scheme. Often visiting the root postorder or inorder leads to the same correct result. Sometimes order *is* important; it depends on the actual application.
2. If the return type of doTreeStuff is not void, be sure to return an appropriate value.

For the following examples assume that trees are implemented with the TreeNode class on page 433.

Example 1

```
/* Precondition:  tree is a binary tree of Integer values.
 * Postcondition: Returns the sum of the values in the tree,
 *                0 if the tree is empty.  */
public int treeSum(TreeNode tree)
{
    if (tree == null)
        return 0;
    else
        return ((Integer) tree.getValue()).intValue()
            + treeSum(tree.getLeft()) + treeSum(tree.getRight());
}
```

Example 2

Two trees are *similar* if they have the same shape and pointer structure. Thus, the following two trees are similar:

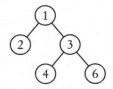 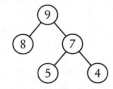

whereas these two trees are not similar:

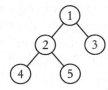 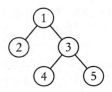

```
//Returns true if tree1 is similar to tree2, false otherwise.
public boolean similar(TreeNode tree1, TreeNode tree2)
{
    if (tree1 == null && tree2 == null)        //both null
        return true;
    else
        if (tree1 == null || tree2 == null)    //one null
            return false;
    else
        return similar(tree1.getLeft(), tree2.getLeft()) &&
            similar(tree1.getRight(), tree2.getRight());
}
```

Example 3

```
/* Precondition:  Binary tree rooted at tree.
 * Postcondition: Creates identical tree and returns reference
 *                to its root node.  */
public TreeNode newTree(TreeNode tree)
{
    if (tree == null)        //base case
        return null;
    else
    {
        TreeNode temp = new TreeNode(tree.getValue());
        temp.setLeft(newTree(tree.getLeft()));      //attach
                                                    //left subtree
        temp.setRight(newTree(tree.getRight()));    //attach
                                                    //right subtree
        return temp;
    }
}
```

NOTE

The `newTree` example is written with several statements to clarify the algorithm. The method can, however, be compacted as follows:

```
public TreeNode newTree(TreeNode tree)
{
    if (tree == null)      //base case
        return null;
    else
        return new TreeNode(tree.getValue(),
            newTree(tree.getLeft()), newTree(tree.getRight()));
}
```

Example 4

Recall that the height of a binary tree is the number of edges on the longest path from the root to a leaf. You may assume that the height of an empty tree is -1. The height of a tree with just one node is 0. The height of any given node is the number of edges on the longest path from that node to a leaf. To write a method that finds the height of a node, you may use the method `Math.max(a, b)`, which returns the larger of a and b.

```
//Return the height of node t.
public int height(TreeNode t)
{
    if (t == null)
        return -1;
    else
        return 1 + Math.max(height(t.getLeft()),
            height(t.getRight()));
}
```

NOTE

The height of node t equals the height of the left or right subtree, whichever is bigger. You must add 1 because the edge from the node to the root is counted in the height of the tree.

Recursion That Alters the Tree Structure

Recursive methods that change the structure of a tree by adding or removing nodes can be tricky. For example, consider using a recursive `insert` method instead of the iterative `insert` provided for the `BinarySearchTree` class (p. 437). Recall that the method inserts a new item into the tree.

A client method would call `insert` with code like the following:

```
BinaryTree tree = new BinarySearchTree();
System.out.println("Enter items to be inserted...");
while (<there are items to insert >)
{
    Object item = IO.readItem();      //read user input
    tree.insert(item);
}
```

If the `insert` method is recursive, the above method call, `tree.insert(item)`, will not work as intended because in order to make recursive calls the method must have a `TreeNode` parameter.

Suppose you modify `insert` so that it includes the required `TreeNode` parameter and change the client statement that invokes `insert` to be

```
tree.insert(tree.getRoot(), item);
```

This *still* won't work because the `TreeNode` parameter is passed by value, so the tree will remain unchanged! The way to change the tree is to *return* the changed `TreeNode`, in addition to having a `TreeNode` as a parameter for the recursive calls.

The problem is solved by making `insert` nonrecursive and having it call a private recursive helper method `recurInsert` that takes a `TreeNode` parameter and returns a `TreeNode` reference. The client method call in the code segment above remains `tree.insert(item)`.

Here is the code for both the `insert` and `recurInsert` methods, which are added to the `BinarySearchTree` class.

```
//Insert item in BinarySearchTree.
public void insert(Comparable item)
{
    setRoot(recurInsert(getRoot(), item));
}


/* private helper method
 * Finds insertion point for new node and attaches it.
 * Returns reference to TreeNode along insertion path. */
private TreeNode recurInsert(TreeNode t, Comparable item)
{
    if (t == null)
        return new TreeNode(item);
    else if (item.compareTo(t.getValue()) < 0)
        t.setLeft(recurInsert(t.getLeft(), item));
    else
        t.setRight(recurInsert(t.getRight(), item));
    return t;
}
```

NOTE

1. If the tree is empty, `recurInsert` simply returns the new `TreeNode` containing `item`. Otherwise, if `item` is less than the value in the current node, the algorithm recursively goes left. If `item` is greater than or equal to the value in the current node, it recursively goes right. When the insertion point is found (base case—`TreeNode` parameter is `null`), a new node is created and attached at that point.

2. The statement in the nonrecursive `insert` method

   ```
   setRoot(recurInsert(getRoot(), item));
   ```

   alters the root node of the tree only if the tree was originally empty or contained just one node. In fact, the recursive method `recurInsert` doesn't alter any nodes of the tree except at the insertion point. The returned node at each previous stage is simply a node along the path to the insertion point.

3. Here is a scheme, in pseudo-code, for a typical recursive helper method that changes the structure of a tree.

```
private TreeNode recurChangeTree(TreeNode t, other parameters ...)
{
    if (t == null)
        return a new TreeNode(...);    //typically
    else if (< some test >)
        t.setLeft(recurChangeTree(t.getLeft(), other parameters...));
    else
        t.setRight(recurChangeTree(t.getRight(), other parameters...));
    return t;        //don't forget this!
}
```

NOTE

For examples of recursive methods that alter a linked list, see Question 22 on p. 397 and Question 23 on p. 670.

BINARY EXPRESSION TREES

Infix, Postfix, and Prefix Expressions

A common application of trees is the storage and evaluation of mathematical expressions. A mathematical expression is made up of *operators* like $+$, $-$, $*$, $/$, and % and *operands*, which are numbers and variables.

There are three different representations of expressions:

infix: $A + B$
prefix: $+AB$
postfix: $AB+$

The "in," "pre," and "post" describe the position of the operator with respect to the operands. To convert the familiar infix form to postfix, for example, convert the pieces of the expression with highest precedence to postfix first. Then continue that way in stages.

Example 1

Convert $(A + B) * (C - D)$ to postfix.

$$(A + B) * (C + D) = (AB+) * (CD-)   \text{//parentheses have highest precedence}$$
$$= AB + CD - *   \text{//treat AB+ and CD- as single operands}$$

Example 2

Convert $(A - B)/C * D$ to prefix.

$$(A - B)/C * D = ((-AB)/C) * D   \text{// * and / have equal precedence. Work}$$
$$\text{// from left to right}$$
$$= (/ - ABC) * D$$
$$= */ - ABCD$$

Example 3

Convert $A - B/(C + D * E)$ to postfix.

$$
\begin{aligned}
A - B/(C + D * E) &= A - B/(C + (DE*)) \\
&= A - (B/CDE * +) \\
&= A - BCDE * +/ \\
&= ABCDE * +/-
\end{aligned}
$$

Example 4

Convert $A - B/(C + D * E)$ to prefix.

$$
\begin{aligned}
A - B/(C + D * E) &= A - B/(C + (*DE)) \\
&= A - (B/(+C * DE)) \\
&= A - /B + C * DE \\
&= -A/B + C * DE
\end{aligned}
$$

Binary Expression Tree

A *binary expression tree* either consists of a single root node containing an operand or stores an expression as follows. The root contains an operator that will be applied to the results of evaluating the expressions in the left and right subtrees, each of which is a binary expression tree.

A node containing an operator must have two nonempty subtrees. A node containing an operand must be a leaf. For example,

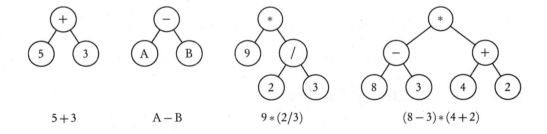

NOTE

1. The level of the nodes indicates the precedence: The operation at the root will always be the *last* operation performed. Operations in the highest level nodes are performed first.
2. An expression can be generated in its infix form by an inorder traversal of the tree. (But *you* must provide the brackets!) A preorder traversal yields the prefix form, whereas a postorder traversal yields the postfix form.

Example 1

Write the infix, prefix, and postfix form of the expression represented by each binary expression tree.

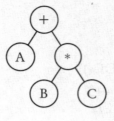

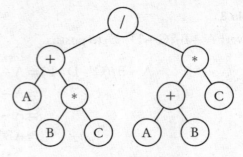

infix: $A + B * C$ infix: $(A + B * C)/((A + B) * C)$

prefix: $+A*BC$ prefix: $/+A*BC*+ABC$

postfix: $ABC*+$ postfix: $ABC*+AB+C*/$

Example 2

Evaluate the expression in the following tree.

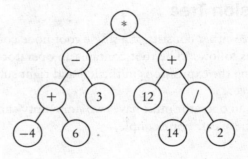

Solution: Do an inorder traversal to get the following infix form:

$$[(-4 + 6) - 3] * [12 + 14/2] = (2 - 3) * (12 + 7) = -19$$

Evaluating a Binary Expression Tree

Consider a program that places an expression in a binary expression tree and then evaluates the tree. For the purposes of this program, assume that a node contains either an operator (like "+", "−", etc.) or an integer value.

For example, a binary expression tree with the expression $(3 + 4) * 6$ would look like this:

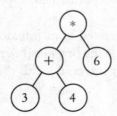

Notice that the left and right subtree of each operator node is an expression:

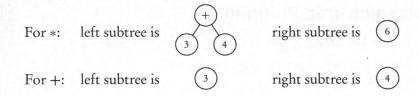

For ∗:   left subtree is   right subtree is   (6)

For +:   left subtree is   (3)   right subtree is   (4)

Each of these quantities is an expression:

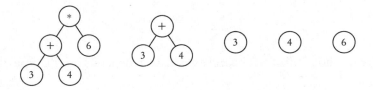

Each of these expressions is a binary operation:

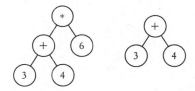

Each of these expressions is a constant:

Each expression that is a binary operation is either a sum, product, quotient, or difference. This all suggests a program that has an `Expression` superclass, with subclasses `BinaryOperation` and `Constant`. Further, `BinaryOperation` should have subclasses `Sum`, `Difference`, `Product`, and `Quotient`.

Evaluating an expression consists of evaluating the left and right subtrees and applying the operator at the root. Thus,

$$(\text{value of tree}) = (\text{value of left subtree}) \bullet (\text{value of right subtree})$$

where • is a binary operation. But

$$(\text{value of left subtree}) = (\text{value of } its \text{ left subtree}) \diamond (\text{value of } its \text{ right subtree})$$

where ◊ is some other binary operation. Clearly the process is recursive. The value obtained from a given subtree depends on whether that subtree is a `Constant` or a `BinaryOperation`. If it's a `Constant`, its value is just that number (base case). If it's a `BinaryOperation`, then, depending on the operator, either a `Sum` is evaluated or a `Product` is, and so on. This procedure extends all the way down to the leaves—polymorphism is applied at each stage, determining which kind of expression to evaluate.

A Binary Expression Tree Program

Here are the classes used in the program[1] for evaluating a binary expression tree:

```
/* An abstract class for arithmetic expressions */
public abstract class Expression
{
    //Postcondition: Returns the value of this Expression.
    public abstract int evaluate();
}
```

NOTE

The evaluate method is abstract because evaluation depends on the type of expression being evaluated.

```
/* A class that defines expressions that are constants */
public class Constant extends Expression
{
    private int myValue;

    public Constant(int value)
    { myValue = value; }

    public int evaluate()
    { return myValue; }

    public String toString()
    { return "" + myValue; }
}
```

NOTE

The Constant class is a concrete (nonabstract) class. The evaluate method is clearly defined for a constant; simply return its value.

```
/* An abstract class that defines expressions
 * that are binary operations */
public abstract class BinaryOperation extends Expression
{
    private Expression myLeft, myRight;
    private String myOp;    //symbolic representation of the operator

    public BinaryOperation(String op, Expression lhs, Expression rhs)
    {
        myLeft = lhs;
        myRight = rhs;
        myOp = op;
    }

    public String toString()
    {
        return "(" + myLeft.toString() + " " + myOp
                   + " " + myRight.toString() + ")";
    }
}
```

---

[1]This program uses the classes shown by David Levine at a workshop at St. Bonaventure and attributed to Scot Drysdale.

```
    public Expression getLeft()
    { return myLeft; }

    public Expression getRight()
    { return myRight; }
}
```

NOTE

The `BinaryOperation` class is abstract because the `evaluate` method cannot be explicitly defined here: It depends on the binary operator.

```
/* A class that defines expressions that are sums */
public class Sum extends BinaryOperation
{
    public Sum(Expression lhs, Expression rhs)
    { super("+", lhs, rhs); }

    public int evaluate()
    { return getLeft().evaluate() + getRight().evaluate(); }
}
```

NOTE

1. For the `Sum` class, the `evaluate` method can be defined without ambiguity:

   (value of left subtree) + (value of right subtree)

2. Similar classes are defined for `Product`, `Quotient`, and `Difference`.

The `ExpressionEvaluator` program looks something like this:

```
public class ExpressionEvaluator
{
    public static void main(String[] args)
    {
        ExpressionHandler h = new ExpressionHandler();
        //create binary expression tree from postfix
        // expression in input file
        Expression expr = h.createTree();
        System.out.println("value of " + expr.toString()
            + " is " + expr.evaluate());
        System.out.println();
    }
}
```

NOTE

1. In case you're wondering how the expression got into the tree, implementation code for the `ExpressionHandler` class and a `FileHandler` class is provided in Appendix B.
2. Notice how polymorphism is applied when `root.evaluate()` is called:

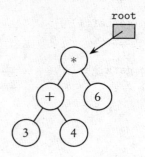

(i) The node with ∗ is encountered. The calling object is therefore a Product, which produces

```
getLeft().evaluate()  *  getRight().evaluate()
```

(ii) For the left-hand side in step (i), the node with + is encountered. The
calling object is therefore a Sum, which produces

```
getLeft().evaluate()  +  getRight().evaluate()
```

(3)   +   (4)

(iii) When the nodes in step (ii) are encountered, and also the right-hand
side in step (i), the controlling object in each case is a Constant. Thus,
a call to evaluate returns the values 3, 4, and 6, respectively.

(iv) Thus, the sum in step (ii) is 7, and the product in step (i) is 7 ∗ 6, which
is 42.

3. As you study this implementation of a binary expression tree, you may be
wondering: Where did the BinaryTree go? The answer is that TreeNode has
been replaced with an Expression. Each node in the tree that's created represents an Expression. Each Expression node contains a value (either a Constant
or BinaryOperation) as well as a left and right pointer field that refers to another Expression. An Expression, like a TreeNode, is self-referential and can
be linked to other Expression objects to form a binary expression tree.

The inheritance hierarchy in this program is an elegant way of representing the
various elements that comprise the binary expression tree.

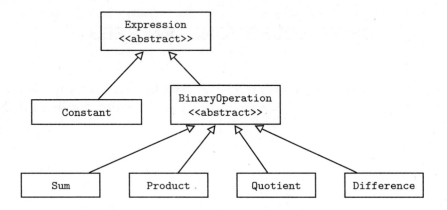

<hr>

RUN TIME OF BINARY SEARCH TREE (BST) ALGORITHMS

<hr>

Operation	Balanced BST	Unbalanced BST	Comment
Insert 1 element into BST	$O(\log n)$	$O(n)$	At most $\log_2 n$ comparisons in balanced BST, n in unbalanced.
Insert n elements into originally empty BST	$O(n \log n)$	$O(n^2)$	Same as above, but for each of n elements.
Search for key	$O(\log n)$	$O(n)$	At most $\log_2 n$ comparisons in balanced BST, n in unbalanced.
Traverse tree	$O(n)$	$O(n)$	Each node visited once.

<hr>

Chapter Summary

<hr>

Know the vocabulary associated with binary trees. You should be able to use the `TreeNode` class to manipulate trees, and also to write code for a `BinaryTree` class.

Understand the definition of a binary search tree (BST)—there are bound to be many questions on this topic. In particular, you should know algorithms that create, traverse, and search a BST. Know the big-O analysis for such algorithms.

Be familiar with the difference between inorder, preorder, postorder, and level order traversals. All are fair game on the AP exam.

You should be able to write recursive algorithms that traverse a tree, including algorithms that alter the structure of a tree. Be familiar with recursive helper methods—in the past few years these have appeared in the free response (part two) questions on the exam.

MULTIPLE-CHOICE QUESTIONS ON TREES

1. A perfect binary tree has every leaf on the same level, and every nonleaf node has two children. A perfect binary tree with k leaves contains how many nodes?
    (A) k
    (B) k^2
    (C) 2^k
    (D) $\log_2 k$
    (E) $2k - 1$

2. The level of a node is the length of the path (or number of edges) from the root to that node. The level of a tree is equal to the level of its deepest leaf. A binary tree has level k. Which represents

    1. The maximum possible number of nodes, and
    2. The minimum possible number of nodes in the tree?

(A)	(1) 2^{k+1}	(2) $2^k + 1$
(B)	(1) 2^{k+1}	(2) k
(C)	(1) $2^{k+1} - 1$	(2) k
(D)	(1) $2^{k+1} - 1$	(2) $k + 1$
(E)	(1) $2^k + 1$	(2) 2^k

3. Which of the following represents (1) inorder, (2) preorder, and (3) postorder traversals of the tree shown?
    (A) (1) GJAPES   (2) JAGPES   (3) GAESPJ
    (B) (1) GJAEPS   (2) JGAPES   (3) GESPAJ
    (C) (1) EPSAJG   (2) PESJGA   (3) ESPGAJ
    (D) (1) GJAEPS   (2) GESPAJ   (3) JGAPES
    (E) (1) GJAPES   (2) GAESPJ   (3) JAGPES

```
        J
       / \
      G   A
           \
            P
           / \
          E   S
```

4. The tree shown is traversed postorder and each element is pushed onto a stack s as it is encountered. The following program fragment is then executed:

    ```
    for (int i = 1; i <= 5; i++)
        x = s.pop();
    ```

    What value is contained in x after the segment is executed?
    (A) M
    (B) G
    (C) K
    (D) F
    (E) P

```
        K
       / \
      P   C
         / \
        M   E
       /     \
      F       G
```

5. Each of the following lists of numbers is inserted, in the order given, into a binary search tree. Which list produces the most balanced tree?
   (A) 2 4 7 5 8 10
   (B) 9 7 2 1 4 0
   (C) 5 1 2 6 3 4
   (D) 2 5 1 4 0 3
   (E) 6 4 1 8 10 5

6. The element 10 is to be inserted into the binary search tree shown.

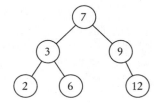

After insertion, the tree is as follows:

(A)
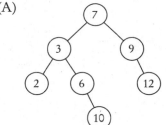

(B)
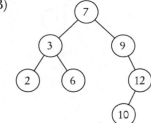

(C)
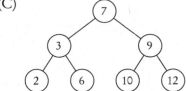

(D)
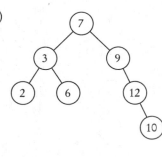

(E)
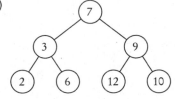

7. Array elements `a[0]`, `a[1]`, ..., `a[n-1]` are inserted into a binary search tree. The tree will then be used to search for a given element. In the *worst* case, the insertion and search, respectively, will be
   (A) $O(n^2)$, $O(n \log n)$
   (B) $O(n \log n)$, $O(n \log n)$
   (C) $O(n^2)$, $O(n)$
   (D) $O(n^2)$, $O(n^2)$
   (E) $O(n)$, $O(n)$

8. Worst case performance of the search for a key in a *balanced* binary search tree is
    (A) $O(n^2)$
    (B) $O(n)$
    (C) $O(\log n)$
    (D) $O(2^n)$
    (E) $O(n \log n)$

9. The value of the binary expression tree shown is
    (A) 1
    (B) 4
    (C) 10
    (D) 11
    (E) 25

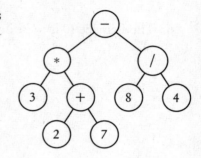

10. Which of the following correctly represents the expression A/B * C % D?

    (A)

    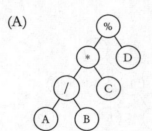

    (B)

    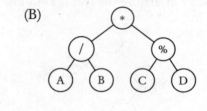

    (C)

    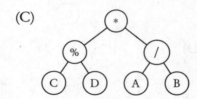

    (D)

    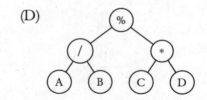

    (E)

    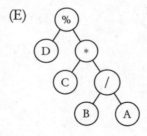

11. The (1) prefix and (2) postfix forms of the expression $P + (Q - R) * A/B$ are
    (A) (1) +P * −QR/AB   (2) PQR − AB/ * +
    (B) (1) PQR − AB/ * +   (2) +P * −QR/AB
    (C) (1) PQR − A * B/+   (2) +P/ * −QRAB
    (D) (1) +P/ * −QRAB   (2) PQR − A * B/+
    (E) (1) + * P − QR/AB   (2) PQRA − * B/+

For Questions 12–22 assume that binary trees are implemented with the TreeNode class on p. 433.

12. Suppose that p refers to a node as shown. Which of the following correctly inserts the Object obj as the right child of the node that p points to?

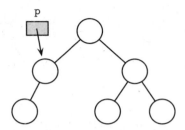

   (A) p.setRight(new TreeNode(obj));
   (B) p = new TreeNode(obj, p.getLeft(), p.getRight());
   (C) p.setRight(new Object(obj));
   (D) p.setRight(new TreeNode(obj, p.getLeft(), p.getRight()));
   (E) p = new TreeNode(obj);

13. Refer to method numNodes:

```
//Returns the number of nodes in tree.
public int numNodes(TreeNode tree)
{
    if (tree == null)
        return 0;
    else
    {
        /* code */
    }
}
```

   Which replacement for /* *code* */ will cause the method to work as intended?

   I return 1 + numNodes(tree.getLeft()) +
             numNodes(tree.getRight());

   II return numNodes(tree) + numNodes(tree.getLeft()) +
             numNodes(tree.getRight());

   III return numNodes(tree.getLeft()) + numNodes(tree.getRight());

   (A) None
   (B) I only
   (C) II only
   (D) III only
   (E) I and II only

14. Two trees are *mirror images* of each other if their roots and left and right subtrees are reflected across a vertical line as shown:

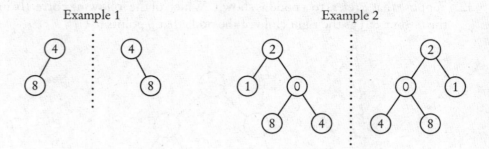

Refer to the following method `mirrorTree`:

```
/* Precondition:  tree refers to the root of a binary tree.
 * Postcondition: A mirror image of tree is created and
 *                a reference to it is returned.  */
public TreeNode mirrorTree(TreeNode tree)
{
    if (tree == null)
        return null;
    else
    {
        /* more code */
    }
}
```

Which of the following replacements for /* *more code* */ correctly achieves the postcondition for method `mirrorTree`?

```
 I  TreeNode temp = new TreeNode(null, null, null);
    temp.setValue(tree.getValue());
    temp.setLeft(mirrorTree(tree.getRight()));
    temp.setRight(mirrorTree(tree.getLeft()));
    return temp;

 II return new TreeNode(tree.getValue(),
               mirrorTree(tree.getRight()),
               mirrorTree(tree.getLeft()));

III return new TreeNode(tree.getValue(),
               mirrorTree(tree.getLeft()),
               mirrorTree(tree.getRight()));
```

(A) I only
(B) II only
(C) III only
(D) I and II only
(E) I and III only

15. Refer to method `leafSum`:

```
//Returns sum of leaves in tree, 0 for empty tree.
public int leafSum(TreeNode tree)
{
    if (tree == null)
        return 0;
    else
    {
        /* code */
    }
}
```

Which replacement for /* *code* */ is correct?

(A) ```
    if (tree.getLeft() == null && tree.getRight() == null)
        return ((Integer) (tree.getValue())).intValue();
    else
        return 1 + leafSum(tree.getLeft()) +
            leafSum(tree.getRight());
```

(B) ```
    if (tree.getLeft() == null || tree.getRight() == null)
        return ((Integer) (tree.getValue())).intValue();
    else
        return 1 + leafSum(tree.getLeft()) +
            leafSum(tree.getRight());
```

(C) ```
    if (tree.getLeft() == null && tree.getRight() == null)
        return ((Integer) (tree.getValue())).intValue();
    else
        return ((Integer) (tree.getValue())).intValue() +
            leafSum(tree.getLeft()) + leafSum(tree.getRight());
```

(D) ```
    if (tree.getLeft() == null || tree.getRight() == null)
        return ((Integer) (tree.getValue())).intValue();
    else
        return leafSum(tree.getLeft()) +
            leafSum(tree.getRight());
```

(E) ```
    if (tree.getLeft() == null && tree.getRight() == null)
        return ((Integer) (tree.getValue())).intValue();
    else
        return leafSum(tree.getLeft()) +
            leafSum(tree.getRight());
```
```

16. Which is true about method `find`?

```
//Return TreeNode with target value,
// or null if target not found.
public TreeNode find(TreeNode root, Comparable target)
{
    if (root == null)
        return null;
    else if (target.compareTo(root.getValue())== 0)
        return root;
    else if (target.compareTo(root.getValue()) < 0)
        return find(root.getLeft(), target);
    else
        return find(root.getRight(), target);
}
```

(A) Method `find` will never work as intended.
(B) Method `find` will always work as intended.
(C) Method `find` will only work as intended if `target` is not in the tree.
(D) Method `find` will always work as intended if the tree is a binary search tree.
(E) Method `find` will only work as intended if the tree is a binary search tree and `target` occurs no more than once in the tree.

17. Refer to method `doSomething`:

```
public Comparable doSomething(TreeNode root)
{
    if (root != null)
        if (root.getRight() == null)
            return (Comparable) root.getValue();
        else
            return doSomething(root.getRight());
    return null;
}
```

Which best describes what `doSomething` does?
(A) It returns the largest element in a nonempty binary search tree.
(B) It returns the largest element in a nonempty tree.
(C) It returns an element at the highest level of a nonempty tree.
(D) It returns the smallest element in a nonempty binary search tree.
(E) It returns the smallest element in a nonempty tree.

18. Refer to method traverse, and to the binary tree of Integer values shown:

```
public void traverse(TreeNode t)
{
    if (t != null)
    {
        /* code */
    }
}
```

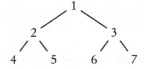

By replacing /* *code* */ with the three statements traverse(t.getLeft()), traverse(t.getRight()), and System.out.print(t.getValue()) in some order, we can cause method traverse to execute one of six traversals. For example, by replacing /* *code* */ with

```
traverse(t.getLeft());
traverse(t.getRight());
System.out.print(t.getValue());
```

we would cause traverse to execute a postorder traversal. Which of the following replacements for /* *code* */ will cause the numbers 1 through 7 to be printed in ascending order when traverse(t) is called?

(A)
```
traverse(t.getLeft());
System.out.print(t.getValue());
traverse(t.getRight());
```

(B)
```
System.out.print(t.getValue());
traverse(t.getLeft());
traverse(t.getRight());
```

(C)
```
traverse(t.getRight());
traverse(t.getLeft());
System.out.print(t.getValue());
```

(D)
```
traverse(t.getRight());
System.out.print(t.getValue());
traverse(t.getLeft());
```

(E) It is impossible to print the numbers 1 through 7 in ascending order using this method.

19. This question uses an object from the following class:

```
/* An Integer object that can be altered */
public class IntObj
{
    private int myValue;

    public IntObj(int value)     //constructor
    { myValue = value; }

    public void increment()      //increments IntObj by 1
    { myValue++; }

    //Returns Integer equivalent of IntObj.
    public Integer getInteger()
    { return new Integer(myValue); }
}
```

Refer to the following method:

```
/* Precondition: tree is at root of binary tree that contains
 *               Integer values.  */
public void number(TreeNode tree, IntObj nextNum)
{
    if (tree != null)
        if (tree.getLeft() == null && tree.getRight() == null)
        {
            tree.setValue(nextNum.getInteger());
            nextNum.increment();
        }
        else
        {
            number(tree.getRight(), nextNum);
            number(tree.getLeft(), nextNum);
        }
}
```

Assuming that a binary tree of Integer values is rooted at tree, which of the following trees is a possible result of executing the next two statements?

```
IntObj nextNum = new IntObj(3);
number(tree, nextNum);
```

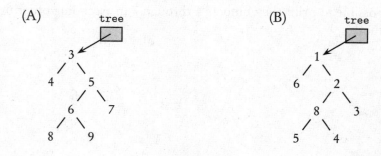

(C) tree

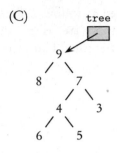

(D) tree

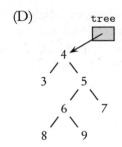

(E) tree

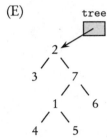

20. Recall that the level of a node is the number of edges from the root to that node. The level of a tree equals the level of its deepest leaf. Thus, the level of a tree with just one node is 0.

    Refer to method `whatsIt`:

    ```
    public int whatsIt(TreeNode tree)
    {
        if (tree == null)
            return -1;
        else
        {
            int x = 1 + whatsIt(tree.getLeft());
            int y = 1 + whatsIt(tree.getRight());
            if (x >= y)
                return x;
            else
                return y;
        }
    }
    ```

    Method `whatsIt` returns −1 for an empty tree. What does method `whatsIt` do when invoked for a nonempty tree?
    (A) It returns the largest value in the tree.
    (B) It returns the number of nodes in the subtree that has the greatest number of nodes.
    (C) It returns the level of the tree.
    (D) It returns 1 plus the level of the tree.
    (E) It returns either the leftmost value or the rightmost value of a tree, whichever is larger.

21. Suppose that the node height of a binary tree is defined as follows: The node height of an empty tree is 0; the node height of a nonempty tree is the number of nodes on the longest path from the root to a leaf of the tree. Thus, the node height of the tree shown is 5.

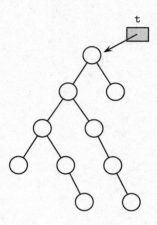

Refer to method f:

```
public int f(TreeNode t)
{
    if (t == null)
        return 0;
    else
        return max(
            nodeHeight(t.getLeft()) + nodeHeight(t.getRight()),
            f(t.getLeft()),
            f(t.getRight()));
}
```

You may assume that method max(a,b,c) returns the largest of its integer arguments and that method nodeHeight returns the node height of its tree argument. What value is returned when f(t) is called for the tree pictured?

(A) 4
(B) 5
(C) 6
(D) 7
(E) 8

22. A recursive method doPostorder is added to a BinaryTree class:

```
public void doPostorder(TreeNode t)
{
    if (t != null)
    {
        doPostorder(t.getLeft());
        doPostorder(t.getRight());
        System.out.print(t.getValue());
    }
}
```

Suppose this method is called for a TreeNode at the root of a tree with n elements. The run-time efficiency of doPostorder is

(A) $O(\log n)$

(B) $O(n)$

(C) $O(n \log n)$

(D) $O(n^2)$

(E) $O(2^n)$

ANSWER KEY

1. **E**	9. **E**	17. **A**
2. **D**	10. **A**	18. **E**
3. **B**	11. **D**	19. **B**
4. **A**	12. **A**	20. **C**
5. **E**	13. **B**	21. **C**
6. **B**	14. **D**	22. **B**
7. **C**	15. **E**	
8. **C**	16. **D**	

ANSWERS EXPLAINED

1. **(E)** Draw some pictures and count!

# of leaves	# of nodes
1	1
2	3
4	7
8	15
16	31
32	63
...	...
k	$2k - 1$

2. **(D)** For the maximum possible number of nodes, each node must have two children. Notice the pattern:

Level	Max possible # of nodes
0	1
1	3
2	7
3	15
...	...
k	$2^{k+1} - 1$

For the minimum possible number of nodes, each node must have no more than one child. Thus, for example, a level 3 tree with the minimum number of nodes will look like this:

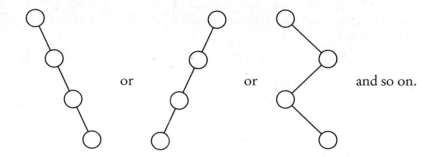

In each case, there will be $k + 1$ nodes.

3. **(B)**
   (1) For inorder think left-root-right (i.e., G-J-right). When you now traverse the right subtree inorder, there is no left, so A comes next. Then traverse the P-E-S subtree inorder, which gives E-P-S.
   (2) For preorder think root-left-right (i.e., J-G-right). When you now traverse the right subtree, A is now the root and comes next. There is no left, so traverse the P-E-S subtree preorder, which gives P-E-S.
   (3) Similarly for postorder, thinking left-right-root produces GESPAJ.

4. **(A)** A postorder traversal yields PFMGECK, so here's the stack:

K
C
E
G
M
F
P

The fifth pop will remove element M.

5. **(E)** In each case, the first number in the list will go into the root node. Subsequent numbers that are less than the first number will go into the left subtree; those greater than or equal to the first will go into the right subtree. Eliminate choices A and B, which are almost in sorted order. Each of these will form trees that are virtually long chains:

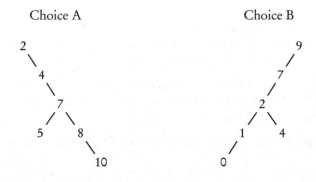

Choice C won't form a balanced tree either: All elements but one will go into the left subtree.

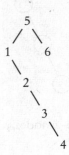

You should be able to eliminate choices A, B, and C by inspection. Comparing the trees in choices D and E shows that E yields the more balanced tree:

Choice D   Choice E

6. **(B)** Starting at the root, compare the new element with the current node. Go left if the element is less than the current node; otherwise go right. Insert at the first available empty slot. For the tree shown, compare 10 with 7. Since $10 > 7$, go right. Then $10 > 9$, so go right. Then $10 < 12$, a leaf, so insert left.

7. **(C)** An example of the worst case for insertion into a binary search tree occurs when the numbers are already sorted. The resulting tree will be unbalanced, a long chain of numbers:

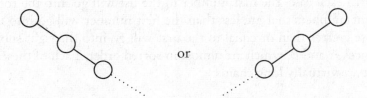

or

Insertion of n elements into the tree requires $0 + 1 + \cdots + n - 1 = n(n-1)/2$ comparisons, which is $O(n^2)$. Searching this tree will require each "link" in the "chain" to be examined, much like a sequential search. This is $O(n)$.

8. **(C)** If the tree is balanced, the worst case occurs when the key is found in a leaf (i.e., at the highest level of the tree). The maximum level of a balanced tree is $\log_2 n$. Therefore, the search is $O(\log n)$.

9. **(E)** The infix form of the expression is $3*(2+7)-8/4$, which equals $(3*9)-2 = 25$.

10. **(A)** The operators /, ∗, and % all have equal precedence and must therefore be performed from left to right. Thus, the order of performing the operations is /, followed by ∗, then %. Now recall the general rule: The earlier an operation is performed, the higher its node level in the tree. In particular, the last operation performed is always the root node. So % must be in the root node, which eliminates choices B and C. Since / is performed before ∗, the node containing / must have a higher level than the node containing ∗, which eliminates choice D. Choice D fails for another reason: C ∗ D is not part of the given expression. Choice E fails because B/A is not part of the given expression. Note that if the given expression had been $(A/B) * (C \% D)$, choice B would have been correct, since / and % would have equal first precedence and ∗ would be the last operation performed.

11. **(D)** For both pre- and postfix, perform the operations in order of precedence, changing each subexpression to prefix or postfix as you go.

    (1) prefix:
    $$P + (Q - R) * A/B = P + [(-QR) * A]/B$$
    $$= P + (* - QRA)/B$$
    $$= P + (/ * -QRAB)$$
    $$= +P/ * -QRAB$$

    To go from the first to the second line, note that ∗ and / have equal precedence, so use the leftmost one first.

    (2) postfix:
    $$P + (Q - R) * A/B = P + [(QR-) * A]/B$$
    $$= P + (QR - A*)/B$$
    $$= P + (QR - A * B/)$$
    $$= PQR - A * B/+$$

12. **(A)** The expression `new TreeNode(obj)` is the correct use of the `TreeNode` constructor that creates a new node with `obj` that has null pointer fields. Calling `p.setRight(...)` with this expression then attaches the new node as the right child of the node that p refers to. Choice C does not create a new `TreeNode`. Choice D is wrong because the pointer fields of the new node must be null. Choices B and E reassign p rather than doing the required attachment to the node that p points to.

13. **(B)** Eliminate segment III; it forgot to count the root node. Segment II calls `numNodes(tree)`, which leads to infinite recursion. Segment I correctly adds 1 for the root node to the number of nodes in the left and right subtrees.

14. **(D)** Segments I and II are equivalent, but segment II, which uses the three-parameter `TreeNode` constructor, is more compact. The order of the pointer parameters in the constructor is left, right, so in segment II the call `mirrorTree(tree.getRight())` will attach as the left subtree of the new tree a duplicate of the right subtree of `tree`. Similarly, the last parameter of the constructor, the call `mirrorTree(tree.getLeft())`, will cause a duplicate of the left subtree of `tree` to be attached as the right subtree of the new tree. Segment III is wrong because it creates an *exact* copy of the tree rather than a mirror image.

15. **(E)** This is an example where you *don't* automatically add the value in the root node. Thus, eliminate choices A, B, and C, which all add something to `leafSum(tree.getLeft()) + leafSum(tree.getRight())`. The correct test for a leaf is that both the left and right pointers must be `null`. Thus, eliminate choice D, which has an "or" in the test instead of an "and."

16. **(D)** The algorithm uses the binary search tree property and searches only the left subtree if `target` is less than the current root value, or only the right subtree if `target` is greater than or equal to the current root value. In a general binary tree (i.e., not a binary search tree), the given algorithm may miss the target. Note that choice E is false; the postcondition specifies that a `TreeNode` with `target` is returned, which the algorithm will do irrespective of the number of times `target` occurs in the tree.

17. **(A)** The algorithm is actually returning the rightmost element of the tree, which is not one of the choices. Note that the rightmost element of a binary search tree is the largest (check it out!), which makes A the best choice. None of the other choices *must* be true. For example, if the tree in choice C looks like the following tree, C will be false.

18. **(E)** Choice A is an inorder traversal yielding 4251637. Choice B is a preorder traversal: 1245367. Choice C is a right-to-left postorder traversal: 7635421. Choice D is a right-to-left inorder traversal: 7361524. Trying the regular postorder and the right-to-left preorder traversals (the two remaining possibilities) does not yield the required output either.

19. **(B)** This method numbers all the leaves of the tree beginning with the right subtree. The starting number given in this case is 3. The rightmost leaf becomes 3, and leaves are numbered in ascending order from right to left.

20. **(C)** In the line `x = 1 + whatsIt(tree.getLeft())`, 1 is added for each recursive call until `tree.getLeft()` is null. Similarly, 1 is added for each recursive call in the line `y = 1 + whatsIt(tree.getRight())`. Look at an example like the following tree:

Here x will end up with value 1 (two recursive calls plus −1 for the base case), whereas y will end up with the value 2 (three recursive calls plus −1 for the base case). The method in this case will return 2, the maximum of x and y, which is the level of the tree.

21. **(C)** The method call f(t) returns the maximum of the following three quantities:
    (1) Sum of node heights of left and right subtrees of root node t. Here $4+1=5$.
    (2) Maximum of sum of node heights of left and right subtrees for *any* node in the left subtree of node t.
    (3) Maximum of sum of node heights of left and right subtrees for *any* node in the right subtree of node t. This is zero because there are no nodes underneath t.getRight().

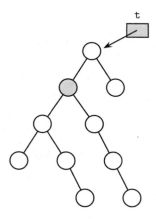

Note that the shaded node in the left subtree of node t has node height of left subtree $= 3$, and node height of right subtree $= 3$. No other node in the subtree returns a higher total, so the method call f(t.getLeft()) returns 6. Since $\max(5, 6, 0) = 6$, f(t) returns 6.

22. **(B)** Each aspect of a postorder traversal is linear, that is, $O(n)$. In a given traversal,

    - Each node is output exactly once, thus printing is $O(n)$.
    - Each if statement is executed once per node, thus testing for null is $O(n)$.
    - The total number of calls to doPostorder is, again, once per node, thus invoking doPostorder is $O(n)$.

    Since each operation of the method is $O(n)$, the total run time is $O(n)$.

Collections

CHAPTER 11

*HASH: There is no definition for this word—
nobody knows what hash is.*
—*Ambrose Bierce*, The Devil's Dictionary *(1911)*

Chapter Goals

- The Java collections API
- The collections hierarchy
- Collections and generics
- Collections and iterators
- The `List<E>` interface
- The `ArrayList<E>` and `LinkedList<E>` classes

- The `Set<E>` interface
- The `HashSet<E>` and `TreeSet<E>` classes
- The `Map<K,V>` interface
- The `HashMap<K,V>` and `TreeMap<K,V>` classes
- Run time of list, set, and map operations

COLLECTIONS IN JAVA

What Is a Collection?

A *collection* is any bunch of objects you can think of: members of a local bridge club, your CD collection, all book titles in the library, the moves in a chess game, the flavors at the ice cream parlor, a sack of toys. Some collections are ordered; some are not. Some allow duplicates; some do not.

The Collections API

When you write a Java program that manipulates a collection, you may use the Collections API (Application Programming Interface), which is a library provided by Java. Most of the API is in `java.util`. This library gives the programmer access to prepackaged data structures and the methods to manipulate them. The implementations of these *container classes* are invisible and should not be of concern to the programmer. The code works. And it is reusable.

All of the collections classes have the following features in common:

- They are designed to be both memory and run-time efficient.
- They provide methods for insertion and removal of items (i.e., they can grow and shrink).
- They provide for iteration over the entire collection.
- In Java 5.0 the collection classes are generic, which means that they have type parameters.

THE COLLECTIONS HIERARCHY

Inheritance is a defining feature of the Collections API. Some of the core interfaces that are used to manipulate the collections follow. They specify the operations that must be defined for any container class that implements that interface.

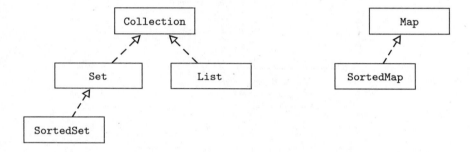

NOTE

1. The diagram shows the `Collection` interface at the root of the collections hierarchy. A `Collection` is simply a group of objects called its *elements*. The `Collection` interface is used to manipulate collections when maximum generality is desired, much like `Object` in the hierarchy of classes.
2. `Set` and `List` are both collections. A `Set` is unordered and cannot contain duplicates. A `List` is ordered and can contain duplicates.
3. A `Map` is not considered to be a true collection and therefore has its own hierarchy tree. A `Map` is an object that maps keys to values. A `Map` cannot contain duplicate keys: each key maps to exactly one value.
4. The `SortedSet` and `SortedMap` interfaces are sorted versions of `Set` and `Map`.

You don't have to know all these interfaces for the AP exam. The only ones you are expected to know are `Set`, `List`, and `Map`. The container classes you are expected to know are `ArrayList`, `LinkedList`, `HashSet`, `TreeSet`, `HashMap`, and `TreeMap`. The diagrams on the next page show which interface is directly implemented by each of these classes:

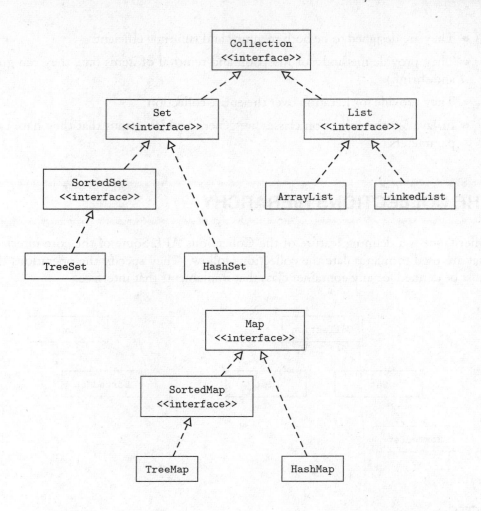

```
                        Collections Classes

        ArrayList and LinkedList implement List.
        HashSet implements Set.
        TreeSet implements SortedSet.
        HashMap implements Map.
        TreeMap implements SortedMap.
```

COLLECTIONS AND GENERICS

The collections classes are generic, with type parameters (see p. 297). Thus, List<E> and Set<E> contain elements of type E, while Map<K,V> maps keys of type K to values of type V.

When a generic class is declared, the type parameter is replaced by an actual object type. For example,

```
private LinkedList<Clown> clowns;
private Map<Clown, Circus> locations;
```

NOTE

1. The `clowns` list must contain only `Clown` objects. An attempt to add an `Acrobat` to the list, for example, will cause a compile-time error.
2. Since the type of objects in a generic class is restricted, the elements can be accessed without casting.
3. There are no primitive types in collections classes. To use primitive types, wrapping and unwrapping must first occur, which is automatically done in Java 5.0 with auto-boxing and -unboxing.
4. All of the type information in a program with generic classes is examined at compile time. After compilation the type information is erased. This feature of generic classes is known as *erasure*. During execution of the program, any attempt at incorrect casting will lead to a `ClassCastException`.

COLLECTIONS AND ITERATORS

Definition of an Iterator

An *iterator* is an object whose sole purpose is to traverse a collection, one element at a time. During iteration, the iterator object maintains a current position in the collection, and is the controlling object in manipulating the elements of the collection.

The `Iterable<E>` Interface

Each of the generic collection classes provides an iterator for traversal of the collection. Each class implements the `Iterable` interface:

```
public interface Iterable<E>
{
    //Returns an iterator over a collection of elements of type E.
    Iterator<E> iterator();
}
```

The `Iterator<E>` Interface

The package `java.util` provides a generic interface, `Iterator<E>`, whose methods are `hasNext`, `next`, and `remove`. A class that implements `Iterator` for a given collection can iterate over that collection, provided the collection implements `Iterable`. The Java Collections API allows iteration over each of its collections classes.

THE METHODS OF `Iterator<E>`

```
boolean hasNext()
```

Returns `true` if there's at least one more element to be examined, `false` otherwise.

```
T next()
```

Returns the next element in the iteration. If no elements remain, the method throws a `NoSuchElementException`.

```
void remove()
```

Deletes from the collection the last element that was returned by `next`. This method can be called only once per call to `next`. It throws an `IllegalStateException` if the `next` method has not yet been called, or if the `remove` method has already been called after the last call to `next`.

Using a Generic Iterator

To iterate over a parameterized collection, you must use a parameterized iterator whose parameter is the same type.

Example 1

```
List<String> list = new ArrayList<String>();
<code to initialize list with strings>
//Print strings in list, one per line.
for (Iterator<String> itr = list.iterator(); itr.hasNext();)
    System.out.println(itr.next());
```

NOTE

1. Only classes that implement the `Iterable` interface can use the for-each loop. This is because the loop operates by using an iterator. Thus, the loop in the above example is equivalent to

```
for (String str : list)    //no iterator in sight!
    System.out.println(str);
```

> Use a for-each loop for accessing and modifying objects in a list. Use an iterator for removal of objects.

2. Recall, however, that a for-each loop cannot be used to remove elements from the list. Thus, the following example *requires* an iterator.

Example 2

```
//Remove all 2-character strings from strList.
//Precondition: strList initialized with String objects.
public static void removeTwos(List<String> strList)
{
    Iterator<String> itr = strList.iterator();
    while (itr.hasNext())
        if (itr.next().length() == 2)
            itr.remove();
}
```

Example 3

```
//Assume a list of integer strings.
//Remove all occurrences of "6" from the list.
for (Iterator<String> itr = list.iterator(); itr.hasNext();)
{
    String num = itr.next();
    if (num.equals("6"))
    {
        itr.remove();
        System.out.println(list);
    }
}
```

If the original list is 2 6 6 3 5 6 the output will be

```
[2, 6, 3, 5, 6]
[2, 3, 5, 6]
[2, 3, 5]
```

Example 4

```
//Illustrate NoSuchElementException.
Iterator<SomeType> itr = list.iterator();
while (true)
    System.out.println(itr.next());
```

The list elements will be printed, one per line. Then an attempt will be made to move past the end of the list, causing a `NoSuchElementException` to be thrown. The loop can be corrected by replacing `true` with `itr.hasNext()`.

Example 5

```
//Illustrate IllegalStateException.
Iterator<SomeType> itr = list.iterator();
SomeType ob = itr.next();
itr.remove();
itr.remove();
```

Every `remove` call must be preceded by a `next`. The second `itr.remove()` statement will therefore cause an `IllegalStateException` to be thrown.

NOTE

In a given program, the declaration

```
itr = list.iterator();
```

must be made every time you need to initialize the iterator to the beginning of the list.

The `ListIterator<E>` Interface

The `List` collections, `ArrayList` and `LinkedList`, provide an expanded iterator, `ListIterator`, that is a subclass of `Iterator`. The `ListIterator` interface allows traversal of the list in either direction, as well as greater capabilities for modifying the list. In addition to `hasNext`, `next`, and `remove`, there are six new methods in `ListIterator`. Of these, you are expected to know just two for the AP exam: `add` and `set`.

METHODS add AND set IN `ListIterator<E>`

```
void add(E item)
```

Inserts the specified element into the list. The insertion point immediately precedes the next element that would be returned by a call to `next`, if any. If the list is empty, the new element becomes the sole element in the list. The method throws a `ClassCastException` if the type of the object added is incompatible with the elements in the list.

NOTE

A subsequent call to `next` would be unaffected by the new element—the "current" element becomes the inserted element.

```
void set(E item)
```

Replaces the last element returned by `next` with the specified element. A call to `set` can only be made if neither `remove` nor `add` have been called after the last call to `next`. The method throws an `IllegalStateException` if `next` has not been called, or if `remove` or `add` have been called after the last call to `next`.

Using the `ListIterator<E>` Interface

To declare a `ListIterator` object for a list `obList` of `ObjectType`, use the `listIterator` method as follows:

```
ListIterator<ObjectType> itr = obList.listIterator();
```

The elements of the list are traversed from beginning to end with this code:

```
while (itr.hasNext())
    < code with call to itr.next() >
```

NOTE

During iteration, a container can be modified using the `remove`, `add`, and `set` methods of the iterator. During iteration, however, *you may not modify the container using non-iterator methods.* A `ConcurrentModificationException` will be thrown. (You don't need to know the name of this exception for the AP exam.)

For each example below, assume that `list` is a `List` of `String` objects.

Example 1

```
//Print elements of list, 1 per line.
for (ListIterator<String> itr = list.listIterator(); itr.hasNext();)
    System.out.println(itr.next());
```

NOTE

This is essentially the same code as when `Iterator` is used.

Example 2

```
//Add element to front of list.
ListIterator<String> itr = list.listIterator();
itr.add("55");
System.out.println(list);
```

If the input for the list is 3 5 7, the output will be [55, 3, 5, 7].

Example 3

```
//Add element to second slot in list.
ListIterator<String> itr = list.listIterator();
String element = itr.next();
itr.add("400");
System.out.println(list);
```

If the input for the list is 3 5 7, the output will be [3, 400, 5, 7].

Use a `ListIterator` for replacing elements in a list. You cannot use a for-each loop.

Example 4

```
//Replace each element in list with "100".
ListIterator<String> itr = list.listIterator();
while (itr.hasNext())
{
    String element = itr.next();
    itr.set("100");
}
```

Example 5

```
//Illustrate IllegalStateException.
ListIterator<String> itr = list.listIterator();
itr.set("55");    //error: set must be preceded by next
```

Each of the following code fragments will also cause the error.

```
String obj = itr.next();
itr.remove();
itr.set("55");    //set must be directly preceded by next

String obj = itr.next();
itr.add("100");
itr.set("55");    //set must be directly preceded by next
```

THE List<E> INTERFACE

A class that implements the List<E> interface is a list of elements of type E. In a list, duplicate elements are allowed. The elements of the list are indexed, with 0 being the index of the first element.

A list allows you to

- Access an element at any position in the list using its integer index.

- Insert an element anywhere in the list.

- Iterate over all elements using ListIterator or Iterator.

NOTE

1. It is generally more run-time efficient to iterate through a list than to cycle through the indexes.
2. For two list objects list1 and list2, list1.equals(list2) returns true if and only if the lists contain the same elements in the same order. This is irrespective of implementation.

The Methods of `List<E>`

Here are the methods in the AP Java subset.

```
boolean add(E obj)
```

Appends `obj` to the end of the list. Always returns `true` (contrast with `add` in `Set`, p. 487). Throws a `ClassCastException` if the specified element is not of type `E`.

```
int size()
```

Returns the number of elements in the list.

```
E get(int index)
```

Returns the element at the specified `index` in the list.

```
E set(int index, E element)
```

Replaces item at specified `index` in the list with specified `element`. Returns the element that was previously at `index`. Throws a `ClassCastException` if the specified element is not of type `E`.

```
void add(int index, E element)
```

Inserts `element` at specified `index`. Elements from position `index` and higher have 1 added to their indices. Size of list is incremented by 1.

```
E remove(int index)
```

Removes and returns the element at the specified `index`. Elements to the right of position `index` have 1 subtracted from their indices. Size of list is decreased by 1.

```
Iterator<E> iterator()
```

Returns an iterator over the elements in the list, in proper sequence, starting at the first element.

```
ListIterator<E> listIterator()
```

Returns a list iterator over the elements in the list, in proper sequence, starting at the first element.

The `ArrayList<E>` Class

This is an array implementation of the `List` interface. The main difference between an array and an `ArrayList` is that an `ArrayList` is resizable during run time, whereas an array has a fixed size at construction.

Shifting of elements, if any, caused by insertion or deletion, is handled automatically by `ArrayList`. Operations to insert or delete at the end of the list are $O(1)$. Be aware, however, that at some point there will be a resizing; but, on average, over time, an insertion at the end of the list is $O(1)$. This is called *amortized constant time*, and will not be tested on the AP exam. In general, insertion or deletion in the middle of an `ArrayList` is $O(n)$, since elements must be shifted to accommodate a new element (`add`), or to close a "hole" (`remove`).

THE METHODS OF `ArrayList<E>`

In addition to the two `add` methods, and `size`, `get`, `set`, `remove`, `iterator`, and `listIterator`, you must know the following constructor.

> `ArrayList()`

Constructs an empty list.

The following constructor, which is *not* in the AP subset, is also worth knowing. It provides neat solutions to certain problems.

> `ArrayList(Collection<? extends E> c)`

Constructs an `ArrayList` containing the elements of `c` in the same order as those in `c`. The parameter is a collection of type `E` or any type that's a subclass of `E`.

NOTE

Each method above that has an `index` parameter—`add`, `get`, `remove`, and `set`—throws an `IndexOutOfBoundsException` if `index` is out of range. For `get`, `remove`, and `set`, `index` is out of range if

```
index < 0 || index >= size()
```

For `add`, however, it is OK to add an element at the end of the list. Therefore `index` is out of range if

```
index < 0 || index > size()
```

Using `ArrayList<E>`

Example 1

```
//Return an ArrayList of random integers from 0 to 100.
public static List<Integer> getRandomIntList()
{
    Random r = new Random();
    List<Integer> list = new ArrayList<Integer>();
    System.out.print("How many integers? ");
    int length = IO.readInt();    //read user input
    for (int i = 0; i < length; i++)
        list.add(new Integer(r.nextInt(101)));
    return list;
}
```

NOTE

1. The variable `list` is declared to be of type `List<Integer>` (the interface) but is instantiated as type `ArrayList<Integer>` (the implementation). This has the advantage of making the code applicable to *any* `List`. For example, the single change

   ```
   List<Integer> list = new LinkedList<Integer>();
   ```

   will produce a `getList` method that creates a linked list of random integers.

2. The `add` method in `getList` is the `List` method that appends its parameter to the end of the list.

Example 2

```
//Swap two values in list, indexed at i and j.
public static void swap(List<E> list, int i, int j)
{
    E temp = list.get(i);
    list.set(i, list.get(j));
    list.set(j, temp);
}
```

NOTE

The `swap` method can be called with an `ArrayList` or a `LinkedList`—in fact, with any list object that implements `List`.

Example 3

```
//Print all negatives in list a.
//Precondition: a contains Integer values.
public static void printNegs(List<Integer> a)
{
    System.out.println("The negative values in the list are: ");
    for (Integer i : a)
        if (i.intValue() < 0)
            System.out.println(i);
}
```

Every call to `remove` must be preceded by `next`.

Example 4

```
//Remove all negatives from intList.
//Precondition: intList contains Integer objects.
public static void removeNegs(List<Integer> intList)
{
    for (Iterator<Integer> itr = intList.iterator(); itr.hasNext();)
        if (itr.next().intValue() < 0)
            itr.remove();
}
```

NOTE

1. In Example 3 a for-each loop is used because each element is accessed without changing the list. An iterator operates unseen in the background. Contrast this with Example 4, where the list is changed by removing elements. Here an iterator *must* be used explicitly.
2. No cast is required for `i.next()`: It is known to be of type `Integer`.
3. To test for a negative value, you could compare the `Integer` `i.next()` to another `Integer` object, namely one with value 0. This has to be constructed with the expression `new Integer(0)`. The test in the `while` loop then becomes

```
if (i.next().compareTo(new Integer(0)) < 0)
```

Example 5

```java
//Change every even-indexed element of strList to the empty string.
//Precondition: strList contains String values.
public static void changeEvenToEmpty(List<String> strList)
{
    boolean even = true;
    ListIterator<String> itr = strList.listIterator();
    while (itr.hasNext())
    {
        itr.next();
        if (even)
            itr.set( "" );
        even = !even;
    }
}
```

NOTE

1. A ListIterator is used because the set method is required: every second element, starting with the first, must be set to the empty string "".
2. The loop must start with a call to next because every call to set must be preceded by next.

> Every call to set must be preceded by next.

The LinkedList<E> Class

This is a linked list implementation of the List interface. The implementation is a doubly linked list with references to the front and back of the list. The AP Java subset, however, does not include the ListIterator methods that allow access to previous elements. This means that for the AP exam, the use of the LinkedList class will be restricted to singly linked lists.

The methods of LinkedList provide easy access to both ends of the list. To access the middle of the list, either an iterator or the get and set methods of the List interface must be used (p. 480).

THE METHODS OF LinkedList<E>

The following methods are in the AP Java subset (in addition to add, size, get, set, iterator, and listIterator).

```java
LinkedList()
```

Constructs an empty list.

```java
void addFirst(E obj)
```

Inserts obj at the front of the list.

```java
void addLast(E obj)
```

Appends obj to the end of the list.

```java
E getFirst()
```

Returns the first element in the list.

```
E getLast()
```

Returns the last element in the list.

```
E removeFirst()
```

Removes and returns the first element in the list.

```
E removeLast()
```

Removes and returns the last element in the list.

NOTE

1. If the list is empty, the getFirst, getLast, removeFirst, and removeLast methods throw a NoSuchElementException.
2. The following constructor, which is *not* in the AP subset, is also worth knowing.

```
LinkedList(Collection<? extends E> c)
```

Constructs a LinkedList containing the elements of c in the same order as those in c. The objects in the Collection parameter are of any type that extends E.

Using LinkedList<E>

The syntax for using a LinkedList is identical to that for using an ArrayList:

- To declare a LinkedList variable, use the interface List on the left side:

  ```
  List<E> b = new LinkedList<E>();
  ```

- To traverse the linked list, use Iterator, ListIterator, or a for-each loop.
- When an object is returned from a generic list, no cast is required before invoking methods with that object.

Writing General Code

Wherever possible try to write code that is general. For example, here is a method that will work for either an ArrayList or a LinkedList of Integer.

```
//Return largest item in list.
//Precondition: list is a nonempty list of Comparable values,
//              in this case, Integers.
public static Comparable findMax(List<Integer> list)
{
    Iterator<Integer> itr = list.iterator();
    Comparable max = itr.next(); //initialize max to first element
    while (itr.hasNext())
    {
        Comparable element = itr.next();
        if (max.compareTo(element) < 0)  //if max < element
            max = element;
    }
    return max;
}
```

The above example can be made even more general if the parameter is a List of any type that is Comparable. The code uses a wildcard, which will not be tested on the AP exam.

```
//Return largest item in list.
//Precondition: list is a nonempty list of Comparable values.
public static Comparable findMax(List<? extends Comparable> list)
{
    Iterator<? extends Comparable> itr = list.iterator();
    Comparable max = itr.next(); //initialize max to first element
    while (itr.hasNext())
    {
        Comparable element = itr.next();
        if (max.compareTo(element) < 0) //if max < element
            max = element;
    }
    return max;
}
```

NOTE

1. The elements of the list must be Comparable so that the compareTo method can be used.
2. In the initialization of max and the assignments to element, the object returned by itr.next() need not be cast to Comparable before compareTo can be called: It is automatically the declared type.

ArrayList VS. LinkedList

Which implementation should you use?

Here are the run times for the various operations:

Operation	ArrayList	LinkedList
Insert at front	add(0, obj) $O(n)$. Must shift all elements to make slot.	addFirst(obj) $O(1)$. A constant number of pointer connections.
Insert at end	add(obj) $O(1)$. May, however, need to resize. $O(n)$ to add n elements.	addLast(obj) $O(1)$. A constant number of pointer connections.
Delete at front	remove(0) $O(n)$. Must shift all elements one unit left.	removeFirst() $O(1)$. A constant number of pointer connections.
Delete at end	remove(size()-1) $O(1)$. Adjust size().	removeLast() $O(1)$. A constant number of pointer connections.

Continued on next page

Operation	ArrayList	LinkedList
Insert in middle	`add(index, obj)` $O(1)$ access to insertion point. $O(n)$ insertion, since elements to right of `index` must be shifted.	`itr.add()` $O(n)$ access to insertion point, using iterator. $O(1)$ insertion.
Delete in middle	`remove(index)` $O(1)$ access to element. $O(n)$ deletion, since elements to right of `index` must be shifted.	`itr.remove()` $O(n)$ access to insertion point, using iterator. $O(1)$ deletion.
Change value in middle	`set(index, obj)` $O(1)$. Fast access.	`itr.set(obj)` $O(n)$ traversal to locate element.

The choice of implementation should be driven by the run-time efficiency of your particular application. Here are some guidelines:

1. For most applications `ArrayList` is faster. This is because

   - `ArrayList` has fast access to any element in the list whose index is known, while `LinkedList` requires an $O(n)$ traversal to reach an interior element.
   - `LinkedList` needs to allocate a node for each element in the list, whereas `ArrayList` does not.

2. There are two cases in which you should consider using `LinkedList`:

   - If your application involves the frequent addition of elements to the front of the list. This is $O(1)$ for `LinkedList` but $O(n)$ for `ArrayList`, which requires copying and shifting elements for insertion.
   - If you must iterate over the list, deleting many elements as you go. This is $O(n)$ for `LinkedList`, a single traversal with a constant number of pointer connections for each deletion. For `ArrayList`, however, the operation is $O(n^2)$: For each deleted element, the entire right side of the list must be shifted.

3. The `LinkedList` methods `addFirst`, `getFirst`, `removeFirst`, `removeLast`, `addLast`, and `getLast` make it convenient to use a `LinkedList` implementation for any program that accesses only the ends of the list. A good example is implementing a queue. What you lose is the advantage of general code—you can no longer easily switch implementations if you decide `ArrayList` will be faster.

THE Set<E> INTERFACE

A *set* is a collection that has no duplicate elements. It may contain a null element. The `Set` interface is based on the idea of a mathematical set.

A set allows you to

- Insert a nonduplicate element into the set.

> A set contains no duplicates.

- Remove an element from the set.
- Test if a given element is in the set.
- Iterate over the elements using `Iterator`.

A class that implements the `Set<E>` interface is a set of elements of type `E`. The two `Set<E>` implementations in the Collections API are

- `HashSet<E>`, which stores its elements in a hash table (see p. 536).
- `TreeSet<E>`, which stores its elements in a balanced binary search tree.

NOTE

Two `Set` objects are equal if and only if they contain the same elements, irrespective of implementation.

The Methods of `Set<E>`

Here are the methods in the AP Java subset:

```
boolean add(E obj)
```

Adds `obj` to the set and returns `true` if `obj` was not already in the set. Leaves the set unchanged and returns `false` if `obj` was already in the set.

```
boolean contains(Object obj)
```

Returns `true` if the set contains `obj`, or if `obj` is `null` and the set contains `null`. Otherwise, the method returns `false`.

```
boolean remove(Object obj)
```

Removes `obj` from the set and returns `true` if `obj` was in the set. Leaves the set unchanged and returns `false` if `obj` was not in the set.

```
int size()
```

Returns the number of elements in the set.

```
Iterator<E> iterator()
```

Returns an iterator over the elements in the set.

The `HashSet<E>` Class

The `HashSet<E>` class implements the `Set<E>` interface. Items are not stored in any particular order and therefore do not need to be `Comparable`.

The methods of `HashSet` in the AP Java subset are the same methods as those given for the `Set` interface: `add`, `contains`, `remove`, `size`, and `iterator`. Additionally, you should know that the iterator returns the elements in no particular order and does not guarantee that the order will stay the same over time.

You should also know the default constructor for `HashSet` objects:

> Use a `HashSet` for fast access and removal of elements.

```
HashSet()
```

Constructs an empty set.

The following constructor, which is *not* in the AP subset, is also worth knowing:

```
HashSet(Collection<? extends E> c)
```

Constructs a new `HashSet` containing the elements in `Collection` c. The new set contains no duplicates, even though c may contain duplicates. The parameter is a collection of type E or any type that's a subclass of E.

The `HashSet` class is implemented with a hash table. As such it offers $O(1)$ run times for the operations `add`, `remove`, and `contains`.

The TreeSet<E> Class

| Use a TreeSet if the elements must be sorted. |

The `TreeSet<E>` class implements the `SortedSet<E>` interface and guarantees that the sorted set will be in ascending order, as determined by `compareTo`. This means that the items of a `TreeSet` are `Comparable`. They must also be *mutually comparable*, which means that you can compare them with each other. (For example, you can't compare a `String` with an `Integer`!)

As with `HashSet`, the `TreeSet` methods in the AP Java subset are those that were specified for the `Set` interface: `add`, `contains`, `remove`, `size`, and `iterator`. Note that the iterator for a `TreeSet` always returns the elements in ascending order.

You should also know the default constructor for `TreeSet` objects:

```
TreeSet()
```

Constructs an empty set.

The following constructor, which is *not* in the AP subset, is also worth knowing:

```
TreeSet(Collection<? extends E> c)
```

Constructs a new set, sorted in ascending order, containing the elements of c without duplicates. The elements of c must be mutually comparable, and their type is E or any type that extends E.

The `TreeSet` class is implemented with a balanced binary search tree. It therefore provides $O(\log n)$ run time for the operations `add`, `remove`, and `contains`.

Examples with HashSet<E> and TreeSet<E>

Example 1

```
Set<String> set = new HashSet<String>();
set.add("Mary");
set.add("Joan");
set.add("Mary");
set.add("Dennis");
set.add("Alan");
System.out.println("Size of set is " + set.size());
```

```
for (String str: set)
    System.out.print(str + " ");
System.out.println();

Set<String> tSet = new TreeSet<String>(set);
for (String str: tSet)
    System.out.print(str + " ");
System.out.println();

Iterator<String> itr = tSet.iterator();
while (itr.hasNext())
    if(itr.next().equals("Joan"))
        itr.remove();
System.out.println(tSet);
```

The output for this code fragment is

```
Size of set is 4
Joan Mary Dennis Alan
Alan Dennis Joan Mary
[Alan, Dennis, Mary]
```

NOTE

1. Again note that the collection variables `set` and `tSet` are declared with their interface type, `Set`, and constructed with their actual type (`HashSet` or `TreeSet`). This maintains flexibility to change implementations by just changing the constructor used.
2. Recall that a set does not allow duplicates. Thus, only one `"Mary"` was added.
3. The names in the second line of output could have been printed in any order.
4. Tossing the elements of a `HashSet` into a `TreeSet` gives a quick method of getting the elements in sorted order. However, the constructor used is not in the AP Java subset. On the exam, the statement

   ```
   Set<String> tSet = new TreeSet<String>(set);
   ```

   is likely to be replaced with a statement like this:

   ```
   Set<String> tSet = copySetToTreeSet(set);
   ```

   where `copySetToTreeSet` is described as a method that returns a `TreeSet` containing all the elements of `Set set`.
5. To access each element of a set without changing the set, use a for-each loop. However, if the set may be changed during the iteration, an iterator must be used.
6. The last line of code,

   ```
   System.out.println(tSet);
   ```

   uses a `toString` method to produce the last line of output.

Example 2

Remove duplicates from an `ArrayList`.

```
/* Precondition:  ArrayList list may contain duplicate items.
 * Postcondition: Returns list with all duplicates removed.
 */
public static ArrayList<String> removeDups(ArrayList<String> list)
{
    Set<String> set = new HashSet<String>(list);
    ArrayList<String> newList = new ArrayList<String>(set);
    return newList;
}
```

If the `list` parameter is created from this file

```
farmer
cat
hen
apple
pear
baboon
cat
hen
cat
```

then the following list of words without duplicates is produced

```
[farmer, pear, apple, baboon, hen, cat]
```

NOTE

1. If the elements in the returned `ArrayList` need to be sorted, replace the first line of the method with

   ```
   Set<String> set = new TreeSet<String>(list);
   ```

   The line

   ```
   ArrayList<String> newList = new ArrayList<String>(set);
   ```

   receives the elements in the same order that they're being stored—for `TreeSet` this is sorted in ascending order.

2. The `removeDups` method can be used in a program as follows:

   ```
   ArrayList<String> words = getWordList();    //read in words
   words = removeDups(words);
   ```

3. Example 2 uses constructors for `ArrayList`, `HashSet`, and `TreeSet` that are not in the AP Java subset. (To achieve the same result without those constructors, you would need to use iterators to copy one collection to another.) If these constructors are used on the AP exam, the statements

   ```
   Set<String> set = new HashSet<String>(list);
   ArrayList<String> newList = new ArrayList<String>(set);
   ```

   will be fully explained or, alternatively, replaced with methods that achieve the same result:

   ```
   Set<String> set = copyListToHashSet(list);
   ArrayList<String> newList = copySetToArrayList(set);
   ```

   where `copyListToHashSet` is described as a method that returns a `HashSet` containing all the elements of `ArrayList` `list`, and `copySetToArrayList` returns an `ArrayList` containing all the elements of `Set` `set`.

Example 3

Consider a `ArrayList` of words, `words`. You need to obtain each of the following:

The total number of words.
The number of *distinct* words (i.e., don't count any duplicates).
A list of words that were duplicates (don't list any more than once!).

Finding the total number of words is trivial. Since `words` is an `ArrayList`, you can simply access its size:

```
int total = words.size();
```

To find the number of *distinct* words, you can use the `removeDups` method of the previous example:

```
ArrayList<String> noDups = removeDups(words);
int numDistinctWords = noDups.size();
```

To get a list of duplicate words, without listing any more than once, suggests using a set of duplicates. How can you generate this set?

Recall that the `add` method returns `false` if the set already contains the element you are trying to add. This gives a way to spot those duplicates. You can iterate through `words`, tossing each word into a set. When you spot a duplicate, add it to the set of duplicates.

```
/* Precondition:  ArrayList list may contain duplicate items.
 * Postcondition: Returns set of duplicates contained in list.
 *                Returns an empty set if there were no duplicates.
 */
public static HashSet<String> getDuplicates(List<String> list)
{
    Set<String> hSet = new HashSet<String>();
    Set<String> duplicates = new HashSet<String>();

    for (String str: list)
        if (!hSet.add(str))
            duplicates.add(str);
    return duplicates;
}
```

If the `List` of words is created from this file

```
farmer
cat
hen
apple
pear
cat
cat
farmer
hen
```

then the set of duplicates produced is

```
[farmer, cat, hen]
```

Using **HashSet** and **TreeSet**

- If ordering of elements is important, use TreeSet.

- If ordering of elements is not important, use HashSet because the run time of the operations is faster.

- After creating an iterator for either Set implementation, don't modify the set with any method other than itr.remove(). You will generate an error if you do.

- The set implementations do not allow duplicates. Two objects e1 and e2 are duplicates if e1.equals(e2) is true, so for user-defined classes you need to override the default equals and hashCode methods to get the correct behavior. Remember two objects that are equal must have the same hashCode (see p. 227). If you do not do this correctly, you could have duplicate elements that are not treated as duplicates!

THE Map<K,V> INTERFACE

A *map* is a collection of key-to-value mappings, where both key and value can be any object. A map cannot contain duplicate keys, which means that each key maps to exactly one value. Different keys, however, can map to the same value. Note that the "value" can itself be a collection.

> In a map, each key can occur only once.

The Map interface allows you to

- Insert a key/value pair into the map.

- Retrieve any value, given its key.

- Remove any key/value pair, given its key.

- Test if a given key is in the map.

- View the elements in the map. (The interface provides three different ways to view the collection: the set of keys, the set of values, and the set of key/value mappings. The AP Java subset requires that you know just one of these, the set of keys, using the keySet method.)

- Iterate over the mapping elements, using Iterator. (The interface allows iteration over keys, values, or key/value pairs. You are required to know iteration over keys only. See Iterating over Maps on p. 494.)

The two Map<K,V> implementations in the AP Java subset are HashMap<K,V> and TreeMap<K,V>.

The Methods of Map<K,V>

Here are the methods in the AP Java subset:

`V put(K key, V value)`

Associates `key` with `value` and inserts the pair in the map. If the map already contained a mapping for this key, the old value is replaced. The method returns either the previous value associated with `key`, or `null` if there was no previous value for this key. Throws a `ClassCastException` if the type of the specified key or value prevents it from being stored in this map.

`V get(Object key)`

Returns the value associated with `key`. Returns `null` if the map contains no mapping for this key. Note that a return value of `null` indicates one of two situations:

1. The map contained no mapping for `key`.
2. This key was explicitly mapped to `null`.

The `containsKey` method can be used to distinguish these cases.

`V remove(Object key)`

Removes the mapping for `key` from this map, if present. Returns the previous value associated with `key`, or `null` if there was no mapping for `key`. Note that a return value of `null` may also indicate that this `key` was previously mapped to a value of `null`.

`boolean containsKey(Object key)`

Returns `true` if the map contains a mapping for `key`, `false` otherwise.

`int size()`

Returns the number of key/value mappings in the map.

`Set<K> keySet()`

Returns the set of keys contained in the map.

The `HashMap<K,V>` Class

The `HashMap<K,V>` class implements the `Map<K,V>` interface with a hash table. There is no particular ordering of elements and no guarantee that any given ordering stays constant over time. The class permits `null` values and the `null` key.

`HashMap` provides $O(1)$ run times for the `get` and `put` operations. This assumes that the keys are uniformly distributed across the hash table. There are two parameters that affect the performance of `HashMap`:

- Initial capacity: the number of slots for keys in the table (called buckets).
- Load factor: how full the table is allowed to get before its capacity is increased. (The default load factor of 0.75 offers a good tradeoff between time and space efficiency.)

You won't be tested on these details of the implementation, but they are helpful to understand how the class works.

Use a `HashMap` for fast insertion and retrieval of elements.

The methods of `HashMap` in the AP Java subset are the same methods as those given for the `Map` interface: `put`, `get`, `remove`, `containsKey`, `size`, and `keySet`. You should also know the following default constructor for `HashMap` objects:

```
HashMap()
```

Constructs an empty map.

The following constructor, which is *not* in the AP subset, is also worth knowing:

```
HashMap(Map<? extends K, ? extends V> m)
```

Constructs a new `HashMap` with the same mappings as `m`. The keys in the parameter `m` can be any type that extends `K`. The values can be any type that extends `V`.

The `TreeMap<K,V>` Class

The `TreeMap<K,V>` class implements the `SortedMap<K,V>` interface using a balanced binary search tree. The class guarantees ascending key order based on the ordering of the key class. `TreeMap` guarantees $O(\log n)$ performance for the `containsKey`, `get`, and `put` operations.

The operations for `TreeMap` that you should know are those described for the `Map` interface: `put`, `get`, `remove`, `containsKey`, `size`, and `keySet`. Additionally, you should know the following default constructor for `TreeMap` objects:

```
TreeMap()
```

> Use a `TreeMap` if the key set must be sorted.

Constructs an empty map.

The following constructor, which is *not* in the AP subset, is also worth knowing:

```
TreeMap(Map<? extends K, ? extends V> m)
```

Constructs a new map with the same mappings as the given map, sorted in ascending order of keys. It assumes that all possible pairs of keys are mutually comparable.

Iterating over Maps

The AP Java subset does not include an iterator method for the `Map` interface. This suggests that you will not be required to iterate over mappings.

You are, however, expected to be able to iterate over sets.

Example 1

To access the set of keys in `map` but not remove any of them, use a for-each loop:

```
for (KeyType key : map.keySet())
    System.out.println(key);
```

Example 2

To filter the map based on some property of its keys, use an iterator:

```
for (Iterator<KeyType> i = map.keySet().iterator(); i.hasNext();)
    if (i.next().isBad())
        i.remove();
```

NOTE

1. Example 1 will print out the *keys only* for map. If map is of type HashMap, the keys will appear in some unknown order. If map is a TreeMap, the keys will be printed in ascending order.
2. The loop in Example 1 causes the keys to be printed one per line. The statement

   ```
   System.out.println(map.keySet());
   ```

   would produce the keys printed on one line.
3. In Example 2, whenever i.remove() is called, the corresponding mapping will be removed from the map.
4. As with all the collections so far, no outside modification is allowed during an iteration.
5. The Map interface allows iteration over the set of keys, the set of values, and the set of key/value pairs. The operations that support the latter two types of iteration are not in the AP Java subset.

Examples with HashMap<K,V> and TreeMap<K,V>

Example 1

Initialize data in a map.

```
Map<String, Employee> employeeMap = new HashMap<String, Employee>();
for (int i = 1; i <= NUM_EMPLOYEES; i++)
{
    Employee emp = new Employee();   //declare a new Employee
    emp.setName(...);                //set the Employee's attributes
    emp.setSalary(...);              // ...
    emp.setID("E" + i);              // ...
    employeeMap.put(emp.getID(), emp);  //add employee to the
                                        //map using ID as the key
}
System.out.println(employeeMap.get("E4"));  //display the employee
                                            //whose key is E4
```

NOTE

1. Both the key and value must be objects. The employee ID is a String object; the corresponding value is an Employee.
2. It is common practice to use one of an object's attributes as a key in a map. You must be careful, however, that the key is unique. For example, using an employee's name as the key would be problematic: Two different employees with the same name could not exist in the same mapping!

Example 2

```
Map<String, String> h = new HashMap<String, String>();
h.put("Othello", "green");
h.put("Macbeth", "red");
h.put("Hamlet", "blue");
if (!h.containsKey("Lear"))
    h.put("Lear", "black");
Map<String, String> t = new TreeMap<String, String>(h);
System.out.println(h.keySet());    //print HashMap keys
System.out.println(t.keySet());    //print TreeMap keys
```

Running this code segment produces the following output:

```
[Othello, MacBeth, Hamlet, Lear]
[Hamlet, Lear, MacBeth, Othello]
```

NOTE

1. The keys are ordered for the `TreeMap`. They are in no particular order for the `HashMap`.
2. To print the set of values, you would need to use the `Map` method `values`, which is not in the AP Java subset. You can print the set of key/value pairs for a `Map` `m` with the statement

   ```
   System.out.println(m);
   ```

3. The statement

   ```
   Map<String, String> t = new TreeMap<String, String>(h);
   ```

   uses a constructor that is not in the AP subset. On the AP exam, the statement is likely to be given as follows:

   ```
   Map<String, String> t = copyMapToTreeMap(h);
   ```

   where `copyMapToTreeMap` is described as a method that returns a `TreeMap` containing all the elements of `HashMap` `h`.

Example 3

Use a `HashMap` to record the frequency of each word in an input file.

```
/* The WordFreqs class represents a mapping of words in a text
 * file to their frequencies.
 */

public class WordFreqs
{
    private Map<String, Integer> m;

    /* default constructor */
    public WordFreqs()
    {
        m = new HashMap<String, Integer>(); //use TreeMap for
                                            // sorted output

        loadMap(m);
    }
```

```
/* Create a HashMap of words from input file.
 * Each key is a lowercase word.
 * Each value is the frequency of the corresponding word.  */
private void loadMap(Map<String, Integer> m)
{
    < code to open input file for reading >
    while  (< there are still words in input file >)
    {
        String word = < next word in file >
        //Get Integer value in Map m associated with word.
        Integer i = m.get(word);
        if (i == null)  //new word found
            m.put(word, new Integer(1));
        else    //update frequency for existing word
            m.put(word, new Integer(i.intValue() + 1));
    }
    < close file >
}

/* Print word frequencies to screen, line by line. */
public void printFrequencies()
{
    System.out.println("Word frequencies: ");
    for (String word : m.keySet())
        System.out.println(word + " " + m.get(word));
        System.out.println();
}

/* Print word frequency mapping to screen, on one line. */
public void printFrequencyMap()
{
    System.out.println("Word frequencies: ");
    System.out.println(m);
    System.out.println();
}

/* Print words to screen. */
public void printKeySet()
{
    System.out.println("Distinct words in file were: ");
    System.out.println(m.keySet());
    System.out.println();
}
}
```

Here is a program that tests the WordFreqs class:

```
public class WordFreqMain
{
    public static void main(String[] args)
    {
        WordFreqs freqs = new WordFreqs();
        freqs.printFrequencies();
        freqs.printKeySet();
        freqs.printFrequencyMap();
    }
}
```

When the input file is

```
apple pear apple orange pear grape orange apple
```

the following output is obtained:

```
Word frequencies:
orange 2
pear 2
apple 3
grape 1

Distinct words in file were
[orange, pear, apple, grape]
Word frequencies:
{orange=2, pear=2, apple=3, grape=1}
```

NOTE

The `while` loop in the `loadMap` method can be written in a simpler form using the auto-boxing and -unboxing feature of Java 5.0. (This feature will not be tested on the AP exam, but you can certainly use it in your answers to the free-response questions.)

```
while  (<there are still words in input file >)
{
    String word =  <next word in file >
    Integer i = m.get(word);
    if (i == null)   //new word found
        m.put(word, 1);
    else             //update frequency for existing word
        m.put(word, i + 1);
}
```

RUN TIME OF SET AND MAP OPERATIONS

Data Structure	Method	Run Time	Comment
HashSet	add(x) remove(x) contains(x)	$O(1)$	Stored in a hash table. Assumes uniform distribution of elements.
TreeSet	add(x) remove(x) contains(x)	$O(\log n)$	Stored in a balanced binary search tree.
HashMap	put(key,x) get(key) remove(key) containsKey(key)	$O(1)$	Keys stored in a hash table.
TreeMap	put(key,x) get(key) remove(key) containsKey(key)	$O(\log n)$	Keys stored in a balanced binary search tree.

Chapter Summary

Be familiar with lists, sets, and maps, and their implementations in the Java API library. In particular, you should know the methods of the AP Java subset for the `ArrayList<E>`, `HashSet<E>`, `TreeSet<E>`, `HashMap<K,V>` and `TreeMap<K,V>` classes.

You should know what type of application calls for the use of a list, set, or map, and you should be able to write code that uses each of these data structures. Know the big-O run time for each method used in manipulating a collection.

You should be able to use iterators to traverse each of these collections, and in particular, you should be familiar with the AP Java subset methods of the `Iterator<E>` and `ListIterator<E>` interfaces.

When traversing an `ArrayList`:

- Use a for-each loop to access each element without changing it, or to modify each object in the list using a mutator method.

- Use an `Iterator` to remove elements.

- Use a `ListIterator` to replace elements.

MULTIPLE-CHOICE QUESTIONS ON COLLECTIONS

For additional questions on the `ArrayList` class, see Questions 22–28 in Chapter 6.

1. Which is a *true* statement about the collections classes?
   (A) `ArrayList` and `LinkedList` extend `List`.
   (B) `HashSet` and `TreeSet` implement `HashMap` and `TreeMap`, respectively.
   (C) `TreeMap` and `HashMap` implement `Map`.
   (D) `TreeSet` implements both `Set` and `Tree`.
   (E) `TreeSet` extends `HashSet`.

2. Which of the following correctly lists all the elements in a set declared as `HashSet<SomeClass> h`? You may assume that `SomeClass` has a `toString` method.

   ```
    I for (ListIterator<SomeClass> i = h.listIterator(); i.hasNext();)
          System.out.println(i.next() + " ");

   II for (Iterator<SomeClass> itr = h.iterator(); itr.hasNext();)
          System.out.println(itr.next() + " ");

  III for (SomeClass element : h)
          System.out.println(element + " ");
   ```

   (A) I only
   (B) II only
   (C) III only
   (D) II and III only
   (E) I, II, and III

3. Which is a correct description of the run times of the given operation for (1) `TreeSet` and (2) `HashSet`?

(A)	Inserting an element (`add`):	(1) $O(1)$	(2) $O(1)$
(B)	Inserting an element (`add`):	(1) $O(1)$	(2) $O(\log n)$
(C)	Removing an element (`remove`):	(1) $O(\log n)$	(2) $O(n)$
(D)	Removing an element (`remove`):	(1) $O(\log n)$	(2) $O(1)$
(E)	Testing if an element is in the set (`contains`):	(1) $O(n)$	(2) $O(n)$

4. A collection of `Comparable` objects is to be maintained in sorted ascending order. The collection can contain duplicates. Individual elements in the collection will be updated frequently. There will be no deletion of elements, and infrequent additions of new elements. The best implementation for this collection is
   (A) An `ArrayList`
   (B) A `LinkedList`
   (C) A `TreeSet`
   (D) A `HashSet`
   (E) A `TreeMap`

5. Consider an `ArrayList list` of `Student` objects. Which of the following correctly adds a `Student s` at position `insertPos`. You may assume that `s` is initialized, and that `insertPos` is of type `int` and is in bounds.

```
  I list.add(insertPos, s)
```

```
 II for (int i = list.size(); i >= insertPos; i--)
        list[i+1] = list[i];
    list[insertPos] = s;
    list.size()++;
```

```
III ListIterator<Student> itr = list.listIterator();
    int index = 0;
    while (index != insertPos)
    {
        itr.next();
        index++;
    }
    itr.add(s);
```

(A) I only
(B) II only
(C) III only
(D) I and III only
(E) II and III only

6. Consider method `replace` below:

```
/* Precondition:   List<E> L is a list of objects, some of which
 *                 could be null.
 * Postcondition: All occurrences of val are replaced
 *                 with newVal, including if val is null.  */
public static void replace(List<E> L, E val, E newVal)
{
    for (ListIterator<E> i = L.listIterator(); i.hasNext();)
        if (val.equals(i.next()))
            i.set(newVal);
}
```

Which is true about the `replace` method?
(A) It always works as specified.
(B) It may cause a `NullPointerException` to be thrown.
(C) It may cause an `IllegalStateException` to be thrown.
(D) It may cause a `NoSuchElementException` to be thrown.
(E) It will never work as specified; it will always cause an exception to be thrown.

7. Consider a map `m`, where `m` is of type `HashMap` or `TreeMap`. Suppose `s1` and `s2` are both sets, of type `HashSet` or `TreeSet`, where `s1` is the set of keys in `m`, and `s2` is the set of corresponding values in `m`. Which *must* be true?
(A) `s1.size() > s2.size()`
(B) `s1.size() >= s2.size()`
(C) `s1.size() == s2.size()`
(D) `s1.size() < s2.size()`
(E) `s1.size() <= s2.size()`

8. Refer to the method `changeEven` below.

```
/* Precondition:  ArrayList<Integer> a contains at least 1 element.
 * Postcondition: Every even-indexed element contains 0, i.e.,
 *                   elements with index 0,2,4,... contain 0.  */
public static void changeEven(ArrayList<Integer> a)
{
    boolean even = true;
    ListIterator<Integer> itr = a.listIterator();
    while (itr.hasNext())
    {
        if (even)
            itr.set(new Integer(0));
        itr.next();
        even = !even;
    }
}
```

Which statement is true about `changeEven`?
(A) It will work as intended for any `ArrayList` a.
(B) It will throw an `IllegalStateException` for every `ArrayList` a.
(C) It will throw an `IllegalStateException` only if `ArrayList` a has an even number of elements.
(D) It will throw an `IllegalStateException` only if `ArrayList` a has an odd number of elements.
(E) It will throw an `IllegalStateException` only if `ArrayList` a has fewer than three elements.

9. Consider the max method below, which is intended to find the largest element in a set.

```
/* Precondition:  s is a nonempty set of String objects.
 * Postcondition: Returns largest element in s.  */
public static Comparable max(Set<String> s)
{
    Iterator<String> itr = s.iterator();
    /* code to find maxValue */
    return maxValue;
}
```

Which replacement for /* *code to find* maxValue */ achieves the desired postcondition?

```
 I String maxValue = itr.next();
   while (itr.hasNext())
   {
       String current = itr.next();
       if (maxValue.compareTo(current) < 0)
           maxValue = current;
   }
```

```
II Comparable maxValue = itr.next();
   while (itr.hasNext())
   {
       Comparable current = itr.next();
       if (maxValue.compareTo(current) < 0)
           maxValue = current;
   }
```

```
III Comparable maxValue = itr.next();
    while (itr.hasNext())
    {
        String current = itr.next();
        if (maxValue.compareTo(current) < 0)
            maxValue = current;
    }
```

(A) I only
(B) II only
(C) III only
(D) II and III only
(E) I, II, and III

10. Consider a `findShortStrings` method that examines the `String` objects in an `ArrayList<String>` and creates a set of strings whose length is less than five.

```
/* Precondition:  list is a nonempty ArrayList of strings.
 * Postcondition: Returns a set of strings whose length is less
 *                than 5.
 */
public static Set<String> findShortStrings(ArrayList<String> list)
{
    Set<String> strSet = new HashSet<String>();
    Iterator<String> itr = list.iterator();

    while (itr.hasNext())
    {
        if (itr.next().length() < 5)
            strSet.add (itr.next());
    }
    return strSet;
}
```

Which is *true* about `findShortStrings`?

(A) It is unlikely to work as intended.

(B) It will always work as intended.

(C) It will work as intended whenever `list` contains an even number of elements.

(D) It will work as intended whenever `list` contains an odd number of elements.

(E) It may throw an `IllegalStateException`.

11. Consider the following code segment:

```
List<Integer> a = new ArrayList<Integer>();
Set<Integer> t = new TreeSet<Integer>();
for (int i = 10; i >= 1; i--)
    a.add(new Integer(i * i));
for (int i = 0; i < a.size(); i++)
{
    Integer intObj = a.get(i);
    int val = (intObj.intValue()) % 3;
    t.add(new Integer(val));
}
System.out.println(t);
```

What will be output as a result of executing this segment?

(A) [1, 0, 1, 1, 0, 1, 1, 0, 1, 1]

(B) [1, 1, 0, 1, 1, 0, 1, 1, 0, 1]

(C) [0, 0, 0, 1, 1, 1, 1, 1, 1, 1]

(D) [1, 0]

(E) [0, 1]

12. Assume that `list` is an array of lowercase words:

```
String[] list = {salad, banana, lettuce, beef, banana,
                      /* more words */}
```

What does this code segment do?

```
public static final Integer ONE = new Integer(1);
Map<String, Integer> m = new HashMap<String, Integer>();
for (int i = 0; i < list.length; i++)
{
    Integer num = m.get(list[i]);
    if (num == null)
        m.put(list[i], ONE);
    else
        m.put(list[i], new Integer(num.intValue() + 1));
}
```

(A) It produces in `m` a count of the *distinct* words in the list.
(B) It produces a table that maps each word in the list to its position in the list.
(C) It produces an alphabetized list of the words in the list and maps each word to its position in the list.
(D) It produces a frequency table that maps each word in the list to the number of times it occurs in the list.
(E) It searches `list` for those words that are already in `m`. When it finds a word in `m`, it updates the frequency for that word.

13. Which of the following correctly removes the first k elements from `LinkedList` L? You may assume that $0 \leq k < L.size()$.

```
 I  int count = 1;
    ListIterator<ElementType> itr = L.listIterator();
    while (itr.hasNext() && count <= k)
    {
        itr.remove();
        count++;
    }
```

```
 II  int count = 1;
     Iterator<ElementType> itr = L.iterator();
     while (count <= k)
     {
         itr.next();
         itr.remove();
         count++;
     }
```

```
 III  for (int i = 1; i <= k; i++)
          L.removeFirst();
```

(A) I only
(B) II only
(C) III only
(D) I and III only
(E) II and III only

14. A certain `LinkedList` `L` may contain duplicates. Which of the following operations removes the duplicates from `L`? (It is not necessary to preserve the order of the elements in the list.)

   (A) Transfer the elements of `L` to a new `HashMap` `m`. Transfer the elements of `m` to a new `LinkedList` `L`.

   (B) Transfer the elements of `L` to a new `HashSet` `h`. Transfer the elements of `h` to a new `LinkedList` `L`.

   (C) Transfer the elements of `L` to a new `ArrayList` `a`. Transfer the elements of `a` to a new `LinkedList` `L`.

   (D) Transfer the elements of `L` to a new `TreeMap` `m`. Assign the key set of `m` to `L`.

   (E) Transfer the elements of `L` to a new `HashMap` `m`. Assign the set of values in `m` to `L`.

15. A new ice cream parlor in a college town is planning to introduce three new flavors: peach chocolate, mango vanilla, and lychee strawberry. The ice cream parlor will do a survey among college students and ask if they would try such flavors. The percentage of students who would be willing to try each flavor will then be tabulated. The raw data of the survey will be stored in a large text file, and a computer program will access the file and calculate percentages. Of the following, which is the most suitable data structure for tabulating the results of the survey in the computer program?

   (A) A `HashMap`

   (B) A `HashSet`

   (C) A priority queue

   (D) An $m \times n$ matrix, where m is the number of flavors and n is the number of people surveyed

   (E) m arrays, where m is the number of flavors

16. Which of the following code fragments will *not* cause an exception to be thrown?

    (A)
    ```
    Map<String, String> m = new HashMap<String, String>();
    String obj = m.get("hello");
    ```

    (B)
    ```
    List<String> l = new LinkedList<String>();
    String obj = l.getFirst();
    ```

    (C)
    ```
    List<String> a = new ArrayList<String>();
    a.add(1, "hello");
    ```

    (D)
    ```
    String str = "";
    Set<String> s = new HashSet<String>();
    s.add("The");
    s.add("rain");
    s.add("in");
    s.add("Spain");
    for (Iterator<String> i = s.iterator(); i.hasNext();)
        str = str + (Integer) i.next();
    ```

    (E)
    ```
    Set<String> t = new TreeSet<String>();
    t.add("The");
    t.add("rain");
    t.add("in");
    t.add("Spain");
    for (Iterator<String> i = t.iterator(); i.hasNext();)
    {
        i.remove();
        i.next():
    }
    ```

17. Consider the following declarations in a program (lines are numbered for reference):

```
1   public class Student
2   {
3       ...
4   }
5   public class GradStudent extends Student
6   {
7       ...
8   }
9   public class UnderGrad extends Student
10  {
11      ...
12  }
13  public class StudentStuff
14  {
15    public void someMethod()
16    {
17      List<GradStudent> grads = new ArrayList<GradStudent>();
18      < code to initialize grads >
19      List<Student> studs = grads;
20        ...
21    }
22      ...
23  }
```

Which lines of code will cause an error?
(A) 5 and 9 only
(B) 17 only
(C) 19 only
(D) 17 and 19 only
(E) 5, 9, 17, and 19 only

18. Consider the following code for creating a new `HashMap`:

```
Map<String, Employee> m = new HashMap<String, Employee>();
< code to initialize m >
```

Which of the following code segments will search the keys of `m` and print each mapping whose key satisfies a given condition?

```
I  for (String s : m.keySet())
   {
       if (s.hasCondition())
           System.out.println(s);
   }
```

```
II  for (String s : m)
    {
        if (s.hasCondition())
            System.out.println(m);
    }
```

```
III  for (String s : m.keySet())
     {
         if (s.hasCondition())
             System.out.println(s + " " m.get(s));
     }
```

(A) None
(B) I only
(C) II only
(D) III only
(E) I and III only

Use the following description of the game of Battleships for Questions 19–22.

A programmer simulates the game of Battleships. The computer will try to sink its opponent's fleet before its own fleet is wiped out. Each player has a grid, hidden from the other player, with ships placed in straight lines, as shown.

Notice that

- No two ships occupy adjacent squares.
- The grid goes from (0, 0) in the top left-hand corner to (SIZE-1, SIZE-1) in the bottom right-hand corner.
- There are five ships of different lengths.

The players take turns shooting at each other's fleet. When a player fires a shot, he communicates the coordinates where the shot lands. His opponent responds "hit" or "miss."

The programmer is considering how the computer should keep track of its opponent's grid. He has defined a Position class and EnemyGrid class as follows:

```
public class Position implements Comparable
{
    private int myRow, myCol;

    public Position(int r, int c)
    {
        myRow = r;
        myCol = c;
    }

    //accessors

    public int row()
    { return myRow; }

    public int col()
    { return myCol; }

    /* Returns Position north of (up from) this position. */
    public Position north()
    { return new Position(myRow - 1, myCol); }

    //similar methods for south, east, and west
        ...
```

```
    /* Compares this Position to another Position object.
     * Returns either -1 (less than), 0 (equals),
     * or 1 (greater than).
     * Ascending order for Positions is row-major, namely start
     * at (0,0) and proceed row by row, left to right.  */
    public int compareTo(Object o)
    {
        Position p = (Position) o;
        if (this.row() < p.row() || this.row() == p.row() &&
                this.col() < p.col())
            return -1;
        if (this.row() > p.row() || this.row() == p.row() &&
                this.col() > p.col())
            return 1;
        return 0;        //row and col both equal
    }

    //equals and hashCode methods not shown ...

    /* Returns string form of Position. */
    public String toString()
    { return "(" + myRow + "," + myCol + ")"; }
}

public class EnemyGrid
{
    //private instance variables not shown ...

    //constructor
    public EnemyGrid()
    { /* implementation not shown */ }

    public void displayGrid()
    { /* implementation not shown */ }

    public Position selectNewPos()
    { /* implementation not shown */ }

    //Update grid with "hit" or "miss" response.
    public void updateGrid(String response, Position pos)
    { /* implementation not shown */ }

    //other methods not shown ...
}
```

19. The private instance variables of the `EnemyGrid` class will depend on the data structure selected to keep track of the grid. Which of the following is the *least suitable* data structure?

    (A) A `TreeMap` in which the keys are `Position` objects that have already been fired at. The corresponding values are the strings `"hit"` or `"miss"`.

    (B) A `SIZE × SIZE` matrix of strings in which each grid element has the value `"hit"`, `"miss"`, or `"untried"`.

    (C) A `LinkedList` of `Position` objects that have been fired at and hit, sorted in increasing order.

    (D) A `TreeSet` called `hitSet`, which is the set of `Position` objects that the computer fired at and hit, and a `TreeSet` called `missSet`, which is the set of `Position` objects that the computer fired at and missed.

    (E) An `ArrayList` of all `Positions` in the grid, and a parallel `ArrayList` of strings in which the *k*th location has value `"hit"`, `"miss"`, or `"untried"`, depending on the status of the *k*th `Position`.

20. The programmer selects a `TreeMap` as the data structure for the `EnemyGrid`. The keys are `Position` objects that have been fired at, and the corresponding values are the strings `"hit"` or `"miss"`. You may assume that `SIZE` is a global constant. The `EnemyGrid` class thus has this private instance variable:

```
private Map<Position, String> posMap;
```

Here is the constructor for the class, and the `updateGrid` method:

```
public EnemyGrid()
{ posMap = new TreeMap<Position, String>();}

/* Precondition:   TreeMap contains Position/String mappings
 *                 for each Position in the grid fired on
 *                 so far. Position pos is in range, and is
 *                 not in the map.
 * Postcondition:  TreeMap contains pos and its corresponding
 *                 response. */
public void updateGrid(Position pos, String response)
{ /* implementation code */ }
```

Which is correct /* *implementation code* */?

```
 I posMap.put(pos, response);

II if (!posMap.containsKey(pos))
       posMap.put(pos, response);

III String str = posMap.get(pos);
    if (str == null)
       posMap.put(pos, response);
```

    (A) I only
    (B) II only
    (C) III only
    (D) I and II only
    (E) I, II, and III

21. Which is a good reason for using TreeMap rather than HashMap in the EnemyGrid class?

    (A) The key set of used positions is displayed in row-major order (top to bottom, left to right), making it easy to see which positions are unused.

    (B) The value set of strings is displayed in order, making it easy to see which positions have been "hit" (or "miss"ed!).

    (C) Searching for any particular key position has faster run time in TreeMap than in HashMap.

    (D) Inserting a Position/String pair into the TreeMap has faster run time than insertion into a HashMap.

    (E) Retrieving a value from TreeMap has faster run time than retrieval from a HashMap.

22. Consider three different implementations for the EnemyGrid class:

    I   A TreeMap in which the keys are a set of Position objects that have already been fired at. The corresponding values are the strings "hit" or "miss".

    II A SIZE × SIZE matrix of strings in which each grid element has the value "hit", "miss", or "untried".

    III A TreeSet called hitSet that is the set of positions fired on and hit, and a TreeSet called missSet that is the set of positions fired on and missed.

    Assuming that the number of positions in the enemy grid is large, and that the most efficient algorithms are used in all cases, which statement is *false*?

    (A) Determining whether a given Position has been tried is more efficient with implementation II than with implementations I or III.

    (B) Updating a new position is more efficient with implementation II than with implementations I or III.

    (C) Listing all of the positions that have been used so far is more efficient with implementation II than implementation III.

    (D) Listing all of the positions, in row-major order, that have been used so far is only slightly more efficient with implementation I than implementation III.

    (E) Listing all of the positions, in row-major order, that have *not yet* been used is more efficient with implementation II than either implementations I or III.

The program description below applies to Questions 23–26.

Every year the Ithaca Bridge Club awards a versatility trophy to the player with the highest final score. A player's final score is the average of his or her top twenty scores in games each with a different partner. Thus, in order to be eligible for this trophy, a player must have played at least twenty games with at least twenty different partners during the year.

Consider writing a program that finds the winner of this trophy. Here are two classes that may be used:

```java
public class Game
{
    private String myPartner;
    private double myScore;

    public Game(String partner, double score)
    {
        myPartner = partner;
        myScore = score;
    }

    public String getPartner()
    { return myPartner; }

    public double getScore()
    { return myScore; }
}

public class Player
{
    private String myName;
    private double myFinalScore;
    private LinkedList<Game> myGames;  //a list of Games for this
                        //Player sorted in decreasing order of score

    public Player(String name)
    {
        myName = name;
        < code to initialize myGames from gameFile >
    }

    public String getName()
    { return myName; }

    //Returns average of elements in arr.
    private double findAverage(double[] arr)
    { < implementation code > }

    //Returns average of top 20 scores for games each with a
    //different partner, or returns -1 if player is ineligible
    //(fewer than 20 games or fewer than 20 partners).
    public double calculateFinalScore()
    { < implementation code > }
}
```

You may assume that every player in the club has a personalized `gameFile` that contains a listing of partners and corresponding scores. For example, Jimmy Carroll's `gameFile` may look like this:

```
Coppola Anthony      46.72
Harmon Mary          71.50
Coppola Anthony      64.27
Smith Jean           50.15
Smith Jean           48.31
Harmon Mary          75.67
    . . .
```

Notice that these scores are not in any particular order. When the data are read in by the `Player` constructor, however, each `Game` is placed in a `LinkedList`, sorted by score in descending order.

23. Consider the algorithm for the `calculateFinalScore` method for a `Player`.
    Traverse the `LinkedList` in order, as follows:

    - Get a `Game`.
    - If the partner has not been used, store the corresponding score, otherwise move on.
    - Stop when you reach the end of the list or you have twenty scores, whichever comes first.
    - If you have fewer than twenty scores, it means that this `Player` either played fewer than twenty games, or had fewer than twenty partners. The player is ineligible and the method should return -1.
    - If the player is eligible, return the average of the twenty scores.

    There are two collections that must be stored during execution of this algorithm:
    (1) the partners that have already been used, and
    (2) the scores that must be counted for the final average.
    Which is the most suitable implementation for
    (1) the partners, and (2) the scores?

    (A) (1) an `ArrayList`   (2) an `ArrayList`

    (B) (1) an `ArrayList`   (2) an array

    (C) (1) a `HashSet`   (2) an array

    (D) (1) a `TreeSet`   (2) an array

    (E) (1) a `HashSet`   (2) an `ArrayList`

24. Here is the implementation code for the `calculateFinalScore` method of the Player class:

```
/* Returns average of top 20 games, each with a different
 * partner. Returns -1 if Player is ineligible (fewer than
 * 20 games or 20 partners).  */
public double calculateFinalScore()
{
    //number of games counted so far
    int count = 0;

    //array of scores to be used in finding average
    double[] scores = new double[20];

    //set of different partners so far
    Set<String> partnerSet = new HashSet()<String>;

    //iterator for LinkedList of Games
    Iterator<Game> itr = myGames.iterator();

    /* code to generate scores array */

    if (count == 20)    //player eligible
        return findAverage(scores);
    else
        return -1;      //player ineligible
}
```

Which is correct /* *code to generate* scores *array* */?

```
I while (myGames.hasNext() && count < 20)
  {
      Game g = myGames.next();
      if (!partnerSet.contains(itr.getPartner()))
      {
          partnerSet.add(itr.getPartner());
          scores[count] = itr.getScore();
          count++;
      }
  }
```

```
II while (itr.hasNext() && count < 20)
   {
       Game g = itr.next();
       if (!partnerSet.contains(g.getPartner()))
       {
           partnerSet.add(g.getPartner());
           scores[count] = g.getScore();
           count++;
       }
   }
```

```
III  while (itr.hasNext() && count < 20)
     {
         Object o = itr.next();
         if (!partnerSet.contains(o.getPartner()))
         {
             partnerSet.add(o.getPartner());
             scores[count] = o.getScore();
             count++;
         }
     }
```

(A) None is correct.
(B) I only
(C) II only
(D) III only
(E) II and III only

25. When the trophy race program is run, the data for all the players are inserted into an `ArrayList`, `players`, of `Player` objects. The list is then traversed, and all players that are eligible have their player name and final score inserted into a `TreeMap<String, Double>`. Recall that an eligible player had his or her final score returned by the method `calculateFinalScore`. The method returned –1 for ineligible players.

    Here is a code segment that traverses the `players` list:

```
for (Player p : players)
{
    if (/* test */) //if this Player is eligible
    {
        /* statement */;   //place (Player name, final score)
                           //pair in TreeMap t
    }
}
```

Which is (1) a correct /* *test* */ and (2) a correct /* *statement* */?

(A) (1) `p.calculateFinalScore() >= 0`
    (2) `t.put(p, p.calculateFinalScore())`

(B) (1) `p.calculateFinalScore() >= 0`
    (2) `t.put(p.getName(), new Double(p.calculateFinalScore()))`

(C) (1) `p.getScore() < 0`
    (2) `t.put(p.getPartner(), new Double(p.getScore()))`

(D) (1) `p.getScore() < 0`
    (2) `t.put(p, new Double(p.getScore()))`

(E) (1) `p >= 0`
    (2) `t.put(p, p.calculateFinalScore())`

26. Having (player name, final score) pairs in a `TreeMap` data structure facilitates which operation?

    I   Listing the final scores in descending order.
    II Listing the names of eligible players in alphabetical order.
    III Listing the eligible players and their corresponding final scores, with the names in alphabetical order.

    (A) I only
    (B) III only
    (C) II and III only
    (D) I and II only
    (E) I, II, and III

27. If `s1` and `s2` are two sets, the *union* of `s1` and `s2`, $s1 \cup s2$, is defined as the set of all elements that are either in `s1` or `s2` or both. For example, if $s1 = \{2, 7, 9\}$ and $s2 = \{7, 2, 5, 1\}$, then $s1 \cup s2 = \{1, 2, 5, 7, 9\}$. Suppose `h1` and `h2` have been declared to be of type `HashSet`, and each has been initialized to contain objects of the same type. Which of the following code segments creates the union of `h1` and `h2` and stores it in `union`? You may assume that each line of code that copies elements into a new collection is correctly implemented as specified.

```
I //Copy the elements of h1 into a new HashSet, union.
  Set<Type> union = new HashSet<Type>(h1);
  for (Type element : h2)
      union.add(element);
```

```
II //Copy the elements of h1 into a new HashSet, union.
   Set<Type> union = new HashSet<Type>(h1);
   for (Type element : h2)
       if(!union.contains(element))
           union.add(element);
```

```
III //Copy the elements of h1 into a new ArrayList, list.
    ArrayList<Type> list = new ArrayList<Type>(h1);
    for (Type element : h2)
        list.add(element);
    //Copy the elements of list into a new HashSet, union.
    Set<Type> union = new HashSet<Type>(list);
```

    (A) I only
    (B) II only
    (C) III only
    (D) II and III only
    (E) I, II, and III

ANSWER KEY

1. C	10. A	19. C
2. D	11. E	20. E
3. D	12. D	21. A
4. A	13. E	22. C
5. D	14. B	23. C
6. B	15. A	24. C
7. B	16. A	25. B
8. B	17. C	26. C
9. E	18. D	27. E

ANSWERS EXPLAINED

1. **(C)** Choice A is false because `ArrayList` and `LinkedList` are not subclasses of `List`; they *implement* the `List` interface. Choice B makes no sense: `HashSet` and `TreeSet` both implement `Set`. Choice D is wrong because there is no standard collections interface called `Tree`. Choice E is wrong: `TreeSet` is not a subclass of `HashSet`; they both are implementations of `Set`.

2. **(D)** Segment I is wrong because `ListIterator` is defined only for classes that implement `List`. If h were an `ArrayList` or `LinkedList`, then segment I would be correct.

3. **(D)** The balanced binary search tree for `TreeSet` provides $O(\log n)$ run times for `add`, `remove`, and `contains` (see the run-time analysis for `insert`, p. 438, and `find`, p. 439). The hash table implementation for `HashSet` provides $O(1)$ run times for `add`, `remove`, and `contains` (see p. 536).

4. **(A)** Accessing individual elements in the list is very efficient with `ArrayList`, $O(1)$. For a `LinkedList`, this operation is $O(n)$. Eliminate choices C and D—a set cannot contain duplicates. Choice E is a poor answer—the given collection is not a mapping.

5. **(D)** Segment I is the best way to do this. The `add` method of `ArrayList` allows instant access at any position in the list. Segment III is not as efficient, but it works! It uses the `ListIterator` method `add` instead of the `ArrayList` method `add`. Note that it is not necessary to include a test of `itr.hasNext()` in the while loop. Since it is given that `insertPos` is in bounds, the algorithm will always find the correct position before running off the end of the list. Segment II is wrong because it's treating the `ArrayList` as if it were an array: There should be no indexing brackets.

6. **(B)** If val is null a `NullPointerException` will be caused by the expression `val.equals(...)`. The problem can be fixed by inserting `if (val == null)` as the first statement in the `for` loop and taking the appropriate action.

7. **(B)** Some keys in m can map to the same value. No two values, however, can match the same key.

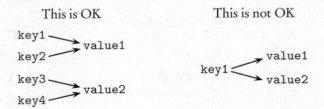

Recall that a set cannot contain duplicates. If the mapping is as shown on the left, s1 will have four elements and s2 will have two elements. If the mapping is one-to-one, then

        s1.size() == s2.size()

In general, however, the relationship will be

        s1.size() >= s2.size()

8. **(B)** The changeEven method throws an IllegalStateException since set is invoked before next on the first pass through the while loop.

9. **(E)** All work! In the declarations for maxValue and current (first and third lines of each segment), itr.next() returns a String, which *is-a* Comparable. Therefore the test if (maxValue.compareTo(...)) is fine.

10. **(A)** The probability of failure is very high because the itr.next() in the test is a different object from the itr.next() added to strSet in the next line! The iterator advances to the next element every time next() is called. The method can be fixed by modifying the while loop as follows:

```
while (itr.hasNext())
{
    String current = itr.next();
    if (current.length() < 5)
        strSet.add (current);
}
```

Note that you can't say definitively that the given code will fail. A fluke list of data may actually end up with the desired outcome! A note about choice E: This method will never throw an IllegalStateException, since itr.remove() is not used (see p. 476). If the iterator runs out of elements during the second itr.next() call in the while loop, the method *may* throw a NoSuchElementException.

11. **(E)** The add method appends new elements to the end of the list. Thus, a contains 100, 81, 64, 49, 36, 25, 16, 9, 4, 1. The second for loop retrieves each element in turn, starting with 100. The remainder when the element is divided by 3 is added to the TreeSet t. The only remainders generated are 1 and 0. Therefore, t contains just these two elements (no duplicates!). The output is 0, 1, since a TreeSet is ordered in ascending order.

12. **(D)** The algorithm traverses the array, starting with the first word. For each word, it checks to see if that word already exists as a key in m. If it does, it increments the corresponding value by 1. If it doesn't, it inserts the word in m and assigns it the value 1. The set of values is thus the frequency for each word.

13. **(E)** Segment I fails because `remove` cannot be called without first calling `next`. Note that it's OK to use either `Iterator` or `ListIterator`, since both are defined for `List` collections. In segment II, notice that you don't need an `itr.hasNext()` test, since you are given that `k` is in range. Segment III repeatedly removes the first element using a method from `LinkedList`.

14. **(B)** Transferring the elements of `L` to a new `HashSet` creates a set containing the elements of `L`, but without the duplicates. The operation of transferring these elements to a new `LinkedList` `L` has the effect of restoring `L` without the duplicates, but not necessarily in the original order. Choices A, D, and E don't make sense: They place the elements of `L` in a map, but there is no mapping! Choice C does not remove the duplicates! It places the elements of `L`, duplicates and all, in an `ArrayList`. Then it restores `L` to its original state.

15. **(A)** For each flavor its corresponding tally must be stored. This suggests that a mapping should be used, with flavors as keys and frequencies as the corresponding values.

16. **(A)** The `get` method of `Map` returns either the value associated with the key or `null` if the map contains no mapping for that key. In the example given, since the `HashMap` is empty, `obj` will be assigned the value `null`. Here are the errors that will be caused by each of the other choices:
B: `NoSuchElementException`: attempting to remove an element from an empty list.
C: `IndexOutOfBoundsException`: If the list is empty, index 1 is out of range. Index 0 would be fine for add.
D: `ClassCastException`: casting a `String` to an `Integer`.
E: `IllegalStateException`: calling `remove` before a call to `next`.

17. **(C)** Here is the point of the question: If `A` is a subclass of `B` and `G` is a generic collection, it is *not* true that `G<A>` is a subclass of `G<B>`. Look at the problems that can develop from line 19. Suppose line 19 is followed by a statement like

```
studs.add(new Student( ... ));
```

Since `studs` and `grads` are aliased (i.e., they refer to the same object), the above line may add a new `Student` to `grads` that is not a `GradStudent`. This is problematic, so the Java compiler will produce a compile-time error at line 19. Note that line 17 is fine: An `ArrayList<GradStudent>` *is-a* `List<GradStudent>`.

18. **(D)** Segment I is wrong because it doesn't print a mapping, only a key. Segment II is wrong because it doesn't examine each key in the key set. It also prints the entire mapping each time it prints. Segment III is correct: It prints the key and the corresponding value.

19. **(C)** There has to be some mechanism in the data structure that keeps track of whether a given position was hit *or missed*. All the data structures except the `LinkedList` in choice C have such a mechanism.

20. **(E)** Segment I associates `pos` with `response` and inserts the pair in the map. Segments II and III contain unnecessary code, but both work. Segment II inserts the `pos`/`response` pair in the map only when it determines that this `pos` is new, which, according to the precondition, it is. Segment III gets the value associated with `pos` in the map. Since `pos` is not in the map, `str` will be `null`, and the `pos`/`response` pair will be inserted in the map.

21. **(A)** Choices B through E are all false statements! Choice B is wrong because only the keys are displayed in order, not the values. (Besides, what does it mean to have "hit" or "miss" in order?) All of the operations in choices C through E are $O(\log n)$ for `TreeMap` and $O(1)$ for `HashMap`, if run time is the most important issue.

22. **(C)** Recall that the `TreeMap` (implementation I) contains only the positions that have been used so far. Thus, listing these is a simple traversal of a tree, requiring no tests. In order to list the used positions in the matrix (implementation II), however, every element in the grid must be inspected so that the "untried" values are omitted. Note that choices A and B are true: Accessing a given element in the matrix is $O(1)$, whereas doing so in a binary search tree is $O(\log n)$. It would appear that choice D is false because positions in the `TreeMap` are already sorted, whereas the positions in the two different `TreeSets`, while individually sorted, would have to be merged. However, in implementation III, a parallel traversal of `hitSet` and `missSet` that compares and prints elements as it goes, traverses the same number of elements as the `TreeSet` in implementation I. For choice E, to list the unused positions is very easy with the matrix implementation. Simply traverse in order and list the positions that are marked "untried". Finding the unused positions in implementations I and III is quite tricky, since these positions are not explicitly included in those structures. Try it!

23. **(C)** *To store the partners:* You want a collection that allows you to test in an efficient and convenient way whether the current partner is already in the collection. The `contains` method of `Set` allows an $O(1)$ test if a `HashSet` is used. A `HashSet` is better than a `TreeSet` because you have no compelling reason to keep the collection sorted. The `contains` method for `TreeSet` is $O(\log n)$, which is slower than $O(1)$. An `ArrayList` for the partners is not as good a choice as a `HashSet` because the search is $O(n)$.

    To store the scores: The length of the list is fixed at 20, and the scores are primitive `doubles`. This suggests that you use a fixed-length array. Using an array eliminates the overhead of wrapping and unwrapping the `double` values during processing.

24. **(C)** Segment II does each of the following correctly:
    - Traverses the list with `itr`, the `Iterator` object.
    - Accesses the partner and score for this `Game`, using `g.getPartner()` and `g.getScore()`.
    - Accesses the `partnerSet` correctly, using `partnerSet.contains` and `partnerSet.add`.

    Segment I uses the `Iterator` and `Game` objects incorrectly. Segment III does not cast the `next` object to `Game`. This is necessary because `getPartner` and `getScore` are `Game`, not `Object`, methods.

25. **(B)** If a player is ineligible, the `calculateFinalScore` method returns `-1`. Therefore the correct test for eligibility is

    ```
    if (p.calculateFinalScore() >= 0)
    ```

    You need `p.getName()` and `p.calculateFinalScore()` to access `Player` p's name and final score. Be careful not to use the `getScore` method from the `Game` class! Note that the test should not be

```
if (p.calculateFinalScore() != -1)
```

Never test whether a floating-point number is exactly equal to or not equal to another number (see the Box on p. 122). Note that in some of the answer choices a `Double` object was created from the final score so that it could be placed in the `TreeMap`:

```
new Double(p.calculateFinalScore());
```

This wrapping is in fact unnecessary since the advent of Java 5.0. The following statement in (2) of choice B would also be correct:

```
t.put(p.getName(), p.calculateFinalScore());
```

You will not, however, see this on the AP exam.

26. **(C)** A `TreeMap` maintains the keys in sorted order, which in this case means that the names are in alphabetical order. Printing the `keySet` gives the names in alphabetical order (operation II). Printing the map `t` gives the (name, score) pairs as described in operation III. Note: it's certainly possible to perform a sort on the set of score values. This operation is not, however, *facilitated* by the `TreeMap` structure, which was the point of the question.

27. **(E)** Segment I places the elements of `h1` in `union`. Then it iterates over `h2`, placing in `union` all the elements of `h2` that are not already in `union`. (Recall that the `Set` method `add` leaves the set unchanged if its `Object` parameter is already contained in the set.) Segment II uses the same idea as segment I. The `contains` test is redundant but not incorrect. Segment III takes a more circuitous route but ends where it should. It places the elements of `h1` in an `ArrayList` and then appends all the elements of `h2` to the list. Note that this list may contain duplicates—the elements that are in both `h1` and `h2`. When `union` is constructed from the `ArrayList`, the duplicates are eliminated, since a set contains no duplicates.

Sorting and Searching

CHAPTER 12

*Critics search for ages for the wrong word, which,
to give them credit, they eventually find.*
—*Peter Ustinov (1952)*

Chapter Goals

- Java implementation of sorting algorithms
- Quadratic sorts: selection and insertion sorts
- Recursive sorts: mergesort and quicksort
- Tree sort: heapsort
- Sequential search and binary search
- Hash coding
- Run time of searching and sorting algorithms

In each of the following sorting algorithms, assume that an array of *n* elements, a[0], a[1], ..., a[n-1], is to be sorted in ascending order.

$O(N^2)$ SORTS: SELECTION AND INSERTION SORTS

Selection Sort

This is a "search-and-swap" algorithm. Here's how it works.

Find the smallest element in the array and exchange it with a[0], the first element. Now find the smallest element in the subarray a[1]...a[n-1] and swap it with a[1], the second element in the array. Continue this process until just the last two elements remain to be sorted, a[n-2] and a[n-1]. The smaller of these two elements is placed in a[n-2]; the larger, in a[n-1]; and the sort is complete.

Trace these steps with a small array of four elements. The unshaded part is the subarray still to be searched.

8	1	4	6	
1	8	4	6	after first pass
1	4	8	6	after second pass
1	4	6	8	after third pass

NOTE

1. For an array of n elements, the array is sorted after $n - 1$ passes.
2. After the kth pass, the first k elements are in their final sorted position.
3. Number of comparisons in first pass: $n - 1$.
   Number of comparisons in second pass: $n - 2$.
   ...and so on.
   Total number of comparisons $= (n - 1) + (n - 2) + \cdots + 2 + 1 = n(n - 1)/2$, which is $O(n^2)$.
4. Irrespective of the initial order of elements, selection sort makes the same number of comparisons. Thus best, worst, and average cases are all $O(n^2)$.

AB ONLY

Insertion Sort

Think of the first element in the array, `a[0]`, as being sorted with respect to itself. The array can now be thought of as consisting of two parts, a sorted list followed by an unsorted list. The idea of insertion sort is to move elements from the unsorted list to the sorted list one at a time; as each item is moved, it is inserted into its correct position in the sorted list. In order to place the new item, some elements may need to be moved down to create a slot.

Here is the array of four elements. In each case, the boxed element is "it," the next element to be inserted into the sorted part of the list. The shaded area is the part of the list sorted so far.

8	1	4	6	
1	8	4	6	after first pass
1	4	8	6	after second pass
1	4	6	8	after third pass

NOTE

1. For an array of n elements, the array is sorted after $n - 1$ passes.
2. After the kth pass, `a[0]`, `a[1]`, ..., `a[k]` are sorted with respect to each other but not necessarily in their final sorted positions.
3. The worst case for insertion sort occurs if the array is initially sorted in reverse order, since this will lead to the maximum possible number of comparisons and moves:
   Number of comparisons in first pass: 1
   Number of comparisons in second pass: 2
   $\vdots$
   Number of comparisons in $(n - 1)$th pass: $n - 1$

   Total number of comparisons $= 1 + 2 + \cdots + (n - 2) + (n - 1) = n(n - 1)/2$, which is $O(n^2)$.
4. The best case for insertion sort occurs if the array is already sorted in increasing order. In this case, each pass through the array will involve just one comparison, which will indicate that "it" is in its correct position with respect to the sorted list. Therefore, no elements will need to be moved.

AB ONLY

Both insertion and selection sorts are inefficient for large n.

Total number of comparisons $= n - 1$, which is $O(n)$.

5. For the average case, insertion sort must still make $n - 1$ passes (i.e., $O(n)$ passes). Each pass makes $O(n)$ comparisons, so the total number of comparisons is $O(n^2)$.

RECURSIVE SORTS: MERGESORT AND QUICKSORT

Selection and insertion sorts are inefficient for large n, requiring approximately n passes through a list of n elements. More efficient algorithms can be devised using a "divide-and-conquer" approach, which is used in all the sorting algorithms that follow.

Mergesort

Here is a recursive description of how mergesort works:

If there is more than one element in the array
      Break the array into two halves.
      Mergesort the left half.
      Mergesort the right half.
      Merge the two subarrays into a sorted array.

> The main disadvantage of mergesort is that it uses a temporary array.

Mergesort uses a `merge` method to merge two sorted pieces of an array into a single sorted array. For example, suppose array `a[0] ... a[n-1]` is such that `a[0] ... a[k]` is sorted and `a[k+1] ... a[n-1]` is sorted, both parts in increasing order. Example:

a[0]	a[1]	a[2]	a[3]	a[4]	a[5]
2	5	8	9	1	6

In this case, `a[0] ... a[3]` and `a[4] ... a[5]` are the two sorted pieces. The method call `merge(a,0,3,5)` should produce the "merged" array:

a[0]	a[1]	a[2]	a[3]	a[4]	a[5]
1	2	5	6	8	9

The middle numerical parameter in `merge` (the 3 in this case) represents the index of the last element in the first "piece" of the array. The first and third numerical parameters are the lowest and highest index, respectively, of array a.

Here's what happens in mergesort:

1. Start with an unsorted list of n elements.
2. The recursive calls break the list into n sublists, each of length 1. Note that these n arrays, each containing just one element, are sorted!
3. Recursively merge adjacent pairs of lists. There are then approximately $n/2$ lists of length 2; then, approximately $n/4$ lists of approximate length 4, and so on, until there is just one list of length n.

An example of mergesort follows:

Break list into
n sublists of
length 1

Merge adjacent
pairs of lists

Analysis of Mergesort:

1. The major disadvantage of mergesort is that it needs a temporary array that is as large as the original array to be sorted. This could be a problem if space is a factor.

2. The merge method compares each element in the subarrays, an $O(n)$ process. It also copies the elements from a temporary array back into the original list, another $O(n)$ process. This total of $2n$ operations makes the merge part of the algorithm $O(n)$.

3. To break the array of *n* elements into *n* arrays of one element each requires $\log_2 n$ divisions, an $O(\log n)$ process. For each of the $\log_2 n$ divisions of the array, the $O(n)$ merge method is called to put it together again. Thus, mergesort is $O(n \log n)$.

4. Mergesort is not affected by the initial ordering of the elements. Thus, best, worst, and average cases are $O(n \log n)$.

Quicksort

For large *n*, quicksort is, on average, the fastest known sorting algorithm. Here is a recursive description of how quicksort works:

If there are at least two elements in the array
      Partition the array.
      Quicksort the left subarray.
      Quicksort the right subarray.

The partition method splits the array into two subarrays as follows: a *pivot* element is chosen at random from the array (often just the first element) and placed so that all items to the left of the pivot are less than or equal to the pivot, whereas those to the right are greater than or equal to it.

For example, if the array is 4, 1, 2, 7, 5, −1, 8, 0, 6, and a[0] = 4 is the pivot, the partition method produces

    −1   1   2   0 | 4 | 5   8   7   6

AB *(continued)*

Here's how the partitioning works: Let a[0], 4 in this case, be the pivot. Markers up and down are initialized to index values 0 and $n - 1$, as shown. Move the up marker until a value less than the pivot is found, or down equals up. Move the down marker until a value greater than the pivot is found, or down equals up. Swap a[up] and a[down]. Continue the process until down equals up. This is the pivot position. Swap a[0] and a[pivotPosition].

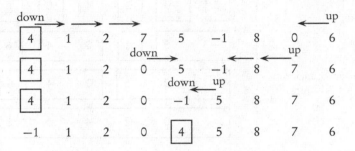

Notice that the pivot element, 4, is in its final sorted position.

Analysis of Quicksort:

1. For the fastest run time, the array should be partitioned into two parts of roughly the same size. In this case, and on average, there are $\log_2 n$ splits. The partition algorithm is $O(n)$. Therefore the best and average case run times are $O(n \log n)$.

2. If the pivot happens to be the smallest or largest element in the array, the split is not much of a split—one of the subarrays is empty! If this happens repeatedly, quicksort degenerates into a slow, recursive version of selection sort and is $O(n^2)$ (worst case).

3. The worst case for quicksort occurs when the partitioning algorithm repeatedly divides the array into pieces of size 1 and $n - 1$. An example is when the array is initially sorted in either order and the first or last element is chosen as the pivot. Some algorithms avoid this situation by initially shuffling up the given array (!) or selecting the pivot by examining several elements of the array (such as first, middle, and last) and then taking the median.

> The main disadvantage of quicksort is that its worst case behavior is $O(n^2)$.

NOTE

For both quicksort and mergesort, when a subarray gets down to some small size m, it becomes faster to sort by straight insertion. The optimal value of m is machine-dependent, but it's approximately equal to 7.

A BINARY TREE SORT: HEAPSORT

AB ONLY

Heapsort is an elegant algorithm that uses an array implementation of a binary tree. Recall the following definitions from Chapter 10:

> A *perfect binary tree* has every leaf on the same level and every nonleaf node has two children.

A *complete binary tree* is either perfect or perfect through the next-to-last level, with the leaves as far left as possible in the last level.

A *heap* (sometimes called a *max heap*) is a complete binary tree in which every node has a value greater than or equal to each of its children.

Example

Is each of the following a heap?

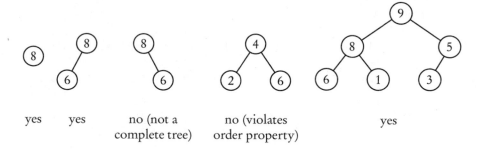

yes	yes	no (not a complete tree)	no (violates order property)	yes

NOTE

1. The largest value in a heap is in the root node.
2. A heap with *n* elements has *n*/2 subtrees that have at least one child. This counts the tree itself.

To sort array `a[0]`, `a[1]`, `a[2]`, ..., `a[n-1]`, heapsort has three main steps:

I. Slot the elements into a "mental" binary tree, level by level, from left to right as shown here. This creates a *complete* binary tree in your head, with the property that if node `a[k]` has children, its left child is `a[2*k+1]` and its right child is `a[2*k+2]`.

a[0]	a[1]	a[2]	a[3]	a[4]	a[5]
2	1	4	9	3	7

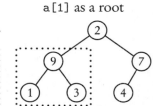

II. Transform the tree into a heap. Note that `a[(n/2)-1]` down to `a[0]` are roots of nonempty subtrees. (Check it out for odd and even values of n.) To form the heap, work from the "bottom" subtree up:

```
for (int rootIndex = (n / 2) - 1; rootIndex >= 0; rootIndex--)
    fixHeap(rootIndex, n - 1);     //n - 1 is the last index
```

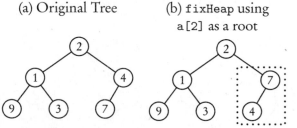

(a) Original Tree   (b) `fixHeap` using `a[2]` as a root   (c) `fixHeap` using `a[1]` as a root

AB *(continued)*

(d) `fixHeap` using `a[0]` as a root   (e) Tree is now a heap

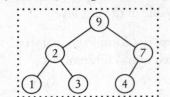 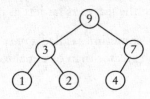

This mental picture gives meaning to what is happening to the array—a sequence of swaps.

	a[0]	a[1]	a[2]	a[3]	a[4]	a[5]
Original array	2	1	4	9	3	7
fixHeap(2,5)	2	1	7	9	3	4
fixHeap(1,5)	2	9	7	1	3	4
fixHeap(0,5)	9	2	7	1	3	4
	9	3	7	1	2	4

III. Sort the array using the heap property that the biggest element is at the top of the tree: Swap `a[0]` and `a[n-1]`. Now `a[n-1]` is in its final sorted position in the array. Reduce the last index by one (think of it as an apple that has dropped off the tree), and restore the heap using one fewer element. Eventually there will be just one element in the tree, at which stage the array will be sorted.

```
while(n > 1)
{
    swap(0, n - 1);        //swap a[0] and a[n-1]
    n--;
    fixHeap(0, n - 1);     //rootIndex is 0 in each case
}
```

(a) Tree is a heap

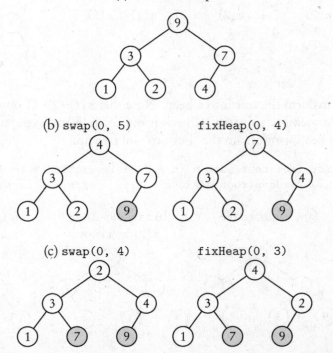

(b) swap(0, 5)   fixHeap(0, 4)

(c) swap(0, 4)   fixHeap(0, 3)

...and so on until `swap(0, 1)` yields

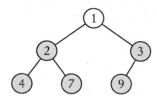

Here is the sequence of swaps in the array, starting after the tree has been formed into a heap.

	a[0]	a[1]	a[2]	a[3]	a[4]	a[5]
heap	9	3	7	1	2	4
swap	4	3	7	1	2	9
fix	7	3	4	1	2	9
swap	2	3	4	1	7	9
fix	4	3	2	1	7	9
swap	1	3	2	4	7	9
fix	3	1	2	4	7	9
swap	2	1	3	4	7	9
sorted!	1	2	3	4	7	9

Note that the `fixHeap` method in parts I and II of this algorithm assumes that the heap property is violated only by the root node (i.e., if you cover the root, the rest of the tree looks like a heap).

Analysis of Heapsort

1. For small n, this is not very efficient because of the initial overhead: Array elements must be rearranged to satisfy the heap property—the largest element must be moved to the "top" of the heap, and then moved again to the end of the array.
2. Heapsort is very efficient for large n.

   a) Building the original heap has $n/2$ iterations, each containing a `fixHeap` call, which, in the worst case, travels to the bottom (highest level) of the tree, $\log_2 n$ iterations. Thus, building the original heap is $O(n \log n)$.
   b) The sorting loop: $(n - 2)$ iterations of an $O(1)$ swap and $O(\log n)$ `fixHeap`-ing. Thus, the sorting piece of the algorithm is also $O(n \log n)$.

3. Heapsort is an "in-place" sort requiring no temporary storage. Its best, average, and worst case run times are all $O(n \log n)$. The worst case is only 20 percent worse than its average run time! This means that the order of the input elements does not significantly affect the run time.

SORTING ALGORITHMS IN JAVA

Unlike the container classes like `ArrayList`, whose elements must be objects, arrays can hold either objects or primitive types like `int` or `double`.

A common way of organizing code for sorting arrays is to create a sorter class with an array private instance variable. The class holds all the methods for a given type of sorting algorithm, and the constructor assigns the user's array to the private array variable.

Example 1

Selection sort for an array of int.

```
/* A class that sorts an array of ints from
 * largest to smallest using selection sort. */

public class SelectionSort
{
    private int[] a;

    //constructor
    public SelectionSort(int[] arr)
    { a = arr; }

    //Swap a[i] and a[j] in array a.
    private void swap(int i, int j)
    {
        int temp = a[i];
        a[i] = a[j];
        a[j] = temp;
    }

    //Sort array a from largest to smallest using selection sort.
    //Precondition: a is an array of ints.
    public void selectionSort()
    {
        int maxPos, max;

        for (int i = 0; i < a.length - 1; i++)
        {
            //find max element in a[i+1] to a[a.length-1]
            max = a[i];
            maxPos = i;
            for (int j = i + 1; j < a.length; j++)
                if (max < a[j])
                {
                    max = a[j];
                    maxPos = j;
                }
            swap(i, maxPos); //swap a[i] and a[maxPos]
        }
    }
}
```

Only Comparable objects can be sorted.

Note that in order to sort *objects*, the elements must be Comparable since you need to be able to compare them.

Example 2

AB ONLY

Heapsort for an array of `Comparable`.

```java
/* A class that sorts an array of Comparable objects
 * from smallest to largest using heapsort. */

public class HeapSort
{
    private Comparable[] a;

    //constructor
    public HeapSort(Comparable[] arr)
    { a = arr; }

    //swap a[i] and a[j] in array a
    private void swap(int i, int j)
    {
        Comparable temp = a[i];
        a[i] = a[j];
        a[j] = temp;
    }

    //Returns index of the maximum child of rootIndex node.
    //The last index of an element in the heap is last,
    // where last <= a.length - 1.
    private int getMaxChildIndex (int rootIndex, int last)
    {
        int leftChildIndex = rootIndex * 2 + 1;
        int rightChildIndex = leftChildIndex + 1;

        if (rightChildIndex > last ||
              a[leftChildIndex].compareTo(a[rightChildIndex]) > 0)
            return leftChildIndex;
        else
            return rightChildIndex;
    }

    //Fixes (sub)heap rooted at a[rootIndex], assuming that all
    // descendants of a[rootIndex] satisfy the heap order property,
    // i.e., order property violated only at the root node.
    //The last index of an element in the heap is last,
    // where last <= a.length - 1.
    private void fixHeap(int rootIndex, int last)
    {
        if (rootIndex * 2 < last)
        {
            int maxChild = getMaxChildIndex (rootIndex, last);
            if (a[maxChild].compareTo(a[rootIndex]) > 0)
            {
                swap(rootIndex, maxChild);
                fixHeap(maxChild, last);
            }
        }
    }
```

AB *(continued)*

```
//Sort array a from smallest to largest using heapsort.
//Precondition: a is an array of Comparable objects.
public void heapSort()
{
    int n = a.length; //number of elements in array

    // Build original heap from unsorted elements.
    for (int rootIndex = (n / 2) - 1; rootIndex >= 0; rootIndex--)
        fixHeap(rootIndex, n - 1);

    //Sort by swapping root value (current largest) in heap
    //with last unsorted value, then fixHeap-ing the
    //remaining part of the array.
    while (n > 1)    //while more than one element in tree
    {
        swap(0, n - 1);
        n--;
        fixHeap(0, n - 1);
    }
}
```

NOTE

The only method in this class other than the constructor that a client would call is heapSort. The swap, getMaxChildIndex, and fixHeap methods are internal to the sorting algorithm and are therefore private.

To sort an array of objects using this class:

```
public class SortTest
{
    < various methods >

    public static void main(String args[])
    {
        //Sort an array of words.
        < fill wordArray with wordList, a list of String objects >
        Comparable[] wordArray = makeArray(wordList);
        HeapSort h1 = new HeapSort(wordArray);
        h1.heapSort();
            . . .

        //Sort an array of Position objects.
        < fill posArray with posList, a list of Position objects >
        Comparable[] posArray = makeArray(posList);
        HeapSort h2 = new HeapSort(posArray);
        h2.heapSort();
            . . .
    }
}
```

NOTE

This code can be used only for objects that implement Comparable. The Java classes Integer, Double, and String all do. The Position class used is on p. 510. All of the Position coordinates are nonnegative. The compareTo method is defined to give

Position objects a row-major ordering, namely top-to-bottom, left-to-right. Thus (1,4) is less than (2,0), and (1,3) is less than (1,4).

AB *(continued)*

SEQUENTIAL SEARCH

Assume that you are searching for a key in a list of n elements. A sequential search starts at the first element and compares the key to each element in turn until the key is found or there are no more elements to examine in the list. If the list is sorted, in ascending order, say, stop searching as soon as the key is less than the current list element.

Analysis:

AB ONLY

1. The best case has key in the first slot, and the search is $O(1)$.
2. The worst case occurs if the key is in the last slot or not in the list. All n elements must be examined, and the algorithm is $O(n)$.
3. On average, there will be $n/2$ comparisons, which is also $O(n)$.

BINARY SEARCH

If the elements are in a *sorted* array, a divide-and-conquer approach provides a much more efficient searching algorithm. The following recursive pseudo-code algorithm shows how the *binary search* works.

Assume that a[low] ... a[high] is sorted in ascending order and that a method binSearch returns the index of key. If key is not in the array, it returns −1.

> Binary search works only if the array is sorted on the search key.

```
if (low > high)    //Base case. No elements left in array.
    return -1;
else
{
    mid = (low + high)/2;
    if (key is equal to a[mid])    //found the key
        return mid;
    else if (key is less than a[mid])  //key in left half of array
        < binSearch for key in a[low] to a[mid-1] >
    else     //key in right half of array
        < binSearch for key in a[mid+1] to a[high] >
}
```

NOTE

When low and high cross, there are no more elements to examine, and key is not in the array.

Example: suppose 5 is the key to be found in the following array:

a[0]	a[1]	a[2]	a[3]	a[4]	a[5]	a[6]	a[7]	a[8]
1	4	5	7	9	12	15	20	21

First pass: `mid = (8+0)/2 = 4.`   Check `a[4]`.
Second pass: `mid = (0+3)/2 = 1.`   Check `a[1]`.
Third pass: `mid = (2+3)/2 = 2.`   Check `a[2]`. Yes! Key is found.

AB ONLY

Analysis of Binary Search:

1. In the best case, the key is found on the first try (i.e., `(low + high)/2` is the index of key.) This is $O(1)$.

2. In the worst case, the key is not in the list or is at either end of a sublist. Here the n elements must be divided by 2 until there is just one element, and then that last element must be tested. This equals $1 + \log_2 n$ comparisons. Thus, in the worst case, the algorithm is $O(\log n)$. An easy way to find the number of comparisons in the worst case is to round n up to the next power of 2 and take the exponent. For example, in the array above, $n = 9$. Suppose 21 were the key. Round 9 up to 16, which equals 2^4. Thus you would need four comparisons to find it. Try it!

3. In the average case, you need about half the comparisons of the worst case, so the algorithm is still $O(\log n)$.

HASH CODING

Description

AB ONLY

Consider the programming problem of maintaining a large database, like patient records in a hospital. *Hash coding* is a technique for providing rapid access to such records that are distinguished by some key field. The coding maps each key to a storage address, and the data are stored in a *hash table*. Each data entry in the table is of some type (`tableElementType`) and has an associated *key field* of type `keyType`. Ideally, a hash table should provide for efficient insertion and retrieval of items.

Here is a simple example of hash coding. A catalog company stores customer orders in an array as follows. The last two digits of the customer's phone number provide the index in the array for that particular customer's order. Thus, two customers with phone numbers 257-3178 and 253-5169 will have their orders stored in `list[78]` and `list[69]`, respectively. In this example, the hash table is an array, the key field is a phone number, the *hash function* is (phone number mod 100), and the *hash address* is the array index.

The simplest implementation of a hash table is an array of data items. To insert or retrieve any given item, a hash function is performed on the key field of the item, which returns the array index or hash address of that item. This method cannot guarantee a unique address for each data item.

For example, suppose a small business maintains employee data in a list called `employeeList`. If the key field is `socialSecurityNo` and the hash function is (`socialSecurityNo % 100`), then 567350347 and 203479247 both hash to the same address: `employeeList[47]`.

A good hash function minimizes such *collisions* by spreading them uniformly through the key field values. A commonly used hash function in Java is

> Use hash coding if speedy insertion and retrieval are required.

```
key.hashCode() % SIZE
```

where `key.hashCode()` is the `hashCode` value of the key object (see p. 227) and `SIZE` is the number of slots in the hash table.

Resolving Collisions

HASH AND SEARCH (OR OPEN ADDRESSING WITH LINEAR PROBING)

Store the colliding element in the next available slot. An example for storing data with `keyValue` 556677003 is shown in the following table.

	employeeList
[00]	empty
[01]	453614001
[02]	empty
[03]	123467003
[04]	689286004
[05]	empty
⋮	
[99]	618272899

The hash function yields hash address 03, but `employeeList[03]` already contains data, so we try slot [04] and so on. In this example, the new data item gets stored in `employeeList[05]`. If the key hashes to the last slot in the array and is filled, treat it as a circular structure and go back to the beginning of the array to search for an empty slot.

In this scheme, searching for a given data item involves

1. Hash and compare.
2. If keys don't match, do a sequential search starting at that slot in the array.
3. Cycle back to the beginning if necessary.

REHASHING

If the first computation causes a collision, compute a new hash address using the old hash address as input. Repeat if necessary. Typically, a rehash function has form

$$(\text{hash address} + <\text{const}>) \% <\text{number of slots}>$$

where "const" and "number of slots" are relatively prime (i.e., no common factors greater than 1). This ensures that every index will be covered.

For example, the hash function for this table is key % 10. The rehash function is (hash address + 3) % 10. (Note that 3 and 10 are relatively prime.) Here are the steps to insert 26402 into the table:

[00]	
[01]	27401
[02]	68902
[03]	
[04]	
[05]	67905
[06]	
[07]	
[08]	
[09]	27309

26402 % 10 = 02   (taken)
(2 + 3) % 10 = 05   (taken)
(5 + 3) % 10 = 08,   which becomes
the hash address
of the new item.

These methods are simple to implement but are less than ideal in resolving collisions. If the table is almost full, an insertion operation becomes $O(n)$. What follows is more elegant.

AB *(continued)*

CHAINING

In chaining, the hash address is the index for an array of linked lists called *buckets*. Each bucket is a linear linked list of data items that share the same hash address.

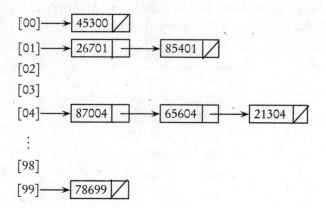

To insert an item, hash to the appropriate bucket and insert at the front of the list. Thus, insertion is $O(1)$. To search for an item, apply the hash function and do a sequential search of the appropriate list. Assuming that items are uniformly distributed in the hash table, a search should occur in constant time, which is $O(1)$.

> A hash table does not provide for sorting of elements.

```
┌──────────────────────────────────────────────────┐
│         Features of a Good Hash Function           │
│                                                    │
│  1. It distributes data items uniformly throughout │
│     the hash table.                                │
│  2. It provides for O(1) insertion and searching.  │
└──────────────────────────────────────────────────┘
```

NOTE ABOUT COLLECTIONS

The Collections API provides several efficient methods for manipulating elements, for example `sort` and `binarySearch`. For the AP exam you are not expected to know the usage of these library methods. You are, however, expected to be familiar with the details of the various sorting and searching algorithms discussed in this chapter.

RUN TIME OF SORTING ALGORITHMS

Assume that the array contains n elements, n large.

AB ONLY

Algorithm	Best Case	Worst Case	Comment
Selection sort	$O(n^2)$	$O(n^2)$	In each case $\approx n$ comparisons and 1 swap in each of $n - 1$ passes. $O(n^2)$
Insertion sort	$O(n)$	$O(n^2)$	Best: already sorted. 1 comparison and no data moves in each of $n - 1$ passes. $O(n)$ Worst: sorted in reverse order. Needs $\approx n$ comparisons and n data moves in each pass. $O(n^2)$
Mergesort	$O(n \log n)$	$O(n \log n)$	$\log_2 n$ splits gives n arrays of 1 element. n elements examined to merge on each level. $O(n \log n)$ irrespective of data.
Quicksort	$O(n \log n)$	$O(n^2)$	Best: $\log_2 n$ partitionings (pivot roughly in middle of each subarray). Partitioning algorithm is $O(n)$, so combination is $O(n \log n)$. Worst: $\approx n$ partitionings (array sorted and pivot at endpoint of each subarray), so combination is $O(n^2)$.
Heapsort	$O(n \log n)$	$O(n \log n)$	Irrespective of data: To fix heap, examine $\log_2 n$ levels. To create original heap, $n/2$ passes with $\log_2 n$ levels: $O(n \log n)$. To sort, $\approx n$ passes making 1 swap and fixing heap on each level: $O(n \log n)$.

RUN TIME OF SEARCHING ALGORITHMS

Assume

AB ONLY

- n elements in each case, n large.
- Sorted array for binary search.
- Uniform distribution of hash addresses in hash table.

AB *(continued)*

Algorithm	Run Time (Average & Worst Case)	Comment
Sequential search	$O(n)$	Examine each element sequentially until key found.
Binary search	$O(\log n)$	"Divide and conquer." $\log_2 n$ splits of array until just 1 element to examine.
Hash coding	$O(1)$	Get hash address (1 move). Find element (constant time).

Chapter Summary

You should not memorize any sorting code. You must, however, be familiar with the mechanism used in each of the sorting algorithms. For example, you should be able to explain each of the following: how the merge method of mergesort works; what the purpose of the pivot element in quicksort is; and how to form a heap in heapsort. You must know the best and worst case situations for each of the sorting algorithms, and the big-O run times in each case. Quicksort and heapsort are for level AB students only.

Be familiar with the sequential and binary search algorithms. You should know that a binary search is more efficient than a sequential search. Level AB students should know the big-O run times of each type of search. All students should know that a binary search can only be used for an array that is sorted on the search key.

Level AB students should know what hash coding is, and the conditions that make a good hash table. Know the various techniques for resolving collisions, and the big-O analysis for insertion and lookup algorithms.

MULTIPLE-CHOICE QUESTIONS ON SORTING AND SEARCHING

1. The decision to choose a particular sorting algorithm should be made based on

    I   Run-time efficiency of the sort
    II Size of the array
    III Space efficiency of the algorithm

    (A) I only
    (B) II only
    (C) III only
    (D) I and II only
    (E) I, II, and III

2. The following code fragment does a sequential search to determine whether a given integer, value, is stored in an array a[0] ... a[n-1].

    ```
    int i = 0;
    while (/* boolean expression */)
    {
        i++;
    }
    if (i == n)
        return -1;     //value not found
    else
        return i;      // value found at location i
    ```

    Which of the following should replace /* *boolean expression* */ so that the algorithm works as intended?
    (A) value != a[i]
    (B) i < n && value == a[i]
    (C) value != a[i] && i < n
    (D) i < n && value != a[i]
    (E) i < n || value != a[i]

3. A feature of data that is used for a binary search but not necessarily used for a sequential search is
    (A) length of list.
    (B) type of data.
    (C) order of data.
    (D) smallest value in the list.
    (E) median value of the data.

4. Array `unsortedArr` contains an unsorted list of integers. Array `sortedArr` contains a sorted list of integers. Which of the following operations is more efficient for `sortedArr` than `unsortedArr`? Assume the most efficient algorithms are used.

    I   Inserting a new element
    II Searching for a given element
    III Computing the mean of the elements

    (A) I only
    (B) II only
    (C) III only
    (D) I and II only
    (E) I, II, and III

5. An algorithm for searching a large sorted array for a specific value x compares every third item in the array to x until it finds one that is greater than or equal to x. When a larger value is found, the algorithm compares x to the previous two items. If the array is sorted in increasing order, which of the following describes all cases when this algorithm uses fewer comparisons to find x than would a binary search?
    (A) It will never use fewer comparisons.
    (B) When x is in the middle position of the array
    (C) When x is very close to the beginning of the array
    (D) When x is very close to the end of the array
    (E) When x is not in the array

6. Assume that `a[0]` ... `a[N-1]` is an array of N positive integers and that the following assertion is true:

    `a[0]` > `a[k]` for all k such that $0 < k < N$

    Which of the following *must* be true?
    (A) The array is sorted in ascending order.
    (B) The array is sorted in descending order.
    (C) All values in the array are different.
    (D) `a[0]` holds the smallest value in the array.
    (E) `a[0]` holds the largest value in the array.

7. The following code is designed to set `index` to the location of the first occurrence of key in array a and to set `index` to −1 if key is not in a.

```
index = 0;
while (a[index] != key)
    index++;
if (a[index] != key)
    index = -1;
```

In which case will this program *definitely* fail to perform the task described?
    (A) When key is the first element of the array
    (B) When key is the last element of the array
    (C) When key is not in the array
    (D) When key equals 0
    (E) When key equals a[key]

8. Refer to method search.

```
/* Precondition:  v[0]...v[v.length-1] are initialized.
 * Postcondition: Returns k such that -1 <= k <= v.length-1.
 *                If k >= 0 then v[k] == key. If k == -1,
 *                then key != any of the elements in v.   */
public static int search(int[] v, int key)
{
    int index = 0;
    while (index < v.length && v[index] < key)
        index++;
    if (index != v.length)
        return index;
    else
        return -1;
}
```

Assuming that the method works as intended, which of the following should be added to the precondition of search?
(A) v is sorted smallest to largest.
(B) v is sorted largest to smallest.
(C) v is unsorted.
(D) There is at least one occurrence of key in v.
(E) key occurs no more than once in v.

Questions 9–14 are based on the binSearch method and the private instance variable a for some class:

```
private int[] a;

/* Does binary search for key in array a[0]...a[a.length-1],
 *      sorted in ascending order.
 * Postcondition: Returns index such that a[index]==key.
 *                If key not in a, returns -1.   */
public int binSearch(int key)
{
    int low = 0;
    int high = a.length - 1;
    while (low <= high)
    {
        int mid = (low + high) / 2;
        if (a[mid] == key)
            return mid;
        else if (a[mid] < key)
            low = mid + 1;
        else
            high = mid - 1;
    }
    return -1;
}
```

A binary search will be performed on the following list.

a[0]	a[1]	a[2]	a[3]	a[4]	a[5]	a[6]	a[7]
4	7	9	11	20	24	30	41

9. To find the key value 27, the search interval *after* the first pass through the `while` loop will be
   (A) `a[0]...a[7]`
   (B) `a[5]...a[6]`
   (C) `a[4]...a[7]`
   (D) `a[2]...a[6]`
   (E) `a[6]...a[7]`

10. How many iterations will be required to determine that 27 is not in the list?
    (A) 1
    (B) 3
    (C) 8
    (D) 27
    (E) An infinite loop since 27 is not found

11. What will be stored in y after executing the following?

    ```
    int y = binSearch(4);
    ```

    (A) 20
    (B) 7
    (C) 4
    (D) 0
    (E) -1

12. If the test for the `while` loop is changed to

    ```
    while (low < high)
    ```

    the `binSearch` method does not work as intended. Which value in the given list will not be found?
    (A) 4
    (B) 7
    (C) 11
    (D) 24
    (E) 30

13. For `binSearch`, which of the following assertions will be true following every iteration of the `while` loop?
    (A) `key = a[mid]` or key is not in a.
    (B) `a[low] ≤ key ≤ a[high]`
    (C) `low ≤ mid ≤ high`
    (D) `key = a[mid]`, or `a[low] ≤ key ≤ a[high]`
    (E) `key = a[mid]`, or `a[low] ≤ key ≤ a[high]`, or key is not in array a.

14. Suppose $n =$ `a.length`. A loop invariant for the `while` loop is: key is not in array a, or
    (A) `a[low] < key < a[high]`, $0 ≤$ `low` $≤$ `high+1` $≤ n$
    (B) `a[low] ≤ key ≤ a[high]`, $0 ≤$ `low` $≤$ `high+1` $≤ n$
    (C) `a[low] ≤ key ≤ a[high]`, $0 ≤$ `low` $≤$ `high` $≤ n$
    (D) `a[low] < key < a[high]`, $0 ≤$ `low` $≤$ `high` $≤ n$
    (E) `a[low] ≤ key ≤ a[high]`, $0 ≤$ `low` $≤$ `high` $≤ n-1$

For Questions 15–19 refer to the `insertionSort` method and the private instance variable a, both in a `Sorter` class.

```
private Comparable[] a;

/* Precondition:  a[0],a[1]...a[a.length-1] is an unsorted array
 *                of Comparable objects.
 * Postcondition: Array a is sorted in descending order.  */
public void insertionSort()
{
    for (int i = 1; i < a.length; i++)
    {
        Comparable temp = a[i];
        int j = i - 1;
        while (j >= 0 && temp.compareTo(a[j]) > 0)
        {
            a[j+1] = a[j];
            j--;
        }
        a[j+1] = temp;
    }
}
```

15. An array of `Integer` is to be sorted biggest to smallest using the `insertionSort` method. If the array originally contains

    $$1 \quad 7 \quad 9 \quad 5 \quad 4 \quad 12$$

    what will it look like after the third pass of the `for` loop?
    (A) 9 7 1 5 4 12
    (B) 9 7 5 1 4 12
    (C) 12 9 7 1 5 4
    (D) 12 9 7 5 4 1
    (E) 9 7 12 5 4 1

16. When sorted biggest to smallest with `insertionSort`, which list will need the fewest changes of position for individual elements?
    (A) 5, 1, 2, 3, 4, 9
    (B) 9, 5, 1, 4, 3, 2
    (C) 9, 4, 2, 5, 1, 3
    (D) 9, 3, 5, 1, 4, 2
    (E) 3, 2, 1, 9, 5, 4

17. When sorted biggest to smallest with `insertionSort`, which list will need the greatest number of changes in position?
    (A) 5, 1, 2, 3, 4, 7, 6, 9
    (B) 9, 5, 1, 4, 3, 2, 1, 0
    (C) 9, 4, 6, 2, 1, 5, 1, 3
    (D) 9, 6, 9, 5, 6, 7, 2, 0
    (E) 3, 2, 1, 0, 9, 6, 5, 4

18. While typing the `insertionSort` method, a programmer by mistake enters

    ```
    while (temp.compareTo( a[j]) > 0)
    ```

    instead of

    ```
    while (j >= 0 && temp.compareTo( a[j]) > 0)
    ```

    Despite this mistake, the method works as intended the first time the programmer enters an array to be sorted in descending order. Which of the following could explain this?

      I The first element in the array was the largest element in the array.
      II The array was already sorted in descending order.
      III The first element was less than or equal to all the other elements in the array.

    (A) I only
    (B) II only
    (C) III only
    (D) I and II only
    (E) II and III only

AB ONLY

19. A loop invariant for the outer loop (the `for` loop) is
    (A) $a[0] \geq a[1] \geq \cdots \geq a[i-1]$, $0 \leq i \leq a.length$
    (B) $a[0] > a[1] > \cdots > a[i-1]$, $1 \leq i \leq a.length$
    (C) $a[0] \geq a[1] \geq \cdots \geq a[i]$, $0 \leq i \leq a.length - 1$
    (D) $a[0] > a[1] > \cdots > a[i]$, $1 \leq i \leq a.length - 1$
    (E) $a[0] \geq a[1] \geq \cdots \geq a[i-1]$, $1 \leq i \leq a.length$

Consider the following class for Questions 20 and 21.

```
/* A class that sorts an array of objects from
 * largest to smallest using a selection sort. */
public class Sorter
{
    private Comparable[] a;

    public Sorter(Comparable[] arr)
    { a = arr; }

    /* Swap a[i] and a[j] in array a. */
    private void swap(int i, int j)
    { /* implementation not shown */ }

    /* Sort array a from largest to smallest using selection sort.
     * Precondition: a is an array of Comparable objects. */
    public void selectionSort()
    {
        for (int i = 0; i < a.length - 1; i++)
        {
            //find max element in a[i+1] to a[n-1]
            Comparable max = a[i];
            int maxPos = i;
            for (int j = i + 1; j < a.length; j++)
                if (max.compareTo(a[j]) < 0) //max less than a[j]
                {
                    max = a[j];
                    maxPos = j;
                }
            swap(i, maxPos);    //swap a[i] and a[maxPos]
        }
    }
}
```

20. If an array of Integer contains the following elements, what would the array look like after the third pass of selectionSort, sorting from high to low?

$$89 \quad 42 \quad -3 \quad 13 \quad 109 \quad 70 \quad 2$$

(A)	109	89	70	13	42	-3	2
(B)	109	89	70	42	13	2	-3
(C)	109	89	70	-3	2	13	42
(D)	89	42	13	-3	109	70	2
(E)	109	89	42	-3	13	70	2

21. A loop invariant for the outer for loop of selectionSort is

(A) $a[0] \geq a[1] \geq \cdots \geq a[i-1],$ $0 \leq i \leq a.length - 1$
(B) $a[0] \geq a[1] \geq \cdots \geq a[i],$ $0 \leq i \leq a.length - 1$
(C) $a[0] \geq a[1] \geq \cdots \geq a[i-1],$ $0 \leq i \leq a.length - 2$
(D) $a[0] \geq a[1] \geq \cdots \geq a[i],$ $0 \leq i \leq a.length - 2$
(E) $a[0] \geq a[1] \geq \cdots \geq a[a.length-1],$ $0 \leq i \leq a.length - 1$

AB ONLY

22. The elements in a long list of integers are roughly sorted in decreasing order. No more than 5 percent of the elements are out of order. Which of the following is a valid reason for using an insertion sort rather than a selection sort to sort this list into decreasing order?

    I There will be fewer comparisons of elements for insertion sort.
    II There will be fewer changes of position of elements for insertion sort.
    III There will be less space required for insertion sort.

  (A) I only
  (B) II only
  (C) III only
  (D) I and II only
  (E) I, II, and III

AB ONLY

23. The code shown sorts array `a[0]...a[a.length-1]` in descending order.

```
public static void sort(Comparable[] a)
{
    for (int i = 0; i < a.length - 1; i++)
        for (int j = 0; j < a.length - i - 1; j++)
            if (a[j].compareTo(a[j+1]) < 0)
                swap(a, j, j + 1);  //swap a[j] and a[j+1]
}
```

This is an example of
  (A) selection sort.
  (B) insertion sort.
  (C) mergesort.
  (D) quicksort.
  (E) none of the above.

24. Which of the following is a valid reason why mergesort is a better sorting algorithm than insertion sort for sorting long lists?

    I Mergesort requires less code than insertion sort.
    II Mergesort requires less storage space than insertion sort.
    III Mergesort runs faster than insertion sort.

  (A) I only
  (B) II only
  (C) III only
  (D) I and II only
  (E) II and III only

25. A large array of lowercase characters is to be searched for the pattern "pqrs." The first step in a very efficient searching algorithm is to look at characters with index
  (A) 0, 1, 2, ... until a "p" is encountered
  (B) 0, 1, 2, ... until any letter in "p" ... "s" is encountered
  (C) 3, 7, 11, ... until an "s" is encountered
  (D) 3, 7, 11, ... until any letter in "p" ... "s" is encountered
  (E) 3, 7, 11, ... until any letter other than "p" ... "s" is encountered

26. The array names[0], names[1], ..., names[9999] is a list of 10,000 name strings. The list is to be searched to determine the location of some name X in the list. Which of the following preconditions is necessary for a binary search?
    (A) There are no duplicate names in the list.
    (B) The number of names N in the list is large.
    (C) The list is in alphabetical order.
    (D) Name X is definitely in the list.
    (E) Name X occurs near the middle of the list.

27. Consider the following method:

```
//Precondition: a[0],a[1]...a[n-1] contain integers.
public static int someMethod(int[] a, int n, int value)
{
    if (n == 0)
        return -1;
    else
    {
        if (a[n-1] == value)
            return n - 1;
        else
            return someMethod(a, n - 1, value);
    }
}
```

    The method shown is an example of
    (A) insertion sort.
    (B) mergesort.
    (C) selection sort.
    (D) binary search.
    (E) sequential search.

28. The partition method for quicksort partitions a list as follows:

    AB ONLY

    (i) A pivot element is selected from the array.
    (ii) The elements of the list are rearranged such that all elements to the left of the pivot are less than or equal to it; all elements to the right of the pivot are greater than or equal to it.

    Partitioning the array requires which of the following?
    (A) A recursive algorithm
    (B) A temporary array
    (C) An external file for the array
    (D) A swap algorithm for interchanging array elements
    (E) A merge method for merging two sorted lists

29. Assume that mergesort will be used to sort an array arr of n integers into increasing order. What is the purpose of the merge method in the mergesort algorithm?
    (A) Partition arr into two parts of roughly equal length, then merge these parts.
    (B) Use a recursive algorithm to sort arr into increasing order.
    (C) Divide arr into n subarrays, each with one element.
    (D) Merge two sorted parts of arr into a single sorted array.
    (E) Merge two sorted arrays into a temporary array that is sorted.

30. A binary search is to be performed on an array with 600 elements. In the *worst* case, which of the following best approximates the number of iterations of the algorithm?
    (A) 6
    (B) 10
    (C) 100
    (D) 300
    (E) 600

31. A worst case situation for insertion sort would be

    I   A list in correct sorted order.
    II A list sorted in reverse order.
    III A list in random order.

    (A) I only
    (B) II only
    (C) III only
    (D) I and II only
    (E) II and III only

AB ONLY

32. Which of the following represents a heap?

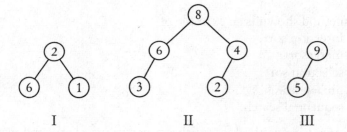

    I   II   III

    (A) I only
    (B) II only
    (C) III only
    (D) I and III only
    (E) II and III only

33. The list

$$17 \quad 9 \quad 2 \quad 7 \quad 21 \quad 18 \quad 4 \quad 5$$

is to be sorted into ascending order using heapsort. What is the level of the binary tree that will be formed, given that the root is at level 0?
    (A) 0
    (B) 1
    (C) 2
    (D) 3
    (E) 4

34. Assume that array a[0]...a[6] = 6 1 5 9 8 4 7 is to be sorted in increasing order using heapsort. Which of the following represents the correct sequence of swaps to be made to form the array into the original heap?

(A) 6 1 7 9 8 4 5
     6 9 7 1 8 4 5
     9 6 7 1 8 4 5
     9 8 7 1 6 4 5

(B) 6 9 5 1 8 4 7
     6 9 7 1 8 4 5
     9 6 7 1 8 4 5
     9 8 7 1 6 4 5

(C) 6 1 7 9 8 4 5
     7 1 6 9 8 4 5
     7 9 6 1 8 4 5
     9 7 6 1 8 4 5
     9 8 6 1 7 4 5

(D) 6 9 5 1 8 4 7
     9 6 5 1 8 4 7
     9 6 7 1 8 4 5
     9 8 7 1 6 4 5

(E) None of these sequences is correct.

35. An array is to be sorted into increasing order using quicksort. If the array is initially sorted in increasing order, which of the following *must* be true?
    (A) The algorithm will be $O(n)$.
    (B) The algorithm will be $O(\log n)$.
    (C) The algorithm will be $O(n \log n)$.
    (D) The algorithm will be $O(n^2)$.
    (E) There is insufficient information to make a prediction about efficiency.

36. The efficiency of hash coding depends on which of the following:

    I   The number of collisions that occur
    II The size of the data items in the list
    III The method of dealing with collisions

    (A) I only
    (B) III only
    (C) I and III only
    (D) I and II only
    (E) I, II, and III

37. The following key values are to be inserted into the hash table shown in the order given:

10   28   2   7   45   25   40   29

array index	0	1	2	3	4	5	6	7	8	9	10
key value											

The hash function is key % 11. Collisions will be resolved with the Open Addressing and Linear Probing ("hash-and-search") method. Which array slot will 29 eventually occupy?
(A) 7
(B) 8
(C) 9
(D) 10
(E) 0

38. An array contains data that was hash coded into it. How should this array be searched for a given item?
(A) A linear search should be used on the key data fields.
(B) If the array is sorted on the key fields, a binary search should be used.
(C) The Java % operation should be applied to the key of the item to obtain the correct array location.
(D) The hashCode method of the item should be applied to the key to obtain the correct array location.
(E) The hash function and a collision resolution algorithm should be applied to the key to find the correct location.

39. A certain hash function $h(x)$ on a key field places records with the following key fields into a hash table.

62   79   81   12   54   97   34

Collisions are handled with a rehashing function $r(x)$, which takes as an argument the result of applying $h(x)$. The key values are entered in the order shown above to produce the following table:

0	1	2	3	4	5	6	7	8	9	10	11	12	13	14	15	16	17	18	19
	81	62						34				12		54			97		79

What are $h(x)$ and $r(x)$, respectively?
(A) key % 20,   (result + 13) % 20
(B) key % 20,   result % 20
(C) key % 30,   (result + 14) % 20
(D) key % 20,   (result + 7) % 20
(E) key % 30,   (result + 7) % 30

Questions 40 and 41 are based on the Sort interface and MergeSort and QuickSort classes shown below.

```java
public interface Sort
{
    void sort();
}

public class MergeSort implements Sort
{
    private Comparable[] a;

    //constructor
    public MergeSort(Comparable[] arr)
    { a = arr; }

    //Merge a[lb] to a[mi] and a[mi+1] to a[ub].
    //Precondition: a[lb] to a[mi] and a[mi+1] to a[ub] both
    //              sorted in increasing order.
    private void merge(int lb, int mi, int ub)
    { /* Implementation not shown. */ }

    //Sort a[first]..a[last] in increasing order using mergesort.
    //Precondition: a is an array of Comparable objects.
    private void sort(int first, int last)
    {
        int mid;

        if (first != last)
        {
            mid = (first + last) / 2;
            sort(first, mid);
            sort(mid + 1, last);
            merge(first, mid, last);
        }
    }

    //Sort array a from smallest to largest using mergesort.
    //Precondition: a is an array of Comparable objects.
    public void sort()
    {
        sort(0, a.length - 1);
    }
}

public class QuickSort implements Sort
{
    private Comparable[] a;

    //constructor
    public QuickSort(Comparable[] arr)
    { a = arr; }

    //Swap a[i] and a[j] in array a.
    private void swap(int i, int j)
    { /* Implementation not shown. */ }
```

```
//Returns the index pivPos such that a[first] to a[last]
//is partitioned.
//a[first..pivPos] <= a[pivPos] and a[pivPos..last] >= a[pivPos]
private int partition(int first, int last)
{ /* Implementation not shown. */ }

//Sort a[first]..a[last] in increasing order using quicksort.
//Precondition: a is an array of Comparable objects.
private void sort(int first, int last)
{
    if (first < last)
    {
        int pivPos = partition(first, last);
        sort(first, pivPos - 1);
        sort(pivPos + 1, last);
    }
}

//Sort array a in increasing order.
public void sort()
{
    sort(0, a.length - 1);
}
}
```

40. Notice that the `MergeSort` and `QuickSort` classes both have a private helper method that implements the recursive sort routine. For this example, which of the following is *not* a valid reason for having a helper method?

    I The helper method hides the implementation details of the sorting algorithm from the user.

   II A method with additional parameters is needed to implement the recursion.

  III Providing a helper method increases the run-time efficiency of the sorting algorithm.

(A) I only
(B) II only
(C) III only
(D) I and II only
(E) I, II, and III

41. A piece of code to test the `QuickSort` and `MergeSort` classes is as follows:

```
//Create an array of Comparable values
Comparable[] strArray = makeArray(strList);
writeList(strArray);
/* more code */
```

where `makeArray` creates an array of `Comparable` from a list `strList`. Which of the following replacements for /* *more code* */ is reasonable code to test `QuickSort` and `MergeSort`? You can assume `writeList` correctly writes out an array of `String`.

(A)
```
Sort q = new QuickSort(strArray);
Sort m = new MergeSort(strArray);
q.sort();
writeList(strArray);
m.sort();
writeList(strArray);
```

(B)
```
QuickSort q = new Sort(strArray);
MergeSort m = new Sort(strArray);
q.sort();
writeList(strArray);
m.sort();
writeList(strArray);
```

(C)
```
Sort q = new QuickSort(strArray);
Sort m = new MergeSort(strArray);
Comparable[] copyArray = makeArray(strList);
q.sort(0, strArray.length - 1);
writeList(strArray);
m.sort(0, copyArray.length - 1);
writeList(copyArray);
```

(D)
```
QuickSort q = new Sort(strArray);
Comparable[] copyArray = makeArray(strList);
MergeSort m = new Sort(strArray);
q.sort();
writeList(strArray);
m.sort();
writeList(copyArray);
```

(E)
```
Sort q = new QuickSort(strArray);
Comparable[] copyArray = makeArray(strList);
Sort m = new MergeSort(copyArray);
q.sort();
writeList(strArray);
m.sort();
writeList(copyArray);
```

42. Which represents the worst case performance of the sequential search and binary search, respectively?
    (A) $O(n^2)$, $O(n \log n)$
    (B) $O(n)$, $O(n \log n)$
    (C) $O(n)$, $O(n)$
    (D) $O(n)$, $O(\log n)$
    (E) $O(n^2)$, $O(\log n)$

43. A typical algorithm to search an ordered list of numbers has an execution time of $O(\log_2 n)$. Which of the following choices is closest to the maximum number of times that such an algorithm will execute its main comparison loop when searching an ordered list of 1 million numbers?
    (A) 6
    (B) 20
    (C) 100
    (D) 120
    (E) 1000

44. A certain algorithm sequentially examines a list of n random integers and then outputs the number of times 8 occurs in the list. Using big-O notation, this algorithm is
    (A) $O(1)$
    (B) $O(\sqrt{n})$
    (C) $O(n)$
    (D) $O(n^2)$
    (E) $O(\log n)$

45. Which represents the worst case performance of mergesort, quicksort, and heapsort, respectively?
    (A) $O(n \log n)$, $O(n \log n)$, $O(n \log n)$
    (B) $O(n \log n)$, $O(n^2)$, $O(n \log n)$
    (C) $O(n^2)$, $O(n^2)$, $O(n^2)$
    (D) $O(\log n)$, $O(n^2)$, $O(\log n)$
    (E) $O(2^n)$, $O(n^2)$, $O(n \log n)$

46. Consider these three tasks:

    I   A sequential search of an array of n names
    II A binary search of an array of n names in alphabetical order
    III A quicksort into alphabetical order of an array of n names that are initially in random order

    For large n, which of the following lists these tasks in order (from least to greatest) of their average case run times?

    (A)   II   I   III
    (B)   I   II   III
    (C)   II   III   I
    (D)   III   I   II
    (E)   III   II   I

ANSWER KEY

1. E	17. A	33. D
2. D	18. D	34. A
3. C	19. E	35. E
4. B	20. A	36. C
5. C	21. A	37. C
6. E	22. A	38. E
7. C	23. E	39. D
8. A	24. C	40. C
9. C	25. D	41. E
10. B	26. C	42. D
11. D	27. E	43. B
12. A	28. D	44. C
13. E	29. D	45. B
14. B	30. B	46. A
15. B	31. B	
16. B	32. C	

ANSWERS EXPLAINED

1. **(E)** The time and space requirements of sorting algorithms are affected by all three of the given factors, so all must be considered when choosing a particular sorting algorithm.

2. **(D)** Choice B doesn't make sense: The loop will be exited as soon as a value is found that does *not* equal a[i]. Eliminate choice A because, if value is not in the array, a[i] will eventually go out of bounds. You need the i < n part of the boolean expression to avoid this. The test i < n, however, must precede value != a[i] so that if i < n fails, the expression will be evaluated as false, the test will be short-circuited, and an out-of-range error will be avoided. Choice C does not avoid this error. Choice E is wrong because both parts of the expression must be true in order to continue the search.

3. **(C)** The binary search algorithm depends on the array being sorted. Sequential search has no ordering requirement. Both depend on choice A, the length of the list, while the other choices are irrelevant to both algorithms.

4. **(B)** Inserting a new element is quick and easy in an unsorted array—just add it to the end of the list. Computing the mean involves finding the sum of the elements and dividing by *n*, the number of elements. The execution time is the same whether the list is sorted or not. Operation II, searching, is inefficient for an unsorted list, since a sequential search must be used. In sortedArr, the efficient binary search algorithm, which involves fewer comparisons, could be used. In fact, in a sorted list, even a sequential search would be more efficient than for an

unsorted list: If the search item were not in the list, the search could stop as soon as the list elements were greater than the search item.

5. **(C)** Suppose the array has 1000 elements and x is somewhere in the first 8 slots. The algorithm described will find x using no more than five comparisons. A binary search, by contrast, will chop the array in half and do a comparison six times before examining elements in the first 15 slots of the array (array size after each chop: 500, 250, 125, 62, 31, 15).

6. **(E)** The assertion states that the first element is greater than all the other elements in the array. This eliminates choices A and D. Choices B and C are incorrect because you have no information about the relative sizes of elements `a[1]...a[N-1]`.

7. **(C)** When `key` is not in the array, `index` will eventually be large enough that `a[index]` will cause an `ArrayIndexOutOfBoundsException`. In choices A and B, the algorithm will find `key` without error. Choice D won't fail if 0 is in the array. Choice E will work if `a[key]` is not out of range.

8. **(A)** The algorithm uses the fact that array `v` is sorted smallest to largest. The `while` loop terminates—which means that the search stops—as soon as `v[index] >= key`.

9. **(C)** The first pass uses the interval `a[0]...a[7]`. Since `mid` $= (0+7)/2 = 3$, `low` gets adjusted to `mid` $+ 1 = 4$, and the second pass uses the interval `a[4]...a[7]`.

10. **(B)** First pass: compare 27 with `a[3]`, since `low` $= 0$ `high` $= 7$ `mid` $= (0+7)/2 = 3$. Second pass: compare 27 with `a[5]`, since `low` $= 4$ `high` $= 7$ `mid` $= (4+7)/2 = 5$. Third pass: compare 27 with `a[6]`, since `low` $= 6$ `high` $= 7$ `mid` $= (6+7)/2 = 6$. The fourth pass doesn't happen, since `low` $= 6$, `high` $= 5$, and therefore the test (`low <= high`) fails. Here's the general rule for finding the number of iterations when `key` is not in the list: If n is the number of elements, round n up to the nearest power of 2, which is 8 in this case. $8 = 2^3$, which implies 3 iterations of the "divide-and-compare" loop.

11. **(D)** The method returns the index of the key parameter, 4. Since `a[0]` contains 4, `binSearch(4)` will return 0.

12. **(A)** Try 4. Here are the values for `low`, `high`, and `mid` when searching for 4:

    First pass: `low` $= 0$,   `high` $= 7$,   `mid` $= 3$
    Second pass: `low` $= 0$,   `high` $= 2$,   `mid` $= 1$

    After this pass, `high` gets adjusted to `mid` -1, which is 0. Now `low` equals `high`, and the test for the `while` loop fails. The method returns -1, indicating that 4 wasn't found.

13. **(E)** When the loop is exited, either `key` $=$ `a[mid]` (and `mid` has been returned) or `key` has not been found, in which case either `a[low]` $\leq$ `key` $\leq$ `a[high]` or `key` is not in the array. The correct assertion must account for all three possibilities.

14. **(B)** Note that `low` is initialized to 0 and `high` is initialized to n - 1. It would appear that $0 \leq$ `low` $\leq$ `high` $\leq$ n - 1. In the algorithm, however, if `key` is not in the array, `low` and `high` cross, which means `low` $>$ `high` in that instance. The correct loop invariant inequality that takes all cases into account is, therefore, $0 \leq$ `low` $\leq$ `high` + 1 $\leq$ n, which eliminates choices C, D, and E. In the algorithm, the endpoints of the new subarray to be considered are adjusted to include

a[mid+1] (if it's the right half) or a[mid-1] (for the left half). This means that key can be at one of the endpoints. Thus, a[low] $\leq$ key $\leq$ a[high] is the correct assertion.

15. **(B)** Start with the second element in the array.

After 1st pass:	7 1	9	5	4	12
After 2nd pass:	9 7 1	5	4	12	
After 3rd pass:	9 7 5 1	4	12		

16. **(B)** An insertion sort compares a[1] and a[0]. If they are not in the correct order, a[0] is moved and a[1] is inserted in its correct position. a[2] is then inserted in its correct position, and a[0] and a[1] are moved if necessary, and so on. Since B has only one element out of order, it will require the fewest changes.

17. **(A)** This list is almost sorted in reverse order, which is the worst case for insertion sort, requiring the greatest number of comparisons and moves.

18. **(D)** j >= 0 is a stopping condition that prevents an element that is larger than all those to the left of it from going off the left end of the array. If no error occurred, it means that the largest element in the array was a[0], which was true in situations I and II. Omitting the j >= 0 test will cause a run-time (out-of-range) error whenever temp is bigger than all elements to the left of it (i.e., the insertion point is 0).

19. **(E)** Note that i is initialized to 1, and after the final pass through the for loop, i equals a.length. Thus, $1 \leq i \leq$ a.length, which eliminates choices A, C, and D. Eliminate choice B since there could be duplicates in the array and a[0] could equal a[1] ....

After initialization: $i = 1$ and a[0] is sorted.
After first pass: $i = 2$ and a[0] $\geq$ a[1].
After second pass: $i = 3$ and a[0] $\geq$ a[1] $\geq$ a[2].

$\vdots$

In general, after initialization and each time the for loop is completed, a[0] $\geq$ a[1] $\geq \cdots \geq$ a[i-1].

20. **(A)**

After 1st pass:	109	42	−3	13	89	70	2
After 2nd pass:	109	89	−3	13	42	70	2
After 3rd pass:	109	89	70	13	42	−3	2

21. **(A)** i is initialized to 0, and after the final pass through the for loop, i equals a.length − 1. Thus, $0 \leq i \leq$ a.length − 1, which eliminates choices C and D. Choice E is wrong because it implies that the whole array is sorted after each pass through the loop.

After initialization: $i = 0$, and no elements are sorted.
After first pass: $i = 1$, and a[0] is sorted.
After second pass: $i = 2$, and a[0] $\geq$ a[1].

$\vdots$

In general, after initialization and each time the for loop is completed, a[0] $\geq$ a[1] $\geq \cdots \geq$ a[i-1]. This rules out choice B.

22. **(A)** Look at a small array that is almost sorted:

    10 8 9 6 2

    For <u>insertion sort</u> you need four passes through this array.
    The first pass compares 8 and 10—one comparison, no moves.
    The second pass compares 9 and 8, then 9 and 10. The array becomes
    10 9 8 6 2—two comparisons, two moves.
    The third and fourth passes compare 6 and 8, and 2 and 6—no moves.
    In summary, there are approximately one or two comparisons per pass and no more than two moves per pass.
    For <u>selection sort</u>, there are four passes too.
    The first pass finds the biggest element in the array and swaps it into the first position.
    The array is still 10 8 9 6 2—four comparisons. There are two moves if your algorithm makes the swap in this case, otherwise no moves.
    The second pass finds the biggest element from a[1] to a[4] and swaps it into the second position: 10 9 8 6 2—three comparisons, two moves.
    For the third pass there are two comparisons, and one for the fourth. There are zero or two moves each time.
    Summary: $4 + 3 + 2 + 1$ total comparisons and a possible two moves per pass.
    Notice that reason I is valid. Selection sort makes the same number of comparisons irrespective of the state of the array. Insertion sort does far fewer comparisons if the array is almost sorted. Reason II is invalid. There are roughly the same number of data movements for insertion and selection. Insertion may even have more changes, depending on how far from their insertion points the unsorted elements are. Reason III is wrong because insertion and selection sorts have the same space requirements.

AB ONLY

23. **(E)** In the first pass through the outer for loop, the smallest element makes its way to the end of the array. In the second pass, the next smallest element moves to the second last slot, and so on. This is different from the sorts in choices A through D; in fact, it is a bubble sort.

24. **(C)** Reject reason I. Mergesort requires both a merge and a mergeSort method—*more* code than the relatively short and simple code for insertion sort. Reject reason II. The merge algorithm uses a temporary array, which means *more* storage space than insertion sort. Reason III is correct. For long lists, the "divide-and-conquer" approach of mergesort gives it a faster run time than insertion sort.

25. **(D)** Since the search is for a four-letter sequence, the idea in this algorithm is that if you examine every fourth slot, you'll find a letter in the required sequence very quickly. When you find one of these letters, you can then examine adjacent slots to check if you have the required sequence. This method will, on average, result in fewer comparisons than the strictly sequential search algorithm in choice A. Choice B is wrong. If you encounter a "q," "r," or "s" without a "p" first, you can't have found "pqrs." Choice C is wrong because you may miss the sequence completely. Choice E doesn't make sense.

26. **(C)** The main precondition for a binary search is that the list is ordered.

27. **(E)** This algorithm is just a recursive implementation of a sequential search. It starts by testing if the last element in the array, a[n-1], is equal to value. If so, it returns the index n - 1. Otherwise, it calls itself with n replaced by n - 1. The net effect is that it examines a[n-1], a[n-2], ... The base case, if (n == 0),

occurs when there are no elements left to examine. In this case, the method returns −1, signifying that `value` was not in the array.

28. **(D)** The `partition` algorithm performs a series of swaps until the pivot element is swapped into its final sorted position (see p. 527). No temporary arrays or external files are used, nor is a recursive algorithm invoked. The `merge` method is used for mergesort, not quicksort.

AB ONLY

29. **(D)** Recall the mergesort algorithm:

> Divide `arr` into two parts.
> Mergesort the left side.
> Mergesort the right side.
> Merge the two sides into a single sorted array.

The `merge` method is used for the last step of the algorithm. It does not do any sorting or partitioning of the array, which eliminates choices A, B, and C. Choice E is wrong because `merge` starts with a *single* array that has two sorted parts.

30. **(B)** Round 600 up to the next power of 2, which is $1024 = 2^{10}$. For the worst case, the array will be split in half $\log_2 1024 = 10$ times.

31. **(B)** If the list is sorted in reverse order, each pass through the array will involve the maximum possible number of comparisons and the maximum possible number of element movements if an insertion sort is used.

32. **(C)** I violates the order property of a heap. II is not a complete binary tree.

AB ONLY

33. **(D)** The elements will be inserted into the tree as shown, so the level of the tree is 3. (Remember that the top level of the tree is 0.)

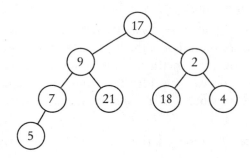

In fact, you don't need the tree or the actual elements!
The first element goes into level 0.
The next two elements go into level 1 (Total = 3).
The next four elements go into level 2 (Total = 7).
The next eight elements go into level 3 (Total = 15).
...and so on.
Since the given array has eight elements, you need a tree that goes to three levels. (Note that the tree shown has not yet been formed into a heap.)

34. **(A)** Assuming that the array contains n elements, the piece of code that forms the original heap is:

```
for (int rootIndex = (n / 2) - 1; rootIndex >= 0; rootIndex--)
    fixHeap(rootIndex, n - 1);
```

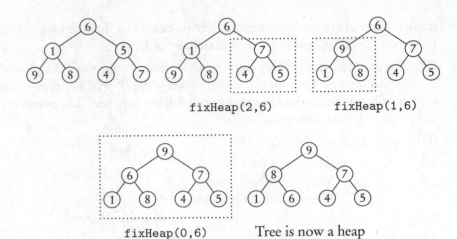

fixHeap(0,6)   Tree is now a heap

The sequence of swaps is
            7 and 5
            9 and 1
            9 and 6
            8 and 6
This leads to choice A.

35. **(E)** The efficiency of the algorithm will depend on how the pivot element is selected. Ideally in quicksort the pivot element should partition the array into two parts of roughly equal size. If the array is sorted and the pivot element is always the first (or last) element in the array, then one section of the array will always be empty after partitioning. This is a worst case for quicksort, $O(n^2)$. On the other hand, if the array is sorted and the pivot element is chosen near the middle of the array, quicksort will be very efficient: $O(n \log n)$.

36. **(C)** An efficient hash coding system must have as few collisions as possible (i.e., the hash addresses should be uniformly distributed throughout the table). When there are collisions, the method of allocating a new hash address should, again, distribute these addresses uniformly throughout the table. The size of the data items is irrelevant since a hash function operates just on a *key field* of the data items.

37. **(C)** Just before 29 is inserted, the table will look like this:

array index	0	1	2	3	4	5	6	7	8	9	10
key value		45	2	25			28	7	40		10

Now 29 % 11 = 7. Slots 7 and 8 are taken, so 29 goes into slot 9.

38. **(E)** Hash coded data must always be searched with a hash function applied to the key field, followed by an algorithm that resolves any collisions.

39. **(D)** In the rehash function, *result* is the current hash address. Choice A works for all numbers except 34. 34 % 20 hashes to 14, which is taken by 54. Then (14 + 13) % 20 rehashes to 7, which is where 34 would go if this were the correct answer. Choice B doesn't successfully resolve collisions: 34 % 20 hashes to 14, which is already taken by 54. 14 % 20 rehashes to 14, the same slot. Recall that a rehash function of the form (result + <const>) % <number of slots> must be such that <const> and <number of slots> are relatively prime (i.e., no common factors other than 1). Otherwise, the method won't generate all the hash table

slots. This eliminates choice C. Choice E produces 30 slots, but the table shown has just 20 slots. Element 81, for example, has no slot under this scheme, since 81 % 30 is 21 and `list[21]` does not exist. Choice D successfully places all the numbers in the table.

40. **(C)** Reason I is valid—it's always desirable to hide implementation details from users of a method. Reason II is valid too—since `QuickSort` and `MergeSort` implement the `Sort` interface, they must have a `sort` method with no parameters. But parameters are needed to make the recursion work. Therefore each `sort` requires a helper method with parameters. Reason III is invalid in this particular example of helper methods. There are many examples in which a helper method enhances efficiency (e.g., Example 2 on p. 344), but the `sort` example is not one of them.

41. **(E)** Since `Sort` is an interface, you can't create an instance of it. This eliminates choices B and D. The `sort` methods alter the contents of `strArray`. Thus invoking `q.sort()` followed by `m.sort()` means that `m.sort` will always operate on a sorted array, assuming quicksort works correctly! In order to test both quicksort and mergesort on unsorted arrays, you need to make a copy of the original array or create a different array. Eliminate choice A (and B again!), which does neither of these. Choice C is wrong because it calls the *private* `sort` methods of the classes. The `Sort` interface has just a single *public* method, `sort`, with no arguments. The two classes shown must provide an implementation for this `sort` method, and it is this method that must be invoked in the client program.

42. **(D)** A sequential search, in the worst case, must examine all n elements—$O(n)$. In the worst case, a binary search will keep splitting the array in half until there is just one element left in the current subarray: $\log_2 n$ splits, which is $O(\log n)$.

43. **(B)** 1 million $= 10^6 = (10^3)^2 \approx (2^{10})^2 = 2^{20}$. Thus, there will be on the order of 20 comparisons.

44. **(C)** This is a sequential search that examines each element and counts the number of occurrences of 8. Since n comparisons are made, the algorithm is $O(n)$.

45. **(B)** Mergesort works by breaking its array of n elements into n arrays of one element each, an $O(\log_2 n)$ process. Then it merges adjacent pairs of arrays until there is one sorted array, an $O(n)$ process. For each split of the array, the `merge` method is called. Thus, mergesort is $O(n \log n)$ irrespective of the original ordering of the elements.

   Quicksort partitions the array into two parts. The algorithm is $O(n \log n)$ only if the two parts of the array are roughly equal in length. In the worst case, this is not true—the pivot is the smallest or largest element in the array. The partition method, an $O(n)$ process, will then be called n times, and the algorithm becomes $O(n^2)$.

   The elements of heapsort are always placed in a balanced binary tree, which gives an $O(\log_2 n)$ process for fixing the heap. $n/2$ passes, each of which restores the heap, leads to an $O(n \log n)$ algorithm irrespective of the original ordering of the elements.

46. **(A)** A sequential search is $O(n)$, a binary search $O(\log n)$, and quicksort $O(n \log n)$. For any large positive n, $\log n < n < n \log n$.

The GridWorld Case Study

CHAPTER 13

> *Man is the only critter who feels the need*
> *to label things as flowers and weeds.*
> —*Anonymous*

Chapter Goals

- The classes in GridWorld: hierarchy and overview
- The Actor class
- The Location class
- The Rock and Flower classes
- The Bug and BoxBug classes
- The Critter class and ChameleonCritter classes
- The Grid interface
- The AbstractGrid class
- The BoundedGrid and UnboundedGrid classes
- Run-time analysis of grid methods

OVERVIEW

The case study is a program that simulates actions and interactions of objects in a two-dimensional grid. The "actors" in the grid are displayed by a GUI (graphical user interface). The GUI can also add new actors to the grid and can invoke methods on all actors.

During a single step of the program, every occupant of the grid gets a chance to act. Each actor acts according to a clearly specified set of behaviors that can include moving, changing color, changing direction, removing other actors from the grid, depositing new actors in specified locations, and so on.

THE CLASSES

The following diagram displays the relationship between the testable classes in the case study.

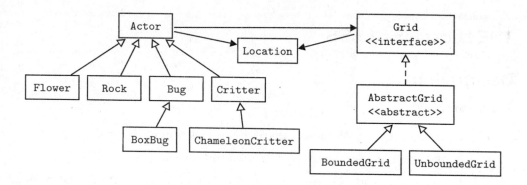

The diagram shows that each of these objects, Flower, Rock, Bug, and Critter *is-an* Actor. A BoxBug *is-a* Bug, and a ChameleonCritter *is-a* Critter. Also, AbstractGrid is an abstract class that implements the Grid interface. Each of BoundedGrid and UnboundedGrid *is-an* AbstractGrid. Every Actor *has-a* Location and Grid, and a Grid *has-a* Location.

NOTE

The Location, Actor, Rock, and Flower classes are "black box" classes whose code is not provided. You are, however, expected to know the specifications of their methods and constants. Code is provided for all of the other classes shown and is testable on the AP exam. While Level A students are expected to be familiar with the method specifications for the grid classes, Level A students will not be tested on any of the code for grid classes.

THE ACTORS

Here is a summary of what each actor does when it acts.

- A Rock does nothing.
- A Flower darkens its color.
- A Bug moves forward when it can. It can move into an empty spot or onto a flower. When it moves, it deposits a flower in its previous location. If it moves to a location occupied by a flower, that flower is removed from the grid. A bug cannot move if it is blocked in front by either another (nonflower) actor or the edge of the grid. When a bug is prevented from moving, it turns 45° to the right.
- A BoxBug moves like a Bug. Additionally, if it encounters no obstacles in its path, it traces out a square of flowers with a given side length. If a BoxBug is blocked from moving, it makes two right turns and starts again.
- A Critter gets a list of its adjacent neighboring actors and processes them by "eating" each actor that is not a rock or another critter. It then randomly selects one of the empty neighboring locations and moves there. If there are no available empty locations, a critter does not move.
- A ChameleonCritter gets a list of its adjacent neighbors, randomly picks one of them, and changes its color to that of the selected actor. The ChameleonCritter moves like a Critter but, additionally, it first changes its direction to face its new location before moving.

THE Location CLASS

Description

The Location class

- Encapsulates row and column values for any position in the grid.
- Provides constants for compass directions and turn angles.
- Provides methods for determining relationships between locations and compass directions.

The flower in the diagram is in row 1, column 2, or Location (1, 2).

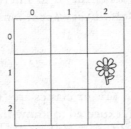

There are eight constants that represent compass directions:

Constant	int Value
Location.NORTH	0
Location.EAST	90
Location.SOUTH	180
Location.WEST	270
Location.NORTHEAST	45
Location.SOUTHEAST	135
Location.SOUTHWEST	225
Location.NORTHWEST	315

The compass directions have integer values starting at 0 (north) and moving clockwise through 360 (degrees). The dotted arrow in the figure below represents a direction of 135 or Location.SOUTHEAST.

N (0°)

135°

There are seven constants representing the most commonly used turn angles:

Constant	int **Value**
Location.LEFT	-90
Location.RIGHT	90
Location.HALF_LEFT	-45
Location.HALF_RIGHT	45
Location.FULL_CIRCLE	360
Location.HALF_CIRCLE	180
Location.AHEAD	0

To get an actor to turn through a given number of degrees, set its direction to the sum of its current direction and the turn angle. For example, to make an actor turn right (through 90°, clockwise)

setDirection (getDirection() + Location.RIGHT) ;

change direction to   current direction   +90°

In general, a class can be represented by a box diagram (shown below) in which private data and methods are completely enclosed within the shaded region, while public methods overlap the shaded region.[1]

The diagram below represents the Location class, and shows that there is one constructor, eight public methods, and two private instance variables.

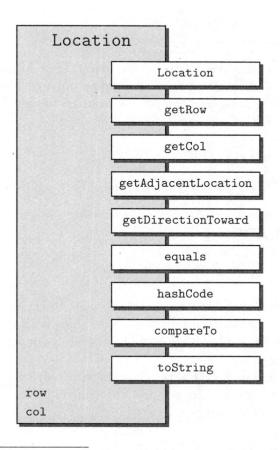

---

[1]The class diagrams are based on diagrams in *A Computer Science Tapestry* by Owen Astrachan and the Marine Biology Case Study narrative by Alyce Brady.

Methods

```
public Location(int r, int c)
```

Constructs a location with given row and column.

```
public int getRow()
public int getCol()
```

Accessor methods that return the row or column of the Location.

```
public Location getAdjacentLocation(int direction)
```

Returns the adjacent location in the compass direction closest to direction.

```
public int getDirectionToward(Location target)
```

Returns the direction, rounded to the nearest compass direction, from this location toward a target location.

```
public int hashCode()
```

Generates and returns a hash code for this Location.

```
public boolean equals(Object other)
public int compareTo(Object other)
```

These methods are used to compare Location objects. Two locations are equal if they have the same row and column values. Ascending order for locations is *row-major*, namely, start at (0, 0) and proceed row by row from left to right. For example, (0, 1) is less than (0, 2) and (1, 8) is less than (3, 0).

```
public String toString()
```

Returns a string representation of this Location in the form (row, col).

THE Actor CLASS

Description

The Actor class is the superclass for every creature or object that appears in the grid.

An Actor has a location, direction, and color, along with the capacity to change each of these instance variables. It has access to its grid. It can put itself in the grid, and also remove itself from it.

Here is the box diagram for the Actor class, showing only its public methods. (Since Actor is a black-box class, you are not privy to its private data and methods, nor the implementation of its methods.)

> Every creature in the grid is coded as a subclass of Actor.

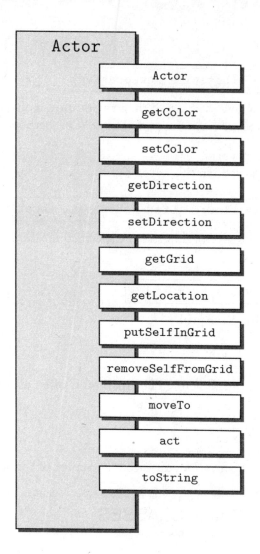

Methods

```
public Actor()
```

Default constructor. Constructs a blue actor facing north.

```
public Color getColor()
public int getDirection()
public Location getLocation()
```

Accessor methods. Return the color, direction, or location of this `Actor`. Note that the direction returned is an `int` from 0 through 359 (degrees).

```
public Grid<Actor> getGrid()
```

Accessor method. Returns the grid of this `Actor`, or `null` if the actor is not in the grid.

```
public void setColor(Color newColor)
public void setDirection(int newDirection)
```

Mutator methods. Change the color or direction of this `Actor` to the new value specified by the parameter.

```
public void moveTo(Location newLocation)
```

Moves this `Actor` to a new location. If the new location is already occupied, the actor in that location is removed from the grid. The `moveTo` method has two preconditions:

1. This `Actor` is in a grid.
2. `newLocation` is valid in this `Actor`'s grid.

```
public void putSelfInGrid(Grid<Actor> gr, Location loc)
```

Puts this `Actor` into the given grid `gr` at the specified location `loc`. A precondition is that `loc` is valid.

```
public void removeSelfFromGrid()
```

Removes this `Actor` from the grid.

```
public void act()
```

Reverses the direction of this actor. (The method is often overridden in sublcasses of `Actor`.)

```
public String toString()
```

Returns a string with the location, direction, and color of this `Actor`.

THE Rock AND Flower CLASSES

The Rock Class

A `Rock` acts by doing nothing. It has a default constructor that creates a black rock, and a second constructor that allows construction of a rock with a specified color. The act method is overridden—it has an empty body!

The Flower Class

A `Flower` acts by darkening its color. It has a default constructor that creates a pink flower, and a second constructor that allows construction of a flower with a specified color. The overridden act method darkens the flower by reducing the values of the red, green, and blue components of its color by a constant factor.

THE Bug CLASS

Description

A `Bug` is an `Actor` that moves forward in a straight line, turning only when it is blocked. A bug can be blocked by either the edge of the grid, or an actor that is not a flower.

As the bug moves, it steps on any flower in its path, causing the removal of that flower from the grid. After each step, the bug places a flower in its previous location.

Here is a box diagram for the Bug class. Methods inherited from Actor are not shown. Overridden methods are indicated with a double frame.

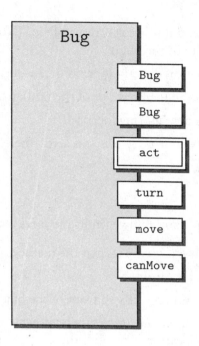

The diagram shows that a Bug has two constructors. The act method is overridden, and there are three additional public methods: turn, move, and canMove. Don't forget that Bug also inherits the following methods from Actor: getColor, setColor, getDirection, setDirection, getGrid, getLocation, putSelfInGrid, removeSelfFromGrid, moveTo, and toString.

Methods

`public Bug()`

Default constructor. Creates a red Bug.

`public Bug(Color bugColor)`

Constructor. Creates a Bug with the specified color.

Note that both of the constructors use the inherited setColor method.

`public void act()`

The Bug moves if it can; otherwise it turns.

Note that this is the only method of the Actor class that is overridden.

`public void turn()`

Turns this Bug 45° to the right without changing its location. It does it by adding Location.HALF_RIGHT to the bug's current direction.

```
public boolean canMove()
```

Returns true if this Bug can move, false otherwise. The bug is able to move if the location directly in front of it (a) is valid and (b) is empty or contains a flower. Here are the steps in the method:

- Get the bug's grid, and if it is null, return false. (Note that a bug's grid is null if another actor removed the bug.)
- Get the adjacent location directly in front of the bug.
- If this location is invalid (namely, out of the grid), return false.
- Get the actor in this neighboring location.
- If the actor is a flower or null (i.e., no actor there!), return true. Otherwise return false.

```
public void move()
```

Moves this Bug forward, placing a flower in its previous location. Here are the steps:

- Get the bug's grid, and if it is null, exit the method.
- Get the bug's current location.
- Get the adjacent location directly in front of the bug.
- If this location is valid, the bug moves there; otherwise it removes itself from the grid. (Note: If this location is invalid, the canMove method will return false, and move will not be called. So the test in this step is redundant, and is probably included as an extra precaution.)
- Create a flower that is the same color as the bug.
- Place the flower in the bug's previous location (which was saved in the second step.)

THE BoxBug CLASS

Description

A BoxBug is a Bug that moves in a square pattern if it is unimpeded. To create the square, a BoxBug has two private instance variables: sideLength, which is the number of steps in a side of its square, and steps, which keeps track of where the BoxBug is in creating a side. Whenever a side has been completed or the bug must start again because it encountered an obstacle, steps gets reset to zero.

Here is the box diagram for the BoxBug class.

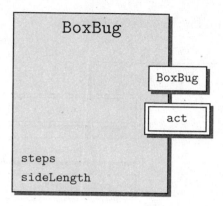

The diagram shows that BoxBug has two private instance variables, one constructor, and an overridden act method. In addition to inheriting all of the public methods of Actor, BoxBug inherits the methods turn, move, and canMove from Bug.

Methods

```
public BoxBug(int length)
```

Constructor. Sets sideLength to the specified length, and initializes steps to 0.

```
public void act()
```

This overridden method performs one step in the creation of the BoxBug's square. First, the method tests whether the bug is still in the process of making a side:

```
if (steps < sideLength...
```

If this is true, and the bug can move, the bug moves and steps is incremented. If the above piece of the test is false, it means that the bug has completed the current side, and must turn so that it can start a new side. It does this by calling turn twice, to create the 90° angle at the vertex of the square. (Recall that a single call to turn turns the bug through 45°.) After the bug has completed the 90° turn, steps is reset to zero in preparation for a new side. Notice that if steps < sideLength is true, but canMove() is false (BoxBug is blocked), the same preparation for a new side must occur (turn, turn, reset steps). If the BoxBug is unimpeded when creating its square, and the sideLength has value k, there will be $k + 1$ flowers on each side of the square.

THE Critter CLASS

Description

A Critter is an Actor with the following pattern of behavior.

- Get a list of neighboring actors.
- Process the actors.
- Get a list of possible locations to move to.
- Select a location from the list.
- Move there.

Here is the box diagram for the `Critter` class.

The diagram shows that the `Critter` class does not have an explicit constructor. This means that the default constructor of the `Actor` superclass will be invoked to create a blue `Critter` facing north. All other methods of `Actor` are inherited, and `act` is overridden. The other five methods are new methods for `Critter`.

Methods

`public void act()`

A `Critter` acts by getting a list of its neighbors, processing them, getting a list of possible locations to move to, selecting one of these, and then moving to the selected location.

`public ArrayList<Actor> getActors()`

Returns a list of adjacent neighboring actors.

`public void processActors(ArrayList<Actor> actors)`

Processes the actors. The `Critter` "eats" all actors that are not rocks or other critters. The actors are processed by iterating through the list of actors. Each actor is examined. If it is neither a rock nor a critter, the actor removes itself from the grid.

`public ArrayList<Location> getMoveLocations()`

Returns a list of valid, adjacent, empty, neighboring locations, which are the possible locations for the next move. The grid method `getEmptyAdjacentLocations` is used, with the critter's current location as its parameter.

```
public Location selectMoveLocation(ArrayList<Location> locs)
```

Selects the location for the next move from `locs`, a list of valid locations. Here are the steps.

- Assign n to be the length of the list.
- If n is zero, which means that there are no available locations, return the current location of the critter.
- Get a random int from 0 to $n - 1$ with the statement

    ```
    int r = (int) (Math.random() * n);
    ```

- Return the location at index r in the `locs` ArrayList.

```
public void makeMove(Location loc)
```

Moveshis `Critter` to the specified location. A precondition is that `loc` is valid. The method is implemented with the statement

```
moveTo(loc);
```

Recall that `moveTo` is inherited from `Actor`.

THE `ChameleonCritter` CLASS

Description

A `ChameleonCritter` is a `Critter`. When it acts, a `ChameleonCritter` gets the same list of actors as a `Critter`, but instead of eating them, it randomly selects one actor and changes its color to that of the selected actor. A `ChameleonCritter` moves like a `Critter`, with one difference: Before it moves, it turns to face its new location.

Here is the box diagram for the `ChameleonCritter` class.

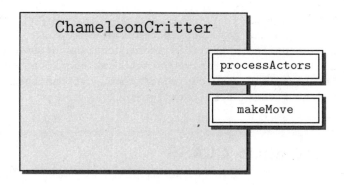

Notice that there is no constructor, which means that when a `ChameleonCritter` is created, the default constructor of `Actor` will be invoked, constructing a blue `ChameleonCritter` facing north.

Methods

```
public void processActors(ArrayList<Actor> actors)
```

Randomly selects an adjacent neighbor, and changes this ChameleonCritter's color to that of the selected actor. Does nothing if there are no neighbors.

```
public void makeMove(Location loc)
```

Moves like a regular Critter, but before it moves, it turns to face its new location. To change direction, the setDirection method is used. The parameter used for the call to setDirection is the direction from the ChameleonCritter's current location to loc:

```
getLocation().getDirectionToward(loc)
```

THE Grid<E> INTERFACE

The interface Grid<E> specifies methods that manipulate a grid of objects of type E. In the case study, Grid<E> is implemented by three classes, AbstractGrid<E>, Bounded-Grid<E>, and UnboundedGrid<E>. When the grid classes are used by clients, type E is replaced by Actor.

Methods

Listed below are the methods in the interface. These methods are commented and discussed in the classes that implement them.

```
public interface Grid<E>
{
    int getNumRows();
    int getNumCols();
    boolean isValid(Location loc);
    E put(Location loc, E obj);
    E remove(Location loc);
    E get(Location loc);
    ArrayList<Location> getOccupiedLocations();
    ArrayList<Location> getValidAdjacentLocations(Location loc);
    ArrayList<Location> getEmptyAdjacentLocations(Location loc);
    ArrayList<Location> getOccupiedAdjacentLocations(Location loc);
    ArrayList<E> getNeighbors(Location loc);
}
```

THE AbstractGrid<E> CLASS

Description

The AbstractGrid<E> class implements five methods of the Grid<E> interface that are common to both the BoundedGrid<E> and UnboundedGrid<E> classes. While no instance of an AbstractGrid<E> can be created, having this class avoids repeated code.

Here is the box diagram for the AbstractGrid class.

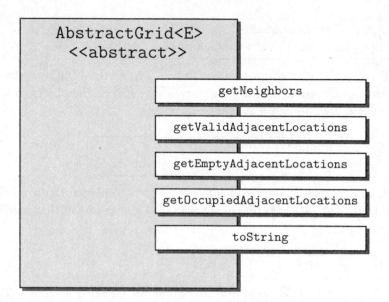

Methods

Note that in every method below that has a `loc` parameter, there is a precondition that `loc` is valid in the grid.

```
public ArrayList<E> getNeighbors(Location loc)
```

Returns a list of all actors in locations adjacent to `loc`. It does this by traversing the locations in `getOccupiedAdjacentLocations(loc)`, and adding the actors in those locations to an initially empty `ArrayList<E>`. Note that if `neighbors` is the `ArrayList` of actors to be returned, and `neighborLoc` is a `Location` in the traversal, the statement

```
neighbors.add(get(neighborLoc));
```

extracts the actor in `neighborLoc` and adds it to the `neighbors` list. Recall that `add` is an `ArrayList` method; but the get method used here is the `Grid` method that returns the object at its `Location` parameter.

```
public ArrayList<Location>
    getValidAdjacentLocations(Location loc)
```

Returns all valid locations adjacent to `loc`. Starting with north (at 0°), and going up in increments of 45, it gets the adjacent location in that direction, and, if that location is in the grid, adds it to an initially empty `ArrayList` of locations. If you do the math, you will see that the line

```
for (int i = 0; i < Location.FULL_CIRCLE / Location.HALF_RIGHT; i++)
```

is equivalent to

```
for (int i = 0; i < 8; i++)
```

The constants `FULL_CIRCLE` and `HALF_RIGHT` are used because they are much more descriptive than "8".

AB *(continued)*

```
public ArrayList<Location>
    getEmptyAdjacentLocations(Location loc)
```

Returns all valid empty locations adjacent to loc. The method traverses the list of loc's valid adjacent locations. If it finds an empty location (i.e., the object in it is null), it adds it to an initially empty ArrayList of locations.

```
public ArrayList<Location>
    getOccupiedAdjacentLocations(Location loc)
```

Returns all valid occupied locations adjacent to loc. Implementation of this method is identical to that of getEmptyAdjacentLocations above, except that it adds locations that contain objects.

```
public String toString()
```

Returns a description of this grid in string form. It does this by traversing the occupied locations in the grid, and concatenating each location and occupying object to an initially empty string. The pieces of information for each location are separated by commas, which is the reason for this segment:

```
if (s.length() > 1)
    s += ", ";
```

What it means is: If there is at least one grid location described, add a comma to the string before starting the information for the next location. The test prevents the string from starting with a comma.

THE BoundedGrid<E> AND UnboundedGrid<E> CLASSES

Description

AB ONLY

The grid classes provide an environment for the actors in GridWorld. A bounded grid is two-dimensional, with a finite number of rows and columns. Creatures in a bounded grid cannot escape its confines. An unbounded grid is also rectangular, but the number of rows and columns is unlimited.

Both BoundedGrid<E> and UnboundedGrid<E> extend AbstractGrid<E> which implements Grid<E>. This means that both of the grid classes inherit the five methods of AbstractGrid<E>, and *must* implement the remaining methods of Grid<E>.

Both the BoundedGrid<E> and UnboundedGrid<E> classes are represented in the following box diagram.

Both
BoundedGrid and
UnboundedGrid
extend
AbstractGrid
and implement
Grid.

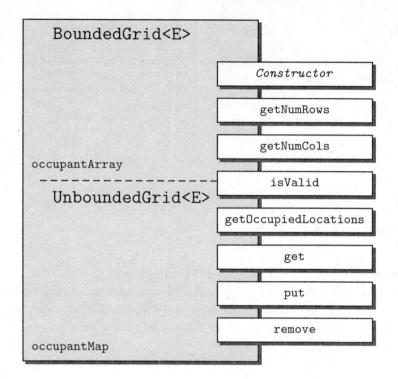

The diagram shows that each class has its own constructor, and each class implements the seven remaining `Grid<E>` methods that are not in `AbstractGrid<E>`. The inherited methods of `AbstractGrid<E>` are not shown: `getValidAdjacentLocations`, `getEmptyAdjacentLocations`, `getOccupiedAdjacentLocations`, `getNeighbors`, and `toString`.

The `BoundedGrid<E>` is implemented with a two-dimensional array of `Object` called `occupantArray`,

```
private Object[][] occupantArray;
```

The element type is `Object`, not `E`, because Java doesn't allow arrays of generic types. Still, all elements of `occupantArray` must be of type `E`, since the method that adds elements to this array, put, requires a parameter of type `E` for the object that is added.

The `UnboundedGrid<E>` is implemented with a map called `occupantMap`, in which a key of the map is a `Location` object and the corresponding value is an object of type `E` in that location:

```
private Map<Location, E> occupantMap;
```

Only those locations that contain an actor are keys of the map.

Methods

THE CONSTRUCTORS

For each class, the constructor creates an empty grid.

AB *(continued)*

BoundedGrid	UnboundedGrid
| ```
public BoundedGrid(
    int rows, int cols)
``` | ```
public UnboundedGrid()
``` |
| Constructs an empty bounded grid with specified number of rows and columns. Throws an `IllegalArgumentException` if either parameter is negative. | Creates an empty unbounded grid. Uses a `HashMap`. |

```
public int getNumRows()
public int getNumCols()
```

BoundedGrid	UnboundedGrid
Returns number of rows or columns in grid. Note that the number of rows is `occupantArray.length` and the number of columns is the length of the 0th row, `occupantArray[0].length`.	Always returns −1, since an `Unbounded-Grid` does not have a specific number of rows or columns.

```
public boolean isValid(Location loc)
```

BoundedGrid	UnboundedGrid
Returns true if `loc` is in bounds, false otherwise.	Always returns true.

```
public ArrayList<Location> getOccupiedLocations()
```

Returns all occupied locations in this grid.

BoundedGrid	UnboundedGrid
• A nested `for` loop traverses the rows and columns of the grid. • Creates new `Location` from current row and column. • Retrieves object at this location (using `get(loc)`). • If object is not `null` (i.e., `loc` occupied), adds this location to `ArrayList`.	• Traverses key set of `occupantMap`, using a for-each loop. • Adds each location in traversal to `ArrayList`. (All the keys are occupied locations.)

```
public E get(Location loc)
```

Returns the object at `loc`, or `null` if `loc` is unoccupied.

BoundedGrid

- An `IllegalArgumentException` is thrown if `loc` is invalid.
- Accesses object at `loc` by using the expression

  ```
  occupantArray[loc.getRow()]
      [loc.getCol()]
  ```

- Before returning this object, cast to E.

UnboundedGrid

- A `NullPointerException` is thrown if `loc` is null.
- Accesses object at `loc` by using the expression

  ```
  occupantMap.get(loc)
  ```

  where get is a `Map` method.

```
public E put(Location loc, E obj)
```

Puts `obj` at location `loc` in this grid, and returns the previous occupant of that location. Returns `null` if `loc` was previously unoccupied.

BoundedGrid

- An `IllegalArgumentException` is thrown if `loc` is invalid.
- A `NullPointerException` is thrown if `obj` is null.
- Saves previous occupant at `loc`.
- Adds `obj` to `loc` using

  ```
  occupantArray[loc.getRow()]
    [loc.getCol()] = obj;
  ```

- Returns previous occupant.

UnboundedGrid

- A `NullPointerException` is thrown if either `obj` or `loc` is null.
- Using the `Map` method put, returns result of

  ```
  occupantMap.put(loc, obj)
  ```

  (This creates a new mapping for `loc`, but returns the previous value that corresponded to `loc`.)

```
public E remove(Location loc)
```

Removes the object at `loc` and returns it. Returns `null` if `loc` is unoccupied.

BoundedGrid

- An `IllegalArgumentException` is thrown if `loc` is invalid.
- Retrieves object from `loc`:

  ```
  E r = get(loc);
  ```

  (Note: get is a `BoundedGrid` method.)
- Sets object in `loc` to null:

  ```
  occupantArray[loc.getRow()]
    [loc.getCol()] = null;
  ```

- Returns r.

UnboundedGrid

- A `NullPointerException` is thrown if `loc` is null.
- Using `Map` method `remove`, removes mapping with `loc` as key, and returns previous object corresponding to `loc`:

  ```
  return occupantMap.remove(loc);
  ```

RUN-TIME ANALYSIS OF GRID METHODS

Bounded Grid

Suppose a bounded grid has r rows, c columns, and n occupied locations, where r, c, and n are large. Any algorithm that requires a traversal of every location will need $r \times c$ "moves" and is therefore $O(rc)$. If you have a list of only those occupied locations, (or the actors in them), processing the actors will be $O(n)$. Accessing any given location in the grid is $O(1)$. An algorithm that processes adjacent neighbors for any location will require no more than eight operations, which is a constant. Therefore the algorithm is $O(1)$.

Unbounded Grid

Rows and columns do not enter into the analysis for an unbounded grid. The map contains only the n locations that are occupied; so big-O run times will all be in terms of n, the number of actors in the grid.

Since keys are stored in a `HashMap`, each of the following operations is $O(1)$: finding a given location (or key), inserting a new actor (or mapping), removing an actor, retrieving a given actor, and so on. These all use the `Map` methods `get`, `put`, and `remove`, which are $O(1)$.

Suppose the implementation of `UnboundedGrid` is changed so that keys are stored in a `TreeMap`. The above `Map` operations now become $O(\log n)$.

In the following examples, you may assume a grid with n occupied locations, and a bounded grid with r rows and c columns.

Example 1

What is the big-O run time for `getOccupiedLocations` in
(1) `BoundedGrid`   (2) `UnboundedGrid`?

(1) $O(rc)$. A nested loop traversal must be done, examining every location. The algorithm depends only on the number of locations in the grid.

(2) $O(n)$. All that is required is a simple traversal through the n locations in the key set of the map.

Example 2

What is the big-O run time for `getNeighbors` in
(1) `BoundedGrid`   (2) `UnboundedGrid`?

(1) $O(1)$.
(2) $O(1)$.
To retrieve the neighbors,

- Get a list of occupied adjacent locations.
- Traverse the list to extract the actors.

In each type of grid, there are no more than eight adjacent locations to be examined, a constant number. Therefore, in each case, the algorithm is $O(1)$.

AB *(continued)*

NOTE

An $O(1)$ operation performed eight times is still $O(1)$. The assumption is that eight is small compared to n.

BIG-O SUMMARY OF GRID METHODS

The run times in the table below assume a grid with n occupied locations, and a bounded grid with r rows and c columns.

AB ONLY

Method	BoundedGrid	UnboundedGrid
getNeighbors	$O(1)$	$O(1)$
getValidAdjacentLocations	$O(1)$	$O(1)$
getEmptyAdjacentLocations	$O(1)$	$O(1)$
getOccupiedAdjacentLocations	$O(1)$	$O(1)$
toString	$O(rc)$	$O(n)$
getOccupiedLocations	$O(rc)$	$O(n)$
get	$O(1)$	$O(1)$
put	$O(1)$	$O(1)$
remove	$O(1)$	$O(1)$

THE CASE STUDY AND THE AP EXAM

Approximately one-fourth of the AP exam will be devoted to questions on the case study. (This means five to ten multiple-choice questions and one free-response question.)

Both level A and AB students will be tested on Chapters 1–4 of the case study. You must be familiar with the Bug, BoxBug, Critter, and ChameleonCritter classes, including their implementations. You should also be familiar with the documentation for the Location, Actor, Rock, and Flower classes, as well as the Grid<E> interface.

On the AP exam, all students will be provided with a Quick Reference that contains a list of methods for the preceding classes and interface. You will also receive source code for the Bug, BoxBug, Critter, and ChameleonCritter classes.

Only level AB students need to know Chapter 5 of the case study. This includes the documentation and implementation for the AbstractGrid<E> abstract class, and the BoundedGrid<E> and UnboundedGrid<E> classes. The Quick Reference for level AB students will include the documentation and source code for all the grid classes.

NOTE

1. The Javadoc comments @param, @return, and @throws are part of the AP Java subset. In this book they are included in the case study questions only. Here is an example.

```
/**
 * Puts obj at location loc in this grid, and returns
 * the object previously at this location.
 * Returns null if loc was previously unoccupied.
 * Precondition: obj is not null, and loc is valid in this grid.
 * @param loc the location where the object will be placed
 * @param obj the object to be placed
 * @return the object previously at the specified location
 * @throws IllegalArgumentException if the location is invalid
 * @throws NullPointerException if the object is null
 */
public E put(Location loc, E obj)
```

This will produce the following Javadoc output:

---

put

`public E ` **`put`** ` (Location loc, E obj)`

> Puts obj at location loc in this grid, and returns
> the object previously at this location.
> Returns null if loc was previously unoccupied.
> Precondition: obj is not null, and loc is valid in this grid.

Parameters:
> `loc` - the location where the object will be placed
> `obj` - the object to be placed

Returns:
> the object previously at the specified location

Throws:
> `IllegalArgumentException` - if the location is invalid
>
> `NullPointerException` - if the object is null

---

2. The GridWorld case study, including documentation, narrative, and code, can be found at *http://www.collegeboard.com/student/testing/ap/subjects.html*.

Chapter Summary

Be thoroughly familiar with each of the actors in this world. Know how they move and act. In particular, you must know the inheritance relationships between the various actors. On the AP exam you are likely to be asked to write subclasses of Bug or Critter, or to write modified methods for some given superclass.

Find GridWorld in the Quick Reference guide, so you can become comfortable referring to this as you write your own code. By the time you get to the AP exam, it should be second nature to you to use the Quick Reference.

Level AB students must be familiar with the Grid interface, and how its methods are implemented in the AbstractGrid class. You must also be able to compare implementations of methods in the BoundedGrid and UnboundedGridclasses. By now it goes without saying that you must know the big-O run times of all of the grid algorithms.

MULTIPLE-CHOICE QUESTIONS ON THE CASE STUDY

Before you begin, note that

- Some of the questions in this section provide code from the case study. On the AP exam, code will not be reproduced in the questions, since you will be provided with a copy of all code to be tested.
- The actors in GridWorld are represented in this book with the pictures shown below. Each actor is shown facing north. These pictures almost certainly will be different from those used on the AP exam!

Actor   Bug   Flower   Rock   Critter   ChameleonCritter

1. Which of the following is a *false* statement about `Rock` and `Flower` behavior?
   (A) When a rock acts, it does nothing.
   (B) When a flower acts, it does nothing.
   (C) A flower never changes its location when it acts.
   (D) A rock never changes its location when it acts.
   (E) When a rock is placed in a location that contains a flower, the flower disappears from the grid.

2. Suppose a `Bug` starts out facing south. If the `turn` method is called for this bug, what will its resulting direction be?
   (A) North
   (B) Northeast
   (C) Northwest
   (D) Southeast
   (E) Southwest

3. Consider the BoxBug in the diagram.

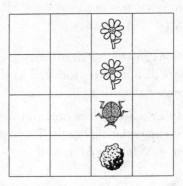

If its sideLength is 3, which represents the result of executing act() once for this BoxBug?

(A)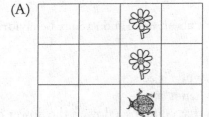

(B)

(C)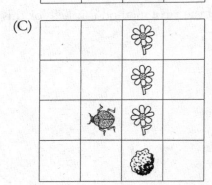

(D)

(E)

4. What will be the effect of executing the following statement in a client class for Bug and BoxBug?

```
Bug bb = new BoxBug();
```

(A) A red BoxBug facing north will be created, with random sideLength.
(B) A red BoxBug facing north will be created, with sideLength = 0.
(C) A red BoxBug with random direction will be created, with sideLength = 0.
(D) A BoxBug with random color and direction will be created, with sideLength = 0.
(E) A compile-time error will occur.

5. Which is a good reason for using the Location class constants for the compass directions and commonly used turn angles?

   I They enhance readability of code.

   II There is no built-in Degree type in Java.

   III They distinguish locations from directions.

(A) I only
(B) II only
(C) III only
(D) I and III only
(E) I, II, and III

6. Which location will the bug occupy after it acts once?

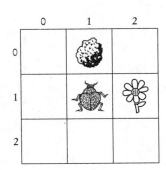

(A) (1, 1)
(B) (0, 1)
(C) (1, 2)
(D) (2, 1)
(E) (1, 0)

7. Suppose you want to modify the behavior of a `Bug` as follows: Every time it moves to a new location, it drops a `Rock` rather than a `Flower` into its old location. Which of the following modifications to the `move` method of the `Bug` class will correctly achieve this?

    I Replace the last two "flower" lines with

```
Rock rock = new Rock();
rock.putSelfInGrid(gr, loc);
```

    II Replace the last two "flower" lines with

```
Rock rock = new Rock();
gr.put(loc, rock);
```

    III Replace the last two "flower" lines with

```
Rock rock = new Rock();
gr[loc.getRow()][loc.getCol()] = rock;
```

(A) I only
(B) II only
(C) III only
(D) I and II only
(E) I, II, and III

8. In which of the following situations will the `canMove` method of `Bug` return true?

I

II

III

(A) I only
(B) II only
(C) III only
(D) I and II only
(E) II and III only

9. What would be the effect of having a subclass of `Actor` called `SubActor` that does not override the act method?

    I A `SubActor` object would always be blue.

    II A `SubActor` object would always face north.

    III A `SubActor` object would remain in its original location when it acts.

(A) I only
(B) II only
(C) III only
(D) I and III only
(E) I, II, and III

10. Consider a 4 × 4 bounded grid that contains a Bug at location (2, 3) facing east. What happens at this bug's turn to act?
    (A) It removes itself from the grid, leaving location (2, 3) empty.
    (B) It removes itself from the grid, leaving a flower in location (2, 3).
    (C) It moves to location (2, 4), leaving a flower in location (2, 3).
    (D) It remains in location (2, 3), and turns to face south.
    (E) It remains in location (2, 3), and turns to face southeast.

11. Suppose a subclass of Critter, SmallCritter, selects its next location by randomly selecting the location of an actor that occupies an adjacent neighboring grid location. The getMoveLocations of the Critter class will need to be overridden. Here is the specification for the overridden method.

    ```
    /**
     * Gets the possible locations for the next move. Returns the
     * occupied neighboring locations.
     * Postcondition: The locations must be valid in the grid of this
     * SmallCritter.
     * @return a list of possible locations for the next move.
     */
    public ArrayList<Location> getMoveLocations()
    { /* implementation code */ }
    ```

    Which of the following is correct /* *implementation code* */ that will satisfy the postcondition?
    (A) `return getGrid().getNeighbors(getLocation());`
    (B) `return getGrid().getValidAdjacentLocations(getLocation());`
    (C) `return getGrid().getOccupiedAdjacentLocations(getLocation());`
    (D) `return getActors();`
    (E) `return getActors().getLocations();`

12. Suppose a `ForwardCritter` extends `Critter`, and exists only in a bounded grid. A `ForwardCritter` has the following behavior when it acts.

    • It eats all actors in the grid (except for rocks and other critters) that are in a straight line in the direction that it is facing.

    • It then moves to a random empty location in the straight line in front of it.

For example, the `ForwardCritter` at (3, 1) would eat the bug at (1, 3) and the flower at (0, 4), then it would randomly move to either (1, 3) or (0, 4). If it were the turn of the `ForwardCritter` at (3, 3) to act, it would eat the bug at (1, 3) and then randomly move to (2, 3), (1, 3), or (0, 3).

In implementing the `ForwardCritter` class, which `Critter` methods would need to be overridden?

   I `getActors`

  II `processActors`

 III `getMoveLocations`

(A) I only
(B) II only
(C) III only
(D) I and III only
(E) I, II, and III

13. Suppose the `Actor` class is modified to add a `Color` parameter to its constructor. If the `Critter` class is not changed, what will happen when the modified constructor is called to create a `Critter` in a client class?
    (A) A compile-time error will occur.
    (B) An exception will be thrown as soon as a color is selected.
    (C) A blue `Critter` will be created.
    (D) A `Critter` will be created with the same color as the `Actor`.
    (E) A dialog box will appear, allowing a `Critter` of any color to be created.

Refer to the grid shown for Questions 14 and 15.

14. Suppose it is the turn of the Critter in location (2, 1) to act. What will be the value of getActors().size() for this Critter?
    (A) 1
    (B) 2
    (C) 3
    (D) 4
    (E) 5

15. Again, suppose it is the turn of the Critter in location (2, 1) to act. What will be the value of getMoveLocations().size() when getMoveLocations is called by this Critter's act method?
    (A) 2
    (B) 3
    (C) 5
    (D) 7
    (E) 8

Refer to the grid shown for Questions 16 and 17.

Location (0, 2) contains a green `Bug`.
Location (2, 0) contains a blue `Bug`.
Location (1, 1) contains a yellow `ChameleonCritter`.
Location (1, 2) contains a pink `Flower`.
Location (2, 2) contains a black `Rock`.
Location (3, 1) contains a red `Critter`.
The `ChameleonCritter` is about to act.

16. After the `ChameleonCritter` has acted, its color could *not* be
    (A) blue.
    (B) green.
    (C) pink.
    (D) black.
    (E) red.

17. After the `ChameleonCritter` has acted, its direction could *not* be
    (A) south.
    (B) southeast.
    (C) north.
    (D) northwest.
    (E) west.

For Questions 18 and 19, refer to the modified act method of the Critter class. The method has been changed by interchanging the lines

```
processActors(actors);
```

and

```
ArrayList<Location> moveLocs = getMoveLocations();
```

Here is the modified method:

```
public void act()
{
    if (getGrid() == null)
        return;
    ArrayList<Actor> actors = getActors();
    ArrayList<Location> moveLocs = getMoveLocations();
    processActors(actors);
    Location loc = selectMoveLocation(moveLocs);
    makeMove(loc);
}
```

18. Suppose that a Critter has at least one adjacent Bug. Which of the following *must* be true as a result of the modified act method for that Critter?
    (A) The Critter would eat a different group of actors.
    (B) The Critter would eat fewer actors.
    (C) There would be fewer locations available for the move.
    (D) The Critter would eat but not move.
    (E) There would be no change.

19. Suppose version 1 is the original version of act, and version 2 is the modified version of act. Let list1 represent the ArrayList<Location> as a result of calling getMoveLocations() in version 1, and let list2 represent the ArrayList<Location> returned by getMoveLocations() in version 2. Which of the following *could* be true, given that nothing is known about the surrounding actors for this Critter?

    I list1.size() == list2.size()

    II list1.size() > list2.size()

    III list1.size() < list2.size()

    (A) I only
    (B) II only
    (C) III only
    (D) I and II only
    (E) I and III only

20. For the 3×3 `BoundedGrid`, grid, shown, refer to the following code segment.

```
Location loc = new Location(1, 2);
ArrayList<Location> list = grid.getValidAdjacentLocations(loc);
System.out.println(list);
```

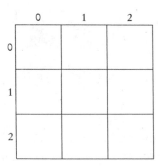

What will be output as a result of executing this code segment?
(A) $[(0, 2), (2, 2), (2, 1), (1, 1), (0, 1)]$
(B) $[(2, 2), (2, 1), (1, 1), (0, 1), (0, 2)]$
(C) $[(1, 1), (0, 1), (0, 2), (2, 2), (2, 1)]$
(D) $[(0, 2), (0, 1), (1, 1), (2, 1), (2, 2)]$
(E) $[(2, 2), (0, 2), (0, 1), (1, 1), (2, 1)]$

21. A method is *deterministic* if, given the inputs to it, you can tell exactly what its result will be. A method is *probabilistic* if, given the inputs, there are various probabilities of different results. Which of the following is *false*?
(A) Setting the original color of any `Actor` is deterministic.
(B) The `getMoveLocations` method in the `Critter` class is probabilistic.
(C) The `processActors` method in the `ChameleonCritter` class is probabilistic.
(D) The `getActors` method in the `Critter` class is deterministic.
(E) The process whereby a `BoxBug` receives its `sideLength` is deterministic.

22. Refer to the following statements concerning a 10×10 bounded grid.

```
Location loc1 = new Location(1, 2);
Location loc2 = loc1.getAdjacentLocation(110);
```

What will `loc2` contain after executing these statements?
(A) `Location.EAST`
(B) `Location.SOUTHEAST`
(C) $(1, 3)$
(D) $(2, 3)$
(E) $(2, 2)$

23. Consider the bounded grid shown.

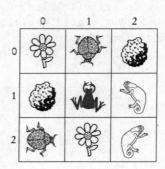

Assume that the `act` method for each actor is invoked with the configuration as shown. Which of the following statements is *false*?

(A) The chameleon critters in locations (1, 2) and (2, 2) will change color but not location.

(B) The bugs in locations (0, 1) and (2, 0) will change direction but not location.

(C) The critter in location (1, 1) will change location.

(D) The flowers in locations (0, 0) and (2, 1) will change color.

(E) The rocks in locations (1, 0) and (0, 2) will change neither color nor location.

Refer to the `BoundedGrid` shown for Questions 24 and 25.

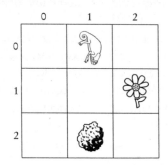

24. The `ChameleonCritter` in location (0, 1) is facing south. After it acts, its direction could *not* be
    (A) `Location.SOUTH`
    (B) `Location.WEST`
    (C) `Location.EAST`
    (D) `Location.SOUTHEAST`
    (E) `Location.SOUTHWEST`

25. Suppose that in the diagram the `ChameleonCritter` is blue, the `Flower` is red, and the `Rock` is black. What is *true* about the color of the `ChameleonCritter` after it acts?
    (A) It is a random color.
    (B) It is red or black, each of which is equally likely.
    (C) It must be red.
    (D) It must be blue.
    (E) It must be black.

26. Suppose a `Critter` has just one empty adjacent location just before its turn to act. What must be *true* after this `Critter` acts?

    I The `Critter` will be in that empty location.

    II The `Critter` will face the same direction that it faced before it acted.

    III After it moves, the only possible adjacent neighbors will be rocks and other critters.

    (A) I only
    (B) II only
    (C) III only
    (D) II and III only
    (E) I, II, and III

27. Suppose a `BoundedGrid` has r rows, c cols, and n occupants. What is the big-O run-time efficiency for the (1) get and (2) put methods?
    (A) (1) $O(rc)$ (2) $O(rc)$
    (B) (1) $O(n)$ (2) $O(n)$
    (C) (1) $O(n)$ (2) $O(1)$
    (D) (1) $O(1)$ (2) $O(n)$
    (E) (1) $O(1)$ (2) $O(1)$

AB ONLY

28. Suppose the data structure for the `UnboundedGrid` were changed to `TreeMap<Location, E>`, instead of `HashMap<Location, E>`. What would be a valid reason for doing this?
    (A) To improve the run time of the `getOccupiedLocations` method.
    (B) To improve the run times of the `get` and `put` methods.
    (C) To simplify the traversal of the map's key set.
    (D) To facilitate the printing of all the actors in the grid in alphabetical order.
    (E) To facilitate the printing of all the occupied locations in the grid in ascending (row-major) order.

29. In order to use a `HashMap` for correct storage of the `UnboundedGrid`, which method(s) must the `Location` class implement?

    I `equals`

    II `hashCode`

    III `compareTo`

    (A) I only
    (B) II only
    (C) III only
    (D) I and II only
    (E) I, II, and III

30. Which is a *false* statement about the grid classes?
    (A) In the `get` method of `BoundedGrid`, the object returned must be cast to `E` because `occupantArray` contains elements of type `Object`.
    (B) In the `UnboundedGrid` class, `getNumRows` and `getNumCols` must be implemented even though they are meaningless in this implementation.
    (C) The element returned by the `get` method of `UnboundedGrid` is not cast to `E` because values in the `Map` are declared to be of type `E`.
    (D) The `AbstractGrid` class must be abstract because it doesn't define all of the methods specified in the `Grid` interface.
    (E) The `occupantArray` of the `BoundedGrid` class contains references of type `Object` rather than type `E` to allow more flexibility in the types of elements that can be inserted into the grid.

31. Which is *true* about the `BoundedGrid` class?

    I It is a two-dimensional grid with a finite number of rows and columns.

    II An occupant of the grid can be an object of any type.

    III Empty locations in the grid have a value of `null`.

    (A) I only
    (B) II only
    (C) III only
    (D) I and III only
    (E) I, II, and III

32. In the `BoundedGrid` class, what would it mean if the following test were *true*?

    ```
    occupantArray[loc.getRow()][loc.getCol()] == null
    ```

    (A) The `occupantArray` has been constructed, but there is no actor in `occupantArray[loc.getRow()][loc.getCol()]`.
    (B) `loc` is an invalid location.
    (C) `loc` has not yet been constructed using `new`.
    (D) `occupantArray` has not yet been constructed using `new`.
    (E) An error has been made and an exception will be thrown.

33. The `isValid(loc)` method of `BoundedGrid` returns false if

    I `loc` is null.

    II `loc` is out of range.

    III The grid has not been constructed.

    (A) I only
    (B) II only
    (C) III only
    (D) I and II only
    (E) I, II, and III

34. The current implementation of the grid classes allows for a given location to have eight adjacent neighbors: those on all four sides, and the four diagonally adjacent neighbors. Suppose the program will be changed so that any given location will have just four adjacent neighbors, those that are north, south, east, and west of the given location. Which of the following methods must be changed in order to achieve the modification described?

    I The constructors of the `BoundedGrid` and `UnboundedGrid` classes.

    II The `isValid` methods of the `BoundedGrid` and `UnboundedGrid` classes.

    III The `getValidAdjacentLocations` method of the `AbstractGrid` class.

    (A) I only
    (B) II only
    (C) III only
    (D) I and II only
    (E) I, II, and III

35. Suppose the GridWorld case study program is run with N actors and M steps in the simulation, where N and M are large. Assume that the grid used is implemented with the `UnboundedGrid` class. The run-time efficiency of M steps of the simulation will be
    (A) $O(N+M)$
    (B) $O(NM)$
    (C) $O(N^2M)$
    (D) $O(M)$
    (E) $O(N)$

36. Suppose a `TreeMap` will be used to implement the `UnboundedGrid` class instead of a `HashMap`. Which method(s) in `UnboundedGrid` will need to be changed?

     I   the constructor

     II `getOccupiedLocations`

     III `get` and `put`

     (A) None
     (B) I only
     (C) II only
     (D) III only
     (E) II and III only

ANSWER KEY

1. B	13. A	25. C
2. E	14. C	26. B
3. A	15. D	27. E
4. E	16. E	28. E
5. A	17. B	29. D
6. A	18. C	30. E
7. A	19. D	31. D
8. E	20. A	32. A
9. C	21. B	33. B
10. E	22. C	34. C
11. C	23. B	35. B
12. D	24. D	36. B

ANSWERS EXPLAINED

1. **(B)** When a flower acts, its color darkens.

2. **(E)** When a bug turns, its resulting direction is its current direction + 45°. In this case:

$$\text{final direction} = \texttt{getDirection()} + \texttt{Location.HALF\_RIGHT}$$
$$= 180 + 45$$
$$= 225$$
$$= \texttt{Location.SOUTHWEST}$$

3. **(A)** When `act()` is called for this `BoxBug`, the test

   ```
   if (steps < sideLength && canMove())
   ```

   will be false, since `canMove()` is false. Thus, the bug will execute two 45° turns, resulting in choice A. Choice B is wrong because it only makes *one* 45° turn. Choice C is the result when act is called *twice*. Choices D and E are wrong because a bug cannot move onto a rock.

4. **(E)** The error message will be

   ```
   The constructor BoxBug() is undefined.
   ```

   This is because the `BoxBug` constructor takes an int parameter representing the `sideLength` for the `BoxBug`. Here are the rules for subclasses and constructors.

   - Constructors are not inherited.
   - If no constructor is provided in a subclass, the default constructor in the superclass is invoked. If there is no default constructor in the superclass, there will be a compile-time error.

- If a constructor with parameters *is* provided in the subclass, but there is no default constructor, as is the case in the BoxBug class, you must use that constructor with parameters; otherwise you will get a compile-time error.

5. **(A)** The constants allow you to visualize directions at a glance. For example, setDirection(Location.WEST) is much clearer than setDirection(270). Reason II is bogus: A Degree type is unnecessary. (There's nothing wrong with representing a direction with an int—it's just more readable to use a constant.) Reason III is also spurious: A location is always easy to recognize because it has both a row and column component. This is easy to distinguish from an int that represents a direction.

6. **(A)** This bug will not change location because it is blocked by a rock. Its canMove method will return false, and the bug will turn instead of moving.

7. **(A)** Segment I is correct: A new rock places itself in the bug's old location and updates its location and direction. Segment II appears to work correctly. However, if the grid adds the rock, the rock does not know that its location and direction have been changed. In general, when adding or removing actors, do not use get and put from the Grid interface, since these methods don't update the location and direction values of the actor. Segment III is egregiously wrong: The variable gr is not a two-dimensional array, it is a Grid object.

8. **(E)** In diagram I the bug can't move because it is at the edge of the grid. In diagram II the bug moves onto the flower. In diagram III the location in front of the bug is empty, and the bug will move there.

9. **(C)** The act method of Actor does not change the location of the actor. A SubActor would inherit this method and exhibit the same behavior. Choice II is wrong because an Actor changes direction when it acts. Choices I and II both fail because an Actor has mutator methods setColor and setDirection, which would be inherited by SubActor.

10. **(E)** The situation before the bug acts is shown. Since the location in front of the bug is not valid, the canMove method for this bug will return false, and the bug will remain in its current location, but turn to face southeast (a half-turn to the right).

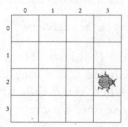

11. **(C)** The method getMoveLocations returns an ArrayList of Location objects; so eliminate choices A and D, which return lists of Actor objects. Choice B is wrong because it will return empty as well as occupied locations, which was not required. Choice E is egregiously wrong: There is no getLocations method in the ArrayList class.

12. **(D)** Method I: getActors must be overridden because you are no longer getting the actors in neighboring locations. Method II: processActors should not be overridden, since once you have the list of actors, the action taken on them is

no different from the action taken by regular critters (namely, they get eaten if they are not rocks or other critters). Method III: getMoveLocations must be overridden since you are no longer getting adjacent locations.

13. **(A)** A subclass does not inherit constructors from the superclass. If there is no constructor provided in the subclass, the compiler will provide a default constructor that calls the superclass default constructor. If the constructor in the superclass (Actor in this case) is not a default constructor, a compile-time error will occur when you try to construct a subclass object. Note that if a parameter is added to the Actor constructor, Actor no longer has a default constructor.

14. **(C)** The getActors method returns a list of adjacent actors. For the grid shown, the list will contain the flower at (2, 2), the rock at (3, 0), and the bug at (1, 1). Therefore the size of the list is 3.

15. **(D)** When the Critter acts it "eats" the nonrock and noncritter actors in the getActors list. Then, getMoveLocations() gets a list of adjacent, empty, neighboring locations. In this case the list contains (1, 0), (1, 1), (1, 2), (2, 2), (3, 2), (3, 1), and (2, 0)—seven elements. Notice that locations (1, 1) and (2, 2) are empty because the previous occupants have been eaten. The rock, however, is still there.

16. **(E)** The actors processed by any Critter must be in adjacent neighboring locations. Since location (3, 1) does not satisfy this condition, the red Critter in (3, 1) is not included in the ChameleonCritter's getActors list.

17. **(B)** The getMoveLocations() method for the ChameleonCritter will contain the following locations: (2, 1), which is south of (1, 1); (0, 1), which is north of (1, 1); (0, 0), which is northwest of (1, 1); and (1, 0), which is west of (1, 1). Thus, the ChameleonCritter will end up facing south, north, northwest, or west. It cannot end up facing southeast because it cannot move to location (2, 2), which is southeast of (1, 1).

18. **(C)** The effect of the change is to get the list of empty adjacent neighboring locations *before* the "edible" neighboring actors have been removed. There would therefore be fewer empty locations available. Notice that choice D *may* be true (if all the neighboring locations were occupied before processing), but it is not necessarily true.

19. **(D)** See the explanation for the previous question on the effect of modifying the act method. Test I would be true if there were no adjacent actors to be eaten. Test II would be true if there were at least one adjacent actor to be eaten. Test III could never be true: The original version of the method creates the biggest possible list of available empty locations, since it removes some of the adjacent actors before the list is created.

20. **(A)** The algorithm in the getValidAdjacentLocations method starts with the adjacent location north of loc (0°) and, going up in increments of 45°, gets the adjacent location in that direction. If that location is in the grid, it adds it to the list.

21. **(B)** There is nothing random about how a Critter gets its list of possible move locations. It simply gets the list of empty neighboring locations. Choices A and E are true: The color and side length values are provided in the constructors. Choice C is true: A ChameleonCritter randomly selects an Actor whose color it will assume. Choice D is true: A Critter gets the list of actors that are in adjacent neighboring locations. There is no probability involved.

22. **(C)** The specification for `getAdjacentLocation` is to return the adjacent location that is in the compass direction nearest to its parameter. Since it does *not* return the nearest compass direction, reject choices A and B. The nearest compass direction to 110 is 90, or east. The adjacent location east of (1, 2) is location (1, 3).

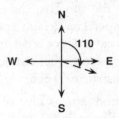

23. **(B)** The bug in (2, 0) will move onto the flower in (2, 1). (The other bug, however, is blocked by the critter in (1, 1), and will turn right.) Each of the other choices is true. Choice A: The chameleon critters have no empty adjacent locations to move to. They will, however, randomly pick one of the neighboring actors and change color. Choice C: The critter will eat the bugs in (0, 1) and (2, 0) and the flowers in (0, 0) and (2, 1), making their locations available. The critter will randomly pick one of these and move. Choice D: Flowers get darker when they act. Choice E: Rocks do nothing when they act.

24. **(D)** The `ChameleonCritter` ends up facing the direction in which it moved. Since it cannot move onto the flower, it cannot end up facing southeast.

25. **(C)** The only actor in the `ChameleonCritter`'s neighborhood is the red `Flower`. Therefore the `ChameleonCritter` ends up red.

26. **(B)** A `Critter` does not change direction when it acts. Statement I is wrong because a `Critter` can end up in the location of an actor that it ate. Statement III is wrong because after a `Critter` moves to a different location, its adjacent neighbors are different from those that it had before the move.

27. **(E)** Each of these methods is given the location that will be accessed. A two-dimensional array allows $O(1)$ access to any location, using

    ```
    occupantArray[loc.getRow()][loc.getCol()]
    ```

    The get method returns the object at that location, and the put method places a new object at that location, while returning the "old" object.

28. **(E)** A `TreeMap` stores the elements of the key set in a balanced binary search tree. To print the keys in ascending order, an inorder traversal of the binary search tree is performed. In a `HashMap`, the keys are stored in a hash table. Printing the keys will not produce them in any predictable order.

    Note that choices A and C are wrong because it is equally easy—and efficient—to traverse the key set of either a `HashMap` or a `TreeMap`. Choice B is wrong because get and put for a `HashMap` are $O(1)$, while for a `TreeMap` they are $O(\log n)$. Choice D is wrong because a `TreeMap` produces the *keys* in order, not the corresponding values. Besides, what does it mean to print the actors in alphabetical order??

29. **(D)** Defining both `equals` and `hashCode` in any class ensures that objects of that class can be stored in a set without allowing duplicates. The condition for `obj1` and `obj2` to be duplicates is

    ```
    obj1.equals(obj2)  ⟹  obj1.hashCode() == obj2.hashCode()
    ```

If hashcode has not been defined for the class, then both obj1 and obj2 may be added to the set (wrongly), even though *you* consider them to be equal. In the HashMap of the UnboundedGrid, it is important that there not be duplicate locations in the key set, which is stored as a HashSet. Note that it's not necessary for the objects in a HashSet to be Comparable (no ordering). Therefore, for the HashMap implementation, Location does not need compareTo.

30. **(E)** The type of elements in the array is Object because Java does not allow arrays of generic types. The following is illegal and will cause a compile-time error:

```
private E[][] occupantArray = new E[rows][cols];
```

31. **(D)** Statement II is false because the grid is declared as BoundedGrid<E>, which means that occupants of the grid must be objects of type E.

32. **(A)** In the constructor, the line

```
occupantArray = new Object[rows][cols];
```

creates a rows × cols two-dimensional array of null objects. Each slot represents an empty location. Notice in the remove method, the line

```
occupantArray[loc.getRow()][loc.getCol()] = null;
```

signifies that loc is now empty.

33. **(B)** The precondition for the method is that loc is not null. If loc is null, an exception is thrown. If the grid has not been constructed, the method call grid.isValid(loc) will throw a NullPointerException before any value can be returned.

34. **(C)** The only method that goes into the details of getting adjacent locations is the getValidAdjacentLocations method of the AbstractGrid class. Every other method that uses some subset of these locations starts by calling the method getValidAdjacentLocations. Note that each of the constructors of BoundedGrid and UnboundedGrid simply creates a grid containing no occupants.

35. **(B)** For each of the N actors to act once is $O(N)$, since getting, putting, and removing objects in a HashMap is $O(1)$. Thus for each actor to act M times is $O(NM)$.

36. **(B)** The implementation of the constructor will need to be changed to

```
occupantMap = new TreeMap<Location, E>();
```

The Map operations required for the methods in II and III are identical for a TreeMap and a HashMap, so nothing else needs to be changed.

Practice
Exams

Answer Sheet: Practice Exam Three

1. Ⓐ Ⓑ Ⓒ Ⓓ Ⓔ
2. Ⓐ Ⓑ Ⓒ Ⓓ Ⓔ
3. Ⓐ Ⓑ Ⓒ Ⓓ Ⓔ
4. Ⓐ Ⓑ Ⓒ Ⓓ Ⓔ
5. Ⓐ Ⓑ Ⓒ Ⓓ Ⓔ
6. Ⓐ Ⓑ Ⓒ Ⓓ Ⓔ
7. Ⓐ Ⓑ Ⓒ Ⓓ Ⓔ
8. Ⓐ Ⓑ Ⓒ Ⓓ Ⓔ
9. Ⓐ Ⓑ Ⓒ Ⓓ Ⓔ
10. Ⓐ Ⓑ Ⓒ Ⓓ Ⓔ
11. Ⓐ Ⓑ Ⓒ Ⓓ Ⓔ
12. Ⓐ Ⓑ Ⓒ Ⓓ Ⓔ
13. Ⓐ Ⓑ Ⓒ Ⓓ Ⓔ
14. Ⓐ Ⓑ Ⓒ Ⓓ Ⓔ

15. Ⓐ Ⓑ Ⓒ Ⓓ Ⓔ
16. Ⓐ Ⓑ Ⓒ Ⓓ Ⓔ
17. Ⓐ Ⓑ Ⓒ Ⓓ Ⓔ
18. Ⓐ Ⓑ Ⓒ Ⓓ Ⓔ
19. Ⓐ Ⓑ Ⓒ Ⓓ Ⓔ
20. Ⓐ Ⓑ Ⓒ Ⓓ Ⓔ
21. Ⓐ Ⓑ Ⓒ Ⓓ Ⓔ
22. Ⓐ Ⓑ Ⓒ Ⓓ Ⓔ
23. Ⓐ Ⓑ Ⓒ Ⓓ Ⓔ
24. Ⓐ Ⓑ Ⓒ Ⓓ Ⓔ
25. Ⓐ Ⓑ Ⓒ Ⓓ Ⓔ
26. Ⓐ Ⓑ Ⓒ Ⓓ Ⓔ
27. Ⓐ Ⓑ Ⓒ Ⓓ Ⓔ
28. Ⓐ Ⓑ Ⓒ Ⓓ Ⓔ

29. Ⓐ Ⓑ Ⓒ Ⓓ Ⓔ
30. Ⓐ Ⓑ Ⓒ Ⓓ Ⓔ
31. Ⓐ Ⓑ Ⓒ Ⓓ Ⓔ
32. Ⓐ Ⓑ Ⓒ Ⓓ Ⓔ
33. Ⓐ Ⓑ Ⓒ Ⓓ Ⓔ
34. Ⓐ Ⓑ Ⓒ Ⓓ Ⓔ
35. Ⓐ Ⓑ Ⓒ Ⓓ Ⓔ
36. Ⓐ Ⓑ Ⓒ Ⓓ Ⓔ
37. Ⓐ Ⓑ Ⓒ Ⓓ Ⓔ
38. Ⓐ Ⓑ Ⓒ Ⓓ Ⓔ
39. Ⓐ Ⓑ Ⓒ Ⓓ Ⓔ
40. Ⓐ Ⓑ Ⓒ Ⓓ Ⓔ

How to Calculate Your (Approximate) AP Score — AP Computer Science Level A

Multiple Choice

Number correct (out of 40)   =   _____

$1/4 \times$ number wrong   =   _____

Raw score = line 1 − line 2   =   _____   ⟸   Multiple-Choice Score
(Do not round. If less than zero, enter zero.)

Free Response

Question 1   _____
(out of 9)

Question 2   _____
(out of 9)

Question 3   _____
(out of 9)

Question 4   _____
(out of 9)

Total   _____   × 1.11 =   _____   ⟸   Free-Response Score
(Do not round.)

Final Score

_____   +   _____   =   _____
Multiple-Choice Score ~~ Free-Response Score ~~ Final Score
(Round to nearest whole number.)

Chart to Convert to AP Grade
Computer Science A

Final Score Range	AP Grade[a]
60–80	5
45–59	4
33–44	3
25–32	2
0–24	1

[a]The score range corresponding to each grade varies from exam to exam and is approximate.

Practice Exam Three
COMPUTER SCIENCE A
SECTION I

Time—1 hour and 15 minutes
Number of questions—40
Percent of total grade—50

Directions: Determine the answer to each of the following questions or incomplete statements, using the available space for any necessary scratchwork. Then decide which is the best of the choices given and fill in the corresponding oval on the answer sheet. Do not spend too much time on any one problem.

Notes:
- Assume that the classes in the Quick Reference have been imported where needed.
- Assume that variables and methods are declared within the context of an enclosing class.
- Assume that method calls that have no object or class name prefixed, and that are not shown within a complete class definition, appear within the context of an enclosing class.
- Assume that parameters in method calls are not `null` unless otherwise stated.

---

1. A large Java program was tested extensively and no errors were found. What can be concluded?
   (A) All of the preconditions in the program are correct.
   (B) All of the postconditions in the program are correct.
   (C) The program may have bugs.
   (D) The program has no bugs.
   (E) Every method in the program may safely be used in other programs.

Questions 2–4 refer to the Worker class below:

```
public class Worker
{
    private String myName;
    private double myHourlyWage;
    private boolean isUnionMember;

    //constructors

    public Worker()
    { /* implementation not shown */ }

    public Worker(String name, double hourlyWage, boolean union)
    { /* implementation not shown */ }

    //accessors getName, getHourlyWage, getUnionStatus not shown ...

    //modifiers

    //Permanently increase hourly wage by amt.
    public void incrementWage(double amt)
    { /* implementation of incrementWage */ }

    //Switch value of isUnionMember from true to false and vice versa.
    public void changeUnionStatus()
    { /* implementation of changeUnionStatus */ }
}
```

2. Refer to the incrementWage method. Which of the following is a correct
   /* implementation of incrementWage */?
   (A) return myHourlyWage + amt;
   (B) return getHourlyWage() + amt;
   (C) myHourlyWage += amt;
   (D) getHourlyWage() += amt;
   (E) myHourlyWage = amt;

3. Consider the method `changeUnionStatus`. Which is a correct
   /* *implementation of* `changeUnionStatus` */?

   ```
    I if (isUnionMember)
           isUnionMember = false;
       else
           isUnionMember = true;

   II isUnionMember = !isUnionMember;

   III if (isUnionMember)
           isUnionMember = !isUnionMember;
   ```

   (A) I only
   (B) II only
   (C) III only
   (D) I and II only
   (E) I, II, and III

4. A client method `computePay` will return a worker's pay based on the number of hours worked.

   ```
   //Precondition:  Worker w has worked the given number of hours.
   //Postcondition: Returns amount of pay for Worker w.
   public static double computePay(Worker w, double hours)
   { /* code */ }
   ```

   Which replacement for /* *code* */ is correct?
   (A) `return myHourlyWage * hours;`
   (B) `return getHourlyWage() * hours;`
   (C) `return w.getHourlyWage() * hours;`
   (D) `return w.myHourlyWage * hours;`
   (E) `return w.getHourlyWage() * w.hours;`

5. Consider this program segment. You may assume that `wordList` has been de-clared as `ArrayList<String>`.

   ```
   for (String s : wordList)
      if (s.length() < 4)
          System.out.println("SHORT WORD");
   ```

   What is the maximum number of times that SHORT WORD can be printed?
   (A) 3
   (B) 4
   (C) `wordList.size()`
   (D) `wordList.size() - 1`
   (E) `s.length()`

6. Refer to the following method.

```
public static int mystery(int n)
{
    if (n == 1)
        return 3;
    else
        return 3 * mystery(n - 1);
}
```

What value does mystery(4) return?

(A) 3
(B) 9
(C) 12
(D) 27
(E) 81

7. Refer to the following declarations:

```
String[] colors = {"red", "green", "black"};
ArrayList<String> colorList = new ArrayList<String>();
```

Which of the following correctly assigns the elements of the colors array to colorList? The final ordering of colors in colorList should be the same as in the colors array.

```
  I for (String col : colors)
        colorList.add(col);

 II for (String col : colorList)
        colors.add(col);

III for (int i = colors.length - 1; i >= 0; i--)
        colorList.add(i, colors[i]);
```

(A) I only
(B) II only
(C) III only
(D) II and III only
(E) I, II, and III

Questions 8 and 9 refer to the classes `Address` and `Customer` given below.

```java
public class Address
{
    private String myStreet;
    private String myCity;
    private String myState;
    private int myZipCode;

    //constructor
    public Address(String street, String city, String state, int zipCode)
    { /* implementation not shown */ }

    //accessors

    public String getStreet()
    { /* implementation not shown */ }

    public String getCity()
    { /* implementation not shown */ }

    public String getState()
    { /* implementation not shown */ }

    public int getZipCode()
    { /* implementation not shown */ }
}

public class Customer
{
    private String myName;
    private String myPhone;
    private Address myAddress;
    private int myID;

    //constructor
    public Customer(String name, String phone, Address addr, int ID)
    { /* implementation not shown */ }

    //accessors

    //Returns address of this customer.
    public Address getAddress()
    { /* implementation not shown */ }

    public String getName()
    { /* implementation not shown */ }

    public String getPhone()
    { /* implementation not shown */ }

    public int getID()
    { /* implementation not shown */ }
}
```

GO ON TO THE NEXT PAGE.

8. Which of the following correctly creates a `Customer` object `c`?

```
I Address a = new Address("125 Bismark St", "Pleasantville",
      "NY", 14850);
  Customer c = new Customer("Jack Spratt", "747-1674", a, 7008);

II Customer c = new Customer("Jack Spratt", "747-1674",
      "125 Bismark St, Pleasantville, NY 14850", 7008);

III Customer c = new Customer("Jack Spratt", "747-1674",
      new Address("125 Bismark St", "Pleasantville", "NY", 14850),
      7008);
```

(A) I only
(B) II only
(C) III only
(D) I and II only
(E) I and III only

9. Consider an `AllCustomers` class that has private instance variable

```
private Customer[] custList;
```

Given the ID number of a particular customer, a method of the class, `locate`, must find the correct `Customer` record and return the name of that customer. Here is the method `locate`:

```
/* Precondition:  custList contains a complete list of Customer
 *                objects. idNum matches the ID number data member
 *                of one of the Customer objects.
 * Postcondition: The name of the customer whose ID number
 *                matches idNum is returned.  */
public String locate(int idNum)
{
    for (Customer c : custList)
        if (c.getID() == idNum)
            return c.getName();
    return null;      //idNum not found
}
```

A more efficient algorithm for finding the matching `Customer` object could be used if
(A) `Customer` objects were in alphabetical order by name.
(B) `Customer` objects were sorted by phone number.
(C) `Customer` objects were sorted by ID number.
(D) the `custList` array had fewer elements.
(E) the `Customer` class did not have an `Address` data member.

GO ON TO THE NEXT PAGE.

10. Often the most efficient computer algorithms use a divide-and-conquer approach, for example, one in which a list is repeatedly split into two pieces until a desired outcome is reached. Which of the following use a divide-and-conquer approach?

> I   Mergesort
> II Insertion sort
> III Binary search

(A) I only
(B) II only
(C) III only
(D) I and III only
(E) I, II, and III

11. In Java, a variable of type `int` is represented internally as a 32-bit signed integer. Suppose that one bit stores the sign, and the other 31 bits store the magnitude of the number in base 2. In this scheme, what is the largest value that can be stored as type `int`?
(A) 2^{32}
(B) $2^{32} - 1$
(C) 2^{31}
(D) $2^{31} - 1$
(E) 2^{30}

12. Refer to method `removeWord`.

```
//Precondition:  wordList is an ArrayList of String objects.
//Postcondition: All occurrences of word have been removed from
                 wordList.
public static void removeWord(ArrayList<String> wordList,
                                              String word)
{
    for (int i = 0; i < wordList.size(); i++)
        if ((wordList.get(i)).equals(word))
            wordList.remove(i);
}
```

The method does not always work as intended. Consider the method call

```
removeWord(wordList, "cat");
```

For which of the following lists will this method call fail?
(A) The cat sat on the mat
(B) The cat cat sat on the mat mat
(C) The cat sat on the cat
(D) cat
(E) The cow sat on the mat

GO ON TO THE NEXT PAGE.

13. What will be output by this code segment?

```
for (int i = 5; i > 0; i--)
{
    for (int j = 1; j <= i; j++)
        System.out.print(j * j + " ");
    System.out.println();
}
```

(A) 1
    1 4
    1 4 9
    1 4 9 16
    1 4 9 16 25

(B) 1 4 9 16 25
    1 4 9 16
    1 4 9
    1 4
    1

(C) 25 16 9 4 1
    25 16 9 4
    25 16 9
    25 16
    25

(D) 25
    25 16
    25 16 9
    25 16 9 4
    25 16 9 4 1

(E) 1 4 9 16 25
    1 4 9 16 25
    1 4 9 16 25
    1 4 9 16 25
    1 4 9 16 25

14. Consider two different ways of storing a set of nonnegative integers in which there are no duplicates.

    Method One: Store the integers explicitly in an array in which the number of elements is known. For example, in this method, the set {6, 2, 1, 8, 9, 0} can be represented as follows:

0	1	2	3	4	5
6	2	1	8	9	0

    6 elements

    Method Two: Suppose that the range of the integers is 0 to MAX. Use a boolean array indexed from 0 to MAX. The index values represent the possible values in the set. In other words, each possible integer from 0 to MAX is represented by a different position in the array. A value of true in the array means that the corresponding integer is in the set, a value of false means that the integer is not in the set. For example, using this method for the same set above, {6, 2, 1, 8, 9, 0}, the representation would be as follows (T = true, F = false):

0	1	2	3	4	5	6	7	8	9	10	...	MAX
T	T	T	F	F	F	T	F	T	T	F	...	F

    The following operations are to be performed on the set of integers:

    I Search for a target value in the set.
    II Print all the elements of the set.
    III Return the number of elements in the set.

    Which statement is *true*?
    (A) Operation I is more efficient if the set is stored using Method One.
    (B) Operation II is more efficient if the set is stored using Method Two.
    (C) Operation III is more efficient if the set is stored using Method One.
    (D) Operation I is equally efficient for Methods One and Two.
    (E) Operation III is equally efficient for Methods One and Two.

15. An algorithm for finding the average of N numbers is

$$\text{average} = \frac{\text{sum}}{N}$$

    where N and sum are both integers. In a program using this algorithm, a programmer forgot to include a test that would check for N equal to zero. If N is zero, when will the error be detected?
    (A) At compile time
    (B) At edit time
    (C) As soon as the value of N is entered
    (D) During run time
    (E) When an incorrect result is output

16. What is wrong with this interface?

```
public interface Bad
{
    void someMethod(String password)
    {
        System.out.println("Psst! The password is " + password);
    }
}
```

    (A) A method in an interface should be declared `public`.
    (B) A method in an interface should be declared `abstract`.
    (C) There should not be a method implementation.
    (D) There should be a class implementation provided.
    (E) There should not be any method parameters.

17. Consider a program that deals with various components of different vehicles. Which of the following is a reasonable representation of the relationships among some classes that may comprise the program? Note that an open up-arrow denotes an inheritance relationship and a down-arrow denotes a composition relationship.

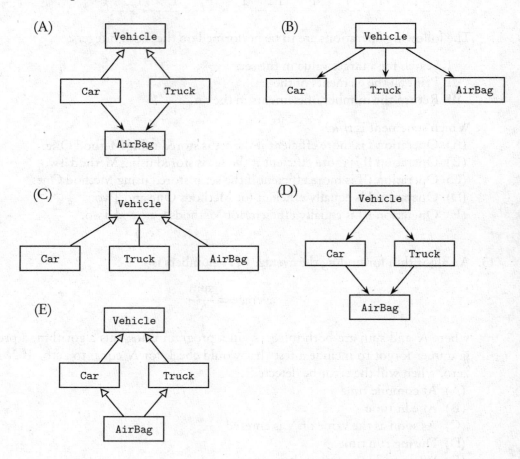

18. Consider the following program segment:

```
//Precondition: a[0]...a[n-1] is an initialized array of
//               integers, 0 < n <= a.length.
    int c = 0;
    for (int i = 0; i < n; i++)
        if (a[i] >= 0)
        {
            a[c] = a[i];
            c++;
        }
    n = c;
```

Which is the best postcondition for the segment?
(A) a[0]...a[n-1] has been stripped of all positive integers.
(B) a[0]...a[n-1] has been stripped of all negative integers.
(C) a[0]...a[n-1] has been stripped of all nonnegative integers.
(D) a[0]...a[n-1] has been stripped of all occurrences of zero.
(E) The updated value of n is less than or equal to the value of n before execution of the segment.

19. If a, b, and c are integers, which of the following conditions is sufficient to *guarantee* that the expression

```
a < c || a < b && !(a == c)
```

evaluates to true?
(A) a < c
(B) a < b
(C) a > b
(D) a == b
(E) a == c

20. Airmail Express charges for shipping small packages by integer values of weight. The charges for a weight w in pounds are as follows:

$$0 < w \le 2 \qquad \$4.00$$
$$2 < w \le 5 \qquad \$8.00$$
$$5 < w \le 20 \qquad \$15.00$$

The company does not accept packages that weigh more than 20 pounds. Which of the following represents the best set of data (weights) to test a program that calculates shipping charges?
(A) 0, 2, 5, 20
(B) 1, 4, 16
(C) −1, 1, 2, 3, 5, 16, 20
(D) −1, 0, 1, 2, 3, 5, 16, 20, 22
(E) All integers from −1 through 22

GO ON TO THE NEXT PAGE.

Questions 21–22 are based on the following class declaration:

```
public class AutoPart
{
    private String myDescription;
    private int myPartNum;
    private double myPrice;

    //constructor
    public AutoPart(String description, int partNum, double price)
    { /* implementation not shown */ }

    //accessors

    public String getDescription()
    { return myDescription; }

    public int getPartNum()
    { return myPartNum; }

    public double getPrice()
    { return myPrice; }
}
```

21. This question refers to the `findCheapest` method below, which occurs in a class that has an array of `AutoPart` as one if its private data fields:

```
private AutoPart[] allParts;
```

The `findCheapest` method examines an array of `AutoPart` and returns the part number of the `AutoPart` with the lowest price whose description matches the `partDescription` parameter. For example, several of the `AutoPart` elements may have "headlight" as their description field. Different headlights will differ in both price and part number. If the `partDescription` parameter is "headlight", then `findCheapest` will return the part number of the cheapest headlight.

```
/* Precondition:   allParts contains at least one element whose
 *                 description matches partDescription.
 * Postcondition: Returns the part number of the cheapest AutoPart
 *                 whose description matches partDescription.  */
public int findCheapest(String partDescription)
{
    AutoPart part = null;       //AutoPart with lowest price so far
    double min = LARGEVALUE;     //larger than any valid price
    for (AutoPart p : allParts)
    {
        /* more code */
    }
}
```

Which of the following replacements for /* *more code* */ will achieve the intended postcondition of the method?

```
I  if (p.getPrice() < min)
   {
       min = p.getPrice();
       part = p;
   }
   return part.getPartNum();

II if (p.getDescription().equals(partDescription))
       if (p.getPrice() < min)
       {
           min = p.getPrice();
           part = p;
       }
   return part.getPartNum();

III if (p.getDescription().equals(partDescription))
       if (p.getPrice() < min)
           return p.getPartNum();
```

(A) I only
(B) II only
(C) III only
(D) I and II only
(E) I and III only

GO ON TO THE NEXT PAGE.

22. Consider the following method:

```
//Precondition: ob1 and ob2 are distinct Comparable objects.
//Return smaller of ob1 and ob2.
public static Comparable min(Comparable ob1, Comparable ob2)
{
    if (ob1.compareTo(ob2) < 0)
        return ob1;
    else
        return ob2;
}
```

A method in the same class has these declarations:

```
AutoPart p1 = new AutoPart(<suitable values>);
AutoPart p2 = new AutoPart(<suitable values>);
```

Which of the following statements will cause an error?

I System.out.println(min(p1.getDescription(),
  p2.getDescription()));

II System.out.println(min(((String) p1).getDescription(),
     ((String) p2).getDescription()));

III System.out.println(min(p1, p2));

(A) None
(B) I only
(C) II only
(D) III only
(E) II and III only

23. This question is based on the following declarations:

```
String strA = "CARROT", strB = "Carrot", strC = "car";
```

Given that all uppercase letters precede all lowercase letters when considering alphabetical order, which is true?
(A) strA.compareTo(strB) < 0 && strB.compareTo(strC) > 0
(B) strC.compareTo(strB) < 0 && strB.compareTo(strA) < 0
(C) strB.compareTo(strC) < 0 && strB.compareTo(strA) > 0
(D) !(strA.compareTo(strB) == 0) && strB.compareTo(strA) < 0
(E) !(strA.compareTo(strB) == 0) && strC.compareTo(strB) < 0

GO ON TO THE NEXT PAGE.

Questions 24–26 refer to the ThreeDigitInteger and ThreeDigitCode classes below.

```
public class ThreeDigitInteger
{
    private int myHundredsDigit;
    private int myTensDigit;
    private int myOnesDigit;
    private int myValue;

    //constructor
    //value is a 3-digit int.
    public ThreeDigitInteger(int value)
    { /* implementation not shown */ }

    //Return sum of digits for this ThreeDigitInteger.
    public int digitSum()
    { /* implementation not shown */ }

    //Return sum of hundreds digit and tens digit.
    public int twoDigitSum()
    { /* implementation not shown */ }

    //other methods not shown
        ...
}

public class ThreeDigitCode extends ThreeDigitInteger
{
    private boolean myIsValid;

    //constructor
    //value is a 3-digit int.
    public ThreeDigitCode(int value)
    { /* implementation code */ }

    /* Returns true if ThreeDigitCode is valid, false otherwise.
     * ThreeDigitCode is valid if and only if the remainder when the
     * sum of the hundreds and tens digits is divided by 7 equals the
     * ones digit. Thus 362 is valid while 364 is not.  */
    public boolean isValid()
    { /* implementation not shown */ }
}
```

24. Which is a *true* statement about the classes shown?
    (A) The `ThreeDigitInteger` class inherits the `isValid` method from the class `ThreeDigitCode`.
    (B) The `ThreeDigitCode` class inherits all of the private instance variables and public accessor methods from the `ThreeDigitInteger` class.
    (C) The `ThreeDigitCode` class inherits the constructor from the class `ThreeDigitInteger`.
    (D) The `ThreeDigitCode` class can directly access all the private variables of the `ThreeDigitInteger` class.
    (E) The `ThreeDigitInteger` class can access the `myIsValid` instance variable of the `ThreeDigitCode` class.

25. Which is correct /* *implementation code* */ for the `ThreeDigitCode` constructor?

    ```
    I  super(value);
       myIsValid = isValid();

    II super(value, valid);

    III super(value);
        myIsValid = twoDigitSum() % 7 == myOnesDigit;
    ```

    (A) I only
    (B) II only
    (C) III only
    (D) I and III only
    (E) I, II, and III

26. Refer to these declarations in a client program:

    ```
    ThreeDigitInteger code = new ThreeDigitCode(127);
    ThreeDigitInteger num = new ThreeDigitInteger(456);
    ```

    Which of the following subsequent tests will *not* cause an error?

    ```
    I   if (code.isValid())
            ...

    II  if (num.isValid())
            ...

    III if (((ThreeDigitCode) code).isValid())
            ...
    ```

    (A) I only
    (B) II only
    (C) III only
    (D) I and II only
    (E) I and III only

27. Consider the following hierarchy of classes:

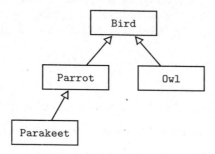

Assuming that each class has a valid default constructor, which of the following declarations in a client program are correct?

```
  I Bird b1 = new Parrot();
    Bird b2 = new Parakeet();
    Bird b3 = new Owl();

 II Parakeet p = new Parrot();
    Owl o = new Bird();

III Parakeet p = new Bird();
```

(A) I only
(B) II only
(C) III only
(D) II and III only
(E) I, II, and III

28. Consider an array `arr` and a list `list` that is an `ArrayList<String>`. Both `arr` and `list` are initialized with string values. Which of the following code segments correctly appends all the strings in `arr` to the end of `list`?

```
  I for (String s : arr)
       list.add(s);

 II for (String s : arr)
       list.add(list.size(), s);

III for (int i = 0; i < arr.length; i++)
       list.add(arr[i]);
```

(A) I only
(B) II only
(C) III only
(D) I and III only
(E) I, II, and III

GO ON TO THE NEXT PAGE.

29. Refer to the `nextIntInRange` method below:

```
/* Postcondition: Returns a random integer in the range
 *                 low to high, inclusive. */
public int nextIntInRange(int low, int high)
{
    return /* expression */
}
```

Which /* *expression* */ will always return a value that satisfies the postcondition?

(A) `(int) (Math.random() * high) + low;`

(B) `(int) (Math.random() * (high - low)) + low;`

(C) `(int) (Math.random() * (high - low + 1)) + low;`

(D) `(int) (Math.random() * (high + low)) + low;`

(E) `(int) (Math.random() * (high + low - 1)) + low;`

30. Consider the following `mergeSort` method and the private instance variable `a` both in the same `Sorter` class:

```
private Comparable[] a;

/* Sorts a[first] to a[last] in increasing order using mergesort. */
public void mergeSort(int first, int last)
{
    if (first != last)
    {
        int mid = (first + last) / 2;
        mergeSort(first, mid);
        mergeSort(mid + 1, last);
        merge(first, mid, last);
    }
}
```

Method `mergeSort` calls method `merge`, which has this header:

```
/* Merge a[lb] to a[mi] and a[mi+1] to a[ub].
 * Precondition: a[lb] to a[mi] and a[mi+1] to a[ub] both
 *               sorted in increasing order. */
private void merge(int lb, int mi, int ub)
```

If the first call to `mergeSort` is `mergeSort(0,3)`, how many *further* calls will there be to `mergeSort` before an array `b[0]...b[3]` is sorted?

(A) 2

(B) 3

(C) 4

(D) 5

(E) 6

31. A programmer has a file of names. She is designing a program that sends junk mail letters to everyone on the list. To make the letters sound personal and friendly, she will extract each person's first name from the name string. She plans to create a parallel file of first names only. For example,

fullName		firstName
Ms.	Anjali DeSouza	Anjali
Dr.	John Roufaiel	John
Mrs.	Mathilda Concia	Mathilda

Here is a method intended to extract the first name from a full name string.

```
/* Precondition:  fullName starts with a title followed by a period.
 *                A single space separates the title, first name,
 *                and last name.
 * Postcondition: Returns the first name only.  */
public static String getFirstName(String fullName)
{
    final String BLANK = " ";
    String temp, firstName;

    /* code to extract first name */

    return firstName;
}
```

Which represents correct /* *code to extract first name* */?

```
I  int k = fullName.indexOf(BLANK);
   temp = fullName.substring(k + 1);
   k = temp.indexOf(BLANK);
   firstName = temp.substring(0, k);
```

```
II  int k = fullName.indexOf(BLANK);
    firstName = fullName.substring(k + 1);
    k = firstName.indexOf(BLANK);
    firstName = firstName.substring(0, k);
```

```
III  int firstBlank = fullName.indexOf(BLANK);
     int secondBlank = fullName.indexOf(BLANK);
     firstName = fullName.substring(firstBlank + 1, secondBlank + 1);
```

(A) I only
(B) II only
(C) III only
(D) I and II only
(E) I, II, and III

GO ON TO THE NEXT PAGE.

32. A large hospital maintains a list of patients' records in no particular order. To find the record of a given patient, which represents the most efficient method that will work?
    (A) Do a sequential search on the name field of the records.
    (B) Do a binary search on the name field of the records.
    (C) Use insertion sort to sort the records alphabetically by name; then do a sequential search on the name field of the records.
    (D) Use mergesort to sort the records alphabetically by name; then do a sequential search on the name field of the records.
    (E) Use mergesort to sort the records alphabetically by name; then do a binary search on the name field of the records.

Use the following information for Questions 33 and 34.

Here is a diagram that shows the relationship between some of the classes that will be used in a program to draw a banner with block letters.

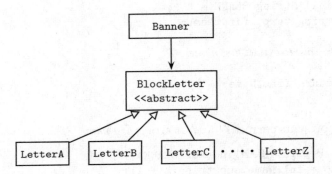

The diagram shows that the `Banner` class uses `BlockLetter` objects, and that the `BlockLetter` class has 26 subclasses, representing block letters from A to Z.

The `BlockLetter` class has an abstract `draw` method

```
public abstract void draw();
```

Each of the subclasses shown implements the `draw` method in a unique way to draw its particular letter. The `Banner` class gets an array of `BlockLetter` and has a method to draw all the letters in this array.

Here is a partial implementation of the `Banner` class:

```
public class Banner
{
    private BlockLetter[] letters;
    private int numLetters;

    //constructor. Gets the letters for the Banner.
    public Banner()
    {
        numLetters = <some integer read from user input>
        letters = getLetters();
    }
```

GO ON TO THE NEXT PAGE.

```
        //Return an array of block letters.
        public BlockLetter[] getLetters()
        {
            String letter;
            letters = new BlockLetter[numLetters];
            for (int i = 0; i < numLetters; i++)
            {
                < read in capital letter >

                if (letter.equals("A"))
                    letters[i] = new LetterA();
                else if (letter.equals("B"))
                    letters[i] = new LetterB();
                    ...             //similar code for C through Y
                else
                    letters[i] = new LetterZ();
            }
            return letters;
        }


        //Draw all the letters in the Banner.
        public void drawLetters()
        {
            for (BlockLetter letter : letters)
                letter.draw();
        }

        //Other methods not shown.
            ...
    }
```

33. You are given the information that `BlockLetter` is an abstract class that is used in the program. Which of the following can you conclude about the class?

    I It *must* have at least one abstract method.

    II It *must* have at least one subclass.

    III No instances of `BlockLetter` can be created.

    (A) I only
    (B) II only
    (C) III only
    (D) II and III only
    (E) I, II, and III

34. Which is a *true* statement about method `drawLetters`?
    (A) It is an overloaded method in the `Banner` class.
    (B) It is an overridden method in the `Banner` class.
    (C) It uses polymorphism to draw the correct letters.
    (D) It will cause a compile-time error because `draw` is not implemented in the `BlockLetter` class.
    (E) It will cause a run-time error because `draw` is not implemented in the `BlockLetter` class.

GO ON TO THE NEXT PAGE.

Questions 35–40 involve reasoning about the code from the GridWorld Case Study. A Quick Reference to the case study is provided as part of this exam. The actors in GridWorld are represented in this book with the pictures shown below. Each actor is shown facing north. These pictures almost certainly will be different from those used on the AP exam!

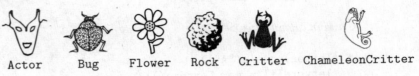

Actor   Bug   Flower   Rock   Critter   ChameleonCritter

35. Suppose a Bug is at the edge of a grid, facing south, as shown.

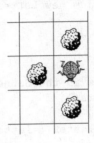

Which of the following correctly represents the state of this part of the grid after the act method has been called twice, assuming no other actors enter it?

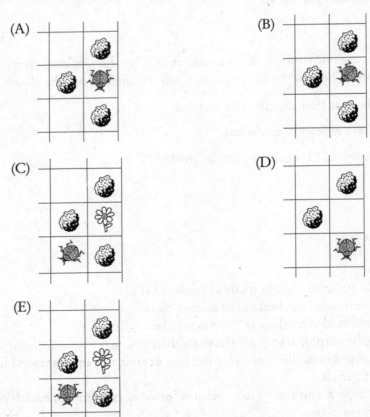

(A)

(B)

(C)

(D)

(E)

36. Which of the following always makes an actor reverse direction?

    I `setDirection(180);`

    II `setDirection(getDirection() + Location.HALF_CIRCLE);`

    III `setDirection(getDirection() - 180);`

    (A) I only
    (B) II only
    (C) III only
    (D) II and III only
    (E) I, II, and III

37. Here is the implementation of the act method in the `Rock` class.

    ```
    public void act()
    { }
    ```

    What would be the effect of omitting this piece of code from the `Rock` class?

    I A `Rock` would change location at its turn to act.

    II A `Rock` would change direction at its turn to act.

    III A `Rock` would change color at its turn to act.

    (A) I only
    (B) II only
    (C) III only
    (D) I and II only
    (E) II and III only

38. Which is (are) *true* about the behavior of a `BoxBug` that moves in a grid with many obstacles?

    I It will make smaller and smaller squares.

    II It will remove itself from the grid when it can no longer move forward.

    III It will step on obstacles until it reaches its `sideLength`.

    (A) None
    (B) I only
    (C) II only
    (D) I and II only
    (E) I and III only

GO ON TO THE NEXT PAGE.

39. Consider a subclass of `Critter` called `CannibalCritter`. A `CannibalCritter` eats only flowers and other critters. Its behavior is otherwise identical to that of a `Critter`. The only method that needs to be overridden in the `CannibalCritter` class is `processActors`. Here is the method.

```
/**
 * Processes the actors.
 * Implemented to "eat" (i.e., remove) all actors that
 * are critters or flowers.
 * @param actors the actors to be processed
 */
public void processActors(ArrayList<Actor> actors)
{
    for (Actor a : actors)
    {
        if ( /* test */ )
            a.removeSelfFromGrid();
    }
}
```

Which replacement for /* *test* */ produces the desired behavior for a `CannibalCritter`?

(A) `a instanceof Critter && a instanceof Flower`
(B) `!(a instanceof Critter) && !(a instanceof Flower)`
(C) `a instanceof Critter || a instanceof Flower`
(D) `!(a instanceof Critter) || !(a instanceof Flower)`
(E) `!(a instanceof Critter || a instanceof Flower)`

40. Refer to the bounded grid shown.

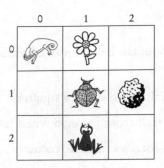

Location (0, 0) contains a `ChameleonCritter` facing southwest.
Location (1, 1) contains a `Bug` facing north.
Location (2, 1) contains a `Critter` facing north.
Which is *true* about the actors in the grid?

(A) If it were the `ChameleonCritter`'s turn to act, it could end up in location (0, 1).
(B) If it were the `Rock`'s turn to act, it could end up in location (1, 1).
(C) If it were the `Bug`'s turn to act, it would end up in location (0, 1).
(D) If it were the `Critter`'s turn to act, it could end up in location (1, 2).
(E) If it were the `Flower`'s turn to act, it would end up in location (0, 2).

END OF SECTION I

COMPUTER SCIENCE A
SECTION II

Time—1 hour and 45 minutes
Number of questions—4
Percent of total grade—50

Directions: SHOW ALL YOUR WORK. REMEMBER THAT
PROGRAM SEGMENTS ARE TO BE WRITTEN IN Java.

Write your answers in pencil only in the booklet provided.

Notes:

- Assume that the classes in the Quick Reference have been imported where needed.

- Unless otherwise stated, assume that parameters in method calls are not null and that methods are called only when their preconditions are satisfied.

- In writing solutions for each question, you may use any of the accessible methods that are listed in classes defined in that question. Writing significant amounts of code that can be replaced by a call to one of these methods may not receive full credit.

---

1. Consider a program that keeps track of transactions in a large department store. Both sales and returns are recorded. Three classes—Transaction, Sale, and Return—are used in the program, related as in the following inheritance hierarchy:

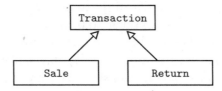

The Transaction class is defined below:

```java
public class Transaction
{
    private String myDescription;
    private int myNumItems;
    private double myItemCost;
    public static final double TAX_RATE = 0.07;
```

GO ON TO THE NEXT PAGE.

```
                    //constructor
                    public Transaction(String description, int numItems,
                                       double itemCost)
                    {
                        myDescription = description;
                        myNumItems = numItems;
                        myItemCost = itemCost;
                    }

                    //accessors
                    public String getDescription()
                    { return myDescription; }

                    public int getNumItems()
                    { return myNumItems; }

                    public double getItemCost()
                    { return myItemCost; }

                    public double getTotal()
                    {
                        double cost = myNumItems * myItemCost;
                        double tax = cost * TAX_RATE;
                        return cost + tax;
                    }
                }
```

(a) Write the code for the Sale class. Each Sale includes

- A description of the item being sold.
- The number of this item being sold.
- The cost of this item.
- Whether the sale is cash or credit, stored as a boolean variable.
- A 10 percent discount for cash, with 10 percent stored as a final variable.

When a new Sale is created, it must be assigned an item description, the number being sold, the cost of this item, and whether the sale is cash or credit. Operations on a Sale include the following:

- Retrieve the description of the item being sold.
- Retrieve the quantity of the item being sold.
- Retrieve the cost of the item being sold.
- Retrieve whether the sale is cash or credit.
- Calculate the total for the sale. In calculating this total, a 10 percent discount for paying cash should be applied to the cost before the tax is calculated.

  (Hint: discount is discount rate × cost.)

Write the code for the Sale class below.

(b) A class called `DailyTransactions` has the following private instance variable:

```
private Transaction[] allTransactions; //contains all transactions
                        //in a single day, including sales and returns
```

Write `findTransactionAverage`, a method for the `DailyTransactions` class, which computes the average of all transactions in a given day. The transactions are contained in the array `allTransactions`, where each object is a `Sale` or `Return`. The method `findTransactionAverage` should
- Compute the total for all transactions.
- Divide by the number of transactions. (You may assume that there's at least one transaction.)
- Return the average.

Note that when an item is returned to the store, the amount paid is returned to the customer. For this reason, the `getTotal` method in the `Return` class returns a *negative* quantity.

Complete `findTransactionAverage` below:

```
//Precondition:  allTransactions contains the day's transactions,
//                   each of which may be a Sale or a Return.
//Postcondition: Average of day's transactions returned.
public double findTransactionAverage()
```

2. Assume that information about candidates in a class election is stored using the `Candidate` and `CandidateList` classes below:

```
public class Candidate
{
    private String myName;
    private int myNumVotes;
    private double myVotePercent;

    //constructor
    //myVotePercent initialized to 0. Actual value set later.
    public Candidate(String name, int numVotes)
    { /* implementation not shown */ }

    //Set myVotePercent equal to votePercent.
    //Precondition: votePercent is a real number between 0.0 and 100.0.
    public void setVotePercent(double votePercent)
    { myVotePercent = votePercent; }

    //accessors

    public String getName()
    { return myName; }

    public int getNumVotes()
    { return myNumVotes; }

    public double getVotePercent()
    { return myVotePercent; }
}
```

GO ON TO THE NEXT PAGE.

```
public class CandidateList
{
    private Candidate[] myCList;

    //constructor
    //Reads name and number of votes for all candidates into myCList.
    public CandidateList()
    { /* implementation not shown */ }

    //Precondition:  myCList contains Candidate objects.
    //Postcondition: The vote percent for each Candidate has been
    //               calculated and updated.
    public void computeVotePercents()
    { /* to be implemented in part (a) */ }

    //Precondition:  myCList contains complete information about
    //               all candidates, including their updated vote
    //               percents. Each vote percent is a real number
    //               between 0.0 and 100.0.
    //Postcondition: Returns a list of viable candidates, namely
    //               those candidates who got at least 10 percent
    //               of the vote.
    public ArrayList<Candidate> getViableList()
    { /* to be implemented in part (b) */ }

    //Precondition:  myCList contains complete information about
    //               all candidates, including their updated vote
    //               percents.
    //Postcondition: The names of viable candidates only have
    //               been printed, one per line, followed by
    //               that candidate's vote percent.
    public void printViable()
    { /* to be implemented in part (c) */ }
}
```

(a) Write the implementation of the computeVotePercents method of the CandidateList class. The computeVotePercents method should fill in the vote percent for each Candidate in myCList. A candidate's vote percent is computed by dividing the number of votes for that candidate by the total number of votes cast for all candidates and then multiplying by 100.

In writing computeVotePercents, you may use any of the accessible methods in the Candidate and CandidateList classes.

Complete method computeVotePercents below.

```
//Precondition:  myCList contains Candidate objects.
//Postcondition: The vote percent for each Candidate has been
//               calculated and updated.
public void computeVotePercents()
```

(b) Write the implementation of the `getViableList` method of the `CandidateList` class. The `getViableList` method should examine the elements in `myCList` and create an `ArrayList` of *viable* candidates only. A viable candidate is one who received at least 10 percent of the vote.

In writing `getViableList`, you may use any of the accessible methods in the `Candidate` and `CandidateList` classes.

Complete method `getViableList` below.

```
//Precondition:  myCList contains complete information about
//               all candidates, including their updated vote
//               percents. Each vote percent is a real number
//               between 0.0 and 100.0.
//Postcondition: Returns a list of viable candidates, namely
//               those candidates who got at least 10 percent
//               of the vote.
public ArrayList<Candidate> getViableList()
```

(c) Write the implementation of the `printViable` method of the `CandidateList` class. The method `printViable` should list the names and vote percents of viable candidates only, one per line. Sample output:

```
Chris Arsenault 42.3278542118662
Anton Kriksunov 15.8023902117245
Lila Fontes 29.7646489012392
```

In writing `printViable` you must call the `getViableList` method specified in part (b), and use the list returned. Assume that `getViableList` works as specified regardless of what you wrote in part (b).
Complete method `printViable` below.

```
//Precondition:  myCList contains complete information about
//               all candidates, including their updated vote
//               percents.
//Postcondition: The names of viable candidates only have
//               been printed, one per line, followed by
//               that candidate's vote percent.
public void printViable()
```

3. Consider the problem of writing a Hi-Lo game in which a user thinks of an integer from 1 to 100 inclusive and the computer tries to guess that number with the smallest number of guesses. Each time the computer makes a guess the user makes one of three responses:

- "lower" (i.e., the number is lower than the computer's guess)
- "higher" (i.e., the number is higher than the computer's guess)
- "you got it in < however many > tries!"

The game will be programmed using the following `HiLoGame` class:

```
public class HiLoGame
{
    private int computerGuess;

    //constructor
    public HiLoGame()
    { computerGuess = 0; }

    //Explain to user how game will work.
    public void giveInstructions()
    { /* implementation not shown */ }

    //Sequence of computer guesses and user responses until computer
    // guesses user's number.
    public void play()
    { /* to be implemented in part (a) */ }
}
```

(a) Write the implementation of the `play` method of the `HiLoGame` class. In writing `play`, the following sequence of steps should be repeated until the computer guesses the user's number:

- Output the computer's guess.
- Prompt the user for a response.
- Read the user's response. You should use the following statement to read the user's response:

```
String response = IO.readString();
```

No error checking is necessary for the response.

In writing the `play` method the computer should use a *binary search* strategy for making its guesses. This is the best strategy for the computer, one that will enable it to find the user's number with the smallest number of guesses on average.

Here's how the binary search strategy works: If the computer's guess is k and the user says "lower," the computer's guess should be midway between 1 and $k - 1$. If the user says "higher," the computer's new guess should be midway between $k + 1$ and 100. Any other response means the computer has guessed the user's number. The initial guess is midway between 1 and 100. With each subsequent guess, the interval of possible numbers is halved from what it was.

Write the `play` method below:

```
//Sequence of computer guesses and user responses until computer
// guesses user's number.
//Computer uses a binary search strategy for its guesses.
//Postcondition: Number of guesses made by the computer is printed.
public void play()
```

(b) Using the binary search strategy, what is the maximum number of guesses the computer could make before guessing the user's number? Explain your answer.

(c) Suppose the computer used a *sequential search* strategy for guessing the user's number. What is the maximum number of guesses the computer could make before guessing the user's number? Explain your answer.

(d) Using a sequential search strategy, how many guesses *on average* would the computer need to guess the number? Explain your answer.

4. This question involves reasoning about the code from the GridWorld Case Study. A Quick Reference to the case study is provided as part of this exam.

Consider a new type of Bug, a JiveBug that dances when it acts. First, it turns. Then, it either stays where it is, or moves forward if it can. Each of these actions is equally likely. Some of the times that it moves forward, it tosses a flower in front of it to the right, according to a specified probability and if the "toss" location is valid.

A partial definition of JiveBug is shown below. Notice that the move method of Bug is overridden: Even though a JiveBug moves like a regular Bug, it no longer drops a flower in its path. Instead, it sometimes tosses a flower. The act and turn methods are also overridden.

```
public class JiveBug extends Bug
{
    private double probOfFlowerToss;
    private int[] myTurns = { /* selection of turns from Location.LEFT,
        Location.RIGHT, Location.HALF_LEFT,
        Location.HALF_RIGHT, Location.FULL_CIRCLE,
        Location.HALF_CIRCLE */ }

    /**
     * Constructs a JiveBug that dances when it acts,
     * and sometimes throws a flower according to the specified
     * probability.
     * @param probToss the probability of tossing a flower
     */
    public JiveBug(double probToss)
    {
        probOfFlowerToss = probToss;
    }

    /**
     * Gets a randomly selected turn from myTurns.
     * @return a randomly selected turn constant
     */
    public int getDanceTurn()
    { /* to be implemented in part (a) */ }
```

GO ON TO THE NEXT PAGE.

```
/**
 * Gets a dance turn, and then turns.
 */
public void turn()
{ /* to be implemented in part (b) */ }


/**
 * Moves forward, like a Bug.
 * Attempts to toss a flower that is the same color as itself.
 */
public void move()
{
    Grid<Actor> gr = getGrid();
    if (gr == null)
        return;
    Location loc = getLocation();
    Location next = loc.getAdjacentLocation(getDirection());
    if (gr.isValid(next))
        moveTo(next);
    else
        removeSelfFromGrid();
    tossFlower();
}


/**
 * Tosses a flower some fraction of the time, given by
 * probOfFlowerToss. A JiveBug tosses a flower in front
 * of itself to the right, if that location is valid.
 * The flower is the same color as the JiveBug.
 */
public void tossFlower()
{ /* to be implemented in part (c) */ }


/**
 * A JiveBug starts by turning when it acts.
 * Then, it is equally likely that it will stay where it is
 * or attempt to move.
 */
public void act()
{ /* to be implemented in part (d) */ }


}
```

(a) Write the getDanceTurn method of JiveBug. This method randomly re-
    turns a turn from the myTurns array.
    Complete method getDanceTurn below.

```
/**
 * Gets a randomly selected turn from myTurns.
 * @return a randomly selected turn constant
 */
public int getDanceTurn()
```

(b) Override the `turn` method from the `Bug` class. The overridden method should get a turn value from its `myTurns` array, and make that turn. Complete the `turn` method below.

```
/**
 * Gets a dance turn, and then turns.
 */
public void turn()
```

(c) Write the `tossFlower` method for `JiveBug`. Method `tossFlower` causes a flower that is the same color as the `JiveBug` to be tossed some fraction of the time, given by `probOfFlowerToss`, if the toss location is valid. When it tosses a flower, a `JiveBug` tosses it into the location that is in front of it and to its right.

Here are some toss locations for a `JiveBug` that has just moved:

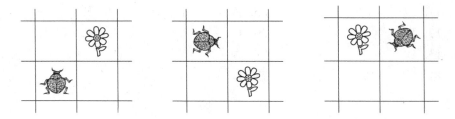

Complete method `tossFlower` below.

```
/**
 * Tosses a flower some fraction of the time, given by
 * probOfFlowerToss. A JiveBug tosses a flower in front
 * of itself to the right, if that location is valid.
 * The flower is the same color as the JiveBug.
 */
public void tossFlower()
```

(d) Override the `act` method of the `Bug` class. A `JiveBug` acts by turning. Then it either stays where it is, or, with equal probability, moves forward if it can. Complete the `act` method below.

```
/**
 * A JiveBug starts by turning when it acts.
 * Then, it is equally likely that it will stay where it is
 * or attempt to move.
 */
public void act()
```

END OF EXAMINATION

ANSWER KEY (Section I)

1. C	15. D	29. C
2. C	16. C	30. E
3. D	17. A	31. D
4. C	18. B	32. A
5. C	19. A	33. D
6. E	20. D	34. C
7. A	21. B	35. C
8. E	22. E	36. D
9. C	23. C	37. B
10. D	24. B	38. A
11. D	25. A	39. C
12. B	26. C	40. C
13. B	27. A	
14. C	28. E	

ANSWERS EXPLAINED (Section I)

1. **(C)** Testing a program thoroughly does not prove that a program is correct. For a large program, it is generally impossible to test every possible set of input data.

2. **(C)** The private instance variable `myHourlyWage` must be incremented by `amt`. Eliminate choice E, which doesn't *increment* `myHourlyWage`; it simply *replaces* it by `amt`. Choice D is wrong because you can't use a method call as the left-hand side of an assignment. Choices A and B are wrong because the `incrementWage` method is void and should not return a value.

3. **(D)** The value of the boolean instance variable `isUnionMember` must be changed to the opposite of what it currently is. Segments I and II both achieve this. Note that `!true` has a value of `false` and `!false` a value of `true`. Segment III fails to do what's required if the current value of `isUnionMember` is `false`.

4. **(C)** `computePay` is a client method and, therefore, cannot access the private variables of the class. This eliminates choices A and D. The method `getHourlyWage()` must be accessed with the dot member construct; thus, choice B is wrong, and choice C is correct. Choice E is way off base—`hours` is not part of the `Worker` class, so `w.hours` is meaningless.

5. **(C)** If `s.length()` < 4 for all strings in `wordList`, then `SHORT WORD` will be printed on each pass through the `for` loop. Since there are `wordList.size()` passes through the loop, the maximum number of times that `SHORT WORD` can be printed is `wordList.size()`.

6. **(E)**

$$\begin{aligned}
\text{mystery}(4) &= 3 * \text{mystery}(3)\\
&= 3 * 3 * \text{mystery}(2)\\
&= 3 * 3 * 3 * \text{mystery}(1)\\
&= 3 * 3 * 3 * 3\\
&= 81
\end{aligned}$$

7. **(A)** The declaration of the `colors` array makes the following assignments: `colors[0] = "red"`, `colors[1] = "green"`, and `colors[2] = "black"`. The loop in segment I adds these values to `colorList` in the correct order. Segment II fails because `colors` is an array and therefore can't use the get method. The code also confuses the lists. Segment III, in its first pass through the loop, attempts to add `colors[2]` to index position 2 of `colorList`. This will cause an `IndexOutOfBoundsException` to be thrown, since index positions 0 and 1 do not yet exist!

8. **(E)** A new `Address` object must be created, to be used as the `Address` parameter in the `Customer` constructor. To do this correctly requires the keyword `new` preceding the `Address` constructor. Segment II omits `new` and does not use the `Address` constructor correctly. (In fact, it inserts a new `String` object in the `Address` slot of the `Customer` constructor.)

9. **(C)** The algorithm used in method `locate` is a sequential search, which may have to examine all the objects to find the matching one. A binary search, which repeatedly discards a chunk of the array that does not contain the key, is more efficient. However, it can only be used if the values being examined—in this case customer ID numbers—are sorted. Note that it doesn't help to have the array sorted by name or phone number since the algorithm doesn't look at these values.

10. **(D)** Mergesort repeatedly splits an array of *n* elements in half until there are *n* arrays containing one element each. Now adjacent arrays are successively merged until there is a single merged, sorted array. A binary search repeatedly splits an array into two, narrowing the region that may contain the key. Insertion sort, however, does no array splitting. It takes elements one at a time and finds their insertion point in the sorted piece of the array. Elements are shifted to allow correct insertion of each element. Even though this algorithm maintains the array in two parts—a sorted part and yet-to-be-sorted part—this is not a divide-and-conquer approach.

11. **(D)** Think of the integer as having 31 slots for storage. If there were just one slot, the maximum binary number would be $1 = 2^1 - 1$. If there were just two slots, the maximum binary number would be $11 = 2^2 - 1 = 3$. If there were just eight slots, the maximum binary number would be $11111111 = 2^8 - 1$. So for 31 slots, the maximum value is $2^{31} - 1$.

12. **(B)** The `remove` method of `ArrayList` removes the indicated element, shifts the remaining elements down one slot (i.e., it does not leave gaps in the list), and adjusts the size of the list. Consider the list in choice B. The index values are shown:

```
The cat cat sat on the mat mat
 0   1   2   3   4  5   6   7
```

After the first occurrence of cat has been removed:

```
The cat sat on the mat mat
 0   1   2   3  4   5   6
```

The value of i, which was 1 when cat was removed, has now been incremented to 2 in the for loop. This means that the word to be considered next is sat. The second occurrence of cat has been missed. Thus, the given code will fail whenever occurrences of the word to be removed are consecutive. You fix it by not allowing the index to increment when a removal occurs:

```
int i = 0;
while (i < wordList.size())
{
    if ((wordList.get(i)).equals(word))
        wordList.remove(i);
    else
        i++;
}
```

13. **(B)** This code translates into

> for five rows (starting at i = 5 and decreasing i)
> > print the first i perfect squares
> > go to a new line

Thus, in the first line, the first five perfect squares will be printed. In the second line, the first four perfect squares will be printed, and so on down to i = 1, with just one perfect square being printed.

14. **(C)** To return the number of elements in the set for Method One requires no more than returning the number of elements in the array. For Method Two, however, the number of cells that contain true must be counted, which requires a test for each of the MAX values. Note that searching for a target value in the set is more efficient for Method Two. For example, to test whether 2 is in the set, simply check if a[2] == true. In Method One, a sequential search must be done, which is less efficient. To print all the elements in Method One, simply loop over the known number of elements and print. Method Two is less efficient because the whole array must be examined: Each cell must be tested for true before printing.

15. **(D)** An ArithmeticException will be thrown at run time. Note that if N were of type double, no exception would be thrown. The variable sum would be assigned the value Infinity, and the error would only be detected in the output.

16. **(C)** An interface should provide method declarations only. No code! Note that the methods are automatically public and abstract, so there is no need to specify this explicitly.

17. **(A)** The correct diagram uses two up arrows to show that a Car *is-a* Vehicle and a Truck *is-a* Vehicle (inheritance relationship). The two down arrows indicate that a Car *has-a* AirBag and a Truck *has-a* AirBag (composition relationship). In each of the incorrect choices, at least one of the relationships does not make sense. For example, in choice B a Vehicle *has-a* Truck, and in choice E an AirBag *is-a* Car.

18. **(B)** The postcondition should be a true assertion about the major action of the segment. The segment overwrites the elements of array a with the nonnegative elements of a. Then n is adjusted so that now the array a[0]...a[n-1] contains just nonnegative integers. Note that even though choice E is a correct assertion

about the program segment, it is not a good postcondition because it doesn't describe the main modification to array a (namely all negative integers have been removed).

19. **(A)** Note the order of precedence for the expressions involved: (1) parentheses, (2) !, (3) <, (4) ==, (5) &&, (6) ||. This means that a < c, a < b, and !(a == b) will all be evaluated before || and && are considered. The given expression then boils down to value1 || (value2 && value3), since && has higher precedence than ||. Notice that if value1 is true, the whole expression is true since (true || any) evaluates to true. Thus, a < c will guarantee that the expression evaluates to true. None of the other conditions will guarantee an outcome of true. For example, suppose a < b (choice B). If a == c, then the whole expression will be false because you get F || F.

20. **(D)** Test data should always include a value from each range in addition to all boundary values. The given program should also handle the cases in which weights over 20 pounds or any negative weights are entered. Note that choice E contains redundant data. There is no new information to be gained in testing two weights from the same range—both 3 and 4 pounds, for example.

21. **(B)** Segment II correctly checks that the part descriptions match and keeps track of the current part with minimum price. If this is not done, the part whose number must be returned will be lost. Segment I is incorrect because it doesn't check that partDescription matches the description of the current part being examined in the array. Thus, it simply finds the AutoPart with the lowest price, which is not what was required. Segment III incorrectly returns the part number of the first part it finds with a matching description.

22. **(E)** Statement I is fine: The parameters are String objects. Statement II will throw a ClassCastException because an AutoPart cannot be cast to a String. Statement III will fail because p1 and p2 are not Comparable objects.

23. **(C)** Ordering of strings involves a character-by-character comparison starting with the leftmost character of each string. Thus, strA precedes strB (since "A" precedes "a") or strA.compareTo(strB) < 0. This eliminates choices B and D. Eliminate choices A and E since strB precedes strC (because "C" precedes "c") and therefore strB.compareTo(strC) < 0. Note that string1.compareTo(string2) == 0 if and only if string1 and string2 are equal strings.

24. **(B)** ThreeDigitCode is a subclass of ThreeDigitInteger and therefore inherits all the instance variables and methods of ThreeDigitInteger except constructors. All of the statements other than B are false. For choice A, ThreeDigitInteger is the superclass and therefore cannot inherit from its subclass. For choice C, constructors are never inherited (see p. 190). For choice D, a subclass can access private variables of the superclass through accessor methods only (see p. 190). For choice E, a superclass cannot access any additional instance variables of its subclass.

25. **(A)** Implementation II is wrong because the constructor has no boolean validity parameter. Implementation III is wrong because a subclass cannot access a private instance variable of its superclass.

26. **(C)** A compile-time error will occur for both tests I and II because at compile time the types of code and num are both ThreeDigitInteger, and the class

ThreeDigitInteger does not have an isValid method. To avoid this error, the code object must be cast to ThreeDigitCode, its actual type. Note that if you try to cast num to ThreeDigitCode, you'll get a run-time error (ClassCastException) because num is not an instance of ThreeDigitCode.

27. (A) The *is-a* relationship must work from right-to-left: a Parrot *is-a* Bird, a Parakeet *is-a* Bird, and an Owl *is-a* Bird. All are correct. This relationship fails in declarations II and III: a Parrot is not necessarily a Parakeet, a Bird is not necessarily an Owl, and a Bird is not necessarily a Parakeet.

28. (E) All three segments traverse the array, accessing one element at a time, and appending it to the end of the ArrayList. In segment II, the first parameter of the add method is the position in list where the next string s will be added. Since list.size() increases by one after each insertion, this index is correctly updated in each pass through the for-each loop.

29. (C) Suppose you want random integers from 2 to 8, that is, low = 2 and high = 8. This is 7 possible integers, so you need

    (int) (Math.random() * 7)

which produces 0, 1, 2, ..., or 6. Therefore the quantity

    (int) (Math.random() * 7) + 2

produces 2, 3, 4, ..., or 8. The only expression that yields the right answer with these values is

    (int) (Math.random() * (high - low + 1)) + low;

30. (E) Here is a "box diagram" for mergeSort(0,3). The boldface numbers 1–6 show the order in which the mergeSort calls are made.

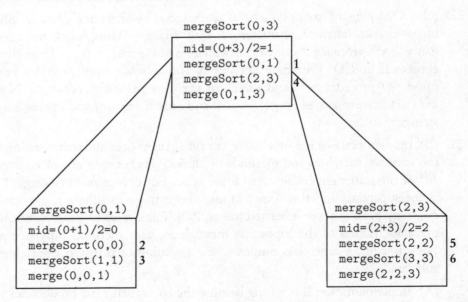

The mergeSort calls in which first == last are base case calls, which means that there will be no further method calls.

31. (D) Suppose fullName is Dr. John Roufaiel. In segment I the expression fullName.indexOf(BLANK) returns 3. Then temp gets assigned the

value of `fullName.substring(4)`, which is `John Roufaiel`. Next k gets assigned the value `temp.indexOf(BLANK)`, namely 4, and `firstName` gets assigned `temp.substring(0, 4)`, which is all the characters from 0 to 3 inclusive, namely `John`. Note that segment II works the same way, except `firstName` gets assigned `John Roufaiel` and then reassigned `John`. This is not good style, since a variable name should document its contents as precisely as possible. Still, the code works. Segment III fails because `indexOf` returns the *first* occurrence of its `String` parameter. Thus, `firstBlank` and `secondBlank` will both contain the same value, 3.

32. **(A)** Since the records are not sorted, the quickest way to find a given name is to start at the beginning of the list and sequentially search for that name. Choices C, D, and E will all work, but it's inefficient to sort and then search because all sorting algorithms take longer than simply inspecting each element. Choice B won't work: A binary search can only be used for a sorted list.

33. **(D)** Statement I *may* be true, but it doesn't have to be. The point about an abstract class is that it represents an abstract concept, and no instance of it will ever be created. The only instances that will be created are instances of its subclasses. Statement II *must* be true, since you are told the abstract class is actually used in the program. Statement III is true because an abstract class cannot be instantiated.

34. **(C)** The `draw` method is polymorphic, which means that it is a superclass method that is overridden in at least one of its subclasses. During run time, there is dynamic binding between the calling object and the method, that is, the actual instance is bound to its particular overridden method. In the `drawLetters` method, the correct version of `draw` is called during each iteration of the `for` loop, and a banner with the appropriate letters is drawn.

35. **(C)** The first time it acts, the bug can't move forward, so it turns 45° right. (Choice B is the situation after it acts once.) The second call to `act` has the bug move forward, leaving a flower in its original location (choice C, the correct answer). Choice A is wrong because if the bug doesn't move, it turns. Choice D fails because a bug cannot move onto a rock. Choice E is wrong because it doesn't reflect the fact that the bug turned to face southwest when it couldn't move the first time. After its second turn it would still be facing southwest.

36. **(D)** Adding 180 to or subtracting 180 from the actor's current direction will reverse that actor's direction. Note that `Location.HALF_CIRCLE` has a value of 180. Statement I is wrong because the method call `setDirection(180)` causes the actor to face south, which does not necessarily reverse its direction.

37. **(B)** With no override of `act`, a `Rock` will do what an `Actor` does, namely change direction.

38. **(A)** Statement I is wrong because the `sideLength` does not get changed when obstacles are encountered. The `BoxBug` tends to make rectangles, rather than squares, since it turns when it cannot move forward. Statement II is false: When a `Bug` cannot move forward, it turns. Statement III is false: A `Bug` steps on flowers, but not on other actors. Its behavior is to turn when it encounters obstacles, not to step on them.

39. **(C)** Here is the logic of choice C: If a is a `Critter` or a `Flower`, remove it. This is what was required. Choice A says: If a is both a `Critter` *and* a `Flower` ...—not possible! Choice B: If a is neither a `Critter` nor a `Flower`, remove it. Wrong

action! Choice E is equivalent to choice B. Choice D: If a is not a `Critter` or a is not a `Flower`, remove it. This test will evaluate to true no matter what a is!

40. **(C)** The `Bug` would move onto the `Flower`. Every other choice is false: Choice A: `ChameleonCritters` do not displace other actors. Choice B: `Rocks` do not move. Choice D: `Critters` do not eat rocks. Choice E: `Flowers` do not move.

Section II

1. (a)
```
public class Sale extends Transaction
{
    private boolean myIsCash;
    private final double CASH_DISCOUNT = 0.1;

    //constructor
    public Sale(String description, int numItems,
        double itemCost, boolean isCash)
    {
        super(description, numItems, itemCost);
        myIsCash = isCash;
    }

    //Return true if Sale is cash, false otherwise.
    public boolean getIsCash()
    { return myIsCash; }

    public double getTotal()
    {
        double cost = getNumItems() * getItemCost();
        if (myIsCash)
        {
            double discount = cost * CASH_DISCOUNT;
            cost = cost - discount;
        }
        double tax = cost * TAX_RATE;
        return cost + tax;
    }
}
```

(b)
```
public double findTransactionAverage()
{
    double sum = 0;
    for (Transaction t : allTransactions)
        sum += t.getTotal();
    return sum / allTransactions.length;
}
```

NOTE

- In part (a), the solution shows some comments. In general, you don't need to provide comments for your code on the exam. However, short comments to clarify what you're doing are fine.
- The Sale class inherits all of the accessors from the Transaction superclass. The getDescription, getNumItems, and getItemCost methods should not be redefined. Their implementation doesn't change. The getTotal method, however, is different in the Sale class and therefore must be overridden.
- In part (b), the fact that getTotal is negative for a Return object means that the correct amount will automatically be added to the sum if the Transaction is a Return. The method is polymorphic and will call the appropriate getTotal method, depending on whether the Transaction t is a Sale or a Return.

2. (a)
```
public void computeVotePercents()
{
    int total = 0;

    //Find total of all votes cast.
    for (Candidate c : myCList)
        total += c.getNumVotes();

    //Set vote percent for each candidate.
    for (Candidate c : myCList)
    {
        double votePercent =
            100 * c.getNumVotes() / (double) total;
        c.setVotePercent(votePercent);
    }
}
```

(b)
```
public ArrayList<Candidate> getViableList()
{
    ArrayList<Candidate> viable = new ArrayList<Candidate>();
    for (Candidate c : myCList)
    {
        if (c.getVotePercent() >= 10)
            viable.add(c);
    }
    return viable;
}
```

(c)
```
public void printViable()
{
    ArrayList<Candidate> list = getViableList();
    for (Candidate c : list)
        System.out.println(c.getName() + " " +
                c.getVotePercent());
}
```

NOTE

In part (a), to get the correct, real-valued votePercent, you have to make sure that your percent calculation doesn't do integer division! You can achieve this either by casting the numerator or denominator to double, or by replacing 100 with 100.0.

3. (a)
```
public void play()
{
    boolean done = false;
    int lo = 1, hi = 100, count = 0;
    while (!done)
    {
        computerGuess = (lo + hi) / 2;
        count++;
        System.out.println("Computer guess is " +
                computerGuess);
        System.out.println("Should computer go higher
                or lower?");
        System.out.println("Or did computer guess right?");
        String response = IO.readString(); //read user input
        if (response.equals("lower"))
            hi = computerGuess - 1;
        else if (response.equals("higher"))
            lo = computerGuess + 1;
        else
        {
            System.out.println("Computer got it in " +
                count + " tries!");
            done = true;
        }
    }
}
```

(b) The computer should find the number in no more than seven tries. This is because the guessing interval is halved on each successive try:

$$
\begin{array}{rl}
(1) & 100 \div 2 = 50 \text{ numbers left to try} \\
(2) & 50 \div 2 = 25 \text{ numbers left to try} \\
(3) & 25 \div 2 = 13 \text{ numbers left to try} \\
(4) & 13 \div 2 = 7 \text{ numbers left to try} \\
(5) & 7 \div 2 = 4 \text{ numbers left to try} \\
(6) & 4 \div 2 = 2 \text{ numbers left to try} \\
(7) & 2 \div 2 = 1 \text{ number left to try}
\end{array}
$$

Seven iterations of the loop leaves just 1 number left to try!

(c) The maximum number of guesses is 100. A sequential search means that the computer starts at the first possible number, namely 1, and tries each successive number until it gets to 100. If the user's number is 100, the computer will take 100 guesses to reach it.

(d) On average the computer will make 50 guesses. The user is equally likely to pick any number between 1 and 100. Half the time it will be less than 50, half the time greater than 50. So on the average the distance of the number from 1 is 50.

4. (a)
```
public int getDanceTurn()
{
    int n = myTurns.length;
    int r = (int) (Math.random() * n);
    return myTurns[r];
}
```

(b)
```
public void turn()
{ setDirection(getDirection() + getDanceTurn()); }
```

(c)
```
public void tossFlower()
{
    if (Math.random() < probOfFlowerToss)
    {
        Grid<Actor> gr = getGrid();
        int tossDirection = getDirection() + Location.HALF_RIGHT;
        Location currentLoc = getLocation();
        Location tossLoc =
                currentLoc.getAdjacentLocation(tossDirection);
        if (gr.isValid(tossLoc))
        {
            Flower flower = new Flower(getColor());
            flower.putSelfInGrid(gr, tossLoc);
        }
    }
}
```

(d)
```
public void act()
{
    turn();
    if (Math.random() < 0.5)
        if (canMove())
            move();
}
```

NOTE

- In part (a), you cannot make assumptions about the number of turns in the myTurns array. You must therefore use myTurns.length.
- In part (b), you must use the method getDanceTurn defined in part (a). You will not get full credit if you reimplement code.

Answer Sheet: Practice Exam Four

1. Ⓐ Ⓑ Ⓒ Ⓓ Ⓔ
2. Ⓐ Ⓑ Ⓒ Ⓓ Ⓔ
3. Ⓐ Ⓑ Ⓒ Ⓓ Ⓔ
4. Ⓐ Ⓑ Ⓒ Ⓓ Ⓔ
5. Ⓐ Ⓑ Ⓒ Ⓓ Ⓔ
6. Ⓐ Ⓑ Ⓒ Ⓓ Ⓔ
7. Ⓐ Ⓑ Ⓒ Ⓓ Ⓔ
8. Ⓐ Ⓑ Ⓒ Ⓓ Ⓔ
9. Ⓐ Ⓑ Ⓒ Ⓓ Ⓔ
10. Ⓐ Ⓑ Ⓒ Ⓓ Ⓔ
11. Ⓐ Ⓑ Ⓒ Ⓓ Ⓔ
12. Ⓐ Ⓑ Ⓒ Ⓓ Ⓔ
13. Ⓐ Ⓑ Ⓒ Ⓓ Ⓔ
14. Ⓐ Ⓑ Ⓒ Ⓓ Ⓔ

15. Ⓐ Ⓑ Ⓒ Ⓓ Ⓔ
16. Ⓐ Ⓑ Ⓒ Ⓓ Ⓔ
17. Ⓐ Ⓑ Ⓒ Ⓓ Ⓔ
18. Ⓐ Ⓑ Ⓒ Ⓓ Ⓔ
19. Ⓐ Ⓑ Ⓒ Ⓓ Ⓔ
20. Ⓐ Ⓑ Ⓒ Ⓓ Ⓔ
21. Ⓐ Ⓑ Ⓒ Ⓓ Ⓔ
22. Ⓐ Ⓑ Ⓒ Ⓓ Ⓔ
23. Ⓐ Ⓑ Ⓒ Ⓓ Ⓔ
24. Ⓐ Ⓑ Ⓒ Ⓓ Ⓔ
25. Ⓐ Ⓑ Ⓒ Ⓓ Ⓔ
26. Ⓐ Ⓑ Ⓒ Ⓓ Ⓔ
27. Ⓐ Ⓑ Ⓒ Ⓓ Ⓔ
28. Ⓐ Ⓑ Ⓒ Ⓓ Ⓔ

29. Ⓐ Ⓑ Ⓒ Ⓓ Ⓔ
30. Ⓐ Ⓑ Ⓒ Ⓓ Ⓔ
31. Ⓐ Ⓑ Ⓒ Ⓓ Ⓔ
32. Ⓐ Ⓑ Ⓒ Ⓓ Ⓔ
33. Ⓐ Ⓑ Ⓒ Ⓓ Ⓔ
34. Ⓐ Ⓑ Ⓒ Ⓓ Ⓔ
35. Ⓐ Ⓑ Ⓒ Ⓓ Ⓔ
36. Ⓐ Ⓑ Ⓒ Ⓓ Ⓔ
37. Ⓐ Ⓑ Ⓒ Ⓓ Ⓔ
38. Ⓐ Ⓑ Ⓒ Ⓓ Ⓔ
39. Ⓐ Ⓑ Ⓒ Ⓓ Ⓔ
40. Ⓐ Ⓑ Ⓒ Ⓓ Ⓔ

How to Calculate Your (Approximate) AP Score — AP Computer Science Level AB

Multiple Choice

Number correct (out of 40)   =   _____

1/4 × number wrong   =   _____

Raw score = line 1 − line 2   =   _____

Raw score × 1.25   =   _____   ⟸ Multiple-Choice Score
(Do not round. If less
than zero, enter zero.)

Free Response

Question 1   _____
(out of 9)

Question 2   _____
(out of 9)

Question 3   _____
(out of 9)

Question 4   _____
(out of 9)

Total   _____   × 1.39 =   _____   ⟸ Free-Response Score
(Do not round.)

Final Score

_____   +   _____   =   _____
Multiple-   Free-   Final Score
Choice   Response   (Round to nearest
Score   Score   whole number.)

Chart to Convert to AP Grade
Computer Science AB

Final Score Range	AP Grade[a]
70–100	5
60–69	4
41–59	3
31–40	2
0–30	1

[a]The score range corresponding to each grade varies from exam to exam and is approximate.

Practice Exam Four
COMPUTER SCIENCE AB
SECTION I

Time—1 hour and 15 minutes
Number of questions—40
Percent of total grade—50

Directions: Determine the answer to each of the following questions or in-complete statements, using the available space for any necessary scratchwork. Then decide which is the best of the choices given and fill in the corresponding oval on the answer sheet. Do not spend too much time on any one problem.

Notes:
- Assume that the classes in the Quick Reference have been imported where needed.
- Assume that the implementation classes `ListNode` and `TreeNode` in the Quick Reference are used for any questions referring to linked lists or trees, unless otherwise stated.
- `ListNode` and `TreeNode` parameters may be `null`. Otherwise, unless noted in the question, assume that parameters in method calls are not `null`, and that methods are called only when their preconditions are satisfied.
- Assume that variables and methods are declared in the context of an en-closing class.
- Assume that method calls that have no object or class name prefixed, and that are not shown within a complete class definition, appear within the context of an enclosing class.

---

1. Which of the following will evaluate to true only if boolean expressions A, B, and C are all false?

   (A) `!A && !(B && !C)`
   (B) `!A || !B || !C`
   (C) `!(A || B || C)`
   (D) `!(A && B && C)`
   (E) `!A || !(B || !C)`

A ALSO

GO ON TO THE NEXT PAGE.

2. The database for a large bookstore has a list of Book objects maintained in sorted order by title. The following operations are performed on this list:

    I   Adding a new book.
    II Updating information for an individual book.
    III Removing a book from the list.

Assuming that the most efficient algorithms are used to perform the operations, which of the following is a *true* statement about using an ArrayList versus a LinkedList to store the database? (Assertions about run time in the choices below should be considered in terms of big-O efficiency.)

(A) Operation I has approximately the same run-time efficiency for a LinkedList as for an ArrayList.

(B) Operation II has faster run-time efficiency for a LinkedList than an ArrayList.

(C) Operation III has faster run-time efficiency for an ArrayList than a LinkedList.

(D) If a new book whose title starts with the letter "A" is to be inserted into the list, inserting into an ArrayList will have faster run time than inserting into a LinkedList.

(E) If the last book in the list must be removed, the run time will be faster for a LinkedList than an ArrayList.

Questions 3–5 are based on the three classes below:

A ALSO

```
public class Employee
{
    private String myName;
    private int myEmployeeNum;
    private double mySalary, myTaxWithheld;

    public Employee(String name, int empNum, double salary,
        double taxWithheld)
    { /* implementation not shown */ }

    //Returns pre-tax salary
    public double getSalary()
    { return mySalary; }

    public String getName()
    { return myName; }

    public int getEmployeeNum()
    { return myEmployeeNum; }

    public double getTax()
    { return myTaxWithheld; }

    public double computePay()
    { return mySalary - myTaxWithheld; }
}

public class PartTimeEmployee extends Employee
{
    private double myPayFraction;

    public PartTimeEmployee(String name, int empNum, double salary,
        double taxWithheld, double payFraction)
    { /* implementation not shown */ }

    public double getPayFraction()
    { return myPayFraction; }

    public double computePay()
    { return getSalary() * myPayFraction - getTax();}
}

public class Consultant extends Employee
{
    private static final double BONUS = 5000;

    public Consultant(String name, int empNum, double salary,
        double taxWithheld)
    { /* implementation not shown */ }

    public double computePay()
    { /* implementation code */ }
}
```

A ALSO

3. The `computePay` method in the `Consultant` class redefines the `computePay` method of the `Employee` class to add a bonus to the salary after subtracting the tax withheld. Which represents correct /* *implementation code* */ of `computePay` for `Consultant`?

  I `return super.computePay() + BONUS;`

  II `super.computePay();`
       `return getSalary() + BONUS;`

  III `return getSalary() - getTax() + BONUS;`

(A) I only
(B) II only
(C) III only
(D) I and III only
(E) I and II only

4. Consider these valid declarations in a client program:

```
Employee e = new Employee("Noreen Rizvi", 304, 65000, 10000);
Employee p = new PartTimeEmployee("Rafael Frongillo", 287, 40000,
    7000, 0.8);
Employee c = new Consultant("Dan Lepage", 694, 55000, 8500);
```

Which of the following method calls will cause an error?
(A) `double x = e.computePay();`
(B) `double y = p.computePay();`
(C) `String n = c.getName();`
(D) `int num = p.getEmployeeNum();`
(E) `double g = p.getPayFraction();`

A ALSO

5. Consider the `writePayInfo` method:

```
//Writes Employee name and pay on one line.
public static void writePayInfo(Employee e)
{ System.out.println(e.getName() + " " + e.computePay()); }
```

The following piece of code invokes this method:

```
Employee[] empList = new Employee[3];
empList[0] = new Employee("Lila Fontes", 1, 10000, 850);
empList[1] = new Consultant("Momo Liu", 2, 50000, 8000);
empList[2] = new PartTimeEmployee("Moses Wilks", 3, 25000, 3750,
    0.6);
for (Employee e : empList)
    writePayInfo(e);
```

What will happen when this code is executed?
(A) A list of employees' names and corresponding pay will be written to the screen.
(B) A `NullPointerException` will be thrown.
(C) A `ClassCastException` will be thrown.
(D) A compile-time error will occur, with the message that the `getName` method is not in the `Consultant` class.
(E) A compile-time error will occur, with the message that an instance of an `Employee` object cannot be created.

A ALSO

Refer to the classes below for Questions 6 and 7.

```java
public class ClassA
{
    //default constructor not shown ...

    public void method1()
    { /* implementation of method1 */ }
}

public class ClassB extends ClassA
{
    //default constructor not shown ...

    public void method1()
    { /* different implementation from method1 in ClassA*/ }


    public void method2()
    { /* implementation of method2 */ }
}
```

6. The `method1` method in `ClassB` is an example of
   (A) method overloading.
   (B) method overriding.
   (C) polymorphism.
   (D) information hiding.
   (E) procedural abstraction.

7. Consider the following declarations in a client class.

   ```java
   ClassA ob1 = new ClassA();
   ClassA ob2 = new ClassB();
   ```

   Which of the following method calls will cause an error?

   I   `ob1.method2();`

   II `ob2.method2();`

   III `((ClassB) ob1).method2();`

   (A) I only
   (B) II only
   (C) III only
   (D) I and III only
   (E) I, II, and III

8. Quicksort is performed on the following array, to sort it in increasing order:

$$45 \quad 40 \quad 77 \quad 20 \quad 65 \quad 52 \quad 90 \quad 15 \quad 95 \quad 79$$

The first element, 45, is used as the pivot. After one iteration of quicksort (i.e., after the first partitioning), which *must* be true?

   I 45 will be the fourth element of the array.
  II All elements to the left of 45 will be sorted.
 III All elements to the right of 45 will be greater than or equal to 45.

(A) I only
(B) II only
(C) III only
(D) I and III only
(E) II and III only

9. A list of numbers in unknown order is inserted into a binary search tree. Which of the following is *true*?
(A) If the tree produced is reasonably balanced, the run time to create the tree is $O(\log n)$.
(B) If the tree is balanced, the run time to search for a given element is $O(n \log n)$.
(C) The worst case run time to insert a new element into the tree is $O(n^2)$.
(D) A postorder traversal of the tree will produce the elements in ascending order.
(E) The run time to print out the elements sorted in ascending order is $O(n)$.

10. Consider the following class declaration:

```
public abstract class AClass
{
    private int v1;
    private double v2;

    //methods of the class
        . . .
}
```

A ALSO

Which is *true* about `AClass`?
(A) Any program using this class will have an error: An abstract class cannot contain private instance variables.
(B) `AClass` *must* have a constructor with two parameters in order to initialize `v1` and `v2`.
(C) At least one method of `AClass` must be abstract.
(D) A client program that uses `AClass` must have another class that is a subclass of `AClass`.
(E) In a client program, more than one instance of `AClass` can be created.

11. Consider the `ObjectList` class and `removeObject` method below.

```
public class ObjectList
{
    private LinkedList<Type> objList;

    //constructor and other methods not shown
        ...

    //Precondition:  objList is a LinkedList of Type objects.
    //Postcondition: All occurrences of obj have been removed
    //               from objList.
    public void removeObject(Type obj)
    {
            /* implementation */
    }
}
```

Which */* implementation */* will produce the required postcondition?

```
I for (Type t : objList)
  {
      if (t.equals(obj))
          objList.remove(obj);
  }
```

```
II for (Iterator<Type> itr = objList.iterator(); itr.hasNext();)
   {
       if (itr.next().equals(obj))
           objList.remove(obj);
   }
```

```
III Iterator<Type> itr = objList.iterator();
    while (itr.hasNext())
    {
        if (itr.next().equals(obj))
            itr.remove();
    }
```

(A) I only
(B) II only
(C) III only
(D) II and III only
(E) I, II, and III

Questions 12 and 13 refer to the `ElapsedTime` class below:

A ALSO

```
public class ElapsedTime implements Comparable
{
    private int myHours, myMins, mySecs;   //0 <= mySecs < 60,
                                           //0 <= myMins < 60

    //constructors

    public ElapsedTime()
    { myHours = 0; myMins = 0; mySecs = 0; }

    public ElapsedTime(int h, int m, int s)
    { myHours = h; myMins = m; mySecs = s; }

    public ElapsedTime(int numSecs)        //numSecs is total number of
    { /* implementation not shown */ }  // seconds of elapsed time

    //Returns number of seconds in ElapsedTime.
    public int convertToSeconds()
    { /* implementation not shown */ }

    //Returns a negative integer if this object is less than obj, 0 if
    // this object is equal to obj, and a positive integer if this
    // object is greater than obj.
    public int compareTo(Object obj)
    { /* implementation */ }

    //accessors getHours, getMins, and getSecs not shown ...
}
```

12. Consider the implementation of the compareTo method for the ElapsedTime class:

```
//Returns a negative integer if this object is less than obj, 0 if
// this object is equal to obj, and a positive integer if this
// object is greater than obj.
public int compareTo(Object obj)
{
    ElapsedTime rhs = (ElapsedTime) obj;
    /* more code */
}
```

Which is a correct replacement for /* *more code* */?

```
I  if (myHours < rhs.myHours && myMins < rhs.myMins &&
                                 mySecs < rhs.mySecs)
        return -1;
   else if (myHours > rhs.myHours && myMins > rhs.myMins &&
                                 mySecs > rhs.mySecs)
        return 1;
   else
        return 0;
```

```
II  if (myHours < rhs.myHours)
        return -1;
    else if (myHours > rhs.myHours)
        return 1;
    else
    {
        if (myMins < rhs.myMins)
            return -1;
        else if (myMins > rhs.myMins)
            return 1;
        else
            return mySecs - rhs.mySecs;
    }
```

```
III  int secs = this.convertToSeconds();
     int rhsSecs = rhs.convertToSeconds();
     return secs - rhsSecs;
```

(A) I only
(B) II only
(C) III only
(D) I and II only
(E) II and III only

13. A client method `timeSum` will find the sum of two `ElapsedTime` objects.

A ALSO

```
//Returns sum of t1 and t2.
public ElapsedTime timeSum(ElapsedTime t1, ElapsedTime t2)
{ /* implementation code */ }
```

Which is correct /* *implementation code* */?

```
 I  int s1 = t1.convertToSeconds();
    int s2 = t2.convertToSeconds();
    return new ElapsedTime(s1 + s2);

 II return new ElapsedTime(t1 + t2);

III int totalSecs = t1.getSecs() + t2.getSecs();
    int seconds = totalSecs % 60;
    int totalMins = t1.getMins() + t2.getMins() + totalSecs / 60;
    int minutes = totalMins % 60;
    int hours = t1.getHours() + t2.getHours() + totalMins / 60;
    return new ElapsedTime(hours, minutes, seconds);
```

(A) I only
(B) II only
(C) III only
(D) I and III only
(E) I, II, and III

14. A program that keeps track of the inventory items for a small store maintains the items in a `HashMap` data structure. The keys are inventory items, where each item is a string, and the corresponding values are quantities of that item that are on the shelf. Thus, some entries in the map could be

Campbells Clam Chowder Soup	11
Kleenex Tissues	35
Extra-strength Bufferin	20

Inventory items are added to and removed from the `HashMap` as needed. When a listing of all inventory items is required, all items of the `HashMap` are inserted into a `TreeMap`, whose `keySet` is then printed. Using the `HashMap` and `TreeMap` data structures as described supports which of the following?

(A) Listing of all current items in alphabetical order, $O(\log n)$ insertion of new items, and $O(\log n)$ retrieval of existing items.
(B) Listing of all current items in alphabetical order, $O(1)$ insertion of new items, and $O(1)$ retrieval of existing items.
(C) Listing of all current items in no particular order, $O(1)$ insertion of new items, and $O(1)$ retrieval of existing items.
(D) Listing of all current items in increasing order of quantities, $O(\log n)$ insertion of new items, and $O(\log n)$ retrieval of existing items.
(E) Listing of all current items in alphabetical order, $O(1)$ insertion of new items, $O(\log n)$ retrieval of existing items.

15. A large sorted array containing about 30,000 elements is to be searched for a value key using an iterative binary search algorithm. Assuming that key is in the array, which of the following is closest to the smallest number of iterations that will guarantee that key is found? Note: $10^3 \approx 2^{10}$.
   - (A) 15
   - (B) 30
   - (C) 100
   - (D) 300
   - (E) 3000

16. Consider the method searchAndStack.

```
//Precondition: v[0]...v[v.length-1] initialized with int values.
//               Stack s is empty. value may or may not be in v.
public static void searchAndStack(int[] v, Stack<Integer> s,
                                                    int value)
{
    for (int i = 0; i < v.length; i++)
    {
        if (v[i] > value % 2)
            s.push(new Integer(v[i]));
        else
        {
            Integer x = s.pop();
        }
    }
}
```

Suppose v initially contains 2 1 6 5 0 9, and searchAndStack(v, s, 5) is invoked. Which of the following will be true after execution of the method?
   - (A) The stack will be empty.
   - (B) The stack will contain three elements with s.peekTop() equal to 9.
   - (C) The stack will contain two elements with s.peekTop() equal to 9.
   - (D) The stack will contain two elements with s.peekTop() equal to 6.
   - (E) An EmptyStackException will have been thrown.

17. Refer to the following code segment:

```
int n = <some positive integer>
for (int i = n; i >= 1; i /= 2)
{
    process(i);
}
```

Given that process(i) has a run time of $O(1)$, what is the run time of the algorithm shown?
   - (A) $O(1)$
   - (B) $O(n)$
   - (C) $O(n^2)$
   - (D) $O(n/2)$
   - (E) $O(\log n)$

18. Assume that linear linked lists are implemented using the `ListNode` class provided. Refer to method `mystery` below.

```
//Precondition: firstNode refers to the first node in a linear
//               linked list.
public static ListNode mystery(ListNode firstNode)
{
    if (firstNode == null)
        return null;
    else
    {
        ListNode p = new ListNode(firstNode.getValue(),
                mystery(firstNode.getNext()));
        return p;
    }
}
```

What does method `mystery` do?
(A) It creates an exact copy of the linear linked list referred to by `firstNode` and returns a reference to this newly created list.
(B) It creates a copy in reverse order of the linear linked list referred to by `firstNode` and returns a reference to this newly created list.
(C) It reverses the pointers of the linear linked list referred to by `firstNode` and returns a reference to the original list, which is now in reverse order.
(D) It leaves the original list unchanged and returns a reference to the original list.
(E) It causes a `NullPointerException` to be thrown.

19. Suppose a queue is implemented with a circular linked list that has just one private instance variable, `lastNode`, that refers to the last element of the list:

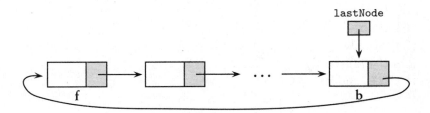

In the diagram, **f** and **b** indicate the front and back of the queue. Which of the following correctly gives the run time of (1) `add` and (2) `remove` in this implementation?

(A) (1) $O(n)$ (2) $O(1)$

(B) (1) $O(1)$ (2) $O(n)$

(C) (1) $O(n)$ (2) $O(n)$

(D) (1) $O(1)$ (2) $O(n^2)$

(E) (1) $O(1)$ (2) $O(1)$

20. Let `list` be an `ArrayList<String>` that contains strings sorted in alphabetical order. Which of the following code segments correctly lists the duplicate values of `list` in alphabetical order? Each duplicate value should be listed just once. You may assume that `list` contains at least one duplicate value, and that the line of code

    ```
    Set<String> set = new TreeSet<String>(list);
    ```
    works correctly as specified.

    ```
    I  //Copy elements of list into a new TreeSet.
       Set<String> set = new TreeSet<String>(list);
       System.out.println(set);
    ```

    ```
    II Set<String> hSet = new HashSet<String>();
       Set<String> kSet = new TreeSet<String>();
       for (String str: list)
           if (!hSet.add(str))
               kSet.add(str);
       System.out.println(kSet);
    ```

    ```
    III //Copy elements of list into a new TreeSet.
        Set<String> set = new TreeSet<String>(list);
        for (String str: set)
        {
            int count = -1;
            for (String s: list)
            {
                if (str.equals(s))
                    count++;
            }
            if (count > 0)
                System.out.print(str + " ");
        }
    ```

    (A) I only
    (B) II only
    (C) III only
    (D) II and III only
    (E) I, II, and III

21. A *binary expression tree* is a binary tree that stores an expression as follows. The root contains an operator that will be applied to the results of evaluating expressions in the left and right subtrees, each of which is a binary expression tree. The *prefix* form of the expression can be generated by a preorder traversal of the binary expression tree that contains the expression. What is the prefix form of the expression in the binary expression tree shown?

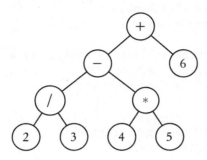

  (A) $+ - /\, 2\, 3 * 4\, 5\, 6$
  (B) $+ * - /\, 2\, 3\, 4\, 5\, 6$
  (C) $+ - * 2 / 3\, 4\, 5\, 6$
  (D) $2\, 3 / 4\, 5 * - 6 +$
  (E) $2\, 3 / 4 - 5 * 6 +$

22. An algorithm to convert a base-10 integer n to base b, where $b < 10$, uses repeated division by b until the quotient is 0. The remainders are stored and then concatenated to form a string, starting with the most recent remainder. This string represents n in base b. For example, to convert 29 to base 3:

3	29		
3	9	rem	2
3	3	rem	0
3	1	rem	0
	0	rem	1

        29 in base 3 is 1002

To convert 53 to base 4:

4	53		
4	13	rem	1
4	3	rem	1
	0	rem	3

        53 in base 4 is 311

Which data structure is most suitable for storing the remainders during the algorithm?
  (A) A String
  (B) An array
  (C) A stack
  (D) A queue
  (E) A priority queue

GO ON TO THE NEXT PAGE.

23. Refer to the `LinearLinkedList` class shown below.

```java
public class LinearLinkedList
{
    private ListNode firstNode;

    //Construct an empty list.
    public LinearLinkedList()
    { firstNode = null; }

    //Return true if list is empty, false otherwise.
    public boolean isEmpty()
    { return firstNode == null; }

    //Return reference to the first node.
    public ListNode getFirstNode()
    { return firstNode; }

    //Change first node of list to newNode.
    public void setFirstNode(ListNode newNode)
    { firstNode = newNode; }

    //other methods not shown...
}
```

Two new methods are added to the class, a public method and a private recursive helper method.

```java
public void method1()
{
    if (!isEmpty() && firstNode.getNext() != null)
        method2(null, firstNode);
}

//Recursive helper method
private void method2(ListNode prev, ListNode cur)
{
    if (cur.getNext() == null)
    {
        setFirstNode(cur);
    }
    else
    {
        method2(cur, cur.getNext());
    }
    cur.setNext(prev);
}
```

Suppose a `LinearLinkedList` object, `list`, is as follows:

What will `list` be as a result of the call `list.method1()`?

(A)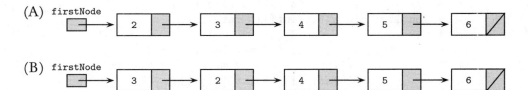

(B)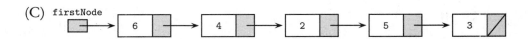

(C)

(D)

(E)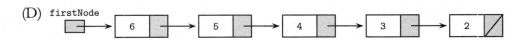

24. Consider a class `MatrixStuff` that has a private instance variable:

```
private int[][] mat;
```

Refer to method `alter` below that occurs in the `MatrixStuff` class. (The lines are numbered for reference.)

```
1   //Precondition:  mat is initialized with integers.
2   //Postcondition: column c has been removed and the last column
3   //               is filled with zeros.
4   public void alter(int[][] mat, int c)
5   {
6       for (int i = 0; i < mat.length; i++)
7           for (int j = c; j < mat[0].length; j++)
8               mat[i][j] = mat[i][j+1];
9       //code to insert zeros in rightmost column
10          ...
11  }
```

The intent of the method `alter` is to remove column c. Thus, if the input matrix mat is

```
2   6   8   9
1   5   4   3
0   7   3   2
```

the method call `mat.alter(1)` should change mat to

```
2   8   9   0
1   4   3   0
0   3   2   0
```

The method does not work as intended. Which of the following changes will correct the problem?

I Change line 7 to

```
for (int j = c; j < mat[0].length - 1; j++)
```

and make no other changes.

II Change lines 7 and 8 to

```
for (int j = c + 1; j < mat[0].length; j++)
    mat[i][j-1] = mat[i][j];
```

and make no other changes.

III Change lines 7 and 8 to

```
for (int j = mat[0].length - 1; j > c; j--)
    mat[i][j-1] = mat[i][j];
```

and make no other changes.

(A) I only
(B) II only
(C) III only
(D) I and II only
(E) I, II, and III

GO ON TO THE NEXT PAGE.

25. A *perfect binary tree* is one with every leaf on the same level; and every nonleaf node has two children. N integers are to be inserted into the *leaves* of a perfect binary tree. The final value of `level` in the following code segment gives the *lowest level* of tree needed to accommodate all N elements in its leaves. Which replacement for /* *boolean expression* */ leads to the correct value of `level`? Note: Start counting levels at the root, which is level 0.

    ```
    int level = 0;
    while (/* boolean expression */)
        level++;
    ```

    (A) N < Math.pow(2, level)
    (B) N >= Math.pow(2, level) && N < Math.pow(2, level + 1)
    (C) N > Math.pow(2, level)
    (D) N > Math.pow(2, level+1)
    (E) N >= Math.pow(2, level)

26. A common use of hexadecimal numerals is to specify colors on web pages. Every color has a red, green, and blue component. In decimal notation, these are denoted with an ordered triple (x, y, z), where x, y, and z are the three components, each an `int` from 0 to 255. For example, a certain shade of red, whose red, green, and blue components are 238, 9, and 63, is represented as $(238, 9, 63)$.

    In hexadecimal, a color is represented in the format #RRGGBB, where RR, GG, and BB are hex values for the red, green, and blue. Using this notation, the color $(238, 9, 63)$ would be coded as #EE093F.

    Which of the following hex codes represents the color $(14, 20, 255)$?
    (A) #1418FE
    (B) #0E20FE
    (C) #0E14FF
    (D) #0FE5FE
    (E) #0D14FF

GO ON TO THE NEXT PAGE.

27. A large club has a membership list of *n* names and phone numbers stored in a text file in random order, as shown:

```
RABKIN ARI 694-8176
HUBBARD JUDITH  583-2199
GOLD JONAH 394-5142
    . . .
```

The text file is edited by hand to add new members to the end of the list and to delete members who leave the club.

A programmer is to write a program that accesses the text file and prints a list of names/phone numbers in alphabetical order. Three methods are considered:

   I Read each line of the file into a string and insert it into a binary search tree. Print the list with an inorder traversal of the tree.

  II Read the lines of the file into an array of strings. Sort the array with a selection sort. Print the list.

 III Read each line of the file into a string and insert it into its correct sorted position in a linear linked list of strings. Thus, the list remains sorted after each insertion. Print the list.

Which is a *false* statement?
(A) Each of methods I, II, and III, if implemented correctly, will work.
(B) Method III, on average, has $O(n)$ run time.
(C) If the names in the text file are approximately in alphabetical order, methods I, II, and III will have the same big-O run times.
(D) If the names in the text file are randomly ordered, method I has the fastest run time.
(E) The part of the algorithm that prints the list of names is $O(n)$ in each of the three methods.

For Questions 28 and 29 refer to customer orders as described below:

Customer orders for a catalog company are stored in a `TreeMap` t, which is declared as follows:

```
private TreeMap<Integer, CustomerOrder> t;
```

The `Integer` key is an invoice number and `CustomerOrder` is the corresponding value in the map. Each `CustomerOrder` object contains the customer's name, address, phone number, a list of items purchased, and the total cost.

28. What will the following code segment do?

```
for (Integer n : t.keySet())
    System.out.println(n);
```

(A) List the invoice numbers in no particular order.
(B) List the invoice numbers in increasing order.
(C) List the customer names in alphabetical order.
(D) List the `CustomerOrder` objects in increasing order by invoice number.
(E) List the `Integer`/`CustomerOrder` pairs in increasing order by invoice number.

GO ON TO THE NEXT PAGE.

29. Instead of an invoice number, the programmer considers using the customer's name as the key and the CustomerOrder as the corresponding value, as before. Why is this a bad idea?

    I It is not possible to store two or more customers with the same name in map t.

    II It is not possible for two or more customers to order the same item.

    III It is not possible for a given customer to have more than one order.

    (A) I only
    (B) II only
    (C) III only
    (D) I and III only
    (E) I, II, and III

30. A class of 30 students rated their computer science teacher on a scale of 1 to 10 (1 means awful and 10 means outstanding). The responses array is a 30-element integer array of the student responses. An 11-element array freq will count the number of occurrences of each response. For example, freq[6] will count the number of students who responded 6. The quantity freq[0] will not be used.

    Here is a program that counts the students' responses and outputs the results.

```
public class StudentEvaluations
{
    public static void main(String args[])
    {
        int[] responses = {6,6,7,8,10,1,5,4,6,7,
                            5,4,3,4,4,9,8,6,7,10,
                            6,7,8,8,9,6,7,8,9,2};
        int[] freq = new int[11];
        for (int i = 0; i < responses.length; i++)
            freq[responses[i]]++;
        //output results
        System.out.print("rating\tfrequency\n");
        for (int rating = 1; rating < freq.length; rating++)
            System.out.print(rating + "\t" +
                freq[rating] + "\n");
    }
}
```

    Suppose the last entry in the initializer list for the responses array was incorrectly typed as 12 instead of 2. What would be the result of running the program?
    (A) A rating of 12 would be listed with a frequency of 1 in the output table.
    (B) A rating of 1 would be listed with a frequency of 12 in the output table.
    (C) An ArrayIndexOutOfBoundsException would be thrown.
    (D) A StringIndexOutOfBoundsException would be thrown.
    (E) A NullPointerException would be thrown.

A ALSO

31. Consider the following method:

```
public static void sketch(int x1, int y1, int x2, int y2, int n)
{
    if (n <= 0)
        drawLine(x1, y1, x2, y2);
    else
    {
        int xm = (x1 + x2 + y1 - y2) / 2;
        int ym = (y1 + y2 + x2 - x1) / 2;
        sketch(x1, y1, xm, ym, n - 1);
        sketch(xm, ym, x2, y2, n - 1);
    }
}
```

Assume that the screen looks like a Cartesian coordinate system with the origin at the center, and that drawLine connects (x1,y1) to (x2,y2). Assume also that x1, y1, x2, and y2 are never too large or too small to cause errors. Which picture best represents the sketch drawn by the method call

```
sketch(a, 0, -a, 0, 2)
```

where a is a positive integer?

(A)
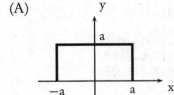

(B)
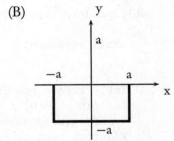

(C)
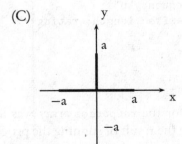

(D)
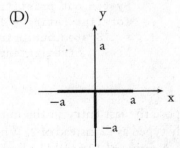

(E)
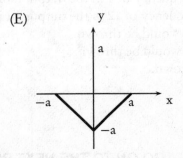

32. Consider the following methods. (You may assume that the `SomeType` class has a default constructor.)

```java
public List<SomeType> method1(int n)
{
    LinkedList<SomeType> list = new LinkedList<SomeType>();
    for (int i = 0; i < n; i++)
        list.addFirst(new SomeType());
    return list;
}

public List<SomeType> method2(int n)
{
    LinkedList<SomeType> list = new LinkedList<SomeType>();
    for (int i = 0; i < n; i++)
        list.addLast(new SomeType());
    return list;
}
```

Which of the following best describes the running time of
    (1) `method1` and (2) `method2`?

(A) (1) $O(1)$ (2) $O(1)$
(B) (1) $O(n)$ (2) $O(n)$
(C) (1) $O(n^2)$ (2) $O(n^2)$
(D) (1) $O(n)$ (2) $O(n^2)$
(E) (1) $O(1)$ (2) $O(n)$

For Questions 33–35, assume that binary trees are implemented with the `TreeNode` class provided.

33. Consider method `printStuff`:

```java
//Precondition: tree refers to the root of a binary tree.
public static void printStuff(TreeNode tree)
{
    if (tree != null)
    {
        if (tree.getLeft() != null)
            System.out.println(tree.getLeft().getValue());
        printStuff(tree.getLeft());
        printStuff(tree.getRight());
    }
}
```

Which best describes what method `printStuff` does?
(A) Prints every element in `tree` except the element in the root node.
(B) Prints every element in `tree`.
(C) Prints the element in the left child of every node in `tree`.
(D) Prints every element in the left subtree of `tree`.
(E) Prints the element in the root node as well as every element in the left subtree of `tree`.

GO ON TO THE NEXT PAGE.

For Questions 34 and 35 consider the `BinaryTree` and `BinarySearchTree` classes below:

```
public abstract class BinaryTree
{
    private TreeNode root;

    public BinaryTree()
    { root = null; }

    public TreeNode getRoot()
    { return root; }

    public void setRoot(TreeNode theNewNode)
    { root = theNewNode; }

    public boolean isEmpty()
    { return root == null; }

    public abstract void insert(Comparable item);

    public abstract TreeNode find(TreeNode p, Comparable key);
}

public class BinarySearchTree extends BinaryTree
{
    //Insert item in BinarySearchTree.
    public void insert(Comparable item)
    { /* implementation not shown */ }

    //Precondition: Binary search tree rooted at p.
    //Returns TreeNode that contains key.
    //If key not in tree, returns null.
    public TreeNode find(TreeNode p, Comparable key)
    { /* implementation code */ }
}
```

34. Which is a *false* statement about these classes?
    (A) The compiler will provide the following default constructor for the
        `BinarySearchTree` class:

        ```
        public BinarySearchTree()
        { super(); }
        ```

    (B) The `insert` and `find` methods in the `BinaryTree` class are abstract because
        their implementation depends on the type of binary tree.
    (C) The `item` and `key` parameters of `insert` and `find` need to be `Comparable`
        since the methods require you to compare objects.
    (D) The private instance variable `root` of the superclass cannot be altered by the
        `BinarySearchTree` class.
    (E) The following statement in a client program will cause an error:

        ```
        BinaryTree tree = new BinarySearchTree(new String("A"));
        ```

35. Which is correct /* *implementation code* */ for the find method?

```
 I if (p == null)
        return null;
    else if (key.compareTo(p.getValue()) == 0)
        return p;
    else if (key.compareTo(p.getValue()) < 0)
        return find(getRoot().getLeft(), key);
    else
        return find(getRoot().getRight(), key);


 II if (p == null)
        return null;
    else if (key.compareTo(p.getValue()) == 0)
        return p;
    else if (key.compareTo(p.getValue()) < 0)
        return find(p.getLeft(), key);
    else
        return find(p.getRight(), key);


 III while (p != null && key.compareTo(p.getValue())!= 0)
    {
        if (key.compareTo(p.getValue()) < 0)
            p = p.getLeft();
        else
            p = p.getRight();
    }
    return p;
```

(A) I only
(B) II only
(C) III only
(D) II and III only
(E) I, II, and III

Questions 36–40 involve reasoning about the code from the GridWorld Case Study. A Quick Reference to the case study is provided as part of this exam. The actors in GridWorld are represented in this book with the pictures shown below. Each actor is shown facing north. These pictures almost certainly will be different from those used on the AP exam!

Actor   Bug   Flower   Rock   Critter   ChameleonCritter

A ALSO

36. Which of the following has *exactly one* possible new location that the Critter in (0, 0) could move to, assuming that it is that Critter's turn to act?

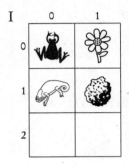

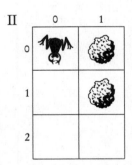

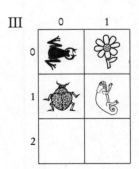

(A) I only
(B) II only
(C) III only
(D) I and II only
(E) I, II, and III

37. Refer to the following statements.

```
Location loc1 = new Location(1, 3);
Location loc2 = new Location(2, 1);
Location loc3 = new Location(3, 2);
Location loc4 = loc1.getAdjacentLocation(40);
Location loc5 = loc2.getAdjacentLocation(200);
```

Which is (are) *true*?

I `loc2.getDirectionToward(loc3)` returns 135.

II `loc1.compareTo(loc5) == 0`

III `loc4.getAdjacentLocation(230).equals(loc1)`

(A) I only
(B) II only
(C) III only
(D) I and III only
(E) I, II, and III

38. The behavior of a Bug is to be modified as follows: Every time it moves to a new location, it will drop a Critter into its old location, instead of a Flower. In order to achieve this change, a programmer modifies the move method of the Bug class as follows. The changes are in boldface.

```
public void move()
{
    Grid<Actor> gr = getGrid();
    if (gr == null)
        return;
    Location loc = getLocation();
    Location next = loc.getAdjacentLocation(getDirection());
    if (gr.isValid(next))
        moveTo(next);
    else
        removeSelfFromGrid();
    Critter critter = new Critter();
    gr.put(loc, critter);
}
```

The program appears to work as intended. However, after a few steps, the programmer notices that the Critter objects are not behaving properly. Flowers and bugs in their neighborhoods are not being "eaten" as specified. Nor are the critters moving as they should. Which of the following is the correct reason for this errant behavior?

(A) The act method of Bug is being called for each critter that is dropped by a bug.
(B) The Actor class is not being correctly accessed by Critter objects.
(C) The Critter class was not imported into the programmer's project.
(D) Each critter being dropped by a bug has no reference to the grid. Therefore, its location is not being updated.
(E) The driver class for the program, a class like BugRunner, is not updating the location of each critter dropped by a bug.

GO ON TO THE NEXT PAGE.

39. The `getValidAdjacentLocations` method of the `AbstractGrid` class is modified as shown below. Changes are in boldface.

```
public ArrayList<Location> getValidAdjacentLocations(Location loc)
{
    ArrayList<Location> locs = new ArrayList<Location>();

    int d = Location.NORTH;
    for (int i = 0; i < Location.FULL_CIRCLE / Location.HALF_RIGHT; i++)
    {
        if (i % 2 == 1)
        {
            Location neighborLoc = loc.getAdjacentLocation(d);
            if (isValid(neighborLoc))
                locs.add(neighborLoc);
        }
        d = d + Location.HALF_RIGHT;
    }
    return locs;
}
```

What is the effect of this change?
(A) The method returns all valid locations whose direction from `loc` is an odd number.
(B) The method returns all valid locations whose direction from `loc` is an even number.
(C) The method returns all valid adjacent locations that share a side with `loc`.
(D) The method returns all valid adjacent locations that share a corner point, but not a side, with `loc`.
(E) The method is equivalent to the original, and returns all valid locations that are adjacent to `loc`.

40. Consider a large, roughly square grid whose dimensions are approximately $n \times n$. The grid is sparsely populated with actors—approximately one actor per row. What is the big-O performance of the `getOccupiedLocations` method if the grid is a
    (1) `BoundedGrid`   (2) `UnboundedGrid`?
    (A) (1) $O(n^2)$ (2) $O(n^2)$
    (B) (1) $O(n^2)$ (2) $O(n)$
    (C) (1) $O(n)$ (2) $O(n)$
    (D) (1) $O(n^2)$ (2) $O(1)$
    (E) (1) $O(n)$ (2) $O(1)$

END OF SECTION I

COMPUTER SCIENCE AB
SECTION II

Time—1 hour and 45 minutes
Number of questions—4
Percent of total grade—50

Directions: SHOW ALL YOUR WORK. REMEMBER THAT
PROGRAM SEGMENTS ARE TO BE WRITTEN IN Java.

Write your answers in <u>pencil only</u> in the booklet provided.

Notes:

- Assume that the classes in the Quick Reference have been imported where needed.

- Assume that the implementation classes `ListNode` and `TreeNode` are used for any questions referring to linked lists or trees, unless otherwise specified.

- `ListNode` and `TreeNode` parameters may be `null`. Otherwise, unless noted in the question, assume that parameters in method calls are not `null`, and that methods are called only when their preconditions are satisfied.

- In writing solutions for each question, you may use any of the accessible methods that are listed in classes defined in that question. Writing significant amounts of code that can be replaced by a call to one of these methods may not receive full credit.

---

1. The following class, `DigitalClock`, is designed to display and manipulate a digital clock. The incomplete class declaration is shown below. You will be asked to write the declaration for a class that stores and manipulates a list of digital clocks.

```java
public class DigitalClock
{
    //private instance variables to represent hours, minutes, and a
    //  display string are not shown...

    //Constructs a DigitalClock set at 12:00.
    public DigitalClock()
    { /* implementation not shown */ }

    //Constructs a DigitalClock set at the specified hour and minute.
    public DigitalClock(int hour, int minute)
    { /* implementation not shown */ }
```

GO ON TO THE NEXT PAGE.

```
                //Advances the time on the DigitalClock by one minute.
                public void advanceTime()
                { /* implementation not shown */ }

                //Returns true if this DigitalClock is defective, false otherwise.
                public boolean isDefective()
                { /* implementation not shown */ }

                //other methods not shown ...
        }
```

Write a complete declaration, including implementation of all methods, for a class called `AllClocks`. This class stores and manipulates a list of `DigitalClock` objects. The `AllClocks` class must have a private instance variable

```
        ArrayList<DigitalClock> clocks
```

and a constructor that creates an empty list of `DigitalClock` objects (i.e., initializes `clocks` to empty).

The `AllClocks` class should have methods that do each of the following:

- Add a new `DigitalClock`, set at 12:00, to `clocks`.
- Advance the time by one minute on all the clocks.
- Remove all defective clocks.
- Replace all defective clocks with a new clock set at 12:30 (hours 12, minutes 30).

Complete the class declaration for `AllClocks` started below:

```
        public class AllClocks
        {
                private ArrayList<DigitalClock> clocks;
```

2. A *color grid* is defined as a two-dimensional array whose elements are character strings having values "b" (blue), "r" (red), "g" (green), or "y" (yellow). The elements are called pixels because they represent pixel locations on a computer screen. For example,

```
                                                        y g r
         b b g r                                         b y g
         g r g r              r r r r                    g r b
                                                        b b g
```

A *connected region* for any pixel is the set of all pixels of the same color that can be reached through a direct path along horizontal or vertical moves starting at that pixel. A connected region can consist of just a single pixel or the entire color grid. For example, if the two-dimensional array is called `pixels`, the connected region for `pixels[1][0]` is as shown here for three different arrays.

```
         b b g r            y g r b             b b
         g r g r            g g y g             b b
                            b g r g
```

The class `ColorGrid`, whose declaration is shown below, is used for storing, displaying, and changing the colors in a color grid.

```
public class ColorGrid
{
    private String[][] myPixels;
    private int myRows;
    private int myCols;

    /* constructor
     * Creates numRows × numCols ColorGrid from String s. */
    public ColorGrid(String s, int numRows, int numCols)
    { /* to be implemented in part (a) */ }

    /* Precondition:   myPixels[row][col] is oldColor, one of "r",
     *                 "b","g", or "y".
     *                 newColor is one of "r","b","g", or "y".
     * Postcondition: if 0 <= row < myRows and 0 <= col < myCols,
     *                 paints the connected region of
     *                 myPixels[row][col] the newColor.
     *                 Does nothing if oldColor is the same as
     *                 newColor. */
    public void paintRegion(int row, int col, String newColor,
        String oldColor)
    { /* to be implemented in part (b) */ }

    //other methods not shown
        ...
}
```

(a) Write the implementation code for the `ColorGrid` constructor. The constructor should initialize the `myPixels` matrix of the `ColorGrid` as follows: The dimensions of `myPixels` are numRows × numCols. String s contains numRows × numCols characters, where each character is one of the colors of the grid—"r", "g", "b", or "y". The characters are contained in s row by row from top to bottom and left to right. For example, given that numRows is 3, and numCols is 4, if s is "brrygrggyyyr", `myPixels` should be initialized to be

```
b r r y
g r g g
y y y r
```

Complete the constructor below:

```
/* constructor
 * Creates numRows × numCols ColorGrid from String s. */
public ColorGrid(String s, int numRows, int numCols)
```

(b) Write the implementation of the `paintRegion` method as started below. **Note: You must write a recursive solution.** The `paintRegion` paints the connected region of the given pixel, specified by row and col, a different color specified by the `newColor` parameter. If `newColor` is the same as `old-Color`, the color of the given pixel, `paintRegion` does nothing. To visualize what `paintRegion` does, imagine that the different colors surrounding the connected region of a given pixel form a boundary. When paint is poured onto the given pixel, the new color will fill the connected region up to the boundary.

For example, the effect of the method call `c.paintRegion(2, 3, "b", "r")` on the ColorGrid `c` is shown here. (The starting pixel is shown in a frame, and its connected region is shaded.)

```
    before              after
r r b g y y         r r b g y y
b r b y r r         b r b y b b
g g r r r b         g g b b b b
y r r y r b         y b b y b b
```

Complete the method `paintRegion` below. **Note: Only a recursive solution will be accepted.**

```
/* Precondition:  myPixels[row][col] is oldColor, one of "r",
 *                "b","g", or "y".
 *                newColor is one of "r","b","g", or "y".
 * Postcondition: if 0 <= row < myRows and 0 <= col < myCols,
 *                paints the connected region of
 *                myPixels[row][col] the newColor.
 *                Does nothing if oldColor is the same as
 *                newColor. */
public void paintRegion(int row, int col, String newColor,
    String oldColor)
```

3. A school newspaper has several students who have each applied to fill at least one of the following editorial positions: News, Arts, Sports, Features, and Photos. For example

Student	Positions Applied For
Mary	News, Features, Sports
Joe	Arts, Photos
Jill	News, Arts, Features
Kay	Photos
Tim	Arts, News, Sports, Photos
Jan	News

GO ON TO THE NEXT PAGE.

The following class, `NewspaperPositions`, manipulates and stores the data described in the table. The class contains two maps for storing data:

- `requestMap`, whose keys are student names, and corresponding values are the sets of positions requested by each student.
- `positionFreqMap`, whose keys are positions, and corresponding values are the numbers of students who requested each position.

```
public class NewspaperPositions
{
    private Map<String, Set<String>> requestMap;
    private Map<String, Integer> positionFreqMap;

    //Postcondition: requestMap contains students and positions
    //               they requested.
    //               positionFreqMap has been created.
    public NewspaperPositions()
    {
        requestMap = loadRequestMap();
        positionFreqMap = createFreqMap();
    }

    //Postcondition: Returns map with student names and
    //               corresponding sets of requested positions.
    private Map<String, Set<String>> loadRequestMap()
    { /* implementation not shown */}

    //Postcondition: Returns map with positions and
    //               corresponding frequencies of requests.
    private Map<String, Integer> createFreqMap()
    { /* to be implemented in part (b) */}

    //Precondition:  student is a key in requestMap.
    //Postcondition: Returns true if student requested the
    //               specified position, false otherwise.
    public boolean didRequest(String student, String position)
    { /* to be implemented in part (a) */}

    //other methods not shown ...
}
```

(a) Write the `NewspaperPositions` method `didRequest`. Method `didRequest` determines whether a given student requested a specified position. For example, using the data in the table on the previous page:

> `didRequest("Tim", "Features")`   will return `false`
>
> `didRequest("Kay", "Photos")`   will return `true`

Complete method `didRequest` below.

```
//Precondition:  student is a key in requestMap.
//Postcondition: Returns true if student requested the
//               specified position, false otherwise.
public boolean didRequest(String student, String position)
```

GO ON TO THE NEXT PAGE.

(b) Write the `NewspaperPositions` method `createFreqMap`. This method creates a frequency map of positions and the corresponding number of requests. For example, if the table shown on p. 686 represents `requestMap`, the statement

```
positionFreqMap = createFreqMap();
```

should create the following mapping.

Position	Number of Requests
News	4
Features	2
Sports	2
Arts	3
Photos	3

Complete method `createFreqMap` below.

```
//Postcondition: Returns map with positions and
//               corresponding frequencies of requests.
private Map<String, Integer> createFreqMap()
```

(c) Suppose you are given the following information:
- `requestMap` is a `HashMap`.
- The values in `requestMap` are `HashSets`.
- There are n students in `requestMap`.
- There is a maximum of c positions being requested.

In terms of n and c, what is the big-O running time of the `didRequest` method, assuming that the most efficient algorithm was used?

4. This question involves reasoning about the code from the GridWorld Case Study. A Quick Reference to the case study is provided as part of this exam.

In this question you will write two of the `BoundedGrid<E>` methods using a linked list implementation of the `BoundedGrid<E>` class. The current version of `BoundedGrid<E>` implements the grid as a two-dimensional array of `Object`. Consider a one-dimensional array of linked lists, where each linked list represents one row of the grid. Thus, each element of the array is a linked list, or `null` if that row is empty. Each index of the array represents a row number.

Each node in each of the linked lists is a `GridNode`, which holds a grid occupant, the location of that occupant, and a link to another `GridNode`. The `GridNode` class is shown below:

```
public class GridNode
{
    private Object occupant;
    private GridNode next;
    private Location myLoc;

    public GridNode(Object initOccupant, GridNode initNext,
                Location initLoc)
    {
        occupant = initOccupant;
        next = initNext;
        myLoc = initLoc;
    }

    public Object getOccupant()
    {return occupant;}

    public GridNode getNext()
    {return next;}

    public Location getLoc()
    {return myLoc;}

    public void setOccupant(Object theNewOccupant)
    {occupant = theNewOccupant;}

    public void setNext(GridNode theNewNext)
    {next = theNewNext;}
}
```

The example below shows how the 4 × 4 `BoundedGrid` shown would be represented in the new implementation. Notice that in each linked list, the locations are maintained in increasing order.

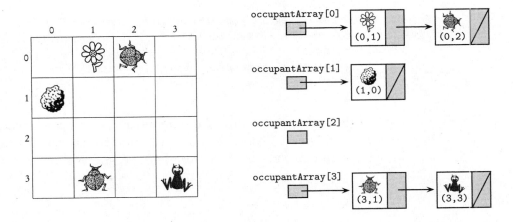

Here are the private instance variables in the modified implementation of `BoundedGrid<E>`.

```
private GridNode[] occupantArray;
private int myNumCols;
```

(a) Write the `getOccupiedLocations` method for the linked list implementation of the `BoundedGrid<E>` class. The method returns all occupied locations in the grid.

Complete method `getOccupiedLocations` below.

```
/**
 * Gets all occupied locations in this grid.
 * @return a list of occupied locations
 */
public ArrayList<Location> getOccupiedLocations()
```

(b) Write the put method for the linked list implementation of the `BoundedGrid<E>` class. Method put inserts object `obj` at location `loc` in the grid, and returns the object that was previously at `loc`, or `null` if that location was unoccupied. Recall that after you have inserted `obj`, the locations in its row must still be in increasing order.

Complete method put below.

```
/**
 * Puts obj at location loc in this grid, and returns
 * the object previously at that location.
 * Returns null if loc was previously unoccupied.
 * Precondition: obj is not null, and loc is valid in this grid.
 * @param loc the location where the object will be placed
 * @param obj the object to be placed
 * @return the object previously at the specified location
 * @throws IllegalArgumentException if the location is invalid
 * @throws NullPointerException if the object is null
 */
public E put(Location loc, E obj)
{
    if (!isValid(loc))
        throw new IllegalArgumentException("Location " + loc
                + " is not valid");
    if (obj == null)
        throw new NullPointerException("obj == null");
```

(c) Suppose that the grid contains r rows, c columns, and n occupants, where r, c, and n are all large. What is the big-O run time for the put method algorithm that you wrote in part (b), in terms of r, c, and n?

END OF EXAMINATION

ANSWER KEY (Section I)

1. C	15. A	29. D
2. A	16. C	30. C
3. D	17. E	31. B
4. E	18. A	32. B
5. A	19. E	33. C
6. B	20. D	34. D
7. E	21. A	35. D
8. D	22. C	36. D
9. E	23. D	37. D
10. D	24. D	38. D
11. C	25. C	39. D
12. E	26. C	40. B
13. D	27. B	
14. B	28. B	

ANSWERS EXPLAINED (Section I)

1. **(C)** In order for !(A || B || C) to be true, (A || B || C) must evaluate to false. This will happen only if A, B, and C are *all* false. Choice A evaluates to true when A and B are false and C is true. In choice B, if any *one* of A, B, or C is false, the boolean expression evaluates to true. In choice D, if any one of A, B, or C is false, the boolean expression evaluates to true since we have !(false). All that's required for choice E to evaluate to true is for A to be false. Since true||(any) evaluates to true, both B and C can be either true or false.

2. **(A)** For adding a book to an ArrayList: Finding the insertion point is $O(\log n)$ (binary search). Insertion is $O(n)$ (requires movement of elements). Overall: $O(n)$. For a LinkedList: Finding the insertion point is $O(n)$. Insertion is $O(1)$. Overall: $O(n)$. Choice B is false: Finding a given book in the ArrayList, which is sorted by title, is $O(\log n)$ (binary search), but $O(n)$ for a LinkedList. Choice C is false: To remove a book requires finding the book and then removing it. For an ArrayList, the search is $O(\log n)$ (binary search) and removal is $O(n)$. On balance, $O(n)$. For a LinkedList, the search is $O(n)$ and removal is $O(1)$. On balance, $O(n)$. Choice D is false: For an ArrayList, finding the insertion point is $O(\log n)$ (binary search). Insertion, however, requires movement of just about all the elements, $O(n)$. In the LinkedList, the sequential search to find the insertion point will be $O(n)$; insertion itself, $O(1)$. So both list implementations will be $O(n)$. Note that knowing that the title begins with "A" doesn't change the run-time efficiency estimate: You don't know where in the A's the title appears, and there are $O(n)$ titles beginning with "A" since you can't assume anything special about the distribution of titles among letters of the alphabet. Choice E is false: To remove the last book from both an ArrayList and a LinkedList is $O(1)$. (Recall

that a `LinkedList` is implemented with a doubly linked list with access at both ends.)

3. **(D)** Implementation I calls `super.computePay()`, which is equivalent to the `computePay` method in the `Employee` superclass. The method returns the quantity `mySalary - myTaxWithheld`. The `BONUS` is then correctly added to this expression, as required. Implementation III correctly uses the public accessor methods `getSalary` and `getTax` that the `Consultant` class has inherited. Note that the `Consultant` class does not have access to the private instance variables `mySalary` and `myTaxWithheld` even though it inherits them from the `Employee` class. Implementation II incorrectly returns the salary plus `BONUS`—there is no tax withheld. The expression `super.computePay()` returns a value equal to salary minus tax. But this is neither stored nor included in the `return` statement.

4. **(E)** Note that p is declared to be of type `Employee`, and the `Employee` class does not have a `getPayFraction` method. To avoid the error, p must be cast to `PartTimeEmployee` as follows:

```
double g = ((PartTimeEmployee) p).getPayFraction();
```

5. **(A)** The code does exactly what it looks like it should. The `writePayInfo` parameter is of type `Employee` and each element of the `empList` array *is-a* `Employee` and therefore does not need to be downcast to its actual instance type. There is no `ClassCastException` (choice C) since nowhere is there an attempt made to cast an object to a class of which it is not an instance. None of the array elements is null; therefore, there is no `NullPointerException` (choice B). Choice D won't happen because the `getName` method is inherited by both the `Consultant` and `PartTimeEmployee` classes. Choice E would occur if the `Employee` superclass were abstract, but it's not.

6. **(B)** Method overriding occurs whenever a method in a superclass is redefined in a subclass. Method overloading is a method in the same class that has the same name but different parameter types. Polymorphism is when the correct overridden method is called for a particular subclass object during run time. Information hiding is the use of `private` to restrict access. Procedural abstraction is the use of helper methods.

7. **(E)** All will cause an error!
I: An object of a superclass does not have access to a new method of its subclass.
II: ob2 is declared to be of type `ClassA`, so a compile-time error will occur with a message indicating that there is no `method2` in `ClassA`. Casting ob2 to `ClassB` would correct the problem.
III: A `ClassCastException` will be thrown, since ob1 is of type `ClassA`, and therefore cannot be cast to `ClassB`.

8. **(D)** During partitioning the array looks like this:

45	40	77	20	65	52	90	15	95	79
45	40	15	20	65	52	90	77	95	79
20	40	15	45	65	52	90	77	95	79

Note that 45, the pivot, is in its final sorted position, the fourth element in the array. All elements to the left of 45 are less than 45 but are not sorted with respect to each other. Similarly, all elements to the right of the pivot are greater than or equal to it but are unsorted.

9. **(E)** An inorder traversal of the tree will produce the elements in ascending order. Whether the tree is balanced or not, each of the n nodes will be visited once during the traversal, which is $O(n)$. Each of the other choices is incorrect. In choice A, *each* of the n elements may require a $\log_2 n$ search to find its slot, so creating the tree is $O(n \log n)$. In choice B, to find a single element in a balanced tree requires no more than one comparison on each of $\log_2 n$ levels. This is $O(\log n)$. In choice C, even if the tree is completely unbalanced and consists of one long linked list (worst case), there will be no more than n comparisons to insert one element. This is $O(n)$. In choice D, a postorder traversal for the binary search tree shown below produces 1, 7, 6, which is not in ascending order. In a binary search tree, the order property causes the leftmost elements to be the smallest and the rightmost the largest. Thus, an *inorder* traversal will produce the elements sorted in ascending order.

10. **(D)** A program that uses an abstract class must have at least one subclass that is *not* abstract, since instances of abstract classes cannot be created. Thus, choice E is false. Choice A is false: An abstract class can contain any number of private instance variables, each of which is inherited by a subclass of `AClass`. Choice B is wrong—for example `v1` and `v2` could be initialized in a default constructor (constructor with no parameters). Choice C is incorrect: The point of an abstract class is that no instances of it will be created. The class does not need to contain any abstract methods.

11. **(C)** When an iterator is used to traverse a list, only the methods of `Iterator` may be used. Implementation II would be correct if the last line were changed to `itr.remove();`. Implementation I fails because a for-each loop cannot be used to remove an object from a collection You *must* use an iterator.

12. **(E)** Implementation I uses faulty logic. For example, it treats an `ElapsedTime` of 5 hours 12 minutes 30 seconds as equal to 12 hours 6 minutes 20 seconds.

13. **(D)** Segment II is wrong because you can't use simple addition to add two objects: The code must be explicitly written. Segment I works because you're adding two `int` values and then invoking the constructor whose argument is the total number of seconds. Segment III works by a brute force computation of hours, minutes, and seconds.

14. **(B)** A `HashMap` stores its elements in a hash table. Therefore, it provides $O(1)$ run times for its `get` and `put` operations. The key set is not stored in any particular order. Constructing a `TreeMap` with the inventory elements places them in a binary search tree and allows printing of the key set in ascending order (which is alphabetic order for `String` objects).

15. **(A)** $30{,}000 = 1000 \times 30 \approx 2^{10} \times 2^5 = 2^{15}$. Since a successful binary search in the worst case requires $\log_2 n$ iterations, 15 iterations will guarantee that key is found. (Note that $30{,}000 < 2^{10} \times 2^5 = 32{,}768$.)

16. **(C)** Since value 5 is odd, value % 2 is 1. Array v is examined sequentially. Each time an element greater than 1 is encountered, it is pushed onto the stack. Each time an element less than or equal to 1 is encountered, the stack is popped. Thus the following sequence of actions will occur: push 2, pop, push 6, push 5, pop, push 9. Four pushes and two pops leave the stack with 2 elements, and 9 on top. Note that an EmptyStackException is thrown if an attempt is made to pop an empty stack.

17. **(E)** The for loop is executed $\log_2 n$ times (i.e., the number of times that i, which is initialized to n, is divided by 2 until it reaches 1).

18. **(A)** If mystery(firstNode) is invoked for the following linear linked list:

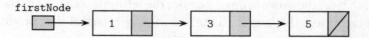

the method will create three new ListNodes whose pointer connections are pending:

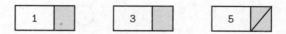

In the method call that creates the last node (containing 5), the expression firstNode.getNext() involves a base case, resulting in

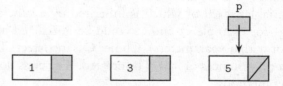

Now each of the previous method calls can be completed, resulting in the following sequence of pointer connections:

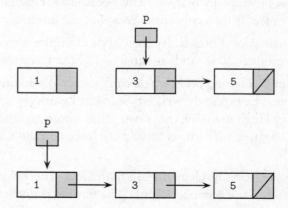

After the execution of the first recursive call has been completed, the final ListNode reference returned refers to the first node of a linear linked list that is identical to the original list.

19. **(E)** Just two pointer adjustments and a reassignment of `lastNode` achieve add: $O(1)$.

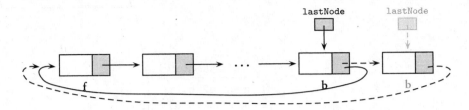

Just one pointer adjustment achieves `remove`: $O(1)$.

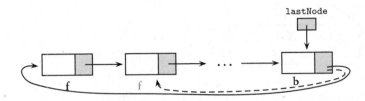

20. **(D)** Segment II places the distinct elements of `list` in `HashSet hSet` and the duplicates in `TreeSet kSet`. The output correctly lists the duplicates in increasing order, since elements of a `TreeSet` are ordered. Segment III places all elements of `list` in a `TreeSet` and then iterates over each element of the `TreeSet` checking for duplicates in `list`. Notice that each element of `list` will be found in `set` at least once. This is why `count` is initialized to -1 and then tested for being *greater than* zero. Segment I prints all the distinct elements of `list`, excluding duplicates, which was not what was required.

21. **(A)** A preorder traversal recursively traverses a tree as follows: root - left - right (see p. 440).

22. **(C)** Notice that the remainders are generated in the opposite order that they must be output. A stack, therefore, is the perfect data structure for storage: The last remainder in will be the first out, as required.

23. **(D)** This is an algorithm for reversing pointers in a linear linked list. Picture what happens to the list below, where `ListNode` references to the three nodes are `a`, `b`, and `c` respectively.

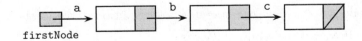

Here is the box diagram that shows the correct sequence of calls, starting with `list.methodr2(null, a)`. The actual order of execution of the statements is numbered 1 through **4**.

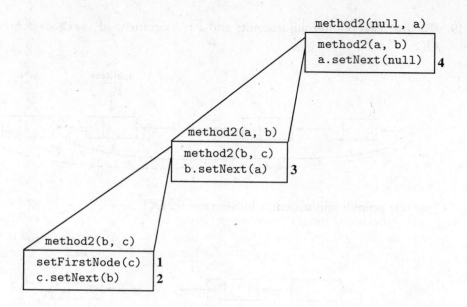

Executing the statements has the following effect on the given linear linked list:

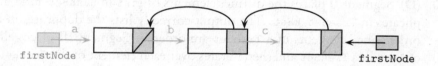

24. **(D)** The method as given will throw an `ArrayIndexOutOfBoundsException`. For the matrix in the example, `mat[0].length` is 4. The call `mat.alter(1)` gives `c` a value of 1. Thus, in the inner `for` loop, `j` goes from 1 to 3. When `j` is 3, the line `mat[i][j] = mat[i][j+1]` becomes `mat[i][3] = mat[i][4]`. Since columns go from 0 to 3, `mat[i][4]` is out of range. The changes in segments I and II both fix this problem. In each case, the correct replacements are made for each row i: `mat[i][1] = mat[i][2]` and `mat[i][2] = mat[i][3]`. Segment III makes the following incorrect replacements as j goes from 3 to 2: `mat[i][2] = mat[i][3]` and `mat[i][1] = mat[i][2]`. This will cause both columns 1 and 2 to be overwritten. Before inserting zeros in the last column, `mat` will be

$$2 \quad 9 \quad 9 \quad 9$$
$$1 \quad 3 \quad 3 \quad 3$$
$$0 \quad 2 \quad 2 \quad 2$$

This does not achieve the intended postcondition of the method.

25. **(C)**   If $N = 1$, the required level is 0
   If $N = 2$, the required level is 1
   If $N = 3$ or 4, the required level is 2
   If $N = 5$–8, the required level is 3
   ...

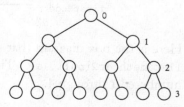

Test each of choices A–E with $N = 4$, where the desired answer is 2. Choice C works. Choices A and B fail the test on the first try and return `level = 0`. Choice D fails on the second try, leaving `level = 1`. Choice E executes the `while` loop one time too many, giving `level` a value of 3 when 2 will suffice. The conditions of the problem specify that the lowest possible level should be found.

26. **(C)**
$$14 = (0)(16^1) + (14)(16^0) = 0E$$
$$20 = (1)(16^1) + (4)(16^0) = 14$$
$$255 = (15)(16^1) + (15)(16^0) = FF$$

Therefore $(14, 20, 255) = \#0E14FF$.

27. **(B)** Method III is $O(n^2)$: For each element in the text file, its insertion point in the linear linked list must be found. For one element, this would be $O(n)$. For n elements, it is $O(n^2)$. Choice A is true: An inorder traversal of a binary search tree accesses the values in ascending order, which is alphabetical order if the elements are strings. Choice C is true: Approximately ordered elements lead to an unbalanced binary search tree (worst case). Number of comparisons to form the tree is $1 + 2 + \cdots + (n-2) + (n-1) = n(n-1)/2$, which is $O(n^2)$. Selection sort is $O(n^2)$ irrespective of the order of the elements. Choice D is true: Random order of the elements generally leads to a balanced binary search tree. Creation of the tree is then $O(n \log n)$, which is faster than the $O(n^2)$ run times of methods II and III. Choice E is true: Traversal of a linear linked list and printing elements of an array are both $O(n)$. An inorder traversal of a binary search tree visits each node once, which is $O(n)$.

28. **(B)** The statement prints the set of keys only, namely the invoice numbers, so eliminate choices C, D, and E. Choice A is wrong because a `TreeMap` stores the elements in a binary search tree and prints the keys in increasing order.

29. **(D)** Recall that the keys in a map must be unique. If a name is entered that already exists in the map, whether it's a new customer with the same name or an existing customer with a new order, the new information will replace the existing entry. Choice II will be OK with this data structure, provided the customers have different names! Different `CustomerOrder` objects *can* contain the same item that was purchased.

30. **(C)** If the `responses` array contained an invalid value like 12, the program would attempt to add 1 to `freq[12]`. This is out of bounds for the `freq` array.

31. **(B)** Here is the "box diagram" for the recursive method calls, showing the order of execution of statements. Notice that the circled statements are the base case calls, the only statements that actually draw a line. Note also that the first time you reach a base case (see circled statement 6), you can get the answer: The picture in choice B is the only one that has a line segment joining `(a,0)` to `(a,-a)`.

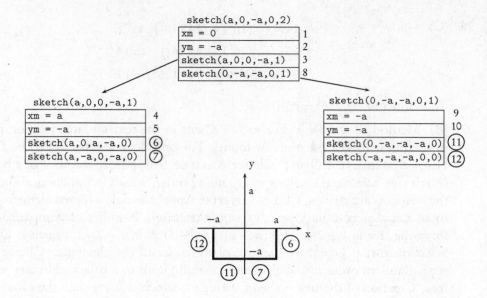

32. **(B)** The `LinkedList` class in the Java Collections library is implemented with a doubly linked list that has a reference to each end. Thus, both `addFirst` and `addLast` are $O(1)$. If n elements are added, the running time becomes $O(n)$ in each case.

33. **(C)** The `System.out.println(tree.getLeft().getValue())` statement indicates that the data in the root node is not printed. This eliminates choices B and E. Notice that there's no `null` test on `tree.getRight()`, nor is there any `System.out.println(tree.getRight().getValue())` statement. This means that no right children are ever printed, which certainly eliminates choice A. It also eliminates choice D, since nodes in the left subtree of `tree` do contain right children.

34. **(D)** The `setRoot` method, which is inherited from the `BinaryTree` class, can be used to change the `root` reference. Note that choice A is true: The `BinarySearchTree` class doesn't inherit any constructors. The compiler does, however, provide the default constructor shown. There is no error since the superclass `BinaryTree` has a default constructor. Choice E is true because the `BinarySearchTree` class does not have a constructor with a parameter.

35. **(D)** Segment II is a correct recursive algorithm, and segment III is a correct iterative algorithm. Segment I fails because making the recursive calls with `getRoot().getLeft()` and `getRoot().getRight()` means that parameter p will not recurse down the tree. The only nodes inspected will be in level 0 and level 1 of the tree!

36. **(D)** In grid I, the `Critter` will end up in location (0, 1) after eating the flower there. In grid II, the `Critter` will end up in location (1, 0), the only location available to it. In grid III, the `Critter` will end up in location (0, 1) or (1, 0), since both of those will be empty after the `Critter` has eaten the flower and bug.

37. **(D)** Locations 1 – 5 are labeled l_1, l_2, l_3, l_4, and l_5.

Notice that `loc4` is adjacent to `loc1` in the direction 45 (the nearest compass direction to 40). Similarly, `loc5` is adjacent to `loc2` in the direction 180 (the nearest compass direction to 200). Statement III gets the adjacent location to `loc4` in the direction 225, the nearest compass direction to 230. This location is (1, 3) or `loc1`. Statement II is false since `Location` (1, 3) is not equal to `Location` (3, 1).

38. **(D)** To add actors to the grid, the `putSelfInGrid` method must be called by that actor, so that location, direction, and other grid variables for that actor can be updated by the actor. The `get` and `put` methods of `Grid` do not automatically do this. With the boldface code given, the grid knows where each actor is, but the actor, without a reference to the grid, does not know where it is.

39. **(D)** Notice that when `i` is 0, 2, 4, or 6, all the `for` loop does is add 45 to `d`. The only locations inspected are those for which `i` is 1, 3, 5, or 7; namely `d` is 45, 135, 225, or 315. These are northeast, southeast, southwest, or northwest. Thus, the valid adjacent locations on the "corners" of `loc` are returned.

40. **(B)** Even though the `getOccupiedLocations` method is creating a list with approximately n objects, in the `BoundedGrid` all n^2 grid positions must be visited to retrieve these actors. This is $O(n^2)$. In the `UnboundedGrid` each location in the key set of `occupantMap` must be visited, approximately n locations. This is $O(n)$. Note that retrieving the actor, in either grid, is $O(1)$.

Section II

```
1.   public class AllClocks
     {
         private ArrayList<DigitalClock> clocks;

         public AllClocks()
         { clocks = new ArrayList<DigitalClock>(); }

         public void add()
         { clocks.add(new DigitalClock()); }

         public void advanceTimeOnAll()
         {
             for (DigitalClock c : clocks)
                 c.advanceTime();
         }

         public void removeDefective()
         {
             Iterator<DigitalClock> itr = clocks.iterator();
             while (itr.hasNext())
             {
                 if (itr.next().isDefective())
                     itr.remove();
             }
         }

         public void replaceDefective()
         {
             ListIterator<DigitalClock> itr = clocks.listIterator();
             while (itr.hasNext())
             {
                 if (itr.next().isDefective())
                     itr.set(new DigitalClock(12, 30));
             }
         }
     }
```

NOTE

- A for-each loop can be used to access and modify each element in a list. Thus, it is OK to use it in advanceTimeOnAll.
- A for-each loop cannot be used for removing or replacing elements in a list. Thus removeDefective and replaceDefective both need iterators.
- Method replaceDefective must use a ListIterator which has a set method that allows replacement. This is not available in Iterator.

2. (a)
```java
public ColorGrid(String s, int numRows, int numCols)
{
    myRows = numRows;
    myCols = numCols;
    myPixels = new String[numRows][numCols];
    int stringIndex = 0;
    for (int r = 0; r < numRows; r++)
        for (int c = 0; c < numCols; c++)
        {
            myPixels[r][c] = s.substring(stringIndex,
                stringIndex + 1);
            stringIndex++;
        }
}
```

(b)
```java
public void paintRegion(int row, int col, String newColor,
        String oldColor)
{
    if (row >= 0 && row < myRows && col >= 0 && col < myCols)
        if (!myPixels[row][col].equals(newColor) &&
            myPixels[row][col].equals(oldColor))
        {
            myPixels[row][col] = newColor;
            paintRegion(row + 1, col, newColor, oldColor);
            paintRegion(row - 1, col, newColor, oldColor);
            paintRegion(row, col + 1, newColor, oldColor);
            paintRegion(row, col - 1, newColor, oldColor);
        }
}
```

NOTE

- In part (a), you don't need to test if `stringIndex` is in range: The precondition states that the number of characters in s is numRows × numCols.
- In part (b), each recursive call must test whether `row` and `col` are in the correct range for the `myPixels` array; otherwise, your algorithm may sail right off the edge!
- Don't forget to test if `newColor` is different from that of the starting pixel. Method `paintRegion` does nothing if the colors are the same.
- Also, don't forget to test if the current pixel is `oldColor`—you don't want to overwrite *all* the colors, just the connected region of `oldColor`!
- The color-change assignment `myPixels[row][col] = newColor` must precede the recursive calls to avoid infinite recursion.

3. (a)
```java
public boolean didRequest(String student, String position)
{
    Set<String> positions = requestMap.get(student);
    return positions.contains(position);
}
```

```
(b) private Map<String, Integer> createFreqMap()
    {
        Map<String, Integer> freqMap =
                    new HashMap<String, Integer>();
        for (String student : requestMap.keySet())
        {
            Set<String> posSet = requestMap.get(student);
            for (String position : posSet)
            {
                Integer i = freqMap.get(position);
                if (i == null) //position not in freqMap
                {
                    freqMap.put(position, new Integer(1));
                }
                else
                {
                    freqMap.put(position,
                        new Integer(i.intValue() + 1));
                }
            }
        }
        return freqMap;
    }
```

(c) $O(1)$

NOTE

- In part (b), you must first create a new freqMap. Then you have to iterate through the key set of requestMap, the map that already exists. For each student key, you need to get the set of positions and iterate through that set. For each position in that set, you need to update its frequency in freqMap. This involves testing whether that position already exists as a key in freqMap. If it does, add 1 to the frequency. Otherwise, simply add that mapping to freqMap with a frequency of 1.
- The solution in part (b) does not use auto-boxing and -unboxing, which is a feature of Java 5.0 that is not in the AP Java subset. In the nested while loop, it would be perfectly OK to use this new feature:

```
if (i == null) //position not in freqMap
{
    freqMap.put(position, 1);
}
else
{
    freqMap.put(position, i + 1);
}
```

- Analysis for part (c): The didRequest method requires two steps:

  1. Locate the given student and corresponding set of positions. In a HashMap this is $O(1)$.
  2. Locate the given position in the set. For a HashSet this is $O(1)$. Therefore the whole algorithm is $O(1)$.

4. (a)
```
     public ArrayList<Location> getOccupiedLocations()
     {
         ArrayList<Location> theLocations =
                 new ArrayList<Location>();

         // Look at all grid locations.
         for (GridNode row : occupantArray)
         {
             GridNode current = row;
             while (current != null)
             {
                 theLocations.add(current.getLoc());
                 current = current.getNext();
             }
         }
         return theLocations;
     }
```

(b)
```
     public E put(Location loc, E obj)
     {
       if (!isValid(loc))
         throw new IllegalArgumentException("Location " + loc
             + " is not valid");
       if (obj == null)
         throw new NullPointerException("obj == null");

       E oldOccupant = get(loc); //save old object at loc

       //Add the object to the grid.
       int rowNum = loc.getRow();
       GridNode current = occupantArray[rowNum];
       if (current == null)//no occupants in that row
       {
         occupantArray[rowNum] = new GridNode(obj, null, loc);
       }
       else
       {
         int frontNodeCol = current.getLoc().getCol();
         if (loc.getCol() < frontNodeCol)  //obj must be inserted
                                     //in first node of this row
         {
           occupantArray[rowNum] = new GridNode(obj, current, loc);
         }
         else  //find insertion point for obj in row
         {
           while (current.getNext() != null &&
               current.getNext().getLoc().getCol() < loc.getCol())
           {
             current = current.getNext();
           }
           current.setNext(new GridNode(obj, current.getNext(),
                                                     loc));
         }
       }
       return oldOccupant;
     }
```

(c) $O(c)$

NOTE

- In part (a), you can use a for-each loop to traverse the array, but you cannot use one for the linked lists because there is no iterator available. (Each linked list is a collection of `GridNodes`. These are not encapsulated in a `LinkedList` object, which could have an iterator defined for it.)
- In part (b), there are three cases to consider:

    1. `obj` must go into an initially empty row.
    2. `obj` must go into the first node of a nonempty row. (This will happen when the column of `loc` is less than the the column in the current first node.)
    3. `obj` must go somewhere after the first node in a nonempty row.

- No casting is needed in the line

    ```
    E oldOccupant = get(loc);
    ```

    since the get method of `BoundedGrid` returns an object of type `E`.
- In part (c), locating any given row is $O(1)$ (accessing an array element). Thus, the required run time depends only on the number of elements in a single row. Since there is a maximum of c columns, there is a maximum of c nodes to traverse, and the algorithm is $O(c)$.

Glossary of Useful Computer Terms

I hate definitions.
—*Benjamin Disraeli*, Vivian Grey *(1826)*

API library: Applications Program Interface library. A library of classes for use in other programs. The library provides standard interfaces that hide the details of the implementations.

Applet: A graphical Java program that runs in a web browser or applet viewer.

Application: A stand-alone Java program stored in and executed on the user's local computer.

Bit: From "binary digit." Smallest unit of computer memory, taking on only two values, 0 or 1.

Buffer: A temporary storage location of limited size. Holds values waiting to be used.

Byte: Eight bits. Similarly, megabyte (MB, 10^6 bytes) and gigabyte (GB, 10^9 bytes).

Bytecode: Portable (machine-independent) code, intermediate between source code and machine language. It is produced by the Java compiler and interpreted (executed) by the Java Virtual Machine.

Cache: A small amount of "fast" memory for the storage of data. Typically, the most recently accessed data from disk storage or "slow" memory is saved in the main memory cache to save time if it's retrieved again.

Compiler: A program that translates source code into object code (machine language).

CPU: The central processing unit (computer's brain). It controls the interpretation and execution of instructions. It consists of the arithmetic/logic unit, the control unit, and some memory, usually called "on-board memory" or cache memory. Physically, the CPU consists of millions of microscopic transistors on a chip.

Debugger: A program that helps find errors by tracing the values of variables in a program.

GUI: Graphical user interface.

Hardware: The physical components of computers. These are the ones you can touch, for example, the keyboard, monitor, printer, CPU chip.

Hertz (Hz): One cycle per second. It refers to the speed of the computer's internal clock and gives a measure of the CPU speed. Similarly, megahertz (MHz, 10^6 Hz) and gigahertz (GHz, 10^9 Hz).

Hexadecimal number system: Base 16.

High-level language: A human-readable programming language that enables instructions that require many machine steps to be coded concisely, for example, Java, C++, Pascal, BASIC, FORTRAN.

HTML: Hypertext Markup Language. The instructions read by web browsers to format web pages, link to other websites, and so on.

IDE: Integrated Development Environment. Provides tools such as an editor, compiler, and debugger that work together, usually with a graphical interface. Used for creating software in a high-level language.

Interpreter: A program that reads instructions that are not in machine language and executes them one at a time.

Javadoc: A program that extracts comments from Java source files and produces documentation files in HTML. These files can then be viewed with a web browser.

JVM (Java Virtual Machine): An interpreter that reads and executes Java bytecode on any local machine.

Linker: A program that links together the different modules of a program into a single executable program after they have been compiled into object code.

Low-level language: Assembly language. This is a human-readable version of machine language, where each machine instruction is coded as one statement. It is translated into machine language by a program called an assembler. Each different kind of CPU has its own assembly language.

Mainframe computer: A large computer, typically used by large institutions, such as government agencies and big businesses.

Microcomputer: Personal computer.

Minicomputer: Small mainframe.

Modem: A device that connects a computer to a phone line or TV cable.

Network: Several computers linked together so that they can communicate with each other and share resources.

Object code: Machine language. Produced by compiling source code.

Operating system: A program that controls access to and manipulation of the various files and programs on the computer. It also provides the interface for user interaction with the computer. Some examples: Windows, MacOS, and Linux.

Primary memory: RAM. This gets erased when you turn off your computer.

RAM: Random Access Memory. This stores the current program and the software to run it.

ROM: Read Only Memory. This is permanent and nonerasable. It contains, for example, programs that boot up the operating system and check various components of the hardware. In particular, ROM contains the BIOS (Basic Input Output System)—a program that handles low-level communication with the keyboard, disk drives, and so on.

SDK: Sun's Java Software Development Kit. A set of tools for developing Java software.

Secondary memory: Hard drive, disk, magnetic tapes, CD-ROM, and so on.

Server: The hub of a network of computers. Stores application programs, data, mail messages, and so on, and makes them available to all computers on the network.

Software: Computer programs written in some computer language and executed on the hardware after conversion to machine language. If you can install it on your hard drive, it's software (e.g., programs, spreadsheets, word processors).

Source code: A program in a high-level language like Java, C++, Pascal, or FORTRAN.

Swing: A Java toolkit for implementing graphical user interfaces.

Transistor: Microscopic semiconductor device that can serve as an on-off switch.

URL: Uniform Resource Locator. An address of a web page.

Workstation: Desktop computer that is faster and more powerful than a microcomputer.

Supplementary Code for Evaluating a Binary Expression Tree

APPENDIX **B**

The ExpressionEvaluator class on p. 451 evaluates binary expression trees. It makes use of an ExpressionHandler class, whose code is given below. This class uses a File-Handler class, also given below.

```java
import java.util.*;

/* A class to create and manipulate expressions */
public class ExpressionHandler
{
    private FileHandler f;
    private Scanner scanner;
    private char ch;
    private Expression exp;
    private Stack<Expression> s; //used to insert expression in tree

    public ExpressionHandler()
    {
        s = new Stack<Expression>();
        f = new FileHandler();
    }

    //Create Constant expression with int value of c.
    //Push this expression onto the stack.
    private void createConstant(char c)
    {
        exp = new Constant(c - '0');
        s.push(exp);
    }

    //Create BinaryOperation depending on operator c.
    //Push this expression onto the stack.
    private void createBinaryOperation(char c)
    {
        Expression right = s.pop();
        Expression left =  s.pop();

        if (c == '+')
            exp = new Sum(left, right);
```

```java
        else if (c == '*')
            exp = new Product(left, right);
        else if (c == '-')
            exp = new Difference(left, right);
        else if (c == '/')
            exp = new Quotient(left, right);
        else
            System.out.println("Error in input file");
        s.push(exp);
    }

    /* Creates binary expression tree from expression in input file.
       Precondition: Input file contains one expression, in postfix form.
       Constants (operands)are single digits.
       The characters of the expression are separated by spaces.
       For example: 9 6 + 4 2 / * represents the expression
       (9 + 6) * (4 / 2). The file should not be terminated with a
       carriage return. */
    public Expression createTree()
    {
        scanner = f.openFileForReading();
        while (scanner.hasNext())
        {
            ch = (scanner.next()).charAt(0);
            if (Character.isDigit(ch)) //constant (operand)
                createConstant(ch);
            else //binary operator
                createBinaryOperation(ch);
        }
        return exp;
    }
}
```

Here is the `FileHandler` class:

```java
import java.io.*;
import java.util.*;

/* A class that manipulates input and output files */
public class FileHandler
{
    private PrintWriter writer;
    private Scanner scanner;

    public FileHandler()
    {}

    //Prompt for fileName, open inFile, create scanner.
    public Scanner openFileForReading()
    {
        Scanner console = new Scanner(System.in);
        System.out.print("Enter input file name: ");
        String fileName = console.next();
        try
        {
            scanner = new Scanner (new File (fileName));
        }
```

```
            catch (FileNotFoundException e)
            {
                System.out.println( "Could not open " +
                        fileName);
                e.printStackTrace();
            }
            return scanner;
        }


        //Prompt for fileName, open outFile, create writer.
        public PrintWriter openFileForWriting()
        {
            Scanner console = new Scanner(System.in);
            System.out.print("Enter output file name: ");
            String fileName = console.next();
            try
            {
                writer = new PrintWriter (new  FileWriter (fileName));
            }
            catch (IOException e)
            {
                System.out.println( "Could not create " +
                        fileName);
                e.printStackTrace();
            }
            return writer;
        }
    }
```

Index